Cognitive Psychology

Cognitive
Psychology

DAVID G. PAYNE

State University of New York at Binghamton

MICHAEL J. WENGER

University of California, Santa Cruz

HOUGHTON MIFFLIN COMPANY   **Boston   New York**

Dedication

To Robyn and Adam—DGP
To Alicia—MJW

Sponsoring Editor: David C. Lee
Senior Associate Editor: Jane Knetzger
Senior Project Editor: Carol Newman
Senior Production/Design Coordinator: Jill Haber
Senior Manufacturing Coordinator: Sally Culler
Marketing Manager: Pamela Laskey

Cover design by Harold Burch Design, New York City

TEXT CREDITS

Chapter 2: p. 63: From VISION by Marr © 1982 by W.H. Freeman and Company. Used with permission.

Chapter 4: p. 106: From *Sensation and Perception* by H.R. Schiffman. Copyright © 1996. Reprinted by permission of John Wiley & Sons, Inc. **p. 123:** Courtesy Eric Mose/Scientific American 1961. Copyright © 1961 Eric Mose. **p. 130:** From I. Biederman, "Human Image Understanding: Recent Research and a Theory," in *Computer Vision, Graphics and Image Processing* by I. Biederman. Copyright © 1985 Academic Press, Inc. Reprinted by permission of the publisher.

Printed in the U.S.A.
Library of Congress Catalog Card Number: 97-72531
ISBN: 0-395-68573-7
1 2 3 4 5 6 7 8 9–DH–02 01 00 99 98

Brief Contents

Contents

Contents

Contents

Part Four: Thought

Preface

We have had the good fortune to work with dozens of talented undergraduate students in our laboratories and many times that number in our cognitive psychology courses. One of the things we learned from these students is that the experience of those who get their hands dirty working in the lab is far different from the experience of those who learn from lectures and textbooks. We have seen how the students in our labs come to appreciate the importance of both theoretical and empirical work in cognitive psychology and how they begin to relate cognitive psychology to other domains in psychology as well as to other academic and professional disciplines. And we have also seen them *get excited* about the scientific study of cognition, an excitement that drew us to this profession and that has maintained us as working scientists. Although it is impractical to provide all students with the opportunity to participate in ongoing research, it is possible to convey some of the excitement and challenges of modern cognitive psychology through our teaching.

We wrote this book because we wanted to convey to students the excitement of the scientific study of the human mind. When we started work on the text, we were not altogether happy with any of the cognitive psychology textbooks on the market, for we did not feel that they adequately conveyed to students the excitement of research, the intellectual framework within which research and theorizing is conducted, or the rapid developments in cognitive neuropsychology. This is a very exciting time to be a cognitive psychologist—it seems as if every week an interesting, novel, and challenging finding is reported in the journals that come across our desks. In this book, we have tried to communicate these aspects of contemporary research to students.

This text is intended for use in undergraduate cognitive psychology courses, although it may also be used in beginning graduate courses, especially survey courses. We have not assumed that the students reading the book have taken either a statistics or a research methods course. We have attempted to present material in a manner that is accessible to undergraduate students while emphasizing the important relations among theory, methods, and data.

SPECIAL FEATURES

Several features of the text were designed to make it as user-friendly as possible and, at the same time, to present good scholarship. These features include the following.

Emphasis on Relating Data and Theory

Students are often confused about the nature of cognitive research and how the data from experiments are used to evaluate theories. We have addressed this problem in two ways. First, the final section of Chapter 1 presents and then answers three questions that students often raise regarding cognitive psychology. These questions address the source of research ideas, the types of research methods used by cognitive psychologists, and what makes specific research topics important at a particular time. Our students have reported that addressing these issues early in the semester helps them to appreciate the topics covered in the course. Second, in the topical chapters (Chapters 3–14), we present both the theories that motivate research on specific topics and the logic by which experiments are designed to test the predictions derived from theories. For example, in Chapter 13, we present the underlying assumptions of the early empirical research on categorization and concept formation and show how these assumptions affect both the types of research done on this topic and the findings obtained. We then use this early work as a springboard for discussing more recent efforts to examine rule-based approaches, information processing views, and connectionist models. In each case, we point out how the theoretical and metatheoretical assumptions of the researchers influence their science. This approach allows students to see how research unfolds and how empirical and theoretical work are related.

Provision of Historical Context

Each chapter places contemporary research and theorizing in an appropriate historical context. This allows the student to see the relation of the current research to previous efforts and also to appreciate the effects of classic earlier work on the topics of interest today. For example, in Chapter 5, we discuss Broadbent's classical filter model and the succession of models that grew out of this pioneering work. This discussion lays the groundwork for topics such as multiple resource models, negative priming, and the development of the concept of automaticity. Chapter 6 describes Atkinson and Shiffrin's classical three-store memory model and then traces the more recent developments in research and theories of memory in the short term. In Chapter 9, we review several major efforts to understand the acquisition of language skills. This discussion touches on materials that date back over 2,500 years, as well as more recent history, such as the influence of Wundt on modern psycholinguistics.

Cutting-Edge Scholarship

We have attempted to balance the need for a historical perspective with the desire to present an up-to-date picture of cognitive psychology. Toward this goal, we have included a great deal of very recent research that is revealing answers to questions that have been asked for quite some time. Examples of this include the recent work on nonverbal measures of infants' memory capabilities (Chapter 11) and discussion of the application of dynamic systems theory to understanding motor development (Chapter 11) and aspects of decision making (Chapter 12).

Coverage of Cognitive Neuropsychology

The study of cognitive processes is being carried out today at both the behavioral and the physiological level. The increasingly interdisciplinary nature of modern cognitive research is reflected in the book in two ways. First, Chapter 2 provides an overview of the physiological bases of cognition, including the basic anatomy and functioning of the nervous system and the methods used to study the structures and functioning of the brain. Second, each chapter contains neuropsychological research related to the cognitive processes discussed in the chapter. Some examples of this type of research are the recent PET studies of the brain processes underlying the production of false memories (Chapter 2), studies examining the involvement of various brain regions in episodic and semantic memory tasks (Chapter 7), and recent fMRI studies of brain regions associated with dyslexia (Chapter 10).

Active Involvement of the Student

Students learn best when they are invited to participate actively in the learning process. For that reason, we have included a number of special pedagogical features designed to foster the reader's active participation. One such feature is the *thought experiment*. In these text passages, we may describe a theory or an experiment and ask the reader to predict the results, or we may present results and ask the reader to try to account for the results using the theory.

We have also included *research report boxes*, which describe in detail actual research that focuses on specific aspects of one or more of the central topics of a chapter. These boxes go beyond the thought experiments in their level of detail and offer one more way of prompting students to actively think through the scientific process. One important example of the type of research discussed in these boxes involves using neuroimaging techniques to ask questions about the relations between cognitive events and brain states. This captivating research leads to important questions about how these relations can be examined with both traditional cognitive tasks and novel neurocognitive technologies. For example, in the chapter on mental expertise and problem solving (Chapter 14), we present recent research examining changes in brain activity as a function of practice in various tasks.

The chapters also feature *experiment boxes*, in which students are invited to conduct mini-experiments related to phenomena described in the chapter. Examples include mini-experiments on false memories (Chapter 1), the blind spot (Chapter 3), the abstraction of complex ideas (Chapter 8), and the availability heuristic (Chapter 12).

Pedagogical Chapter Structure

The chapters include a number of organizational features designed to help students acquire the information presented in the chapter and review the material before examinations. Each chapter begins with a detailed *chapter outline*, which lays out the chapter's conceptual structure. At the end of each section in the chapter, a *section summary* reiterates the section's main points. The *concept review* at the end of the chapter contains short essay questions that students can use to test their mastery of the material. In addition, a *key terms* list appears at the end of each chapter, and a full *glossary* is provided at the end of the text. Each chapter also features a list of *suggested readings* for additional sources of information.

ORGANIZATION AND COVERAGE

We were trained in the human information processing tradition, and this is reflected in the selection and ordering of the topics in the text. We assume that cognition involves stages of information processing in which people take in information from the world around them, store and retain the information in memory, and then use the information, along with new information, to think and to communicate ideas with others.

This view is reflected in the four major sections that follow the introductory chapter. Part One, Cognitive Foundations, discusses the neuropsychological bases of cognition, how humans create internal codes for the objects and events in their environment, and how attention affects the overall processing of information. Part Two, Memory, discusses memory in the short term and in the long term. Part Three, Language and Cognitive Development, includes materials on the perception, production, and comprehension of language and the way in which cognition changes across the life span. Finally, Part Four, Thinking, covers so-called higher mental processes, including judgment and decision making, categorization and concept formation, and mental expertise and problem solving.

Within the organizational framework provided by an information processing perspective, we have striven to present a balance of competing theoretical views. We discuss theories that predate the information processing perspective as well as more recent connectionist and dynamic systems approaches. The individual chapters in each section discuss research and theories concerning key topics within the specific domains.

Chapter 1 outlines the intellectual antecedents of cognitive psychology and some of the major facets of modern cognitive research and theorizing. This chapter describes the importance of considering the historical context in which research takes place and the need for studying the mind at various levels (e.g., physiological, behavioral). This leads into Chapter 2, which presents an overview of the functioning of the brain and nervous system and also discusses how the human mind and the brain are being studied at many different levels. This chapter emphasizes that there is no one "right" way to study the mind and that good science involves utilizing many methods while keeping in mind the limitations of the various approaches.

Chapters 3 and 4 describe how people obtain information about the world around them via the brain and sensory and perceptual systems. In addition to reviewing important findings and theories, these chapters investigate the relation between sensory and perceptual processes and the "higher" mental processes associated with cognition. Chapter 3 illustrates the importance of converging evidence and the distinction between laboratory and real-world research. Chapter 4 presents a variety of approaches to understanding visual perception and object recognition. Like the other chapters, Chapter 4 stresses the importance of different research approaches (e.g., physiological, behavioral) and types of theories (e.g., computational, connectionist) and how these various aspects of cognitive research influence one another.

Chapter 5 discusses divided and selective attention, as well as the development of automaticity. In addition to providing a bridge between the chapters dealing with sensation and perception and those dealing with memory and higher cognitive processes, Chapter 5 illustrates the importance of historical perspective in understanding modern research and the utility of using converging operations to study unobservable cognitive processes.

Chapters 6–8 discuss various aspects of memory performance. Chapter 6 focuses on the retention of information over short periods of time, while Chapters 7 and 8 are concerned with how event-specific and general knowledge are retained for longer periods of time. The distinction between event-specific and general knowledge corresponds to Tulving's distinction between episodic and semantic memory, and this distinction provides a useful framework for organizing the materials in these two chapters.

Chapters 9 and 10 deal with the production and comprehension of language. In these chapters, we present both the case for language as a specialized form of cognitive processing and the view that language can be treated as another form of information processing. Both chapters include materials on topics that students find particularly interesting, including language disorders, language in nonhuman species, bilingualism, and writing as a form of language. These topics are closely interwoven with the major theoretical models of language production and comprehension.

Chapter 11 discusses changes in cognitive processes across the life span from several theoretical perspectives (e.g., Piagetian, information processing). It also includes sections emphasizing development in specific domains, such as perception, memory, and language. These topics are ordered in parallel with the corresponding earlier chapters in the text to emphasize the utility of considering cognition from an information processing perspective.

The final three chapters build on the information presented in Parts One through Three. These chapters deal with complex cognitive processes that rely on perception, attention, memory, and so forth. Chapter 12 shows how human decision making can be viewed from a number of different perspectives, including motivational aspects of decision making, a utility theory view, and the role of expertise in decision making. Chapter 13 discusses the ubiquitous nature of categorization and concept formation. This chapter traces research on these topics from the early 1900s through modern connectionist accounts and demonstrates how the theoretical perspectives adopted by researchers affect both their experimental methods and the results they obtain. Mental expertise and problem solving are topics that can only be fully appreciated by considering the contributions of all perceptual and cognitive processes. In Chapter 14, we use these two topics to integrate the materials presented in the earlier chapters. These topics serve as an excellent capstone for the course, and students find them inherently interesting.

We have arranged these chapters in order from lower-level to higher-level processes, but instructors may vary the order in which the chapters are assigned. Each chapter is largely self-contained and may be read without detailed knowledge of the materials in previous chapters. Still, there are some constraints on how much the chapter order can be varied. Specifically, Chapters 3 and 4 should be read in order, as Chapter 4 makes frequent reference to the information presented in Chapter 3. Similarly, Chapters 7 and 8 are best read in order. Finally, if the instructor plans to cover cognitive neuropsychological research during the course, then Chapter 2 should be assigned early in the term.

ANCILLARIES

Several resources have been created to accompany the text and assist the instructor. The *Instructor's Resource Manual and Test Bank*, developed by Alicia J. Knoedler of San Jose State University, provides materials that can be used to supplement and expand on the contents of the chapters. These include in-class demonstrations, supplemental lecture materials, suggestions for other supplemental media (videos, articles available in the popular press, etc.), and a list of sites on the World Wide Web containing relevant and interesting information. The manual also provides approximately fifty multiple-choice questions (factual, conceptual, and applied) and five essay and short-answer questions per chapter.

In addition, Houghton Mifflin's website provides access to useful and innovative teaching and learning resources that support this book. You can reach this location by going to the Houghton Mifflin home page at http://www.hmco.com/ and then to the College Division psychology page.

ACKNOWLEDGMENTS

Many people have contributed in a variety of ways to this text. The staff at Houghton Mifflin has been outstanding, and we could not have completed this text without their skillful assistance. David Lee, Sponsoring Editor, has supported the project from the outset, and his talented and energetic staff has provided excellent assistance throughout the project. Our Senior Associate Editor, Jane Knetzger, has been extremely helpful and patient. We thank Jane for her unending enthusiasm for the project and patience in dealing with our constantly evolving schedules. Barbara Brooks provided an incredible amount of help as our developmental editor; we have learned a tremendous amount from Barbara, and we hope that the text you now have in your hands meets or exceeds her high standards for excellence in scholarship and clarity of presentation. Our Senior Project Editor, Carol Newman, provided outstanding assistance in many ways as the chapters wound their way from draft form to final pages. Charlotte Miller did a fantastic job with the line art for the text; we continue to be amazed at how she was able to take our rough ideas for illustrations and turn them into high-quality art that adds significantly to the prose materials. Maryam Fakouri, our photo researcher, did a wonderful job of finding appropriate photos; we especially appreciate her diligence in finding photos that were difficult to obtain. In addition, we would like to thank Diane Kraut at DK Research for her help in tracking down permissions for the text and Beverly Peavler for her considerable copyediting skills. We also thank our secretaries, Janice Kellar and Roxanne Anderson, for their assistance in typing and revising chapters and handling correspondence during the review process.

We are fortunate to have had an outstanding set of experts review drafts of each chapter. The reviewers, listed in alphabetical order below, provided detailed and valuable comments that were extremely useful in producing the final chapters. We appreciate their help and acknowledge that the final product reflects their many contributions.

Corlene Ankrum, Washington State University at Vancouver
Jack B. Arnold, St. Mary's College of California
David J. Bryant, Northeastern University
John C. Jahnke, Miami University
Gary J. Klatsky, State University of New York at Oswego
David Kreiner, Central Missouri State University
Doug Needham, Redeemer College
Raymond J. Shaw, West Virginia University
Aimée Surprenant, Purdue University
Jyotsna Vaid, Texas A & M University
Lori R. Van Wallendael, University of North Carolina at Charlotte
John W. Webster, Towson State University
Daniel B. Willingham, University of Virginia
Rolf A. Zwaan, Florida State University

We would also like to thank the following colleagues (listed alphabetically) for providing invaluable discussions, reviews, and commentaries that helped shape the materials presented in the text: Cynthia Connine (Binghamton University–SUNY), Sonya Dougal (University of Massachusetts–Amherst), Celia Klin (Binghamton University–SUNY), Albrecht Inhoff (Binghamton University–SUNY), Erik Reichle (University of Massachusetts–Amherst), Lael Schooler (The Pennsylvania State University), Kam Silva (Indiana University), Norman E. Spear (Binghamton University–SUNY), and Debra Titone (Brandeis University). Of especially notable help were Danny Hager (Binghamton University–SUNY) and Alicia Knoedler (San Jose State University), who provided extensive developmental assistance with several chapters.

We would like to acknowledge the deep debt of gratitude we owe to our mentors (alphabetically): John F. Catalano, James H. Neely, David G. Payne, Henry L. Roediger III, Jan H. Spyridakis, Michael P. Toglia, and James T. Townsend. We hope that our presentation of their work, as well as the work of all of the scientists represented in the pages that follow, is consistent with the integrity, thoughtfulness, comprehensiveness, and honesty that they have taught (and continue to teach) us to value.

Finally, we want to thank our families for bearing with us through missed meals, late nights, and lost weekends. Their grace is our supreme good fortune.

KEEPING IN CONTACT

If you would like to learn a little more about us and the places where we work, you can visit these web sites:

http://psychology.binghamton.edu/
http://zzyx.ucsc.edu/psych/psych.html

We would also sincerely appreciate receiving your thoughts on our book and how we might change and improve it. You can reach us by e-mail at:

dpayne@Binghamton.edu
mjwenger@cats.ucsc.edu

David G. Payne

Michael J. Wenger

Cognitive Psychology

> *It is a supreme challenge* for the popularizer of science to make clear the actual, tortuous history of its great discoveries and the misapprehensions and occasional stubborn refusal by its practitioners to change course. Many, perhaps most, science textbooks for budding scientists tread lightly here. It is enormously easier to present in an appealing way the wisdom distilled from centuries of patient and collective interrogation of Nature than to detail the messy distillation apparatus. The method of science, as stogy and grumpy as it may seem, is far more important than the findings of science.—Carl Sagan (1995, p. 22)

WHEN RAJAN SRINIVASAN MAHADEVAN was five years old, his parents had a party for his sister's first birthday. There were quite a few guests at the party, and they arrived in over twenty different vehicles. Rajan surprised his parents and their guests by memorizing the license plate number of each vehicle, as well as who owned the vehicle. Years later, Rajan earned a place in the *Guinness Book of World Records* by reciting from memory the first 31,811 digits of the number pi (Thompson et al., 1991).

November 28, 1988, is a day that Paul Ingram will probably never forget, for on that day Ingram was confronted with the fact that his two grown daughters had accused him of sexually assaulting them when they were young girls. In the weeks and months after Ingram was accused, he confessed to these crimes and gave investigators detailed accounts of the incidents (Ofshe & Watters, 1994).

A researcher, Richard Ofshe, wondered if Paul Ingram might be responding to pressures to confess rather than recovering memories of actual events. To find out, Ofshe told Ingram that his children had accused him of forcing them to have sex while he watched. This accusation had in fact been fabricated by Ofshe to test Ingram's memory. Over the course of several days, Paul Ingram began to "remember" these incidents in vivid detail.

When confronted with the information that the incident had been fabricated, Paul Ingram clung to his belief that his memory of these events was as real as his memory of the other incidents of which his children had accused him (Ofshe & Watters, 1994).

Early in 1996, Garry Kasparov, the world chess champion, sat down for a match against a formidable foe, a supercomputer that could calculate more than 100 million moves per second. The IBM supercomputer, dubbed Deep Blue, won the first game of the match, but Kasparov was not easily vanquished. Kasparov learned from each game he played against Deep Blue and managed to win the six-game match. In the final game, Kasparov required only 43 moves to defeat the supercomputer. In May 1997 Kasparov lost a six-game match to a revised version of Deep Blue that had double the computing power of the first version. Kasparov believes that he can beat Deep Blue if he is given the chance to play more games against the machine and learn its strengths and weaknesses. Regardless of the final outcome of this rivalry, the fact that Kasparov beat the machine the first time attests to the power of the human mind.

STUDYING THE HUMAN MIND

The three scenarios we just described reveal glimpses of how the human mind works. The mind has long been the object of inquiry, and we are going to examine one of the primary contemporary disciplines devoted to this inquiry—the discipline of cognitive psychology.

Cognitive psychology is an empirical research science that has as its primary goal understanding the processes that underlie the workings of the human mind. An *empirical re-*

search science is one that relies on observations, and cognitive psychologists use a variety of research techniques for collecting these observations. Cognitive psychologists study a wide range of psychological processes, including sensation and perception, attention, learning, memory, reasoning and decision making, language, categorization, and mental expertise.

In this chapter, we provide an overview of the historical antecedents of cognitive psychology as well as some facts about contemporary cognitive psychology. We begin by considering one of the hallmarks of cognitive psychology—its research methodology.

How Cognitive Psychologists Conduct Research

One thing that differentiates cognitive psychologists from researchers in other disciplines who are also interested in the mind (e.g., philosophers) is that cognitive psychologists conduct controlled experiments to test their ideas. In the following chapters, we describe some of the research, findings, and applications that have come from this work. One benefit of studying the human mind through controlled experiments, rather than relying on other means of gaining knowledge, is that experiments provide objective data that can be compared against our intuitions concerning how the mind and brain function.

Although our intuitions are often correct, in some situations they are at odds with reality. For example, how do you think your eyes move across the page as you read this sentence? Most people report that it seems that their eyes move smoothly and continuously from left to right. However, research has shown that the eyes actually move in short jumps (known as *saccades*) from one fixation point to the next (Rayner, 1978). Researchers have measured saccades in controlled experiments, and the results of these studies have provided important insights into the reading process. For example, studies have found that there are differences in the saccades made by good and poor readers (Buswell, 1937) and that eye movements are different for easy versus difficult passages (Rayner and Pollatsek, 1989). We will have more to say about reading in Chapter 10.

Another advantage of conducting experiments is that they allow us to test alternative accounts of the phenomena of interest. For example, does Rajan have a very unusual

Cognitive psychologists employ scientific methods to study the human mind. In the experiment presented here, the woman on the left is seated at an eyetracker, which records her eye movements. The researcher on the right is monitoring the subject's responses.

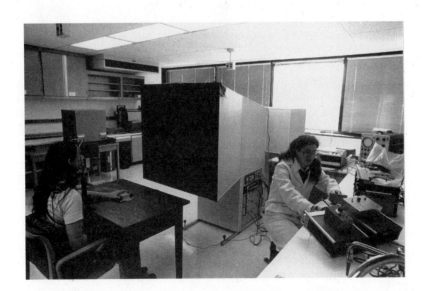

memory system, or does his ability to memorize over 30,000 digits of pi reflect the use of effective memorization strategies? Does Garry Kasparov have some innate (i.e., genetic) ability to play chess at an expert level, or have his years of experience taught him things that were not captured by the software running the original Deep Blue supercomputer? Is the confession of Paul Ingram to an event that never happened (the one fabricated by Richard Ofshe) an anomaly, or do people regularly mis-remember and come to remember events that did not occur?

Throughout this book, you will learn how cognitive psychologists attempt to answer these and other questions concerning human cognition. We begin by considering two aspects of human cognition that have important real-world implications: (a) how memory changes over time and (b) the accuracy of human memory.

Memory after the Fact

We turn first to changes in memory over time. In this example, we introduce an exercise that we use throughout the book. We refer to these exercises as **thought experiments.** A thought experiment is a mental exercise in which you consider what might happen in a specific hypothetical situation. In our thought experiments, we describe a hypothetical situation and either ask you to predict what will happen or tell you what happens and ask you to try to explain the results. Our students find these exercises very useful means for developing an understanding of the principles described in the text, and we hope that you will actively participate in these exercises.

Now, imagine that you are a juror in a trial involving a robbery that occurred a year ago. One of the key witnesses watched the robbery through a window from a distance of about 80 feet. One of the men involved in the crime was in view for approximately three seconds. At a preliminary hearing three weeks after the incident, this witness testified that she was not certain if the man charged with the crime was the man she had seen from her window. A great deal of media attention has been focused on the crime, and the accused person has been pictured frequently on the news and in newspapers. At the trial, the witness provides a detailed description of the man she saw during the crime, including details such as the length of the man's hair, his weight, the clothing he was wearing, and that he was clean shaven at the time of the crime. As a juror, what do you conclude? Do you believe the witness is telling the truth and that her memory has improved in the year following the crime?

Before you start to ponder this question, we should tell you that this hypothetical case is quite similar to the actual case of Sacco and Vanzetti (Frankfurter, 1927). In this real case, the witness saw the accused several times between the crime and the trial. Despite the fact that Sacco and Vanzetti had multiple alibis, they were convicted of robbery and murder and were executed for the crimes.

Can a person's memory improve during the retention interval following a brief glimpse of an event? Memory researchers (Erdelyi & Becker, 1974; Scrivner & Safer, 1988) have shown that under certain circumstances a person's memory for an event can actually improve across the retention interval. This increase in recall performance is called *hypermnesia,* and it is a reliable and robust memory phenomenon (Payne, 1987).

However, eyewitness memory researchers have also shown that what happens during the retention interval can greatly affect what a person reports having seen during a crime (e.g., Belli et al., 1994; Loftus & Palmer, 1974). For example, if during the retention interval a witness sees someone other than the person who actually committed the crime, the witness may erroneously come to "remember" this other person as the one who committed the crime (Loftus, 1979b). Scientists are working to discover the factors that cause people to make these types of errors (e.g., Ross, Ceci, Dunning, & Toglia, 1994; Whittlesea, 1993).

We have briefly described one line of research that shows that memory can improve across a retention interval *and* one line of research that shows that sometimes memory gets worse as time goes by. Surely the witness in our thought experiment could have been influenced by other factors that we have not considered, such as stress and the exact conditions under which she viewed the crime. Without a more complete understanding of the conditions under which the witness attempted to recall the crime, we cannot know exactly what caused the change in her memory.

You might be thinking that this is a poor "thought experiment" if it has no right answer. We would argue that it is a great thought exercise, because it highlights other questions to ask. As you will see, research is an active process in which the answers we find generally raise new sets of questions. In later chapters, we discuss many factors that could have affected this witness's memory.

Repressed and Recovered Memories

Repressed memories refer to memories that a person cannot bring into conscious awareness. Some (e.g., Bass & Davis, 1988) have argued that under certain conditions it is possible to "recover" these repressed memories and recall the original event. Others (e.g., Loftus & Ketchum, 1994) have argued that there is no firm scientific evidence for repressed memories and that some recovered memories may be false.

Repressed and recovered memories have taken on new importance as many adults have reported that they have recovered repressed memories dealing with childhood abuse, crimes against others, and so forth. In 1990, George Franklin became the first person convicted solely on the basis of his accuser's recalling a repressed memory (Horn, 1993). Franklin's daughter Eileen claimed to have recovered the memory of witnessing her father rape and murder her eight-year-old friend 20 years earlier. George Franklin has maintained that he is innocent.

In another case, Melody Gavigan entered psychotherapy to deal with depression and while in therapy reported what she thought were repressed memories of her father molesting her as an infant. She confronted her father with her accusations and severed her relationship with him. She later concluded that the memories were false and begged her father for forgiveness (Jaroff, 1993). In a number of other cases, too, people who initially claimed to have remembered an event from their past later came to believe that these memories were not accurate (Goldstein & Farmer, 1993).

As the cases of George and Eileen Franklin and Melody Gavigan demonstrate, accepting recovered memories as accurate records of previous events can have significant implications. Melody Gavigan appears to have remembered an event that never occurred. It seems that Paul Ingram, whom we met at the beginning of the chapter, had a similar experience. How can a person "remember" something that never happened? Does this occur only under very specific circumstances (e.g., when the person is very nervous or when the memories involve childhood experiences)? If "remembering" events that never occurred actually happens in the real world, can this phenomenon be studied in the laboratory?

One way that researchers study memory is to use word lists, under the assumption that reading a word constitutes an event in a person's life. To see how researchers have used this approach to try to assess the accuracy of memory, read Experiment 1A and complete the task described there before reading further.

George Franklin
As an adult, Eileen Franklin claimed that she had recovered memories of her father, George Franklin, murdering a childhood friend. George Franklin was convicted of the murder on the basis of his daughter's testimony. The conviction was overturned in 1995, and the prosecutor declined to bring the case to a new trial. Interestingly, the judge ruled that the defense in the original case had been unfairly prohibited from introducing evidence showing that most of the details of Eileen's memory had been previously reported in local news accounts of the crime.

EXPERIMENT 1A: Memory for Common Words

Presented below is a list of 50 words. Before looking at this list, please read the following instructions:

Read the words in the list one at a time. After you read each word, rate how pleasant the word is on a scale of 1 to 7, with 1 being *extremely unpleasant* and 7 being *extremely pleasant*. You can record your ratings next to the words or on a piece of paper numbered from 1 to 50. As you read and rate each word, also try to remember the word. After you finish reading and rating the pleasantness of each word, turn to Experiment 1B and follow the instructions there.

Word	Rating	Word	Rating
1. queen	_____	27. snooze	_____
2. England	_____	28. blanket	_____
3. crown	_____	29. doze	_____
4. prince	_____	30. slumber	_____
5. George	_____	31. table	_____
6. dictator	_____	32. sit	_____
7. palace	_____	33. legs	_____
8. throne	_____	34. seat	_____
9. chess	_____	35. couch	_____
10. rule	_____	36. desk	_____
11. shoe	_____	37. recliner	_____
12. hand	_____	38. sofa	_____
13. toe	_____	39. wood	_____
14. kick	_____	40. cushion	_____
15. sandals	_____	41. sour	_____
16. soccer	_____	42. candy	_____
17. yard	_____	43. sugar	_____
18. walk	_____	44. bitter	_____
19. ankle	_____	45. good	_____
20. arm	_____	46. taste	_____
21. bed	_____	47. tooth	_____
22. rest	_____	48. nice	_____
23. awake	_____	49. honey	_____
24. tired	_____	50. soda	_____
25. dream	_____	Stop. Now turn to Experiment 1B	
26. wake	_____	and follow the instructions.	

EXPERIMENT 1B: Assessing Memory Accuracy

Listed below are 25 words. Read each word and decide if it was on the list you read in Experiment 1A or was not on that list. Place a check in the appropriate column to mark your answer, or record your answers on a sheet of paper numbered from 1 to 25.

Word	On List	Not on List	Word	On List	Not on List
1. piano	_____	_____	14. sandals	_____	_____
2. hand	_____	_____	15. king	_____	_____
3. sit	_____	_____	16. frigid	_____	_____
4. tough	_____	_____	17. throne	_____	_____
5. foot	_____	_____	18. desk	_____	_____
6. blanket	_____	_____	19. hospital	_____	_____
7. boat	_____	_____	20. sweet	_____	_____
8. crown	_____	_____	21. awake	_____	_____
9. loud	_____	_____	22. pear	_____	_____
10. sleep	_____	_____	23. taste	_____	_____
11. climb	_____	_____	24. creek	_____	_____
12. winter	_____	_____	25. chair	_____	_____
13. sour	_____	_____			

Ecological Validity

Here are the correct answers to the memory test you just completed. Items 2, 3, 6, 8, 13, 14, 17, 18, 21, and 23 were on the study list, and Items 1, 4, 7, 9, 11, 12, 16, 19, 22, and 24 were not on the list. How accurate were you at identifying the items from the list and rejecting the items that were not on the list?

The interesting part of the demonstration comes from five items that you have not scored yet. Items 5, 10, 15, 20, and 25 were *not* on the study list. Were you able to reject these items as accurately as you rejected the other ten new words, or did you falsely recognize these items as having been on the list? Studies similar to this demonstration (e.g., Payne et al., 1996; Roediger & McDermott, 1995) have shown that people often falsely recognize these items as having appeared in the study list. This phenomenon has been termed a **false memory,** a memory for an event (in this case, a word on a list) that never occurred.

Laboratory studies may shed some light on why people might experience false memories in the real world. Still, there is controversy over whether experiments with word lists are relevant to the recovered/false memory controversy, because the "events" in the laboratory studies—words in a list—are very different from the types of events that people recover in the real world (Freyd & Gleaves, 1996; Roediger & McDermott, 1996).

This raises the issue of **ecological validity,** the extent to which processes studied in a laboratory task capture important aspects of the real-world task of interest. In the case of false memories, some researchers (e.g., Loftus & Pickerell, 1995) are using different procedures to examine situations in which people remember more complex events that did not occur, such as getting lost in a mall.

Ecological validity is primarily concerned with the extent to which results from laboratory research can be used to explain what happens in the real world. If a task has high ecological validity, then the cognitive processes employed in performing the task are similar to those used in the real world. Under these conditions, it would be appropriate to generalize the results from the lab to make predictions about the real world. Note that ecological validity does not require that the real-world task be used in the laboratory. Rather, what is essential is that the same cognitive underlying processes are at work in the two situations.

Section Summary: Studying the Human Mind

Cognitive psychologists are interested in identifying the processes that underlie the workings of the human mind. They use controlled experiments to test ideas about the mind, and this approach has several advantages. Although some topics cannot be studied by use of controlled experiments, it is still possible to try to create situations and tasks that mimic important aspects of the real-world phenomenon of interest. The false-memory demonstration illustrates one such situation. Still, we need to exercise caution when generalizing the results of these laboratory studies to life beyond the laboratory. Important factors may be operating in the real world (e.g., extreme stress) that we cannot mimic in the laboratory.

HISTORICAL ANTECEDENTS OF MODERN COGNITIVE PSYCHOLOGY

As Carl Sagan noted in the quote at the beginning of the chapter, understanding the processes scientists employ to advance knowledge is actually more important than memorizing experimental findings. That is why a central premise of this text is that contemporary cognitive psychological research and theories can only be fully understood when they are viewed within the *context* in which the research was conducted and the theories were developed. This premise is based on the simple fact that science does not occur in a vacuum; it occurs within a larger historical and social context. This context exerts considerable influence on the activities of the researchers in a field.

We turn now to a consideration of the historical context of cognitive psychology. Developing an appreciation for these earlier efforts helps us to see how the questions asked by cognitive psychologists are related to the larger goal of understanding the human mind. Another reason for placing cognitive psychological research in a historical context is that much of the contemporary research examining human cognition is highly interdisciplinary. Hence, it helps to consider where and how cognitive psychology fits in with other areas of inquiry.

Early Studies of the Human Mind

Scholars have long debated issues concerning the human mind, and many of these debates continue today. The debates have relied on a wide range of approaches to studying the human mind, from casual introspection about how our minds seem to work through controlled experiments using trained observers. We start our review with some of the oldest writings on the nature of the human mind.

Relating Physical Stimuli and Psychological Phenomena   One of the most important developments in any scientific enterprise is the ability to classify and measure the events and phenomena of interest. Pythagoras (584–495 B.C.), a Greek mathematician, was one of the first to apply mathematical theory to psychological experience. In Pythagoras' time, it was well known that if one took a string from a musical instrument such as a harp and plucked it, it produced a *ground note,* a note with a specific pitch. Pythagoras discovered that if the string was cut into halves or quarters and one of the pieces was plucked, the note produced was harmonious with the ground note; other divisions of the string yielded notes that were not harmonious with the ground note.

An important implication of Pythagoras' finding was that it is possible to relate measurements of the physical world to unobservable psychological events—in this case, the perception of sounds as being either harmonious or not harmonious. This is especially important for cognitive psychology because the mental processes that underlie intelligent behavior are unobservable. Researchers can only infer them from the effects of varying the information or tasks given to the subjects in a study.

Early Philosophical Views on the Mind   The early Greek philosophers also made important contributions to the way we view the human mind. Socrates (469–399 B.C.) held firmly that it is essential to question life and that what we learn during life is to a large extent determined by the types of questions we ask. Socrates was so convinced of the importance of this questioning attitude that he developed an approach to education that has come to be known as the *Socratic method* of instruction (Klein, 1975; Teagle, 1986). In this method, the teacher guides the learner to the solution to a problem rather than simply presenting the solution. Interest in the utility of this type of learning (often referred to as *discovery learning;* McDaniel & Schlager, 1990) has continued over the years. Another interesting notion about the human mind that can be traced to Socrates is the view that the human mind plays an active role in transforming and manipulating the products of perception rather than passively responding to external events.

A major contribution made by Socrates' student Plato (427–347 B.C.) is the distinction between sensations as they arise from our sensory systems and what Plato called *forms,* the internal representations revealed to us through our rational thoughts. The notion that different forms of information may be represented in the human mind is one of the cornerstones of modern cognitive psychology.

A third Greek philosopher whose ideas had an impact on cognitive psychology was Aristotle (384–322 B.C.). Socrates and Plato stressed that the human senses were imperfect and that therefore reality could only be known through the application of logic and reason. In contrast, Aristotle emphasized an inductive, empirical approach. Aristotle's approach was *empirical* in that he relied on observations rather than strictly rational analysis, and it was *inductive* in that he believed that from many specific observations one could ascertain general truths. As we noted earlier, modern cognitive psychology relies heavily on empirical methods.

The work of Socrates, Plato and Aristotle is important because it addresses a core issue faced by cognitive psychologists: How do people acquire knowledge? We will consider this issue further in Chapter 4 when we discuss how we perceive the world around us. Another important issue addressed in these philosophical works concerned memory: Once we have acquired knowledge how do we maintain that knowledge over time? Aristotle also exerted a tremendous influence on later psychologists through his treatise *De Memoria* ("Concerning Memory"). In this work, Aristotle outlined a theory that presumed that memory results from associations that are formed and stored in the human mind. This type of associative model is still prevalent in our everyday, informal theories of memory as well as in the scientific theories offered and tested by cognitive psychologists.

British Empiricists and Associationists   During the period 1600–1900, many philosophers thought about issues such as how people acquire knowledge and how they represent the external world in their minds. Some of the most influential philosophers during this period were the early British empiricists and associationists Thomas Hobbes (1588–1679), John Locke (1623–1704), James Mill (1773–1836), and John Stuart Mill (1806–1873). These scholars held that knowledge is gained through experience with the world and that experiences with the world are stored in the mind as associations.

The issues of the day for these scholars included what types of associations could be stored in the mind and how these associations were organized and related to one another. For example, James Mill, and later his son John Stuart Mill, described in considerable detail the manner in which events in the environment can give rise to thoughts. James Mill described the process as follows:

> If our senses are awake, we are continually receiving sensations, of the eye, ear, the touch, and so forth; but not sensations alone. After sensations, ideas are perpetually excited of sensations formerly received; after those ideas, other ideas; and during the whole of our lives, a series of these two states of consciousness, called sensations, and ideas, is constantly going on. I see a horse; that is a sensation. Immediately I think of his master; that is an idea. The idea of his master makes me think of this office; he is a minister of the state: that is another idea. (Mill, 1829, cited in Rand, 1912, p. 463, and in Hothersall, 1984, p. 49)

James Mill also distinguished among different types of sensations and ideas. For example, he proposed that simple ideas serve as the building blocks for more complex ideas. John Stuart Mill later developed an elaborate approach for describing how simple ideas could be formed into more complex ideas. The ideas that the younger Mill proposed were based in the developing physical science of chemistry, and his approach came to be described as *mental chemistry.*

Early Studies of the Brain and Nervous System   A number of significant advances made during the 1800s in biology and medicine contributed to our current understanding of mental processes. Physiologists made considerable progress in describing the gross anatomy of the nervous system. This knowledge allowed researchers to begin to understand the connections among various parts of the nervous system. Other advances involved the functioning of the nervous system. One such advance was the doctrine of *specific nerve energies,* proposed by Johannes Mueller (1801–1858).

Mueller argued that in order for the sensory systems and the brain to be able to distinguish, say, information arising from the eyes from information arising from the ears, either the sensory systems must convey different types of information *(nerve energy)* to the brain or the sensory systems must send their information to different regions of the brain. As you will see in Chapter 2, we now know that the sensory systems accomplish their tasks in part through the projection of information to different areas in the brain and in part through the specialization of the nervous system for performing certain types of tasks.

Several discoveries in the middle 1800s showed that specific areas of the brain are involved in processing different kinds of sensory information and in controlling different cognitive processes. For example, Paul Broca (1824–1880) reported that persons who suffered damage to a localized area of the left side of the brain were not able to speak but could still understand spoken language. Carl Wernicke later showed that damage to another area on the left side of the brain resulted in difficulty in speaking meaningful sentences. Other studies demonstrated that the normal functioning of the intact human nervous system could be studied with behavioral measures. For example, Hermann von Helmholtz (1821–1894) devised several simple yet clever ways to demonstrate that it was possible to measure the speed of a neural impulse.

The findings of researchers working during the 1800s are important because they revealed fundamental physiological properties of the nervous system. They also demonstrated that through careful observation we can discern how the workings of the human nervous system are related to mental processes. Modern clinical work continuing this tradition has yielded many important and interesting facts. Some of this work and the research techniques used to study the human brain are presented in Chapter 2.

Structuralism and Gestalt Psychology

In 1879, in Leipzig, Germany, Wilhelm Wundt (1832–1920) established the first psychological laboratory and set the stage for much of the early experimental research in the newly developing field of psychology. The school of thought established by Wundt is known as **structuralism.** Structuralism holds that the primary goal of psychology is to specify the nature of conscious experience through the use of introspection.

Wundt argued that psychologists must address three basic questions (Marx & Hillix, 1973):

1. What are the components of consciousness? For example, what sensations give rise to the feeling of wetness or to an apple's appearance of redness?
2. How are these elemental parts connected? If cold and pressure are the basic units that give rise to the feeling of wetness, for example, then how do these individual sensations combine to produce the feeling of wetness?
3. What are the laws governing the ways in which these elements come to be connected? Can all basic sensations be combined, or are there classes of sensations that interact in specific ways?

As you may have noticed, the questions posed by the structuralists are quite similar to the issues addressed by the Mills and especially John Stuart Mill in his "mental chemistry." What separates the approach of the philosophers from that of scientists such as Wundt and his followers is their research strategy. Whereas the philosophers were comfortable with casual introspection—thinking about what they were sensing, thinking, or feeling—Wundt embraced a procedure known as **analytical introspection.**

Analytical introspection involves having trained observers report on the contents of their conscious, moment-to-moment experience as they perceive an object or event. Wundt trained his observers to report the basic sensations they experienced rather than their interpretations of these experiences. For example, if asked about the experience of viewing an apple, an observer might report "red, round" but not "an apple." *Red* and *round* represent basic descriptions of the stimulus, whereas *apple* signifies how these basic properties of the stimulus are interpreted and classified.

For a variety of reasons (e.g., lack of agreement among observers), the analytical introspection technique, as well as Wundt's structuralist approach, eventually fell into disfavor. Still, the work of the early structuralists served to establish psychology as an empirical science, and that tradition continues today. An interesting long-term consequence of the criticisms leveled at the method of analytical introspection was that for decades verbal reports of personal experiences were viewed as unacceptable forms of scientific data. In more recent times, this view has been challenged (e.g., Ericsson & Simon, 1984), and verbal reports are now taken as evidence in a number of areas of cognitive psychology (e.g., Crutcher, 1994; Long & Bourg, 1996; Predebon & Woolley, 1994).

Soon after the structuralists began the task of decomposing the stream of consciousness, another group of German psychologists, including Max Wertheimer (1880–1943), Kurt Koffka (1886–1941), and Wolfgang Köhler (1887–1967), reported a series of intriguing demonstrations of phenomena that they argued could not be accounted for by the structuralist approach. One such phenomenon, called the phi phenomenon, is illustrated in Figure 1.1.

Based on their demonstrations, Wertheimer and the other German psychologists formed a school known as **Gestalt psychology.** Gestalt psychology emphasizes the importance of whole patterns in perception as opposed to the reduction of perception into constituent parts. One of the main contributions of the Gestalt psychologists has been their argument that the mind cannot be viewed as a collection of individual elements. In the words of the Gestalt psychologists, the whole is different from the sum of the parts. That is, many of the properties we experience when we perceive a whole stimulus (e.g., a barking dog) are actually *emergent* properties—properties that do not belong to any single part or component of the object but that emerge when the parts are perceived as a whole (Boring, 1950, p. 588). These ideas have had a tremendous impact on many cognitive psychologists and have led researchers to look for interrelations among mental processes rather than simply breaking down mental processes into smaller and smaller subprocesses.

Behaviorism and the Associationist Tradition

By the early 1900s, many psychologists had grown unhappy with the rather murky mentalistic concepts (i.e., subjective and not open to public scrutiny) of the structuralists and

FIGURE 1.1   **The Phi Phenomenon**   When two adjacent lights blink on and off at a rate of about 20 times per second, what the observer experiences is not two lights blinking but a single light moving between the two locations. Wertheimer (1912) argued that, because there is no sensory input that corresponds to the light perceived as being between the two lights' actual locations, the phi phenomenon cannot be accounted for by the structuralist approach. The phi phenomenon allows us to perceive displays like that on the New York Stock Exchange "ticker tape" display not as a set of lights flashing on and off but rather as a moving message.

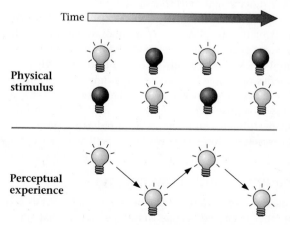

Gestalt psychologists. These psychologists argued that psychology needed to change its emphasis from unobservable mental processes to observable events and behaviors. This sentiment formed part of the basis of **behaviorism,** the dominant approach to psychology in America beginning in the early 1900s and continuing until the 1960s. One of the main tenets of behaviorism is that learning consists of the development of associations between stimuli and responses. This focus on associations places the behaviorists clearly within the associationistic tradition of the philosophers Hobbes, Locke, and Mills.

In an influential series of articles and textbooks, John B. Watson (1878–1958) laid out the fundamental assumptions on which the school of behaviorism was established. One of the main points Watson made was that psychology should concern itself with events and observations that are objective and open to public scrutiny. A major problem that had arisen within the structuralist school was that disagreements often arose among the trained introspectionists; given the same stimulus, different observers would report that they experienced different sensations. This, Watson argued, was unacceptable if psychology was a science, because one of the hallmarks of all sciences is that, to be accepted as a scientific fact, an observation must be *replicable,* or repeatable.

To focus on observable phenomena, the behaviorists set out to discern the relations between stimuli and the responses of organisms to those stimuli. The behaviorists explicitly rejected the investigation of such concepts as consciousness, imagery, and attention, arguing that such phenomena are not directly observable and hence, fall outside the bounds of scientific psychology.

Researchers working in the behaviorist tradition identified a number of important principles of learning and memory. These well-documented findings were of great use to the psychologists who began the cognitive revolution in the late 1950s. (We return to the cognitive revolution in the next section.) In addition, after the cognitive revolution began, many behaviorists "changed hats" and considered themselves cognitive psychologists. Furthermore, many of the concepts employed by the behaviorists (e.g., associations between events) are used extensively today in cognitive psychology.

A final point regarding the behaviorists concerns the types of theoretical mechanisms these theorists proposed. History shows us that some of the ideas of the "new" cognitive psychology of the late 1950s were in fact foreshadowed by the work of behaviorist researchers of the early 1930s. For example, Edward C. Tolman (1886–1959) was a behaviorist who studied, among other things, how hungry rats learn to navigate a maze to find food in a goal box. According to a strictly associationistic account of this learning, the animal learns a series of responses (e.g., left, left, right, left) that are reinforced by the food.

To see if what the animals had learned was a series of simple associations, Tolman blocked off part of the maze, thus making it impossible for the animals to reach the goal box by the series of responses it had supposedly learned. Tolman (1948) showed that under these conditions the animal would quickly learn a new path to the goal box. He proposed that, rather than learning a series of simple responses, the animals had actually developed what he called a **cognitive map**—in essence, an internal representation of the shape of the maze. Today, cognitive psychologists such as Barbara Tversky (1996) continue to study topics related to cognitive maps. Tolman thus made an important theoretical contribution—the notion of an internal representation of the world—as well as establishing an area of active research.

The Emergence of Contemporary Cognitive Psychology

Beginning in the late 1950s, psychologists began to reject the behaviorists' emphasis on observable stimuli and the responses they elicit and instead came to embrace what Ulric

Edward C. Tolman
Edward C. Tolman (1886–1959) received his Ph.D. from Harvard University and spent most of his academic career at the University of California, Berkeley. Tolman is credited with blending the behaviorists' focus on careful, objective observations of behavior with his own interest in cognition. He discovered that rats that learned to navigate through mazes developed cognitive maps, or internal representations of the spatial arrangements of the mazes.

Neisser (1967) later termed *cognitive psychology.* Unlike behaviorism, which avoids terms and concepts that are subjective and unobservable, cognitive psychology as Neisser defined it clearly embraces a number of concepts that cannot be directly observed:

> cognition refers to all processes by which the sensory input is transformed, reduced, elaborated, stored, recovered, and used. It is concerned with these processes even when they operate in the absence of relevant stimulation as in images and hallucinations. Such terms as *sensations, perception, imagery, retention, recall, problem solving,* and *thinking* among many others, refer to hypothetical stages or aspects of cognition. (Neisser, 1967, p. 4)

In this section, we briefly review several disciplines that contributed to the reemergence of the study of the mind following behaviorism's reign. Each of these disciplines includes numerous theories and aspects of the scientific approach. Cognitive psychologists incorporated some of these theories and aspects of the scientific approach into their own theorizing and research and rejected others.

Verbal Learning   A very influential branch of experimental psychology from the 1930s through the 1950s was **verbal learning,** a subdiscipline of behaviorism concerned with how people acquire, retain, and form associations among verbal units such as letters, words, and nonsense syllables. Nonsense syllables (e.g., KIB) were often used because it was assumed that these items did not have meaning for experimental subjects and hence enabled researchers to study how novel items were learned and associated over repeated study trials.

Many very productive researchers worked in the verbal learning tradition, and these researchers established a number of important findings, as well as many research techniques for studying learning and memory. The verbal learning researchers generally made an easy transition into cognitive psychology and brought with them their focus on memory as a critical issue for study, their empirical data base, and their skill in and knowledge of experimental methodology.

One aspect of the verbal learning tradition was a reliance on simple acquired associations as a means to account for human language capabilities. As described next, cognitive psychologists rejected this aspect of the tradition.

Linguistics   In 1957, the famous behaviorist B. F. Skinner published a book entitled *Verbal Behavior* in which he attempted to account for human language acquisition in terms of reinforcement principles. Skinner's book attracted considerable attention. Soon after it was published, Noam Chomsky, a linguist, presented a detailed critique of this behavioristic approach to language in a journal article (Chomsky, 1959). Although in the title of his article Chomsky identified Skinner's theory as the object of his critique, in fact Chomsky was arguing against all similar accounts of language acquisition and use, including those of linguists who had embraced the behaviorist tradition (e.g., Bloomfield, 1933).

Chomsky argued, in essence, that behavioristic accounts fail to explain many aspects of language acquisition and use. We examine the differences between Skinner's and Chomsky's views in more detail in Chapter 9. For now, we simply note that, in general, Chomsky's view can be said to have prevailed. This outcome was not determined strictly on the basis of the scientific merits of Chomsky's arguments, however. Numerous changes in the scientific community in the late 1950s contributed to many psychologists' embracing the main points of Chomsky's arguments and, as a result, shifting the focus of research on the psychology of language (see Carroll, 1986, pp. 15–22, and Lachman, Lachman, & Butterfield, 1979, pp. 75–87, for a review of some of these factors). Finally, although it is sometimes implied that Skinner's approach to language was incapable of capturing the creative aspect of language use, Skinner in fact devoted several pages of his text to this issue (Skinner, 1957, pp. 456–460). Skinner's arguments may not have won the battle, but he certainly was aware of the issues involved.

Linguistics offered a great deal to the development of cognitive psychology. It provided a host of reasons for rejecting the behaviorist approach to accounting for complex mental phenomena such as language. It also offered language as an important topic area for study. Along with that came a reason to reject the animal research that had prevailed in the behaviorist tradition. Finally, linguists pointed to many examples in which human behavior (in this case, speech) reveals both *ruliness* (behavior that appears to follow high-level rules) and significant creativity. Accounting for ruliness and creativity became one of the goals of cognitive psychology. We discuss this issue further in Chapter 9 when we review how humans produce language.

Human Factors   An interesting fact sometimes lost in science education is that scientists are part of the society they live in and are affected by events in society just as all other citizens are. During World War II, experimental psychologists were called on to address problems that were arising in the military. One of these problems was that soldiers were being asked to use increasingly sophisticated pieces of equipment (e.g., radar and aircraft), and many tragic occurrences involving equipment were being attributed to human error. For example, in many instances, pilots were pulling up their landing gear just before landing—not a good thing to do! These pilots were often required to fly many different types of aircraft, and these aircraft had not been standardized as to the shape and location of the controls used for various functions. Thus, a response that was appropriate in one aircraft might lead to an accidental raising of the landing gear in another aircraft.

Experimental psychologists were thus drawn into the developing field of **human factors,** a discipline that deals with the interaction of persons and machines. This movement had several important consequences. First, psychologists came into direct contact with scientists from the physical sciences and engineering, resulting in a healthy exchange of ideas across disciplines. We will see one excellent example of the benefits of such an exchange when we consider the theory of signal detection in Chapter 3.

A second consequence of psychologists' human factors experience during World War II was that it became clear that many of the theories developed by the behaviorists could not be applied to the types of tasks that human operators were being asked to perform. As a result, human factors psychologists began to develop views of the human operator that highlighted cognitive processes such as attention, decision making, and problem solving. After World War II, many of the researchers who had been involved with human factors research returned to university and industrial laboratories and took with them the experience and knowledge gained from trying to solve real-world problems.

Finally, the wartime efforts of psychologists demonstrated that psychological research could produce data and theory that had real-world applications. In consequence, after the war, the federal governments of several countries (e.g., Great Britain and the United States) provided considerable support for continued psychological research.

Computer Science and Communications Engineering   Two disciplines—computer science and communications engineering—have contributed to cognitive psychology in similar ways. Both provide analogies on which to build cognitive models as well as experimental and theoretical concepts on which to ground research.

From computer science, cognitive psychology borrowed the analogy of humans as sym-

The human factors field has contributed in many ways to the development of modern devices that are regularly used at home, at work, and in leisure activities.

bol manipulators. In the 1940s and 1950s, computer scientists had considerable success in getting machines to exhibit behavior that appeared intelligent. These developments came about through the use of computers as manipulators of abstract symbols. Psychologists began to view humans in a similar fashion. Cognitive psychologists also began to view humans as analogous to computers in the sense that both humans and computers must take in information from the outside world, store that information over time, and use the information to make responses or produce output. This analogy between the computer and the human mind was the dominant one throughout the early history of cognitive psychology, and it still serves a useful purpose. It is important to keep in mind, however, that in many ways the human brain still far exceeds the computer in its capabilities—a point well illustrated by the victory of Garry Kasparov over Deep Blue described earlier.

From communications engineering, cognitive psychology borrowed a number of concepts that shared as a common theme the notion that stimuli in the environment can be viewed as messages and that what humans do is transmit these messages via the nervous system to the "destination" manifest in specific responses. For example, you might consider the handwritten notes for this chapter as signals that are transmitted to the destination of the keys on a computer keyboard by a typist. Using this analogy, you can meaningfully ask questions such as how efficiently the information is transmitted from the source to the destination. Communications engineering developed an impressive array of theories and measurement techniques that psychologists applied to the study of human performance.

Section Summary: Historical Antecedents

Many disciplines contributed to the development of cognitive psychology. Furthermore, cognitive psychologists are concerned with issues that have been debated by scholars for centuries, and the scientific investigations of cognitive psychologists must be evaluated in the context of these earlier investigations. One component of the historical context of cognitive philosophy is philosophy. Cognitive psychology drew upon ideas proposed by philosophers but differs from philosophy in its reliance on empirical methods to evaluate accounts of the human mind. Cognitive psychology also benefited from many early biological and medical studies of the nervous system. The end of the nineteenth century saw the emergence of the new field of psychology, clearly a vital contributor to cognitive psychology. Structuralism and Gestalt psychology, early schools of psychological thought, emphasized subjective methods of research. Behaviorism rejected subjectivity to focus on objective events and observations. Starting in the latter half of the twentieth century, developments in verbal learning, linguistics, human factors, computer science, and communications engineering contributed to a return of psychologists' interest from the behaviorists' focus on observable events to questions concerning the mind and mental processes.

BASIC ASSUMPTIONS IN COGNITIVE PSYCHOLOGY

Cognitive psychologists vary considerably in the approaches they take to studying human mental processes and the theories they embrace. Despite these differences, cognitive psychologists share three basic assumptions that serve to unite them and to differentiate the cognitive approach from other approaches in psychology (e.g., behaviorism). These three assumptions are that (a) mental processes exist, (b) humans are active information processors, and (c) mental processes can be identified through the use of behavioral measures such as reaction times and patterns of correct and incorrect responses.

Existence of Mental Processes

The most fundamental assumption made by cognitive psychologists is that mental processes not only exist but also are appropriate subject matter for scientific investigation. Mental processes are viewed as systematic and lawful in nature. The goal of cognitive psychology is to identify what these processes are, how they function, and how they work together to give rise to the human mind.

As we have discussed, earlier schools of psychology either attempted to study the human mind (e.g., the structuralists) or rejected the notion that the human mind could be studied scientifically (e.g., the behaviorists). One of the criticisms raised against the earlier attempts to study the mind was that the methods employed in these efforts did not meet accepted scientific standards, such as reliability and replicability. Cognitive psychologists, mindful of these lessons, have strived to devise research methods that will withstand close scrutiny. Cognitive psychologists are also aware that some of the criticisms of early studies raised by the behaviorists (e.g., lack of precise definitions of terms such as *imagery* and *attention*) are valid and must be addressed by researchers dealing with unobservable mental processes. As a consequence, cognitive psychologists strive to employ objective and reliable measures and to state their assumptions concerning mental processes in a manner that is not influenced by subjective biases.

Humans as Active Information Processors

Early behaviorists viewed humans as largely passive organisms who respond to the environment as a consequence of prior conditioning. In contrast, cognitive psychologists assume that humans are active information processors. That is, humans do not simply wait to form associations between stimuli and responses. Rather, human mental processes are actively involved in selecting information from the environment, forming hypotheses during problem solving, reflecting on the consequences of actions, and so forth.

One simple but elegant demonstration of the active role mental processes play in cognitive tasks is provided by the phenomenon of **subjective organization,** a process by which people organize lists of randomly organized items (Tulving, 1962). In studies of subjective organization, people are given multiple opportunities to study a list of words. On each presentation of the list, the words are presented in a new random order. After each list presentation, subjects are asked to recall the words in any order they choose, but they tend to recall the items in a similar order on all tests. The list organization differs from person to person, and hence the name *subjective* organization. Despite the facts that (a) they are not required to organize the list and (b) the list is presented in a new order each time, people nonetheless impose an order on the list, and this order differs across subjects—a subjective organization.

The assumptions that mental processes exist and that humans are active information processors are central to cognitive psychology. In fact, these assumptions are so central that they are never explicitly stated in cognitive theories; they are simply accepted as valid by cognitive psychologists. Assumptions that have this status are referred to as **metatheoretical assumptions,** assumptions that go beyond the specifics of any individual theory. These two assumptions together lead to the third basic assumption made by cognitive psychologists, which involves how they can study these active mental processes.

Inferring Mental Processes from Behavior

Cognitive psychologists assume that mental processes can be inferred from two general aspects of human behavior: (a) the time it takes to make a response and (b) the patterns of responses people make in specific situations. Cognitive psychologists rely quite heavily on reaction-time measures. **Reaction time** refers to the length of time between the presentation of a stimulus and a subject's response. It is assumed that mental processes use a finite amount of time in processing information (either information conveyed through a stimulus or information stored in memory) and that by carefully examining the patterns of reaction times across various conditions, we can discern the nature of the mental processes involved in performing a task.

Reaction-Time Measures Over a hundred years ago, the Dutch physiologist Donders developed a simple, clever technique for measuring the duration of various mental processes by using the three conditions illustrated in the upper panel of Figure 1.2. Donders' method is called the *subtractive method* because it involves measuring the reaction time of subjects performing several tasks and then using subtraction to compute the time required for individual processes.

In a Donders A task, a light goes on, and the subject responds by pressing a response key. A real-world example of a simple reaction-time task is the start of a 100-meter dash. There is a single stimulus, the crack from the starter's gun, and there is one response: start running!

A Donders B task requires the person to observe two stimuli and make a different response depending on which stimulus is presented. A good example of such a reaction-time task is approaching an intersection with a traffic light. After seeing the traffic signal, you make one response if the light is red (pressing on the brake pedal) and another if the light is green (pressing on the accelerator pedal).

Finally, in a Donders C task, more than one stimulus may appear, but the person makes a response only to one specific stimulus. You have experienced this type of task if you have ever been at a fast-food restaurant or a deli where you take a number before you place your order. As the numbers of others are read off, you wait until your number is called, and only then do you give the clerk your order. In this case, there are many stimuli—the numbers being called out—but you only make the single response of ordering your food when your number is called. Let's see how the method works using Donders' simple tasks. Donders proposed that it is possible to use the reaction times from the Donders A, B, and C tasks to estimate the time required to identify a stimulus (mental identification) and to select a response (mental selection). The time required for mental identification is estimated by subtracting the reaction time for the A task from the reaction time for the C task. Subtracting the reaction time for the B task from the reaction time for the C task gives the time required for mental selection. Donders' subtractive method showed that by using behavioral measures researchers can estimate the amount of time required for various mental processes.

Although the logic underlying Donders' subtractive method is straightforward, it turns out that some subtle problems with this approach have limited its application as a modern research tool. To illustrate, one of the problems concerns the A task: If subjects can predict when the stimulus is going to be presented, then they can prepare to make the response shortly after the time when the stimulus is to be presented, rather than in response to the actual stimulus. For this reason, in many track and field contests, race officials vary the interval between the "get ready" signal and the shooting of the starting gun. In world-class running events, they also measure the time between when the starter's pistol goes off and when the runners leave the starting block. Runners who leave too soon after the gun goes off are assumed to have started before they heard the gun go off, and the start is ruled a misstart. Such a mistake can have disastrous consequences: In the 1996

FIGURE 1.2

Donders A, B, and C Reaction-Time Tasks (a) In the A reaction-time task, there is one stimulus and one response. The B task involves multiple stimuli and multiple responses. The C task involves multiple stimuli, but only one of these stimuli requires a response.

(b) The subtractive method. By using the reaction times from the Donders A, B, and C reaction times it is possible to estimate the time required to identify a stimulus (mental identification) and to select a response (mental selection). See text for description of the subtractive method.

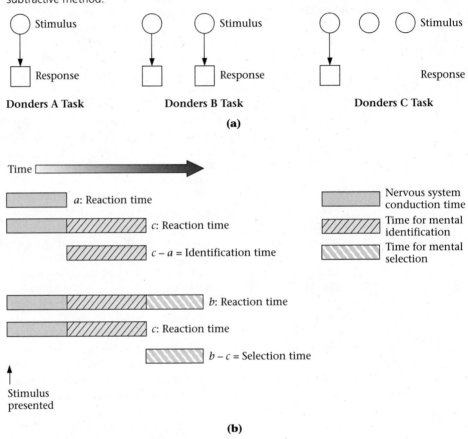

Source: Adapted from Kantowitz & Sorkin (1983).

Summer Olympics in Atlanta, Linford Christie, the defending champion in the event, was disqualified from the finals of the 100-meter race because he started too quickly on two attempts.

Although we now have more complex and sophisticated methods for attempting to estimate the durations and nature of mental processes (e.g., Dutta, Schweickert, Choi, & Proctor, R. W., 1995; Sternberg, 1966, 1975; Townsend & Schweickert, 1989), we should not overlook the historical importance of Donders' contributions. His method was important in showing that behavioral measures could be used to estimate the durations of unobservable mental processes.

Response Patterns Cognitive psychologists also use subjects' response patterns to gain insights into the nature of mental processes. The data that led to the discovery of the subjective organization phenomenon, described earlier, represents an example of how response patterns can help identify mental processes. Cognitive psychologists also frequently use error rates as an important index of mental processes. Error rates are often used in conjunction with reaction-time measures to compare performance across different conditions of interest.

Finally, cognitive psychologists analyze the nature of errors that subjects make. For example, a subject in a memory experiment who recalls an item that was not on the original study list is said to have made an *intrusion error.* This error might involve incorrectly recalling a word that is associated with a studied item (e.g., incorrectly recalling the word *chair* when *table* was on the list) or a word that rhymes with a studied word (e.g., recalling *cable* instead of *table*). The nature of the errors people make can provide important information concerning how a task is being performed. For example, if a subject's intrusion errors are associated with the study items, then this suggests that what the subject is storing in memory is the meaning of the study items. If the errors rhyme with the study items, then presumably what the subject has stored in memory is what the items sound like rather than what they mean.

Section Summary: Basic Assumptions

Cognitive psychologists make three assumptions that influence how they study the human mind. They assume, first, that mental processes exist and furthermore that they are appropriate subject matter for scientific investigation. Cognitive psychologists also assume that humans are active information processors rather than passive organisms whose behaviors are shaped through reinforcement. These first two assumptions are rarely made explicit in the theories used by cognitive psychologists, yet they provide the basis for many of the approaches used to understand the functioning of the human mind. Finally, cognitive psychologists assume that they can identify mental processes by examining how people respond as they perform specific tasks. Many different techniques, such as reaction-time measures and studies of response patterns, help cognitive psychologists to draw inferences about the human mind based on such responses.

EXPLANATIONS IN COGNITIVE PSYCHOLOGY

The three general goals of science are to describe, predict, and explain the phenomena of interest. Cognitive psychologists use a variety of theoretical tools in working toward these three goals. In this section, we review the main types of theoretical explanations used in cognitive psychology. In later chapters we will describe how the types of theoretical explanations used by scientists affect the types of data they collect and the research strategies they use.

Metaphors and Analogies

When people are confronted with phenomena that they do not understand or that are extremely complex, a common response is to try to explain these phenomena by comparing or relating them to more familiar things. Metaphors and analogies are frequently used in science to make complex ideas more understandable. For example, in physics, we might compare sound waves to waves on water. In psychology, we might say that memory is like

Linford Christie
After two false starts, Linford Christie was disqualified from the finals of the 100-meter dash in the 1996 Summer Olympics in Atlanta. Sensors on the starting blocks indicated that he had left the blocks too soon after the starter's gun went off, indicating that he was anticipating the gunshot rather than starting to run when he heard it.

a filing cabinet and when we learn things we place them into this cabinet according to some filing scheme (Roediger, 1980a).

Using metaphors to try to explain cognitive processes presents both advantages and disadvantages (Payne & Blackwell, 1998). For purposes of conveying basic ideas, such as many of the concepts we will be discussing in the following chapters, metaphors and analogies are extremely useful, and we will make extensive use of them. As rigorous scientific explanations, however, metaphors are limited. Scientists prefer to work with explanations that are more precise and less tied to appeals to other objects and phenomena. Saying that memory is like a filing cabinet is a nice way to convey the notion that information in memory is organized, but it does not readily lend itself to generating new ideas for research.

Theories and Models

In lay terms, when we say that some statement is true "in theory," we generally mean that the statement is probably not true. This is *not* what cognitive psychologists mean when they refer to a theory. For our purposes a **theory** is a set of related statements proposed to explain phenomena of interest. A theory may be represented in terms of a set of verbal descriptions, systems of mathematical equations, or computer programs. The vast majority of theories in cognitive psychology are stated in terms of verbal descriptions. It is becoming increasingly common, however, for cognitive theories to be stated as computer simulations or as mathematical equations, for these quantitative theories are more precise and subject to empirical tests.

Theories in cognitive psychology serve two main purposes. First, theories allow scientists to organize their data. That is, as more and more research is done within any content area, empirical findings accumulate. Rather than view the results of individual experiments as being unrelated to one another, scientists can use a theory to organize the experiments according both to the results of the experiments and to the portion of the theory related to the experiment (e.g., Posner, 1982).

Second, theories allow researchers to generate predictions for situations in which no data have yet been obtained. This aspect of theory use has two important components. The first is related to the application of theories to real-world phenomena. Theories that are supported by findings from laboratory experiments can be used to make predictions about how humans will behave in the real world (e.g., Butter, Glisky, & Schacter, 1993; Glisky, 1992; Krishnan & Shapiro, 1996).

The second component of using the predictions derived from theories goes to the core of how experimental science operates. Basic scientific research is conducted to evaluate the adequacy of theoretical accounts of the phenomena of interest. The way that scientists evaluate a theory is to derive predictions from the theory and then test the predictions in controlled experiments. If the results of the research are consistent with, or support, the predictions of the theory, then our confidence in the theory increases. If, however, the predictions of the theory are not borne out in the data, then the theory needs to be either modified or abandoned. Theories and experimental research thus go hand-in-hand in the scientific process: Theories help identify the types of questions that scientists ask in their research, and the results of the research inform the scientist as to the adequacy of the theory. Figure 1.3 illustrates how research and theorizing go hand-in-hand in the scientific process.

Another common theoretical device used in cognitive psychology is a **model,** which is basically a description or analogy used to account for some limited set of phenomena. Generally speaking, models tend to account for a smaller range of observations than do

FIGURE 1.3   **Relations among Theories, Predictions, Experiments, and Data** This cycle of scientific research allows us to identify weaknesses in theoretical accounts and also to provide evidence that will increase our confidence in the theory.

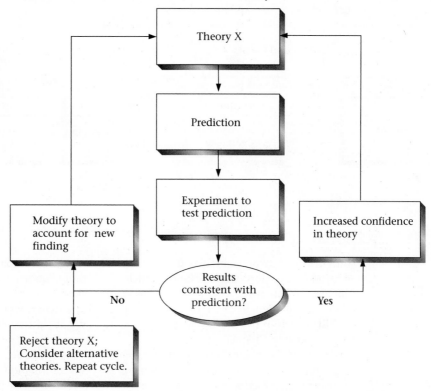

theories. Models also tend to be used more to organize data than to generate predictions. Models tend to be offered as analogies that help us to understand something complex in terms of something simpler and better understood. Saying that memory is like a filing cabinet is a good example of a simple model. It highlights the fact that memories are organized and does so using something that people are quite familiar with. Finally, models tend to be less precise than theories.

Information Processing Models   Cognitive psychology has employed many metaphors and models to try to explain the human mind (Roediger, 1980a). For most of cognitive psychology's history, the **information processing model** has been primary among them. This type of model assumes that information is processed through a series of stages, with each stage performing unique operations on the information. The goal of an information processing model is to capture important aspects of how information is encoded, stored in the human mind, and used to perform cognitive tasks. Figure 1.4 presents a simple information processing model that might be used to account for how people take in information, store it, and then use the stored information to make responses.

Connectionist Models   A more recent development in cognitive psychology is the class of models known as **connectionist models** (e.g., Rumelhart & McClelland, 1986). Like

FIGURE 1.4
Simple Human Information Processing Model This model shows the various stages through which information from the environment can be encoded (or taken in) by a person, stored in memory, and used to make responses. Models of this type are used to account for performance in various types of tasks.

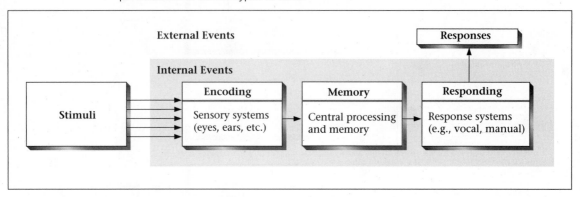

information networks, these models consist of many simple computing units linked in a network architecture. Connectionist models are becoming quite popular in cognitive psychology as well as in many applied areas (e.g., artificial intelligence). James McClelland and David E. Rumelhart are two of the influential researchers who popularized connectionist models in the 1980s. We will have more to say about the historical precedents of these models in Chapter 2.

An example of a simple connectionist model is presented in Figure 1.5. In this model, input units encode stimulus information and pass this information forward to a group of units known as *hidden units* (they are called hidden units because in our research all we "see" are the stimuli and the responses). The hidden units then pass information along to response units. The pattern of responses in the output units represents the response of the model. Connectionist models have been successfully applied to a number of areas in cognitive psychology, and we consider several examples in later chapters.

Section Summary: Explanations in Cognitive Psychology

The three general goals of science are to describe, predict, and explain the phenomena of interest. Cognitive psychologists use a variety of theoretical tools to describe, predict, and explain how the human mind operates. Some of the simpler tools, such as metaphors and analogies, provide explanations by comparing something complex (e.g., memory) to things we are more familiar with (e.g., a filing cabinet). Other types of theoretical tools include theories and models. Theories and models vary along several dimensions, including the scope of the phenomena being accounted for (e.g., theories account for a broader range than do models) and the precision of the predictions of the accounts (e.g., mathematical models are more precise than verbal models). Finally, all theoretical accounts serve to organize results, explain the phenomena of interest, and allow researchers to derive and test predictions.

FIGURE 1.5   **A Simple Connectionist Model**   Stimuli are represented as patterns of activation on the input units. Stimulus information is passed along to the hidden units according to the patterns of connections between the input units and the hidden units. Activation from the hidden units is then passed on to the output units. Responses correspond to patterns of activation on the output units.

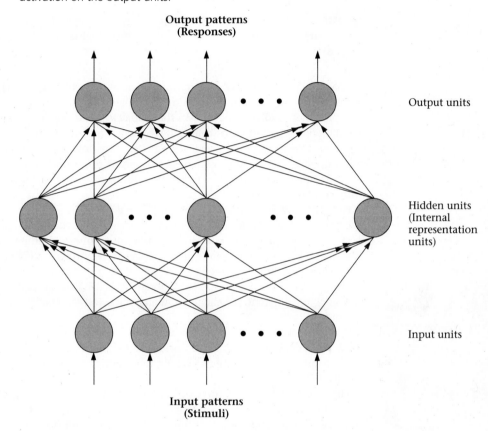

THREE QUESTIONS STUDENTS COMMONLY ASK ABOUT COGNITIVE PSYCHOLOGY

We often find that working in the field of cognitive psychology is like trying to piece together a giant three-dimensional jigsaw puzzle. This jigsaw puzzle, however, is different from other puzzles, because as we learn more about cognitive processes, new pieces are made for the puzzle, and the shape of the puzzle changes. Much of the excitement of our work comes from the process of working on the puzzle, but keep in mind that we are a long way from putting the whole puzzle together. To help you gain an understanding of the research and theories cognitive psychologists use in the puzzle-solving process, we next present three questions that our students frequently raise. These three questions and their answers will help you build a conceptual framework for the information presented in the remainder of the text.

The Source of Research Ideas

Question   "Research in cognitive psychology often seems far removed from anything of interest in the real world. How do cognitive psychologists come up with the ideas for these studies?"

Answer   One of the basic assumptions made by cognitive psychologists is that they can study mental processes by conducting controlled laboratory research in which the cognitive processes involved in the tasks that subjects are asked to perform are related to the mental processes of interest. That is, if researchers are interested in how people in the real world are able to carry on several tasks at the same time (e.g., carrying on a conversation while driving an automobile), then they can study this process in the laboratory by setting up experiments in which they carefully monitor people's behaviors as these people perform two tasks.

Note that this approach does not require that the tasks used in the laboratory look like the tasks that people perform in the real world, only that the mental processes involved in performing the laboratory tasks share important features with the tasks of interest in the real world. This is, of course, the approach taken in many scientific disciplines. For example, a complex chemical process that takes place in the real world can be studied under tightly controlled conditions in the laboratory. In this case the real world and the laboratory are quite different, but the phenomena of interest—chemical reactions—are the same in both contexts.

This general research approach is as effective in psychology as it is in physics or chemistry, and it does relate to the real world because the cognitive processes studied in the lab (e.g., memory, attention, language comprehension) are the processes we use in our everyday lives.

The question of how cognitive psychologists come up with the ideas for the studies that they conduct is more difficult to answer. The simple answer, and the one typically given in research methods courses, is that research grows out of previous research findings and science proceeds by accumulating knowledge. This answer is partially true: Scientific research does proceed as more data are accumulated. However, this progress is not nearly as linear (i.e., Finding A leads to Experiment B, which leads to Finding B, which leads to Experiment C, etc.) as research methods courses would have you believe. Furthermore, many "rules of the game" in science are not written down but are simply shared by members of the scientific discipline. For example, there is no explicit rule that determines what specific topic or phenomenon will attract the attention of researchers in a particular field at a given point in time. There are always more questions that can be asked than we have time to answer, and over time, the focus of interest in a field changes. It is often difficult to discern why Topic X is "hot" now, whereas three years ago Topic Q attracted attention. Like it or not, explaining why certain research topics attract attention is similar to explaining why certain styles of clothing are trendy: We can watch the changes and make up stories about why our tastes and interests change, but the causes of these changes are not to be found in the literature.

Students sometimes use music as a way to avoid distractions. This student might remember more if she were not listening to music, though. Laboratory research has shown that in many situations, presenting a person with an auditory stimulus such as music can actually hinder performance.

Research Methodologies

Question   "The experimental methods used by cognitive psychologists appear so complex. It almost seems as if the research methods are more complex than the ideas being tested. Why?"

Answer   We believe that there are several reasons why students find research in cognitive psychology to be complex. All are related to the fact that cognitive psychology deals with unobservable mental processes that are inferred from how humans respond to various combinations of tasks, stimuli, learning histories, and so on. In order to test hypotheses concerning mental processes, researchers must set up conditions in which they can manipulate one or more aspects of the experimental setting that they presume to be related to the unobservable mental processes. But since the mental processes are themselves unobservable, researchers must be cautious in drawing simple conclusions about how the conditions varied in the experiment and the behavioral measures collected relate to these processes.

Independent variables are the factors controlled or manipulated by the researcher, and **dependent variables** are the measures of performance collected during the study. A third class of variables involves entities not directly observed but rather inferred and involves two subclasses of variables known as intervening variables and hypothetical constructs. An **intervening variable** is a variable used to conveniently summarize several related concepts using a single term. MacCorquodale and Meehl (1948) suggested that these variables be distinguished from other theoretical concepts in which the theoretical terms imply something more "real." For example, suppose we use the term *memory* to refer simply to retention of information over time without assuming that memory involves any specific sort of underlying brain structure or manner of representing information. In this use, memory is an *intervening variable*; presumably, a variety of processes are responsible for, say, allowing you to remember a telephone number long enough to dial it. In contrast, suppose that by *memory* a researcher is referring to a specific memory system that is presumed to store all of our knowledge about the words of the language(s) that we can speak. In this case, the term *memory* is being used as a **hypothetical construct.** A hypothetical construct describes an unobservable factor or variable that is able to account for existing data (or knowledge) as well as providing implications for new observations. Presumably the researcher using the term *memory* in this latter case is making certain assumptions about the nature and operation of this word-information memory system.

Intervening variables and hypothetical constructs are unobservable and closely tied to the independent and dependent variables used in research. Because intervening variables and hypothetical constructs are in large part specified and defined by the experimental conditions used to study them, we need to be careful in how we set up our experiments. In order to precisely specify the nature of intervening variables and hypothetical constructs it is important that researchers employ experimental conditions that examine different aspects of these theoretical entities. As a consequence, scientists have employed two main approaches for studying the mind. The behavioral approach relies on detailed measurement of how people perform tasks that require cognitive processes. The biological approach aims to understand how the brain and nervous system carry out cognitive processes. Cognitive neuropsychology uses both of these approaches for studying cognitive processes. Cognitive psychologists have developed rather elaborate and complex methodologies to meet these needs.

RESEARCH REPORT 1:   PET Studies of False Memories

Earlier in this chapter, you saw one of the ways in which cognitive psychologists are studying false memories. There has been a great deal of interest in the similarities and differences between false and true memories, but until recently we have not been able to study which portions of the brain might be related to these two different types of memories. By "different types of memories," we mean people's recall or recognition of, on the one hand, events that did not occur (false memories) and, on the other hand, events that did occur (true memories).

Daniel Schacter and his colleagues recently reported one of the first studies designed to examine the neuroanatomical correlates of false and true memories (Schacter et al., 1996). Specifically, they wanted to find out which areas of the brain seem to be active when people falsely recognize something that did not occur in an experiment and which areas seem to be active when they recognize something that did occur in the experiment. They presented their subjects with lists similar to the one you studied in Experiment 1A and then gave them a recognition test like the one you completed in Experiment 1B. While subjects were taking the recognition tests, the researchers measured the amount of blood flowing through various parts of the subjects' brains using a technique known as positron emission tomography, or PET. As you will learn in Chapter 2, the PET procedure allows researchers to determine which areas of the brain are most active at any point in time by recording how much blood is flowing through those regions.

Presented in Figure 1A are the results of scans that correspond to trials on which a subject had a false memory (right-hand panel) and a true memory. These figures show that the patterns of cerebral blood flow associated with true and false memories differ significantly. In Chapter 2, we discuss the use of PET scans and other techniques for examining how the brain

In the remaining chapters of this text, we will provide you with some of the historical background for the topic areas we will be discussing. This background will help you to appreciate why researchers use the methods they do.

What Makes a Topic Important

Question   "It seems unclear why some experiments were conducted in the first place. Some aspects of the previous research seem to attract a great deal of attention, whereas no one appears to care about other aspects. How is this determined?"

Answer   This question goes to a core fact about cognitive psychology. As you now know, cognitive psychology has been around for only about forty years. One consequence of being a young science is that many fundamental issues have not been completely resolved, and this is reflected in the research that is conducted and the theories that are developed. For example, in the 1970s, the predominant information processing models attempted to

FIGURE 1A   **Increased Blood Flow**   The PET scans in this figure show the relative increases in blood flow when subjects were presented with a studied item (a) and an item that was related to the studied items but not actually presented in the list (b). There was a significant difference in the locations of the brain regions that responded to true memories versus false memories.

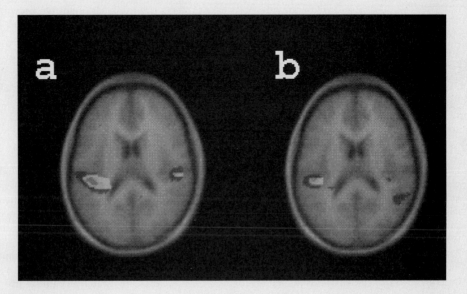

operates while performing various cognitive tasks. The results of Schacter's study are exciting, and we will learn more about the false memory phenomenon as other behavioral and neuropsychological investigations are completed.

capture the notion that humans had different memory systems and that these different memory systems seemed to follow different laws. Today, little of this type of research is going on owing to changes in the interests of members of the field as well as the development of newer models.

Researchers and theorists need to decide which phenomena to examine and what types of models and theories hold the greatest promise for providing useful explanations of these phenomena. There are no hard-and-fast rules about how these decisions are made, but the reality of cognitive psychology today is that diversity of topics and approaches is the rule rather than the exception. This makes things interesting for cognitive psychologists, who constantly learn new facts. We hope to convey some of this excitement to you in the following chapters.

Finally, an important development that has greatly added to our understanding of the human mind in recent years involves advances in **cognitive neuropsychology,** the interdisciplinary study of the physiological underpinnings of cognitive processes. We discuss this area in Chapter 2. Research Report 1 describes some exciting recent work in this area that is related to the false memory effect you read about earlier in the chapter.

Section Summary: Three Questions Students Commonly Ask about Cognitive Psychology

Many factors affect the specific questions asked by cognitive psychologists, and few of these factors are described in books or journal articles. For one, the community of cognitive psychologists shares certain preferences, and these change over time. The nature of the questions asked affects the methods cognitive psychologists use. Most of these methods are elaborate.

REVIEWING   INTRODUCTION TO COGNITIVE PSYCHOLOGY

CONCEPT REVIEW

1. What factors distinguish cognitive psychology from other disciplines that are interested in how the human mind operates? What role does research methodology play in cognitive psychology?

2. What are some of the pros and cons of conducting laboratory experiments to study the human mind?

3. Describe the main contributions to modern cognitive psychology of (a) the early Greek scholars and (b) the philosophers, scientists, and physicians of the 1800s. Be sure to discuss (a) the ideas and findings of these workers and (b) how these ideas and findings affected cognitive psychology.

4. What were the primary contributions of the structuralist and Gestalt schools of psychology? What were the shortcomings of these schools?

5. The behaviorists rejected many mentalistic concepts that were used by earlier workers (e.g., the structuralists). Why? Explain why Tolman argued against a strictly associationistic account of results of his studies of rats learning to run through mazes to obtain food.

6. Indicate which aspects of the following disciplines were accepted by, and which were rejected by, cognitive psychology: verbal learning theory, linguistics, human factors, computer science, and communications engineering.

7. What are the three basic assumptions shared by cognitive psychologists? Describe a simple hypothetical experiment that a cognitive psychologist might run, and then show how these three assumptions are related to the experiment.

8. What sorts of explanatory mechanisms are used by cognitive psychologists? What is the difference between a theory and a model?

9. Modern cognitive psychology employs specialized research procedures, and the phenomena that are studied by cognitive psychologists may seem quite far removed from the "real world." How would a cognitive psychologist explain why she or he uses specific methods and tasks to study the human mind?

KEY TERMS

analytical introspection (p. 12)
behaviorism (p. 14)
cognitive map (p. 14)

cognitive neuropsychology (p. 29)
cognitive psychology (p. 3)
connectionist model (p. 23)

dependent variable (p. 27)
ecological validity (p. 8)
false memory (p. 8)

KEY TERMS (*continued*)

Gestalt psychology (p. 13)   intervening variable (p. 27)   structuralism (p. 12)
human factors (p. 16)   metatheoretical assumption (p. 18)   subjective organization (p. 18)
hypothetical construct (p. 27)   model (p. 22)   theory (p. 22)
independent variable (p. 27)   reaction time (p. 19)   thought experiment (p. 5)
information processing model (p. 23) repressed memory (p. 6)   verbal learning (p. 15)

SUGGESTED READINGS

A very good source of information on the history of the cognitive approach to the study of the human mind is Howard Gardner's (1985) *The mind's new science: A history of the cognitive revolution* (New York: Basic Books). A somewhat shorter historical survey can be found in a paperback book by George Mandler (1985) titled *Cognitive psychology: An essay in cognitive science* (Hillsdale, NJ: Lawrence Erlbaum). The first five chapters in Lachman, Lachman, and Butterfield's (1979) text *Cognitive psychology and information processing: An introduction* (Hillsdale, NJ: Lawrence) provide an excellent description of the many historical antecedents of the information processing approach to cognitive psychology. Ulric Neisser's (1967) book *Cognitive psychology* (New York: Appleton-Century-Crofts), generally considered the first textbook on cognitive psychology, is still worth reading. Michael Posner's (1989) *Foundations of cognitive science* (Cambridge, MA: MIT Press) contains an excellent collection of surveys on various aspects of cognitive psychology written by experts in the field.

The hope that biological and cognitive levels of investigation might be integrated has had a long history. Once it became evident that the operations of the brain were essential for thoughts and actions, discovering the biological basis for mental functions was an abiding objective. . . . Translating that goal into reality has been far from straightforward, however, because nervous systems are notoriously difficult to study. Until quite recently the hope often seemed frustratingly remote and unattainable. —Terrence J. Sejnowski & Patricia S. Churchland (1989).

COGNITIVE PSYCHOLOGISTS study the mental processes that underlie the workings of the human mind. One question that immediately arises when we start to study unobservable mental processes is how to go about this task. Generally speaking, we can use two fundamentally different approaches. First, we can study behavior—how people perform on tasks that require cognitive processes. As mentioned in Chapter 1, Helmholtz's studies of the speed of neural conduction and Donders' subtractive method showed that behavioral approaches could be used to study unobservable cognitive processes. The second approach to studying the human mind is biological—we can attempt to understand how the brain and nervous system carry out cognitive processes. For example, in Chapter 1, we pointed out that Broca's and Wernicke's discoveries of specific brain regions related to language processing showed how studies of the nervous system could aid our understanding of cognitive processes.

COGNITIVE NEUROPSYCHOLOGY

In the past two decades, an explosion of new findings has integrated biological and behavioral methods of studying the mind. *Cognitive neuropsychology* is the interdisciplinary approach that uses both behavioral and physiological methods to study cognitive processes. The study you read about in Chapter 1 that used PET scans to examine real and false memories employed this approach (Schacter et al., 1996; see Research Report 1).

RELATING THE BRAIN AND THE MIND

This chapter provides a broad overview of modern cognitive neuropsychology. We start with a review of some of the historical events that led to the development of cognitive neuropsychology. The remainder of the chapter focuses on five basic issues concerning the relation between the brain and the mind and how these issues relate to cognitive neuropsychology. The first four issues deal with basic aspects of the anatomy and physiology of the nervous system.

1. How do the cells of the nervous system function, and how can studying the functioning of these cells inform us about cognitive processes?
2. How is the nervous system able to learn, remember, and make decisions? Learning and memory are two important capabilities exhibited by virtually all animals, and these capabilities must be accomplished through some means of changing the responses of the cells within the nervous system. Decision making is also a fundamental skill that must be accomplished by the nervous system.
3. How is the nervous system organized? Specifically, what are the major structures and systems within the brain, and how are they related to performing cognitive tasks?

4. How do scientists study the functioning and structures of the brain, and how does this help us to understand the processes that underlie the human mind? Many of the scientific methods used to study the brain depend on knowledge of the structure and functioning of the nervous system, so understanding how these techniques work depends on facts we will review in discussing the first three issues.

These first four issues, as noted, all deal with basic aspects of the anatomy and physiology of the nervous system. As cognitive psychologists, however, we are interested in how behavior reflects the workings of the mind. Although it is true that behaviors ultimately reflect the functioning of biological structures and processes, it is also true that these biological structures and processes depend on brain chemistry, which depends on physics, and so on. Thus, there are many different "levels" at which we could attempt to study the processes that give rise to the mind. As scientists, we must keep an open mind and look for many different ways to study the mind. At the same time, we must exercise caution when trying to draw conclusions from one level (e.g., the biological) and apply them to another level (e.g., the psychological). In the final section of the chapter, we discuss the fifth issue: how the concepts and knowledge gained from studying the nervous system contribute to our understanding of cognitive processes.

Intellectual Precursors to Cognitive Neuropsychology

Some of the earliest recorded speculations on the relation between the functioning of the human body and the mind date back to the ancient Egyptians, who held that the heart was the organ that controlled mental life, or the mind. In the centuries following, there were many proponents of this *cardiocentric* (heart-centered) view.

An alternative explanation was the *cerebrocentric* (brain-centered) view, which held that the brain and nervous system were related to the mind. During the seventeenth century, scholars such as René Descartes proposed accounts of human thought and behavior in which the brain played an important role. Descartes' views are unsophisticated by today's standards, but remember that these ideas were proposed when knowledge of the anatomy of the nervous system was extremely primitive. More important than the details of these ideas was their role in focusing attention on the brain and nervous system.

Following the eventual acceptance of the cerebrocentric view, researchers demonstrated many important functional relations between the nervous system and behavior. For example, research with animals revealed separate and identifiable pathways for perception and motor movement (Feinberg & Farah, 1997). This experimental work with animals laid the groundwork for later clinical investigations of humans and studies of the relation between the brain and cognitive processes such as memory and language.

As researchers learned more about the nervous system, a major debate developed concerning whether the mind and thought processes reflected the functioning of local areas within the brain (localism) or the entire brain working in concert (holism). Proponents of the localist view argued that specific regions of the brain are responsible for various mental processes. Perhaps the best-known member of this camp was Franz Josef Gall (1758–1828), who developed an elaborate system for relating human abilities (faculties) to specific brain sites (see Figure 2.1). Gall argued that brain development at these sites could affect the shape of the skull, and thus the various faculties could be measured by examination of the shape of the head. Gall identified over 25 distinct human abilities and pointed to places on the skull where these abilities could be measured.

Gall's view, which came to be known as **phrenology,** came under strong attack by scholars who thought that the notion that the human mind could be studied by measuring the bumps on a person's head was ridiculous. Although Gall's ideas were later dis-

FIGURE 2.1   **Phrenology**   Franz Josef Gall promoted phrenology, the idea that mental abilities could be assessed through measurement of bumps on the head. Gall eventually identified more than 25 different abilities that he thought were reflected in the shape of the skull.

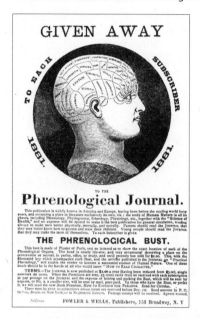

counted, his work did serve an important historical function, and that was to mobilize critics who argued against the localist view and in favor of the holistic position. According to the holistic view, great flexibility characterizes the human brain, and specific regions are not dedicated to specific types of cognitive processes.

The debates between those who favored the localist view and those who favored the holist view dominated research for many decades. Starting in the 1860s, several important discoveries—such as Broca's and Wernicke's identification of specific regions of the brain that played important roles in language processing—tipped the balance in favor of the localist view. These discoveries also broadened the localism/holism debate to include the notion of **hemispheric specialization,** the idea that the right and left halves of the brain are differentially involved in performing certain types of tasks. The debate over whether the brain functions as a collection of separate modules or in a more unified fashion continues today (e.g., Anderson, 1983; Farah, 1994; Fodor, 1983; Kosslyn & Koenig, 1995).

The debates on localist versus holist views of the brain, as well as the concept of hemispheric specialization, set the stage for a number of important developments that directly contributed to the rise of modern cognitive neuropsychology. The debates on localization of function expanded to cover other domains (e.g., memory, problem solving). At the same time, the technologies and methods available for studying the brain and nervous system underwent significant improvements. Along with these advances in techniques came a flood of empirical data and efforts to provide theoretical accounts of these data. Scientists made great strides in studying the nervous systems of animals and conducted many important clinical studies with humans. For example, studies showed that the behavior and thought processes of a person who has sustained extensive damage to the brain may not be as affected as one might expect. (See Research Report 2.)

RESEARCH REPORT 2:   Phineas Gage:
Heterogeneous Effects of a Traumatic Brain Injury

On September 13, 1848, Phineas Gage, a 25-year-old railroad construction foreman, was the victim of an incredible industrial accident. Gage was working with an assistant, using explosives to remove rocks. The task required the men to drill holes in the rock, partially fill the holes with explosive powder and sand, and then use a fuse and tamping iron to trigger an explosion. On the day of the accident, Gage was momentarily distracted and began tamping directly over the powder before his assistant had covered it with sand. The powder exploded, hurling the metal tamping rod through Gage's face, skull, and brain. The rod exited near the top of his head—an unbelievably bad accident. More unbelievable is the fact that, although he was momentarily stunned, Gage regained full consciousness soon after the accident, and with the help of his men, he was able to walk. Damasio and colleagues (1994) recently created a computer model of the injury suffered by Gage (see Figure 2A).

In many ways, Gage recovered fully from his accident. He remained able-bodied and apparently as intelligent as before the accident. However, in many other ways, Gage was drastically changed. Before the accident, he was a responsible and socially well-adapted young man. After the accident, his behavior changed profoundly. He showed no respect for social conventions, he used profanity, and he showed a general lack of social responsibility. (See Damasio et al., 1994, for a fuller description of the changes in Gage's behavior.)

Although his accident made headlines in the newspapers, when Gage died in San Francisco 12 years later, his death went largely unnoticed. Although there was some speculation as to what areas of the nervous system were involved in Gage's injury and how these related to his changed behavior, these speculations did not attract much attention in the scientific community. Using modern neuroimaging techniques and measurements from Gage's skull, Damasio and colleagues recently concluded that Gage suffered damage in an area of the brain now known to be related to rational decision making and the processing of emotions.

Section Summary: Relating the Brain and the Mind

Scientists have employed two main approaches for studying the mind. The behavioral approach relies on detailed measurement of how people perform tasks that require cognitive processes. The biological approach aims to understand how the brain and nervous system carry out cognitive processes. Cognitive neuropsychology uses both of these approaches for studying cognitive processes. The earliest theorists on the relation between the body and the mind debated whether the heart or the brain controlled the mind. Later, the localism/holism debate contrasted two views of the relation between brain and cognition. The localist view held that local areas in the brain were responsible for specific cognitive processes. The holist view held that cognitive processes reflected the workings of a unified brain. This debate continues today, and further improvements in the techniques available for studying the brain will allow researchers to paint an ever more detailed picture of how the brain supports human cognition.

FIGURE 2A   The Damage Suffered by Phineas Gage as the Result of a Rail-
                   road Accident

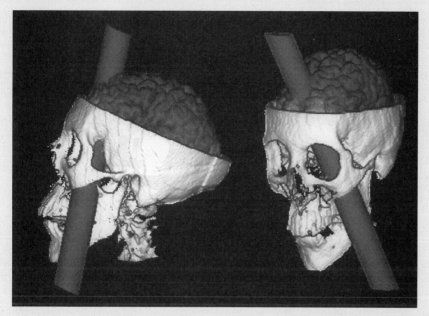

It is interesting to note that whereas the work of Broca and Wernicke attracted a great deal of attention, Gage's case was largely ignored by neuroscientists and physicians. Damasio and colleagues argue that these different responses may have been due to the fact that there were autopsy reports in the cases reported by Broca and Wernicke but not in Gage's case. Without specific information concerning the nature and extent of the damage Gage suffered, it was impossible to draw any meaningful conclusions concerning how the affected areas of the brain related to the observed behavior changes.

INFORMATION PROCESSING MECHANISMS IN THE NERVOUS SYSTEM

To survive, an animal must be able to sense changes or events in the environment, respond appropriately to these events, and somehow learn from these experiences. To achieve these goals, an organism's nervous system must be able to (a) *encode,* or take in through its sensory systems, information from the environment, (b) integrate and store the encoded information with previously acquired knowledge, and (c) use this information to select and execute responses. These three general functions—encoding information, storing and processing internally represented knowledge, and selecting and executing responses—are accomplished by the coordinated activity of billions of cells in the nervous system. In this section, we review how these functions are achieved by the human nervous system.

Cells in the Nervous System

The human nervous system is comprised of two primary types of cells, neurons and glial cells. Glial cells provide various types of physiological support to neurons, such as physically holding neurons together and absorbing dead cells in the nervous system. For our purposes, however, **neurons** are the most important cells of the central nervous system, for they serve as the basic building blocks of the nervous system. The human brain contains about 180 billion neurons, and it is estimated that 50 billion of these neurons are engaged in information processing related to cognitive processes (Kolb & Wishaw, 1990).

Neurons are remarkably diverse in size, shape, and functional properties. This diversity reflects the fact that neurons are specialized for a wide range of different information processing tasks. Fortunately for us, some fundamental structural properties are characteristic of all neurons. Most neurons have three distinct structures: (a) the cell body and the cell membrane that surrounds the cell body, (b) branching filaments from the cell body called **dendrites,** and (c) a projection from the cell body called the **axon** (see Figure 2.2). These three structures are specialized for accomplishing the basic information processing tasks illustrated in Table 2.1.

Transmitting Information Between Cells

Neurons transmit information, but they do not act as simple relays that passively transmit the same message, or information, they receive. Rather, neurons collect information from many other neurons and then integrate and transform this information before sending messages along to still other neurons. If we view the three primary tasks of neurons as (a) collecting information from other neurons, (b) processing the messages from these neurons, and (c) sending information to still other neurons, then we can organize our description of the structure and functional properties of neurons along these three tasks (see

TABLE 2 . 1   Major Processes in Communication Within and Between Neurons

Component	Function	Information Communicated
Dendrite and cell body	Carry information to the axon	A graded, excitatory, or inhibitory change is made in resting potential.
Axon	Carries signal away from the cell body	An all-or-none action potential is carried the length of the axon to the axon terminal.
Synapse	Allows transfer of signals between adjacent cells	Chemicals (neurotransmitters) are released into the synapse and alter the resting potential of adjacent cells.
Neurotransmitter	Alters resting potential of postsynaptic cells	Resting potential is increased or decreased, which affects the chances that an action potential will fire.

FIGURE 2.2   **The Main Anatomical Features of a Neuron**   The dendrites and the axon are projections from the cell body. The dendrites and cell body collect messages from other neurons at sites called synapses. The axon hillock is the point at which the axon extends away from the cell body. Action potentials are carried away from the neuron and down the axon, where they cause the release of neurotransmitters that affect nearby neurons.

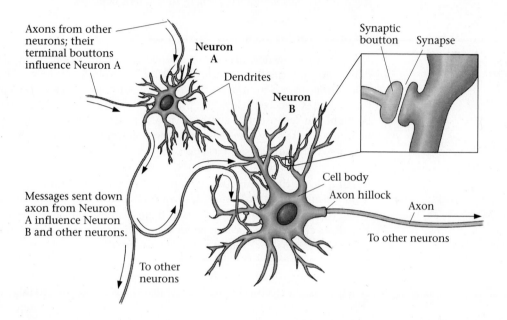

Table 2.1). After we review the main structures involved in collecting, processing, and sending information, we describe in more detail how these processes are accomplished.

The first component of the process of communication between neurons involves the axon. On the axon of a neuron that is sending a message is a structure called the *synaptic boutton* ("button") which contains chemicals that are released from the sending neuron. These chemicals carry a message to the receiving neuron. The chemicals are released into the second component of this communication process, the *synaptic cleft,* a small space between the sending and receiving neurons. The point at which these chemical messengers operate is called the **synapse.** Chemicals travel across the synaptic cleft and come in contact with the third component of this communication process, the *postsynaptic membrane.* The chemicals that are released into the synapse are called **neurotransmitters.** When these neurotransmitters reach the postsynaptic membrane, they cause chemical changes there that affect the type of message that the receiving neuron will transmit to other neurons. This message will be carried toward other neurons by axons that extend from the cell body of the receiving cell. It is the message sent along the axon that results in the release of neurotransmitters in the next synapse.

To summarize, the entire process of communication between neurons involves several structures and processes. At the most general level, the main structures are the *presynaptic neuron,* the synapse, and the *postsynaptic neuron.* The pre- and postsynaptic neuron are terms given to the neurons that release neurotransmitters into the synapse (presynaptic neuron) and the neurons that are affected by neurotransmitters released into the synapse (postsynaptic neuron). These three structures give rise to several processes that allow communication to take place. First, neurotransmitters are released from the synaptic bouttons of presynaptic neurons. Next, these neurotransmitters cross the synaptic cleft and affect postsynaptic neurons. Any given neuron receives many messages in the form of neurotransmitters from other neurons that release neurotransmitters into synaptic clefts. These messages are combined and then, based on the overall information it receives, the receiving neuron sends a message along to subsequent neurons.

Information Processing Within a Cell

Now that we know how neurons communicate with one another, the next question to address is how information is processed within a neuron. A neuron's cell body and dendrites collect information from other neurons via neurotransmitters that come in contact with the dendrites and cell body. The three main components of the synapse, the synaptic boutton, the synapse, and the postsynaptic neuron, can be thought of in terms of the sending and receiving of messages from one neuron to the next. In this section we will discuss how the neurotransmitters affect the functioning of a neuron.

Resting Potentials   An essential aspect of neuronal functioning is related to the *membrane potential,* which is a difference in the electrical charge inside and outside a neuron. When the neuron is in its resting state, there is an imbalance between the positively and negatively charged chemicals (known as ions) inside the neuron and the ions outside the neuron. This imbalance causes a difference in electrical charge between the inside and the outside of the neuron. During the resting state, the inside of the neuron has an electrical charge of about –70 millivolts (mV). (A millivolt equals one thousandth of a volt.) This relatively constant electrical potential is called the **resting potential.** In the resting state, then, a –70 mV charge is built up across the neuron's cell membrane, and the neuron is said to be *polarized.*

As we noted earlier, neurons communicate with one another through a chemical process involving neurotransmitters. When a neurotransmitter comes in contact with a neuron's cell membrane at the synapse, it can have one of two effects on the resting potential of the neuron. First, the neurotransmitter can decrease the resting potential—for example, changing it from –70 to –68 mV. The process of decreasing the resting potential is referred to as *depolarizing* the neuron. Second, the neurotransmitters may *hyperpolarize* the neuron, causing the resting membrane potential to increase from, say, -70 to -72 mV.

If the neurotransmitter causes the neuron to depolarize, an *excitatory postsynaptic potential* (EPSP) is created. As we will see in a moment, EPSPs increase the chances that the neuron will communicate through neurotransmitters with its neighboring neurons. In contrast, if the neurotransmitter causes the neuron to hyperpolarize, the result is an *inhibitory postsynaptic potential* (IPSP), which decreases the chances that the neuron will fire.

When an excitatory neurotransmitter comes in contact with a neuron's cell membrane, then, it causes the resting potential to decrease. Similarly, an inhibitory neurotransmitter causes a cell's resting potential to increase. EPSPs and IPSPs are both *graded responses*. This means that the magnitudes, or amplitudes, of the EPSPs and IPSPs are related to the relative intensity of the signals that cause them; weak signals result in small changes in the resting potential, whereas strong signals result in large changes in the resting potential.

One last point we want to make here concerns the relation between concepts used to account for the structure and functioning of the nervous system and concepts used in cognitive psychology. Many concepts used to explain the functioning of the nervous system have been incorporated into cognitive psychological theories. The concepts of excitatory and inhibitory processes and thresholds are excellent examples, as these concepts play a major role in many theories and models in cognitive psychology (e.g., information processing models and models of visual attention). Note, however, that the use of these concepts in cognitive theories does not mean that the cognitive theories presume that these aspects of the model reflect the operation of a similar process at the physiological level. That is, if a cognitive theory proposes that there is an excitatory process operating at the cognitive level, this does not mean that the theory assumes that there is a one-to-one correspondence between the excitatory process used in the cognitive theory and the excitatory processes used in physiological models of the brain. We will have more to say about relating concepts across different levels (e.g., the physiological and psychological) later in the chapter.

Action Potentials   A second form of communication within a neuron occurs along its axon. The graded EPSPs and IPSPs that result from the action of neurotransmitters are conducted decrementally along the neuron's cell membrane to a location known as the *axon hillock* (see Figure 2.2). By *decremental,* we mean that the magnitude of the change in the cell membrane potential decreases as it moves along the cell.

If the total effect of all the hyperpolarizations and depolarizations reaching the axon hillock is a depolarization of the cell membrane to approximately -65 mV, then an **action potential** is generated at the axon hillock (see Figure 2.3). The action potential is the result of a series of sudden chemical changes that cause the polarity of the cell membrane potential to very quickly reverse and become positive, followed by a return to a negative potential. The action potential takes about 1 millisecond (ms), and during this time the membrane potential changes from -65 to $+50$ and then back to slightly more than -70 mV. Once fired, action potentials travel the length of the axon and result in the release of neurotransmitters into the synaptic cleft, thereby affecting other neurons.

In contrast to the changes in membrane potential produced by neurotransmitters affecting the dendrites and cell body, the action potential is not a graded response. That is, action potentials follow an *all-or-none principle*; an action potential either fires or does not fire. Furthermore, the action potential (at least in terms of its amplitude, or strength) is unrelated to the magnitude of the depolarization at the axon hillock. If the depolarization exceeds the threshold, an action potential fires; if the depolarization does not exceed the threshold, no action potential fires.

The all-or-none response of the action potential can be likened to the firing of a gun. If the total amount of pressure applied to the trigger exceeds some threshold, a bullet fires. In neurons, if the depolarization exceeds the threshold, an action potential fires. Note, however, that once the threshold is crossed, the action has no further effect. Only one bullet is fired at a time, no matter how hard the trigger is pulled. Similarly, only one action potential is fired for each depolarization that exceeds the threshold.

This gun analogy can also help us to understand how the graded responses produced by excitatory and inhibitory neurotransmitters result in the all-or-none response of the action potential. Imagine that instead of one person handling the gun, two people have their fingers on the trigger, one person pulling in one direction to try to fire the gun and the other person pulling in the opposite direction to prevent the gun from firing. The person trying to fire the gun is like an excitatory neurotransmitter, and the person trying to stop the gun from being fired is like an inhibitory neurotransmitter. The total pressure on the trigger is graded; it can be greater in the direction of firing the gun (more excitatory neurotransmitter) or in the direction of not firing the gun (more inhibitory neurotrans-

FIGURE 2.3   **The Firing of an Action Potential**   This schematic shows changes in cell membrane potential during the firing of an action potential. The stimulus in the figure refers to the release of neurotransmitters that cause the membrane potential to depolarize to the threshold for firing an action potential.

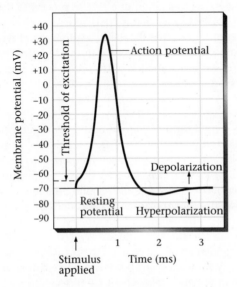

mitter). Once the pressure in the direction of firing the gun exceeds the threshold for the trigger, a bullet is fired. The same holds for neurons and action potentials.

Section Summary: Information Processing in the Nervous System

Neurons are the basic building blocks of the nervous system. Neurons process information and communicate with each other through complex chemical and electrical processes. Communication among neurons is accomplished when neurotransmitters released from the presynaptic neuron cross the synaptic cleft and increase or decrease the polarity of the postsynaptic neuron's resting potential. The total effect of all excitatory and inhibitory neurotransmitters affecting a given neuron determines whether the neuron will fire an action potential. Once fired, action potentials travel the length of the axon and result in the release of neurotransmitters into the synaptic cleft, thereby affecting other neurons.

COMPUTATION, LEARNING, AND MEMORY IN THE NERVOUS SYSTEM

Although communication among neurons in the sensory systems, the brain, and the response systems (e.g., muscles) is certainly important, our nervous systems must also be able to make decisions and to learn and remember. Scientists have long sought to understand how neurons might alter their structure and functioning to accomplish these two goals: *computing,* or making the types of logical decisions that underlie cognition, and *learning,* or changing as a consequence of experience. In this section, we review three landmarks of cognitive research that help to explain how the nervous system supports these functions.

Computing: The McCulloch and Pitts Neuron

The first contribution comes from McCulloch and Pitts (1943), who combined knowledge of basic neural functioning with mathematical logic to show how groups of neurons could "compute." To appreciate these researchers' insights, let us start with a concrete example of how decisions are made.

Imagine that you are taking a course on a pass/fail basis, and two exams will determine your grade. Imagine further that the exam scores are weighted. Let's say that the midterm counts for 40 percent of your grade and the final exam counts for 60 percent. Your teacher specifies that you need an overall average of 75 or greater to pass the course. If each test is worth 100 points, then to get your final grade, you would multiply your midterm grade by .40 and your final exam score by .60 and then add these two numbers together. If the total is 75 or above, you pass the course; if less than 75, you fail.

We can understand the basic idea behind McCulloch and Pitts's proposal by using a similar weighting of neural excitation. Consider first the three neurons shown in the top panel of Figure 2.4. Assume that Neuron A receives excitatory input from two other neurons, X and Y. As we noted earlier, the amount of excitation (or inhibition) a neuron receives is graded, and we can capture this notion in the weight given to the excitation from Neurons X and Y. Assume for the moment that Neurons X and Y each provide 1.5 "units" of excitation and that the weight given to that excitation can be a number between 0 and 1. To know how much excitation Neuron A receives, we simply multiply the input from Neurons X and Y by the weights given to that input and add these two numbers together.

Neuron A has some threshold for firing an action potential, and let us assume for the moment that this threshold can vary. If the total input to Neuron A exceeds this threshold, then Neuron A fires; if the total input is less than the threshold, then the neuron does not fire. This arrangement is similar to the hypothetical example we described earlier with two exams and an overall final grade. Neurons X and Y are analogous to the midterm and final exam, whether Neuron A fires an action potential is similar to the "decision" that the teacher makes (pass/fail), and the threshold for Neuron A's firing is like the cutoff for pass/fail.

McCulloch and Pitts showed that simple arrangements of neurons could "compute" various types of decisions. Two of the simplest types of decisions involve AND rules and OR rules. An example of an AND rule is that a spark and a flammable substance coming together will cause a fire. A spark alone will not cause a fire, and neither will a flammable substance without a spark. You need both a spark *and* a flammable substance.

The top panel of Figure 2.4 shows how Neurons A, X, and Y can perform an AND decision in which Neuron A fires only if both X *and* Y provide input to Neuron A. The lower panel of the figure shows how these three neurons can make an OR decision in which Neuron A will fire if either Neuron X *or* Neuron Y provides input.

McCulloch and Pitts's work was important because it showed how arrangements of neurons could accomplish simple computing tasks. By linking these simple neuron groups in larger and larger arrangements, it is possible to achieve very sophisticated information processing systems. The approach of linking many simple computing devices together to achieve sophisticated information processing devices is evidenced in many of the cognitive psychology theories that have been proposed in recent years.

Learning and Memory: Hebb's Contributions

Another key development in the cognitive neuropsychology of learning and memory came from the Canadian psychologist Donald O. Hebb (1904–1985). Hebb was one of the first researchers to explicitly state the conditions that might allow a change at the synap-

FIGURE 2.4   **The McCulloch and Pitts Model**   The model describes how a collection of neurons could compute simple decisions. In the illustrations here, Neuron A receives input from Neurons X and Y, and these inputs are weighted equally at 1. The top panel shows how this arrangement of neurons could make an AND decision, with Neuron A firing an action potential only if both Neuron X *and* Neuron Y provide input to Neuron A. The lower panel shows an OR arrangement, with Neuron A firing an action potential if either Neuron X or Neuron Y provides input. As illustrated, Neuron X provides an input and Neuron Y does not; this is sufficient to allow Neuron A to fire.

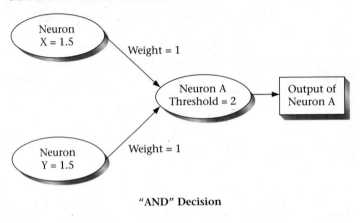

tic level to reflect learning and memory. Hebb (1949) suggested a functional relationship between a presynaptic neuron (A) and a postsynaptic neuron (B) that could change as a consequence of cell A's frequently exciting cell B (that is, releasing an excitatory neurotransmitter into the synapse): "When an axon of cell A is near enough to excite a cell B and repeatedly or persistently takes part in firing it, some growth process or metabolic change takes place in one or both cells such that A's efficacy, as one of the cells firing [cell] B is increased" (p. 62).

Mechanisms for Storing Information   One way in which we could imagine a change in the efficacy of one cell in causing another cell to fire would involve changing the weights given to the inputs from one cell to another (see Figure 2.4). This is a logical possibility, but is there any evidence for something like a change in the weights given to the input from a cell?

In the years following Hebb's work, scientists have identified a number of mechanisms that can, in effect, make such changes. Consider for a moment that Cell A releases an excitatory neurotransmitter that affects Cell B. Figure 2.5 illustrates three ways in which learning can occur at the synaptic level. First, if Cell A is repeatedly stimulated, the

FIGURE 2.5   **Three Ways Neurons Can Change to Support Learning**   The schematics on the left represent the neurons before learning, and those on the right show the changes after learning. In Panel 1, the change is an increase in the neurotransmitter released when an action potential is fired. In Panel 2, the size of the synaptic region increases with learning; and in Panel 3, more synapses are formed after repeated exposure to some learning event.

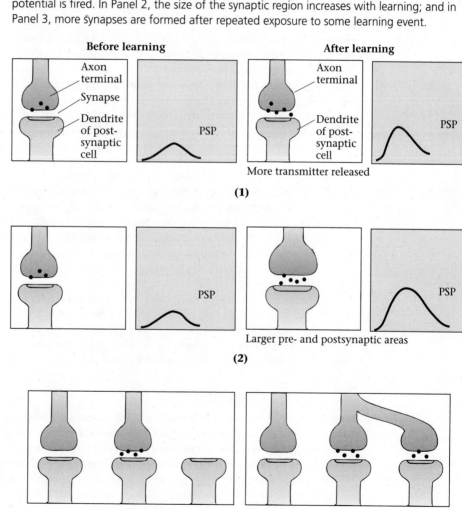

amount of neurotransmitter released with each action potential may be altered. This can lead to a greater postsynaptic potential, or a greater likelihood that the postsynaptic neuron will fire an action potential. This is similar to saying that a greater weight is given to the input from Cell A. Second, the area of the postsynaptic region on Cell B that responds to the neurotransmitter from Cell A can increase in size. (It is also possible that both the amount of neurotransmitter released *and* the sensitive area of Cell B that responds to the neurotransmitter experience increases.) Third, new synapses can be formed between Cells A and B.

Neuroscientists have discovered many ways in which the communication between cells changes as a function of experience. Several of the basic ideas behind these mechanisms, such as the change in weights given to the inputs from various neurons, have been incorporated into cognitive psychology theories such as the connectionist models discussed in Chapter 1. Here again, we see that the knowledge gained from studying the functioning of the nervous system can be used in attempting to account for the processes of the mind.

Dual Trace Hypothesis   Hebb (1949) proposed a theory about how changes in synaptic transmission might occur, and this account is similar in many ways to theories of memory proposed by psychologists over the years (e.g., Atkinson & Shiffrin, 1968; James, 1890; see Chapters 6 and 7). According to Hebb's **dual trace hypothesis,** the formation of a memory requires two processes. The first is a relatively short-term process: The learning experience sets up neural activity that tends to reverberate through collections of neurons known as *neural circuits.* This reverberatory process keeps the memory "alive" for a short time. If the reverberatory process lasts long enough, or is repeated a sufficient number of times, the result is a stable (i.e., long-term) change in the nervous system—a **memory trace.** Such changes underlie both learning and memory.

One approach to studying memory traces in the mammalian brain involves a phenomenon known as *long-term potentiation,* a stable and long-lasting increase in the magnitude of neural response after neurons have been repeatedly stimulated with a series of electrical stimuli at fairly high frequencies. Scientists have studied this phenomenon by stimulating nerve cells with small electrical currents. When this is done under the right conditions, the cells show a prolonged and elevated response to further stimuli—they have "learned" to respond to these stimuli (Hawkins & Kandel, 1984).

The final point to consider concerning memory at the neural level is how neurons might be arranged to store the types of memories that we acquire. Various terms are used to describe the arrangements of cells that store information, including (in increasing orders of complexity) *cell assemblies, neural circuits,* and *systems.* In general, the more complex the learning and memory processes, the more cells required to store the information.

Rosenblatt's Perceptron

Finally, we briefly consider the work of Frank Rosenblatt (1958, 1962). Rosenblatt made several contributions that laid the groundwork for later cognitive models that attempted to incorporate information concerning the functioning of the nervous system. Rosenblatt developed a mechanism called a **perceptron** for recognizing letters and other visual patterns, and the device had some initial success. The perceptron was basically a grid of 400 photocells that detected light energy that fell on the grid. The outputs of these photocells were passed along to a simple logical device. The overall collection of input devices (photocells) and logical devices, and the manner in which these two components were wired together, allowed the system to recognize patterns rather well. Importantly, the perceptron worked by presenting the device with patterns to recognize and then providing "feedback" as to whether the response of the device was correct or not. With practice and feedback, the perceptron "learned" to identify patterns.

For our purposes, Rosenblatt's work had two important consequences. First, it demonstrated that collections of simple processing units could, when placed in the appropriate architecture, or arrangement, perform fairly complex tasks—in this case, recognizing visual patterns. Second, unfortunately for Rosenblatt, his work attracted considerable attention from critics, who argued that his approach in building the perceptron had fundamental flaws. For example, Minsky and Papert (1968) published a book in which they demonstrated convincingly some of the limitations of the perceptron approach of using simple processing units that learn as a consequence of experience.

One result of these criticisms was that many researchers lost faith in attempts to model cognitive processes using simple processing devices that functioned similarly to neurons. For example, the cognitive theories proposed in the 1960s and 1970s were primarily of the information processing style. The theorists who proposed these models did not worry about the extent to which the theories accorded with what was known about the nervous system. It was not until the 1980s, when connectionist models such as those mentioned in Chapter 1 began to appear, that cognitive psychologists again begin to take notice of the advantages to be gained from considering advances in the neurosciences.

Section Summary: Computation, Learning, and Memory

Basic communication within and between neurons might appear to suggest that these cells serve primarily as information relays. Research has shown, however, that neurons can modify their connections with each other. This ability makes it possible for neurons both to learn through experience and to behave like simple decision-making devices. McCulloch and Pitts showed how cells could compute by making simple decisions such as AND and OR decisions. Hebb and Rosenblatt suggested ways in which collections of neurons might learn and remember. Hebb's ideas stimulated a great deal of research into the basis of various types of learning and memory. Rosenblatt's work with the perceptron helped to provide the basis for the development of connectionist models, although at the time his work was reported, researchers underestimated the importance of his ideas.

THE BRAIN

We have now discussed how neurons communicate, how they can act as simple computing devices, and how they can exhibit learning from experience and memory. As impressive as these accomplishments are, they are not adequate for explaining human cognitive processes. A great deal of the "computing power" of the human brain comes from the fact that the brain contains many billions of cells arranged in a highly structured manner. In this section, we review some of the main organizational properties of the brain.

Major Anatomical Subdivisions

The three main divisions of the brain are the hindbrain, the midbrain, and the forebrain. Within these three major divisions, a number of subdivisions and principal structures can be identified, as shown in Figure 2.6.

FIGURE 2.6   **The Human Brain**   This diagram shows the three major subdivisions of the human brain along with some of the major structures in each of these subdivisions.

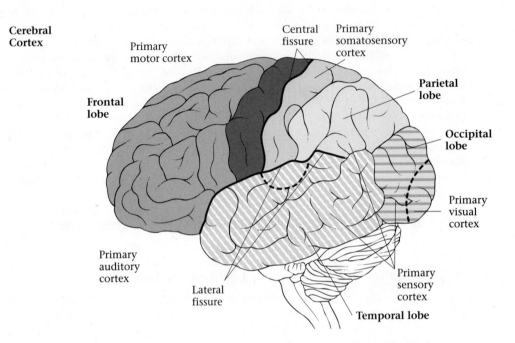

Cerebral Cortex

Primary motor cortex
Central fissure
Primary somatosensory cortex
Parietal lobe
Frontal lobe
Occipital lobe
Primary visual cortex
Primary auditory cortex
Lateral fissure
Primary sensory cortex
Temporal lobe

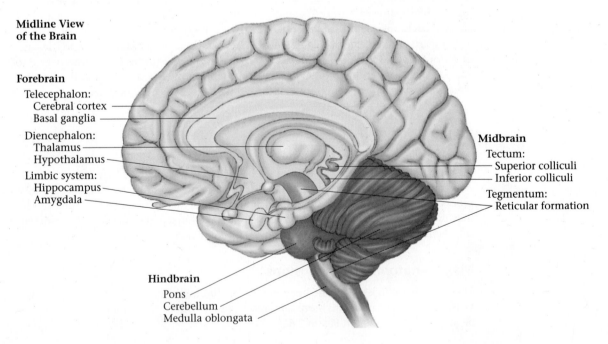

Midline View of the Brain

Forebrain
  Telecephalon:
    Cerebral cortex
    Basal ganglia
  Diencephalon:
    Thalamus
    Hypothalamus
  Limbic system:
    Hippocampus
    Amygdala

Midbrain
  Tectum:
    Superior colliculi
    Inferior colliculi
  Tegmentum:
    Reticular formation

Hindbrain
  Pons
  Cerebellum
  Medulla oblongata

Hindbrain   In terms of evolution, the hindbrain is the oldest part of the brain. It contains three major structures. The *cerebellum* ("little brain") plays a major role in the planning, timing, and overall patterning of skilled movement. The cerebellum receives information from various sensory systems (e.g., visual, auditory, and somatosensory), as well as from other portions of the brain that control motor movement. An important function of the cerebellum is to integrate inputs from these various sources and allow us to perform motor movements smoothly. Damage to the cerebellum can result in jerky or poorly coordinated movements. The *pons* and the *medulla oblongata* are the other two principal structures in the hindbrain. These two structures are concerned with important physiological functions controlling sleep, arousal, and the functioning of the cardiovascular system.

Midbrain   The midbrain, located above the hindbrain, consists of two major subdivisions, the *tectum* and the *tegmentum*. The tectum contains two important sets of structures, the *superior colliculi* and the *inferior colliculi*. The superior colliculi play an important role in the processing of visual information, and the inferior colliculi are involved in the processing of auditory information. The tegmentum includes a portion of the *reticular formation*, which is involved in attention, sleep and arousal, and several basic reflexes.

Forebrain   Above the midbrain is the forebrain, which is the largest and, from an evolutionary perspective, the most recently developed structure in the brain. The forebrain is subdivided into two major parts, the *telencephalon* and the *diencephalon*. The telencephalon, the largest subdivision of the human brain, includes the two *cerebral hemispheres* and other important structures. The cerebral hemispheres are covered by a cortex, or layer of neural tissue (*cortex* is from Latin, meaning "bark"). This **cerebral cortex** surrounds the cerebral hemispheres as bark surrounds a tree. The cerebral cortex has expanded considerably during human evolution and now comprises about 80 percent of the mass of the human brain (Kolb & Wishaw, 1990). The cortex is highly convoluted and consists of *sulci* (small grooves) and *fissures* (large grooves) that permit a much larger surface area than would be possible with a smooth brain of comparable dimensions. The cerebral hemispheres are involved in virtually all cognitive processes. We describe the major divisions of the cerebral cortex in detail in the next section.

Another important portion of the telencephalon that is closely tied with cognitive processes is the *limbic system*. Two primary structures of this system are the *hippocampus* and the *amygdala*. Early researchers (e.g., MacLean, 1949) noted that the development of the limbic system coincided with the emergence of emotional responses, suggesting that the limbic system is involved with emotion. Subsequent research has shown that the limbic system plays an important role in the formation of memories.

The other major division of the forebrain is the diencephalon. The two principle structures of the diencephalon are the *thalamus* and the *hypothalamus*. Most of the neural information received by the cerebral cortex comes from the thalamus. Large areas of the cerebral cortex receive inputs from specific parts of the thalamus. Neurons within the thalamus receive sensory information from the sensory receptor systems (e.g., the eye and the ear) and then relay the sensory information to sensory projection areas in the cerebral cortex. The other major structure of the diencephalon, the hypothalamus, organizes and controls behaviors related to the survival of the species. The hypothalamus controls four important classes of behaviors: feeding, fighting, fleeing, and mating.

Major Divisions of the Cerebral Cortex

The cerebral cortex contains a number of important fissures. One of these, the *longitudinal fissure,* serves to almost completely separate the two cerebral hemispheres. The two hemispheres are connected by several bands of fibers called *commisures.* The largest of these commisures is the **corpus callosum,** which plays an important role in transmitting information from one cerebral hemisphere to the other. On each cerebral hemisphere are two deep fissures that divide it into four lobes, each named after the bones in the skull that surround these lobes. These four lobes are the *frontal, parietal, temporal,* and *occipital.* These lobes can be identified by the grooves that divide the lobes. The *central fissure* divides the frontal lobe from the parietal lobe, and the *lateral fissure* divides the temporal lobe from the frontal and parietal lobes.

Each lobe of the brain is specialized to perform different functions, and each receives input from and sends output to different portions of the nervous system. The frontal lobes are involved with the planning, execution, and control of movement. An especially important region of the frontal lobe is the area immediately in front of the central fissure separating the frontal lobe from the parietal lobe. This area, known as the *primary motor cortex,* contains neurons directly involved with motor movements.

The remaining three lobes (parietal, occipital, and temporal) play important roles in perception, and here again there is a considerable degree of specialization. The *primary somatosensory cortex* lies adjacent to the central fissure that separates the frontal and parietal lobes. The *primary sensory cortex* lies within the parietal lobe and receives input from the various senses (e.g., vision, hearing, taste, touch). Located in the occipital lobe near the back of the head is the *primary visual cortex,* which receives input from the visual sensory system. Finally, located in the temporal lobe is the *primary auditory cortex,* which receives input from the auditory sensory system.

The remainder of the cerebral cortex is referred to as *association cortex.* In the frontal lobe, the association cortex plays a major role in the planning of motor movements. The association cortex in the remaining three lobes receives information from the primary sensory areas and is heavily involved in perception and memory processes. Damage to the association cortex in any of these three lobes results in a deficit in the ability to process sensory information. For example, a person with damage to the visual association cortex may be unable to identify common objects through sight alone, although the person might be able to identify the object if allowed to touch it.

Organization of the Cerebral Hemispheres

Two interesting principles concerning the organization of the cerebral hemispheres are important to keep in mind as we study human cognition. First, each of the cerebral hemispheres is concerned primarily with sensory and motor processes on the *contralateral,* or opposite, side of the body. That is, the primary motor cortex in the left hemisphere controls movements on the right side of the body, and the primary visual cortex in the right hemisphere receives input from the left side of the scene the person is viewing. There is also evidence of contralateral dominance in the auditory system; that is, the left temporal lobe plays the greatest role in processing information from the right ear, and vice versa.

The second principle concerning the organization of the cerebral hemispheres is that, although on the surface the two cerebral hemispheres appear to be mirror images of one another, they are in fact quite different both in terms of their structure and, more importantly for our purposes, the types of information processing tasks they perform. Although we are far from having a complete understanding of hemispheric specialization, a great deal of evidence supports the idea that different portions of the brain are involved in different information processing tasks (see Springer & Deutsch, 1993). For example, a general pattern that has emerged is that the left hemisphere is heavily involved with language processing, including both production and reception/understanding of speech. In contrast, the right hemisphere is heavily involved with perceptual/spatial processing tasks.

A term that captures the notion that different portions of the brain are involved with different types of information processing tasks is **localization of function.** Localization of function means that certain areas of the brain are more closely involved with one kind of function (e.g., memory, strategic planning) than with other functions. Localization of function does *not* mean that a specific function is controlled exclusively by one region of the brain. Experiment 2 describes a simple demonstration that shows the differential role of the two hemispheres in a language task.

What results did you obtain from Experiment 2, and are they consistent with your prediction? Here is what is typically found in this experiment, and why. Spelling words backwards is a language task. Hence, for a right-handed participant, it should require mainly left-hemisphere processes. Because the balancing task involves contralateral control of the movement of the hands, the left hemisphere is required to control the right hand, and vice versa. Thus, when a person is spelling and balancing the stick on the right hand, both the spelling and balancing tasks are using left-hemisphere processes. Since there is a limit to the amount of information processing the hemispheres can achieve at one time, the difference score should be larger for the right hand than the left hand. That is, the spelling task should overload the left hemisphere when the person is balancing the stick with the right hand (which is controlled by the left hemisphere), with the result being relatively poor performance. We present evidence consistent with this prediction when we discuss theories of attention in Chapter 5.

Section Summary: The Brain

The human brain contains several anatomically distinct areas that play important roles in cognition. Its three major divisions are the hindbrain, midbrain, and forebrain. The forebrain is the structure most recently evolved, and many cognitive processes depend on structures in the forebrain. The cerebral cortex, part of the forebrain, comprises about 80 percent of the mass of the human brain. The cerebral cortex is divided into four distinct lobes: frontal, temporal, parietal, and occipital. These lobes are involved in different types of processes. Two separate hemispheres make up the brain, and although the left and right hemispheres look similar in overall structure, they differ in important ways in the information processing tasks they control. Evidence indicates, for example, that the left hemisphere is heavily involved with language processing, whereas the right hemisphere is heavily involved with perceptual/spatial tasks. Important principles relating to the organization of the brain include contralaterality, hemispheric specialization, and localization of function.

RESEARCH METHODS IN COGNITIVE NEUROPSYCHOLOGY

In this section, we review some of the techniques used to study the brain as it engages in cognitive processes. Several aspects of the human brain make studying its structure and functioning difficult. For example, the human brain is tremendously complex, with billions of cells arranged in systems, subsystems, assemblies, and so forth. The complexity of the relationships *among* systems and structures in the brain, as well as the relationships *be-*

The electrical activity in this subject's brain is being measured with 64 small electrodes arranged around his head. The three electrodes attached to the face record the activity of facial muscles, which can produce electrical signals that add noise to the brain-activity data collected from the scalp. If the electrodes measuring facial muscle activity show that the facial muscles were active during a trial, the data from that trial are discarded.

EXPERIMENT 2:   Hemispheric Specialization

In Chapter 1, we mentioned research by Broca and Wernicke that showed that damage to the left hemisphere of the brain can result in difficulty in performing language tasks. Subsequent research has shown that for about 95 percent of right-handed people, the left hemisphere is dominant for language, meaning that the left hemisphere does most of the information processing in language tasks. In left-handed people the figure is some what lower, around 70 percent (Carlson, 1994).

You can easily demonstrate the dominance of the left hemisphere in language tasks with a simple experiment. All you will need is a yardstick (or any other sturdy, light object about three feet long), a watch that can time in seconds, and a volunteer to participate in the experiment. We recommend that you find a right-handed volunteer, as left hemisphere dominance is more likely with a right-handed person.

In the experiment, your volunteer is going to try to balance the yardstick first with her left hand and then with her right. Also, the volunteer will do the balancing task either alone or while performing a verbal task—spelling words backwards.

Begin the experiment by giving the person four minutes to practice balancing the yardstick, two minutes with each hand. After this practice, have the person complete 11 trials under each of four conditions. For each trial, record how long the person can balance the stick without moving her feet and without having the stick touch her body. If she balances the stick for 45 seconds, record a 45 for that trial and start a new trial.

In the first condition, ask the person to balance the yardstick with her left hand for 11 trials. In the second, have her repeat this with her right hand for 11 trials. The last two conditions will be exactly the same, except that as the person is balancing the stick, you are going to read a word aloud from the list below. The person will try to spell the word backwards as quickly as

tween brain structures and processes and observable behaviors, present many conceptual difficulties. Furthermore, nature has placed several interesting barriers between the scientists who wish to study the brain and the object of their interest. For example, the brain is encased in a rock-hard bony enclosure, it floats in a viscous fluid, and it is surrounded by several layers of tissue. Let's see what techniques scientists have come up with to try and get around these problems.

Scalp Electroencephalography

The brain is composed of billions of neurons that communicate through changes in electrical charge (e.g., action potentials), and it is possible to measure the electrical potentials of these cells at the scalp on the surface of the skull. The collective electrical activity of large groups of cells can be measured with an **electroencephalogram (EEG)**, which provides an overall measure of the electrical activity of the brain. Recording an EEG requires placing a number of small electrodes on a person's scalp. These electrodes record the sum, or total, of the electrical events occurring throughout the person's head.

possible while also balancing the yardstick. If the person finishes spelling a word, give her the next word in the list. Again, record how long she can balance the stick.

Once the person has completed all 44 trials, compute the median balancing time for each of the four conditions. The median is the middlemost score when the scores are arranged from smallest to largest, so it is simply the sixth longest time for each condition. Finally, for both the left and the right hand, compute the difference between the median balancing time for the condition with no spelling and the condition with spelling.

You now have two difference scores, one for each hand. These difference scores tell you how much the spelling task interfered with the balancing task. Given what you have read about hemispheric specialization, which hand should have the largest difference score, and why? After you have made your predictions and computed the scores, finish reading this section of the chapter.

Words to be Spelled Backwards

location	memory	concentrate	experiment
continue	telephone	strawberry	factory
procedure	computer	geometry	barbecue
chocolate	magazine	microscope	digital
hospital	newspaper	energize	safety
cassette	playmate	buffalo	zebra
participate	alphabet	epidemic	repression
character	imagination	celebration	downsize
evacuate	hamburger	baseball	psychology
electric	sailboat	vacation	videotape

Spontaneous EEGs   Researchers use two types of EEG measures. The first is an EEG recording obtained without specific types of external stimulation. These *spontaneous EEGs* are quite useful to researchers. EEG data are plotted on graphs that have *voltage* on the y-axis and *time* on the x-axis. These plots are referred to as *waves* or *waveforms*. A number of EEG waveforms are associated with specific states of consciousness and certain types of neural damage. If an individual is experiencing difficulty with certain types of cognitive tasks, then an EEG can help to identify which portions of the brain may be damaged.

   Although the overall spontaneous EEG procedure has proved to be a useful clinical diagnostic tool, it has not resulted in as many insights into brain functioning as was once hoped. The reason is that the spontaneous EEG represents the total electrical activity arising from many different parts of the brain. There are billions of neurons in the brain, all constantly varying in their membrane potentials, so the patterns of activity recorded are only loosely related to events of interest in the brain. Furthermore, because the researcher has no control over what the person is thinking or perceiving, it is difficult to relate these brain-wave activities to underlying thought processes.

Event-Related Potentials (ERPs)   This latter problem is reduced in the second type of EEG, which records **event-related potentials (ERPs)**. When EEGs are measured, there is a great deal of background noise that is unrelated to the cognitive process of interest. With the ERP technique, each subject is presented with a given type of stimulus many times, and the EEG is recorded for each of these stimulus presentations. The EEGs are averaged across many repetitions of the stimulus presentation, so the background noise averages out, and what is left is a representation of the average response of the brain to the external stimulus. When the event-related potential is averaged over many stimulus presentations, the average brain wave that results is referred to as the **average evoked potential (AEP).** Each AEP wave is characterized by its change in voltage (either positive or negative) and by its latency, the time between the stimulus and the appearance of the wave. By tracing the time course of the AEPs, researchers have been able to relate these brain-wave signals to underlying cognitive processes.

ERPs have been used successfully in studying a wide variety of cognitive processes. The basic approach, as mentioned, is to present the subject with a specific type of stimulus and take an EEG recording each time the stimulus is presented. For example, on each trial, a subject might be asked to read a sentence stem (e.g., "The pizza was too hot to") followed by a single word. On some trials, the word given after the sentence stem fits the sentence (e.g., "eat"), and on others, it does not (e.g., "cry"). When the EEG recordings from trials of each type are averaged, we see significant differences between the ERPs from trials in which the word fits and the ERPs from trials in which the word does not fit.

By carefully varying the types of stimuli and instructions given to subjects, researchers can correlate certain aspects of the ERP wave with perceptual and cognitive processes. For example, at about 300 ms after a surprising or unexpected stimulus is presented, a large, positive-voltage waveform is obtained. A large negative waveform is obtained at about 400 ms when the stimulus is incongruous in meaning, as when "cry" is presented after "The pizza was too hot to" (Kutas & Van Petten, 1988).

Computerized Tomographic Scans

Recent technological advances and increasingly powerful computer systems have led to the development of a number of methods for studying the structure of the intact human brain. The first such procedure developed was the **computerized axial tomography (CAT)** scan, a computerized x-ray procedure that produces a two-dimensional picture of the structure of the human brain. The CAT scan procedure basically involves taking a series of x-ray images of different horizontal sections of the living brain, which a computer then combines to yield a series of two-dimensional images.

A person having a CAT scan lies with his or her head inside a large cylinder. On one side of the cylinder is a source of x-ray beams, and on the opposite side is an x-ray detector. As the subject lies still within the CAT scan device, the x-ray source and detector are rotated around the cylinder, taking a series of individual images as they rotate. After taking images of one "slice" of the brain, the x-ray source and detector are moved either up or down so as to take another series of images at a different location in the brain. This process is usually repeated to yield eight or nine horizontal images from each subject. After the scan is complete, the computer takes the information extracted from the scan and plots a series of two-dimensional pictures of a horizontal section of the patient's brain (see Figure 2.7).

CAT scans have been extremely useful in the diagnosis of neurological damage. The CAT scan technique has also been used effectively by neuroscientists to relate cognitive and behavioral deficits to damage within specific locations in the human brain.

FIGURE 2.7   **CAT Scan Results**   (Top) Illustration of the computerized axial tomography (CAT) scan technique. The CAT scan device moves a source of x-rays around the person's head at different heights and the x-rays are measured as they pass through the person's head. These data are processed by a computer that produces detailed images of the structures in the person's head. (Bottom) CAT scans from a normal individual (left) and an individual who had sustained a stroke. The stroke lesion is visible as a large white area.

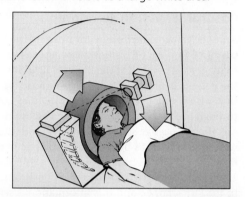

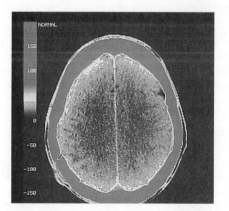
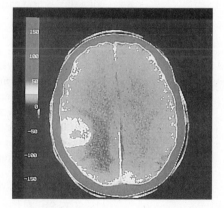

Magnetic Resonance Imaging

Another useful imaging technique is **magnetic resonance imaging (MRI)**. Unlike a CAT scanner, an MRI scanner does not use x-rays. Rather, it produces an extremely strong magnetic field. As with the CAT scan procedure, the patient's head lies within the scanning device. When tissue is placed in a strong magnetic field, the nuclei of some molecules in the tissue spin in a particular spatial orientation. The MRI procedure takes advantage of the fact that hydrogen atoms emit energy at a specific frequency when activated by radio frequency waves in the magnetic field produced by the MRI. Because the concentration of hydrogen atoms varies considerably and predictably in different neural structures, the MRI procedure produces an image of the brain that is of much higher spatial resolution than that yielded by the CAT scan procedure. (We return to the issue of spatial resolution later in this chapter.)

MRI scans yield important data concerning the structure of the human brain. In addition, recent technological advances have allowed researchers to use the MRI procedure to examine the activity levels in given brain structures. In one procedure, known as *functional MRI*, the MRI works indirectly by detecting blood flow. Blood cells give up their oxygen to active brain cells, and the MRI traces this process. Functional MRI promises to yield important new insights relating brain structure to brain activity (see Cohen, Noll & Schneider, 1993).

Positron Emission Tomography

Another valuable technique for imaging the brain is the **positron emission tomography (PET)** scan. PET scans allow researchers to determine the amount of metabolic activity in various areas of the living brain. In the most common type of PET scan procedure, the patient is first injected with a radioactive substance similar to glucose. Communication within and between neurons requires considerable energy, which must be supplied through the blood system. Because glucose is the primary source of energy for neural tissue, the radioactive substance injected into the patient is taken up by the most active neurons in the patient's brain. As this radioactive substance is being taken into active neural tissue, the patient's head is placed in a PET scanner. As the radioactive material decays, it emits subatomic particles known as positrons. These positrons are measured by detectors in the PET scanner, and this information is sent to a computer, which produces an image of a slice of the patient's brain. This image thus represents the relative activity level of various regions within the brain.

PET scans are quite useful because they allow researchers to investigate dynamic processes that take place in real time. By varying the stimuli and tasks given to people and then examining which regions of the brain increase (or decrease) in activity levels, we can determine which areas are involved in performing the various tasks. Let us consider how PET scans have been used to study the activity you are engaged in right now—reading.

In reading, very small differences in physical stimuli can signal important information about the intended meaning of the letter strings. For example, *bead* and *head* differ only slightly in terms of physical stimuli, and yet these items are perceived by readers of English to mean quite different things. These differences clearly are learned, which means that in some way the nervous system has acquired the ability to discern small differences, including the fact that some letter strings correspond to meaningful words in a given language, whereas others (e.g., *xrtuzq*) do not.

Peterson and his colleagues (1988) began with the assumption that as visual stimuli, words can be represented by four different types of codes, or internal representations. First, words are made up of combinations of connected lines and curves in various spatial arrangements; these codes are called *visual features*. Second, a subset of all possible visual features comprises the 26 letters in the English language. This set of features corresponds to the *letter* codes for English. Third, rules within the English language determine the permissible orders in which the 26 letters can be arranged to make pronounceable letter strings. These rules represent the *orthographic* codes for the language. Finally, words have specific meanings that are understood by speakers of the language; these can be referred to as the *word meaning* codes.

Given this set of four codes, how can we identify which part (or parts) of the nervous system is (or are) responsible for processing each code? If we were to present a subject with English words and measure his or her brain's responses to these words, these responses should be the response to all four codes. So how can we determine if different areas are responsible for, say, processing visual features and processing word meaning?

To answer this question, Peterson and his colleagues presented various types of visual stimuli to their subjects and monitored brain activity using a PET scan procedure. In order to separate the overall response of the nervous system to English words, they used items that corresponded to different types of codes. The types of stimuli used in the experiment are presented in Table 2.2. As the table indicates, these four sets of stimuli can be arranged so that each higher-level set includes all the codes of the lower set plus one additional code. Peterson and his colleagues conducted PET scans of a group of normal English-speaking adults as they were passively observing these four types of stimuli. The average PET scan results are presented in Figure 2.8. As this figure indicates, the nervous system responds in a very different manner to these four classes of stimuli.

By combining appropriate experimental methodology with powerful brain-imaging techniques, Peterson and his colleagues demonstrated that the brain responds in very discernible ways to stimuli with different characteristics. Subsequent research along these lines has expanded this methodology by requiring subjects to actively process the visual items as they are presented.

Assessing Neuropsychological Recording Methods

Neuroscientists are actively pursuing many different ways to explore the relations among brain, behavior, and thought. One way to characterize the relative strengths and weaknesses of the various research techniques employed by neuroscientists is to consider them in terms of spatial resolution (i.e., how finely the technique can identify a structure or

TABLE 2.2   **Examples of the Four Types of Stimuli Used by Peterson, Fox, Posner, Mintum, and Raichle (1988)**

Stimuli			
False Fonts	**Letterstrings**	**Pseudowords**	**Words**
₥НƎ	VSFFHT	GEEL	ANT
Ɉ၅ɈU	TBBL	IOB	RAZOR
४၅ᎢU	TSTFS	RELD	DUST
⊦⌐ᎠႮ	JBBT	BLERCE	FURNACE
ႮႮᎫႱჵ	STB	CHELDINABE	FARM
Codes			
Visual	Visual	Visual	Visual
Features	Features	Features	Features
	Letter code	Letter code	Letter code
		Orthographic	Orthographic
			Word meaning

FIGURE 2.8   **PET Scan Results from Peterson et al.**   Peterson and his colleagues studied the brain's response to different types of visual stimuli. Note that different regions of the brain responded most vigorously to different types of stimuli. By contrasting these different patterns of responses, Peterson and his colleagues were able to identify different types of internal codes processed during reading.

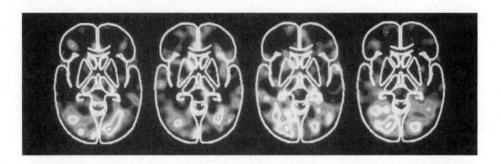

process in the brain) and temporal resolution (i.e., over what time span the technique is appropriate).

Churchland and Sejnowski (1991) reviewed the available techniques and noted several important facts concerning these techniques. First, each is relatively limited in terms of both spatial and temporal resolution. For example, a PET scan may be useful for studying processes that occur over several minutes, but it cannot be used to study processes that occur within several seconds. Second, the spatial and temporal resolutions of the various techniques overlap only slightly. One consequence of this fact is that different techniques are useful for studying different processes or structures.

To appreciate the implications of these limitations, let us consider the types of information we can get from more familiar devices. If you are looking at objects with a microscope, you can see very small details, but if you want to look at a larger field of view or at more distant objects, you might want to use binoculars. These two devices differ in their spatial resolution; microscopes are good at showing small details, and binoculars are better for looking at larger objects. Similarly, if you want to capture an image of a very rapid event (e.g., a raindrop landing on a table), you might want to use a high-speed camera that takes single photos. If, however, you want to record something that takes longer (e.g., your parents' wedding anniversary celebration), then you might want to use a video recorder. These two imaging devices differ greatly in the time, or temporal, domains for which they are well suited. The neuropsychological recording methods available today are subject to similar limitations.

A further limitation is that some structures and processes are beyond the scope of current neuropsychological research techniques. These structures and processes somehow exceed these techniques' spatial or temporal resolution.

As a consequence of the various limitations of current research tools, neuroscientists need to make inferences across wide ranges of different types of observations. This situation is nicely captured by an analogy developed by Professor John Mazziotta. Mazziotta (cited in Crease, 1993) likened the task of building an understanding of brain functioning from the observations of various imaging techniques to drawing pictures using the pointillist style of painting. In discussing brain imaging technologies in behavioral research, Mazziotta (1993) presented a slide of a pointillist painting like the one in Figure 2.9 and made this observation:

> I use this slide to illustrate the current state of brain and behavioral research techniques. Individual investigators have each been working on their own dots, developing their own techniques to optimize the precision, accuracy, and reliability of each. But we're just at the stage where we can begin to step back from the canvas and look at the emerging big picture that is the integrated sum of all methods. And what we are beginning to see is something much greater than what we've been able to see before—more than the sum of each of the parts.

Finally, these various limitations will probably not prove to be insurmountable. For example, a number of advances have been made recently that combine existing techniques

---

FIGURE 2.9   **A Pointillist Painting**   Note that the entire picture consists of dots spread across the page. The picture emerges only when you consider all of the dots together.

in creative ways. One of the newest of these is a technique that combines EEG and MRI technologies (Gevins et al., 1994). To record the EEG signals, as many as 128 electrodes are attached to the person's head. A computer is then used to map the ongoing brain activity recorded from the scalp onto a three-dimensional MRI image of the brain. When these two imaging techniques are combined, the results provide a view that is like a videotape of on-going changes in brain-cell activity (see Figure 2.10).

Clinical Case Studies

The imaging and recording techniques we have just reviewed allow researchers to conduct controlled experiments using normal subjects or subjects with some neurological damage. But there are ethical limitations on the types of research that can be conducted using human subjects. For example, it is not possible to remove portions of the brain simply to see what effect this will have on behavior and mental processes. In some cases, however, individuals suffer damage to the brain and sensory systems, and we can study these cases to try to discern the effects of the damage on behavior.

   Clinical neurological case studies are investigations of individuals who have suffered damage to the nervous system either as a result of accident (e.g., stroke) or through surgical interventions designed to deal with neurological problems. The description of Phineas Gage given in Research Report 2 is an example of a clinical case study. In such

---

FIGURE 2.10   **Combining EEG and MRI**   Researchers have recently combined EEG and MRI technologies that allow them to monitor moment-by-moment changes in electrical charges from cells in different regions of the brain. The models in this figure show the changes that occur on the brain's surface as a person compares the location of a new stimulus with the location of one recently presented. Different regions of the brain are activated over time as the person performs this task.

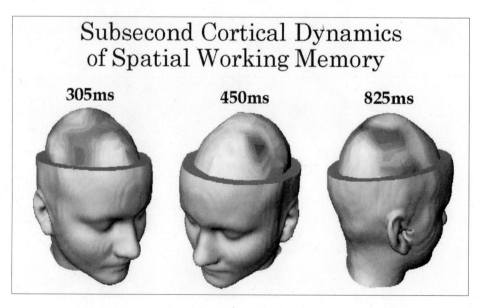

studies, investigators attempt to determine the relation between cognitive functions and damage to specific brain areas in specific individuals. These studies can be quite important and can reveal information that would not be readily obtainable with noninvasive research techniques such as those described earlier. Still, a healthy dose of skepticism is called for in interpreting the results of case studies, especially those involving single subjects. One general problem with single-subject clinical case studies is that it is difficult to determine how representative the individual case is with regard to the population at large. Another problem is that it is often difficult to know the exact source and extent of damage suffered by the individual. Note, however, that not all clinical case studies involve single subjects. Many types of brain damage, unfortunately, affect many individuals. In these cases, interpreting the results of studies does not involve the problems associated with single cases.

Another problem with interpreting the results of clinical case studies involves combining data from different sources. Imagine that (1) a brain scan shows that some region of the brain is damaged and (2) observations of the individual show impairment in the performance of some types of cognitive tasks. Can we interpret these data as indicating that the processes necessary for performing these types of tasks are localized at the damaged brain site? Not really, for there are alternative interpretations. For example, perhaps the processing is actually performed in another region of the brain but the information is normally conveyed through the damaged region. This interpretive problem is not specific to clinical studies, but it is especially important to consider alternative interpretations when only a single subject is available for study. Still, with rapid improvements being made in brain-imaging techniques, this interpretive problem should decrease in the future.

Section Summary: Research Methods

Scalp electroencephalography (EEG, ERP) allows researchers to study changes in overall patterns of electrical activity in the intact brain. CAT scans and MRI scans provide fairly detailed images of the structure of the brain; CAT scans use x-ray imaging, whereas MRI scans use magnetic fields to produce images of the brain. PET scans offer a powerful means for studying brain activity by measuring patterns of metabolic activity. Information regarding the activity levels and structure of the brain can provide important insights into the neuropsychological underpinnings of the mind. However, the types of conclusions that can be drawn based on the existing types of brain-imaging procedures are limited by the spatial and temporal resolution that can be achieved with these procedures. Another way to conduct research is through clinical neurological case studies. However, the conclusions that can be drawn from such studies are also limited, especially when they involve a single subject.

ANALYSIS AND EXPLANATION OF COGNITION

Earlier we described John Mazziotta's analogy between brain-imaging techniques and pointillist painting. We would add that what one sees—a single point, a group of points arranged in a line, or an entire image—depends entirely on whether one is focusing on a small part of the image or the entire canvas. Similarly, the answers to questions about brain-behavior relations often depend on what level of the nervous system a researcher is interested in. In this final section, we discuss how to put the various approaches, methods, and results into a proper perspective.

Levels of Analysis

Up to this point, we have focused mainly on the functioning of individual neurons and the gross anatomical structure of the brain. We can, however, consider the brain's structure and functioning on other levels. For example, we might consider chemical processes that underlie the workings of neurons, collections of neurons arranged in networks, larger collections of neurons that act as separate systems (e.g., the visual system, the auditory system), and so forth.

The important point to note here is that the nervous system is organized on many levels and each of these levels relates in important ways to aspects of cognition. Since each level plays a role in producing mental activity and behavior, an interesting question that arises is how the various levels relate to one another. Once we acknowledge that the nervous system is organized at many different levels and in many different ways, it becomes evident that a complete understanding of brain-behavior relations requires not only that we understand the workings of the nervous system at many levels but also that we specify the relations *across* levels. We consider this important fact in the next section.

Levels of Explanation

One important issue that we have not addressed thus far is how the various types of empirical observations we have discussed relate to various types of theories accounting for human cognition. It turns out that different theorists have offered quite distinct views on this issue.

Marr's View on Theories   David Marr (1982) was a vision researcher whose writings on how to develop theories have had a tremendous impact on cognitive scientists. Marr was concerned with how we can understand any machine (or organism) that carries out an information processing task (e.g., recognizing an object in a visual scene). Marr argued that this understanding can be framed at three fundamentally different levels: computational theory, representation and algorithm, and hardware implementation. These levels are presented in Table 2.3. Although Marr was concerned with how the visual system could be understood, his insights have important implications for theories of human cognition and also for how physiological and behavioral research relate to one another.

A few words of explanation are in order before we discuss how Marr's ideas relate to studying cognition. First, Marr's term *computational theory* refers to an abstract level of problem (or task) analysis in which the task of interest is broken down into its main components. For example, a problem in visual perception might involve determining the three-dimensional structure of a moving object from a series of views of that object. Second, *algorithm level* refers to a formal procedure (or set of rules) for performing the task by providing a correct output from a given input. Finally, *implementation level* refers to the actual physical "hardware" that performs the information processing task using the specified algorithm.

Marr argued that each higher level is largely independent of the levels below it. To make this point concrete, consider the following example of an information processing task. Imagine that you have as a goal being able to compute daily and yearly return rates on investments based on an annual interest rate. This goal is analogous to Marr's top, abstract level, the computational theory, for it specifies the inputs to the task and the appropriate outputs based on those inputs. A set of mathematical formulas can be used to achieve the goal. The formulas represent the algorithm for achieving the computational goal of taking a given set of inputs (e.g., interest rate, amount of money invested) and producing correct

TABLE 2.3   **Marr's Three Levels at which a Machine Carrying Out an Information Processing Task Must Be Understood**

Computational Theory	Representation and Algorithm	Hardware Implementation
What is the goal of the computation? Why is the computation appropriate? What is the logic by which this strategy can be carried out?	How can this computational theory be achieved? What is the nature of the information input to and output from the theory? What rules are used to transform inputs into outputs?	How can the inputs and outputs, as well as the rules of transformation, be realized in a physical device?

Source: Adapted from Marr (1982).

output. Note, however, that these formulas are in a sense independent of both the goal and the use or implementation of the formulas. They are not entirely determined by the goal because other formulas could be used to achieve the goal. They are not specific to the hardware used to carry out the computations, either; they will produce the correct output regardless of whether they are used in paper-and-pencil calculations, with a calculator, or as a computer program.

By analogy, then, if the goal of understanding human cognition is to specify how cognitive tasks are performed, we can attempt to understand cognition at the level of computational theory ("What is the exact task we are interested in? What are the inputs to the task, the outputs, and any other constraints on how the task is performed?"), at the algorithmic level ("Given these inputs, outputs, and associated constraints, what are the functional relationships that yield the correct outputs given the inputs?"), or at the hardware level ("How are these algorithms performed by the sensory and nervous systems?").

Marr's argument that each higher level is independent of the lower levels suggests that we can develop abstract theories of human cognition without being overly concerned with how the information processing task is accomplished by the sensory and nervous systems. Taken at face value, this approach has considerable merit, and some have suggested that cognitive psychology can proceed to develop theories without specifying the manner in which the processes postulated by the theories are accomplished by the sensory and nervous systems.

Churchland and Sejnowski's Proposal   Churchland and Sejnowski (1991) have argued that although Marr's views are correct in a strictly abstract, formal sense, in another sense, they are flawed. Since the algorithms specified by a given theory are abstract, they may be carried out by microcomputers or groups of neurons. Thus, an algorithm may be embodied in any one of an almost infinite set of possible physical systems. In this case, how are we to discover the algorithm used by the particular machine or organism in which we are primarily interested? Cognitive psychologists and cognitive neuroscientists are interested in how humans perform various tasks; thus, the fact that other machines could utilize algorithms different from the ones used by the human brain is of little consequence. Deciding which view (Marr's or Churchland and Sejnowski's) is "correct" depends upon your goal. If you wish to formulate a theory that can account for intelligent behavior in general (that is, not just human behavior), then Marr's view has merit. If, on the other hand, you are interested in accounting for human behavior, then Churchland and Sejnowski's view seems more reasonable. As cognitive psychologists we want to learn how the *brain* supports intelligent *behavior,* and hence we are well advised to use *both* behavioral and physiological approaches for studying human cognition. We offer the following three points to support this conclusion.

First, understanding how the nervous system operates can place important limitations on psychological theories. For example, if two competing theories attempt to account for the same set of phenomena, then it is reasonable to ask whether one of them seems more plausible given what we know about the operation of the nervous system. If one of these theories makes assumptions that are neurologically implausible, then that theory is less likely to be accepted by psychologists as an adequate theoretical account than is a theory that is consistent with known facts about the brain and sensory systems.

Second, as our understanding of brain functioning becomes more detailed, the facts obtained from studies of the brain can serve to guide theory development in cognitive psychology and to suggest areas for further behavioral research. For most of the history of scientific psychology, studies of behavior and studies of the nervous system have operated more or less in parallel. Although both the neuroscientific and cognitive approaches have produced considerable success, recent theoretical, empirical, and technological developments have made it possible to pursue the study of cognition in a different manner. Polster, Nadel, and Schacter (1991) refer to these newer approaches as follows:

> **Complementary relations** are observed when the analysis of a phenomenon in one discipline can usefully supplement the analysis of a similar phenomenon in another discipline. . . . **Convergent relations** refer to situations in which scientists in two or more disciplines coordinate their research programs so as to investigate a particular issue or phenomenon with the tools and ideas of each of the disciplines. (Polster et al., 1991, p. 196)

Churchland and Sejnowski (1991) argue that this type of convergent-relations approach involving different scientific disciplines can be used in a **coevolutionary research approach** where behavioral analyses of cognitive processes proceed hand in hand with more physiological analyses of the functioning of the nervous system (e.g., Cohen, Noll & Schneider, 1993; Peterson et al., 1988).

Finally, findings from studies of the functioning of the nervous system and behavior patterns of humans and other animals can be important sources of converging operations (Garner, Hake & Eriksen, 1956). **Converging operations** are situations in which manipulation of two or more independent variables converge upon, or provide support for, a specific hypothesis or theory. Converging operations involve the evaluation of hypotheses and theories on the basis of multiple, independent lines of evidence. Converging operations are an important research tool for investigators concerned with unobservable events such as cognitive processes.

Section Summary: Analysis and Explanation of Cognition

The human mind can be studied on many different levels (e.g., physiological, behavioral). Each of these levels relates to human cognition and research is rapidly moving ahead on many different levels. One critical problem that needs to be addressed in studying the human mind is how to relate the findings from studies across different levels of analysis. David Marr argued that information processing systems can be understood at three different levels (computational theory level, algorithm level, implementation level) and that these three levels were logically independent of one another. Churchland and Sejnowski (1991) have argued that researchers interested in understanding human cognition need to be concerned with facts about how the human brain functions because this information can help scientists understand the human mind. Although there is no one "right" level at which to study human cognition, results from studies that utilize different levels of analysis are important sources of converging operations that can help refine theories and models of human cognition.

REVIEWING THE NEUROPSYCHOLOGICAL BASES OF COGNITION

CONCEPT REVIEW

1. What are the localist and holist views of brain function? Which of these views is more in line with findings of specific cognitive deficits following brain damage? Is the notion of hemispheric specialization more consistent with a localist or a holist view?

2. What are the major structures of a neuron? How are they involved in communication processes within and between cells?

3. Communication within and between cells involves graded and all-or-none responses. Describe which responses are graded and which are all-or-none. How are these concepts used in cognitive psychology theories?

4. How can the McCulloch and Pitts neuron "compute," or make decisions?

5. What processes and mechanisms support learning and memory at the neural level?

6. What are the three major divisions of the brain? What are the primary functions performed by the structures within these divisions?

7. Describe the major divisions of the cerebral cortex and the types of functions performed by cells within these divisions. What are the two main principles of organization within the cerebral hemispheres?

8. The research methods used by cognitive neuropsychologists involve several types of brain-imaging techniques. Describe these techniques, noting whether each is used more to study the structure of the brain or the processes in the brain.

9. What are clinical neurological case studies? What are their strengths and weaknesses?

10. Describe the three levels at which Marr argued we can understand a computing system. According to Marr, how are these levels related? What are the arguments against using Marr's theoretical approach to understand brain-behavior relations in humans?

KEY TERMS

action potential (p. 41)
average evoked potential (AEP) (p. 54)
axon (p. 38)
cerebral cortex (p. 49)
clinical neurological case study (p. 60)
coevolutionary research approach
    (p. 64)
complementary relations (p. 64)
computerized axial tomography (CAT)
    (p. 54)
convergent relations (p. 64)

converging operations (p. 64)
corpus callosum (p. 50)
dendrite (p. 38)
dual trace hypothesis (p. 46)
electroencephalogram (EEG) (p. 52)
event-related potential (ERP) (p. 54)
hemispheric specialization (p. 35)
localization of function (p. 51)
magnetic resonance imaging (MRI)
    (p. 55)

memory trace (p. 46)
neuron (p. 38)
neurotransmitter (p. 39)
perceptron (p. 46)
phrenology (p. 34)
positron emission tomography (PET)
    (p. 56)
resting potential (p. 40)
synapse (p. 39)

SUGGESTED READINGS

A good source for a brief review of neuroscience principles is Richard Thompson's (1993) *The brain: A neuroscience primer* (New York: W. H. Freeman). A somewhat more detailed, although still very readable, overview of physiological psychology is given in Neil Carlson's (1994) text *Physiology of behavior* (Needham Heights, MA: Allyn and Bacon). An excellent overview of cognitive neuroscience can be found in Stephen Kosslyn and Olivier Koenig's text *Wet mind: The new cognitive neuroscience* (New York: Free Press). The 1995 edition of this text includes an epilogue on recent research as well as interesting comments on the 1992 edition of the book. Patricia Churchland and Terrence Sejnowski's (1989) book *The computational brain* (Cambridge, MA: MIT Press) gives an in-depth review of research on how the brain functions and how this research can inform theories that seek to explain cognitive processes. A good source for original research on cognitive neuropsychology is *Journal of Cognitive Neuroscience*.

3 Sensing and Perceiving

We are so familiar with seeing, that it takes a leap of imagination to realize that there are problems to be solved. But consider it. We are given tiny distorted upside-down images in the eyes, and we separate solid objects in surrounding space. From the patterns of stimulation on the retinas we perceive the world as objects, and this is nothing short of a miracle. —R. L. Gregory (1973)

AKE A MOMENT AND LOOK AROUND YOU. Move your head quickly from side to side. You will experience a stable, three-dimensional world that does not move when you shake your head. This is no simple feat. From a rapidly moving pattern of light falling on your retinas, your sensory and perceptual processes determine, among other things, what objects are in the room, the color of these objects, and which objects are closer to you than others.

In this and the following chapter, we explore how we develop internal representations of the world around us. Chapter 3 explains how our sensory systems function, and Chapter 4 describes how we identify patterns and objects in the environment. Why is this knowledge important for cognitive psychologists?

Quite simply, the answer is that sensory and perceptual processes are closely linked to how we think. Because cognitive psychology is concerned with the mind, cognitive psychologists must be aware of the abilities and limitations of the sensory and perceptual systems that provide information about the world. As we discussed in Chapter 2, cognitive psychologists will not seriously consider a theory whose assumptions are invalid based on what is known about how the nervous system functions. Similarly, they do not want to propose theories of the mind that are at odds with how the sensory and perceptual systems represent the world around us.

We begin our discussion by examining how we extract stimulus information from the world. In the remainder of the chapter, we review how sensory and perceptual systems begin the process of creating internal representations that can be used in various cognitive processes. In Chapter 4, we discuss how these initial representations are interpreted so that we experience an organized, meaningful world rather than a jumble of individual sensations. Then, in the remaining chapters, we focus on the higher-level cognitive processes that underlie the human mind. It is important to remember, however, that these "higher" cognitive processes rely on the sensory and perceptual systems' establishing fairly accurate representations of the world around us. If we misperceive a tennis ball's speed, the movement of a car ahead of us on the highway, or the letters printed on this page, this error will influence our behaviors and thoughts.

DETECTING STIMULI

The methods that scientists use generally reflect their assumptions about the phenomena they are studying. Early sensory researchers assumed that the sensory systems would respond consistently to a given physical stimulus presented on two occasions, and the methods they developed to study the responses of the sensory systems reflect this view. Later, researchers realized that the responses a person makes to a stimulus can be affected by many factors. Once scientists accepted this new view that the sensory and perceptual systems are very flexible, they developed theories and methods consistent with this view.

A Generic Model of Sensory and Perceptual Processes

Our sensory and perceptual systems allow us to perform three main functions: (a) detecting that a stimulus is present, (b) detecting a change in a stimulus, and (c) identifying what objects or events gave rise to the stimulus. As the quote from Gregory at the start of the chapter indicates, these sensory and perceptual abilities normally work so well that it is easy to overlook the difficulty of, for example, perceiving a three-dimensional world from a two-dimensional image in the eye or understanding a conversation in a noisy room. A good way to begin to appreciate the complexity of these systems is to consider a simple model of how these processes operate.

Figure 3.1 presents the major parts of a generic information processing model of sensory and perceptual processes. This model provides a good overview of the main stages involved in creating an internal representation of the external world. The stages in this model do not necessarily correspond to physical structures involved in processing information (e.g., receptors in the eye, neural pathways connecting the sensory receptors and the central nervous system). Rather, they represent information processing stages that have been postulated by researchers to account for sensing and perceiving.

According to the model in Figure 3.1, objects and events in the environment give rise to stimulus energy, which is registered in the sensory organs—the receptors in the eyes and ears. The energy that strikes the sensory receptors undergoes **transduction,** a process by which the physical energy from the stimulus is translated into a change in activity in the nervous system. The transduced stimulus energy is then registered in a sensory memory system, which maintains a representation of the stimulus's physical characteristics for a brief period of time. One of the main questions we consider in this chapter is how these sensory memory systems function. That is, what type of information do we obtain from stimuli, and how long does this information last?

In the next stage, information from the sensory receptors is conveyed to higher areas of the central nervous system. In the central nervous system, the stimulus representation is further processed and coded, so as to represent the various properties of the stimulus (e.g., color, shape, motion). The stimulus may also be classified according to learned categories (e.g., a volleyball, a tune by Aerosmith), and the nervous system can store this representation as well. Finally, the information extracted from the stimulus is represented in memory and may be transformed in other ways as necessary to perform various tasks.

FIGURE 3.1 **Information Processing Model of Sensation and Perception** The model illustrates both observable external phenomena and unobservable internal stages and processes.

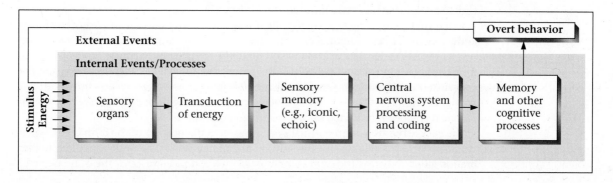

Although the model in Figure 3.1 does not contain a "dividing line" between sensation and perception, we have implied that some distinction exists between sensing and perceiving. Historically, *sensations* have been thought of as simple experiences elicited by simple stimuli, whereas *perception* has been said to involve the interpretation of these sensations. Thus, we refer to "sensing" the presence of a light or a tone and "perceiving" a face or a voice. This distinction between sensation and perception may appear straightforward, but in practice the division between the two is very unclear. Because we have no method for distinguishing between a sensation and a perception, the distinction is more one of convenience than of scientific fact.

Visual Sensory System

We turn next to a consideration of the visual sensory system. The manner in which the eye and the nervous system respond to light affects the quantity and type of information we can obtain through the visual modality. In addition, the connections between the eye and the brain affect how the nervous system processes visual information.

Sensory Receptors   The stimulus we call light comes from a small band of electromagnetic energy to which our visual system is sensitive. This energy travels in waves, which can vary in intensity and in wavelength. Intensity, the amount of energy in a unit of time, is a major factor determining how bright the light is perceived to be. A 100-watt light bulb has more energy and is perceived as brighter than a 70-watt bulb. Wavelength is the distance between two successive waves. It is a major determinant of perceived color.

Presented in Figure 3.2 are the major structures of the eye and the cells in the eye that respond to light. When light enters the eye, it is focused and inverted by the cornea and lens, and the inverted image is projected onto the *retina* at the back of the eye. Visual system transduction—the point at which the nervous system codes, or represents, the external stimulus—begins at the retina.

The nervous system's response to light begins in the *photoreceptor layer,* where chemical processes in photoreceptor cells known as *rods* and *cones* convert patterns of light stimulation into changes in cell membrane potentials. Rods are specialized for responding to very low levels of light, and cones are involved in color perception. Action potentials fired in these cells begin the process that allows information about the stimulus to be conveyed to the brain. The rods and cones share synapses with *bipolar cells,* which collect information from these receptors. The bipolar cells in turn pass information along to *ganglion cells,* whose axons convey information via the optic nerve to higher centers in the brain. The point at which the optic nerve leaves the retina is referred to as the **blind spot,** because it contains no photoreceptors. Although we are normally not aware of the blind spot, it is easy to demonstrate its existence (see Experiment 3).

When we look directly at an object, light from that object falls on an area of the retina known as the **fovea.** Visual acuity, or how precisely we can discriminate between two nearby objects, is greatest at the fovea. The fovea contains only cones, but as we move from the fovea toward the periphery of the retina, the number of cones decreases, and the concentration of rods increases. This distribution of rods and cones creates important differences in how the visual system responds to light coming from different areas of the visual field and being projected onto different areas of the retina.

The **receptive field** in the visual system refers to the portion of the retina that, when stimulated, causes a change in the activity level of neurons in the optic nerve and higher brain regions. Whereas the retina contains 127 million receptor cells, the optic nerve of

FIGURE 3.2 **The Human Eye** The diagram shows the gross structure of the eye, including the cornea, lens, retina, fovea, blind spot, and optic nerve. Detail from the retina shows the main layers of cells, including the photoreceptor layer (rods and cones), bipolar cell layer, and ganglion cell layer.

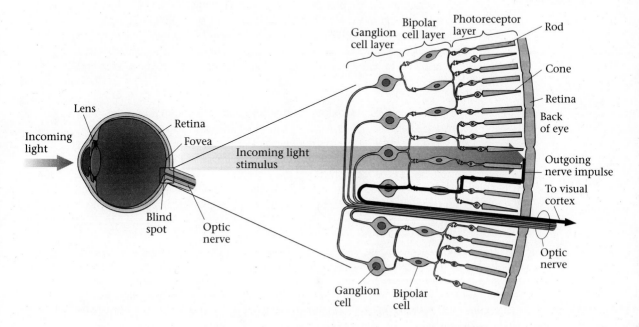

each eye contains only about 800,000 ganglion cells. This means that a single ganglion cell conveys information from many photoreceptors. The receptive fields of rods are much larger than those of cones, which means that, in general, a ganglion cell that collects information from rods collects information from more photoreceptors than a ganglion cell that collects information from cones. This is one reason why our visual acuity is greatest for objects projecting light onto the fovea, where cones are highly concentrated.

Connections Between the Eyes and the Brain Information from the photoreceptors is projected along a complex neural pathway from the optic nerve of each eye to the **primary visual cortex** in the occipital lobe. The optic nerves meet at the *optic chiasm*. At that point, axons from cells in the outer portion of the retina continue on to the same side of the brain, whereas axons from the inner portion of the retina cross at the chiasm and continue on to the opposite side of the brain. An interesting consequence of this arrangement is that each hemisphere of the brain receives information from the *contralateral* (or opposite) half of the visual field. Thus, if you are looking straight at the middle of a movie screen, the images on the left edge of the screen are being processed by the right side of the brain, and vice versa. This contralateral processing of visual information is similar to the contralateral control of motor movements you encountered in Experiment 2.

An analogy is often made between the human eye and a camera. Producing images with a camera, however, involves a passive process in which chemicals respond to light projected onto film at the back of the camera. In contrast, the visual systems of humans and

EXPERIMENT 3:   The Blind Spot

The area of the retina at which the optic nerve leaves the eye is functionally blind because it contains no photoreceptor cells (rods or cones). You can use the images presented here to demonstrate the existence of this blind spot. Before you try this exercise, answer this question: What do you think you will see when light from the word *Cat* is projected onto your blind spot? If your perception of the world depended on just the response of your sensory systems, then you should see nothing. Let's find out if that is what happens.

Using the top row in Figure 3A, close your left eye and with your right eye focus on the word Dog. Keep your left eye closed and move the page toward you. At some point the word Cat disappears. This happens because the image of the word Cat is falling on your blind spot, which demonstrates the existence of the blind spot. But do we see "nothing" at the location where the word Cat had been? No. Although the word Cat seems to disappear from the page, the line that connects the boxes but does not go through them now appears to continue unbroken across the area where Cat appeared.

This phenomenon indicates that the visual system somehow automatically "fills in" the missing information. Furthermore, the visual system will fill in more complex shapes. To demonstrate this, repeat the steps described above using either the wavy-line version or the patterned version of the demonstration. In both cases, the nervous system uses the information surrounding the blind spot—the context—to construct an image that appears at the blind spot. Perception and pattern recognition are far more complicated than simple, passive responses to the patterns of stimulus information that fall upon the receptor cells. Researchers have used perception at the blind

other animals do not respond passively to visual stimulation. Rather, as you saw in Experiment 3, vision involves an active and complex set of processes that respond selectively to specific aspects of the patterns of light that fall on the retina. We have described some of the basic aspects of how the visual sensory system operates, but a host of other perceptual and cognitive processes (e.g., pattern recognition, imagination, visual imagery) both rely on and extend beyond these more basic sensory processes. Research Report 3 describes two phenomena that illustrate some of the complexities of visual perception.

Auditory Sensory System

As with the visual system, how the auditory receptors and the brain respond to sounds affects our representations of the world around us. The process of hearing begins with the translation of sound waves into vibrations of structures in the ear. These vibrations are then transduced into a neural response.

spot as a powerful technique for assessing how the visual system operates (Kawabata, 1984, 1990).

FIGURE 3A   Blind Spot Demonstration

Follow the instructions to demonstrate the existence of the blind spot and also to experience how the sensory and perceptual system "fills in" the blind spot from the context.

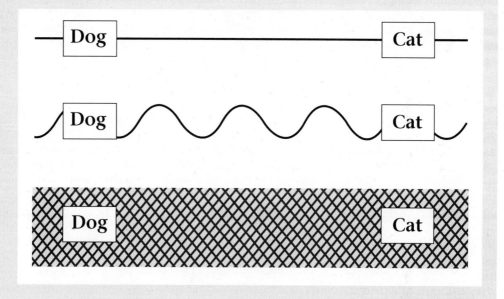

Sensory Receptors and Auditory Stimuli Hearing is the psychological response to sound waves that travel through the air (or water, if you happen to be swimming) and strike the eardrum. To understand how the auditory system functions, we need to consider (a) the properties of the physical stimuli that give rise to sounds and (b) the sensory mechanisms that transduce these stimuli into a neural response. We can appreciate several important fundamental properties of complex sound waves by considering the simplest sound wave, that of a pure tone. A pure tone is a specific type of sound wave known as a sine wave (see Figure 3.3). Complex sound waves can be formed by combining sine waves of differing dimensions.

The *frequency* of a sine wave is the number of complete cycles of the wave per unit of time. Frequency is generally measured in terms of cycles per second (cps) or Hertz (Hz; 1 Hz = 1 cps). Frequency is related to the psychological dimension of pitch. Humans are sensitive to sounds from approximately 20 cps to 20,000 cps, although our ability to hear sounds at the higher frequencies decreases as we get older.

RESEARCH REPORT 3:   Subtleties in Visual Perception Illustrated by Breakdowns in Normal Vision

Individual case studies of persons with various types of damage to the sensory and perceptual systems can provide important knowledge of how the systems operate in normal individuals. In Experiment 3, we demonstrated both that the blind spot exists and that the visual system fills in visual information so that we are unaware of the blind spot. Damage to the visual cortex can also lead to areas of blindness; such an area is known as a *scotoma*. Many patients with scotomas are completely unaware of their visual deficits, as you are unaware of the blind spot. One of the main reasons for these patients' unawareness is the phenomenon of completion: When presented with a complex display, the patients report seeing the entire display.

Completion phenomena can also occur in individuals with no permanent damage to the visual system. One condition that can produce a temporary scotoma is the decrease in blood flow to the visual cortex associated with migraine headaches. A noted psychologist, Karl Lashley (1941), reported his own experience with a large scotoma to the left of the fovea that accompanied a migraine headache. Lashley wrote that when he looked to the left of a friend's head, the head disappeared because light reflected from the head landed on the affected area. Interestingly, what Lashley perceived was not a "hole" in his visual field. Rather, the vertical stripes on the wallpaper behind his friend appeared to extend down to his friend's necktie!

Oliver Sacks (1995), a neurologist, described another interesting case of an individual with unusual vision—in this case a painter whom Sacks referred to as Mr. I. Mr. I. suffered damage to an area of the visual cortex responsible for color vision. More important for our purposes was the fact that Mr. I. appeared to have little or no visual deficits other than in his color vision. His ability to recognize forms and textures was unimpaired, which demonstrates the extreme specificity of the damage he suffered to his visual cortex. The case of Mr. I. also demonstrates that while we normally think of vision as being a unitary experience, distinct areas of the nervous system are responsible for the perception of color, motion, and so on.

Another important property of sound waves is the amount of energy in a wave. This property determines the intensity, or loudness, of the sound. The energy in sound waves is measured on the decibel (dB) scale. Figure 3.3 presents some representative sounds and their dB ratings.

Figure 3.4 presents the major anatomical structures of the ear and a close-up view of the structures of the middle and inner ear. The part of the ear we are most familiar with, the *pinna,* or external ear flap, serves to direct sound waves into the auditory canal. Sound is carried down the auditory canal until it strikes the eardrum, or *tympanic membrane.* Vibration of the eardrum causes three small bones of the middle ear, the *hammer, anvil,* and *stirrup,* to vibrate. The stirrup is connected to a membrane (*oval window*) on the *cochlea,* the major structure of the inner ear. Displacement of this membrane causes motion in the fluid within the cochlea, which in turn causes hair cells along the basal membrane to vibrate. The motion of these hair cells results in the transduction of the mechanical energy

FIGURE 3.3 **Sine Waves and the Loudness of Real-World Events** (a) A simple sine wave Air pressure changes over time, and we can measure the wavelength, which is the distance between one peak of the wave and the next. The frequency of the wave is the number of cycles the wave completes per second. The difference in air pressure between the highest and lowest points of the wave is related to the intensity, or loudness, of the wave. (b) Representative sounds and their dB ratings.

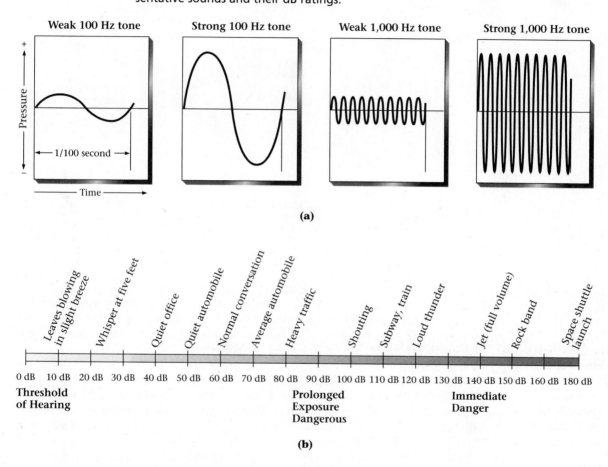

(a)

(b)

of sound waves into a neural response. This neural response is transmitted by the auditory nerve to the thalamus and then to the auditory cortex of the temporal lobe.

Human Auditory Abilities Although we generally refer to hearing as though it were a unitary skill, hearing actually involves a number of impressive abilities for using the information arising from sound waves (Bregman, 1990). For example, people with normal hearing are able to discriminate between sounds produced by string versus horn instruments (Coren & Ward, 1989), to identify a person simply on the basis of what his or her voice sounds like (e.g., Yarmey, 1994; Yarmey & Matthys, 1992), and to accurately locate objects in the environment based on the sounds coming from the objects (Coren & Ward, 1989). Our hearing is extraordinarily sensitive to detecting the presence of sound. In a

FIGURE 3.4   **The Human Ear**   Hearing involves processes in all three parts of the ear (outer, middle, and inner). Sound waves that strike the eardrum result in a neural response in the auditory nerve, which is relayed to the auditory cortex.

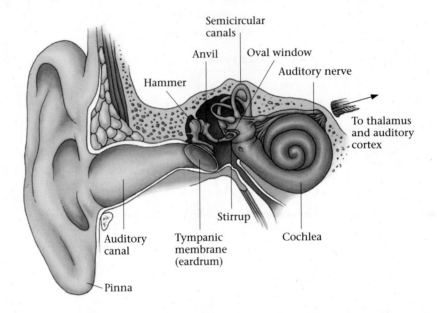

quiet room, humans are able to detect the tick of a watch from 20 feet away (Galanter, 1962). Von Bekesy (1957) estimated that if human hearing were any more sensitive, we would be able to hear individual air molecules bouncing off the eardrum as well as the low-frequency sounds produced by the muscles and organs of our bodies.

Interestingly, many of our auditory abilities are present at a very early age. If you stand to one side of an infant and shake a rattle, the child will turn her head in the direction of the sound. Infants are also particularly sensitive to high-frequency sounds, melodies, and the human voice (Aslin, 1989). Infants show a preference for their mothers' voices over the voices of other women (DeCasper & Fifer, 1980). Some sensory preferences may even be acquired before birth. DeCasper and Spence (1986) asked pregnant women to read aloud Dr. Seuss's classic story *The Cat in the Hat* during the last six weeks of their pregnancies. When the children were born, they showed a preference for *The Cat in the Hat* over another story with a different rhythm and pace.

Although these sensory abilities are certainly impressive, another human auditory capability is in a sense even more amazing. When we listen to someone speak, we are converting a continuous stream of sound waves into a message that we can comprehend (see Figure 10.1 on p. 313 for an illustration of the continuous nature of speech). An interesting aspect of this process is that we are able to recognize speech despite (a) tremendous variations in speakers, listening conditions, and the like and (b) the fact that no single portion of the speech signal contains all of the information needed to identify the words we hear. Furthermore, the speech recognition process can occur even when words are produced at a rate of two to three *per second!* We examine auditory language processing in more detail in Chapter 10.

The Relations Among Stimulus Factors, Perception, and Cognition

Our experience of events that happen around us is a complex interaction involving the nature of the physical stimuli, our nervous systems' responses to those stimuli, our abilities, and the tasks we are trying to perform. For example, imagine that you are trying to listen to two tape-recorded messages at the same time and you want to follow the instructions given in one of these messages. Imagine further that you can only vary the loudness of one of these messages, the one that you want to listen to.

Most of us would probably expect that if you made that message louder, it would be easier for you to hear what was being said. But what if you cannot make that message louder than the other message, the one you are trying to ignore? Do you think that turning the message that you want to hear *down* in volume would help? It turns out that having a difference in loudness between two messages does help in situations such as this, even if the message that you want to listen to is played at a lower volume. We discuss this finding further in Chapter 5.

It also turns out that the meaning of the messages we are trying to listen to affects our performance. Parents with a newborn infant often hear even a faint whimper from the baby's room, even if there is plenty of other noise. In such cases, the physical stimulus is not the sole determinant of what we experience; what we are trying to accomplish also plays a role. Parents will thus hear their baby's cry better than they will hear a sound that is more intense but not as important (e.g., the horn of a truck in the street outside).

The point of all this is that, as cognitive psychologists, we need to know about how the physical aspects of stimuli can affect performance, how the sensory systems respond to these stimuli, and how people's goals and experiences interact with these factors. As a colleague once put it, if you want to catch the attention of a person you find attractive, wearing the most intense perfume or cologne will do it, but you might achieve your goal with a better long-term effect through subtler means. Cognitive psychologists are interested in issues such as how the intensity of a stimulus affects people and what messages are conveyed by different types of stimuli.

Section Summary: Detecting Stimuli

Sensory and perceptual processes function to create internal representations of objects and events. The process of creating these representations begins with the transduction of stimulus energies into neural responses. The neural response to light begins in the retina at the back of the eye. Photoreceptors known as rods and cones transduce the energy from light into changes in the firing rates of neurons in the visual system. Information from the rods and cones is transmitted by the optic nerve to the primary visual cortex of the occipital lobe. Each hemisphere of the brain receives information from the contralateral (or opposite) half of the visual field. Auditory perception involves analyzing sound waves that strike our eardrums. The energy from these sound waves is transduced in the cochlea, and the neural response to these stimuli is transmitted to the auditory cortex. Cognitive psychologists are interested in the physical aspects of stimuli, the sensory systems' responses to these stimuli, and the effects of goals and experiences.

PSYCHOPHYSICS

Psychophysics is a subdiscipline in psychology that examines how changes in physical stimulation from the environment are translated into psychological experience. One of the earliest questions asked by psychophysicists concerned the **absolute threshold,** the weakest level of physical stimulation that a person can detect.

To determine the absolute threshold for, say, a 1,000-Hz tone, we might present subjects with a series of trials in which we start with either a faint or a loud tone. On each trial, we either increase or decrease the intensity of the tone. The subject's task is to report whether he or she can hear the tone on each trial. We repeat these ascending and descending trial sequences many times to ensure that we have a reliable estimate. The absolute threshold is the physical intensity of the tone that the subject reports detecting on 50 percent of the trials.

Assumptions Implicit in Determining an Absolute Threshold

One assumption underlying the notion of an absolute threshold is that the threshold represents a boundary between stimuli that are imperceptible and stimuli that can be perceived. The conception of a threshold implies that sensations are all-or-none: The person either does or does not perceive the presence of the stimulus. This assumption is an important aspect of both the concept of an absolute threshold and the psychophysical methods used to measure the absolute threshold.

Despite the fact that this all-or-none assumption seems reasonable, it creates several problems. One of these is illustrated in Figure 3.5, which shows how the data from the tone detection experiment we just described are plotted and how the absolute threshold is determined from this psychophysical function. Although the absolute threshold is defined as the intensity at which subjects report detecting the stimulus 50 percent of the time, there are stimuli below the threshold that subjects report hearing and stimuli above the threshold that subjects say they cannot hear. If the threshold were an all-or-none boundary, subjects should detect none of the stimuli below the threshold and all the stimuli above the threshold. This corresponds to a response pattern like the dotted line in Figure 3.5.

Why do you suppose people report that they detect a stimulus below the absolute threshold? One possibility is that the subjects are not reporting accurately. According to this logic, the threshold is an all-or-none phenomenon, but subjects are not completely correct in their reporting. To test this, researchers often include trials in which no stimulus is presented. If a subject reports hearing a tone on one of these "catch trials," it is obvious that the subject is not reporting accurately for one reason or another. Reporting that a stimulus has been presented when there was no stimulus is called a **false alarm.**

But is it indeed obvious that a false alarm represents an inaccurate report? This idea is itself based on the all-or-none assumption, and this assumption turns out to be invalid. Sensory experiences, such as seeing a very dim star in the sky, are not all-or-none phenomena. You have probably experienced this yourself. For example, have you ever thought that you heard the telephone ring while watching TV or listening to music, only to find when you turned the sound down that the telephone was not ringing? This example illustrates one problem with the concept of a fixed threshold—people can vary in their responses in many ways, and we cannot assume that a stimulus of a given intensity will always be either detected or not detected. Because absolute thresholds are not in fact absolute, we need more than a statistical criterion (e.g., 50 percent "stimulus present" responses) to account for how people detect stimuli.

Signal Detection Theory

Signal detection theory (Green & Swets, 1966; Macmillan & Creelman, 1991) provides a formal approach for dealing with some of the problems associated with the classical psy-

FIGURE 3.5   **Results from a Tone Detection Experiment**   In this hypothetical experiment, a subject is presented with tones of varying intensities (arbitrary units). The points in the figure represent the percentages of trials in which the person reports detecting the stimulus at each intensity. The dotted line represents the absolute threshold as determined by classical psychophysical methods. The dashed line represents how an ideal subject should respond, assuming that thresholds are all-or-none.

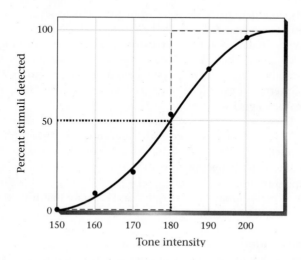

chophysical notion of a fixed absolute threshold. One of the problems with the threshold view is that it does not take into account people's bias to respond "yes" or "no" in a detection experiment. For example, perhaps the subject wants to impress the experimenter with his sensitive hearing. One way to ensure that he detects all the tones that are presented is to respond "yes" on every trial. Doing so guarantees that he will never miss a tone that is presented, but it also means that he will make many false alarms. To return to our telephone example, if you are waiting for an important call, you are more likely to "hear" the phone ringing (even if it is not) than if you are not awaiting a call.

In order to describe performance in a detection task accurately, then, we need to be able to separate subjects' biases to say "yes" or "no" from their ability to discriminate the presence or absence of a tone. Signal detection theory provides a framework for achieving this goal. As we will see, although signal detection theory is based on relatively few assumptions, it has proved applicable to a wide range of both laboratory and real-world situations (e.g., Kanwisher, Kim & Wickens, 1996; Matthews, 1996; Merickle, 1988).

Basic Features of Signal Detection Theory   Signal detection theory assumes that two states of the world are possible: Either the signal is present, or it is not present. Subjects can make two possible responses, saying either "Yes, the signal was presented" or "No, the signal was not presented." The combination of two states and two possible responses yields a 2×2 matrix consisting of four types of events (see Figure 3.6). The four possible events in a simple detection trial are: (a) a **hit,** when a subject responds that a signal was present, and a signal was present; (b) a *false alarm,* when a subject responds that a signal was present, but no signal was present; (c) a **miss,** when a subject responds that no signal was present, but a signal was present; and (d) a **correct rejection,** when a subject indicates that no signal was present, and no signal was present.

Much early work using signal detection theory in psychology examined detection of auditory signals (e.g., Green & Swets, 1966). To make the detection task more difficult, the signals were presented embedded in a background of white noise. (White noise sounds like the static from an AM radio that is not tuned to a station.) Under these conditions, we can call the trials in which no tone was presented Noise Alone and the trials containing a tone Signals + Noise.

The noise component need not come from an external source. It is assumed that in any situation, the signals that are presented are perceived against background "noise" in the nervous system. That is, even when no external noise is presented (or when the detection task involves signals other than auditory events), an ever-present background level of spontaneous activity in the nervous system produces internal noise. Regardless of whether the noise is internal or external, the subject is faced with the same task—discriminating Noise Alone from Signal + Noise.

In a detection experiment, if a subject responds perfectly, there are only two events: hits (responding "yes" when a tone is presented) and correct rejections (responding "no" when no tone is presented). In most detection experiments, however, the task is very difficult, and we seldom obtain perfect performance. Instead, we see all four possible events. The important question then is: How do we take the data from such a study, obtain estimates of the subjects' biases to say "yes" or "no," and separate that from their sensitivity in detecting the presence of a signal?

Assumptions Underlying Signal Detection Theory Signal detection theory assumes that detecting a stimulus involves two processes. First, sensory evidence is gathered concerning the presence or absence of a signal. Second, this sensory evidence is used to make a decision about whether a signal was present. According to this view, presenting a signal results in increased neural activity in the brain. This neural activity represents the sensory

---

FIGURE 3.6 **A Signal Detection Theory Matrix** In a simple signal detection trial, there are two possible states of the world (signal present or no signal present) and two possible responses from the subject (signal present or no signal present). The four possible combinations of these two sets of events define the four possible outcomes in a signal detection trial: hit, false alarm, miss, and correct rejection.

Response from Subject	State of the World: Signal present	State of the World: No signal present
Signal present	Hit	False alarm
No signal present	Miss	Correct rejection

evidence; note, however, that external noise may be presented, and internal noise is always present in the nervous system. The additional neural activity provided by the external stimulus is then added to the internal noise in the system. The decision process involves deciding whether the amount of neural activity is enough to exceed a threshold (or response criterion) for responding that a signal was present. If the neural activity exceeds the threshold, then the subject responds "yes"; otherwise, he or she responds "no."

We can represent the amount of sensory evidence present in Noise Alone and Signal + Noise trials using two distributions (see Figure 3.7). Because the signal adds sensory information to the noise, the distribution for the Signal + Noise trials is shifted in the direction of greater evidence, or more neural activity. Signal detection theory allows us to identify two aspects of performance in this situation: how well the person can discriminate between signal and noise trials (sensitivity) and the person's bias to respond that a signal is present (response bias). In signal detection theory, **d′ (d-prime)** is the measure of sensitivity and **ß (beta)** is the measure of response bias, or the response criterion.

We measure sensitivity, or d′, by determining the distance between the means of the Signal + Noise and Noise Alone distributions. If the two distributions overlap very little, as in Figure 3.7b, the subject is very sensitive to detecting the signal. The performance here is analogous to hearing a loud smoke detector while listening to soft music. Whereas the signal is strong in Figure 3.7b, it is weak in Figure 3.7a (e.g., similar to a telephone ringing). In signal detection theory, an intense signal shifts the Signal + Noise distribution farther away from the Noise Alone distribution. Remember, the larger the value of d′, the more sensitive the subject is to detecting the presence or absence of the signal.

Although signal detection theory employs a threshold concept, it is not assumed that the threshold is fixed. Subjects can adopt a liberal response criterion, which will produce many hits but also many false alarms (see Figure 3.7c). Alternatively, they can adopt a conservative response criterion, which will result in fewer hits and fewer false alarms (see Figure 3.7d).

Furthermore, we can independently measure (and manipulate) (a) the subjects' sensitivity to detecting the stimulus and (b) their bias to respond "yes" or "no." β determines the threshold for responding "yes" versus "no," and it is related to several factors. One is the relative cost of false alarms and gains from hits. For example, the cost of missing an alarm from a smoke detector is much greater than the cost of missing a telephone call, which is one reason why different types of sounds are used with these two devices. Another factor is the probability of signal versus no signal. For example, if you live in a house where the telephone often rings, you are far more likely to think that the telephone is ringing than you would be if the telephone rarely rang. Research has shown that d′ and β can be independently manipulated (Green & Swets, 1966), and there is strong evidence to support the two-process model of detection proposed by signal detection theory.

Applications of Signal Detection Theory Cognitive psychologists are interested in how stimulus factors, as well as a person's knowledge and goals, determine how the person experiences different stimuli. The hope is that studying people's responses in a variety of situations will yield important principles that relate events in the environment to our conscious experience of these events.

Signal detection is a good example of a theory that was developed in the laboratory using very highly controlled experiments but that identified important factors that affect how people perform in a wide range of everyday tasks. Signal detection theory has been used in many basic and applied research areas (e.g., Park, Lee, & Lee, 1996; Pastore &

FIGURE 3.7   **Noise Alone and Signal + Noise Distributions**   The two distributions represent the sensory evidence present on Noise Alone and Signal + Noise trials. Also shown are the four possible outcomes in a signal detection trial (hit, false alarm, miss, and correct rejection) that result as a function of where subjects set their response criteria. Parts a and b of the figure differ in terms of the strength of the signal. When the signal is very weak (Part a), the Noise and Signal + Noise distributions overlap a great deal; hence, d′ is small. When the signal is strong (Part b), there is little overlap of the Noise and Signal + Noise distributions, and d′ is large. Performance can also vary depending on whether the subject adopts a liberal response criterion (Part c) or a conservative criterion (Part d).

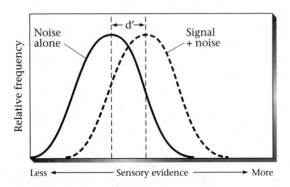

(a) Weak Signal

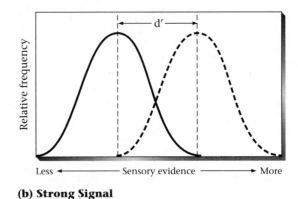

(b) Strong Signal

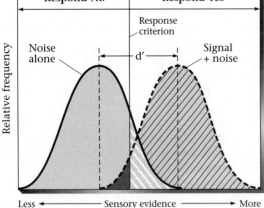

(c) Lenient Response Criterion

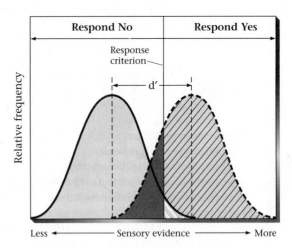

(d) Conservative Response Criterion

☐ Correct rejection   ■ Miss   ◨ False alarm   ▨ Hit

Scheirer, 1974; Scurfield, 1996; Yonelinas, Regeher, & Jacoby, 1996). In essence, any situation in which there are two states (signal versus no signal) and two possible responses (signal present versus signal absent) can be conceptualized within the theoretical framework of signal detection theory.

For example, researchers investigating eyewitness memory are interested in the eyewitness's decision as to whether the individual on trial matches the eyewitness's memory of the person seen committing the crime. In the case of a suspect lineup, there may be one "signal"—the person who actually committed the crime—and several "noise" stimuli—people not suspected of committing the crime. The eyewitness's task is to try to make a "hit" and avoid making a "false alarm." Eyewitness memory research has identified a number of factors that affect both accuracy and response bias in eyewitnesses (e.g., Buckhout, 1974; Ellison & Buckhout, 1981).

The signal detection framework has also been applied to the task facing radiologists reading x-rays (e.g., Parasuraman, 1985). Here, the task is to determine whether the shadows on the films are indicative of disease (signal) or merely reflect differences in patients' physiology (noise). Although one might hope that radiologists are extremely sensitive in making these decisions, studies have shown that the accuracy of radiologists' judgments in these tasks rarely exceeds 70 percent (Lusted, 1971). As predicted by signal detection theory, many factors affect the response criterion (β) used to make these decisions. For example, β is affected by whether the radiologist believes that the x-rays come from a totally healthy individual (and hence the probability of a tumor is small) or a person with other symptoms of disease (and a greater likelihood of having a tumor present) (Norman et al., 1992; Swets & Pickett, 1982). Signal detection theory has also been applied to real-world topics such as recovering memories of childhood sexual abuse (e.g., Lindsay & Read, 1994; Pezdek, 1994), performance changes in Sonar operators over time (e.g., Mackie, Wylie, & Smith, 1994), and group decision making (e.g., Sorkin & Dai, 1994).

Section Summary: Psychophysics

Detecting the presence of stimuli is one of the most fundamental tasks performed by the sensory and perceptual systems. Traditional research in psychophysics sought to determine absolute thresholds for various modalities. The notion of a fixed absolute threshold was called into question by findings showing that subjects could vary their response biases for detecting the presence or absence of stimuli. Signal detection theory assumes that a person's performance in detection tasks depends on the sensitivity of the individual in detecting stimuli as well as the individual's response bias. Research using the signal detection theory framework demonstrated that many tasks that require people to categorize items or events into different groups really involve not one but rather two processes. One process determines sensitivity and involves the accumulation of evidence concerning the membership of the item or event along one or more dimensions. Once this information is gathered, the person must make a decision as to the class to which this item or event belongs. This decision process involves the second process of setting a response criterion. By noting that these are two separate processes, we can study which variables affect sensitivity and which affect response bias.

VISUAL SENSORY STORE

People have known for centuries that visual sensation persists after the offset, or termination, of the physical stimulus. According to Allen (1926), Aristotle's (384–322 B.C.) writings contain the first known reference to this *visual persistence* phenomenon. You may have experienced this phenomenon yourself: When we view a flash from a camera, we "see" the aftereffect of the flash long after the light from the flash is gone. This raises an important question: What evidence is there that, under viewing conditions that more closely approximate the intensity of stimuli normally experienced in the real world, we continue to

Sonar operators are required to discriminate blips on the screen that correspond to objects of interest (signals) from noise. In real-world situations such as this, signal detection theory can be used to predict human performance.

experience a stimulus after it has been presented and is no longer physically "there"? If we do have experiences that extend beyond the duration of the stimulus, what are the limitations on this phenomenon? Is the phenomenon limited to the visual system? We begin to consider these issues by describing some early research designed to answer these questions.

Span of Apprehension

The issue of how much information can be taken in during a single brief visual presentation is very old. Some early evidence came from Sir William Hamilton (1859), who conducted simple experiments with marbles as stimuli. On each trial, Hamilton would toss several marbles in front of himself, glance briefly at them, and then try to estimate how many marbles were there. Hamilton noted that unless there were only a few marbles, he was unable to make accurate estimates. With larger sets of marbles, he could note that there were a number of marbles, but he was unable to count them.

At the end of the last century, several researchers conducted more tightly controlled experiments. In these studies, subjects were presented with visual displays containing, say, 12 numbers or letters. The subjects' task was to report all of the items in the display. Subjects could usually report around 4 or 5 items (e.g., Whipple, 1914), with the exact number depending on factors such as the nature of the items in the display and the physical characteristics of the visual displays. The number of items subjects could report was termed the **span of apprehension** or span of immediate memory (Averbach & Sperling, 1960), and this measure was thought to reflect the amount of information that a person could take in (or apprehend) in a single glance.

Let's use a thought experiment to begin exploring some of the important aspects of these experiments. Imagine that you are presented with a 50 ms display containing 12 random letters and are asked to report what letters are in the display. To perform this task, you will have to categorize the items in the display and then either write down or pronounce the names of these items. The process of categorizing the items is not instantaneous, and it is reasonable to assume that it will take more than 50 ms to identify and report all 12 letters. Because the time required for categorization and reporting is longer than the time during which the actual physical stimulus is present, in order to report the items in the display, you must have some memory system or systems that can maintain a representation of the physical stimulus until the items are categorized and reported.

Since you will be able to report some of these items, the systems must be working. Still, we know that you will not be able to report all of the items. Hence, the question of interest becomes: What might be responsible for your failure to report all of the items in the display? The answer to this question was identified in some important experiments performed in the 1960s.

Iconic Store

Ulric Neisser (1967) coined the labels **iconic store** and **echoic store** to refer to brief sensory memory stores for vision and audition, respectively. In this and the following section, we consider evidence for and against the existence of such stores. These **precategorical sensory stores** maintain a relatively accurate representation of the physical characteristics of stimuli encoded by the sensory systems. By *precategorical,* we mean that the information represented in these systems corresponds to a fairly *veridical,* or accurate, representation of the physical stimulus and not to the category to which the item is assigned after it is identified. In the case of vision, for example, the iconic store is presumed to maintain a representation of the physical properties of the stimulus before we identify it as a letter, number, or symbol (e.g., @, $).

We discuss the processes by which we identify complex visual stimuli in the next chapter. For now, the important point is that before the items are identified they are represented by something like a description of what the physical stimulus looked like—the letter A, for example, might be coded as "two upright lines arranged to form an angle and a horizontal line midway between these two lines." Assuming that the identification process takes time, an interesting question we can ask is this: What happens while we are attempting to identify and report the items in the display?

A common finding from many of the early studies of span of apprehension (e.g., Cattell, 1883; Erdmann & Dodge, 1898) was that subjects often claimed they could see more items than they were able to report. Subjects said that it seemed as if items that were available for report faded away while they were reporting the initial items.

These subjective reports present an interesting paradox: Subjects are claiming to be aware of the presence of some items in the display, yet they cannot report what these items are. It is almost as if the subjects are reporting both what they know (the items from the display that they can correctly report) and what they do not know (the items they claim to be aware of and yet cannot report).

Two very different types of data are involved in these subjective reports. For items that subjects are able to report, we have strong evidence that the subjects actually perceived the items—we can compare their reports against what was presented in the display. In contrast, the evidence for the items that subjects claim to be aware of and yet cannot report is simply their subjective reports. How do we know that subjects are actually aware of more items than they can report? Maybe they were told that there were 12 items in the display, and when they could report only 5, they simply claimed that they could see the other 7. If subjects are actually aware of items that they cannot report, then we need to find a way to test this using objective measures. Fortunately, researchers have provided a solution to this problem.

Sperling's Partial Report Technique

George Sperling (1960) reasoned that the procedure used in the span of apprehension experiments may tell us more about what subjects *remember* from the visual displays than about what they *perceive*. Prior to Sperling's study, subjects in span of apprehension experiments were required to report all of the items in the display. Because the displays were very brief and it takes time to identify and then report the items, what these subjects were reporting was necessarily what they remembered from the display, which could be different from what they perceived when the display was initially presented. To appreciate this distinction, consider a simple thought experiment.

Imagine that we presented you with a list of 30 words at a rate of 2 seconds per word. If after the list was presented we asked you to report all the items in the list, you could probably report less than half. Could we conclude from this that you had perceived (or apprehended) only 10 to 15 items? Of course not! Certainly, if we had asked you to report the 20th item right after it was displayed, you could have done so easily. We thus know that you perceived the item—how else could you tell us what it was? Still, chances are you would not be able to recall this item on a test given after the whole list was presented. If we wanted to verify that you had perceived the items, we could require you to pronounce each item as it was presented. Even under these conditions, though, you would still probably recall only a small subset of the list of items on the final test.

George Sperling
Sperling's pioneering research using the partial report technique helped to demonstrate the existence of a visual sensory store.

This is in essence what was being done in the span of apprehension experiments. Subjects in these experiments were presented with a fairly large set of items and asked to report all of them. Sperling (1960) devised an ingenious procedure to partially circumvent the limitation in reporting that such experiments involve. If we are interested in what is available for report—that is, what was perceived from a display rather than what is remembered—then we can minimize the role of memory by decreasing how many items need to be remembered. Sperling's insight was that asking people to report only a subset of the items from the display will decrease both the number of items subjects have to remember and the length of time subjects spend reporting items.

Sperling used a device known as a **tachistoscope** (or **T-scope**) to present arrays of letters and digits to subjects for very brief intervals. The T-scope allows the researcher to control the timing of stimulus presentation precisely. In several experiments, Sperling used a 3×4 array of letters (i.e., three rows of four letters each) as the stimulus display. Each array was presented for 50 milliseconds and was followed by a blank postexposure field. The subjects' task was to report the items from the display.

Two main conditions were defined by how subjects reported the items. In both conditions, at the start of the trials, subjects were required to focus on a fixation point located where the middle of the stimulus display would appear. In the **whole report** condition, subjects were asked to report all the letters from the display (see Figure 3.8). This condition is similar to the procedure used in the span of apprehension studies.

The ingenious twist in Sperling's study involved the second condition, the **partial report** condition, illustrated in Figure 3.8. Here, after the visual display ended, a tone was presented that signaled to the subject which row of the display to report (high frequency signaled top row, middle frequency indicated middle row, low frequency signaled bottom row).

The logic behind the partial report technique is similar to that used in assessing students' knowledge on exams: Professors ask questions that test students' knowledge of some of the information to which they were exposed through lectures and readings. It is assumed that a student who can answer 80 percent of the test questions correctly has learned 80 percent of the target information. Similarly, in Sperling's experiment, it was assumed that whatever percentage of the target row of letters the subjects could report represented an estimate of the number of letters available for report from the whole display soon after the display was presented. An explanation of Sperling's results should clarify this point.

Sperling found that in the whole report condition, his subjects reported on average about 4.3 letters. Furthermore, the number of letters that subjects could report was not affected very much by the number of letters in the display. Subjects reported about the same number of items from 5-item displays as from 12-item displays. This indicates how many items people can report. But how many can they perceive?

To answer this question, consider the results from the partial report condition. Sperling used the number of items that subjects could report from one row to estimate the total number of items available for report. For example, if subjects could report 3.03 items from a display of three rows of four items each, this number was multiplied by the number of rows in the display (three) to give the total number of items available for report, about 9.1 items. These data suggest that about 75 percent of the items in the display (9.1 of 12 items) were available after the initial display.

The upper curve in Figure 3.9 represents the estimated number of items available for report when the tone signaling which row to report was presented immediately after the display was presented—the partial report condition. As you can see, the number of items

FIGURE 3.8 **Whole Report Versus Partial Report Trials of a Span Apprehension Experiment**
Each trial begins with the subject looking at a fixation point. The fixation point is then replaced with a 12-item display. In the whole report trials, as soon as the display is presented,
the subject attempts to report all of the items. In the partial report trials, after the display
goes off, a tone cues the subject to report the items from either the top, middle, or bottom
row.

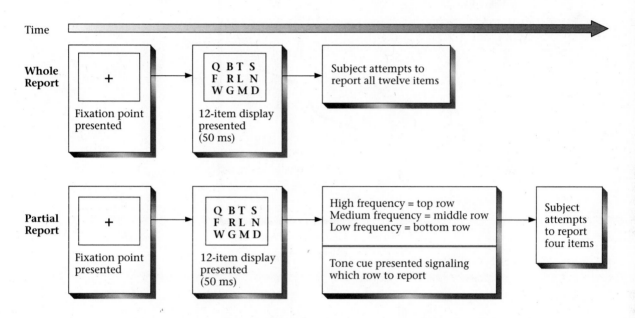

available for report was much larger than in the whole report condition, and the estimated
number of items available increased with increases in the number of items in the display.

What conclusions can we draw from the data presented in Figure 3.9? According to the
logic described above, the difference between the partial and whole report conditions reflects a difference in the number of items *perceived* from the display (as indicated by the
partial report data) versus the number of items that subjects *remember* from the entire display (as indicated by the whole report data). In other words, under the whole report condition, subjects rapidly forget some items that they initially perceive. Before we accept this
conclusion, however, we need to rule out an alternative explanation for the differences between the partial and whole report conditions.

Alternative Accounts of the Partial Report Results   One major difference between
the two conditions concerns the number of items that subjects are required to report. Relevant here is a general phenomenon known as **output interference** (Tulving & Arbuckle, 1963), which refers to the fact that when people recall items from memory, the
more items they recall, the less likely they are to be able to recall additional items. In the
whole report condition, the opportunity is greater for output interference to affect performance, because subjects have more items to attempt to report than in the partial report
condition.

FIGURE 3.9   **Results of Sperling's (1960) Study**   The lines represent the number of items subjects in the study reported in partial and whole report conditions with displays ranging from 3 to 12 items. The dotted line shows the number of items subjects reported in the whole report trials. The solid line indicates the number of items estimated to be available in the partial report trials.

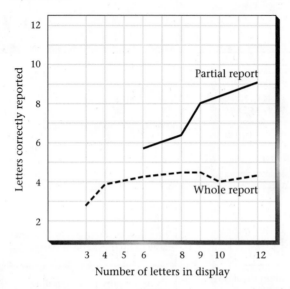

Source: Adapted from Sperling, 1960.

One way to contrast the output interference interpretation with the rapid forgetting view is to set up conditions in which the two explanations make opposing predictions and then test to see which prediction is supported. Sperling did just that in an experiment in which he varied the time interval between when the display ended and when the subject was signaled as to which row to report. On the one hand, if the difference between the partial report estimate and the whole report data is due to rapid forgetting in the whole report condition, then with an increasing interval between display offset and signal onset, the superiority of the partial report results evident in Figure 3.9 should disappear. On the other hand, the output interference hypothesis predicts that the superiority of the partial report results should be unaffected by the delay of the signal, because regardless of when the signal is presented, the partial report condition still requires fewer items to be reported than the whole report condition.

Figure 3.10 shows the results of an experiment in which Sperling presented the tone signaling which row to report either 100 ms before the display offset, at the same time as the display offset, or following a delay of 150, 300, or 1,000 ms. The bar on the right side of the figure represents the number of items reported by subjects in the whole report condition, and the circles represent the estimated number of items available in the partial report condition as a function of the delay of the signal. As predicted by the rapid forgetting hypothesis, the superiority of partial report results declined as the interval between display offset and signal onset was increased. These results have been replicated by many other re-

FIGURE 3.10   **Results of Delaying the Partial Report Cue**   In this study, Sperling varied the delay of the partial report cue. Data presented are the estimated number of items available in the partial report trials (left side) and the percent correct recall in the whole report trials (right side).

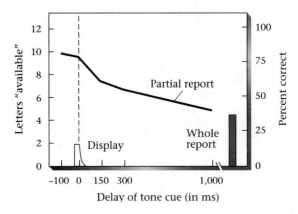

Source: Adapted from Crowder, 1976.

searchers (e.g., Averbach & Coriell, 1961), and the decline in the superiority of partial report results with delay of the signal is now well established. This finding provides converging evidence in favor of the rapid forgetting view and against the output interference explanation (but see Holding, 1975a, 1975b, for a different view on this issue).

What Type of Information Is Maintained in Iconic Store?   Earlier, we suggested that the information held in the iconic store is precategorical—that is, that the visual information has not yet been categorized. If the information in iconic store is closely related to the physical characteristics of the stimulus items (e.g., their color, brightness, location in visual space), then we might expect that only these types of physical dimensions could be used to cue subjects as to which items to report in a partial report superiority condition. That is, if the subject has information available about the physical characteristics of the items, then this information can be used to select which items to report. If this information is truly precategorical, then the subject could not be cued to report items from one category (e.g., letters), since the information has not yet been categorized. In this case the subject does not know if a given item is a letter, a number, or some other symbol.

Sperling reported an experiment that tested these ideas using displays containing two rows of two letters and two numbers each. There were two partial report conditions. In one, the tone signaled whether the subject was to report from the top row or the bottom row; and in the other, the tone signaled the subject to report either letters or numbers. There was also a whole report condition against which the performance of the partial report conditions was compared. Sperling found that when the subjects were asked to report based on a physical characteristic of the display, the spatial location of the items (top versus bottom row), the partial report conditions yielded a sizeable superiority effect. In contrast, when the tone signaled subjects to report on the basis of categories of items, either the numbers or the letters, the partial report results showed no superiority. In fact, the partial report results showed no superiority under this cueing condition even when the signal was given 100 ms before the end of the visual display.

Coltheart, Lea, and Thompson (1974) used a somewhat different procedure to test whether the information in iconic store was precategorical. These researchers used a partial report cue to signal subjects to report only letters that ended in specific sounds (e.g., a long *ee* sound, as in B or C). Their research showed that under these conditions, partial report results evidenced no superiority. Still other studies have shown a superiority effect for partial report data using color (e.g., Clark, 1969), brightness (e.g., Von Wright, 1968), and shape (e.g., Turvey & Kravetz, 1970) as the partial report cues. Taken together, these results indicate that the information that persists following a brief visual display has visual but not phonological or semantic characteristics. This suggests that information in iconic store is indeed precategorical—subjects are aware of the location and color of items, but the items have not yet been classified as, for example, being letters or numbers or having a long *ee* sound.

Arguments Concerning Iconic Store

Sperling's (1960) study, along with a great deal of subsequent research using the partial report technique, appeared to provide a firm empirical basis for the existence of an iconic store. These initial demonstrations complemented earlier work examining visual persistence (cf. Cowan, 1984). Based on this evidence, most cognitive psychologists came to view iconic store as the first stage in visual information processing.

However, as is often the case with new ideas, not everyone agreed with the interpretation of the visual persistence and partial report data we have presented here. Specifically, some researchers questioned the view than an iconic representation is a necessary part of normal visual perception. The most vocal proponent of the view that icons—the precategorical representations of stimuli—and iconic memory may have nothing to do with visual perception in the real world was Ralph Norman Haber (1983). Haber summarized his views in an article titled "The Impending Demise of the Icon: A Critique of the Concept of Iconic Storage in Visual Information Processing." In this article, Haber reviewed the evidence for visual persistence and agreed that there was good evidence for this phenomenon. He also acknowledged that the partial report studies had provided good evidence for iconic memory. What Haber disagreed with was the view that the laboratory studies that had provided the evidence for visual persistence and iconic memory told us anything about how human perception operates in the real world. As Haber put it, the "notion of an icon as a brief storage of information persisting after stimulus termination cannot possibly be useful in any typical visual information-processing task except reading in a lightning storm" (Haber, 1983, p. 1).

Laboratory Research Versus the "Real World"

Haber's criticisms were based in large part on the notion of *ecological validity*. Recall from Chapter 1 that ecological validity concerns the extent to which results from laboratory studies generalize to the real world. If a research procedure is ecologically valid, then the results obtained in the laboratory can be used to make predictions about performance in real-world tasks. Haber argued that the laboratory studies he was discussing did not exhibit ecological validity—that is, what subjects do in, say, a partial report experiment is greatly different from what they do in the real world. According to this view, then, performance in partial report experiments tells us nothing about real-world perception.

Given the constant availability of real-world visual scenes, Haber argued, why would people need an internal storage mechanism to maintain a representation of a scene? According to this line of reasoning, even though good evidence has been presented that such a storage mechanism is at work in visual information processing tasks involving brief visual displays, these situations are quite different from our real-world experience. Thus, we need not invoke the concepts of icons and iconic store to explain visual perception as it occurs in the real world.

The journal in which Haber's article appeared (*The Behavioral and Brain Sciences*) invites other experts to comment on articles; and in the case of Haber's article, 32 commentaries appeared. Some authors agreed with at least some of Haber's general points (e.g., Banks, 1983). Still, as Geoffrey Loftus (1985) noted, 30 of the 32 commentators took issue with Haber's position, and some authors offered specific rebuttals to Haber's conclusions. We consider here two aspects of Haber's commentary that attracted criticism from other experts in the field.

First, consider the notion of ecological validity. Haber argued that viewing a stimulus in a T-scope bears so little resemblance to real-world viewing conditions that we cannot generalize the results from these laboratory studies to real-world information processing tasks. Loftus (1983) and others have criticized this view by arguing that science has made great advances by studying phenomena under conditions that are quite discrepant from those in the real world. For example, physicists have studied gravity by observing objects falling in near-vacuums and ball bearings rolling down nearly frictionless inclined planes. These laboratory conditions are obviously vastly different from the conditions under which an egg dropped from a nest plummets to the ground or a rock bounces down a hillside. Still, we can use what we have learned about gravity in the laboratory to predict the behavior of the egg or the rock in the real world.

The general point here is that by studying the phenomenon of interest under controlled conditions, scientists can identify important principles that can then be tested for the extent to which they generalize to the real world. According to this view, if visual persistence is a characteristic of the visual information processing system, then the task of cognitive psychologists is to determine the conditions under which iconic memory plays a role in normal visual perception.

A second criticism Haber raised concerns the fact that in most real-world situations, we do not keep our eyes and head fixed in space as we view the world around us. Rather, we are constantly moving our eyes as well as our heads and bodies. Haber argued that valuable sources of information are available to us as a consequence of these movements. By restricting the viewing conditions in laboratory studies to static "snapshots," or fixed displays viewed while the head and eyes are motionless, we have created an artificial viewing task that tells us little about normal perception.

An interesting question raised by this second criticism is whether representations of anything other than static items might be maintained in iconic store. Although it is true that Sperling and many others used displays of items in fixed positions, this does not mean that iconic store is incapable of representing movement. To test whether iconic store—or, more accurately, the partial report superiority effect—is limited to viewing static displays, researchers have presented subjects with brief displays of moving dots. The subjects' task is to report the direction of movement. Note that this procedure assesses a very different aspect of iconic store than did the Sperling procedure. In Sperling's studies, subjects had to report the *identity* of the items in the display. In the moving dots procedure, the identity of the items is not in question, but the *direction of movement* is critical. Results from several studies have indicated that people do maintain a brief representation of motion information (e.g., Shiori & Cavanagh, 1992; Treisman, Russell & Green, 1975).

Section Summary: Visual Sensory Store

A great deal of evidence supports the idea that a visual sensory store (iconic store) maintains a brief representation of a visual stimulus that persists after the physical stimulus ends. Sperling's work with the partial report technique provided much of the early evidence, and subsequent research has added converging evidence. It now appears that the iconic store maintains a representation of the physical characteristics of visual stimuli (e.g., location, color). Although some theorists (e.g., Haber, 1983) have questioned the ecological validity of research examining iconic store, others have argued that controlled laboratory studies provide important and useful insights into the functioning of the visual system.

AUDITORY SENSORY STORE

Recall that the *echoic store* (Neisser, 1967) refers to the memory system that maintains a representation of an auditory stimulus for a brief time following the presentation of the stimulus. One aspect of auditory stimuli makes it quite likely that there is a brief memory store for auditory information. Whereas visual stimuli are distributed spatially, auditory stimuli are temporally distributed—that is, the sounds are spread out in time. To take speech as an example, producing one word takes about 250 ms. Because no single portion of the sound wave for speech fully specifies the word that is being produced (see Figure 10.1, p. 313), we must have a means for maintaining a representation of the early part of the sound while the later portions are being processed. The echoic store is believed to serve this function.

Partial Report Studies

Moray, Bates, and Barnett (1965) developed an auditory analog of the Sperling procedure using an experimental preparation they referred to as the "four-eared man." As in the studies of iconic store, subjects in these experiments were presented with a fairly large number of letters. The researchers used stereo equipment to present auditory items that appeared to be coming from one of four spatial locations. You have probably experienced a similar effect listening to stereo music or attending a movie theater with a sophisticated sound system; if the sound tracks are mixed appropriately, different sounds (e.g., a trumpet and a guitar) appear to coming from different locations. Moray and colleagues used a similar technique to make the sounds appear to be coming from four different locations.

In the experiment, after the target items were presented, subjects either were required to report all the items presented in the four spatial locations (analogous to the whole report condition used by Sperling) or were cued with a light as to which of the four spatial locations they were to report. The results showed that the estimated number of items available for report was higher in this latter condition—the partial report condition—than in the whole report condition. This superiority effect provided some of the early evidence for the existence of the echoic store.

Refinements to the Initial Demonstrations of Echoic Store

One shortcoming of the study just described is that the partial report advantage might have been due to greater output interference in the whole report condition than in the partial report condition. Furthermore, the study did not assess how information was coded in the echoic store. Unlike the Sperling study, there was no comparison of cueing with precategorical versus postcategorical cues.

These two limitations were addressed in a subsequent study by Darwin, Turvey, and Crowder (1972), who presented subjects with lists of digits and numbers at each of three apparent spatial locations. To test the output interference question, Darwin and colleagues varied the interval between the offset of the auditory items and the presentation of the visual cue (a bar of light) signaling which location to report. Under a condition involving a short delay, results showed a partial report superiority effect. More importantly, the superiority of partial report results decreased as the interval between the offset of the list items and the presentation of the report cue increased. This latter result indicates that the partial report advantage obtained by Moray and colleagues could not have been due simply to a difference in the number of items subjects had to report in the whole report and partial report conditions, for this was constant regardless of the delay preceding the report cue in the partial report condition.

The second question Darwin and colleagues asked was whether the information that supported performance in this task was precategorical—that is, sensory in nature rather than reflecting classification according to some learned scheme. In one of their experiments, these researchers told subjects that particular bars of light signaled that they should report only the digits or only the letters in the display. Although this condition produced a very small partial report advantage, it appeared only when the delay between the list items and the report cue was very short. The researchers concluded that the codes representing physical aspects of the stimulus items (e.g., their spatial locations) were at least much more accessible in the echoic store than was information representing categorical dimensions (e.g., digits versus letters) of the stimuli.

Converging Evidence for Echoic Store

Researchers have used procedures other than the partial report technique to study the echoic store, and the results obtained with these other techniques provide evidence that converges with the results from the partial report studies. These studies also revealed some intriguing characteristics of echoic store. One line of evidence consistent with the notion of echoic store comes from memory studies comparing recall of items presented visually versus auditorally.

Conrad and Hull (1968) presented subjects with lists of seven items and required them to recall the items in the order in which they had been presented—a *serial recall* task. The list items were presented visually, and subjects were required either to read the items silently as they were presented or to read the items aloud as they were presented. The data from this study are presented in Figure 3.11. This *serial position curve* shows the number of errors subjects made in attempting to recall the list items as a function of the serial position of the items in the study list. These data indicate an advantage for auditory input (the subjects hear their voices as they read the items aloud), but this advantage is limited to the last few items in the list. This advantage of auditory presentation over visual presentation is called the **modality effect.**

What causes the modality effect? According to one view, information presumably persists in the echoic store longer than in the iconic store. Subjects can use this auditory in-

FIGURE 3.11   **The Modality Effect in Serial Recall**   The dependent variable is the number of errors made at each serial position, so better performance is shown by lower error rates. Data are from an experimental condition in which subjects vocalized the items aloud and a control condition in which subjects read the items silently.

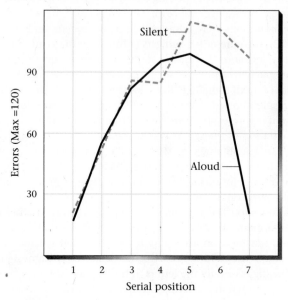

Source: Adapted from Crowder, 1976.

formation when they are recalling the list items. Because subjects are required to recall the items in the order in which they are presented, this advantage of echoic store is evident at the end of the list—that is, after subjects have already spent time recalling the initial items. The modality effect is very robust, and it has been obtained in a number of other memory tasks (e.g., Duis, Dean & Derks, 1994; Murdock, 1967). Because the modality effect is both reliable and generalizable across tasks, it appears to reflect an important fundamental difference between the two sensory systems, or at least in the information derived from these systems.

A second memory task that provides evidence concerning the echoic store also uses short lists and a serial recall task. In these experiments, a list of items (e.g., 7, 4, 3, 8, 6, 9, 1) is presented aurally, and the subjects' task is to recall the items in order. In the control condition, the last item is followed by either silence or a meaningless sound, such as a tone. In the experimental condition, a word (e.g., "recall") is spoken at the end of the list. This so-called *stimulus suffix* appears at the end of the list just as a suffix appears at the end of a word. In both the control and suffix conditions, subjects are told to ignore any sound that comes after the end of the list. They are instructed that this cue is simply included as a signal to tell them when to begin recalling the list items.

Figure 3.12 presents results from one study employing a stimulus suffix. As these data indicate, the stimulus suffix causes subjects to make more errors on the last few items on the list, compared with the control condition. This difference, referred to as the **suffix effect,** presumably occurs because the suffix interferes with, or masks, the echoic representation

FIGURE 3.12   **The Effect of a Verbal Suffix on Serial Recall**   The dependent variable is the number of errors made at each serial position, so better performance is shown by lower error rates. Data presented are the number of errors made at each serial position for a condition in which a suffix (the word *zero*) was presented at the end of the nine-item list and a control condition in which a buzzer was sounded at the end of the list.

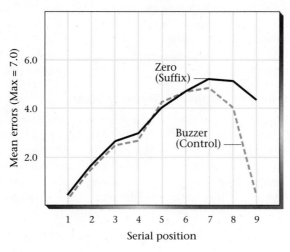

Source: Adapted from Crowder, 1976.

of the last few items in the list. We should point out, however, that there is some debate over whether it is the precategorical representation of information in echoic store or the postcategorical interpretation of the suffix sound made by the subject that causes the suffix effect (see Ayres et al., 1979; Neath, Surprenant & Crowder, 1993).

Overall, then, studies of the partial report superiority effect, the modality effect, and the suffix effect all converge on the view that echoic store serves to preserve a brief precategorical representation of the physical characteristics of auditory stimuli. These data parallel findings on iconic store.

A Final Word on Sensory Store Studies

We conclude with three additional points concerning the results of the iconic and echoic store studies. First, estimates of how long information persists in these two stores indicate a substantial difference between the two. In general, it appears that information lasts for about a quarter of a second in iconic store, whereas information in echoic store lasts about 4 seconds, or 16 times longer. Some studies (e.g., Watkins & Watkins, 1980) have yielded estimates as long as 20 seconds for the duration of information in echoic store. Differences across experiments in estimates of how long information persists are very likely due to the specific procedures used in the studies. The point remains that, in terms of the persistence of information, the studies have found large differences between iconic store and echoic store. Given the fact that auditory information is spread out in time whereas visual information is spread out in space, it seems reasonable that information would last longer in the echoic store.

The second point to note is that large differences also exist in the estimated number of items available for report in the two modalities. In studies of the visual modality, Sperling and others have obtained estimates of 75 percent or more, whereas in the two auditory studies reviewed here, the percentages were much lower. Even with no delay, Darwin and colleagues estimated that only about five of the nine items presented were available for report. This may reflect a difference in the amount of information needed to identify visual versus auditory items.

Third, debate continues regarding the appropriate theoretical interpretation of results from tasks such as those reviewed here (e.g., Chow, 1991; Crowder, 1986; Nairne, 1988). These ongoing debates deal with aspects of iconic and echoic store that are beyond the scope of this text, but it is important for you to realize that we are still learning about the details of these perceptual/cognitive stores and how they affect performance.

Section Summary: Auditory Sensory Store

Research on the echoic store has revealed that this system maintains a representation of the physical stimulus that extends beyond the duration of the external stimulus. The partial report technique that provided evidence for the iconic store has also been applied to echoic store, with additional evidence coming from studies of the modality and suffix effects. Comparisons between the visual and auditory modalities suggest that these two systems differ in terms of the operation and duration of their respective sensory stores.

REVIEWING SENSING AND PERCEIVING

CONCEPT REVIEW

1. Describe the main stages of the generic information processing model of sensory and perceptual processes. Using this model, briefly describe how the model applies to the visual and auditory systems.

2. Discuss how the visual system responds to light that falls on the retina. What are the pathways by which this information is passed along to the visual cortex?

3. How is the physical energy present in sound waves converted to a neural response in the auditory system?

4. Describe an experiment for determining the absolute threshold for detecting a faint light presented to subjects. Using the same conditions, describe how d' and β would be determined in a signal detection application. Be sure to describe the four types of trials involved in a signal detection analysis.

5. Describe the whole report and partial report conditions used by Sperling. How are the data from the partial report conditions used to determine the number of items available? What lines of converging evidence support the existence of iconic store?

6. What evidence supports the proposal that iconic store maintains a precategorical representation of a stimulus?

7. Describe Haber's criticisms of the laboratory studies of iconic store. For each, what is the counterargument made in favor of laboratory studies?

8. Describe three findings that argue in favor of echoic store. Indicate for each finding the task(s) involved and the data that support the notion of a precategorical store.

KEY TERMS

absolute threshold (p. 78)
β (beta) (p. 81)
blind spot (p. 70)
correct rejection (p. 80)
d' (d-prime) (p. 81)
echoic store (p. 84)
false alarm (p. 78)
fovea (p. 70)

hit (p. 79)
iconic store (p. 84)
miss (p. 79)
modality effect (p. 93)
output interference (p. 87)
partial report (p. 86)
precategorical sensory store (p. 84)
primary visual cortex (p. 71)

psychophysics (p. 77)
receptive field (p. 70)
span of apprehension (p. 84)
suffix effect (p. 94)
tachistoscope (T-scope) (p. 86)
transduction (p. 69)
whole report (p. 86)

SUGGESTED READINGS

Coren, Ward, and Enns (1994) provide in-depth coverage of sensation and perception, as well as many interesting sample demonstrations that can be used to experience different aspects of sensory and perceptual processes, in their book *Sensation and perception* (New York: Harcourt Brace). In *Perception* (Boston: Allyn and Bacon, 1993), Margaret Matlin presents a very readable overview of sensation and perception. A 1984 article by Nelson Cowan (On short and long auditory stores, *Psychological Bulletin, 96,* 341–370) reviews much of the evidence on echoic store and suggests that there may, in fact, be not one but two types of acoustic sensory store. In two well-written books, *The man who mistook his wife for a hat* (New York: HarperCollins, 1985) and *An an-*thropologist on Mars (New York: Alfred A. Knopf, 1995), Oliver Sacks presents a number of interesting clinical case studies of sensory and perceptual difficulties that arise from damage to the sensory receptors and the central nervous system. Pinel (1993) presents an excellent overview of the physiological underpinnings of sensation and perception in *Biopsychology* (Boston: Allyn and Bacon). For a discussion of applications of knowledge about sensation and perception, see Proctor and Van Zandt's *Human factors in simple and complex systems* (Boston: Allyn and Bacon, 1994) or Wickens' *Engineering psychology and human performance* (New York: Harper-Collins, 1992).

Visual Perception and Object Recognition

I N   C H A P T E R   3 , we discussed how people sense stimuli in the environment, and we described some of the limitations of our sensory systems in extracting information from visual and auditory displays. Although sensory processes play an important role in allowing us to perceive the world, our experience of the world requires more than simply sensing environmental stimulation and sending this sensory information to the brain. In this chapter, we discuss the processes involved in creating an internal representation of the world around us using the visual system.

PERCEPTION: THE LINK BETWEEN SENSATION AND COGNITION

Perceiving the many aspects of the world around us involves many complex and interrelated processes. One good way to understand these processes and how they interact is to subdivide perceiving into three stages: sensation, perception, and identification/recognition, as shown in the information processing model in Figure 4.1.

Sensation refers to the processes whereby physical energy from the environment is transduced into neural responses that code, or represent, basic information about the stimulation received by the sensory receptors. **Perception** refers to the processes that create internal representations of objects and events in the environment. Such an internal representation is known as a **percept,** and it can be thought of as the observer's working description of the nature of an object. Thus, three lines might be perceived as a triangle, an H, or an A, depending on the arrangement of the lines and the context in which they are viewed. The third stage, **identification/recognition,** involves categorizing or assigning meaning to the percept. Whereas the second stage addresses the issue of what an object looks like, the third stage deals with identification (e.g., "What is this object?") and recognition (e.g., "Is this object a living thing?"). We discussed the basics of sensation in Chapter 3. In this chapter, we focus on the latter two stages.

Before we begin to discuss the last two stages of perceiving the world, we should comment on why it is important to discuss perception in a cognitive psychology text. First, just as there is no fixed line separating sensation from perception (see Figure 3.1), there is no line that identifies where perceiving ends and cognition begins. Perception is not a separate, "lower-level" process that simply provides input to cognitive processes. Rather, perception and cognition involve many related and interactive processes, and it is important to appreciate how these two functions of the mind are related.

Second, many of the concepts used in theories of perception (e.g., stimulus features, templates, recognition processes) are also used in theories of cognitive processes. Understanding these concepts as they pertain to perceptual processes will help you when you encounter these processes in later chapters.

FIGURE 4.1   **An Information Processing Model of Visual Perception**   The three primary stages are sensation, perception, and identification/recognition. Top-down processes are those in which higher-level perceptual or cognitive processes affect lower-level processes. Bottom-up processes are those that depend on information extracted from stimuli.

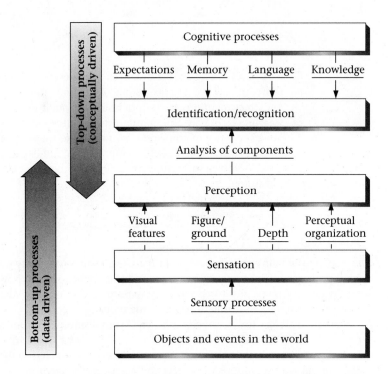

Third, understanding some of the basics of visual perception will help you appreciate both the complexity and the interrelated nature of the cognitive processes we discuss in later chapters (e.g., attention, memory, categorization). Finally, our students have found that understanding how people develop internal codes that represent objects and events helps them understand the types of information processing tasks and theories used by cognitive psychologists.

Normal Perception and the Experience Error

As the quote from McCloskey and Palmer (1996) at the beginning of the chapter indicates, we normally perceive objects in the environment almost effortlessly. When we look out a window, we do not experience discrete, simple sensations like lights, colors, lines, and curves. Rather, we see cars on the road, pedestrians standing or walking, and leaves blowing in the wind. Because perception of objects and scenes is so effortless, it is easy to make the **experience error,** which refers to the mistake of assuming that one's *perceptual experience* in viewing a stimulus is directly available in, or given by, the stimulus itself. The experience error can lead one to think that experiencing the world does not require an explanation in terms of perceptual and cognitive mechanisms. To appreciate the experience error, look at Figure 4.2 and see if you can identify the objects depicted there.

FIGURE 4.2   **The Experience Error**   (a) This drawing illustrates that when we attempt to recognize objects, we do not simply determine which areas of the visual field have the same luminance, or brightness. If we did, then we would see dozens of objects here rather than a zebra against a background. (b) We perceive this figure as a white triangle on top of a black triangle and three circles. Although it appears as if the borders of the white triangle extend across the white space, in fact no edge is there. (c) Can you identify the object depicted here?

(a)

(b)   (c)

Source: Part a, Gregory et al., 1995; Part b, Kanizsa, 1976; Part c, after Daniel Sloat.

Most people are able to identify the zebra in Figure 4.2a and the triangles and circles in Figure 4.2b. We can also "tell" that the zebra is in front of the patterned backdrop and that the white triangle is in front of the black triangle. Because of the ease with which we perceive these objects, it is easy to think that the zebra and triangles are simply "there" and we are responding only to the information in the display. That is the experience error: The objects are not "in" the figure; we create a representation of these objects by organizing and interpreting the light from the figure that falls on our retinas. If we did not organize and interpret the patterns of light and dark in Figure 4.2a all we would see would be dozens of light and dark shapes.

Perception, then, does not depend on simply sensing patterns that arise from a stimulus. In many situations, the perceiver's perceptual and cognitive systems play an important and active role in creating a meaningful percept. To appreciate this point, look at Figure 4.2c. Often, when people first look at this figure, they cannot see what is depicted there. If you have not perceived the object in the figure, take a look at Figure 4.3 and then look back at Figure 4.2c. After seeing the simple line drawing in Figure 4.3, most people can easily perceive the rabbit in Figure 4.2c.

Intellectual Antecedents to Modern Research on Perception

Visual perception was one of the first topics studied in scientific psychology. As with many aspects of cognition, however, psychologists were not the first to think about the relations between sensing, perceiving, and thought. Before modern experimental studies of perception were undertaken, scholars had speculated for centuries about the roles of, for example, experience and innate knowledge; and early scientific investigations of visual perception were conducted against the backdrop of these speculations.

Philosophical Views on Perception and Cognition   Democritus (460–370 B.C.), a Greek philosopher, thought that all matter (including the human mind) was made up of tiny, atomic particles in constant motion. Democritus also believed that objects in the world emit beams of atoms and that these beams affect the observer's mind in such a way as to produce the observer's perception of these objects. Interestingly, he also argued that the atomic beam is a representation of the object itself; thus, a round object emits a circular beam, a rectangular object a rectangular beam, and so forth. Although these ideas may seem quaint, at least one modern theoretical approach to visual perception—the direct perception view (Gibson, 1966, 1979)—suggests that light reflected or emitted from an object provides a great deal of information about the object. Later, we contrast the direct perception view with modern information processing theories that attempt to specify how the visual perceptual system uses different types of information extracted from the light falling on the retina to identify patterns and recognize objects.

Whereas Democritus focused on how people establish an internal representation of objects in the environment, other scholars pondered the relation between perceptual experience and knowledge. Socrates (469–399 B.C.) held that truth and knowledge lie in the mind of the individual and that the role of experience is to facilitate the emergence of this knowledge. Thus, according to Socrates, our experience with the world teaches by allowing us to uncover preexisting knowledge. We perceive objects and events in the world, and this allows us to uncover innate knowledge.

A very different proposal was put forth by Plato (427–347 B.C.). Plato stressed a fundamental distinction between sensations that arise from the senses and "forms," which are revealed through rational thought processes. Plato argued that sensations are short-lived

FIGURE 4.3   **Drawing of a Rabbit**   This line drawing should help you to identify Figure 4.2c.

Source: After Daniel Sloat.

and not always accurate representations of the world. Forms, on the other hand, are stable and accurate.

Plato used an analogy to illustrate the distinction between senses and forms: Imagine you are chained within a cave, so that all you can see is the shadows cast by the flames of a fire outside the cave. The shadows formed by the fire are analogous to sensations, and Plato's forms are analogous to the objects outside the cave. Because the flames flicker and dance, the shadows are imperfect representations of the forms in the outside world. In Plato's view, the senses provide an imperfect representation of the external world.

Modern theorists agree with Plato's notion that what we perceive is not a simple reflection of what is "really out there." As we will see, our perception of the world depends on many processes that help us to interpret the signals coming from the sensory receptors. Two of the main goals for cognitive psychologists interested in perception are (a) to identify what factors affect our perception of the external world and (b) to specify how our perception of the world affects our thinking (and vice versa).

Finally, Aristotle (384–322 B.C.) took quite a different view from Plato concerning the relation between perception and knowledge. Aristotle argued that all knowledge and ideas are the result of experience. The view that all knowledge comes from the senses is called an *empiricist view*. In the centuries following Aristotle, many scholars embraced Aristotle's empiricist views, and these views have had a major impact on the scientific study of perception.

Empirical Approaches to Studying Perception   Herrmann von Helmholtz (1821–1894) made an important theoretical proposal that greatly affected the way perception was viewed by scientists. Helmholtz took the view that all perceptions are acquired through experience and that people also acquire certain "rules" that they use when interpreting sensory information. In one series of clever experiments, Helmholtz demonstrated how perception of the spatial location of objects can be altered by experience.

Helmholtz had subjects wear goggles that contained lenses that distorted the visual field. For example, let's assume that the lenses shift the images of objects several degrees to the right. Helmholtz asked his subjects to look at an object and then close their eyes and reach for the object. Subjects' first attempts at reaching were always to the right of the object—that is, toward the apparent as opposed to the actual position.

More important for present purposes was what happened when Helmholtz gave his subjects several minutes to reach for and handle objects. After this experience, when subjects were asked to repeat the original task—look at an object, then close their eyes and reach for the object—they did so perfectly. Subjects reported that when they first put on the goggles, they had to consciously instruct themselves to compensate when they reached; but with practice, the reaching became quite natural and effortless. Helmholtz called this shift in perception a *perceptual adaptation.* Interestingly, when subjects took the goggles off after wearing them for some time and tried the same reaching task, they again made errors, but now the errors were in the opposite direction—reaching to the left of the object.

Helmholtz argued that many perceptual phenomena such as perceptual adaptation could arise from a process he termed **unconscious inference.** Basically, Helmholtz argued that through experience we learn to make inferences when we perceive and these inferences reflect the rules we use when we interpret sensory information. Helmholtz called these inferences *unconscious* because, in his view, the rules are so well learned that they have become automatic, and applying them requires no conscious effort. Note that, in contrast to the view of Democritus that objects in the world determine our perceptions, Helmholtz argued that our perceptions are affected by what we have learned through perceiving similar events and objects.

Helmholtz's research and his concept of unconscious inference are important in several ways for modern research and theories of perception and cognition. First, Helmholtz's research showed that it is possible to study perceptual processes using behavioral methods. In the next section, we will see that although modern researchers differ in the types of theories they prefer, they agree that empirical methods are a necessary tool in studying perception. Second, the unconscious inferences that Helmholtz proposed are analogous to the stages of information processing in modern theories. Helmholtz and modern theorists would agree that we must interpret the elementary sensations arising from the sensory receptors before we can understand the world around us. In spite of differences in the language used to describe how these sensations are interpreted (Helmholtz used the notion of inferences, and modern theories propose stages and processes), the basic ideas are quite similar. As often happens in the history of science, good ideas are maintained, but the language used to express those ideas changes over time.

Modern Theoretical Approaches to Perception

Today, researchers investigating perception use many approaches, including physiological studies, computational approaches, and studies of machine perception. However, two general theoretical approaches dominate behavioral research and theorizing on human perception. Both approaches attempt to explain how our perception of the world is derived from sensations provided by the sensory system. As noted in Chapter 1, researchers working within a specific theoretical framework share a number of common metatheoretical assumptions. Often, these assumptions are not put to an empirical test; rather, they serve as starting points for the theoretical explanations offered by members of the various theoretical camps.

The two dominant theoretical approaches to perception that we will consider differ greatly in their underlying assumptions. We will review these assumptions as they pertain to the task of perceiving an organized three-dimensional world from the two-dimensional image that falls on the retina. As you will see, these modern theories are similar in many ways to the proposals offered by the early philosophers. The main thing that differentiates the efforts of the philosophers from those of modern researchers are the methods used to test ideas. The early philosophers relied on logic and logical arguments, whereas modern researchers use empirical methods.

The Direct Perception Approach

The **direct perception approach** (Michaels & Carello, 1981) holds that much of what we perceive about the world is directly available in the stimulus information that strikes the sensory systems. This approach grew out of pioneering work by J. J. Gibson (1979). Note that the direct perception view is similar in spirit to Democritus' notion that tiny particles from objects in the world come in contact with our eyes, giving rise to our perceptions.

Proponents of the direct perception view share three main assumptions. First, all the information that is needed to see a three-dimensional world is present in the retinal image or in relations among the parts of the retinal image. One good example of how this might work can be seen in the notion of the **optical flow pattern**—the changes in the retinal image that occur as an observer moves through the world or as objects move past the observer (see Figure 4.4). As we move about, the retinal image is continuously changing. The flow of the parts of the retinal image gives cues as to the location, distance, and movement of objects in the environment.

Second, the perceptual system analyzes the visual scene in terms of surfaces and entire objects rather than more elementary units such as edges, shapes, and locations. Third, perceptual features such as distance and motion arise directly in the observer and are not dependent on processes, computations, or inferences made by the observer. Taken together, these three assumptions help guide the research of proponents of the direct perception view. They also serve to separate members of this camp from the second main approach.

The Human Information Processing Approach

The direct perception view stands in stark contrast to the **human information processing approach.** According to this view, perception and cognition involve stages of information processing that take as their input information from the senses and have as their product perception of the world. Human information processing theories assume that perception and cognition involve transforming information across various stages in order to perceive and think. There are many different types of human information processing theories (e.g., flowchart models, connectionist models), but they all share several assumptions that place them at odds with researchers from the direct perception camp. First, human information processing theories assume that the sensory systems extract information about basic features of objects in the environment, such as edges, color, location, and movement. Second, these basic features are used by perceptual and cognitive processes to create perceptual experience. Whereas the direct perception view holds that perception arises directly from sensory information, human information processing theories maintain that complex processes use information extracted from a stimulus, along with knowledge and memory, to create an internal representation of the external world.

FIGURE 4.4   **Optical Flow Patterns**   These patterns would be present when an observer moved forward while focusing on Point F. The contours in the figure would continue to flow toward the periphery as the observer moved forward.

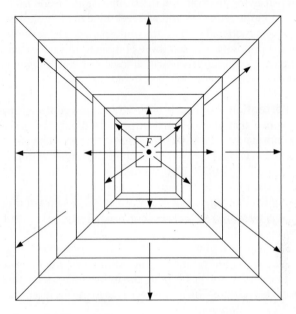

Source: Schiffman, 1996.

The differences between the direct perception and human information processing views are substantial, and they affect every aspect of the research and theorizing carried out by members of these groups: the types of questions asked by researchers, the research methodologies used, and the form of the theoretical explanations favored. For example, a researcher who assumes that optical flow is an important aspect of normal perception will conduct research in such a way that optical flow information is available to the perceivers. In contrast, a researcher who adheres to the information processing view will present subjects with stimuli in such a way that the researcher can identify what basic features of the stimuli the observers are sensitive to. The difference between these two theoretical approaches is a clear example of the effect of metatheoretical assumptions on scientific research.

Although workers in the direct perception tradition have made many excellent points, the human information processing approach is more compatible with modern cognitive psychology. Furthermore, most research conducted today falls within this tradition. As a result, we focus here on the human information processing approach to perception. Keep in mind, however, that it is not the only viable approach.

The theories we discuss in the remainder of the chapter, then, are information processing theories. Given what you have just read about these types of theories, what questions do you think these theories must answer? Generally speaking, the two main questions these theories must address are: (1) What are the units of information that the senses extract from a stimulus and that are used by perceptual and cognitive processes? (2) How do perceptual and cognitive processes combine sensory information with knowledge from prior experience to create our perception of the world?

Section Summary: The Link Between Sensation and Cognition

Perception is the link between sensing stimuli in the environment and thinking about those stimuli. Because perception works so well, many people make the experience error—that is, they assume perceptual experience is directly given by the stimulus. Scholars have thought about the relations between sensing, perceiving, and thinking for centuries. Early philosophical views on perception focused on how people create their perceptions of the world and how knowledge and experience affect perception. Modern theoretical approaches to perception build on these early philosophical ideas but rely on empirical methods for testing theories. The two dominant theoretical approaches to the behavioral study of perception are the direct perception view and the human information processing view. The human information processing view is the one adopted by most cognitive psychologists.

BASIC PROCESSES IN VISUAL PERCEPTION

We noted earlier that perceiving the world can be divided into three stages: sensation, perception, and identification/recognition. In this section, we review three basic processes involved in the second stage, perception. These three processes are segmenting the visual field, locating objects in space, and organizing perceptions.

Segmenting the Visual Field

One of the first tasks facing the perceptual system is how to divide the visual field into *shapes* separated or divided by *contours*. The shapes identified by the visual system are sometimes called **blobs,** to highlight the fact that these shapes have not been classified as squares, rectangles, and so forth. Rather, they are simply identified as areas that "go together" as some part of an object. In addition to being defined as specific regions in the retinal image, shapes can have other attributes or features, such as color and motion.

Visual Features Many attempts have been made to identify how perceptual processes use basic stimulus features in identifying or recognizing an object (e.g., Boring, 1950). Identifying the basic features to which the visual system responds is important because these features serve as the foundation for pattern and object recognition. Unless the visual system responds to a specific attribute or feature of a stimulus, it is unclear how this attribute or feature could be a part of the percept that results from the stimulus.

One method used to identify features is a **visual search task** (e.g., Treisman & Gelade, 1980), in which subjects are asked to detect the presence of one or more target items among a set of distracter items. Treisman and Gelade asked subjects to search for either a color (blue) or a shape (the letter S) among a set of distracter items that were different in both color (green and brown) and shape (the letters X and T) from the targets. The researchers presented from 1 to 30 letters on each trial and examined how the number of letters in the display affected the time it took subjects to detect the presence of a target item. In another set of conditions, Treisman and Gelade asked subjects to detect a T in a display containing either Ys and Is or Zs and Is (see Figure 4.5a and 4.5b on page 110).

The two main questions of interest in these experiments are whether the number and type of distracter items affect how long it takes to search for a target. It turns out that both

EXPERIMENT 4:   Visual Search

You can demonstrate the effects of the type and number of distracters on people's ability to locate target items using the displays in Figure 4A. To complete this demonstration you will need several volunteers and a watch or timer that will allow you to time in seconds. In this experiment, volunteers will search through four displays in each of four conditions. You will test all participants in the manner described below. After testing is completed, compute the average search time for each of the four conditions.

Tell participants their task is to search for the capital letter T in a series of displays, each containing one T among a number of other distracter letters. There are four different conditions, and volunteers should search through each display in each condition as quickly as possible until they find the target T. (Use sheets of paper to cover up the three conditions not being searched.) Ask the volunteers to continue searching until they have gone through all four displays for a particular condition and say "done" when they are finished. Record how long it takes each person to complete the search.

Conditions 1 and 2 contain more items than Conditions 3 and 4. In addition, the distracter items differ across Conditions 1 and 3 versus Conditions 2 and 4. What was the difference in time required to search through Condition 1 as compared to searching through Condition 3? Was the difference smaller or larger than the difference between searching through Conditions 2 and 4? What do these results tell you about the similarity of the features between the letters I and Z versus the letter T (Conditions 1 and 3) as compared to the similarity of features between letters Y and I versus the letter T. (Conditions 2 and 4)? Are your results consistent with what you would have predicted based on the results described in the text?

of these factors affect performance. In the case of targets that are defined by a single dimension, such as color or shape, the time it takes a person to detect the target is not greatly affected by the number of distracters (see Figure 4.5c). Searching for a T among Ys and Is is very easy because there is one feature, a horizontal line, that differentiates the target (T) from the distracters (Y, I). Under these conditions, people can search multielement displays as quickly as they can search single-element displays. You can appreciate this by noting how easy it is to detect the T in the display containing Ys and Is relative to the display containing Zs and Is. In situations such as this, the target is said to "pop out" of the display, and the dimension that defines the target (e.g., color, shape) is said to constitute a basic visual feature.

In other circumstances, however, the number of distracter items greatly affects reaction time. When people are searching for a T in a display containing Zs and Is, there is no single stimulus feature that differentiates the target from the distracters—both targets and distracters have vertical and horizontal lines. Under these conditions the target is defined by the combination of these two features, and adding extra distracters to the display slows reaction time (see Figure 4.5c). Results such as these help researchers identify the basic features used to perceive objects. Experiment 4 will allow you to demonstrate these basic findings.

Figure 4A Four Conditions

Condition 1

```
I Z Z Z I Z Z Z     I Z Z Z I Z I T     I I I I Z Z I I     I I Z Z I Z I Z
Z Z Z I I I I Z     Z Z Z Z I Z I I     Z Z Z T I I Z Z     I Z Z Z I Z Z I
I I I Z I I Z Z     I Z I Z Z Z Z I     I Z Z Z Z I I Z     I I I I T Z Z Z
I Z I I Z T I Z     I Z Z I I Z I I     I I Z Z Z I I Z     Z I Z I I Z I Z
Z I Z Z I I Z I     I Z I I Z I I Z     Z I Z Z I I I Z     Z I Z I Z I I I
```

Condition 2

```
Y Y I I I I I I     Y I Y I Y Y Y I     I Y Y I I Y I Y     Y I Y Y I Y I I
Y I I Y Y Y I Y     I I I Y I Y I Y     I Y I Y Y Y Y Y     I I Y Y Y Y I I
Y I I Y Y Y I I     Y I Y I I I Y I     Y Y I I I Y Y I     I Y I I I Y I I
T Y Y I I I I Y     Y Y Y I I T I Y     T I I Y I Y Y Y     T I Y Y Y Y I Y
Y Y I Y Y I I Y     Y Y Y I Y I I Y     I I Y I I I I I     Y I I Y Y I Y I
```

Condition 3

```
I   Z   Z   Z     I   Z   I   T     I   I   I   I     I   Z   I   Z
I   I   I   Z     I   Z   I   I     Z   Z   Z   T     I   Z   Z   I
I   I   Z   Z     Z   Z   Z   I     I   Z   Z   Z     T   Z   Z   Z
Z   T   I   Z     I   Z   I   I     I   I   Z   Z     I   Z   I   Z
I   I   Z   I     Z   I   I   Z     Z   I   Z   Z     Z   I   I   I
```

Condition 4

```
Y   Y   I   I     Y   Y   Y   I     I   Y   Y   I     Y   I   Y   Y
Y   I   I   Y     I   Y   I   Y     I   Y   I   Y     I   I   Y   Y
Y   I   I   Y     I   I   Y   I     Y   Y   I   I     I   Y   I   I
T   Y   Y   I     I   T   I   Y     T   I   I   Y     T   I   Y   Y
Y   Y   I   Y     Y   I   I   Y     I   I   Y   I     Y   I   I   Y
```

Another task used to identify visual features is the **texture segregation task.** Here, subjects are presented with displays containing many elements, and their task is to identify which part of the display is different from the rest. If observers are able to identify the "odd" areas when the displays are presented very quickly, then the feature that differentiates the odd area from the rest of the display is considered to be a basic visual element.

Research using these and other tasks has identified many basic stimulus features to which the visual system responds. These features include brightness, color, spatial orientation, length, and curved versus straight contours (e.g., Cavanagh, 1988; Julesz, 1984; Neisser, 1967). These features play a prominent role in the theories of pattern and object recognition discussed later in the chapter.

Figure/Ground Differentiation   Another important step in visual perception involves segregating the visual field into two parts: a distinct shape in the foreground (called the **figure**) and the remainder of the field (the **ground**). For example, as you read this text,

FIGURE 4.5   **Stimuli and Results from Treisman and Gelade (1980)**   The subjects' task was to detect a T in a display containing either (a) Ys and Is or (b) Zs and Is. The graph (c) shows the mean reaction times to detect a T as a function of the type of display used and the number of items in each display.

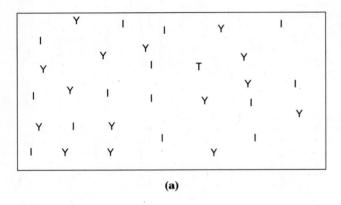

(a)

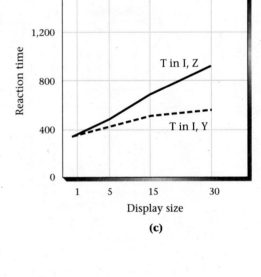

(c)

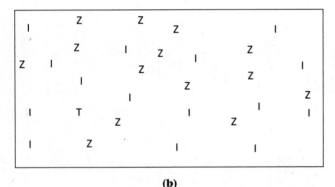

(b)

Source: Data from Treisman & Gelade, 1980.

the page appears as the figure and the desktop on which the book rests becomes the ground.

The Danish psychologist Rubin made the figure/ground distinction in 1915 (Rubin, 1915/1958), and psychologists continue to study the factors that affect the division of the visual field into figure and ground (e.g., Peterson, 1994). In any visual display containing two or more regions, there is some ambiguity as to which regions constitute the figure and which constitute the ground. For example, in a famous ambiguous figure—the Rubin face/vase figure (see Figure 4.6)—you can see either a pair of faces gazing toward each other or an ornate vase. An important fact concerning figure/ground differentiation is that it is a psychological phenomenon, as opposed to a process that depends completely on the stimulus presented to the observer. This can be seen in the fact that the organization of Figure 4.6 will change if you look at the figure for a few moments, despite the fact that the display has not changed. If perception depended simply on the physical stimulus, then we would not perceive two different organizations.

FIGURE 4.6   **A Reversible Figure and Ground**   The displays can be viewed as either a pair of black faces or a white vase. In general, when the white area is smaller, the vase is easier to perceive; and when the black area is smaller, the faces are easier to perceive.

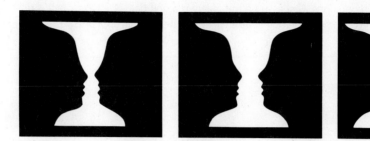

Researchers investigating how figure/ground distinctions are made have achieved great strides. We now have a fairly good understanding of the factors that affect figure/ground differentiation. For example, the shape that tends to be identified as the figure is generally symmetrical, convex (i.e., bowing outward) in shape, smaller in size than the ground, and either vertical or horizontal in orientation (Goldstein, 1984). This knowledge serves as part of the foundation on which theories of higher-order visual processes such as pattern and object recognition are built.

Locating Objects in Space

Look around the room and see if you can tell how far various objects are from you. Can you also tell which objects are closer to you and which are farther? When you judge the distance between you and an object, you are making an estimate of *absolute distance*; when you notice that the pen on your desk is closer than the stapler you are judging *relative distance*. Perceiving these types of spatial relations involves perceiving the dimension of *depth*. There are two general classes of depth cues, *monocular cues* and *binocular cues*.

Monocular Depth Cues   Monocular cues are available even when the stimulus is presented to only one eye (*mono* means "one," and *ocular* refers to the eye). These cues are also known as *pictorial depth cues* because they can be used in representing a three-dimensional scene in a painting or some other two-dimensional format (e.g., a movie).

One important monocular depth cue is **relative size.** As an object moves closer to you, the retinal image cast by that object increases in size, as illustrated in Figure 4.7a. Changes or differences in the relative size of the retinal image can be used to judge distance, especially for familiar objects. Figure 4.7 illustrates how we can use relative size to judge distance and also how our familiarity with the objects we are viewing can affect the way in which we interpret retinal image size.

Linear perspective is a monocular depth cue that has been used by artists for centuries. You may have noticed this phenomenon when driving down a long straight road or looking down railroad tracks. The sides of the road or the railroad tracks are parallel— that is, the same distance apart—but as their distance from you increases, they appear to move closer together. Artists make use of linear perspective to give the sense of a scene extending out away from the viewer (see Figure 4.8a).

FIGURE 4.7   **The Monocular Depth Cue of Relative Size**   (a) Because the size of the retinal images cast by the pictures decreases from left to right, we perceive the cats as receding into the distance as we look from left to right. (b) You can appreciate the effect of familiarity on distance perception by trying to estimate which cat the circular object is closest to under two conditions: First assume the object is a golf ball. Then assume it is really a volleyball. When you look at the object as a volleyball, it suddenly appears farther away.

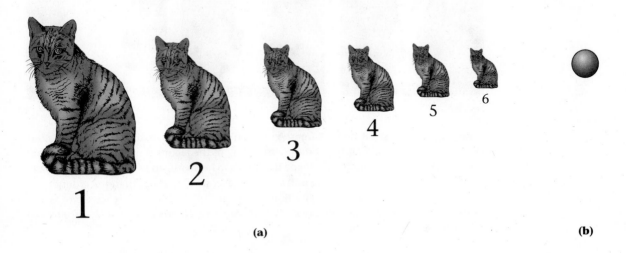

(a)   (b)

Another monocular cue comes from *texture gradient,* the relative density of the texture of items in the environment. As objects recede into the distance, the features that make up their texture become smaller and closer together (see Figure 4.8b). *Interposition,* or overlap, is a monocular depth cue that arises from the fact that nearer objects tend to block, or occlude, our view of more distant objects. Interposition provides an important source of information for relative distance, but it provides no information about absolute distance (see Figure 4.8c).

The monocular cues we have discussed thus far can be depicted in static images such as photographs and paintings. However, depth perception normally takes place as we are moving about in the world, the objects we are watching are moving, or both. Motion provides the final monocular cue we will discuss, *motion parallax.* When you move, the images of nearby objects move across your field of view faster than do more distant objects. Thus, if you are riding a bicycle, the trees near your path appear to whiz by whereas those further away move much slower. Motion parallax and the other monocular cues are used extensively in many computer and video games.

Binocular Depth Cues   The fact that we have two eyes gives rise to two additional cues we can use in judging distance. One of these cues has to do with the fact that the eyes must move to focus on objects at different distances. The second cue depends on the separation of the two eyes, which is about 6cm.

As you may recall from Chapter 3, visual acuity is best for images that are focused on the fovea. If an object moves closer to you and you wish to keep that object in focus, your eyes must converge, or rotate to focus closer together. When the object recedes away from you,

FIGURE 4.8   **Monocular Depth Cues**   The cues shown are (a) linear perspective, (b) texture gradient, and (c) interposition.

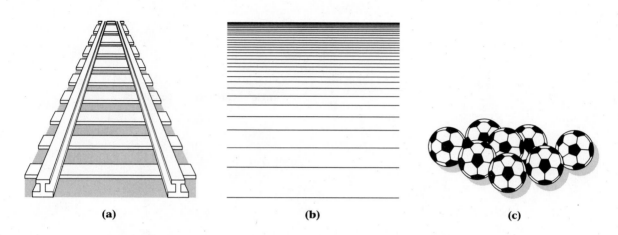

(a)   (b)   (c)

your eyes must diverge, or rotate to focus farther apart (see Figure 4.9). The muscles that control the positioning of the eyes provide the nervous system with information about the eye's *vergence* movements (convergence and divergence), and this provides another cue concerning how far away the object is from you.

The second binocular cue arises from the fact that, because the two eyes are in different locations in space, they provide slightly different images of the same object. The brain fuses these two images into a single image that represents the three-dimensional object that gave rise to the images in the two eyes. The relative discrepancy between the images in the two eyes is used as an indicator of how close the object is to the observer.

Perceptual Organization

We have seen that our visual systems respond to basic features of stimuli and that we are able to locate objects in space. But how do we go from simple visual features and the location of objects to the perception of objects and organized scenes? In this section, we consider part of the answer to this question. Specifically, we consider how we organize our perception of simple visual displays.

Gestalt Principles of Organization   The Gestalt psychologists, most notably Max Wertheimer (Wertheimer, 1923), Kurt Koffka (Koffka, 1935), and Wolfgang Kohler (Kohler, 1947), studied how people organize and classify sets of stimuli. The principles discovered by the Gestalt psychologists are referred to as the **Gestalt principles of organization.** These principles are important because they illustrate how the perceptual system takes sensory information and actively imposes an organization on that information. Figure 4.10 illustrates four of the Gestalt principles:

1. *Principle of proximity.* Stimulus elements that are close together (in the figure, spatially close) tend to be organized into units. We see four sets of pairs of circles in Figure 4.10a rather than eight separate circles.

FIGURE 4.9   **The Binocular Depth Cue of Convergence**   As we focus on objects at different distances, the angle of convergence between the two eyes changes.

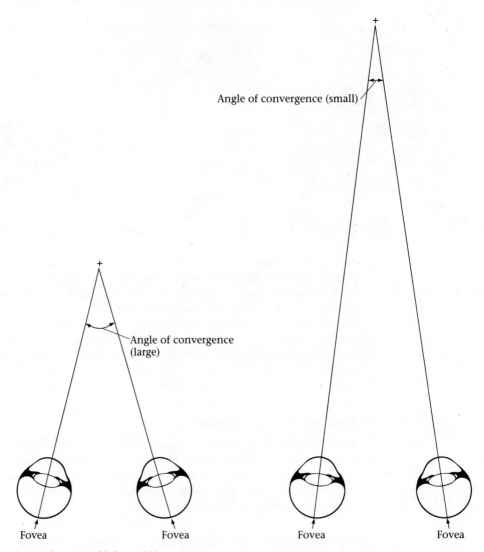

Source: Coren, Ward & Enns, 1994.

2. *Principle of similarity.* Elements that look alike tend to be grouped together. We see Figure 4.10b as containing alternating pairs of filled circles and open circles.

3. *Principle of good continuation.* Elements that form a straight line or a smooth curve tend to be grouped together. In Figure 4.10c, we perceive two curved segments crossing one another. Note here that this combined set of lines could just have easily been made up of the components in Figure 4.10d, and yet this is not the way we organize

FIGURE 4.10 **Gestalt Principles of Perceptual Organization** The principles illustrated are the (a) principle of proximity, (b) principle of similarity, (c) and (d) principle of good continuation, and (e) principle of closure.

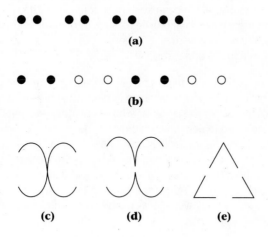

these lines perceptually. We see two continuous lines rather than two "V-shaped" lines.

4. *Principle of closure.* When a stimulus contains a break, or gap, we tend to perceive the figure as a closed, complete figure (Figure 4.10e).

The Gestalt principles exert a powerful influence on visual perception. They also affect perception from an early age. Researchers have shown that even infants tend to group, or organize, stimuli according to the Gestalt principles (e.g., Quinn, Burke & Rush 1993).

We have now described research showing that a number of very basic processes are involved in visual perception. It is also clear, however, that more is required for perceiving objects and events in the world. We turn next to some additional processes that use information about basic features to create our organized perception of the world. Research Report 4 describes several phenomena related to faulty higher perceptual processes.

Section Summary: Basic Processes in Visual Perception

Before we can identify patterns and objects in the environment, we need to identify the basic visual features used to build these percepts. Visual perception begins with several basic processes that identify features of stimuli. Segmenting the visual field into separate areas that correspond to different objects requires identifying visual features and separating the display into figure and ground. To locate an object in space, the visual system uses both monocular and binocular cues. Another important aspect of visual perception is the organization of stimuli into objects and groups. The Gestalt psychologists identified many important principles of organization. These principles help to specify how the visual system processes different types of information in order to create an organized perception of the world.

RESEARCH REPORT 4:   Visual Agnosia

People who sustain damage to areas of the brain involved in visual perception sometimes suffer from *visual agnosia*. In this disorder, recognition and identification of visual stimuli are impaired, even though elementary perceptual processes, such as discrimination of light from dark, remain intact and visual acuity is normal. Lissauer (1890) described two main forms of visual agnosia, *apperceptive agnosia* and *associative agnosia*.

Apperceptive agnosia involves the early stages of visual processing; here, the individual is unable to recognize objects because of a breakdown in perceptual processes. An interesting example of apperceptive agnosia involves a soldier who accidentally experienced carbon monoxide poisoning that resulted in permanent brain damage (Benson & Greenberg, 1969). After he recovered from a coma, the soldier was able to discriminate light intensities, colors, and the direction in which an object was moving; this indicates that he was able to sense visual stimuli. Interestingly, though, he could not identify simple shapes (circle, square, etc.), nor could he recognize faces or letters. Despite the fact that his sensory system was able to process visual information, his nervous system was unable to organize that visual information into a meaningful perceptual experience.

The second form of visual agnosia described by Lissauer is *associative agnosia*. A person with associative agnosia has virtually normal basic perceptual abilities but cannot associate the perceived object with meaning. This form of agnosia derives its name from the fact that it was

PATTERN RECOGNITION

Perceiving visual features, organizing those features, and locating objects in space are important visual processes. In this section, we describe another important process, identifying visual patterns.

Theories about how we identify patterns fall into two main classes: template matching theories and feature comparison theories (Crowder, 1982b; Neisser, 1967). Both classes are examples of **bottom-up theories,** which assume that the processing of information begins with low-level information, which is passed along to "higher" cognitive processes (see Figure 4.1). Such theories can be contrasted with **top-down theories,** in which information and knowledge are used to guide the lower-level perceptual processes. We return to the distinction between bottom-up and top-down theories when we discuss context effects later in this chapter.

Template Matching Theories

According to **template matching theories,** we identify patterns such as the letters in the alphabet by comparing the pattern of neural excitation arising from the retina with patterns—*templates*—stored in our memories. Template theories suggest that rather than analyzing a letter in terms of its features (e.g., two long angled lines and a short horizontal line for the letter A), we perform a wholistic match between stimuli and the representations of letters in memory.

Figure 4.11 illustrates how such a template matching process might work. In this figure, identifying a letter is a process involving finding a match between patterns of neural exci-

originally thought to be caused by an inability to associate visual information with knowledge stored in memory. Farah (1992) reported on a patient (L. H.) who suffered from associative agnosia. When L. H. was presented with simple line drawings of objects and was asked to name them, he was unable to do so, despite the fact that he could copy the drawings. The fact that he could accurately copy the drawings indicates that his sensory system was functioning adequately. L.H.'s difficulty came from not being able to perceive the patterns in visual stimuli.

Associative agnosia does not always affect a person's ability to recognize all classes of stimuli equally. For example, *pure alexia* involves an impairment in printed word recognition, and *prosopagnosia* involves a disruption in the ability to perceive faces. These selective impairments in object recognition can be quite disruptive to the individual. Farah (1992) describes a prosopagnosic who told of sitting in a social club and wondering why another member was staring at him. When he asked one of the waiters to see what was going on, he was told that he had been looking at himself in the mirror!

Mixed forms of agnosia have also been reported. For example, Behrmann, Moscovitch, and Winocur (1994) reported data from C. K., who had sustained a closed-head injury in a motor vehicle accident. C. K. was able to recognize famous faces, and he could discriminate unfamiliar faces. He was also able to perform a number of simple visual tasks, such as copying geometric patterns. However, he suffered profound deficits in other object recognition tasks. In one experiment, he was unable to name many common objects (e.g., safety pin, toothbrush). He was also quite poor at naming common objects when they were presented as simple line drawings, and he did not appear to be able to identify printed letters, although he was able to copy handwritten messages.

tation from the retina and stored patterns of excitation in memory. As the figure shows, when there is a good match between the excitation caused by the stimulus and the template stored in memory, the system can identify what the pattern is—say, an A or an L.

Template matching works very well in pattern recognition machines that read letters and numbers in very constrained contexts, such as the equipment that scans the account number from your checks. However, for human pattern recognition, the template matching procedure has too many limitations to be a viable account of how patterns are perceived. For example, as Figure 4.11 suggests, slight deviations in shape, size, orientation, and so forth would keep a template matching system from being able to recognize even the limited number of stimuli that make up the written language. In its most literal form, a template matching system could only identify the variations in letter patterns that we can perceive by having a huge number of templates for each letter, with the different templates corresponding to differences in type font, size, angular orientation, and so forth. Such a system would be unwieldy because it would need to store a huge number of templates.

Template matching theory could be modified to deal with this problem by the addition of a step preceding the comparison, or template matching, process. This additional step would involve "normalizing," or "cleaning up" the input pattern before it is matched to the stored template. It seems reasonable to assume that differences in the size of stimuli, as well as their orientation, might be accomplished by such a normalization process.

Still, people are able to recognize a huge range of written messages, which contain gaps in the letters, variations in the writing instruments, and many other variations. While nor-

FIGURE 4.11   **The Template Matching Process for Letters**   The letter must match the template exactly, as in (a). The template matching procedure can fail because of (b) change in position, (c) change in size, and (d) change in orientation.

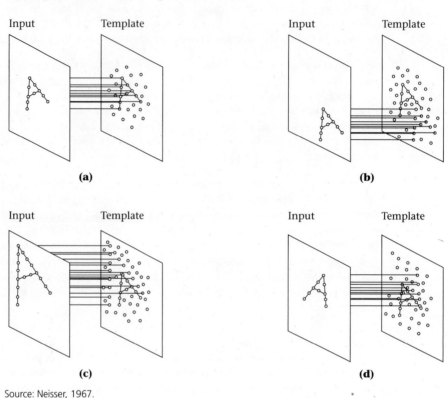

Source: Neisser, 1967.

malization could account for some of the variability in stimuli that are recognized, if all pattern recognition depended on a "normalization + template matching" process, we would need a tremendous number of normalization procedures, not to mention processes to handle other aspects of human pattern recognition. Still, the concept of normalization has proven useful in accounting for some types of complex pattern recognition such as identifying a speaker based on his or her voice (e.g., Legge, Grossman & Pieper, 1984).

Feature Comparison Theories

As a consequence of the many problems with template matching theories, researchers now generally favor the second class of theories, **feature comparison theories.** Here, we discuss two different types of feature comparison models: feature detection models and feature analysis models. Both assume that elementary features are used to identify patterns, but they differ in the assumptions they make about how these features are processed. **Feature detection models** assume that the perceptual system detects the presence or absence of specific features and uses this information to determine what stimulus the person is perceiving. **Feature analysis models** also assume that the system an-

FIGURE 4.12 **Features of Letters** The figure shows one scheme for identifying 26 letters using distinct features. Notice that letters that share many features tend to look very similar and thus might be confused.

Features	A	E	F	H	I	L	T	K	M	N	V	W	X	Y	Z	B	C	D	G	J	O	P	R	Q	S	U
Straight																										
Horizontal	+	+	+	+		+	+								+				+							
Vertical		+	+	+	+	+	+	+	+	+						+		+				+	+			
Diagonal/	+		+					+	+		+	+	+	+	+											
Diagonal\	+		+					+	+	+	+	+	+	+	+							+	+			
Curve																										
Closed																+		+			+	+	+	+		
Open V														+												+
Open H																	+		+	+						
Intersection	+	+	+	+			+	+								+						+	+	+		
Redundancy																										
Cyclic change		+						+	+							+									+	
Symmetry	+	+	+	+		+	+	+			+	+	+	+		+	+	+			+					+
Discontinuity																										
Vertical	+		+	+		+	+	+	+						+							+	+			
Horizontal		+	+			+	+								+											

Source: Gibson, 1969, p. 88.

alyzes a stimulus for features, but the features are not necessarily assumed to be either definitely present or definitely absent. There can be strong evidence that a feature is present or weak evidence for the presence of a feature.

One fact that led to the development of feature comparison theories is that many common elements are shared by different stimuli. For example, the letters b, d, p, and q are all rather similar, as are the letter pairs O and Q and B and P. Whereas template matching theories postulate that we store a wholistic template for each letter, feature comparison theories suggest that letters can be described by their elemental features. Figure 4.12 shows one scheme that could be used to describe the letters of the English language in terms of their constituent features.

Human pattern recognition is very flexible, and an adequate theory of human pattern recognition must be able to account for this flexibility. Feature detection models are a step toward this goal, but they are limited by problems similar to those that face template models. For example, while the features in Figure 4.12 will work to let the system identify block letters, we can identify letters in a wide range of styles, typefaces, and sizes (e.g., B, **B**, *B*, ʙ). A theory that assumes that the perceptual system simply works like a checklist to see if the features are present or absent is going to have trouble with letters that are not "perfectly" written. As a consequence, theorists in the late 1950s began considering a different sort of model, the feature analysis model.

Feature Analysis Models   Feature analysis models are similar to feature detection models in that they assume that the sensory and perceptual systems function by analyzing stimuli for the presence of specific visual features. However, rather than assume that a feature is either present or absent, these models assume that the feature can be present in varying degrees.

One of the earliest and most influential feature analysis models was Selfridge's (1959) **pandemonium model.** Whereas template models involve only two stages—one to detect the presence of a signal and one to compare the stimulus against a stored template—feature analysis models involve several stages. In Selfridge's pandemonium model of letter recognition, there are four stages (see Figure 4.13). Each stage involves "demons" that perform specific tasks.

The tasks performed by the demons are illustrated in Figure 4.13a. The letter R at the left of the figure is the pattern to be recognized. The first set of demons, the *image demons,* record the image that falls on the retina and pass this information along to the *feature demons.* The feature demons analyze the image for the presence of features such as specific types of lines, curves, contours, and angles. Figure 4.13a shows only seven feature demons, but the model assumes that there are a much larger number, each of which tests for a different feature. If a feature demon detects the presence of the target feature, the demon responds and passes this information along to the next set of demons, the *cognitive demons.* These demons determine which group of features are present. Each cognitive demon is responsible for identifying one pattern. Thus, to identify the uppercase letters of the English alphabet, 26 cognitive demons would be needed.

You might be wondering how this model got the name *pandemonium.* The name comes from the next process. Each cognitive demon that detects one or more of the features it is looking for begins to yell. The more of its features it detects, the louder it yells. The final demon is the *decision demon,* and this demon listens to the pandemonium caused by all of this yelling. The decision demon selects the cognitive demon that is yelling the loudest and decides that the pattern searched for by that cognitive demon is the most likely pattern in the real world to have produced the image falling on the retina.

Advantages of Feature Comparison Theories   Feature comparison models have many advantages over template matching theories. First, it is possible to identify the relations among features that are critical for identifying a given letter. Thus, a capital A might be described as "two lines that are joined at the top to form an acute angle and that are crossed by a horizontal line." With this type of a description, A, **A**, *A*, and A are all valid As.

A second advantage is that, since the features identified by the model are simpler than the templates used by template matching models, the models can more easily account for variability in stimuli. Thus, if **A** is identified as an A by observers, we can change the description of the necessary relations among features to be "two lines that are joined in some fashion at the top and that that are crossed by a horizontal line."

A third advantage of feature comparison models stems from the units that make up the descriptions of patterns in the two classes of theories. Template matching theories assume that we have a template corresponding to each pattern we can recognize. Feature comparison models assume that we store the basic features of stimuli in memory, along with descriptions of how these features need to be arranged to form particular patterns. This gives feature comparison models the advantage of not needing to store as much information in memory as would be required by template matching theories. Template matching theories would require one template for every pattern to be identified; feature comparison models can use a small set of features plus the arrangement of features to recognize many diverse patterns.

FIGURE 4.13   **Selfridge's Pandemonium Model of Visual Word Perception**   The image, feature, letter, and cognitive demons all respond to different types of information and perform different tasks. In (a) the system is presented with the letter R, and in (b) the letter T is the target. The arrows between the feature demons and the cognitive demons are solid for inputs to the correct target and dashed for inputs to other letters.

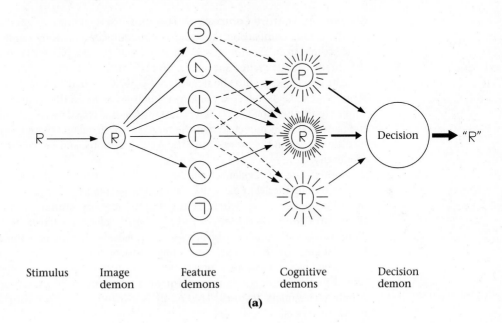

(a)

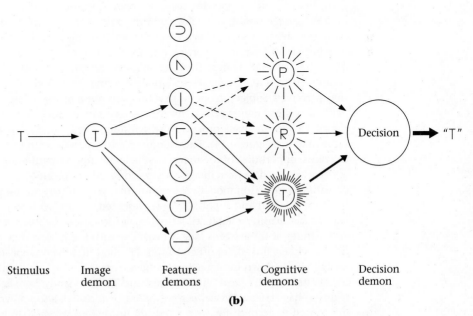

(b)

Source: Goldstein, 1984.

Note that the processes by which stimuli are compared to information stored in memory are also quite different for the two theories. Template matching theories involve a *wholistic process* in which an entire stimulus is compared with a template stored in memory. Feature comparison models involve an *analytical process* in which the stimulus is analyzed in terms of its basic features, and these are then used in the pattern recognition process.

Support for Feature Comparison Theories   Several lines of experimental evidence favor the feature comparison models over the template matching models. One line of evidence comes from experiments using visual search tasks. Neisser (1964) asked subjects to search for a target letter such as Z embedded in distracters that either shared many straight-line features with the target (e.g., X, W, V) or had curved features (e.g., O, C). He found that subjects detected the target much faster when the distracters had features dissimilar to those of the target. Note that this result is exactly what one would predict from the pandemonium model. When the targets and distracters share few features, there will be little overlap in the output from the feature demons, and hence the targets will be easy to identify.

Another line of evidence consistent with feature comparison models, and the pandemonium model in particular, comes from experiments that have looked at the types of errors people make when attempting to identify stimuli. Kinney, Marsetta, and Showman (1966) flashed letters and numbers briefly on a screen and asked subjects to identify what stimulus had been presented. Results showed that the more features two letters shared, the more likely the subject was to confuse the two letters. For example, when they were shown a C, subjects were 26 times more likely to report that it was a G than a B. The pandemonium model predicts that such errors are more likely when the stimuli share many features. This result is difficult to explain with a simple template matching model.

Further evidence supporting feature comparison theories comes from studies of stabilized images. Normally, there are slight movements or tremors in our eyes (called *nystagmus*), even when we try to keep them fixated on a specific location. Such movements are very important for normal perception, because if an image is stabilized on the retina, the image gradually fades out so that one no longer sees it. Pritchard (1961) used sophisticated equipment to stabilize images on subjects' retinas and then asked them to report what they perceived. Subjects reported that the perception of the fading of a stabilized image is neither a general fading nor an instantaneous disappearance of the image. Rather, the fading appears to involve a process in which lines at the same orientation disappear at the same time (see Figure 4.14). These findings are consistent with feature detection theories; the units, or portions, of the image that fade out are the features of the object.

There are also data from image stabilization studies that are inconsistent with one aspect of feature comparison models, the notion that pattern recognition is primarily a bottom-up process. Inhoff and Topolski (1994) presented subjects with compound words like *cowboy* and *teacup* using a stabilized retinal image procedure. Of interest here is how the letters and features of these words fade. Consistent with the notion that perception and cognition are closely linked, Inhoff and Topolski found that the disappearing images were more likely to break down into meaningful fragments (e.g., *cow, cup*) than into nonmeaningful fragments (e.g., *owb, acu*). In the Inhoff and Topolski study, knowledge of word meaning seems to have affected visual perception—a clear case of a top-down influence. This finding is hard to account for with a bottom-up theory like the pandemonium model. The study shows the strong link between perceptual and cognitive processes, in this case visual

FIGURE 4.14   **Perceptual Fragmentation in Stabilized Images**   The four figures at the left are the original stimuli presented to subjects in Pritchard's (1961) study; the remaining items in each row illustrate what subjects reported they perceived after the stimuli had been stabilized on their retinas.

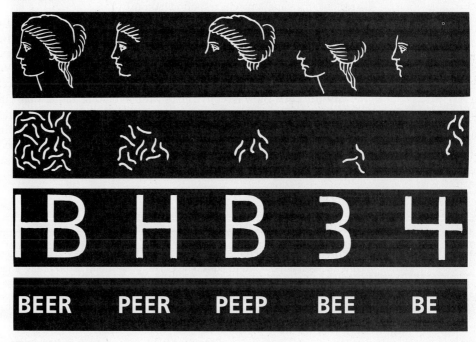

Source: Pritchard, 1961.

word recognition and knowledge of language. Later we will discuss models that are designed to account for both bottom-up and top-down influences on perception.

Physiological Evidence Consistent with Feature Comparison Theories   In Chapter 3, we pointed out that the rods and cones respond to the relative amounts of light falling on the retina. However, simply detecting the presence or absence of light is insufficient for pattern or object recognition. The information provided by the photoreceptors must be processed further to support these functions.

A key source of information used to identify and recognize objects is the contours, or edges and borders, of the objects. Kuffler (1953) discovered an important fact about how the visual system detects contours. He found that a given ganglion cell fires action potentials at a fairly constant base rate when the receptive field of the cell is not being stimulated. More importantly, the cell's rate of activity can be selectively increased or decreased through stimulation of different areas within the cell's receptive field. Kuffler found that the receptive fields of many ganglion cells contain two distinct regions. For the *on* region, the ganglion cell's activity increases when light is present; and for the *off* region, the cell's activity decreases when light is present.

An important consequence of the arrangement of neural connections between the photoreceptors and the ganglion cells is that the *on* and *off* regions of a receptive field are mutually antagonistic: If light is shone on both an *on* and an *off* area of the same receptive field, the two effects tend to cancel one another, with the result being a very weak *on* or *off* response. However, if the light falls only on one region, there is a large neural response. Because of the antagonistic effects of *on* and *off* regions, the ganglion cells are very responsive to contrasts. Thus when the edge of a stimulus falls at the boundary of *on* and *off* regions, the ganglion cells respond vigorously.

Hubel and Wiesel (1962) extended Kuffler's work and examined the responses of the cells in the visual cortex to stimuli projected onto the retina. They found that cells in the visual cortex respond most rigorously to light or dark bars and edges of stimuli. Based on the responses of these cells to different types of stimuli, Hubel and Wiesel identified three main types of cells: simple cells, complex cells, and hypercomplex cells.

Simple cells show receptive fields with an oblong, rather than circular, shape (see Figure 4.15). These cells have *on* and *off* areas that are arranged in parallel along the axis of the oblong. Simple cells are quite specific in terms of the type of stimulus to which they will respond. For example, some simple cells will fire in response to a line at a 45-degree angle in the middle of the visual field but not in response to a vertical line or a line at the side of the visual field.

FIGURE 4.15   Retinal Receptive Fields for Cells of the Visual Cortex   The ovals represent areas of the retina that respond to light. The pluses correspond to *on* areas, which increase the level of activity of their simple cells in response to light falls. Minuses represent *off* areas, in which the activity of simple cells decreases in response to light. The stimuli on the right are the best stimuli for eliciting a high rate of response from the receptive field.

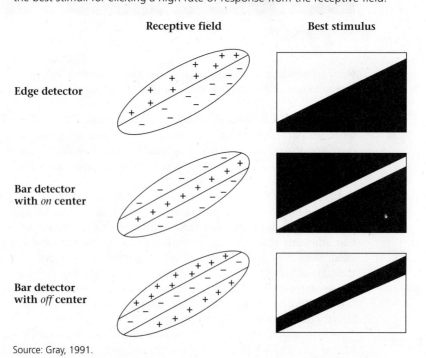

Source: Gray, 1991.

Several types of simple cells have been identified. *Edge detectors* respond best when the edge of the light and dark areas on the retina are arranged along the edge of the *on* and *off* regions of the receptive field. *Bar detectors* respond most vigorously to bars of light or dark.

Whereas the receptive fields of simple cells are arranged into discrete *on* and *off* areas, **complex cells** are most responsive to edges at particular orientations, regardless of where they occur in the receptive field. Thus, the responses of complex cells are tuned to the angle of an edge, and they do not require that the edge occur at a specific retinal location. These cells provide important information concerning contours that is independent of the location of the stimulus on the retina.

Finally, **hypercomplex cells** respond to edges or bars located within the receptive fields, but they are also sensitive to the length of the stimuli and their angular orientation. Some hypercomplex cells respond most rigorously to specific shapes, such as two lines set at an angle. Hypercomplex cells receive their input from complex cells. Thus, for example, if one simple cell responds to a /, a second to a \, and a third to a —, then a hypercomplex cell that receives inputs from these cells might respond to the letter A, which has all three of these features. Note that this is a physiological analog of the assumptions underlying feature detection theories.

Considerable debate has raged over whether some arrangements of hypercomplex cells might be specialized for recognizing more complex classes of objects (e.g., Mollon, 1982). Some data suggest that there are collections of cells that respond actively to biologically relevant classes of stimuli (e.g., faces, hands) and not to other complex stimuli (e.g., Desimone & Ungerleider, 1989). These cells may show remarkable specificity in what they respond to. Perrett and his colleagues (1990) reported evidence of a cell that fired most vigorously for a face only when the eyes in the face were pointed in a specific direction! There are, of course, limits to how specialized these cells might be, if for no other reason than at some point the specialization would require too many cells. As Mollon (1982) put it, "It would be no good having a system in which there were, say, single units specific to chartreuse-colored Volkswagens moving left at a distance of 10 meters" (p. 80).

Section Summary: Pattern Recognition

Features identified by the visual system are used to perceive patterns in stimuli. The two main types of theories of pattern recognition are template matching theories and feature comparison theories. Template matching theories assume that a wholistic match is made between patterns of activation on the retina and templates stored in memory. Because this type of pattern recognition would require that a huge number of templates be stored in memory, researchers generally favor the feature comparison approach. According to this view, pattern recognition involves identifying the constituent features in a stimulus and then determining what stimuli have these features. Two types of feature comparison models are feature detection models and feature analysis models; the latter type provides for more flexibility in pattern recognition. Selfridge's (1959) pandemonium theory is an influential early feature analysis model. Feature detection theories are supported by both behavioral and physiological data.

OBJECT RECOGNITION

Pattern recognition is an important perceptual skill, but we also need to be able to recognize three-dimensional objects in the environment. In this section, we describe the dominant theoretical approaches to object recognition. Our focus is on the logic behind the types of representations and processes proposed by these theories.

Marr's Computational Theory

David Marr (1982) proposed a very influential theory of object recognition. According to Marr's theory, three basic types of representations are constructed during object recognition.

1. The first representation formed, called a **primal sketch,** provides a two-dimensional representation of the patterns of light energy present on the retina. More specifically, the primal sketch is a description of the changes in the patterns of light intensity across the retina. This representation contains information about edges, contours, and blobs, or closed contours. The primal sketch is used to form the second representation, the 2½-D sketch.
2. The **2½-D sketch** contains information about the depth and orientation of the surfaces of objects. A number of cues to depth and orientation are used to form this representation, including binocular disparity, texture, motion, and shading. The 2½-D sketch is used to form the final representation of the object, the 3-D sketch.
3. The **3-D sketch** contains a description of the shapes of objects and the relative positions of these objects in the visual field.

Marr's theory uses many of the principles and findings that we have reviewed in this chapter, and it takes a substantial step toward providing an integrated theory of object recognition. Marr's theory is called a **computational theory** because it seeks to specify the mathematical functions that the perceptual system might compute using the information available to identify objects. Let us examine why this theory is described as computational.

According to the theory, the primal sketch provides information about edges and the shapes of objects. How is this information obtained? To take the simplest example, how could one determine the location of a line based simply on the patterns of light intensities across the retina? Marr and Hildreth (1980) proposed one means for computing the location of lines, and Marr incorporated this algorithm, or set of formal rules, into his theory. Although Marr used a precise mathematical formulation for this algorithm, we can convey its essence in a nonmathematical format.

In Marr's theory, the patterns of light intensity from the retinal image are used to form a *gray-level representation* of the retinal image. Basically, this representation consists of the light intensities at very small areas of the retina. The higher the light intensity, the larger the value in this representation. Thus, each area of the retina is assigned a number, and we can think of these numbers as being stored in a table of numbers, with rows and columns corresponding to locations in two dimensions across the retina.

The Marr-Hildreth algorithm for detecting edges in this gray-level representation uncovers what are known as *zero crossings*. Here is how the process works. Assume that the light intensity at a specific location on the retina changes, and this change corresponds to a transition from dark to light. This is what you would find if you were to draw a line with a pen on a white piece of paper and then compare the intensity of light reflected from the line with the intensity of light reflected from the paper. This change in intensities produced by a line drawn on paper is what we would expect if we were to measure the intensity of light on the retina as we look at the paper and line.

Figure 4.16a illustrates the change in light intensity from the black line to the white paper. Figure 4.16b illustrates the first derivative of the rate of change. The first derivative simply indicates how quickly the intensity changes from Point 1 to Point 4 in Figure 4.16a. As you see, the rate of change is zero from Point 1 to Point 2 (because the light intensity is

FIGURE 4.16   **A Marr-Hildreth Zero Crossing**   A change in light intensity is shown in (a), the first derivative of the change in (b), and the second derivative in (c).

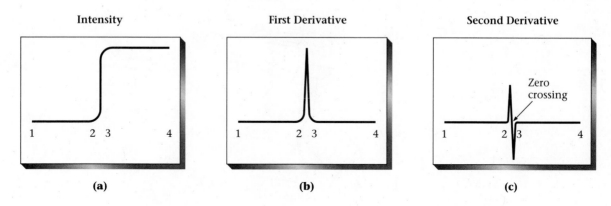

Intensity	First Derivative	Second Derivative
(a)	**(b)**	**(c)**

the same at these points), rapid between Points 2 and 3, and finally zero again from Point 3 to Point 4.

Figure 4.16c shows the second derivative of the intensity change—in other words, the rate of change in the derivative shown in Figure 4.16b. Note that in Figure 4.16b, the rate of change between Points 2 and 3 is positive at first and then negative. Thus, in Figure 4.16c (which depicts this rate of change), there is a point at which the second derivative changes from rapidly increasing to rapidly decreasing. The point at which the second derivative crosses the horizontal midline is the zero crossing.

The Marr-Hildreth algorithm describes how the perceptual system could determine where there is a line, or a rapid change in the intensity in the gray-level representation. The next step is to identify *zero-crossing segments,* which are simply zero crossings with the same spatial orientation in the gray-level representation. The zero crossings and zero-crossing segments are then used along with depth cues to compute the 2½-D sketch, and this representation is used to form the 3-D sketch.

Biederman's Recognition by Components

Another influential computational theory is the **recognition by components (RBC) theory** proposed by Biederman (1987). Like feature comparison theories, Biederman's RBC theory holds that we recognize objects by identifying a relatively small number of basic components and then specifying the relations among these components.

Take a look at Figure 4.17. Can you "recognize" this image as an object? Despite the fact that nothing that looks like this exists in the real world, there is almost unanimous agreement that it could be a real object and that we can identify its parts. Biederman's RBC theory proposes that we recognize objects like this by first detecting the edges present in the visual image.

An important aspect of Biederman's theory is the notion of **nonaccidental properties.** These are arrangements of lines or edges that "would only rarely be produced by accidental alignments of viewpoints and object features and consequently are generally unaffected by slight variations in viewpoint" (Biederman, 1987, p. 119). Figure 4.18a pre-

Irving Biederman
Irving Biederman developed an influential theory of object recognition known as *recognition by components.* This model assumes that we recognize objects by identifying basic geometric shapes and then noting the spatial arrangement of these shapes.

FIGURE 4.17   Nonsense Object

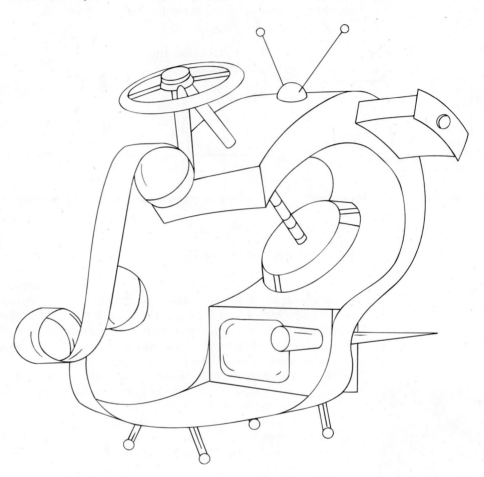

sents five nonaccidental properties of three-dimensional objects, and Figure 4.18b illustrates how these nonaccidental properties could be used to discriminate a cylinder from a
brick.

Biederman proposed that a small set of 36 **geons** (for *geometrical ions*) can be identified
on the basis of, among other things, the nonaccidental properties of lines in the retinal
image. Geons are essentially three-dimensional volumes such as cones, cylinders, and
wedges. Just as feature detection theory can account for how we identify a large number of
patterns using only a small set of features, RBC theory argues that we identify objects by
first identifying geons and then noting the spatial relations among these geons. The importance of the spatial relations among geons is illustrated in Figure 4.19.

Biederman's theory assumes that the nonaccidental properties of objects are critical in
object recognition. Biederman (1987) tested this hypothesis by presenting subjects with
line drawings of objects from which some of the line segments had been removed (see Figure 4.20). In the "recoverable" versions of these stimuli, line segments had been removed
from regions where the line segments could be replaced or "filled in" with straight or

FIGURE 4.18 **Nonaccidental Properties** Biederman's recognition by components model assumes that nonaccidental properties play a critical role in visual perception. Examples of nonaccidental properties that can be used in object recognition appear in (a). A demonstration of how nonaccidental properties can be used to discriminate between a brick and a cylinder appears in (b).

Three Space Inference from Image Features		
2-D Relation	**3-D Inference**	**Examples**
1. Collinearity of points or lines	Collinearity in 3-Space	
2. Curvilinearity of points of arcs	Curvilinearity in 3-Space	
3. Symmetry	Symmetry in 3-Space	
4. Parallel Curves (Over Small Visual Angles)	Curves are parallel in 3-Space	
5. Vertices—two or more terminations at a common point	Curves terminate at a common point in 3-Space	"L" "Fork" "Arrow"

(a)

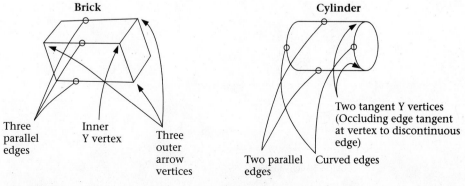

Brick

Three parallel edges

Inner Y vertex

Three outer arrow vertices

Cylinder

Two tangent Y vertices (Occluding edge tangent at vertex to discontinuous edge)

Two parallel edges   Curved edges

(b)

Source: Biederman, 1987.

FIGURE 4.19   **Spatial Relations of Geons**   Different spatial arrangements of the same component geons can result in different objects.

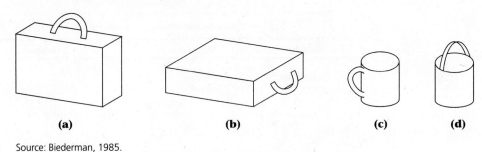

(a)   (b)   (c)   (d)

Source: Biederman, 1985.

FIGURE 4.20   **Recoverable and Nonrecoverable Stimuli**   The five figures on the left are original stimuli used in Biederman's (1987) experiment. The middle column presents the recoverable versions of these stimuli, and the right column shows the nonrecoverable versions.

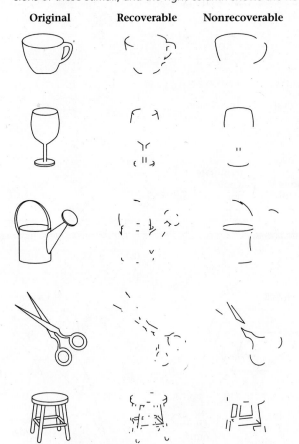

Source: Biederman, 1987.

curved lines, leaving the nonaccidental properties intact. In the "nonrecoverable" versions, the line segments had been removed from locations that contained nonaccidental properties.

Subjects were presented with recoverable and nonrecoverable stimuli and were asked to identify what object was depicted in the drawing. When the stimuli were presented very quickly, subjects were much better able to identify the recoverable stimuli than the nonrecoverable stimuli. Furthermore, with longer exposures, the advantage of the recoverable over the nonrecoverable stimuli increased. When the stimuli were exposed for 5 seconds, almost all of the recoverable stimuli were identified, but only about 40 percent of the nonrecoverable stimuli were identified.

Section Summary: Object Recognition

Object recognition theories attempt to specify what types of information are used to identify objects and how this information is processed. Most modern theories of object recognition specify in detail how sensory information is processed to determine what object gave rise to the patterns of light on the retina. Marr's computational theory assumes that three basic types of representations are constructed during object recognition: a primal sketch, a 2½-D sketch, and a 3-D sketch. Each includes different types of information (e.g., edges, depth cues, descriptions of shapes) about an object. Biederman's recognition by components (RBC) theory assumes that the visual system identifies geons, which are three-dimensional volumes. The spatial arrangements of geons then determine what object gave rise to the retinal image.

CONTEXT EFFECTS

Thus far in the chapter, we have been concerned mainly with identifying patterns and objects in isolation. However, most of the time, we perceive things within a meaningful context, and this context can exert a powerful influence on how we perceive. For example, read the following two lines:

THE CAT
24 13 76 81 A 13 C D

Did you read "THE CAT" and "24, 13, 76, 81, A, B, C, D"? In these examples, the letters A and H in the first line are physically identical, and so are the number 13 and the letter B in the second line. Despite the fact that these stimuli are physically identical, you still perceived them as being very distinct because of the contexts provided. We can, then, perceive the same physical stimulus in very different ways, depending on the context.

The effect of context extends beyond single letters and numbers. For example, read the following two series of words as quickly as you can:

RAT, OWL, SNAKE, SQUIRREL, RABBIT, SWAN, D*CK
DAVE, BOB, BILL, HENRY, MIKE, STEVE, D*CK

Did you have any trouble reading the final word in each list? Did you read "DUCK" in the first list and "DICK" in the second? In this case, you used your knowledge of categories (animals and male names) to perceive what otherwise would have been an ambiguous stimulus.

Context Effects for Pictorial and Verbal Materials

The theories of pattern recognition we have discussed thus far have a difficult time dealing with context effects such as the ones you just experienced. Experimental evidence has shown that context effects are obtained in a wide variety of situations. Palmer (1975) asked subjects to identify a target object such as a loaf of bread, a mailbox, or a drum. These items were presented after subjects had viewed an appropriate or an inappropriate context for the target item. Thus, a kitchen scene was appropriate for a loaf of bread but inappropriate for a drum. Palmer found that people recognized the objects more quickly after they had viewed an appropriate scene than an inappropriate scene. Similar results have been obtained in several studies using slightly different procedures (e.g., Biederman, Glass & Stacy, 1973; Biederman et al., 1974).

Researchers have also shown that providing a context can aid in the recognition of written words. Tulving and Gold (1963) asked subjects to identify words that were briefly flashed on the screen of a tachistoscope. Subjects were able to recognize target words more quickly when they were preceded by an appropriate verbal context (e.g., the context "The people were killed in a terrible highway . . ." for the target word COLLISION) than when no context was provided. Subjects were also slower to recognize target words when an inappropriate context preceded the target word (e.g., TREASON following "The people were killed in a terrible highway . . ."). Context can thus both help and hinder perception.

Another striking context effect shows that sometimes it is easier to perceive a more complex stimulus than a simple one. This is the **configural superiority effect** (Pomerantz, 1981), shown in Figure 4.21. This effect describes the finding that observers are able to perceive a difference among stimuli that are integrated more readily than they are able to perceive the same difference among simple stimuli.

FIGURE 4.21   **The Configural Superiority Effect**   Observers perceive differences among stimuli that are integrated (a) more readily than they perceive differences among single stimuli (b). Note that the feature that differs is the same in both sets of stimuli, yet subjects are better able to detect the difference in the more complex set.

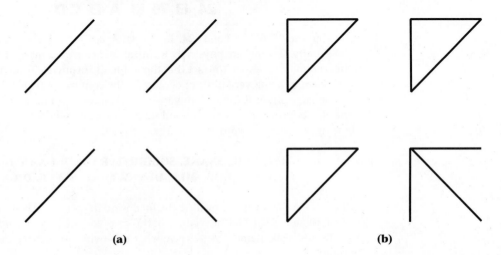

(a)   (b)

Word Superiority Effect

A verbal analog of the configural superiority effect has attracted a great deal of attention, and in this final section we review this effect and one of the explanations that has been offered for it. The **word superiority effect** (Cattell, 1886) refers to the finding that it is easier to identify letters when they are presented in words than when they are presented individually. Modern studies of the effect (e.g., Reicher, 1969; Wheeler, 1970) have used a forced-choice procedure in which subjects are first presented with either a word (e.g., WORK) or a single letter (e.g., K). Following the brief presentation of these target items, subjects are asked to identify, in the case of the word condition, which of two letters appeared in a specific location (e.g., - - - D versus - - - K). In the single-letter condition, subjects are given two letters (e.g., D versus K) and are asked which one is the target stimulus. Studies have shown that under a wide range of conditions, subjects are more accurate at identifying the target letter in the word condition than in the single-letter condition. This is a very counterintuitive finding, because we usually think that embedding a target among other items will serve to make perception of the target more difficult.

Interactive Activation Model of Word Recognition

All of the context effects we have described show that in certain situations, having a context aids perception. You may have experienced this yourself if you have ever made a photocopy of a textbook page and the copy turned out to be of poor quality for the part of the page close to the binding. When this happens, we can often read what is printed on the low-quality portion of the page if we can read the words that came before and after the blurred part of the copy. If you were to try to read these same blurred words without the help of context, it would be much more difficult.

One very influential model that has been proposed to account for context effects is the **interactive activation model** of McClelland and Rumelhart (1981). This connectionist model assumes that there are both bottom-up and top-down influences on word recognition. The model is similar in some ways to Selfridge's pandemonium model. Let us consider how the model can account for context effects in visual word recognition.

McClelland and Rumelhart's model makes a number of specific assumptions about how word recognition takes place. First, the model assumes that visual word perception takes place within an information processing system that involves processing at three different levels: feature, letter, and word (see Figure 4.22a). Furthermore, higher levels of processing provide top-down input to the word level.

Second, perceptual processes occur in parallel within these different levels. While the system is processing information regarding the features of the target stimulus, it is also processing the letters within the stimulus, as well as which possible word the stimulus might represent.

Third, the model is an interactive activation model, which means that it includes both bottom-up, or data-driven, processes and top-down, or conceptually driven, processes. These processes interact to provide constraints on what words the system will perceive. For example, knowledge of English words will operate in a top-down manner at the same time incoming information about the features in a target word will operate in a bottom-up manner. Knowledge of English and information about what features are present in the word will constrain what word the system will select as the perceived stimulus.

To appreciate how this model works, it is important to understand the model at two dif-

FIGURE 4.22   **Macrostructure and Microstructure of the Interactive Activation Model**   The arrows
ending with points represent excitatory connections, and the arrows ending with dots represent inhibitory connections. (a) The organization, or macrostructure, includes three levels of
analysis. (b) The microstructure features connections among nodes. The nodes at the bottom respond to features of letters; those in the middle to letters within words; and those at
the top to words.

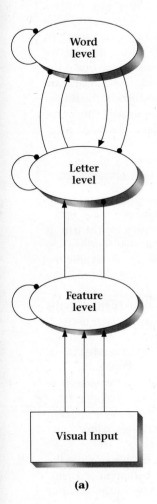

(a)

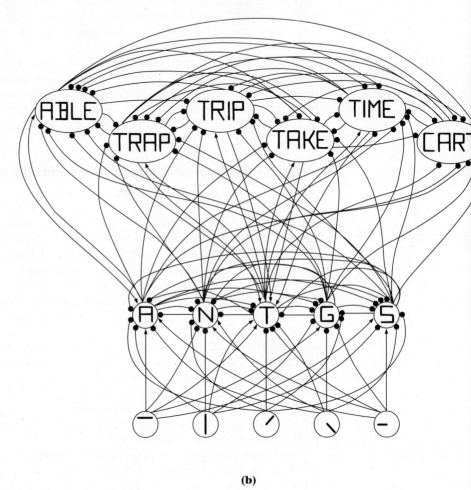

(b)

Source: McClelland & Rumelhart, 1981.

ferent levels, the *macrostructure* and the *microstructure*. The macrostructure specifies how
the levels of the model are organized and how information is passed between the levels.
The microstructure specifies in detail how the information is processed by the nodes

within the system. The macrostructure of the model is shown in Figure 4.22a, and the microstructure is shown in Figure 4.22b.

Within the model there are two types of connections, *inhibitory connections* and *excitatory connections*. Connections may occur within and between adjacent levels. Connections within a level are inhibitory. For example, if there is evidence to suggest that a letter in the target stimulus is a T, then the letter cannot also be a Z; therefore, there are inhibitory connections between letter nodes. Connections between levels can be either excitatory or inhibitory. As shown in Figure 4.22b, for example, there are excitatory connections between the node for the letter A and the word ABLE, since there is an A in ABLE. The connections between the A letter node and the TRIP word node are inhibitory, because there is no A in TRIP. Thus, information at the letter level suggesting that there is an A in the target word supports the hypothesis that the word could be ABLE and provides evidence against the hypothesis that the word could be TRIP.

McClelland and Rumelhart present a computer simulation that captures how word recognition is accomplished by the model. Imagine that a subject has been shown a stimulus like the one in Figure 4.23a. From this stimulus, the subject has extracted the features for the letters W, O, and R. The features extracted from the fourth letter are consistent with the letters R and K. How does the model come to recognize the stimulus as the word WORK?

Recall that in the pandemonium model, the cognitive demon listens to the letter demons shouting. Whichever letter demon is shouting the loudest is the one that the cognitive demon decides corresponds to the target letter. A similar logic is used in McClelland and Rumelhart's interactive activation model, although the concept of shouting is replaced with the concept of activation. Activation occurs at each of the levels within the model, and the node with the highest activation is presumed to correspond to the target stimulus.

Figure 4.23b shows the activation levels for word and letter nodes over time. Over time, the activation level at the node for WORK increases, and the activation levels for other word nodes decrease. The activation levels at the letter nodes show that the highest activation is for the K node, with the R node the next highest. Because the activation level for the WORK node is the highest, the system recognizes the target stimulus as WORK.

It is easy to see how this model can account for context effects such as the word superiority effect. Recall that the word superiority effect shows that subjects are better able to identify letters when they are presented in the context of a word than when they are presented alone. According to the model, when a word is presented, activation from the word level feeds into the letter level. When single letters are presented, this input from the word level is missing; as a result, the overall activation level at the letter nodes will be higher in the word condition than in the single-letter condition.

The interactive activation model has been applied to a wide range of perceptual and cognitive tasks, and it does quite a good job of accounting for the results of behavioral studies (e.g., McClelland & Rumelhart, 1981; Rumelhart & McClelland, 1982). Results from brain-imaging studies provide converging support for the general notion of discrete levels of information processing corresponding to different features of stimuli (e.g., features of letters, words; Peterson et al., 1988; Posner et al., 1988). These and other lines of research on the interactive activation model have established clear connections between perceptual processes, such as feature detection and analysis and word recognition, and higher-level cognitive processes, such as memory and language. The remaining chapters in the book build on this foundation.

FIGURE 4.23   **Word Recognition in the Interactive Activation Model**   (a) A subject shown this stimulus will extract the features W, O, and R. (b) Activation at the word and letter levels over time shows how the subject eventually recognizes the stimulus as WORK.

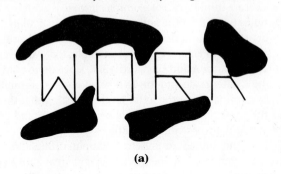

(a)

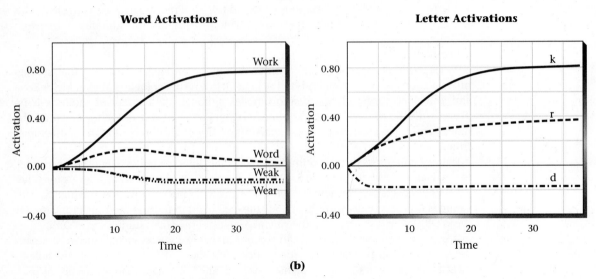

(b)

Source: McClelland & Rumelhart, 1981.

Section Summary: Context Effects

Context plays an important role in visual perception. Context effects can be demonstrated across a wide range of tasks, materials, and so forth. Context can either help or hinder perception. If the context is consistent with the appropriate perception of an object, then context helps. When there is a mismatch between context and how an object should be perceived, context hinders perception. Context also affects the types of perceptual and cognitive processes that are used in performing tasks. Context effects are both general, in the sense that they occur frequently, and specific, in the sense that they are limited to the specific stimuli and contexts that a person experiences. McClelland and Rumelhart's (1981) interactive activation model assumes that both bottom-up and top-down processes affect perception. This model has been applied to a wide range of perceptual phenomena. Finally, context effects illustrate the close relation between perceptual and cognitive processes.

REVIEWING # REVIEWING VISUAL PERCEPTION AND OBJECT RECOGNITION

CONCEPT REVIEW

1. What is the experience error, and how is this error relevant to visual perception and pattern recognition?

2. Briefly describe the views of Democritus, Socrates, Plato, and Aristotle on the relation between knowledge and experience. Indicate the position of each of these scholars as to whether knowledge is innate or acquired through experience.

3. Describe Helmholtz's experiments on perceptual adaptation. What did Helmholtz mean when he argued that perception involves unconscious inferences?

4. Briefly describe the main assumptions underlying the direct perception view and the human information processing approach to perception. Which of these two approaches is favored by most cognitive psychologists, and why?

5. What are visual search tasks and texture segregation tasks? How are these tasks used to identify visual features?

6. Briefly describe each of the following depth cues and indicate whether it is a monocular or a binocular cue: convergence, interposition, linear perspective, motion parallax, texture gradient, and relative size.

7. What is figure/ground differentiation? Why is it important to visual perception?

8. Describe the Gestalt principles of perceptual organization.

9. According to template matching theories, how do we perceive patterns? How does this differ from the way feature comparison theories say we perceive patterns? What is the difference between feature detection theories and feature comparison theories?

10. What evidence supports feature comparison theories?

11. What are simple cells, complex cells, and hypercomplex cells, and how do they relate to the notion of feature detectors?

12. Describe the basic stages of information processing according to Marr's theory.

13. How are objects recognized according to Biederman's recognition by components theory?

14. Briefly describe some of the evidence indicating that context affects visual perception.

15. What is the difference between bottom-up processing and top-down processing?

16. Describe the microstructure and macrostructure of McClelland and Rumelhart's model.

KEY TERMS

blob (p. 107)
bottom-up theory (p. 116)
complex cell (p. 125)
computational theory (p. 126)
configural superiority effect (p. 132)
direct perception approach (p. 105)
experience error (p. 100)
feature analysis model (p. 118)

feature comparison theory (p. 118)
feature detection model (p. 118)
figure (p. 109)
geon (p. 128)
Gestalt principles of organization (p. 113)
ground (p. 109)

human information processing approach (p. 105)
hypercomplex cell (p. 125)
identification/recognition (p. 99)
interactive activation model (p. 133)
linear perspective (p. 111)
nonaccidental property (p. 127)
optical flow pattern (p. 105)

KEY TERMS (*continued*)

pandemonium model (p. 120)
percept (p. 99)
perception (p. 99)
primal sketch (p. 126)
recognition by components (RBC)
  theory (p. 127)

relative size (p. 111)
sensation (p. 99)
simple cell (p. 124)
template matching theory (p. 116)
3-D sketch (p. 126)
texture segregation task (p. 109)

top-down theory (p. 116)
2½-D sketch (p. 126)
unconscious inference (p. 104)
visual search task (p. 107)
word superiority effect (p. 133)

SUGGESTED READINGS

In addition to the materials listed at the end of Chapter 3, there are many other excellent sources of information on visual perception and pattern recognition. Roger N. Shepard's wonderful book *Mind sights* deals with illusions and ambiguous figures that Shepard drew over the course of his distinguished career (W. H. Freeman and Company, 1990). *The perception of illusory contours,* edited by Susan Petry and Glenn E. Myer, contains excellent information and dozens of interesting figures and photographs (New York: Springer-Verlag, 1987). Richard F. Thompson's book *The brain: A neuroscience primer* (2nd Ed.) (W. H. Freeman and Company, 1993) has a very good chapter on the physiological underpinnings of sensory and perceptual processes. For a psychologist's view of the types of distortions used in art, we recommend J. B. Deregowski's book *Distortions in art: The eye and the mind* (Routledge & Kegan Paul, 1984).

W E ARE CONTINUALLY EXPOSED to more information than we can possibly process, and we often try to perform more than one task at a time. As you read this sentence, perhaps the clock on the wall is ticking, or a person seated nearby is wearing perfume, or the TV is flickering across the room. If you are attending to reading the words on the page, then you are probably not aware of these other events. However, if you attend to the other events, you easily become aware of them. You also might be trying to do two things at the same time, dividing your attention between reading and listening to music, for example. In this chapter we will discuss research examining the ways in which attention affects cognitive processes. We will consider both how attention limits performance in cognitive tasks and how attention allows us to process various types of information.

BASIC RESEARCH ON ATTENTION

Common experience tells us that there is a limit on the amount of information we attend to at any one time, as William James observed in the quote above. Although we could be aware of many stimuli in the world around us, in fact we process only a selected portion. Presumably you are not aware of the pressure of your shoes on your feet at this time, but if you "switch" your attention to your feet, you can easily perceive this pressure.

A series of important studies reported in the late 1950s showed that attentional processes play a major role both in what people perceive and in what they remember. In this section, we review studies that used auditory or visual events to examine subjects' attentional processes. After we describe these studies, we consider three classes of modern cognitive theories proposed to account for performance limits attributed to attention: structural models, capacity/resource models, and process models. Each is intended to account for different attentional phenomena, and each has underlying assumptions different from those of the others.

A Bit of History: The Cocktail Party Phenomenon

E. Colin Cherry (1953) set the stage for the modern study of attention by describing the **cocktail party phenomenon,** which describes how people respond when confronted with several simultaneous conversations, as they are at a cocktail party or in similar situations. As you have probably noticed, you can selectively attend to one among many conversations going on around you. But at the same time, while seeming to ignore other conversations, you sometimes notice things, such as your name being mentioned, in one of the "ignored" conversations.

The first aspect of the cocktail party phenomenon reflects a process of **selective attention**—the ability to attend to one of several possible streams of information, as we do when we listen to a specific conversation and ignore others going on nearby. The second aspect of the phenomenon reflects **divided attention**—the processing of more than one stream of information at a time. Divided attention is revealed when we suddenly are aware of personally relevant information, such as our name, in a conversation we thought we were ignoring. This chapter deals with each of these aspects of attentional processes.

Auditory Events

In an important early study of selective attention in the auditory domain, Cherry (1953) used a **dichotic listening task,** in which researchers present different auditory stimuli to subjects' two ears through stereo headphones. In one version, a **speech-shadowing task,** subjects are required to attend to one of the messages and repeat, or "shadow," this message as quickly and accurately as possible (see Figure 5.1). The message the subject shadows is called the *attended message,* and the other message is called the *unattended message.*

Cherry's experiments, as well as subsequent research (Broadbent, 1958; Cowan, 1995), reveal several interesting facts about the relationship between the messages in the attended and unattended ears. If the physical characteristics of the two messages are different (e.g., a male voice and a female voice), subjects' performance is better than when the same voice presents the two messages. The intensity of the two messages also plays an important role. Shadowing is easier if either message is slightly louder than the other (Egan, Carterette & Thwing, 1954). Taken together, these results demonstrate that the physical nature of the auditory message affects subjects' ability to selectively attend to just one message.

Another interesting finding from early shadowing studies concerns subjects' responses to the unattended message. Subjects appear to be quite unaware of many changes in the unattended message. For example, if midway through the shadowing task the language of the unattended message changes from English to German, but the speaker remains the same, subjects are often unable to report this change at the end of the trial. Cherry also re-

FIGURE 5.1   **A Dichotic Listening Task**   In the speech-shadowing task used by Cherry (1953), the two messages are played to the listener at the same time, and the listener's task is to repeat word for word the message in the attended ear.

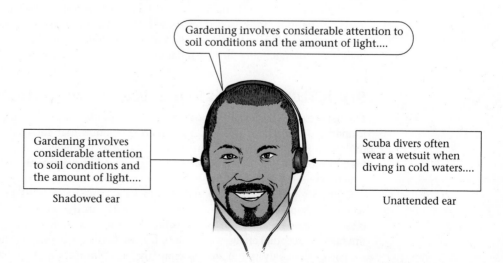

Gardening involves considerable attention to soil conditions and the amount of light....

Gardening involves considerable attention to soil conditions and the amount of light....

Scuba divers often wear a wetsuit when diving in cold waters....

Shadowed ear

Unattended ear

ported that most subjects do not notice when the unattended message changes from English to English played backward (see also Wood & Cowan, 1995). In contrast, if the voice speaking the unattended message changes from male to female, or if the message is replaced by a non-speech tone, subjects can almost always note the change after the trial ends.

Perhaps the most surprising result reported by Cherry was that subjects are extremely poor at recalling the content of the unattended message. In many cases, the listeners in Cherry's study were not able to report a single word or phrase from the unattended message! Neville Moray (1959) went so far as to repeat words 35 times in the unattended ear and then ask subjects to recall the words after the trial was over. Even under these conditions, subjects' memory for the items in the unattended ear is very poor. The overall pattern that emerged from early studies on attention was that subjects are aware of basic sensory attributes of items in the unattended message, but they cannot report the identity of the words presented in the unattended channel.

Visual Events

Neisser and Becklen (1975) created a visual task similar to the speech-shadowing task by videotaping two very different events and then combining them into a single video in which the two events were superimposed (see Figure 5.2). Subjects presented with this video were asked to follow the action in one of the events. To focus their attention on one scene, subjects were instructed to press a button whenever an unusual event occurred in the scene they were watching.

Results showed that when subjects attend to one scene, they do not notice what is going on in the other scene. For example, only one subject of the 24 who focused on the basketball scene noticed that midway through the tape the players of the hand-slapping game stopped their game and shook hands. As in the speech-shadowing experiments, then, people attend selectively to one stream of information and ignore another. You can see this for yourself in Experiment 5A.

Section Summary: Basic Research on Attention

Research examining the cocktail party phenomenon identified many basic limitations of selective attention and divided attention. Studies using the speech-shadowing task showed that the physical characteristics of auditory messages affect people's ability to selectively attend to one of several messages. Results also showed that people are very poor at remembering information presented in an unattended message, even when the information is repeated many times. Similar results have been found for the auditory modality.

STRUCTURAL MODELS OF SELECTIVE ATTENTION

The data reviewed thus far support the idea of a fundamental limit on the amount of information humans can process. A general explanation that emerged to account for this limitation proposed that it is caused by a structural "bottleneck" somewhere in the information processing system. We consider next the structural models of selective attention, which take this view.

Figure 5.3 presents the two general types of structural models proposed to identify where the bottleneck, or capacity limitation, exists in the sequence of information processing stages. According to **early selection models,** attention is the bottleneck that limits the perceptual analysis of stimuli. If items are not attended to, they are not selected for perceptual analysis and are subsequently "lost" from the system. In contrast, **late se-**

EXPERIMENT 5A: A Selective Reading Task

Begin with the top line and read every line in **bold** type.

Selective attention allows a person to process one message and ignore, or not

Information to which we are not attending can sometimes "capture" our attention. For example,

attend to, another. The ability to selectively attend allows us to deal with the

words that have special meanings, such as *sex* and *murder,* sometimes work this way.

information overload that we would experience if we were conscious of all the

Physical aspects of stimuli may also capture our attention, as in a series of digits (333-653-4271)

events that take place around us. Psychologists have been studying selective

or words that are printed in ALL CAPITAL LETTERS. In some situations, we may

attention for almost the entire history of experimental psychology. Attentional

find it difficult to ignore a message; material about experimental psychology and attention here

processes play a role in almost every perceptual and cognitive process. In this

may be hard for you to ignore when you are reading about a similar topic in bold print.

and the remaining chapters, we discuss research and theories on these topics.

Were you able to read the passage in bold type and ignore the passage in regular type? Did you find that any of the words or phrases in regular type were hard to ignore, like *sex,* the digits 333-653-4271, or the words in ALL CAPITAL LETTERS? How about the phrase "experimental psychology and attention"?

lection models suggest that all stimuli are initially encoded and perceptually analyzed. These models hold that the limit on attention occurs after perceptual analysis, when the person uses the information from perceptual analysis to select a response. As we review these two structural models, we consider evidence for and against each model.

Early Selection Models

A number of influential early selection models were proposed in the 1950s and 1960s. These models exerted a tremendous influence both on the study of attention in particular and on the developing science of cognitive psychology more generally.

Broadbent's Filter Theory   Donald Broadbent (1958) proposed one influential model of selective attention. Two important characteristics contributed to this model's significant impact in psychology. One is that Broadbent's model was the first flowchart model of

FIGURE 5.2   **A Selective Looking Task**   Neisser and Becklen (1975) used video displays to study selective looking. Original scenes of (a) a hand-slapping game and (b) a basketball game were superimposed (c).

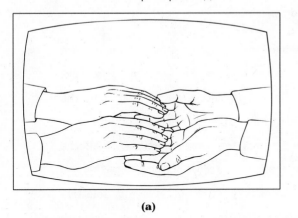

(a)

(b)

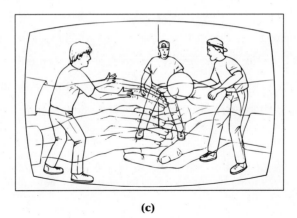

(c)

Source: Neisser & Becklen, 1975.

human information processing (see Figure 1.4) and thus represented a major conceptual departure from previous psychological models. Before Broadbent introduced his model, most psychological theories accounted for human behavior in behaviorist terms, by trying to specify the associations between stimuli and responses that are learned with experience. Broadbent's model attempted to show how information might be transmitted from the sensory receptors to the perceptual and cognitive systems and then to the response systems.

   The second important aspect of Broadbent's model is that it contains the seeds of its own destruction. Broadbent's model is both testable and falsifiable, and researchers were soon able to show that important aspects of the model were wrong. Although it might seem strange, having one's model proved incorrect is actually quite a positive accomplishment for a scientist, for it shows that the model is viewed as important enough to warrant

FIGURE 5.3   **Structural Models of Selective Attention**   In the early selection model of selective attention, the bottleneck, or locus of selective attention, occurs prior to perceptual analysis. In the late selection model, the bottleneck occurs after perceptual analysis. For both types of models, the shaded box represents the locus of selective attention.

Early Selection Model

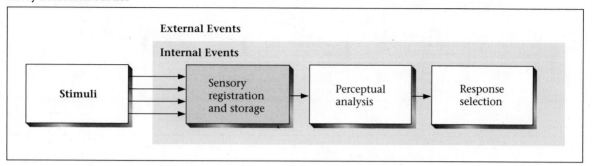

Late Selection Model

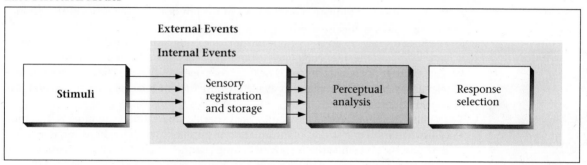

Source: Adapted from Lachman, Lachman, & Butterfield, 1979.

close scrutiny. A model can suffer no more ignoble fate than to languish in libraries and not attract the attention of other scientists.

Broadbent's model, called **filter theory,** assumes that the human cognitive system can be viewed as a communications channel that takes in messages from the environment, processes the messages through the channel defined by the human nervous system, and then transmits the messages to a destination—in this case, the response system (e.g., manual or spoken responses; see Figure 5.4).

According to filter theory, the first main component of the system, the sensory stores, maintain fairly accurate representations of stimuli for a short time after the stimuli are presented. (Recall from Chapter 3 that Neisser [1967] later dubbed the visual and auditory sensory stores the *iconic store* and *echoic store,* respectively.)

The second main component of the model is the filter, which serves to select one stream of information from all the streams available in the sensory stores. If a message is selected by the filter, then it can be processed completely. Messages that are not selected are blocked from further processing and are soon lost.

The filter in Broadbent's model has several important characteristics:

FIGURE 5.4   Broadbent's Filter Model of Selective Attention

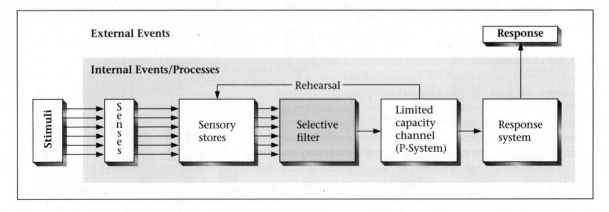

Source: Based on Broadbent, 1958.

1. The filter selects information on the basis of the physical characteristics of the stimulus (e.g., pitch, spatial location).
2. The filter operates in an all-or-none fashion, meaning that only the selected stimulus passes through the filter completely. Stimulus events that are not attended to are blocked from further processing. The filter thus operates like the channel selector on a television: Of the many channels available, only the one selected is processed and displayed on the screen.
3. The filter is under conscious control. People decide what stimulus to process, and they can switch from one stream of information to another. Switching, however, is a rather slow process; and while the filter is switching channels, no information is passed along from the sensory stores. This process is similar to the SEEK function on a digital radio: While the radio is switching from one radio station to another, no further signals are processed and played on the speakers.
4. After a stimulus is selected for further processing, it is passed along to the limited-capacity *P-system* (perceptual system). The P-system functions to identify the items being attended to (e.g., words in a shadowed message).

Evidence Supporting Filter Theory   How well does filter theory account for the results of the early speech-shadowing experiments? One important finding was that listeners are not able to recall the content of unattended passages. According to filter theory, when subjects are shadowing a message presented to one ear, the filter passes information from that source along for further processing, such as identifying the words in the message. Because the filter operates in an all-or-none fashion, the message from the unattended ear is blocked by the filter, and so the listener cannot report the unattended message.

Filter theory also accounts for how various changes in the unattended message affect performance. For example, filter theory defines channels in terms of physical characteristics of stimuli. Thus, making the auditory messages more distinct (e.g., a male versus a female voice, a soft versus a loud message) would be expected to improve performance.

Donald Broadbent
Donald Broadbent was a productive and influential researcher and theorist who worked at the Applied Psychology Research Unit of the Medical Research Council in Cambridge, England and Oxford University. His filter theory of attention is an important early selection model.

Finally, once a listener begins to shadow a message, the filter should block the information in the unattended ear. This would account for why listeners do not notice or report changes in the unattended message.

Filter theory can also explain several other findings from dichotic listening studies. One such finding comes from experiments using a **split-span task,** in which subjects are presented with a small series of items in pairs, with one member of each pair presented to each ear (see Figure 5.5). The listener's job is to report all the items presented to the two ears. When the item pairs are presented at a rapid rate (e.g., 0.5 second per pair) and subjects are allowed to report items in any order, subjects tend to report the items from one ear first and then attempt to report the items from the other ear (e.g., Broadbent, 1954).

This result makes sense in terms of the characteristics of Broadbent's filter. Since the filter is slow to switch from one ear to the other, subjects attend to items from only one ear during item presentation. After all items are presented, subjects switch their attention to the other ear and attempt to recover items from the sensory store.

Further support seems to come from split-span experiments in which items are presented at a rapid rate and subjects are asked to report the items pair by pair (i.e., reporting the items from the first pair, then the second pair, then the third pair) rather than ear by ear (reporting all the items from one ear followed by all the items from the other ear). Under these conditions, subjects make many more errors than when reporting ear by ear. According to filter theory, this is because the filter is too slow to switch ears. Consistent with this analysis, when the items are presented at a slower rate, pair-by-pair reporting is as accurate as ear-by-ear reporting (Broadbent, 1954).

FIGURE 5.5 **A Split-Span Task** Pairs of items are presented simultaneously in the two ears. After the items have been presented, the listener's task is to report all of the presented items.

Evidence Against Filter Theory   Moray (1959) reported a clever experiment that called into question the filter theory account of speech shadowing. In Moray's experiment, at various times during a shadowing task, subjects were instructed to stop shadowing the message in the attended ear and switch to shadowing the message in the unattended ear. These instructions were presented in either the attended or the unattended ear.

As predicted by filter theory, the subjects frequently followed the instructions when the instructions were presented in the attended ear but virtually never switched when the instructions were given in the unattended ear. The interesting twist in Moray's study concerns trials in which the instruction to switch ears was preceded by the subject's name (e.g., "Robyn, switch ears"). Under these conditions, subjects often followed the instructions, even when the instructions were given in the unattended ear. But if the filter blocked all information from the unattended ear from perceptual analysis, then subjects should never have followed the instructions given in that ear.

Another early study that showed a problem with filter theory was reported by two Oxford University undergraduates. Gray and Wedderburn (1960) tested the all-or-none aspect of the filter by presenting subjects with items that could be grouped on the basis of the nature of the items (e.g., Dear, Aunt, Jane, 9, 7, 6). The items from the two sets were presented in alternating fashion to the two ears (e.g., Dear, 7, Jane in one ear and 9, Aunt, 6 in the other, as shown in Figure 5.6), and the subject's task was to report all of the presented items.

If the filter completely blocked the message in the unattended ear, then under the conditions just described, subjects should not have been able to follow one full set of items (e.g., Dear, Aunt, Jane). Gray and Wedderburn's results, however, showed that subjects

---

FIGURE 5.6   **Gray and Wedderburn's Procedure**   In Gray and Wedderburn's (1960) study, subjects tended to report items on the basis of their relation to one another despite the fact that the related items were presented in different ears.

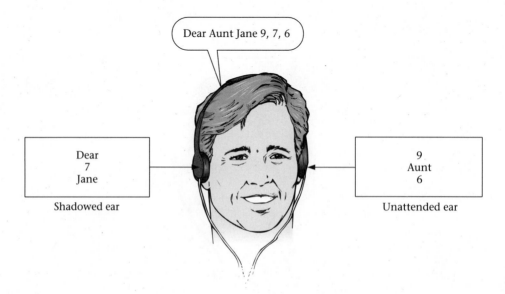

Dear Aunt Jane 9, 7, 6

Dear
7
Jane

Shadowed ear

9
Aunt
6

Unattended ear

Anne Treisman
Anne Treisman is a professor of psychology at Princeton University. She has made numerous important contributions to the fields of attention and perception. Her modification of Broadbent's (1958) filter theory was an influential early selection model.

were able to follow the two sets of items and were able to report them as two distinct groups.

Other research also showed that subjects do not completely block out the message in the unattended ear. Treisman (1960, 1964) reported studies in which, midway through the shadowing task, the messages were switched between ears. For example, at the start of the trial, the left headphone might be presenting information about a baseball game, and the right headphone, a message about the stock market. Later, the messages were reversed so that the left headphone presented stock market information and the right headphone, baseball information. Under these conditions, subjects sometimes "followed" the message from the attended ear to the unattended ear and repeated a word or two from the unattended ear but then reverted to shadowing the message in the attended ear.

Treisman's Attenuation Model   To account for these and other results, Anne Treisman (1960) proposed a modification to filter theory—the **attenuation model**. Treisman suggested that rather than an all-or-none filter, selective attention at the early stages of information processing operates as an *attenuator*, allowing the attended message to be passed along intact and allowing the unattended message to be passed along in an attenuated, or weakened, form (see Figure 5.7).

Treisman's model assumes that a series of analytical tests are performed on the incoming materials. If the attended message can be discriminated from the unattended message on the basis of physical cues, then selection can occur very early in the information processing system. However, the unattended message is not completely blocked by a filter, and hence a word in the unattended ear that is consistent with the meaning of the message in the attended ear can intrude into awareness and affect performance. Treisman's model can easily account for results such as those of Gray and Wedderburn (1960). If the items presented in the unattended ear are processed sufficiently that subjects know what these items are, then the subjects can easily notice that the items form a meaningful set.

FIGURE 5.7.   **The Attenuation Model of Selective Attention**   In Treisman's (1960) attenuation model, the attenuator allows one message to pass through intact and other messages to pass through in a weakened, or attenuated, form.

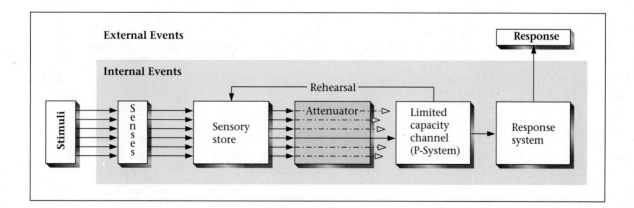

Late Selection Models of Selective Attention

In early selection models, such as Broadbent's filter theory and Treisman's attenuation model, the locus of selective attention (i.e., the place in the system where selective attention exerts its influence) is early in the information processing system. In contrast, late selection models assume that the selection of a stimulus for further processing occurs after the stimulus has been processed to the level of a short-term memory store (Deutsch & Deutsch, 1963; Norman, 1968). We next consider Donald Norman's late selection model in some detail.

Norman's Model   According to Norman's model (see Figure 5.8), incoming stimuli are processed sufficiently to be compared with representations stored in memory. That is, when a listener hears a person speak the word *apple*, this information is processed by the sensory system, and the resulting internal representation contacts a representation of *apple* in the listener's memory. Information corresponding to items that are seen or heard is then available in a short-term memory system that maintains the information for a brief time.

An important aspect of Norman's model is the concept of **pertinence value.** The pertinence value serves to weight the relative importance of incoming stimuli. Some stimuli are very important to a listener (e.g., the listener's name), and hence these stimuli should attract attention even if the physical stimulus is weak. In Norman's model, the incoming stimulus that has the greatest overall activation, as determined by the sensory input and the pertinence value, is selected for further processing.

Note that in Norman's model, the process of selective attention occurs *after* the stimulus has undergone extensive processing. Furthermore, there is no filtering or attenuating of stimuli prior to selection. The items that we become aware of are those with the greatest combination of sensory activation and pertinence value, but all stimuli access their representations in memory regardless of whether they are selected.

It is easy to see how a late selection model such as Norman's can account for the results we have reviewed thus far. For example, in Moray's "switch ears" experiment, subjects often followed the instruction to switch ears when the instruction was preceded by their names. According to Norman's model, this occurs because a subject's own name has a high pertinence value.

Evidence Supporting Late Selection   A general form of evidence consistent with late selection comes from studies showing that subjects can access the meaning of unattended items. For example, MacKay (1973) used a speech-shadowing task in which some of the sentences presented in the attended ear included a word with two meanings—for example, "They were standing near the bank." In the unattended ear, MacKay presented either the word *money* or the word *river*. Subjects interpreted the word *bank* as either "river bank" or "financial bank," depending on which word was presented in the unattended ear. Thus, the subjects must have processed whether *money* or *river* was presented in the unattended ear. If the meaning of an item can be accessed, clearly the item could not have been filtered out before perceptual processing occurred, as the early selection models suggest.

The type of result obtained in MacKay's experiment is referred to as a **priming effect.** Priming occurs when one stimulus, the prime item, affects the processing of a target stimulus. In this case, *river* and *money* are primes and *bank* is the target stimulus.

Priming of attended target items by unattended primes have been reported by many researchers. Balota (1983) and Marcel (1983a, 1983b) visually presented words that were below the threshold for identification (see Chapter 3 for a discussion of thresholds). These

FIGURE 5.8   **Norman's Late Selection Model of Selective Attention**   In this illustration of Norman's (1968) model, five male names—one of them Adam—are spoken to a subject named Adam. The model includes a pertinence value (π), which increases the weight given to inputs from the senses (σ). Since Adam has a high pertinence value for this subject, it will tend to be selected and attended to.

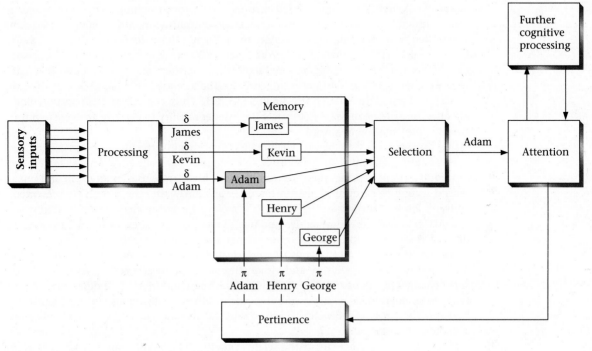

Source: Adapted from Norman (1968).

briefly presented items primed subjects' responses to target items (see Holender, 1986 for a critical discussion of the methods used in these studies).

Eich (1984) used a selective listening task in which subjects attended to items in one channel and ignored the word pairs presented in the other channel. The unattended items consisted of word pairs in which the first word provided a context for interpreting the second word (e.g., taxi, fare). After the listening task, subjects were asked to spell various words as they were spoken, including the words from the unattended word pairs. Subjects spelled the words more often in the manner consistent with the context in which the words had been presented in the unattended channel (e.g., "fare" rather than "fair"). Importantly, this spelling bias was even larger when subjects attended to the word pairs, suggesting that the processing of the word pairs was more complete when subjects attended to these pairs.

Evaluation of Early and Late Selection Models

The evidence that led to the development of late selection models argued against the notion of early selection. But evidence against late selection models also exists. For example, late selection theories assume that attention does not play a role until after an item has undergone perceptual analysis. If this is correct, then there should be no difference in subjects' ability to perceive and recognize items presented in attended and unattended channels in a selective attention experiment. Both behavioral and physiological data reveal that there is a difference, however.

Treisman and Geffen (1967) tested the prediction that attention at an early stage of information processing has no effect on perception by presenting target words in both the attended channel and the unattended channel in a dichotic listening experiment. Subjects were instructed to respond whenever a target word occurred in either channel. Treisman and Geffen measured subjects' sensitivity to perceiving these items using the d' measure from signal detection theory. Recall from Chapter 3 that d' measures how well a person can differentiate target trials from nontarget trials. Treisman and Geffen found that subjects were more sensitive to items presented in the attended channel (d' = 4.2) than to items presented in the unattended channel (d' = 1.8). Thus, contrary to late selection models, attending to one message does affect the listener's ability to perceive an event—in this case, the presentation of a word.

Cognitive neuropsychological evidence also argues against the notion that selection occurs only after perceptual analysis. If selective attention exerts its effect only at a late stage of information processing, then we would expect brain responses to attended and unattended stimuli to be quite similar in the interval shortly after the stimuli are presented. Hillyard, Hink, Schwent, and Picton (1973) recorded event-related potentials (ERPs; see Chapter 2) associated with attended and unattended stimuli. They found that these ERPs differed as soon as 50 milliseconds after the items had been presented.

Hackley, Woldorff, and Hillyard (1990) replicated this finding and also showed that the effect occurs for both auditory and visual stimuli. Woldorff and colleagues (1993) measured changes in the neuromagnetic fields of the brain and found that differences for attended and unattended auditory stimuli occur within 20 milliseconds of the presentation of items. These results show clear effects of selective attention occurring very shortly after a stimulus is presented.

What can we conclude about the relative merits of early selection and late selection models? Neither can account for all the available data. It would seem that behavioral evidence and physiological evidence converge on the conclusion that selection occurs at multiple places in the human information processing system.

The Neuropsychology of Selective Attention: Event-Related Potentials

Researchers have used the ERP technique to examine a host of applied questions concerning how people process information. In one study, Weinstein (1995) examined how anxious college students process threat words (e.g., horror, assault) compared with neutral words (e.g., hand, program). According to an influential model of anxiety (Beck & Emery, 1979), anxious individuals selectively attend to and process information that is related to the things that make them anxious. Although this hypothesis seems reasonable, the behavioral evidence to support it is rather mixed. You might expect that anxious people would better remember information to which they attended, but there is little behavioral evidence that clinically anxious people recall threatening materials any better than nonanxious control subjects.

Weinstein presented subjects with sentences followed by words (e.g., "The boy on the bed was tortured" followed by "fear"). The subjects were instructed to press one button if the sentence and the word matched and to press another button if they did not match. Weinstein used both a behavioral measure, the reaction time for deciding if the sentences and words matched, and the ERPs elicited by the words presented after the sentences. Results showed no differences in the reaction times to threatening, neutral, and positive words. Importantly, there were differences in the ERPs for these items, however, and these differences depended on whether the subjects were anxious or not. Several of the differences emerged soon after the words were presented, thus suggesting a difference at an early stage of information processing. Weinstein argued that the differences in the ERPs for anxious and nonanxious subjects reflect the fact that highly anxious subjects process threatening information more completely than do nonanxious subjects.

Kramer, Trejo, and Humphrey (1995) used the ERP technique to examine **cognitive workload,** the extent to which the information processing system is involved in performing a task. The subjects in this experiment were highly trained Navy radar operators. Subjects monitored a display looking for various target items, such as specific types of aircraft. Kramer and his colleagues measured the ERPs associated with auditory stimuli that the operators were instructed to ignore and found that these ERPs could be used as an effective measure of cognitive workload.

The basic notion of using brain waves as a measure of mental processes is well established, and the results of Kramer and his colleagues suggests that some combination of ERP measures and behavioral indices could be used to estimate how mentally "overworked" a person is. It is likely that in the future, we will see efforts to apply these techniques in real-world situations where errors are very costly (e.g., in aircraft and air-traffic control towers).

Section Summary: Structural Models of Selective Attention

The two primary types of structural models of selective attention are early selection and late selection models. Both assume that a structural bottleneck in the information processing system is responsible for the fact that people cannot process all the information that is available. Early selection models, which include Broadbent's filter theory and Treisman's attenuation model, assume this limitation occurs at an early stage of information processing, before items are perceptually analyzed. Late selection models, such as that of Norman, assume that selection occurs after perceptual processing. Neither early nor late selection models can accommodate all the available data. Behavioral evidence and physiological evidence converge on the conclusion that selection occurs at multiple places in the human information processing system.

CAPACITY AND RESOURCE MODELS OF DIVIDED ATTENTION

Models of selective attention deal primarily with one aspect of the cocktail party phenomenon—attending to one stimulus while ignoring others. In this section, we discuss the flip side of this effect—dividing attention to perform more than one task at a time. For example, how can you notice your name spoken in one of those "ignored" conversations? In discussing divided attention, we consider the second general class of attentional models, capacity models and resource models.

Single Capacity Models

Daniel Kahneman (1973) pointed out that real-world tasks frequently require the concurrent operation of many perceptual and cognitive processes. A core assumption of Kahneman's model (see Figure 5.9a) is that mental processes compete for access to a limited pool

Kahneman's Single Capacity Model of Attention   (a) The flowchart illustrates the relations among capacity demands, arousal, and responses. (b) The graph illustrates the relation between task demands and resources/capacity supplied to the task. Performance levels show a decrement whenever the resources demanded exceed the resources/capacity supplied.

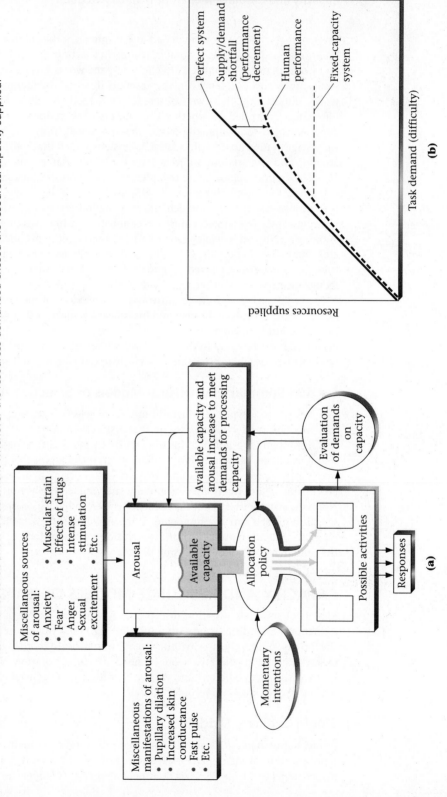

Source: Kahneman, 1973.

of attentional resources, or **capacity.** Capacity is a hypothetical construct that can be viewed as serving an energizing function for the system. In order for a process to operate, it must be supplied with adequate capacity. We might consider capacity as being like electricity and mental processes as being like devices that require electricity to function (e.g., an electric pencil sharpener, a desk lamp). If there is adequate electricity (capacity), then several devices (mental processes) can operate simultaneously.

Whereas early and late selection models attempt to identify the *structure* (e.g., filter) responsible for poor performance, capacity models such as Kahneman's point to limitations in capacity as the cause of performance deficits. Kahneman's model is a **single capacity model** because it assumes that there is one source, or pool, of capacity to be allocated to the available perceptual and cognitive processes. The model is also a *variable capacity model* in that several factors can increase or decrease the amount of capacity available. Kahneman suggested that the amount of capacity available is related to the individual's arousal level and that a number of physiological indices (e.g., pupil dilation) can be used to measure arousal level.

Kahneman's model also assumes that an "allocation policy" apportions capacity to the tasks that require it. The allocation policy is controlled by several factors. One factor is the changing momentary intentions of the individual. This factor is reflected in shadowing tasks in which the listener allocates capacity to processing the message in one ear. Another factor is the evaluation of demands on capacity. This factor is related to monitoring performance levels in the tasks to which capacity is being allocated. For example, if we are attempting to complete two tasks at once (e.g., reading a homework assignment and listening to a favorite musical piece) and performing neither task very well, we may decide to allocate more capacity to one task in order to ensure we complete that task adequately.

Studying Capacity Limitations   Kahneman's model makes several easily testable predictions. One is that performance deficits should be observed when (a) two tasks are performed simultaneously and (b) the total demands of the tasks exceed the available capacity. Figure 5.9b illustrates how the variable capacity aspect of Kahneman's model is reflected in performance. According to Kahneman's model, as noted, capacity is variable, which means that as task demands increase, so can the available capacity. Note, however, that capacity cannot continue to increase forever. Hence, as task demands increase, a performance decrement appears, and the decrement increases in magnitude with continued increases in task demands.

A **dual-task methodology** has been used to study the single capacity model account of when two tasks should compete for capacity. As its name implies, in a dual-task experiment, subjects are asked to perform two tasks, either singly or at the same time. If the instructions given to subjects emphasize that they should perform one of these tasks to the best of their abilities, then presumably they will allocate sufficient capacity to that task. The task that is to be performed at the maximal level is referred to as the *primary task,* and the other task is the *secondary task*. It is assumed that any capacity remaining after the primary task is performed will be allocated to the secondary task. Thus, performance levels on the secondary task are used as an indirect measure of the capacity required to perform the primary task.

The dual-task methodology has been used to study a variety of cognitive processes, such as encoding in a memory task (e.g., Tyler et al., 1979). It has been used to examine the cognitive demands of more complex tasks such as reading (e.g., Britton et al., 1982; Britton & Tessler, 1982) and has proved useful in a number of applied studies involving human factors issues (e.g., Payne et al., 1994; Wickens, 1976). For example, Payne and his colleagues

(1994) used the methodology to see what effect varying the quality of an auditory message would have on performance of other tasks. They found that when the auditory signal was poor, performance decreased in visual tasks that required the person to make decisions or to recall information. These results have implications for real-world situations such as driving while talking on a cellular telephone.

Selective Interference   An important prediction of single capacity theory is that *any* two tasks can interfere with each other as long as the total capacity required to perform the tasks exceeds the amount of capacity available. In other words, if two tasks require considerable capacity, then a performance deficit should occur in one or both of the tasks when they are performed at the same time. Although the results from a number of studies are consistent with this prediction, there is also considerable evidence to the contrary.

Two patterns of results are inconsistent with single capacity theory. One pattern comes from studies in which subjects are able to perform two demanding tasks with no deficit in performance on either task, compared with performance in single-task control conditions. For example, Allport, Antonis, and Reynolds (1972) had subjects perform an auditory shadowing task at the same time they were sight-reading music. Despite the fact that both of these tasks are quite demanding, the two tasks were performed together with little loss in performance levels. Similarly, Shaffer (1975) reported a study in which a skilled typist could transcribe a written message while engaging in a shadowing task with no performance decrement in either task.

The second pattern involves **selective interference,** the situation in which performing one task interferes with performing another, similar task. For example, Brooks (1968) required subjects to perform two tasks, both of which involved making a series of yes/no decisions based on information held in short-term memory. One task was a verbal task in which subjects first memorized a simple sentence and then decided whether or not each word in the sentence was a noun. The second task required subjects to decide whether angles in a block letter were closed or open angles (see Figure 5.10a).

Brooks required his subjects to use several modes of responding in his experiment, and we will consider two of these. On some trials, subjects responded verbally, with either yes or no. A second form of responding involved pointing. Subjects were given a display containing a series of Ys and Ns (for yes and no), and they responded by pointing to the appropriate letter. The Ys and Ns in the display were placed in an irregular arrangement on the response page, so this task required the subjects to pay continuous attention to the display as they worked their way down the page. The data from the four conditions we are interested in are presented in Figure 5.10b.

Results from Brooks's study showed that the response times depended on both what types of items subjects were maintaining in memory and how subjects made their responses. When the memory load involved verbal materials, subjects responded much faster by pointing to the Ys and Ns. This difference does not mean the pointing response mode was simply easier than the verbal mode, however. When the memory task involved keeping the shape of a block letter in memory, subjects responded faster in the verbal condition than in the pointing condition. These results are difficult to interpret in terms of a single capacity model, since performance is assumed to reflect the overall difficulty of the tasks and not the specific nature of the tasks.

The results of the Brooks (1968) study indicate that the nature of required responses can play an important role in determining performance levels. Other studies (e.g., Wickens, Sandry, & Vidulich, 1983) have indicated that when two tasks are performed simultaneously, the similarity of the two tasks can affect performance levels. Results such as these

FIGURE 5.10 **Selective Interference** (a) The letter diagram is like those used in Brooks's (1968) study. The subject's task is to start at the location indicated by the * and proceed around the letter, deciding whether each angle is an open or a closed angle. (b) The graph of data from Brooks's study shows mean time (in seconds) required to complete the sentence and letter-matching tasks as a function of the type of memory item and the mode of responding.

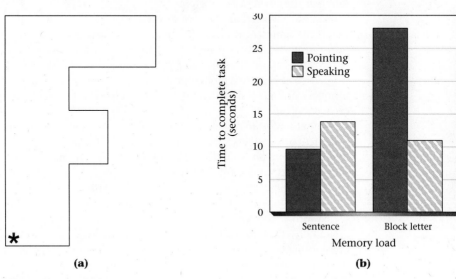

(a) (b)

Source: Data from Brooks, 1968.

indicate that one or more of the assumptions underlying the single capacity model of Kahneman (1973) are invalid.

Multiple Resource Models

One possible explanation for why two tasks might not interfere with one another is that the tasks do not draw from a single pool of capacity. Rather, separate sources of capacity may be specialized for particular processes. This notion has given rise to **multiple resource models,** models of attention that assume the existence of separate pools of perceptual and cognitive resources that can be applied to different processes.

Navon and Gopher (1979) developed an influential multiple resource model of attention that differs from single capacity theory on two dimensions: (a) how much tasks interfere with one another and (b) whether performance levels on one task can be traded for performance levels on another task. Whereas Kahneman's model assumes that capacity can be allocated among any tasks that require it, Navon and Gopher's idea of "mental resources" is more specialized. Resources here are "processing facilities," and the performance on a task is normally "positively related to the amount of resources available to [the task]" (Navon & Gopher, 1979, p. 215).

Cognitive Resources Navon and Gopher employed the economic concepts of supply and demand to outline a number of factors that can affect performance levels in dual-task situations. They likened the human cognitive system to a manufacturer producing one or more goods. In order to produce these goods, the manufacturer can employ a wide range of tools, equipment, and other economic resources. Raw materials serve as input to the process, and goods are generated as output.

In the case of the human cognitive system, the inputs are generally stimuli in the environment, the manufacturing process involves various transformations of the internal codes used to represent these stimuli, and the outputs are the responses that the person makes. The manner in which the components of the manufacturing process are used determines the efficiency of the process.

Imagine that a certain tool or process is needed to produce a manufacturing plant's output. If the supply of these tools or processes meets or exceeds the demand, then production can move ahead without delay. However, if the demand for the tools or resources exceeds the supply, then the manufacturing process will slow down. In a similar fashion, if a particular cognitive process or resource is required to complete certain tasks, then performance of these tasks will be slowed down when demand for the process or resource exceeds supply.

Another important aspect of Navon and Gopher's model concerns the ability to substitute mental resources. Suppose that, in a manufacturing plant, a drill press is normally used to perform an operation. When the drill press is unavailable, a portable drill may be substituted. However, this substituted tool may not be as efficient as the normally used tool, and hence performance may suffer. Furthermore, other tools that are available cannot be substituted for the needed tool—tasks performed with a drill press cannot be completed with a table saw.

Similarly, in the human cognitive system, the extent to which two tasks interfere with one another depends not only on the *amount* of resources the tasks require but also on the *types* of resources they require. Two tasks that require exactly the same resources can interfere with one another completely, whereas two tasks that require totally different sets of resources should not interfere with one another. According to multiple resource models, the *resource composition* of two tasks—that is, the specific resources required to complete the tasks—plays a major role in determining performance levels in a dual-task situation.

Testing Multiple Resource Theory   Multiple resource theory can account for the selective interference observed in dual-task situations. Interference among tasks occurs when the tasks compete for the same resources, and no interference occurs when the tasks require different resources. One obvious potential problem here concerns the specification of what constitutes a resource, for without an *a priori* specification, the logic behind multiple resource theory becomes circular: If one obtains dual-task interference, then the two tasks require similar resources; if not, then the tasks require different or separate resources. Unless the resources required to perform a task can be identified before data are collected, multiple resource theory cannot be proved wrong and hence is of little scientific use.

Two general approaches have been used to avoid this circularity. One approach views the two cerebral hemispheres as comprising separate pools of resources, each specialized for different types of processes. Models using this approach (e.g., Kinsbourne & Hicks, 1978) utilize findings from studies of hemispheric specialization (cf. Springer & Deutsch, 1993) to identify what types of processes might be performed most efficiently by each hemisphere. A second approach (Wickens, 1980, 1984) examines the dual-task literature and attempts to determine what types of tasks seem to interfere with one another. These patterns of interference are then used to discern the resources involved in performing the tasks.

Let us consider research that illustrates some of the logic behind multiple resource theories, as well as how these theories make predictions that go beyond those of single capacity theory. Dawson and Schell (1982) reported a study involving the presentation of classically conditioned words in the unattended channel during a shadowing task. In this study, subjects were first presented with a series of words paired with a mild electric shock. This classical conditioning phase was designed to create stimuli that later, when the stimuli were presented alone, would elicit an autonomic nervous system response from subjects. After the conditioning phase, subjects completed a selective listening task. Of primary interest here was whether subjects would show an autonomic response to items presented in the unattended ear, items of which they were presumably unaware.

Before briefly reviewing Dawson and Schell's study and the model they proposed, we should note two important points about this work. First, although Dawson and Schell made a number of simplifying assumptions in developing their physiological model, their work shows how an understanding of the physiological underpinnings of perception and cognition can form the basis of an understanding of how tasks are performed. Second, the Dawson and Schell model fits nicely within the multiple resource framework and shows how the basic concepts of this approach can guide both research and theorizing about performance in dual-task situations.

In conducting their study, Dawson and Schell went to considerable lengths to ensure that subjects were actually not aware of the items in the unattended ear. This is important because if the subjects were able to momentarily shift their attention from the attended to the unattended ear during the trial, then an autonomic response would not reflect a response to an unattended item.

Dawson and Schell also varied which ear the unattended messages were presented in—the left ear for some subjects, and the right ear for others. When the researchers analyzed their data for subjects who received the classically conditioned items in the left ear, the results replicated those from previous studies (e.g., Corteen & Wood, 1972; Corteen & Dunn, 1974). In these studies, unattended items had been presented in the left ear only, and subjects had shown an autonomic nervous system response to the classically conditioned stimuli. In the Dawson and Schell study, however, on trials in which the subjects did not shift their attention to the unattended ear, no significant autonomic response was found for subjects who received the unattended information in the *right* ear.

Dawson and Schell's differential findings for the left-ear and right-ear trials would be difficult to interpret within a single capacity framework. However, the researchers were able to interpret their results using a neuropsychological model, presented in Figure 5.11, that is compatible with the multiple resource approach. This model is based in part on a well-known fact concerning the projection of information from the sensory receptors to higher-level cortical areas: When auditory stimuli are presented for dichotic listening, there are both *ipsilateral* (same-side) and *contralateral* (opposite-side) projections from the sensory receptors to the auditory cortex. However, the contralateral projections are both more numerous and functionally stronger than the ipsilateral projections. Furthermore, in a dichotic listening task, competition may occur between the stronger, contralateral messages and the weaker, ipsilateral messages. Although this is something of a simplification, we can view each ear as primarily sending information to the contralateral hemisphere. We must also note that the two hemispheres are not equally facile at performing different types of information processing tasks.

Now consider what occurred in Dawson and Schell's study when the attended message was presented in the right ear. This message is projected to the left hemisphere. Because the left hemisphere is specialized for both speech reception and speech production, it can perform the speech-shadowing task. This leaves the right hemisphere free to process the unattended message. Because the right hemisphere appears capable of analyzing speech

FIGURE 5.11   **Dawson and Schell's Neuropsychological Model**   In the conditioning phase of the experiment, the word "dog" is paired with a mild electric shock. In the second part of the experiment, which involves a shadowing task, the subject attends to a message in one ear and ignores the information in the other ear. Of interest is whether the unattended message will elicit an autonomic response. (a) For subjects who attend to the right-ear message, the unattended message is processed by the left hemisphere, which is presumed to perceive speech. (b) For subjects who attend to the left-ear message, the attended message is projected to the right hemisphere but is also sent to the left hemisphere (because the left hemisphere is responsible for speech production). Since the left hemisphere is engaged in processing the information from the attended ear, it is not able to process the information from the unattended ear.

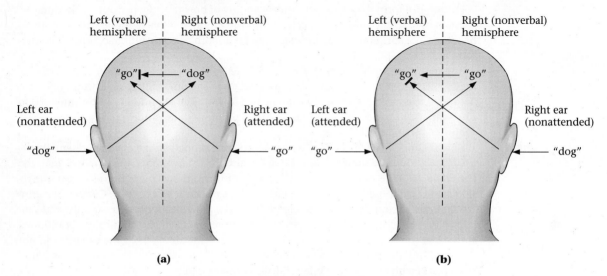

Source: Adapted from Dawson & Schell, 1982.

signals (Searleman, 1977), it can identify the words in the unattended message. If identifying the words is sufficient to retrieve the classically conditioned response, then we should observe an autonomic response to these items.

Consider next the trials in which the attended information was presented in the left ear and thus projected to the right hemisphere. Recall that the subject's task is to shadow this message. Evidence indicates that language production is primarily a left-hemisphere process, and so in order for this message to be shadowed, the information from the right hemisphere must be conveyed to the left hemisphere via the corpus callosum. However, since the information in the unattended message is also projected to the left hemisphere, the left hemisphere is required both to perform the shadowing task and to process the items in the unattended message. These requirements may exceed the resources available. Since the subject's primary task is to shadow the message in the attended ear, resources should be allocated to this task. If the task requires most of the available resources, then we should not expect to observe an autonomic response to the classically conditioned words in the unattended ear. Thus, although the results of the Dawson and Schell study are difficult to interpret within a single capacity model, a multiple resource model can easily account for these data.

Section Summary: Capacity and Resource Models of Divided Attention

In addition to selectively attending to some events and ignoring others, people can divide their attention among two or more tasks. The single capacity model proposed by Kahneman (1973) assumes a limited amount of capacity that must be shared among any tasks that a person attempts to perform. The idea that capacity is limited has received a great deal of support, but the notion that there is a single pool of capacity is less well accepted. The multiple resource approach (Navon & Gopher, 1979) assumes that separate pools of perceptual and cognitive resources can be applied to different processes. This approach has proved useful as an explanatory framework and has also been a source of predictions for the types of tasks that should and should not interfere with one another.

PROCESS MODELS OF SELECTIVE AND DIVIDED ATTENTION

The research discussed thus far suggests that the cognitive system is very flexible in dealing with input from different sources. This flexibility points out the shortcomings of both the structural models and the capacity and resource models described earlier. It also has given rise to a new class of models that focus on the processes that underlie selective attention. In this section, we review the third general class of models: the process models. We consider two specific process models, one that focuses on resolving the debate on early-versus-late selection (Johnston & Heinz, 1978) and a second that questions the assumption that unattended items are simply not processed (Tipper, 1992).

A Capacity Model of Selective Attention

Johnston and Heinz (1978) proposed a capacity model of selective attention designed to account for its flexibility. The Johnston and Heinz model makes two assumptions. First, selective attention—that is, selecting a set or subset of items to process—requires capacity. Like Kahneman, Johnston and Heinz assumed that a limited amount of capacity is available. This imposes a limit on how many items we can attend to, or process. The second assumption of the Johnston and Heinz model is that early selection, or selection based on sensory or perceptual properties, requires less capacity than does late selection, or selection based on identity or meaning. The Johnston and Heinz model is a process model because it seeks to identify the processes in the human cognitive system that affect performance in selective and divided attention tasks. The model does not assume that there is only one structure responsible for the effects of selective and divided attention, as did the early and late selection models. The Johnston and Heinz model focuses on how capacity affects different perceptual and cognitive processes, and how these different processes require different amounts of capacity.

Johnston and Heinz tested their model using a dual-task methodology. In their study, the primary task was a selective listening task involving one or more messages presented to both ears. Subjects were instructed to listen to a target message and ignore any other message. The messages differed in terms of either a perceptual dimension (male versus female speaker) or a semantic dimension (different topics, such as tennis versus meteorology). According to the model, selection based on the perceptual dimension involves processes early in the system, and selection based on the semantic dimension involves processes late in the system.

While subjects performed the selective listening task, they also performed a secondary visual reaction-time task. In this task, lights appeared on a screen and subjects pressed a button as quickly as possible when they detected a light. If the listening task requires very little capacity, then there should be plenty of spare capacity available to perform the visual task, and hence, reaction times in the visual task should be short. If the listening task requires a great deal of capacity, however, then reaction times on the visual task should be long.

Johnston and Heinz's results provide strong support for their capacity model of selective attention. First, subjects performed the visual task slower when they were listening to two messages than when they were listening to one message. This shows that the process of selecting a message to attend to requires capacity. Second, when subjects were listening to two messages, less capacity was required when the two messages differed on a perceptual dimension (speaker's voice) than when they differed on a semantic dimension (meaning of the messages). This shows that less capacity is required for the processes involved in early selection than for those involved in late selection.

The Johnston and Heinz model is a significant improvement over the structural models described earlier. The model can account for the early data on selective attention and also for the more recent data showing evidence of late selection. For example, recall the Eich (1984) study in which subjects listened to word pairs (e.g., taxi, fare) and later performed a spelling test. Eich found that the context provided by the first word in the pair affected how subjects performed in the spelling test. This context bias was larger when subjects attended to the word pairs than when the word pairs were in the unattended channel. The Johnston and Heinz model can account for this difference by assuming that less capacity is available in the unattended condition, resulting in less complete processing of the word pairs. The fact that the spelling bias still occurs when the word pairs are presented in the unattended channel, however, also indicates that the words are not completely "filtered out." This raises another issue: What are the effects of "ignoring" information in the unattended channel?

Inhibitory Mechanisms in Selective Attention

Imagine that you are driving down a road with many street signs, billboards, and so on along the roadsides. You cannot read all of these signs, so you focus your attention on a subset of them and ignore the others. To use the terminology of the structural models, you could say that you are filtering out the ignored signs. But how do we know that you are simply "filtering out" some signs and attending to others? Perhaps you are somehow inhibiting internal representations of the ignored stimuli. Indeed, recent research supports the view that inhibitory processes act on unattended stimuli.

According to *dual-process models,* selective attention involves two separate mechanisms, a *facilitatory* mechanism that works to process attended stimuli and an *inhibitory* mechanism that serves to block the representations of ignored stimuli. Steven Tipper and his colleagues have reported important experiments that demonstrate inhibitory mechanisms in selective attention. These experiments use a priming procedure in which subjects are presented with prime stimuli and target stimuli. The critical question is whether the prime stimuli will facilitate or inhibit the processing of the target stimuli.

In one experiment, Tipper and Driver (1988) presented subjects with a series of trials, each containing a prime display and a target display. The prime items were presented in green and the target items in red (see Figure 5.12). Tipper and Driver were interested in how reaction time to target items would vary depending on the nature of the primes and targets in the displays. They measured how long it took subjects to name the items in red

FIGURE 5.12 **Negative Priming** In Tipper and Driver's (1988) study of negative priming, each display contained two items, one in red (depicted here as a solid line) and one in green (broken line). Subjects were required to attend to the items in red and ignore the items in green. Subjects identified the red items in the prime displays and named the red items in the target displays.

Condition	Prime	Probe
Attended repetition		DOG FOOT
Attended semantic		DOG FOOT
Control		DOG FOOT
Ignored semantic		DOG FOOT
Ignored repetition	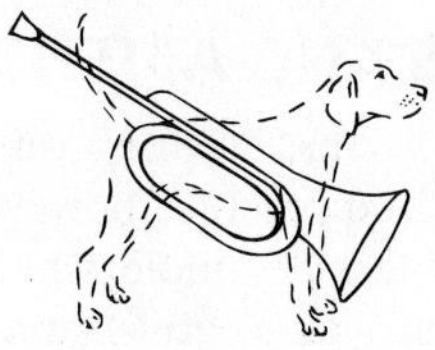	DOG FOOT

Source: Tipper & Driver, 1988.

from the target displays. When these attended-to items were the same on two successive displays, subjects named the target item faster than when the attended-to items in two successive trials were unrelated (the control items in Figure 5.12). This is a **positive priming** effect, and it has been obtained in hundreds of experiments. A similar positive priming effect was obtained when the attended-to items in successive displays were semantically related (e.g., the words "cat" and "dog").

The novel finding from this study concerns the trials in which the *ignored* item in one display was the same as or related to the attended-to item in the next display (see the ignored semantic and ignored repetition conditions in Figure 5.12). Under these conditions, subjects were actually slower to name the target item than they were in the control condition. This slower response rate is called **negative priming,** and it has been interpreted as indicating that the unattended-to prime is not simply ignored but actively inhibited.

Another important finding from the Tipper and Driver study is that negative priming is not limited to conditions in which the prime and the target are presented in the same format (e.g., both pictures, as in Figure 5.12). Negative priming occurs when the prime is presented as a word and the target as a picture, and vice versa. That is, negative priming occurs when items share the same conceptual representation (DOG) but different surface features (a picture of a dog and the word "dog"). This shows that the inhibitory mechanism does not operate simply to block a particular physical stimulus from being processed.

Negative priming effects have been reported in a number of domains. The negative priming paradigm has also shown that inhibitory effects can operate at different levels in the information processing system (e.g., Neill, 1977, 1979, 1985; Neill & Valdes, 1992; Neill et al., 1992; Tipper, 1985, 1992; Yee, 1991). Here, "levels" refer to the range of internal representations from low-level sensory features of an item to high-level conceptual representations. Research Report 5 describes examples of the negative priming procedure.

Section Summary: Process Models of Selective and Divided Attention

The Johnston and Heinz capacity model of selective attention assumes that capacity effects can be observed at different stages in the information processing system. According to this model, early selection involves selection based on the sensory or perceptual properties of stimuli. Late selection involves selection based on the identity or meaning of stimuli. The model assumes that early selection involves less capacity than late selection. The dual-process model of selective attention proposed by Tipper and others suggests that attention serves both to facilitate the processing of attended-to items and to inhibit the processing of unattended-to items. In contrast to the fixed, structural accounts of the early and late selection models, the dual-process theory assumes great flexibility in how these facilitatory and inhibitory mechanisms operate.

PRACTICE EFFECTS AND ATTENTIONAL PROCESSES

Many complex behaviors, such as driving a car, require all our attention when we are first learning them. With time and practice, however, these tasks can become relatively automatic. To use a loose "dual-task" example, when we first start driving, it is all we can do to control the car. We can't carry on a conversation or listen to music, as this "overloads" us. With practice, driving appears to require less capacity, and we can easily talk with a passenger while driving.

RESEARCH REPORT 5:   Negative Priming

The negative priming paradigm has been used to investigate several interesting questions about human information processing. For example, in Chapters 3 and 4, we discussed the various levels at which stimuli can be represented (e.g., features versus shape versus identity of the object). What effect does attending to or ignoring a stimulus have on the level at which various types of stimuli are processed?

Murray (1995) asked whether visual objects that are rotated from their normal upright positions are encoded when they are ignored. She presented subjects with prime and target displays that contained red and green line drawings of objects and animals. Subjects were presented with pairs of displays, a prime display followed by a target display (see Figure 5A). The subjects' task was to identify the red (solid line in our figure) item in the prime display and ignore the green (broken line) item. After the prime was presented, subjects were shown the target display and asked to name the red drawing as quickly as possible and then report the name of the green item in the target display.

Murray's study included three conditions. In the *attended semantic* condition, the attended prime item was semantically related to the target item to be named. In the *control* condition, none of the selected or ignored items in any display were related. Finally, in the *ignored semantic* condition, the ignored prime was related to the attended-to target item.

The question of interest in Murray's study was whether subjects would identify the ignored prime item when it was rotated. Murray used the time it took subjects to name the green item in the target display as her index of whether the rotated and ignored items were identified. She found both positive and negative priming (see Figure 5B). Subjects named the target item faster when the prime item they attended to was related to the target (positive priming). More importantly, subjects named the target slower when it was related to the ignored prime. This indicates that subjects encoded the ignored items at least to the level of categorizing them. If subjects had simply ignored the rotated items, then the time required to name the items should have been the same in the control condition as in the ignored semantic condition.

Researchers have used the negative priming paradigm to investigate how attentional processes vary across the lifespan. Conventional wisdom suggests that elderly people are easily distractible and suffer in terms of their ability to focus attention on a task. On the face of it, it seems reasonable to assume that this distractibility reflects a problem of selective attention. However, a great deal of evidence now suggests that the effects of aging have more to do with a loss of the ability to inhibit information. In other words, the inhibitory processes observed in the negative priming paradigm are less effective in older adults than in younger adults.

Hasher, Stoltzfus, Zacks, and Rypma (1991) had young and old adults complete a letter-naming task using the negative priming procedure. On each trial, subjects were presented with two letters in two different colors. Subjects were instructed to read the target letters in one color (e.g., red) and ignore the letters in the other color.

The researchers found the typical negative priming effect for the young adults. These subjects were slower to name a letter that had previously served as an ignored item than they were to name a control item that had not been presented earlier. In contrast, older adults showed no

(Research Report 5 continued on p. 166)

such negative priming. Similar findings have been reported by several other researchers (e.g., Kane et al., 1994; McDowd & Oseas-Kreger, 1991; Tipper, 1991). These developmental changes in negative priming have significantly altered the way in which researchers conceptualize changes in selective attention across the lifespan.

FIGURE 5A   **Stimuli Used in Murray's (1995) Study**   The solid lines were red in the display, and the dashed lines were green.

FIGURE 5B   **Negative and Positive Priming in the Upright and Rotated Conditions**

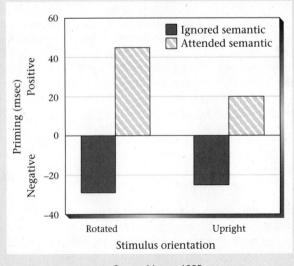

Source: Murray, 1995.

Experimental evidence supports the idea that practice on difficult tasks can lead to significant improvements in performance. For example, Underwood (1974) examined subjects' performance in a digit-detection task performed at the same time as a shadowing task. One of the subjects' tasks was to shadow a message presented in the attended ear. The second task was to respond whenever a digit was presented in either the attended or the unattended ear. Naive (unpracticed) subjects were able to detect only 8 percent of the digits presented in the unattended ear. One subject in the experiment was Neville Moray, a prominent attention researcher whose work you read about earlier. In contrast to the unpracticed subjects, Moray detected nearly 70 percent of the digits in the unattended channel. Moray presumably had had extensive practice with speech shadowing, and this practice allowed him to be quite efficient at the task.

In this section, we examine research on the development of such *automaticity*. The study of automaticity is closely related to capacity and resource models of attention. As we have seen, according to these models, perceptual and cognitive processes must draw on a limited amount of capacity. A general assumption held by a number of researchers is that what differentiates many tasks is the extent to which the tasks demand capacity. Tasks on which we have not had much practice require a great deal of attention; but with increasing experience, the processes underlying performance in these tasks become "automatic" and they require less and less capacity.

Controlled and Automatic Processes

Tasks that require conscious attention are referred to as **controlled processing tasks,** and tasks that do not require attention are called **automatic tasks** (Posner & Snyder, 1975). Controlled and automatic tasks are sometimes viewed as distinct types of tasks that reflect the operation of qualitatively different processes. For example, controlled processing tasks involve processes that are slow, that are limited by the available capacity, and that require conscious attention, whereas automatic tasks may require little if any capacity. It is probably more accurate to view controlled and automatic processes as the two end points on a continuum specified by the amount of capacity required to complete the processing (MacLeod & Dunbar, 1988). Furthermore, a complex real-world task such as driving a car in an unfamiliar city may involve several processes, some automatic and some controlled.

Some of the differences between controlled and automatic processes can be viewed from a capacity or resource approach. First, automatic processes are fast relative to controlled processes. This difference in processing time reflects the fact that controlled processes are limited by the availability of capacity whereas automatic processes do not require capacity. Second, automatic processes are viewed as effortless in the sense that they do not require conscious control. Third, automatic processes are obligatory, or uncontrollable, because once they are started no attention is required in order for them to run to completion. Automatic processes presumably operate on stimuli by processing the stimuli completely as soon as they are presented. Controlled processes, in contrast, require that we pay continuous attention to the stimuli in order to process them.

Interference Between Controlled and Automatic Tasks

John Ridley Stroop (1935) introduced a task that shows the effects of automatic and controlled processes in a single task. In the original Stroop task, subjects name the color of a patch or of the ink used to print words. In one control condition, subjects are required to name the colors of the ink used to print neutral, or non-color-related, words (e.g., "book," "cup," and "watch" printed in red, green, and yellow ink). In the compatible-word condition, the colors of the ink match the words (e.g., the word "red" printed in red ink). Finally, in the incompatible condition, there is a mismatch between the color words and the ink colors (e.g., the word "red" printed in green ink). In all cases, subjects are required to name the color of the ink, ignoring any words printed on the page. Experiment 5B presents a numerical analog of the Stroop task that you can try for yourself.

More than 700 studies have been published dealing with the Stroop task (MacLeod, 1992), and there are many well-documented findings in the literature (MacLeod, 1991). For our purposes, two of the most important basic findings to emerge from studies using the Stroop task concern reaction times in the various conditions used to study the Stroop effect. First, facilitation occurs in the compatible condition. That is, subjects are faster and make fewer errors when the ink colors match the color words than in the control condition. Second, interference occurs in the incompatible condition. Subjects take longer to name the ink colors when they are incompatible with the color words than in the control condition.

These two findings can be interpreted in terms of two processes, a controlled process and an automatic process (MacLeod, 1997). As adults, we have been reading for many years; reading is thus a relatively automatic process. Color naming, on the other hand, is something we have less practice with, and hence, color naming is a relatively controlled process. The facilitation effect occurs when both the word-reading process and the color-naming process are activating the same response. The interference effect occurs when the automatic process of reading interferes with the controlled process of color naming. Imagine that a subject is presented with the word "red" printed in green ink. The automatic process of reading quickly accesses the word "red." But meanwhile, the controlled process of color naming accesses the response "green." According to this analysis, the response activated by the color word interferes with making the required response based on the color of the ink.

Before we move on to discuss the development of automaticity, we should note here that despite its intuitive appeal, the speed-of-processing account of the Stroop effect that we have just described cannot account for all of the available data on the Stroop task (e.g., Dunbar and MacLeod, 1984). As with many phenomena, what initially appears to be quite simple turns out upon closer inspection to be very complex. Researchers are continuing to learn more about various aspects of the Stroop effect (e.g., Schooler et al., 1997) and to consider the implications of new findings for theoretical accounts of the Stroop effect (e.g., Cohen et al., 1997). Despite these controversies, the Stroop task remains a classic example of the differences between automatic and controlled processes.

Development of Automaticity

One of the largest and most influential programs of research investigating the development of automaticity is that of Schneider and Shiffrin (1977; Shiffrin & Schneider, 1977). These researchers used a visual search task to study the factors that affect the transition from controlled task to automatic task. In this task, subjects are required to search for a specific target item or items among a series of briefly presented displays.

On each trial, subjects are presented with the set of target items for that trial. For instance, subjects might be asked to search for the letters J and D. After the subjects have committed these items to memory, they are presented with a visual fixation point fol-

EXPERIMENT 5B: Stroop Task Number Analog

The panels below present a numerical analog of the Stroop color-word interference task. Count the number of digits in each of the 16 boxes in Panel A out loud, as quickly as possible. Then count the number of letters in each box in Panel B out loud, as quickly as you can.

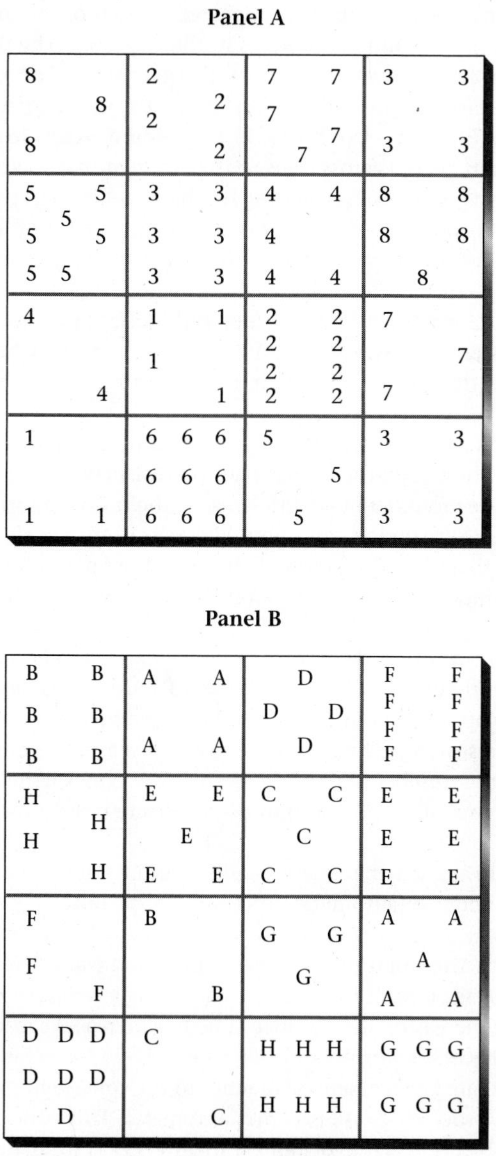

FIGURE 5 C
Numerical Analog of Stroop Color-Word Interference Task

Panel A

8	8	2	2 2	7	7 7	3	3
8		2	2	7		3	3
5 5	5 5 5	3 3 3	3 3 3	4 4 4	4 4	8 8 8	8 8 8
4	4	1 1	1 1	2 2 2 2	2 2 2 2	7 7	7
1	1	6 6 6 6 6 6 6 6 6		5 5 5		3 3 3	3

Panel B

B B B	B B B	A	A A	D	D D D	F F F F	F F F F
H H	H H	E E E	E E	C C C	C C	E E E	E E E
F F	F	B	B	G G G	G	A A A	A A
D D D D D D D		C	C	H H H H H H		G G G G G G	

Was it harder to count the digits in Panel A aloud than to count the letters in Panel B aloud? Since college students are well practiced at reading numbers, the number information that comes from reading the digits interferes with the counting task. This is similar to what happens when the automatic reading of the color word in the Stroop task interferes with the naming of the color of the stimulus.

lowed by a series of displays containing various letters. These displays are called frames, and the speed at which the frames are presented is varied across trials.

Two main types of trials were used in Schneider and Shiffrin's study. On positive trials, a letter from the target set appeared in one of the frames, and on negative trials, no target was presented in any of the frames. The subjects' task was to decide whether a target item appeared in any of the frames. The dependent variables were the subjects' reaction times to respond either yes (a target was present) or no (no target was present) and the accuracy of these responses.

Schneider and Shiffrin manipulated three things in their study. The first was *frame size,* the number of items (one, two, or four) that appeared in each of the display frames. The second was *memory-set size,* the number of items in the target set. The third was the mapping of targets and distracters (nontarget items). In the **consistent mapping condition,** in all trials, the target items were drawn from the same set of items, and the distracters came from a different set of items. In the **varied mapping condition,** the targets and distracters were mixed across trials so that an item that was a distracter on one trial could be a target on another trial. Searching for the target item in the consistent mapping condition is something like looking for numbers among a set of letters, and searching in the varied mapping condition is like looking for one or more letters among other letters.

One of the main questions asked by Schneider and Shiffrin was how quickly subjects could learn to perform the visual search task. Another question was whether performance would differ in the consistent and varied mapping conditions as a function of frame size and memory-set size.

To compare performance in the consistent and varied mapping conditions, Schneider and Shiffrin determined how long the frames had to be displayed in order for subjects to be 95 percent correct. They found a huge difference in the presentation durations needed to reach this goal in the two mapping conditions. Subjects in the consistent mapping condition could perform with a high accuracy rate after very brief presentations (e.g., 70 to 80 ms per frame), whereas much longer presentations (e.g., 210 ms) were required in the varied mapping condition.

A second main finding was that the effects of frame size and memory-set size differed widely in the two mapping conditions (see Figure 5.13). After considerable practice, subjects in the consistent mapping condition were not affected by the number of items in the memory set—they could search for four items almost as fast as they could search for a single item. Furthermore, the number of items in the display frames had little effect. In contrast, both the memory-set size and the frame size affected performance in the varied mapping condition.

Schneider and Shiffrin argued that these results demonstrate three important points concerning the development of automatic processing. First, during the initial portion of the experiment, the visual search task is a controlled processing task. Performance in these trials is affected by both the duration of frame presentation and the number of target items. Presumably, subjects perform the task by completing a serial search of all items in a frame as it is presented. Increasing the number of targets increases capacity demands, and therefore performance becomes worse.

Second, when subjects are given extended practice in the consistent mapping condition, this initially controlled processing task becomes automatic. This conclusion is supported by the fact that, after subjects in Schneider and Shiffrin's (1977) study had been given considerable practice, the slope of the reaction time function for the consistent mapping

FIGURE 5.13   **Data from Schneider and Shiffrin (1977)**   The graphs show mean reaction times and percentages of errors as a function of the memory-set size and frame size for both the consistent and varied mapping conditions in Schneider and Shiffrin's Experiment 2.

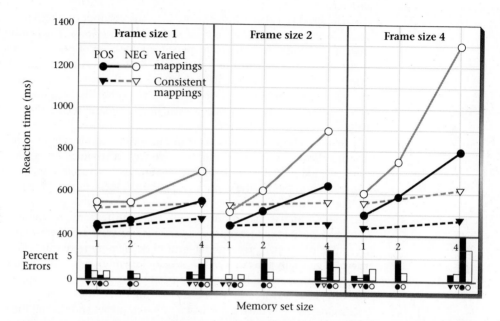

group approaches zero (see Figure 5.13). That is, reaction time increases only slightly as the number of items in the memory set increases. Furthermore, this near-zero slope is obtained even with larger frame sizes. If the search task is still a controlled processing task, then longer reaction times should be obtained with increases in memory-set size and frame size. This is exactly the result obtained with the varied mapping condition, and this difference between the consistent and varied mapping conditions points to the third major conclusion drawn by Schneider and Shiffrin.

Schneider and Shiffrin argued that in order for a controlled processing task to develop into an automatic task, it is necessary that there be consistent mapping between the stimuli presented and the responses made to those stimuli. The varied mapping condition does not meet this requirement. Across trials, subjects respond to the same stimulus in different ways: The letter T might be a target on Trial 20 and a distracter on Trial 21.

The difference in performance in Schneider and Shiffrin's consistent versus varied mapping conditions has been replicated many times (e.g., Fisk & Hodge, 1992; Schneider, Dumais & Shiffrin, 1984), and it is an important fact that must be accounted for by any adequate theory of automaticity. Several theorists (e.g., Cheng, 1985; Logan, 1988) have questioned whether these results indicate differences in capacity requirements. We consider next an interesting alternative account of the development of automaticity.

Instance Theory

Gordon Logan (1988; Logan & Etherton, 1994) has developed an alternative account of the data from experiments such as those of Schneider and Shiffrin. Logan's theory is referred to as **instance theory,** because one of its main assumptions is that each en-counter a person has with a given stimulus is stored in memory as an instance. Rather than invoke differences in capacity requirements to explain performance in the consis-tent and varied mapping conditions, Logan points to memory as a possible basis for the differences.

At the heart of Logan's instance model is the assumption that, in a task such as a visual search, a person can make a correct response in two ways. The first involves what Logan refers to as an *algorithm*; here, the person applies a set of rules to decide what response to make. Applying an algorithm is a relatively slow process, and it also seems to be rather de-liberate in nature. Using an algorithm in a visual search task is like saying to oneself, "If there is a **T** or a **B** in the display, respond yes; otherwise, respond no." According to Lo-gan, performance in tasks that appear nonautomatic reflect the operation of an algo-rithm.

The second basis on which a person can perform a task is *memory retrieval*. According to Logan's theory, every encounter we have with a stimulus set is stored in memory, and when we are presented with the same stimulus later on, an obligatory retrieval process commences as soon as the stimulus is presented. If the retrieval process locates an instance in memory, then that instance contains the response that was associated with the stimu-lus, and we can use that information to make our response on this occasion.

Logan's model is an example of a *horse race model,* in that performance is said to depend on which of the two processes (algorithm or memory retrieval) finishes first. Memory re-trieval is generally the faster of the two, and memory retrieval time decreases as the num-ber of instances stored in memory increases. The reason for this speed-up is complex, but you can get a feel for it through the following thought exercise.

Imagine that you have a stable of a hundred horses and that all the horses run at differ-ent speeds. Now assume that you are going to run two types of races, one with two horses and a second with twenty horses. If we let the time it takes the first horse to cross the fin-ish line represent the speed for the race, then which type of race is likely *on average* to pro-duce the fastest time? Your intuition probably tells you that if you run the two-horse and twenty-horse versions over and over, the chances are that you will more often have a faster horse in the twenty-horse version than in the two-horse version. Similarly, in Logan's model, the speed of retrieving instances varies, and the more instances you have, the greater the chances that the memory retrieval process will be faster than the algorithm process.

Logan's model makes a number of specific predictions, and Logan has tested some of them (1988; 1990; Logan & Etherton, 1994; Logan, Taylor, & Etherton, 1996). To appreci-ate how this model can account for the difference in consistent versus varied mapping conditions, recall that the pool of targets is the same across trials in a consistent mapping condition but is changed in the varied mapping condition. Thus, in general, for a given number of trials, more instances are stored for each target in the consistent mapping con-dition than in the varied mapping condition. With more instances of each stimulus and the appropriate response stored, it is more likely that the memory retrieval process will "win the race" with the algorithm, and hence performance will depend on this process rather than the slower algorithm process. Furthermore, retrieval from memory is obliga-tory and can operate in a parallel fashion (e.g., retrieving instances of T and B simultane-ously), so we would not expect memory-set size to have a major impact on performance in the consistent mapping condition.

Section Summary: Practice Effects and Attentional Processes

Practicing a task has a number of important consequences on the task's attentional demands. Controlled processes are assumed to require capacity, and automatic processes are said to not be limited by capacity. Schneider and Shiffrin showed that, with practice, controlled tasks in which there is consistent mapping between stimuli and responses will become automatic tasks. They interpreted these results as showing that the tasks eventually require less and less capacity. Logan, in his instance theory, argued that what changes with practice is not the capacity demanded by the processes but rather how the tasks are completed. According to instance theory, practice creates many memories of instances in which the task was performed. As more instances are stored in memory, it becomes more likely that the task can be performed by retrieval of an instance from memory.

REVIEWING ATTENTION

CONCEPT REVIEW

1. What physical characteristics of a spoken message are likely to affect how well a listener can selectively attend to that message?

2. How do early and late selection models of selective attention differ? Describe three lines of evidence that are consistent with each type of model and three findings that are inconsistent with each type of model.

3. What are the primary assumptions of Broadbent's filter theory? Which one of these assumptions was modified in Treisman's attenuation model?

4. What role does pertinence value play in Norman's late selection model? How can this concept account for hearing one's name in a distant conversation in a noisy room?

5. What do we mean when we say that unattended information can have a priming effect? How does the finding of priming by unattended information affect the validity of early and late selection models?

6. Discuss some neuropsychological findings that have implications for early and late selection models.

7. What are the main assumptions of Kahneman's single capacity model of divided attention? How can these assumptions be tested with the dual-task methodology?

8. What is the primary difference between single capacity models and multiple resource models? What findings are inconsistent with single capacity models but consistent with multiple resource models? Are there any data that multiple resource models cannot explain?

9. Describe Johnston and Heinz's capacity model of selective attention. How can this model account for some of the data that you reviewed in Question 2?

10. What is negative priming, and how does this phenomenon relate to studies of divided attention?

11. Describe the Schneider and Shiffrin studies of the development of automaticity. What is the instance theory of automaticity, and how does it relate to the explanation offered by Schneider and Shiffrin?

KEY TERMS

attenutation model (p. 149)

automatic task (p. 167)

capacity (p. 155)

cocktail party phenomenon (p. 140)

cognitive workload (p. 153)

consistent mapping condition (p. 170)

controlled processing task (p. 167)

dichotic listening task (p. 141)

divided attention (p. 141)

dual-task methodology (p. 155)

early selection model (p. 142)

filter theory (p. 145)

instance theory (p. 172)

late selection model (p. 142)

multiple resource model (p. 157)

negative priming (p. 164)

pertinence value (p. 150)

positive priming (p. 164)

priming effect (p. 150)

selective attention (p. 140)

selective interference (p. 156)

single capacity model (p. 155)

speech-shadowing task (p. 141)

split-span task (p. 147)

varied mapping (p. 170)

SUGGESTED READINGS

Nelson Cowan's 1988 journal article, "Evolving conceptions of memory storage, selective attention, and their mutual constraints within the human information processing system" (*Psychological Bulletin, 104,* 163-191), provides a good overview of selective attention and models of selective attention. Cowan's text *Attention and memory: An integrated framework* (New York: Oxford University Press, 1995) expands on the earlier article and also includes recent neuropsychological findings. *Attentional processing: The brain's art of mindfulness* (Cambridge, MA: Harvard University Press, 1995), by David LaBerge, is an excellent overview of modern research on attentional processes written by one of the leading researchers in the field. For readers interested in clinical investigations of attentional processes, we recommend *Clinical neuropsychology of attention* by Adriaan H. van Zomeren and Wiebo H. Brouwer (New York: Oxford University Press, 1994). Somewhat more detailed discussions of the neuropsychology of attention can be found in the text *Behavioral neurology and neuropsychology,* edited by Todd E. Feinberg and Martha J. Farah (New York: McGraw-Hill, 1997).

Memory in the Short Term

Between the two boundary episodes that allow public observation of information in memory—when at first the person receives the information to be stored and when later he overtly retrieves it—there is a complicated invisible history of transformation, abstraction, and elaboration.—Robert G. Crowder (1976, p. 29)

A few years ago I was taken aback when a colleague asked me, "Whatever happened to short-term memory? Didn't people used to study that?"
—Richard M. Shiffrin (1993, p. 193)

CONSIDER THIS TASK: You are at the library, looking up material for a paper you need to write. In the card catalog, you find two books that look like great references. One of them is shelved on the floor you are presently on, and the other is on a different floor. To find these books, you need to remember their call numbers, but you have no paper to write on, and you have forgotten to bring a pen. You know that you can get to one of the books quickly, but getting to the second is going to involve walking to another part of the library and then finding the book. How are you going remember these two call numbers?

To remember the first call number, you can probably do something simple. For example, you can just repeat the call number to yourself until you locate the book. But you probably are going to need a different strategy for the second call number—one that will allow you to remember that call number after having focused your efforts on locating the first book. You might start thinking about how the call number reminds you of something meaningful. In a similar situation, one of us used to remember call numbers for books in psychology by noting that many of the call numbers started with the letters BF, the first two initials of the famous psychologist B. F. Skinner. You might go on to find something meaningful in the numbers that go along with the letters. For example, the numbers might be close to the current time (e.g., 311 could be 3:11 P.M.).

Here we have two memory tasks. One requires the use of memory over a reasonably short period of time, and the other requires the use of memory over a slightly longer period of time. Some aspects of the two tasks are similar; others are different. On the basis of this simple analysis of a pair of memory tasks, how willing would you be to conclude that we have two *different types* of memory?

You probably have been exposed to the idea—in fact you may believe—that there are at least two distinct types of memory: short-term and long-term memory. But, as you may have guessed from our analysis of the library task, while it is apparent that we humans have the need to maintain information over different spans of time, that does not necessarily mean that we have different types of memory.

To get a better understanding of this logical distinction, imagine that instead of studying memory, we are studying trees. Imagine that you and a friend are given the task of scientifically describing trees to the rest of the world. And imagine that the rest of the world knows very little about trees. You decide to study trees using a high-powered microscope and measure detailed aspects of the tree's cell structure. Your friend decides to observe trees from a distance and measure the types of materials the trees exchange with the environment. After a while, you are both called on to present your research findings. You illustrate your work with the picture shown in Figure 6.1a, while your friend illustrates her work with the picture in Figure 6.1b. In the absence of much knowledge about trees, some people in your audience may conclude that you and your friend are studying different things.

The notion of short-term memory has become familiar and accepted even outside psychology.

Drawing by Ed Fisher; © 1983 *New Yorker Magazine* Inc.

"*The matters about which I'm being questioned, Your Honor, are all things I should have included in my long-term memory but which I mistakenly inserted in my short-term memory.*"

FIGURE 6.1   **Tree Research Findings**   A microscopic cross-section of a beech tree (left). A beech tree from a distance (right). If people did not already know that both these images were beech trees, they might be tempted to conclude that the photos represent very different things.

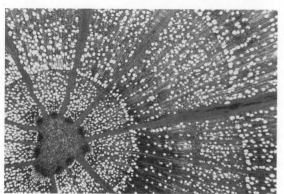

Source: (left) *Scientific American,* December 1994.

But, as you and your friend know, you are studying the same thing—just at different levels of analysis on the size dimension.

While it makes some sense to consider different levels of analysis with respect to the *size* of memory (e.g., how much we can remember), another important dimension is that of *time* (Crowder, 1993; Crowder & Neath, 1991). Studying how memory works over very short periods of time is much like studying how trees work by looking at their individual cells. Focusing the "microscope" of experimental techniques on memory over short time intervals has given psychologists a very detailed view of the various ways in which we retain and process information when the time between being exposed to it and needing to use it is relatively short. As you will see, this detailed view of memory suggested to a number of psychologists that memory in these kinds of situations might be distinct from other types of memory. However, you will also see that although memory may look different at different levels of time, the basic processes of memory can be very similar in the short and the long term.

Beginning with this chapter, we focus on the study of memory—what it is and how we use it. We concentrate primarily on the "how we use it" part. Much of what we know about memory comes from the study of specific tasks performed with memory. In this chapter, we discuss things we do with memory in brief periods of time. In Chapter 7, we discuss things we need to do with memory when the time between storing the information and calling it up again (retrieving it) is much longer. Finally, in Chapter 8, we deal with tasks that require the retrieval of very general types of information—information that is typically not specific to the situation in which it was learned.

A LITTLE HISTORY: PRIMACY IN THE RESEARCH ON MEMORY IN THE SHORT TERM

Think about the library task again. At a minimum, you have to do three things with your memory to perform this task. First, you have to get the information (the call numbers) into memory. Second, you have to maintain or preserve that information in memory while you take care of other parts of the task (like waiting for the elevators, wandering through the stacks, etc.). Finally, you have to get the information out of memory, perhaps more than once.

This analysis suggests that there are three logically separable parts of any memory task. The first is **acquisition,** the process of putting information into memory. *Acquisition* is sometimes used as a synonym for learning and is also referred to as **encoding.** The second part of the task is called **retention,** the process of holding on to information once it has been stored in memory. The final part is **retrieval,** the actions required to get information out of memory. The distinction among acquisition, retention, and retrieval is generally attributed to Köhler (1947) and Melton (1963).

Consider how your ability to perform the library task offers insight into how acquisition, retention, and retrieval might work. If your performance on that task is perfect, then you can be reasonably safe in assuming that you have successfully acquired, retained, and retrieved the information needed. But what if you make a mistake at some point during the task? What if you get to the stacks and cannot remember what you are looking for? Which of the three processes—acquisition, retention, or retrieval—do you think is most likely at fault? What types of experiments could you design to test your ideas?

Our concern for the moment is with tasks that require the encoding, retention, and retrieval of information over short periods of time. Ideas about the operation of memory in tasks like these have come to play important roles in theories about other aspects of cognition. For example, short-term memory performance has been strongly equated with basic measures of intelligence (Sattler, 1982). Memory for recently processed information has also been suggested as the basic limitation in cognition (Miller, 1956; Shiffrin, 1975, 1976). Memory in the short term may be one of the most critical processes involved in language comprehension (Crowder, 1982a). Furthermore, the notion of a short-term memory has become so pervasive in the psychological literature that it is often implicitly equated with consciousness and cognition in general (see Shiffrin, 1993 for a critical discussion). Although there have been some serious theoretical and empirical challenges to these views (Nairne, 1992; Schweickert & Boruff, 1986), it is safe to say that memory in the short term, be it a distinct type of memory or simply a distinct manifestation of the way memory in general is used, has come to play a central role in the way both scientists and nonscientists think about cognition.

Early Suggestions for a Distinct Form of Memory

As we discussed in Chapter 3, as early as 1859, Sir William Hamilton (1859) noted that, after quickly viewing a set of marbles, he could not accurately recall how many marbles there were (Searleman & Herrmann, 1994). Hamilton was interested in measuring how much information can be acquired in a single glance—something he called the *span of apprehension* (see Chapter 3)—and in how retention of that information changes over short periods of time. About 30 years later, the American psychologist William James (1890) proposed that a "primary" memory system was closely related to consciousness and was different in important ways from memory for general knowledge.

James based his ideas on informal introspection, but psychologists employing physiological measures were thinking along similar lines. For example, around the beginning of the twentieth century, two German scientists (Muller & Pilzecker, 1900, cited in Bower & Hilgard, 1981) proposed that experiencing an event causes neural activity that persists for some time after the event. As time elapses after the original event, the neural changes become either more pronounced or more permanent. This general idea was given more precise formulation by a Canadian psychologist, Donald O. Hebb (1949).

In its most general sense, Hebb's **consolidation hypothesis** holds that, as a function of experiencing and encoding an event, the physical state of the nervous system changes. If you could compare the nervous system just before and just after the experiencing and encoding of the event, then you could observe evidence of the nature of this change. Tulving (1983, p. 158) noted that this idea is similar to the definition of the soul proposed by the sixteenth century physician Jean Fernel: the difference one would observe by comparing an organism just before and just after death.

Central to the importance of the consolidation hypothesis to the modern study of memory is the notion of a **memory trace** (discussed in Chapter 2) and the related notion of an **engram,** the physical record left in memory by an experience. You can think of a memory trace (or an engram) as a "track" laid down in memory, as musical tracks are laid down on CDs.

The modern notion of a memory trace dates back nearly a hundred years, when the term *engram* was introduced by the German psychologist Richard Semon. Semon believed that experience is directly recorded in the physical matter of the nervous system, referring to the "engraphic action of a stimulus, because a permanent record has been written or engraved on the irritable substance" (Semon, 1921, p. 24).

Although Semon may have coined the term, its most influential use came in the work of Karl Lashley. Lashley began his work in the early 1900s, searching for the anatomical changes in the nervous system that might result from classical conditioning (Lashley, 1929). He was following closely in the footsteps of the famous Russian physiologist Ivan Pavlov (1927), who also believed that classical conditioning produces changes in the structure of the nervous system.

Later, Hebb based his consolidation hypothesis on the idea of an "activity trace." He suggested that this trace consists of the neural activity of cells or groups of cells involved in perceiving an event. A common metaphor for the activity that results in a memory trace is that of reverberations, or resonance, in the nervous system that result from experiencing some event. According to Hebb, the longer the activity (the reverberations) of these cells continues, the higher the probability that actual structural changes will take place in the brain.

In more modern terms, the activity trace corresponds to memory in the short term; and the pattern of changes in neural structure that were proposed to result from those reverberations corresponds to memory in the long term. Many of Hebb's original ideas about memory have been forgotten, and some have been rejected (even, in fact, by Hebb himself; Hebb, 1961), but the idea that physical and neural changes can represent memory storage has been used in many contemporary theories (e.g., Miller, Kasparow & Schactman, 1986; Ratcliff, 1978).

Interference, Trace Decay, and Multiple Stores

Around the time that Hebb was proposing types of memory traces, a number of American psychologists were working with a conception of memory that did *not* require different types of neural activity. These psychologists approached memory from the associationist view, which had grown out of the behaviorist tradition (see Chapter 1). Memory, from this perspective, is a set of stimulus-response associations; and memory performance on tests with any materials (often referred to as *to-be-remembered,* or *TBR,* items) is a function of the strength of these associations. In addition, similarity between stimulus-response associations for the TBR items and stimulus-response associations learned *before* the TBR items are presented for study can actually affect memory for the TBR items, as can similarity between stimulus-response associations for the TBR items and stimulus-response associations learned *after* the TBR items are presented but before the memory test.

The general way in which these similar associations can affect memory for the TBR items is referred to as **interference** (Melton & Irwin, 1940). The impairment of memory for TBR items due to similar associations learned *before* the TBR items is referred to as **proactive interference.** In contrast, the impairment of memory for TBR items due to similar associations learned *after* the TBR items is referred to as **retroactive interference.**

You should note two things about these definitions. First, although two types of interference are possible, both are happening in one "place"—memory. That is, the two types of interference do not require two types of memory. Second, the type of interference is specified only with respect to when the interfering associations are learned (either before or after the TBR items) and how similar the interfering associations are to the TBR items.

In the late 1950s, however, a pair of simple and elegant studies caused scientists to question whether it was possible to explain interference using the idea of a single memory system. To understand the impact of these ground-breaking experiments, let us consider in a little more detail the metaphor of reverberations in memory.

Find something that will ring like a bell when it is struck (a metal bowl or a glass will work). Try striking the object with a pencil or ruler and listen to what happens. More than likely, what you will hear is an initial ringing that quickly dies down. If you do not strike the object again, the ringing—the reverberation—dies down, or decays. However, if you strike the object repeatedly, then you can keep the ringing at a reasonably loud level and keep it from decaying.

If we think about memory activity as reverberations, then we can think about forgetting as a decrease in those reverberations. Given this metaphor, it might surprise you to learn that, even though psychologists were using the idea of reverberations to conceptualize memory, many of them were surprised when two independently conducted studies demonstrated that if subjects studied very short lists of items, and were prevented from rehearsing those items, the lists were quickly forgotten (Brown, 1958; Peterson & Peterson, 1959). In terms of the reverberation metaphor, this (very simply) is equivalent to showing that if you do not keep hitting the ringing object, the ringing will die down.

The procedure that was used in these two studies has come to be called the **Brown-Peterson distractor task,** in honor of the two sets of researchers who independently developed it: John Brown, working in England (Brown, 1958), and the husband-and-wife team of Lloyd Peterson and Margaret Intons-Peterson, working in the United States (Peterson & Peterson, 1959). The procedure is a simple one. The experimenter presents subjects with three-consonant trigrams, such as B J K. Immediately after the last consonant is presented, the experimenter gives subjects a number, like 665, and tells them to quickly count backward by threes (e.g., 665, 662, 659, 656, . . .). Subjects keep counting until the experimenter tells them to stop. The time spent counting (called the *retention interval*) is varied, for example, from 0 to 18 seconds.

The original results showed that, by the time 6 seconds had elapsed, subjects could remember only one or two letters; and by the time 18 seconds had elapsed, forgetting was almost complete (see Figure 6.2a). A great deal of research was inspired by this finding, and the basic effect was shown to be quite robust, even when more meaningful stimuli (like

FIGURE 6.2   **Results from the Brown-Peterson Task**   (a) The percentage of letters correctly recalled as a function of time spent counting backward in the Brown-Peterson task falls off rapidly as the retention interval increases from 0 to 18 seconds. (b) A strikingly similar pattern occurs when words rather than trigrams are used in the studied list.

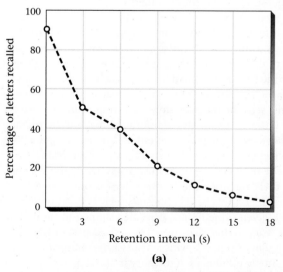
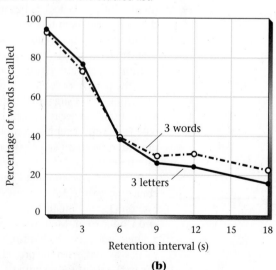

(a)   (b)

Source: (a) Ashcraft, 1989. (b) Lachman, Lachman & Butterfield, 1979.

words) were used in the studied list (see Figure 6.2b, which presents results from Murdock, 1961).

The findings of Brown and the Petersons were published in the midst of a rather heated debate. On the one side were those scientists who were committed to interference theory and its notion that there was only a single type of memory. On the opposing side were those who, inspired by developments in computer science, proposed that there were multiple types of memory (Houston, 1991; Schwartz & Reisberg, 1991; Searleman & Herrmann, 1994). The data from the Brown-Peterson task suggested that something other than interference was at work. Specifically, it suggested that some way of maintaining the activity of a trace (i.e., to keep it from rapidly decaying) was required to keep information available in the short term. Since this rapid decay was not observed in memory performance over longer time intervals, the Brown-Peterson data pointed toward some important functional difference between memory in the short term and memory in the long term.

It was not long, however, before other researchers began to report results that contradicted this conclusion. As in many research areas, it turned out that the methods used in these early studies played a crucial role in determining the nature of the evidence. The key to understanding this evidence is to realize that when psychologists collect data, an *average* is computed of all the responses made in a particular condition for each individual subject. Those averages are then subjected to statistical analysis.

To make this problem concrete, imagine that you are conducting a memory experiment using the Brown-Peterson task. For simplicity, you decide to test different retention intervals using different groups of subjects: For some subjects, the retention interval is 0 seconds, for others it is 3 seconds, and so forth. To make sure that you have a stable measure of each subject's performance, you have each go through a number of trials (say 20) in which he or she hears trigrams, counts backward, and then tries to recall the trigrams. After the experiment is complete, you calculate the average proportion of items recalled across trials for each subject and then perform your statistical analysis.

What you have done, by averaging across all the trials for each subject, is to assume that no important changes in performance occur across trials. It was this assumption that a number of psychologists began to question. What they thought might be happening in the Brown-Peterson task was that proactive interference was building up across trials. Keppel and Underwood (1962) tested this hypothesis and demonstrated that, on the very first trial, there was *very little* forgetting as a function of the amount of time subjects spent counting backward. On the second trial, performance began to decline; and by the third trial, the pattern of forgetting was at the level represented in Figure 6.2. Essentially, Keppel and Underwood suggested that a *general* mechanism of memory, proactive interference—rather than the decay of a trace from a separate memory store—was responsible for the effect. Each time a subject completed a trial, he or she stored information about the trigram presented on that trial. As the number of trials increased, so did the chances for proactive interference, and this interference effect was largest at the long retention intervals.

Another major argument against the notion of separate memory systems, and another challenge to the interpretation of the data from the Brown-Peterson task, came from Melton (1963). The first part of his argument was based on results such as those of Keppel and Underwood. Melton argued that, given these results, it seemed simpler to think that a single memory mechanism was at work, rather than two. The second part of his argument was that, with the proper manipulations, performance on a task depending on memory in the short term could show dramatic influences of memory in the long term.

Baddeley (1986) has provided a clever example of how this might work. Imagine that you are conducting an experiment using a Brown-Peterson task but that you are using the months of the year as stimuli rather than consonant trigrams. For each trial, you randomly select three months for subjects to study, and you put these three months in a random order. After presenting the months, you give subjects a number and ask them to count backward by threes. You will probably observe a pattern across trials similar to what Keppel and Underwood observed.

But now imagine that on some of the trials the three months by chance appear in their proper order. What do you think performance will be like on those trials? Most likely, even if the trials occur later in the experimental session, you will see very little forgetting. Essentially, your subjects can rely on their background knowledge (i.e., their knowledge of the correct order for the months) to help them perform your task.

If you thought there were two distinct memory systems, then a finding like this would require that you specify some way for these systems to exchange information. You would also need to explain why a system that supposedly was important (or specialized) for long-term tasks could influence a system that was specialized for short-term tasks. So your theory would quickly start to get complicated. If, on the other hand, you did not think there were two distinct memory systems, then a finding like this would not be too difficult to explain and would not require additional complications.

During the 1960s and 1970s, evidence accumulated supporting both theoretical positions. Research in this period showed that a variety of factors could contribute to performance on the Brown-Peterson task. Many studies showed how switching from one type (or category) of item to another could prevent interference and thus prevent forgetting (Loess, 1968; Wickens, 1970; Wickens, Born & Allen, 1963). This effect has been referred to as **release from proactive interference.** Experiment 6 offers instructions for demonstrating this impressive effect.

Other studies showed that the degree of forgetting (or degree of interference) depends on the amount of time that elapses between trials, implying that some decay is possible along with interference (Conrad, 1967; Peterson & Gentile, 1963). Finally, Baddeley and Scott (1971) tested more than 900 subjects in a single-trial Brown-Peterson task across a variety of conditions and showed that, even on a single trial, it was possible to observe some forgetting and that this forgetting reached a maximal point after about 5 seconds. This finding was particularly hard to account for with the explanation offered by Keppel and Underwood, since there was only one trial.

The situation ended up being quite confusing. There were plenty of logical arguments and plenty of data to support either a single-system or a multiple-system view of memory. The shift in the debate came from a rather unremarkable memory phenomenon and what has come to be a rather remarkable and influential theoretical conception of memory.

Serial Position Effects and Multiple Stores   Frequently, memory experiments use lists of things (words, pictures, etc.). Since each item occurs in a particular position in the list, it is possible to look at performance with items as a function of position. The general label given to differences in memory performance as a function of position in a list is the **serial position effect.** Serial position effects have been examined in a number of domains. For example, we discussed a serial position effect when we explored the modality effect in Chapter 3.

By the early 1960s, serial position effects in recall tasks had been well documented. For example, Figure 6.3 shows data reported by Murdock (1962), illustrating serial position ef-

EXPERIMENT 6:   Release from Proactive Interference

The build-up of interference in a Brown-Peterson task and the disappearance of that interference are easy to demonstrate. To do this, you will need at least four willing friends to serve as subjects. Make sure that you tell your subjects only that you will be performing an experiment designed to explore how memory works. Tell them that few if any risks are involved in the experiment and that they can quit at any time. Essentially, make sure that your subjects voluntarily consent to being in your experiment. Performing an experiment without this type of voluntary consent is unethical. It can also cause you to lose friends.

Read through all these instructions before you start. You will need to test each subject separately. Tell the subject that he will listen to four lists of words, with each list composed of three words. After each list, you will give him a number and have him count backward by threes for 15 seconds. Then you will ask him to write down all the words he remembers.

Make sure the subject has blank paper and a pen or pencil and that you have a stopwatch. When you and your subject are ready, begin by reading List 1 to the subject, at the rate of about 1 word per second. Then read the number and have the subject count backward by threes. Continue through List 2 and List 3 as described below.

> *List 1:* apple, banana, honeydew
> *Number:* 176 (count backward by threes for 15 seconds)
> *Recall:* Give the subject 1 minute to write down as many words as possible. Then go on to List 2.

> *List 2:* peach, pineapple, strawberry
> *Number:* 993 (count backward by threes for 15 seconds)
> *Recall:* Again, give each subject 1 minute to write down as many words as possible. Then go on to List 3.

> *List 3:* cherry, grape, pear
> *Number:* 547 (count backward by threes for 15 seconds)
> *Recall:* As before, give each subject 1 minute to write down as many words as possible.

For List 4, you will use a separate list for each subject. But you will use the same procedure as for the first three lists.

> *Subject 1:* doctor, lawyer, dentist
> *Subject 2:* rose, daffodil, gardenia
> *Subject 3:* asparagus, broccoli, peas

Subject 4: orange, watermelon, grapefruit
Number: 720 (count backward by threes for 15 seconds)
Recall: As before, give each subject 1 minute to write down as many words as possible.

After all your subjects have completed the experiment, count the number of words that each recalled on each trial, divide the total by 3 (the number of words in each list), and multiply by 100 to get the percent recall on each trial for each subject. Then plot a graph of your results with percentages on the vertical axis and list numbers on the horizontal axis. What you should see is a set of data that looks like Figure 6A. These are data from a study reported by Wickens (1972) that used these same types of items.

FIGURE 6A   **Release from Proactive Interference**   This pattern illustrates the release from PI you probably observed in your own experiment. Note how, when subjects changed categories, their memory performance improved markedly. Also notice that when subjects changed to a category (vegetables) that was very similar to the category used on the initial three lists (fruits), the improvement was much less dramatic than when they worked with very different categories.

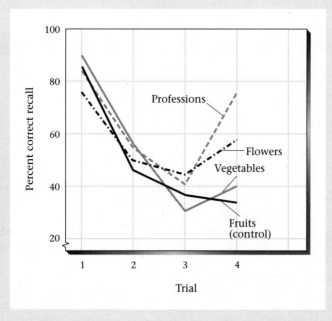

FIGURE 6.3   **Serial Position Effects**   These effects show recall for lists of 10, 20, 30, and 40 items.

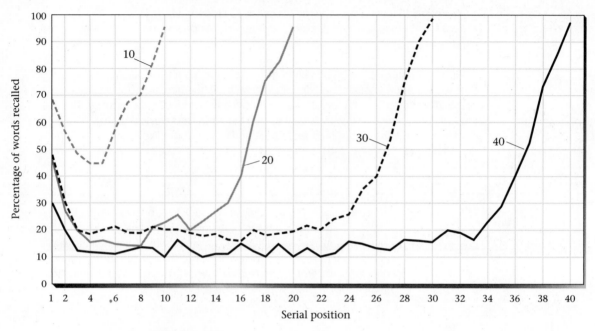

Source: Murdock, 1962.

fects in recall for lists of 20, 30, and 40 items. The initial portion of each curve—the left arm of the U—is referred to as the *primacy portion* of the curve, and the last portion—the right arm of the U—is referred to as the *recency portion.*

If the left arm of the U is present (if performance is better for early items than middle items), the data are said to show a **primacy effect.** If the right arm of the U is present (if performance is better for late items than middle items), the data are said to show a **recency effect.** The shape of serial position curves seemed to many psychologists powerful evidence for the existence of two memory systems. The primacy portion of the curve seemed to reflect long-term memory, with the best performance observed for the items most likely to have "made it into" long-term memory (the initial items in the list). The recency portion of the curve seemed to reflect short-term memory, with the best performance observed for the items that had had the least amount of time to decay (the last items in the list).

Although serial position curves were thoroughly studied (and presumably well understood), they actually contributed to the debate over how many subsystems of memory might exist. How could this be? The answer came from experiments designed to independently change or eliminate the primacy and recency portions. The logic was that if manipulations could be identified that would affect one portion but leave the other unaffected, then this would be evidence supporting distinct memory systems. Such effects would not be easy to explain if memory is a single, unitary thing, since any manipulation would be able to affect only one type of memory.

FIGURE 6.4   **Results from Rundus (1971)**   The probability of correctly recalling an item was highly correlated with the number of times it was overtly rehearsed, but this correlation was restricted to the initial (primacy) portion of the list.

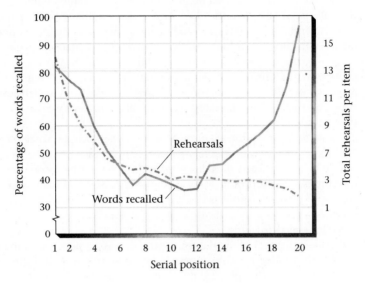

Source: Rundus, 1971.

In fact, researchers were able to provide just this type of challenging evidence. For example, Glanzer and Cunitz (1966) showed that the primacy portion alone was affected by the amount or type of rehearsal allowed per item. Other researchers took a different approach but provided corroborating evidence: When rehearsal was minimized or eliminated, the primacy portion of the function could be eliminated without affecting the recency portion (Brodie & Prytulak, 1975; Marshal & Werder, 1972; Seamon & Murray, 1976). Finally, Rundus (1971) asked subjects to "think aloud" during list presentation. Results from this study (see Figure 6.4) showed that the number of times an item is rehearsed out loud is highly correlated with the probability of its later recall, but only for items at the beginning of the list.

There was also a rehearsal manipulation that affected recency without affecting primacy: the Brown-Peterson task. When Glanzer and Cunitz (1966) varied the amount of backward counting time from 0 to 10 to 30 seconds, they dramatically diminished the recency portion of the curve while having no effect on the primacy portion. These and other selective effects (Glanzer, 1972) suggested to many psychologists that separate types or mechanisms of memory were responsible for the two portions of the curve. One was specific to the degree of initial learning, and one was specific to the immediate strength of the memory for the most recently presented information.

Atkinson-Shiffrin: The Modal Multistore Model   With serial position effects and the debates about the mechanisms involved in the Brown-Peterson task, it seemed that a wealth of data was swinging the debate in favor of the multiple-system view of memory.

But at this point, no theory existed to tie all the data together. This need was met by a flow-chart model of memory, one that represented the flow of memory information among distinct memory subsystems. Although this flowchart description was reasonably general, it was considerably more precise than most of its predecessors. The model was able to tie together much of the data that existed at the time, including data on decay and serial position effects. In fact, over the years since it was originally proposed, it has been so useful and influential that it has come to be called the *modal* (the most common, or consensus) model of memory (Murdock, 1974). A general representation appears in Figure 6.5.

The original version of this model, and the one that has had the greatest impact on psychologists' thinking about memory, is that proposed by Atkinson and Shiffrin (1968). The Atkinson-Shiffrin model has two important aspects: (a) an **architecture,** comprising the structures that make up memory, and (b) a set of **control processes** that operate on these structures.

The architecture of the Atkinson-Shiffrin model includes three memory structures. The first is a set of very transient memories specific to each of the senses. These are similar to the iconic and echoic stores described in Chapter 3. The second memory structure is referred to as the short-term store. Waugh and Norman (1965) had referred to this as the "primary" memory, and it is this part of the architecture that has come to be known as short-term memory. The third memory structure is the long-term store, now commonly called long-term memory.

The second aspect of the model, control processes**,** determines the flow of information among the various memory structures (the sensory store, the short-term store, and the long-term store). The first of these control processes can roughly be thought of as attention. It delimits the amount and types of information that are transferred from the sensory registers to the short-term store. You will remember from our discussion in Chapter 3 that information is preserved in the sensory registers for only a very short time. Thus, if attention does not or cannot allow this information to move to the short-term store, it will be lost and unavailable for later processing. This view of attention is similar to the "bottleneck" in attention discussed in Chapter 5.

FIGURE 6.5 **The Modal Model of Memory** This general representation is based on the Atkinson-Shiffrin (1968) model.

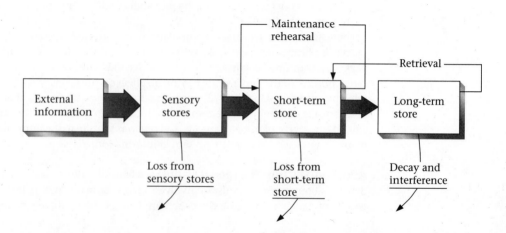

If attention is directed at items in the sensory registers, then this information can pass into the short-term store. Once this happens, *rehearsal processes* take over. Rehearsal processes are necessary to preserve the information within the short-term store. Anything that prevents rehearsal will cause the information in the short-term store to be lost, or to decay. (Here is where the evidence from the Brown-Peterson task and the manipulation of the two portions of the serial position curve comes into play.) Information can also be brought into the short-term store from the long-term store by way of *retrieval*. Finally, information can be transferred to the long-term store as a result of various types of rehearsal and the interacting effects of new information and retrieved information.

The Atkinson-Shiffrin model has a variety of properties that make it important. Probably the most significant, at least from a historical perspective, is that it provided a coherent way of organizing the large amount of memory research that had accumulated during the debates between those favoring interference theory and those interested in developing theories incorporating multiple subsystems in memory. For example, using the model, we can explain the forgetting that can be observed even on a single trial of the Brown-Peterson task (Baddeley & Scott, 1971) by saying that backward counting disrupts the rehearsal processes necessary for maintaining the activation of information in the short-term store.

Similarly, we can explain the serial position findings as reflecting contributions from the long-term and short-term stores. In this view, the primacy portion of the serial position curve is due to the activity of the long-term store. These items are the first to be presented and can be rehearsed while some of the items that follow are being presented. This rehearsal allows them to be transferred to the long-term store. The recency portion is due to the activity of the short-term store. The last items in the list are still present and maintained in this store when subjects reach the end of the list (and the beginning of the memory test).

The Atkinson-Shiffrin model also appeared to tie together ideas about different aspects of memory in the short term. For example, the model explicitly included a set of brief duration stores for each of the senses (vision, audition, etc.). This was because Atkinson and Shiffrin were careful to consider the data on sensory memory that had been collected prior to their work. By including these ideas in their model, Atkinson and Shiffrin gave researchers interested in sensory memory a "big picture" within which to place their work.

Since the model specified interactions among the sensory and short-term stores, and between the short-term and long-term stores, questions about these types of interactions could also be considered within a "big picture" of memory. One of these questions concerns the *form* in which information is presented in short-term memory. For example, since each of the sensory stores provides input to the short-term store, it is reasonable to ask whether the information in the short-term store somehow preserves important sensory characteristics of the original information. Before the Atkinson-Shiffrin model was proposed, a number of studies had demonstrated that memory can represent information in terms of both its visual (Posner & Keele, 1967; Postman, 1975) and its acoustic properties (Conrad, 1964; Kintsch & Buschke, 1969; Wickelgren, 1965). Although acoustic information appeared to be the most important, the Atkinson-Shiffrin model forced researchers to consider that multiple forms of information might be represented in memory (Brandimonte, Hitch & Bishop, 1992; Crowder, 1982).

The Atkinson-Shiffrin model also took into account many important ideas from the study of attention. In particular, note in Figure 6.5 that the model assumes that information can be lost from the sensory stores. This reflects ideas about a bottleneck in attention that were being considered around the time that Atkinson and Shiffrin were developing their model. In terms of memory, the possibility for a processing bottleneck, or a limitation that could lead to a loss of information, was seen as imposing a limit on the *capacity* of memory in the short term (Shiffrin, 1975, 1976).

Considering the capacity of the short-term store allowed the model to take into account the influential ideas of Miller (1956), who had proposed almost 20 years earlier a fundamental limit on the number of "things" that can be held in memory over short time periods. The general idea was that the maximum number of items we can hold in memory at any one time is 7 ± 2—referred to as the "magical" number. The "magical" part of the description came from Miller's observation that this limitation showed up in a wide variety of tasks. The important point for our discussion is that, by explicitly considering capacity, the Atkinson-Shiffrin model was able to deal with another important aspect of memory while still providing a "big picture."

Finally, the general strength of the Atkinson-Shiffrin model was reinforced by data from a variety of studies of patients with different types of amnesia. These studies suggested that it might be possible to find individuals with damage to the brain that corresponded to damage to specific parts of the model. For example, Baddeley and Warrington (1970) documented that amnesic patients who had severe difficulties with tasks requiring memory in the long term still showed recency effects, suggesting that some aspect of memory in the short term was preserved. A similar pattern was documented by Milner (1966) for an amnesic patient who performed well on a digit-span task (demonstrating memory in the short term) but who was unable to learn new information (i.e., transfer information to the long-term store). In addition, Shallice and Warrington (1970; Warrington & Shallice, 1969) demonstrated that amnesic patients who performed poorly on tasks requiring memory in the short term failed to show recency effects.

Difficulties with the Short-Term/Long-Term Distinction

In spite of the usefulness of the Atkinson-Shiffrin model, over the years a great deal of evidence has accumulated suggesting that its architectural distinction between the short- and long-term stores is either flawed in some way or unnecessary. For example, although the data from the Warrington and Shallice (1969) study were consistent to some extent with the predictions of the Atkinson-Shiffrin model, other aspects of the data from that study created problems for the model.

Specifically, the Atkinson-Shiffrin model held that active rehearsal of information in the short-term store was required in order for information to be transferred to the long-term store. The amnesic patient studied by Warrington and Shallice showed diminished abilities on short-term tasks and showed no recency effects, all suggesting that there were problems with the short-term store. However, this same patient was able to retain language information acquired in paired-associate and list-learning tasks. Remember that, according to the Atkinson-Shiffrin model, for information to be transferred to the long-term store, the control processes of the short-term store must work properly. If, as the data suggested, the amnesic patient's short-term store was damaged, then learning *any* type of information (including language information) should have been impossible.

In addition, some of the data that were originally interpreted as supporting the architectural distinctions of the Atkinson-Shiffrin model actually presented problems as well. Consider, for example, Keppel and Underwood's (1962) demonstration that the rapid forgetting observed in the Brown-Peterson task was to some extent an artifact of averaging the data across trials: Performance on the first of the series of trials frequently showed no forgetting. If the backward counting is disrupting rehearsal, then the information that otherwise would have been rehearsed should decay and be lost from short-term memory.

If this is the case, then the Atkinson-Shiffrin model could explain the *lack* of forgetting only by assuming that the target items in the Brown-Peterson task were *active* in the long-term store. But this feature of being active, even though supposedly in the long-term store, is something most psychologists would think of as a feature of the short-term store (Crowder, 1993).

A third, and related, problem was the finding that manipulations that, according to the Atkinson-Shiffrin model, should disrupt the recency portion of the serial position curve by preventing rehearsal often have little effect. For example, Baddeley and Hitch (1977) demonstrated that a recency effect could be observed even when the subject was prevented from rehearsing the items to be learned. Even greater difficulties were presented by results showing recency effects for information that *had* to be stored in the long-term store. Roediger and Crowder (1976) asked students to recall the names of the presidents of the United States. Their data showed striking primacy and recency effects (see Figure 6.6a). Furthermore, in a follow-up study (reported in Crowder, 1993) conducted more than 15 years later with different subjects, those presidents who had initially shown the benefit of a recency effect (Nixon and Ford) now showed levels of recall appropriate for items in the middle of the list (see Figure 6.6b).

Although the primacy effects in these data could be predicted by the Atkinson-Shiffrin model, the recency effects could not be accounted for. This is because the model explains recency effects as reflecting material that is active and maintained in the short-term store. But it is highly unlikely that subjects in the Roediger and Crowder studies were spending much time rehearsing the names of the most recent presidents.

Other studies also showed recency effects for information that could not have been in short-term memory. For example, Baddeley and Hitch (1977) asked patrons of pubs in England to name the rugby teams that had competed against the local team. These recall data showed strong recency effects. Pinto and Baddeley (1991) asked people parking at a university building to recall where they had parked weeks and months before, and these data showed strong recency effects. Finally, Watkins and Peynircioglu (1983) showed that, in cued recall, up to *three* separate recency effects could be produced when the list contained items from different categories and the cue used to signal which items to recall was the category name. That is, the last few items in each category were recalled better than the items from the middle of the category, independent of their absolute position in the list.

In spite of data like these, however, the architectural distinction between the short- and long-term stores is still going strong in some circles in scientific psychology (Cowan, 1993; Koppenaal & Glanzer, 1990). Perhaps one of the strongest logical arguments for the continued usefulness of the distinction comes from one of its authors (Shiffrin, 1993). Shiffrin argues that the fact that memory in the short term and memory in the long term show similar functional characteristics does not necessarily imply that there is really only one memory system.

In the first place, the idea that the short- and long-term stores contribute separately to performance is really a simplification that was not inherent in the original model. In fact, the Atkinson-Shiffrin model holds that performance will probably show contributions from both stores, meaning that aspects of short- and long-term memory tasks will be highly related. In the second place, if one assumes that the passage of time can reduce the ability of a given situation to cue recall of specific information (such as parking places), then the Atkinson-Shiffrin model can actually predict long-term recency effects. As the retention interval gets longer, retrieval will be less effective, which will depress performance on information learned very long ago. Finally, if activation in the short-term store is nec-

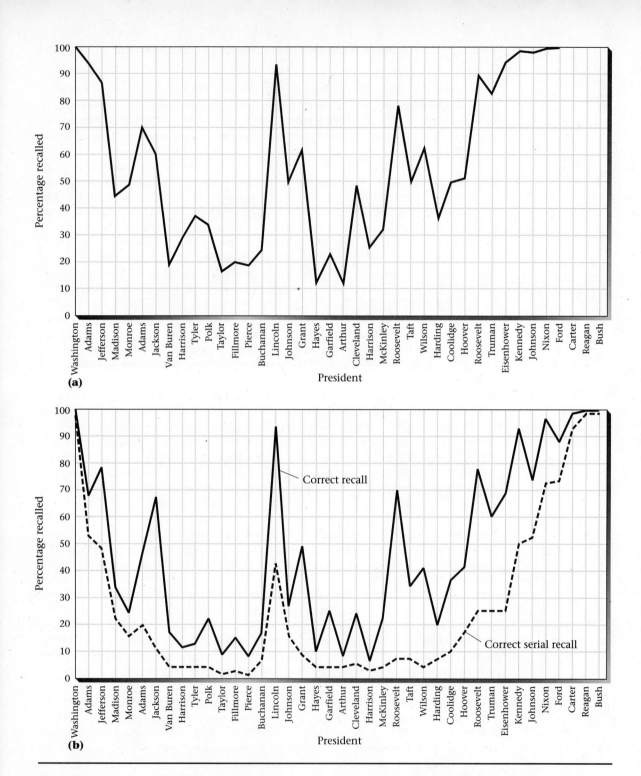

FIGURE 6.6   Serial Position Effects in Long-term Memory   (a) Roediger and Crowder (1976) observed serial position effects in long-term memory when they tested college students' recall of the names of the presidents of the United States. (b) When the Roediger and Crowder (1976) experiment was followed up after more than 15 years, names that had originally shown the benefit of recency were now at levels of recall appropriate to their position toward the interior of the historical list. Source: (a) Roediger & Crowder, 1976; (b) Crowder, 1993.

essary for information to enter long-term memory, then the information in long-term memory will probably show some of the effects of being in short-term memory, meaning that the functional characteristics of the two types of memory are highly related.

Section Summary: Primacy in the Research on Memory in the Short Term

We can identify three logically separable parts of any memory task: acquisition (or encoding), retention, and retrieval. Although this simple analysis might suggest that memory is a single "thing," hypotheses proposing distinct types of memory have a long history. One early example is Hebb's proposal of different types of memory traces in the nervous system. At about the time Hebb was developing this idea, American psychologists were developing the notion of interference within a single unitary memory. However, in the late 1950s, data collected by Brown and the Petersons suggested the existence of some type of memory specialized for tasks in the short term. In addition, data from experiments examining serial position effects (particularly experiments designed to selectively affect primacy and recency) suggested to many that there were indeed distinct types of memory specialized for different time scales. Many of these ideas came together in the Atkinson-Shiffrin model, which was based in large part on the distinction between short-term and long-term storage in memory. The necessity and validity of this distinction has come under question, and debate and research on this issue continue.

CURRENT THEMES AND ISSUES: RECENCY IN THE RESEARCH ON MEMORY IN THE SHORT TERM

The current literature on memory in the short term contains three themes that reflect the history of research in this area (Shiffrin, 1993). These themes concern (a) changes in the ability to access memory information over short time intervals, (b) capacity limitations in memory performance over short time intervals, and (c) memory control processes revealed in tasks requiring memory in the short term.

Changes in the Ability to Access Memory Information

We mentioned earlier that recency effects can be observed over both short and long time intervals. The Atkinson-Shiffrin model has difficulty accounting for these effects at long time intervals, since recency effects, according to the model, reflect information that is active in the short-term store. This suggests that it may be important to consider not just the time between seeing (or hearing) *each* of the items and seeing (or hearing) the next item but also the time between learning *all* of the items and using that information.

In other words, if we can get serial position effects at many different retention intervals, including very long ones, then there are probably some interesting interactions going on between factors important to (a) the order in which items were learned and (b) the overall ability to retain the information. In this section, we present two approaches to explaining these interesting empirical facts.

Changes in Distinctiveness Across Time   If you ever took car trips as a child, you probably spent some time staring out the window, watching the telephone poles disappear behind you (see Figure 6.7a). One thing that you may have noticed about the poles is that it was relatively easy to discriminate among the poles that were closest to you, but it became more and more difficult the farther down the road you looked (this involves the

FIGURE 6.7   **The Temporal Distinctiveness Model**   The telephone poles that are nearest to you in this picture are the easiest ones to tell apart (discriminate). But as you look farther and farther down the road, it becomes harder and harder to tell the individual poles apart. This is the metaphor behind the temporal distinctiveness model. The Interpresentation Interval (IPI) can be thought of as the distance between the poles, and the Retention Interval (RI) can be thought of as the distance between the last pole and you.

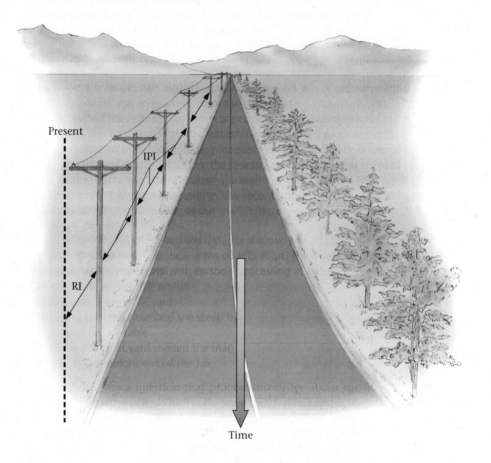

depth cue of texture gradient discussed in Chapter 4). In addition, as you continued down the road, the poles that just a moment ago were the easiest to discriminate became harder and harder to tell apart as you continued to move away from them.

Instead of telephone poles and distance, now consider items going into memory and time. It is easy to see that the ability to tell any of the poles apart (the *discriminability* of the poles) is a function of two distances: (a) the distances between the poles and (b) the distance between you and the poles. When we consider memory, perhaps a similar relationship holds, with the important "distances" being (a) the time between the presentation of one list item and the next and (b) the time between the presentation of the list and the test of memory.

A number of researchers have proposed this very idea—that the discriminability of items in memory is a function of the ratio of the time between presentation of items in the list and the time that elapses before the memory test. This function has been referred to as the **discrimination ratio** (Baddeley & Hitch, 1993; Glenberg et al., 1980; Glenberg et al., 1983). This basic idea may sound intuitively appealing to you, but how would you translate it into *predictions* about memory performance?

One way that psychologists have approached the task of going from intuition to prediction is by way of models (see Chapter 1). And one type of model that is particularly useful is a type that has been extremely important in other sciences: mathematical models (Townsend & Kadlec, 1990). Mathematical models are just statements of theories. But instead of using the language of scientific conversation, they use the language of mathematics. To give you a sense of how mathematical models work, we next consider a model originally proposed by Murdock (1960) and further developed and extended by Neath (1993a; 1993b). We refer to this model as the *temporal distinctiveness model*.

To understand how this model works, we need to define several terms (see Figure 6.7b). First, there is the time that goes by between the presentation of the last item and the beginning of the memory test. This is called the **retention interval (RI)**. In terms of our example of passing telephone poles, imagine that you are driving down a road that has only 10 telephone poles alongside it; these are analogous to 10 items in a list you are trying to remember in a memory experiment. The RI can be thought of as the distance between you and the last telephone pole in that set, or the overall distance between you and the *set* of poles.

Second, there is the time between the presentation of one individual item and the presentation of the next item. This is the **interpresentation interval (IPI)**. The IPI can be thought of as the distance between any two neighboring telephone poles. In the temporal distinctiveness model, the specific values of the IPI and the RI in any experiment are combined to produce a value (called s) for each item. This value indicates the abstract "distance" in time from the beginning of the memory test back to the presentation of that item.

An s value can be calculated for each item in the list. But this is just the first step. For technical reasons (Helson, 1964; Neath, 1993a, 1993b), these s values next undergo a logarithmic transformation to produce an initial estimate of the discriminability (d) of each item in the list. A benefit of using a log transformation is that it can turn a "curvy" function into more of a straight-line function; and mathematically, straight-line functions are usually easier to work with than curvy functions. Finally, the actual estimate of each item's distinctiveness (δ) in time is calculated using sequential pairs of items from the list.

All of this might sound complex, but you can actually make precise predictions about serial position memory with this model using nothing more complex than your calculator—as long as it has log and square root functions, that is. In fact, you will soon get a chance to set up this model and predict a serial position curve.

This brings up an important strength of the temporal distinctiveness model. Although apparently simple (you will see that there are only a handful of easy equations to deal with), this model has been able to describe a great deal of data. It has been used successfully to account for free recall of words (Neath, 1993a), recognition of different parts of complex sentences (Neath & Knoedler, 1994), and recognition of snowflakes (Neath, 1993b). And the distinctiveness model can work *without* assuming two distinct types of memory.

Now it is your turn to create a mathematical model to predict memory performance. Research Report 6 presents a set of data from an imaginary memory experiment and takes

RESEARCH REPORT 6: A Simple Mathematical Model of Memory

In this exercise, you will put together a mathematical model of serial position effects using a simplified version of the temporal distinctiveness model of Neath (1993a, 1993b). To complete this exercise, all you will need is a calculator with logarithmic and square root functions. The task you will model is the study and recognition of a four-item list. This might seem like an awfully short list, making the task extremely easy. But consider this: the items in the list are high-quality black-and-white photographs of snowflakes. Stop and think about this for a moment: Snowflakes are not items that can be easily rehearsed. So if information about the snowflakes could not be kept active in memory, how could we obtain a serial position effect? *Would we expect to obtain a serial position effect?* What would the Atkinson-Shiffrin model predict?

To see what the predictions of the temporal distinctiveness model are, we will complete Table 6A. We have left a number of the places blank for you to fill in during this exercise (but the answers are available in Table 6B at the end of the chapter).

TABLE 6A		**Calculations for Research Report 6: IPI = 1, RI = 1**			
(1) Item (k)	**(2) Initial** Value (I)	**(3)** s	**(4)** $d = \log(s_k)$	**(5)** ∂_k	**(6)** $\partial_k / \Sigma \partial_k$
1	1	4 (I × IPI + s2)	.602	1.028	
2	1	3 (I × IPI + s3)		.778	
3	1	2 (I × IPI + s4)			
4	1	1 (I × RI)	.000	————	
				(SUM)	

To begin, we need to establish values for IPI and RI. Let us assume that the time between the presentation of one item and the presentation of the next (the IPI) is 1 second and that the length of the retention interval (RI) is 1 second. Now we can start constructing predictions about performance in this task.

Step 1. List the items by serial position, in the first column, and give each item an initial value of 1 (in the second column).

Step 2. Calculate the estimate of the distance in time (s) from the subject, starting with the last item and working your way back to the first. (Why is it logical to do this?) To calculate s for Item 4, we multiply the initial value (1) by the value of the RI. For the rest of the items, we multiply I by the value of the IPI and add that to the s value for the item that follows it.

Step 3. Calculate the initial estimate of discriminability (*d*) for each item by taking the logarithm of the s value. We have done this for Items 1 and 4. You should do the same now for Items 2 and 3.

Step 4. Calculate the distinctiveness (*∂*) of each item. To start, we calculate the following quantity:

$$\sum_{j=1}^{n}\sqrt{\left(d_k-d_j\right)^2}$$

In this equation, the subscripts j and k refer to items in the list. The term n refers to the total number of items in the list and the symbol $\sum_{j=1}^{n}$ tells us to sum, or add up, all of the values in $\sqrt{\left(d_k-d_j\right)^2}$ for the entire list. Thus, to calculate this quantity, for each item (k), we in turn subtract the d value of every item in the list (the js) from the d value for the item, square the difference, take the square root of the result, and add all of those together. Here is how to do it:

For item 1:

$$\sum_{j=1}^{n}\sqrt{\left(d_k-d_j\right)^2}=\sqrt{(.602-.602)^2}+\sqrt{(.602-.477)^2}+\sqrt{(.602-.301)^2}+\sqrt{(.602-.000)^2}$$

$$\sum_{j=1}^{n}\sqrt{\left(d_k-d_j\right)^2}=.000+.125+.301+.602$$

$$\sum_{j=1}^{n}\sqrt{\left(d_k-d_j\right)^2}=1.028$$

For item 2:

$$\sum_{j=1}^{n}\sqrt{\left(d_k-d_j\right)^2}=\sqrt{(.477-.602)^2}+\sqrt{(.477-.477)^2}+\sqrt{(.477-.301)^2}+\sqrt{(.477-.000)^2}$$

$$\sum_{j=1}^{n}\sqrt{\left(d_k-d_j\right)^2}=.778$$

For item 3:

$$\sum_{j=1}^{n}\sqrt{\left(d_k-d_j\right)^2}=\sqrt{(.301-.602)^2}+\sqrt{(.301-.477)^2}+\sqrt{(.301-.301)^2}+\sqrt{(.301-.000)^2}$$

$$\sum_{j=1}^{n}\sqrt{\left(d_k-d_j\right)^2}=$$

For item 4:

$$\sum_{j=1}^{n}\sqrt{\left(d_k-d_j\right)^2}=\sqrt{(.000-.602)^2}+\sqrt{(.000-.477)^2}+\sqrt{(.000-.301)^2}+\sqrt{(.000-.000)^2}$$

$$\sum_{j=1}^{n}\sqrt{\left(d_k-d_j\right)^2}=$$

Again, the values we just calculated are the distinctiveness values. Enter the values you calculated for these items in the proper places in the table. We are almost done—only two steps left.

Step 5. Add up all the ∂ values and enter the result at the bottom of Column 5 in the table.

Step 6. Calculate the predicted proportion correct by dividing each item's distinctiveness value by the sum of all the distinctiveness values. Enter each result in Column 6.

You have just made predictions about performance in this recognition task by using a simple quantitative model. To check how well your model performs, graph the values you obtained. How well do you think the model did in capturing a serial position curve? As an extra exercise, you might try changing the values of the IPI and RI and see how your predictions change.

you step-by-step through setting up and producing predictions for performance using the temporal distinctiveness model. We think this exercise will help you see how transforming a model from metaphor to math can allow you to make reasonably precise predictions with relative ease.

Changes in Precision Across Time   The temporal distinctiveness model deals with what at one time would have been called the level of activation, or the strength of the memory information. *Activation* and *strength* are metaphorical terms similar to the resonance metaphor described earlier in this chapter. Intuitively, all three of these metaphors (activation, strength, and resonance) seem positively related to memory performance. Basically, the higher the level of activation, strength, or resonance, the greater the likelihood of recognizing or recalling the information. Conversely, as the activation, strength, or resonance dies down, the likelihood of recognizing or recalling the information should go down as well. Looked at another way, as activation, strength, or resonance dies down, the likelihood of an *error* should *increase*. Actually, errors increase as time passes in very regular ways. One of these ways involves the decreasing precision of memory.

To get a sense of what this relationship might look like, consider this simple experiment: Subjects are presented with a list of items to learn; and then, after some retention interval, the items are presented again. The subjects' task is to put the items in their original order. If we think of each item in the studied list as a sort of "mini-event," then we can see that this task requires memory for both the mini-events and the order in which the mini-events occurred. This requirement is like needing to remember what things occurred within a larger event (such as the specific things that happened during a bank robbery) as well as the order in which those things occurred.

In experiments like this, we find two things. First, not surprisingly, people make mistakes. Second, and more importantly, these mistakes most often involve placing an item *near* but not *at* its correct position. In terms of our bank robbery example, a person making this sort of mistake might say that the second thing that happened was that the robbers shouted "Hands in the air!" when in reality this was the third thing that happened. In fact, we notice this pattern of errors whether we test subjects after only 30 seconds or after as long as 4 hours.

Another consistent finding in these experiments is that the positions with the fewest errors are the initial and final positions in the list. Here again, the pattern shows up for both short and long retention intervals. What we might conclude from these patterns is that people seem to be reasonably good at remembering the *relative* positions of items they learn, but some confusion occurs as the retention interval increases, and this confusion seems to occur less for items at the beginning and end of the list.

One way of thinking about how this might happen is to imagine a model in which the individual items in a list are represented as ping-pong balls and the list itself as an egg carton with very high sides, particularly at the ends. Each of the balls is numbered. Each of the indentations in the egg carton is also numbered, and the numbering represents the actual positions of the items. Thus, studying the list of items can be modeled as putting Ball 1 into Indentation 1, Ball 2 into Indentation 2, and so on.

At the end of the list presentation, the retention interval begins. But imagine that for the duration of the retention interval, we shake the egg carton. What do you think will happen to the balls? Some of the balls will pop out of their indentations and go into the indentations next to them. At the end of the RI, when we stop shaking the carton, some of the balls will not be in their correct positions.

The process of moving the balls around is referred to technically as *perturbation,* because the items are perturbed (that is, in general terms, shaken up), and we refer to this model as the *perturbation model*. The general idea behind the notion of perturbation is that position changes across time. Such changes can be produced by some active process (like shaking the egg carton) or by a more passive process. For example, instead of thinking of the list items as balls in an egg carton, we can think of them as helium balloons in a drafty gymnasium. In this case, the random breezes inside the gymnasium perturb the balloons and change their positions.

An original use of the idea of perturbation of memory was presented by Estes (1972; Lee & Estes, 1977, 1981) with later applications and refinements by Nairne (1991, 1992). As with the temporal distinctiveness model, the actual mathematics needed to transform the metaphor into quantitative predictions is reasonably simple. In the simplest case, we need only one unspecified number: the probability that memory for any item in any position will undergo a perturbation and shift into a neighboring position. This is equivalent to knowing the overall probability that any one of the balls will bounce out of its indentation and go into a neighboring indentation.

Using this method, we can predict the probability of recalling each item in its correct position and the probability of recalling each item in an incorrect position. Nairne (1992) did this for five-item lists at retention intervals of 30 seconds, 4 hours, and 24 hours, and the perturbation model predicted the pattern of recall by position quite well (see Figure 6.8a). Because of this, the model also predicted the *overall* level of recall at each of the different retention intervals quite well (see Figure 6.8b). Several things are important to note. One is that the perturbation model worked for a retention interval that would usually define a short-term task (30 seconds) and for retention intervals that would usually define long-term tasks (4 hours and 24 hours). And it did this without an assumption of two different types of memory for these different retention intervals. It was also able to account for memory for both item information and order information.

Capacity Limitations

As we mentioned earlier, one of the most basic questions concerning attention and memory in the short term is the amount of information that can be retained or processed in a given unit of time (Miller, 1956; Townsend & Ashby, 1983). This is a question about the **capacity** of the cognitive system.

One important aspect of memory in the short term is that the amount of information that can be used at any one point in time is variable. That is, a definition of the capacity of memory in the short term needs to take into account two things: the amount of information that can be held in memory and the amount of work that can be done with that information. In this section, we consider how psychologists have explored these two aspects of capacity of memory in the short term.

Measuring the Span of Memory in the Short Term   One common metaphor for memory is the storehouse—a place we put and store information (see Roediger, 1980, and Chapter 1 for more on metaphors in cognitive psychology). According to this metaphor, the question of capacity is a question about how much can be stored in the storehouse. The question is complicated a little by the fact that the items we are storing have a reasonably short "shelf life." That is, they seem to decay or become less usable as time goes by. So to get an accurate sense of capacity, we need to be able to measure it with reference to the time during which the stored items are the most usable.

The simplest way of figuring out how many items a storehouse can hold is simply to count the number of items that are there. In terms of a memory experiment, we might do

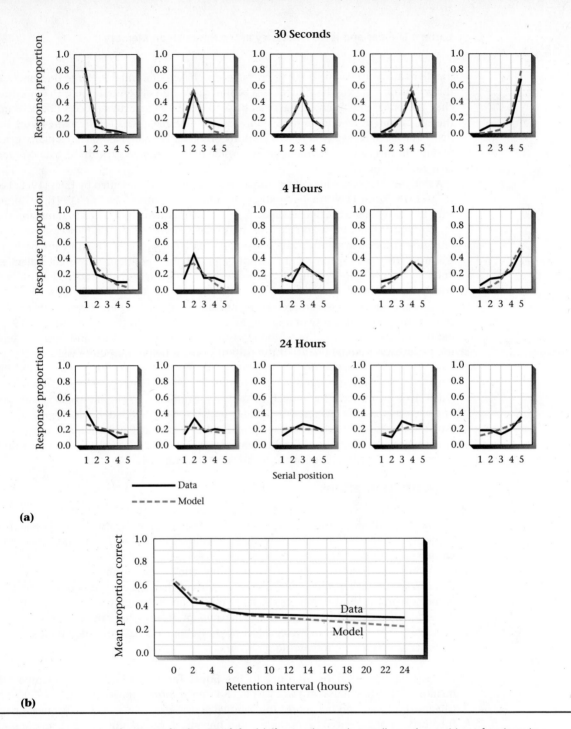

FIGURE 6.8 **The Perturbation Model** (a) If you ask people to tell you the position of an item in a studied list, most of their responses will be centered on the actual position. This pattern shows up whether testing occurs soon after the study session or after a reasonably long period of time has gone by. The perturbation model predicts this pattern of performance quite well. (b) The perturbation model that predicts the specific patterns of recall is also able to predict the overall level of performance quite well. Source: Nairne, 1992.

this by having subjects report how much they remember. But that might not be as simple as it sounds.

To get a sense of some possible complications, imagine that you are a subject in a memory experiment. The experimenter begins the trial by having a computer display the letter strings KAC, GIF, and BUV one at a time, in order. Then, after some predetermined amount of time has passed, the experimenter asks you to repeat the strings. Now think about what might be happening to your memory for the letter strings as time passes, including the time required to repeat each string. You might have the sense that your memory is getting "fuzzier." Psychologists have taken into account this sense of increasing "fuzziness" as a function of time in their definition of the span of memory.

The *span* of memory in the short term is generally defined as the number of items in a list that, half of the time, can be recalled in correct order immediately after being presented (Schweickert, 1993). As illustrated by our discussion of the distinctiveness and perturbation models, however, it is important to consider not only how much information is presented (in this case, the total number of items) but also what is going on as time goes by. In the case of a span test, what is going on is that the subject is saying the words being recalled. If the subject says the items quickly, a short amount of time passes. If the subject says the words slowly, a long amount of time passes. It should come as no surprise, then, to realize that the measure of span needs to take into account the rate at which the items can be spoken or pronounced.

A model for memory span that takes these factors into account was proposed by Baddeley, Thomson, and Buchanan (1975). Let s represent the measure of span (in items), r represent the rate at which these items can be pronounced (in items per second), and t represent the time required to pronounce s items in t seconds (a measure of the time it takes for the information to decay to unusable levels). Then span can be calculated as follows:

$$s = rt$$

The relationship is sometimes stated another way:

$$s = rt + c$$

In this second equation, c represents what we might think of as the absolute minimum number of items that will be reported. Some researchers have suggested that c represents a contribution from memory in the long term (Hulme, Maughan & Brown, 1991), while others have suggested that a non-zero value of c is simply something that results from averaging the performance of a number of subjects (Schweickert, Guentert, & Hersberger, 1990).

A great many studies have found that, over a wide variety of types of materials and under a range of experimental conditions, the estimate of t comes out consistently to be about two seconds (Baddeley, Thomson & Buchanan, 1975; Hulme et al., 1984). This means that memory information in these tasks decays in about two seconds. It also means that one of the major things that determines the span of memory in the short term is the rate at which the items can be pronounced.

Recent research suggests that it *is* possible to affect span by changing the value of t (the useful lifetime of the information). For example, Hulme and Tordoff (1989) and Schweickert and colleagues (1990) found that if the items to be remembered sound very similar to each other, the value of t is reduced (and thus span is reduced) without affecting r, the rate at which the items can be pronounced. And this happens without changing the relationship described by the equations above.

The Neurology of Memory Span and Sentence Processing A number of researchers have suggested that the limitations of memory in the short term are critical in the comprehension and use of language (e.g., Crowder, 1982; Shiffrin, 1993). Humans use language in various forms—for example, spoken and written. In fact, some neuropsychological evidence suggests that certain memory abilities or processes may be specialized for visual and auditory language information.

For example, in some cases, amnesic individuals have deficits that are specific to phonological (sound-based) information. That is, their memory spans are reduced only for phonological information and not for visual information (Martin, 1993; Shallice & Vallar, 1990). Some research done in the 1970s and 1980s suggested that this phonological storage deficit was related in some way to the ability to find and use the semantic (meaningful) information in a sentence (we discuss sentence and language processing further in later chapters). For example, studies of patients who appeared to have deficits that were specific to phonological information indicated that these individuals also had trouble remembering both the structure and the meaning of sentences (Caramazza et al., 1981; Saffran & Marin, 1975).

More recent research, however, raises questions about whether a memory deficit for phonological information is related to any more general memory deficit in processing language. For example, Martin (1993; Martin, Shelton & Yaffee, 1993) reported a series of intensive studies with a single patient who showed an impairment in memory for phonological information. This patient displayed essentially normal levels of performance on tasks that required the detection of a number of subtle changes in language and was also able to repeat with a high degree of accuracy the "gist," or meaning, of sentences. These findings are consistent with those of other studies of patients with specific types of memory deficits (e.g., Baddeley et al., 1988; Butterworth, Campbell & Howard, 1986; Waters, Caplan & Hildebrandt, 1991). In general, it appears that whatever deficit these individuals might have is restricted to memory for phonological information; their performance on language tasks is impaired only to the degree that the tasks require memory for phonological information.

The interesting thing to note about these conclusions is that they suggest the possible existence of specific subsystems of memory dedicated to different types of information. It might seem surprising that we point this out, given that we have argued that there is no reason to think there are specialized subsystems of memory (as least insofar as time scales are concerned). But data such as those presented by Martin are intriguing and could provide strong evidence for specific subsystems of memory. So while we do suggest postponing any strong conclusions about the numbers and types of memory systems, we also suggest that you keep an open mind.

Control Processes

Up to now, we have not discussed how a person might retrieve information from memory in the short term. Only a few explicit models address how retrieval, or any other process of memory in the short term, is controlled (Shiffrin, 1993). In this section, we present three models that deal with retrieval: one that deals with how retrieval might take place as the information in memory is becoming less usable, one that attempts to provide a comprehensive account of how memory in the short term is controlled, and one that is based on emerging knowledge about how the brain might represent and control memory in the short term.

Redintegration in Recall   Earlier, when we defined the basic measure of memory span, we mentioned that this measure depends on the rate at which items can be pronounced. We saw that the upper limit on memory span is, in part, determined by the time it takes for the information in memory to become so degraded that it is not usable. However, it is possible to recall information that is degraded if, for example, something can be done to reconstruct or refresh the degraded information. One such process of reconstruction is referred to as **redintegration** (pronounced "re-dintegration" rather than "red-integration").

Relatively little information is available on how redintegration might work (Cowan & Morse, 1986). Recently, however, Schweickert (1993) has proposed a simple model for redintegration in short-term memory tasks. The model he developed is presented as a processing tree diagram (see Figure 6.9). To read a processing tree diagram, you begin on the left side. A path through the diagram comprises a series of branches by which you go from the left side to a point on the right side. Making it to the far right side of the diagram means that processing is complete for a single trial. Because of the structure of the diagram, it is possible to assign a probability to each branch. The probability of taking any path from the left side to the right side is the product of the probabilities of the branches traveled on that path.

Now, assume we are considering a memory task in which a subject reads and then recalls a short list of words. According to this model, at the beginning of the memory test, there are only two possibilities for the information in memory: The information can be either intact enough to directly support responding or not. Thus, if we let I represent the probability that the information is intact enough, then the probability that the information is *not* intact enough is $1 - I$. These two possibilities form the first two branches of the tree diagram in Figure 6.9.

FIGURE 6.9   **A Processing Tree Model of Redintegration**   The model represents the process of redintegration in memory in the short term. Each possible path from the left to the right side is a way in which a correct or incorrect response can be produced in a memory task. The branch labeled I represents processing when the memory information is intact enough to support a correct response. The branch labeled R indicates that the redintegration, or recovery, process is being used to support a correct response.

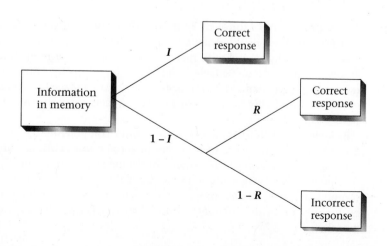

We have already noted that we seem to be able to recover or rebuild memory information when it has been diminished. Consequently, the model would be incomplete if it stopped at the ends of the first two branches. Specifically, it must include a way for us to get a correct response if we end up traveling down the branch in Figure 6.9 that represents the probability that the memory information is not intact enough (the branch labeled $1 - I$).

To do this, Schweickert's model proposes that a *reconstructive* process can be used. This process is represented in the model by the branch labeled R, where R is the probability that the reconstructive process can recover or rebuild the information to allow for a correct response. If the reconstructive process fails, as represented by the branch labeled $1 - R$, then an incorrect response is produced.

We now have two ways of getting a correct response, one using intact information and the other using a reconstructive process. This latter probability can be expressed as $(1 - I) \times R$, and the overall probability of getting a correct response can be expressed as $I + [(1 - I) \times R]$. The overall probability of getting an incorrect response is expressed as $(1 - I) \times (1 - R)$, which represents the probability that the information is not intact enough *and* the reconstructive process fails.

We have presented here a simplified version of Schweickert's model. Schweickert (1993) used refined versions of the model to predict the outcomes of an experiment conducted by Besner and Davelaar (1982), who were able to affect memory span by manipulating the degree of phonological similarity among the words to be remembered. In addition to accounting for the outcomes of this experiment, Schweickert demonstrated how the general approach represented in Figure 6.9 can be used to develop alternative models for redintegration. In doing this, Schweickert obtained a set of contrasting predictions for a set of alternative models. Since he was able to obtain contrasting predictions, he was able to *reject* some of the alternative models, because the observed data did not correspond to their predictions.

Two aspects of this work are important. First, like the distinctiveness and perturbation models, Schweickert's approach has no need for a specialized short-term memory. Although the model has not been applied to long-term tasks, it assumes nothing that precludes such an application. Second, Schweickert was able to confidently reject some models on the basis of precise predictions made by the models. This would have been much more difficult (perhaps impossible) if the models had not been put into mathematical form.

A Comprehensive Model of Working Memory   The model we present in this section was proposed by Baddeley and Hitch (1974) and described in detail by Baddeley (1986) specifically to deal with memory as something that both stores information *and* processes information. Baddeley and Hitch intentionally chose the term **working memory,** rather than *short-term memory* or *primary memory,* to emphasize the fact that they were considering the processing aspects of memory in the short term along with the storage aspects.

Baddeley and Hitch's model consists of three components. The first is a *central executive,* which directs the use of resources in specific tasks (Just & Carpenter, 1992). This component of the model can roughly be thought of as attention. The central executive is responsible for integrating sound and visual information from each of the other two component systems. In addition, it provides the link to stored information—what might be thought of as the long-term store from the perspective of the Atkinson-Shiffrin model.

The remaining two components are specific to the modality (i.e., visual or auditory) of the information on which they work. The first is the *articulatory loop,* which operates on sound information. The articulatory loop itself consists of two component subsystems. The first is a *phonological store,* similar to the phonological memory discussed earlier (Martin, 1993). The second is an *articulatory control process*. The store and the process that controls it have the capacity to work with only a limited amount of information and to preserve that information for only about two seconds. This makes Baddeley and Hitch's model consistent with the span data that we reviewed earlier.

The second of the two modality-specific systems is called the *visuo-spatial scratchpad*. This component of working memory is specialized to visual information. It operates on information such as abstract images and pictures (Baddeley & Lieberman, 1980; Sadoski, Paivio & Goetz, 1991). Like the phonological store, the visuo-spatial scratchpad is assumed to have a limited capacity in terms of both the number of items that can be held and the duration of the information (Brandimonte, Hitch & Bishop, 1992).

Baddeley and Hitch's model has been very influential. It has seen useful application in a variety of domains, such as general models of language comprehension (Just & Carpenter, 1992), neuropsychological investigations of language processing (Martin, 1993, sentence processing), and comprehension of computer-based text (Wenger & Payne, 1996). The model has also inspired efforts to link the various components to structures in the nervous system by way of connectionist models (Schneider & Detweiler, 1987; 1988).

To be sure, problems have arisen. For example, the reality of the specific subsystems has been questioned, along with their modality- or stimulus-specific nature (Turner & Engle, 1989). However, just as the Atkinson-Shiffrin model was extremely useful in directing research that, eventually, called it into question, so has Baddeley and Hitch's model of working memory been useful in helping researchers frame interesting research questions. It remains to be seen whether the data that result will put the model of working memory in a historical position similar to that of the Atkinson-Shiffrin model in terms of its impact on cognitive psychology.

Memory in the Short Term and the Nervous System   Two aspects of the biology of the nervous system seem important for memory in the short term. First, an aspect of *activity decay* is associated with all biological signals (recall the notions of activation, strength, and resonance we discussed earlier). That is, for any type of biological signal, such as an action potential or neurotransmitter, a period of decay follows the initial action. For example, each of the neurotransmitters produces a change in the membrane potential of the receiving cell. Following the initial change, the level of the potential returns to the resting level. The time required for this decay ranges from milliseconds to seconds, depending on the specific type of neurotransmitter (Hille, 1992; McCormick, 1990). A number of scientists have taken note of the fact that this range of decay times corresponds quite well to the range of decay times observed for the various sensory memories (Long, 1980; Schneider, 1993).

The second important biological aspect of the nervous system that is important for memory in the short term is the notion of *sustained recurrent activation*. Basically, it appears that certain areas of the cortex can be maintained in active states over short time periods (less than 10 seconds) (Brown, Wilson & Riches, 1987; Bruce & Goldberg, 1985; Funahashi, Bruce & Goldman-Rakic, 1989; Gnadt & Andersen, 1988; Miyashita & Chang, 1988). These sustained levels of activity appear to support performance on a variety of tasks in which the activated regions are involved in the initial presentation of a stimulus. When these regions are maintained in active states, responses to subsequent presentations of the same or a related stimulus are much less error-prone than when the activity in these regions dies down before presentation of the stimulus.

Findings like these have inspired a number of scientists working with computational models based on nervous system structure. For example, Zipser (1991) and Shedden and Schneider (1990) have used connectionist systems to model the effects of sustained activation in cerebral regions. The success such approaches suggests that models inspired by the basic biology and activity of the nervous system can capture important aspects of cognition. We consider these connectionist models in more detail in Chapter 13.

Section Summary: Recency in Research on Memory in the Short Term

Current research explores three themes concerning memory in the short term, each linked in important ways to the history of study in this field. The first theme has to do with changes in the ability to access information across short time intervals, an ability that can be described in terms of the relative distinctiveness of items as a function of two aspects of time (the time between items and the time from the last item to the test of memory) and how this might produce serial position functions. The temporal distinctiveness model can predict these serial position effects on the basis of a precise relationship between the retention interval and the item interpresentation interval. And it can make these predictions for a wide range of materials, including sentences and snowflakes. Another source for serial position effects might be decreases in the precision of memory for the ordering of items across time. The perturbation model shows how these types of changes might produce serial position effects and (along with the temporal distinctiveness model) show how such effects can be predicted without the need to assume distinct types of memory (e.g., short-term and long-term).

The second theme has to do with research probing aspects of the capacity of memory in the short term. An important measure of capacity is the span of memory, generally defined as the number of items in a list that, half of the time, can be recalled in correct order immediately after being presented. Recent neurological evidence suggests that capacity in the short term may be specific to different types of information.

The third theme has to do with the types of processes that might control memory in the short term. Information that may have become degraded over time might still be able to support memory through a process called redintegration. A simplified model for redintegration shows how this process might work, without the assumption of specialized subsystems of memory. In contrast, a comprehensive model of working memory, one that explicitly assumes different subsystems, has proven to be very influential in understanding how memory in the short term might be controlled. Consideration of basic physiological characteristics of the nervous system also provides important clues as to how memory in the short term might be controlled.

REVIEWING MEMORY IN THE SHORT TERM

CONCEPT REVIEW

1. Define *acquisition, retention,* and *retrieval.* Provide some examples of how each has been studied relative to memory in the short term.

2. Define *engram* and review the history of the search for the engram in the nervous system. Does the idea of an engram relate more to how information is stored or how it is processed? Why would it be important to consider this distinction?

3. Describe the two types of interference that can be observed in memory tasks. Describe the Brown-Peterson task and explain how the results of experiments using this task relate to interference and the hypothesis of distinct types of memory.

4. Describe and define the parts of a serial position curve. How did the study of the serial position effect influence the debate over the number and types of memory systems?

5. Describe the architecture and control processes of the Atkinson-Shiffrin model. Explain how the model accounts for a wide variety of phenomena, including serial position effects, performance in the Brown-Peterson task, sensory memory, and capacity. What are some problems with this model?

6. Describe the temporal distinctiveness and perturbation models. What types of data are each model designed to predict and explain? How and why are the models different from earlier theories of decay and interference?

7. How is the span of memory in the short term defined? What aspects of performance seem to be important in determining this span?

8. Define *redintegration,* and explain why it might be important to propose such an idea.

9. Describe Baddeley's model for working memory. In particular, explain how the model describes how memory information is stored and how it is processed.

10. What two important aspects of the nervous system may be responsible for producing the results observed in experiments on memory in the short term? How do these aspects relate to the general debate over the possibility that there might be distinct types of memory?

11. A central theme that runs through this chapter is whether memory in the short term is distinct from memory in the long term. To understand the evidence for and against each view, try this simple activity. Put "memory" on trial. That is, imagine that someone has accused "memory" of being composed of two parts: a short-term part and a long-term part. You will need to recruit three groups of students: one to act as prosecutors, one to act as defense counsels, and a third to act as a jury. The prosecutors are responsible for presenting evidence (from this chapter and possibly from other chapters) to support the accusation. The defense counsels are responsible for presenting evidence (from this and possibly other chapters) to refute the accusation. After the cases have been presented, let the jury decide: On the basis of the evidence, does it appear that there are two types of memory? Or is there a reasonable doubt that this is the case? This exercise should give you some sense of the issues that working scientists are considering concerning memory in the short term.

KEY TERMS

acquisition (p. 178)
architecture (p. 188)
Brown-Peterson distractor task (p. 181)

capacity (p. 199)
consolidation hypothesis (p. 179)
control process (p. 188)

discrimination ratio (p. 195)
encoding (p. 178)
engram (p. 179)

KEY TERMS (*continued*)

interference (p. 180)
interpresentation interval (IPI)
  (p. 195)
memory trace (p. 179)
primacy effect (p. 186)
proactive interference (p. 180)

recency effect (p. 186)
redintegration (p. 203)
release from proactive interference
  (p. 183)
retention (p. 178)

retention interval (RI) (p. 195)
retrieval (p. 178)
retroactive interference (p. 180)
serial position effect (p. 183)
working memory (p. 204)

SUGGESTED READINGS

Alan Baddeley (1986) offers, in the initial chapters of *Working memory* (Oxford: Clarendon Press), a readable and balanced review of the research that suggested the need for an alternative to the modal model. This book also covers, in detail, the development of the working memory model. In "The demise of short-term memory" (*Acta Psychologica, 50,* 291–323), Robert Crowder (1982a) presents a concise set of arguments to support the lack of necessity for a distinct short-term memory. This article is one of the most cited papers in the literature on the distinction. The papers collected in the September 1993 issue of the journal *Memory and Cognition*

offer a fascinating set of contrasting views on current research on memory in the short term. The story of Richard Semon, the scientist who coined the term "engram," is related by Daniel Schacter, in his book, *Stranger behind the engram,* Hillsdale, NJ: Erlbaum, 1982. Finally, if you are interested in the general ways in which mathematics relates to and is applied in psychological research, James Townsend and Helena Kadlec (1990) provide a readable and intriguing introduction in a book chapter entitled "Psychology and mathematics" (pp. 224–248 in R. E. Mickens, Ed., *Mathematics and science,* Singapore: World Scientific).

TABLE 6B   **Solutions for Research Report 6**

(1) Item (k)	(2) Initial Value (I)	(3) s	(4) $d = \log(s_k)$	(5) ∂_k	(6) $\partial_k/\Sigma\partial_k$
1	1	4 (I × IPI + s2)	.602	1.028	.259
2	1	3 (I × IPI + s3)	.477	.778	.196
3	1	2 (I × IPI + s4)	.301	.778	.196
4	1	1 (I × RI)	.000	1.380	.348
				3.964 (SUM)	

7 Memory in the Long Term: Episodic Memory

I began thinking of words that subjects learned as to-be-remembered *events*, rather than, as conventional wisdom had it, to-be-remembered *items*. . . . One of the immediate consequences of thinking of word-events in memory experiments was my "discovery" of what many wise philosophers from Heraclitus on had known all the time: events do not repeat themselves, there is never another event exactly like a given one.—Endel Tulving (1983, p. 19)

ITH THIS CHAPTER, we begin a two-part study of how we use memory in the long term. We start by considering tasks that depend on memory for information that is in some way specific to the event during which it was learned. We are concerned here with memory for the *details* of things we have experienced.

In Chapter 6, we discussed a distinction between types of memory that was based on the amount of time involved between encoding and retrieval. In this chapter and the next, we take up another distinction: the distinction between *episodic* and *semantic memory* (Tulving, 1972; Tulving, 1983). Although these terms are probably not as familiar to you as *short-term* and *long-term memory,* we think you will come to understand why they have been almost as important.

Journalists are trained to ask six questions about any story they cover: What? Who? Where? When? Why? How? If they can get the people they interview to answer these questions, then they will know most of the critical information about the event. For example, suppose a reporter is covering a bank robbery. Witnesses to the robbery might provide the following answers to the reporter's first four questions: "a bank robbery," "by a gang wearing clown masks," "at the First Intergalactic Bank on Main Street," "at 3:15 this afternoon."

The first question and answer define *what* the event was (a bank robbery). In order to label the event as a bank robbery (rather than a circus or some other event), the witnesses must use knowledge that is not specific to the particular bank robbery they witnessed; they must rely on memory for general information, such as the meaningful characteristics of different types of events. This type of memory information is referred to as **semantic memory information**—information that has general meaning and is not specific to any particular event.

In contrast, other questions and answers require information that *is* specific to the event. For example, in order to answer questions about who, where, and when, witnesses *must* rely on their memories of the specific event (the bank robbery). This type of memory information is referred to as **episodic memory information**—information that is specific to a particular event.

The logical distinction between episodic and semantic memory information relies on a distinction between memory *tasks.* This is the same logic that we encountered in Chapter 6, when we discussed the differences between memory in the short term and memory in the long term. Given that we are dealing with the same type of logic, we need to be careful that we do not make a logical error similar to the one discussed in Chapter 6. That is, the fact that we need to remember general (semantic) and event-specific (episodic) information does not mean we have two different types of *memory.* What we can say is that we seem to be able to identify two logically distinct types of *information;* and as you will soon see, we can do different things with these two types of information. We begin by reviewing how the distinction between episodic and semantic information came to be important.

A HISTORY OF MEMORY DISTINCTIONS

The scientific study of memory is commonly traced to Herrmann von Ebbinghaus, a German scientist working around the same time (the late nineteenth century) as Wilhelm Wundt, the first scientist to establish a psychology laboratory (Slamecka, 1985). Ebbinghaus was familiar with Wundt's work, but he never worked with Wundt (Watson, 1968). Whereas Wundt believed that "higher" processes (such as memory) were not amenable to scientific study, Ebbinghaus believed that scientific methods could be used to study these higher processes.

Ebbinghaus and the Types of Information in Memory

Ebbinghaus did not work in an established laboratory, so he did not have access to subjects and equipment. Consequently, he was forced to be creative. He had to develop new experimental tasks, new materials, and new ways of quantifying the outcomes of his experiments. And he had to do all this while being the *only* subject in his experiments.

Ebbinghaus was interested in the fundamental properties of memory, independent of the type of information placed in memory. He noted that items that have meaning by themselves or in combination (like words) would exert "a multiplicity of influences which change without regularity and are therefore disturbing" (Ebbinghaus, 1885/1913, p. 23). Essentially, he knew that unless he could control what was already in memory, he would not have experimental control over all the factors involved in the acquisition, retention, and retrieval of new information.

So he invented new stimuli and a new task. The stimuli were nonsense syllables made up of a consonant, a vowel, and another consonant, such as BIM and KAJ. The experimental task that Ebbinghaus used is now called a **relearning task.** To perform this task, Ebbinghaus practiced a list of nonsense syllables until he could recall the entire list to a specified level of accuracy. Then he allowed a certain amount of time to go by, after which he relearned the list to the original level of accuracy. By removing meaning and prior knowledge as confounding factors, carefully specifying the degree of initial learning, controlling the time between original learning and later test, and carefully relating the conditions of the later test to the original learning, Ebbinghaus brought aspects of acquisition, retention, and retrieval under a high degree of experimental control.

Ebbinghaus called the dependent measure in the relearning task a **savings score.** He counted the number of trials he originally needed to learn a list to some criterion level (say, 100 percent correct recall), then counted the number of trials he later needed to relearn the list to the same level. Assume, for example, that 10 trials were required to learn the list the first time and, later, 8 trials were required to relearn the list. If we take the difference (10 − 8 = 2), divide by the original number of trials required (2 ÷ 10 = .20), and then multiply by 100 percent, we get the amount of original learning that was saved (20 percent).

Ebbinghaus tracked savings as a function of the elapsed time between original learning and relearning. The result is the famous "forgetting curve," shown in Figure 7.1. Note that the major amount of forgetting appears to occur shortly after relearning, reaching its maximum after about six days.

Ebbinghaus's careful control of the conditions of his experiment, his concern for the type of information with which he was working, his development of new methods and

Herrmann von Ebbinghaus
The modern scientific study of memory owes much to the pioneering efforts of Hermann von Ebbinghaus, whose methods and results were summarized in a book published in 1885. Ebbinghaus was a contemporary of Wilhelm Wundt but, unlike Wundt, believed that "higher" cognitive processes (such as memory) could be studied scientifically. *Archives of the History of American Psychology, University of Akron, Akron, Ohio 44325-4302.*

tools, and his remarkable dedication to his work set standards for all memory researchers who have followed him (Murdock, 1985).

Types of Information in Memory in the Long Term

Although Ebbinghaus did not make an explicit distinction between episodic and semantic memory information, he did note that existing memory for meaning could easily disturb his experimental results. Endel Tulving (1972; 1983), working at the University of Toronto, is commonly given credit for focusing psychologists' attention on the differences between episodic and semantic memory. However, there are several historical precedents for the distinction (Herrmann, 1982; Hintzman, 1978). In this section, we concentrate on some of the work that contributed to the development of the distinction between episodic and semantic memory information.

Episodic and Semantic Information   Imagine a simple memory experiment. In this experiment, you ask a friend to remember five words: *bashful, cheetah, dog, burrito,* and *treasure*. Your friend studies these words; then, some time later, you ask her to recall the words that she studied. Since you are asking her to remember something (the list of words) that is specific to an event (the study episode), we can consider this an episodic memory task. But is all the knowledge needed to perform on the test really acquired during the study episode? The answer to this question, obviously, is no. Your friend's performance on the test depends in large part on information she has in memory before she participates in your experiment (e.g., knowing what the words in the list mean).

Now consider a second question: Would the information originally acquired be equally likely to be retrieved in different settings? For example, assuming your friend knows what

---

FIGURE 7.1   **The Forgetting Curve of Ebbinghaus**   The figure shows the amount of original learning that was saved at relearning as a function of the amount of time between original learning and relearning.

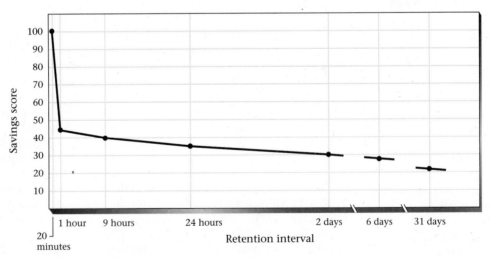

Source: Ashcraft, 1989.

a taco is, could you affect her ability to recall the list term *burrito* in response to the cue *taco* by testing her in a Mexican restaurant? The answer to this second question is, more than likely, yes. Your friend is probably more likely to remember *burrito* in response to *taco* in a Mexican restaurant than in your dorm room.

Observations like these were critical to the development of the distinction between episodic and semantic memory. Tulving (1983) pointed out that in the 1950s and 1960s most psychologists who were studying human memory made the assumption that, under the proper acquisition conditions, information acquired during an experiment and information acquired before the experiment could be thought of in the same way. In contrast, Tulving identified five issues logically separating episodic and semantic memory information.

The first issue concerns information about the co-occurrence of events in time. Episodic memory information includes such information, while semantic memory information does not. The second issue in the distinction between episodic and semantic memory concerns the types of associations involved in each. Particularly important here are associations specific to a person's life experiences. Episodic memories have some type of autobiographical reference, in Tulving's view, while semantic memories do not (Tulving, 1983, p. 24).

The third issue has to do with the conditions required for retrieval and the consequences of retrieving the two types of memories. For semantic memories, aspects of the learning situation are not especially important for retrieval, according to this view. For episodic memories, these same aspects are very important. Retrieving a semantic memory does not change the amount or strength of the information in memory, while retrieving an episodic memory leads to an increase in or a strengthening of the information.

The fourth issue involves the degree to which interference affects the two types of memory information. According to this view, semantic memory is less susceptible to associative interference. Semantic memory information has reasonably high levels of strength and so can be retrieved equally well with a variety of associated cues. In fact, a reasonable amount of evidence in the literature seemed to support this conclusion (Bower & Reitman, 1972; Slamecka, 1966). In contrast, episodic memory information was thought to be highly susceptible to interference. As we saw in Chapter 6 when we discussed the Brown-Peterson task, interference for items with little meaning could be shown to be very susceptible to interference.

The final issue concerns the degree to which semantic and episodic memory information can be dealt with independently of each other. Although Tulving noted that episodic and semantic memory need to work together, he assumed that they can be treated as nearly distinct systems. With this assumption, he was free to treat semantic and episodic memory as independent, or at the least as varying between a high degree of independence and a high degree of dependence. Basically, semantic and episodic memory in this view are two distinct types of memory in the long term.

About ten years after he made his original proposal, Tulving (1983, p. 27) acknowledged that one of the things he may have overlooked in his 1972 proposal was the fact that memories for information specific to some episode also have semantic content, and memories with semantic content can have a great deal of associated episodic content. An easy demonstration of this is the fact that many people can remember what they were doing when they learned that President John Kennedy had been shot. Many people, too, can remember where they were when the space shuttle Challenger blew up. Such memories, which have been called **flashbulb memories,** have distinct meaningful and situational components (Brown & Kulik, 1977)

Endel Tulving
Born in Estonia in 1927, Endel Tulving studied medicine at the University of Heidelberg before emigrating to Canada in 1949. After doing honors work at the University of Toronto, he completed his doctorate at Harvard University, where he studied with eminent psychologists such as E. G. Boring, G. A. Miller, and B. F. Skinner. He spent much of his professional career at the University of Toronto and was a founding member of the Ebbinghaus empire. Recently, he has turned his attention to the study of brain processes that are important to memory.

In the decade following Tulving's proposal, researchers carefully investigated the possible differences between episodic and semantic memories. A number of these studies looked for a dissociation between episodic and semantic memory. A **dissociation** occurs when an experimental variable has certain effects on one type of memory and distinct and different effects on another type of memory. For example, Jacoby (1983b) documented a dissociation between two measures of memory as a function of the type of study task. In brief, the study task that produced the *best* performance on one of the tasks produced the *worst* performance on the other.

Strong evidence for a dissociation between episodic and semantic memory requires the use of two tests of memory equated on all variables *except* the type of information to be retrieved or worked with (Neely, 1989; Neely & Payne, 1983). This might sound easy, but take a look at Table 7.1, where we list some of the things necessary to meet these conditions. As an exercise, see if you can list everything you would need to do to meet the conditions for the test introduced at the beginning of this section, "Episodic and Semantic Information" (good luck!).

Although a number of studies supported Tulving's episodic/semantic distinction, some did not. Nevertheless, because the distinction promoted much important and previously unimagined research (Ratcliff & McKoon, 1986), it has been suggested that the distinction is a good **heuristic.** That is, it is a good rule of thumb that can help psychologists in their investigations of aspects of memory (Neely, 1989) without necessarily being literally correct.

Item, Associative, and Order Information   The attention paid to Tulving's (1972) distinction in a sense overshadowed another important distinction made at about the same time by another important psychologist at the University of Toronto: Bennet Murdock. (So much memory research has been done at the University of Toronto that it is sometimes called the "Ebbinghaus empire"; Murdock, 1974, p. x.) Murdock (1974) suggested that memory operates using three different types of information: *item information, associative information,* and *order information.*

TABLE 7.1   **Testing for Dissociations**   Here are the things you would need to do to properly test for dissociations between episodic and semantic memory tasks.

1. Equate the items to be encoded and retrieved in each of the two tasks.
2. Equate the original encoding conditions for at least some of the test items in each of the tasks.
3. Equate the original encoding for the studied items using an instruction that tells subjects they will be tested (intentional encoding) and instructions that make no mention of a memory test (incidental encoding).
4. Use identical test lists.
5. Equate the way materials are presented.
6. Equate the ways subjects respond and the number of response alternatives.
7. Make certain that the episodic information and the semantic information are not correlated.

Source: Based on Neely, 1989.

To place Murdock's suggestion in historical context, remember that in 1974 the Atkinson-Shiffrin model of short-term and long-term stores in memory (discussed in Chapter 6) was only six years old, a theoretical "baby." Tulving's distinction between episodic and semantic memory, like Atkinson and Shiffrin's model, depended on temporal distinctions between types of memory systems or memory information. So at this point in history, two prominent distinctions relating to memory were based in some way on time. Murdock's proposal was radical in this context, because it was not based on specific temporal aspects of information. To understand how this is so, consider the following example.

Figure 7.2 is a picture of J. Danforth "Dan" Quayle, former vice president of the United

FIGURE 7.2   **Item, Associative, and Order Information**   We can use the picture of Dan Quayle, former vice president, to retrieve item, associative, and order information from memory.

| Item Information | Associative Information | Order Information |

States. This picture, if used as a retrieval cue, can allow us to retrieve a good deal of information from memory. For example, we can retrieve the name *Dan Quayle*. This involves using the picture to retrieve **item information**—information about the specific identity of the item. Quayle's picture might also cause us to remember that, not too long before he and President George Bush ran for reelection in 1992, Quayle gained some unfortunate fame for misspelling *potato* in a spelling bee. In this instance, we are using the picture to retrieve **associative information**—information associated with the item but not the item's specific identity. Finally, we can use the picture to remember that the vice-president who followed Dan Quayle is Al Gore. This involves using the picture to retrieve **order information**—information about the item's place in a series of items. Of these three types of information, only order information makes specific reference to time.

Although Murdock's distinction has not been used as widely as Tulving's, it has motivated significant and interesting research. In addition, it formed the basis for a prominent computer model of memory, Murdock's own *theory of distributed associative memory,* otherwise known as *TODAM* (Murdock, 1983; 1993). Like Tulving's proposal, Murdock's distinction serves a heuristic function, in that it and the computer model continue to inspire interesting questions and controversies (Lewandowsky & Li, 1994; Nairne & Neath, 1994).

Encoding Specificity   The research and theorizing of Ebbinghaus, Tulving, Murdock and others suggested that memory performance depends to varying degrees on relationships among the types of information to be processed. If that is the case, what do you think would be the general characteristics of the most effective memory *retrieval cues?* If you say that such cues would include references to all possible types of information used when the memory information was originally encoded, then you are proposing a hypothesis similar to what Tulving and his associates called *encoding specificity* (Tulving & Thomson, 1973).

In its simplest form, the **encoding specificity hypothesis** states that the best conditions at retrieval are those that are most similar to the conditions at encoding. To get an idea of the types of evidence supporting encoding specificity and how such evidence led to some of the ideas we will explore later, consider two experiments.

First, imagine that you are conducting a simple memory experiment. You have all your subjects learn a categorized list of words. Then you test half your subjects using a *cued recall test,* where you provide category labels for the words in the list and the subjects provide the list words associated with those categories. You test the other half of your subjects using a *free recall test,* where the subjects must recall the words in the list without any cues. Which group do you predict will have the highest level of performance?

You probably predicted that the cued recall group would show higher levels of performance than the free recall group. This is a logical prediction, since the cued recall group receives more information at testing than the free recall group. It is also a prediction that is generally consistent with encoding specificity. That is, it is consistent *if* we assume that the cues provided at testing correspond to the category labels in the study list. But what if the subjects studied a list containing the word *squash* along with other sports (the category label) but were tested with the category label *vegetables?*

Even though the word *squash* is easily associated with the vegetable category label, it was not associated with that label in the study list. So encoding specificity predicts that cued recall of *squash* with the retrieval cue *vegetable* (if it was studied with *sports*) will be poor, possibly even worse than in free recall. This is because the study and test cues do not agree. In comparison, subjects in the free recall condition could conceivably remember the category labels they saw while studying and use those to help them recall the items in the list.

And if they did this, they would be giving themselves cues that would agree with the cues provided during study.

Roediger and Payne (1983) tested this interesting prediction. In their study, subjects learned one of two lists of words. Each list contained a set of homographs (two words that are spelled the same but have different meanings, like *squash* the sport and *squash* the vegetable). In one list, the critical items appeared with the category labels for one of their meanings (e.g., *squash* with the category label *sports*); and in the other list, with the category labels for their other meanings (e.g., *squash* with the category label *vegetables*).

After learning the lists, subjects were given one of two tests. For the *congruous* test, most of the category labels referred to the categories that were studied. For the *incongruous* test, most of the category labels referred to the alternative (unstudied) categories. The results of this study are presented in Table 7.2. As you can see, when the test cues were congruent with the study cues, cued recall performance was better than free recall. But when the test cues were incongruent with the study cues, cued recall performance was far worse than free recall. This is exactly what the encoding specificity principle would predict.

Now consider a second experiment, which shows the same importance of match between acquisition and retrieval conditions but uses a recognition rather than a recall test. Thomson (1972) had subjects study a list of words, with the words that would later be tested presented either alone or with a semantically unrelated word. In the testing conditions, the words that required the recognition decision were presented either alone or paired with the words they had been paired with during study. The results of this experiment are presented in Table 7.3. If the logic we used with the Roediger and Payne (1983) data is correct, we should see encoding specificity effects for all the conditions in Thomson's (1972) data. And, in fact, we do: Subjects who studied items singly did best when the

TABLE 7.2 **Effects of Congruous and Incongruous Cues** Data show the proportion of critical items correctly recalled in a free recall test, a cued recall test in which the study and test cues were congruous, and a cued recall test in which the study and test cues were incongruous.

			Recall test	
	Acquisition list	Free recall	Congruous cued recall	Incongruous cued recall
Experiment 1	List A	0.31	0.44	0.03
	List B	0.22	0.36	0.06
	M	0.27	0.40	0.05
Experiment 2	List A	0.29	0.57	0.09
	List B	0.33	0.57	0.13
	M	0.31	0.57	0.11

Source: Roediger & Payne, 1983.

TABLE 7.3   **Acquisition and Retrieval Conditions in a Recognition Test**   Data show recognition performance as a function of the type of item pairing at test and the type of item presentation at acquisition.

	Item Presentation at Retrieval	
Acquisition Condition	**Single**	**Paired**
Single Item	.68	.54
Paired Item	.71	.80

Source: Data from Thomson, 1972.

test involved single-item presentation. Subjects who studied items in pairs did best when the test involved the same pairing.

These two experiments illustrate how performance at retrieval is determined by the interaction of the information as it was originally learned and the information available at retrieval. In addition, they demonstrate that the effect of the match between acquisition and retrieval conditions can be found in a variety of different tests of memory.

Types of Processes in Memory in the Long Term

Around the time Tulving and Murdock proposed distinctions among types of memory information, a number of proposals were made for distinctions among memory processes. One of the most influential ideas concerned the level (depth) of processing, and another involved retrieval operations.

Levels of Processing   If your grandmother asked you what she could do to improve her memory for something (perhaps her shopping list), what types of things would you recommend (other than writing down the items to be remembered)? More than likely, a number of your recommendations would involve various ways of rehearsing the items to be learned.

One of your recommendations might be simply to spend more time studying each individual item or thinking about the items to be remembered. This idea corresponds to a hypothesis prominent prior to the 1970s: the **total-time hypothesis** (Bugelski, 1962). This hypothesis says, very simply, that the more time you spend rehearsing an item, the better your memory for that item will be. The Atkinson-Shiffrin model discussed in Chapter 6 is to some extent consistent with this hypothesis, since it proposes that the longer an item is rehearsed in the short-term store, the higher is the probability that it will be transferred to the long-term store.

But in the early 1970s, psychologists at the University of Toronto (members of the Ebbinghaus empire) made the radical proposal that what one did during rehearsal might be more important than how long one rehearsed. The name given to this proposal was the **levels-of-processing hypothesis** (Craik & Lockhart, 1972). To illustrate this idea, consider an experiment conducted by Craik and Tulving (1975). In this experiment, subjects were asked a simple question that they could answer using the word that was to be shown next. A question that emphasized surface characteristics of the item (such as whether or not the word was presented in capital letters) was referred to as involving a "shallow" level of processing. (This is a similar sense of *shallow* that you might apply to someone who is only interested in the physical characteristics of other people.) A question that relied heavily on the meaning of the item, such as whether or not it fit in a sentence, was referred to as involving a "deep" level of processing. (This is the same sense of *deep* that you might apply to someone who is very philosophical or thoughtful.)

The levels-of-processing hypothesis predicts that reliance on meaningful aspects of the stimulus will improve memory for the item. Craik and Tulving designed their experiment in such a way that, if this hypothesis was correct, the effect could be present without subjects' consciously doing anything to bias the results in favor of the hypothesis (such as spending more time or placing more emphasis on certain words). The subjects in Craik and Tulving's experiment were not told that there was going to be a test for their memory of the words. They thought they were participating in an experiment on perception of words that were presented for very short times. (They were informed about the true nature of the experiment at the end of the experimental session.)

The results of this experiment showed that subjects' recognition memory performance was directly related to the level of processing apparently required by the question presented before the word. The words that were processed at a deep level at study were remembered better than the words that were studied at a shallow level. And since the different levels of memory performance were observed after equal amounts of study time (200 milliseconds), the data provided strong evidence against the total-time hypothesis. In fact, in one of the tasks that Craik and Tulving used, the task at the *shallowest* level of processing required the *most* processing time yet produced some of the lowest levels of performance.

History has been both kind and unkind to the levels-of-processing hypothesis. The general idea of using levels of processing as a task manipulation has remained useful, with researchers still relying on the notion to manipulate levels of performance (Brown & Mitchell, 1994; Wenger & Payne, 1996). However, the idea of a ranked set of levels of processing is not sufficient to explain details from a variety of memory tasks (Bransford et al., 1979). Consider also the logical problem that the definition of a "level" of processing is circular (Baddeley, 1978): Good memory performance is due to deeper levels of processing, and the evidence for deeper levels of processing is good memory performance. Essentially, there is no way to define the level of processing independent of the performance observed.

Nevertheless, the levels-of-processing hypothesis (itself another example of a heuristic) has had a dramatic impact on scientific psychology. Indeed, like the episodic/semantic distinction, it may have had a greater effect than many more completely worked-out theories have had. Consider the data plotted in Figure 7.3, which shows the number of times that each of three published works was cited in other published research between 1973 and 1994. The three works are Tulving's (1972) original paper containing the proposed distinction between episodic and semantic memory, the levels of processing paper by Craik and Lockhart (1972), and a major theoretical work on memory written at about the same time (Anderson and Bower, 1973). As you can see, the two heuristics have been cited much more than the contemporary formal theory of human memory.

Part of the impact of these heuristics stems from their intuitive appeal. To get a sense of the potency of the levels-of-processing hypothesis, try the demonstration in Experiment 7. We think that the results you obtain will give you an idea why scientists were convinced of the usefulness of this hypothesis, in spite of its relative lack of theoretical precision.

FIGURE 7.3   **Citations to Three Important Works**   The graph shows the number of times each of three important works were cited in the psychological literature between 1973 and 1994. Two of these papers present heuristics: the distinction between episodic and semantic memory (Tulving, 1972) and the notion of levels of processing (Craik & Lockhart, 1972). The third describes a formal theory of memory (Anderson & Bower, 1973).

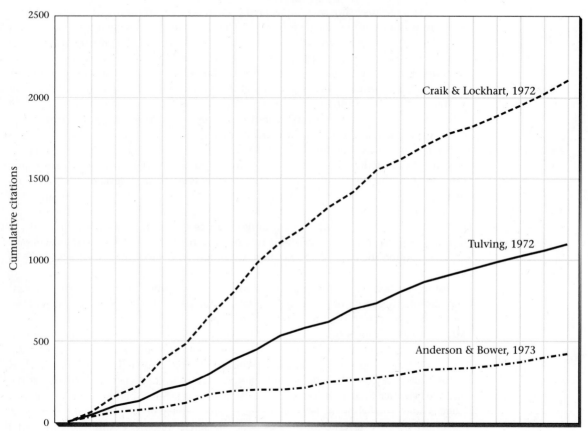

Dual Process Theories   Return for a moment to an imaginary experiment described earlier in the chapter. In that experiment, we had our subject learn five words and then tested her memory. Imagine that we test her memory in two ways. We will begin with a general knowledge test (e.g., cue *dog* with the question, "what kind of animal was Lassie?") followed by a recognition test, in that order, with the recognition test following immediately after the general knowledge test. Do you think that the subject's memory will operate* well in these conditions? In particular, do you think that performance on the recognition test would be different in this situation if we tested without presenting the general knowledge questions first?

     If you think that this situation will produce high levels of performance, then you agree with a general approach to memory retrieval that was prominent at the time Tulving proposed the episodic/semantic distinction. **Generate-recognize theories** hold that retrieval is comprised of two processes: the generation of a set of possible response items (as in the general knowledge test) and then the selection or recognition of the "best" or most likely response (Anderson & Bower, 1972a, 1973; Bahrick, 1970; Kintsch & van Dijk, 1978). Generate-recognize theories have a long history, going back at least as far as the philosopher John Locke and Ebbinghaus's pioneering studies (Tulving, 1983). Perhaps the first complete treatment of the idea can be found in a paper presented to the Psychological Society of Great Britain in 1845 (Tulving, 1983, p. 244).

Although generate-recognize theories seem to have history on their side, they present at least three serious problems. First, such theories generally assume that the generation process operates primarily on semantic memory while recognition operates primarily on episodic information (Bahrick, 1970; Kintsch, 1970a). Yet data show that recall performance with certain cues is much better than would be predicted on the basis of how semantic memory alone would respond to those cues (Tulving, 1983). Second, the operation of the recognition process assumes to some degree that subjects know what they want to remember before they remember it. The third problem concerns whether recognition should always be better than recall, as these theories imply. We consider this issue a little later in the chapter, when we talk about episodic retrieval processes.

A similar but more formal treatment of the idea that two processes operate in retrieval became prominent in the early 1970s and has been called the **dual process theory** of retrieval (Juola et al., 1971; Mandler, 1991). As originally conceived, only one of the two processes in dual process theory actually requires retrieval of information from memory, while the other relies simply on the general level of activation of memory (recall the resonance metaphor mentioned in Chapter 6).

The first of the two processes is a recall process similar to the generation of response alternatives. This process is generally thought of as involving a search of the contents of memory along with (possibly) some type of decision process that operates on the output from recall (e.g., is the retrieved item the one that is needed?). The second process is a familiarity process that depends on the activation of memory in response to the cues. Essentially, this familiarity process does not involve any active processing of the information; the presentation of the cue results in some degree of activation in memory, and the level of this activation is what helps determine responding.

While generate-recognize theories assume that both processes contribute to performance in almost all cases, dual process theory does not. In dual process theory, the familiarity process is generally equated with recognition performance, and the search process corresponds in general to recall performance.

The idea that the familiarity process is distinct from retrieval was supported by evidence from experiments examining the organization of information in memory using accuracy as the principal dependent variable. The logic of these experiments was that if retrieval is dependent on the organization of memory, only tasks involving retrieval (like recall) should be affected by the organization of information. Tasks that do not involve retrieval (like recognition) should not be affected by organization.

The idea that recall would be affected by organization whereas recognition would not be was appealing to researchers working in the late 1960s, but the data from experiments testing this idea were contradictory (Mandler, 1970; 1972). At about the same time that Mandler and his colleagues were asking these questions using response accuracy and confidence as dependent variables, Atkinson and his colleagues were examining similar questions using reaction times (Juola et al., 1971). This work led Atkinson and his colleagues to frame

EXPERIMENT 7:   Checking Out Levels of Processing

You can observe directly the powerful effects of different levels of processing. You will need two groups of subjects, with between three and five subjects in each group. One group will perform a "shallow" processing task and the other will perform a "deep" processing task. You will need to work separately with the groups, asking each group to look at a list of words, then solve some simple math problems, then perform a recall test. But you are *not* going to tell the subjects in advance about the recall test.

Follow these steps with each group of subjects:

1. Write the following list of words as a two-column list, with 13 words in the first column and 12 words in the second. Leave enough space to the side of each word to allow subjects to write two or three words (see step 5). At the bottom of the page, write a set of 10 multiplication problems involving two-digit numbers (e.g., $25 \times 14 =$), without providing the answers. Copy this sheet, and give each subject a separate sheet.

bottle	nuclear
solar	vegetable
water	belly
animal	school
blossom	sandwich
fabric	jewel
vacation	airport
dough	chicken
judge	piano
popcorn	daisy
forest	hurricane
guitar	reporter
typewriter	

the recognition process in the language of signal detection theory (Atkinson, Herrmann & Westcourt, 1974; Atkinson & Juola, 1973; Atkinson & Juola, 1974). (For a discussion of signal detection theory, see Chapter 3.)

   Their proposal relied on two response criteria with which the actual level of memory activation was compared. If activation was above the high criterion, the item was recognized (the subject responded that the item was "old," or previously studied). If activation was below the low criterion, the item was not recognized (the subject responded that the item was "new," or not previously studied). Figure 7.4 shows these possible situations as a function of the activation produced by a probe item relative to some low-activation distribution such as might be produced by new or unstudied items.

   But this only defines the high and low extremes of activation. Activation can also occur *between* the high and low criteria (the middle distribution in Figure 7.4). Atkinson and

2. As noted, you will work with one group at a time. One group will perform a shallow processing task and the other will perform a deep processing task. As you begin work with each group, tell subjects you are going to ask them to help you with a *two* simple psychology experiments that require them to perform a task with words and then perform a task with numbers. You will tell them it was only *one* experiment when you are done.

3. Ask the subjects performing the shallow task to write the letter S at the top of their sheets. Ask the subjects performing the deep task to write the letter D at the top of their sheets.

4. Ask the subjects performing the shallow task to count the number of *vowels* in each word and write this number to the left of the word. Tell subjects that you will be giving them one minute per word and that they should not go on to the next word until you tell them. Use a watch or stopwatch to pace the subjects. (Why do you think it is important to control the amount of time spent on each word?)

5. Ask the subjects performing the deep task to go through the list and write down two or three words that are closely related to the word in the list. Tell subjects that you will be giving them one minute per word and that they should not go on to the next word until you tell them. Use a watch or stopwatch to pace the subjects.

6. When they complete all the words in the list, tell the subjects to work through as many multiplication problems as they can in two minutes. Keep track of the time, and stop the subjects as soon as two minutes have passed.

7. Ask the subjects turn their sheets over and write down as many words as they can remember from the list. Give them a total of two minutes.

8. Calculate the percentage of words each subject in each group recalled. Then calculate an *average* percentage for each group by taking the average of the percentages for all the subjects in each group. Which group recalled a higher percentage of the list?

If things went well, you should see the best performance in the group that performed the deep processing task. Since you controlled the total time spent on each word, the time that passed between when subjects saw the words and when they were tested, and the cues you provided at test, what seems to be the source of the difference in performance between the two groups?

Juola (1973, 1974) proposed that, if activation falls into this middle region, then the subject will have to search memory. Thus, an active retrieval process can be part of recognition, if some aspect of the cue results in an intermediate level of activation. Evidence supporting the presence of this additional processing step takes the form of long reaction times for items assumed to produce intermediate levels of activation, as opposed to short reaction times for items falling either below the low criterion or above the high criterion.

Since its proposal, dual process theory has been modified and extended to deal with a number of different theoretical questions and empirical phenomena, including studies of different types of amnesia (Jacoby & Dallas, 1981; Jacoby & Witherspoon, 1982; Mandler, 1980; Mandler et al., 1990). Dual process theory has also been influential in the development of contemporary formal models of memory retrieval (Gillund & Shiffrin, 1984; Raaijmakers, 1981).

FIGURE 7.4   **Critical Response Regions for Dual Process Theory**   The strength distributions correspond to critical response regions. If strength is low (in the left-most distribution), the item
can easily be rejected as "new," and if strength is high, the item can easily be identified as
"old." But if strength is intermediate, a search process is required to determine the item's
status.

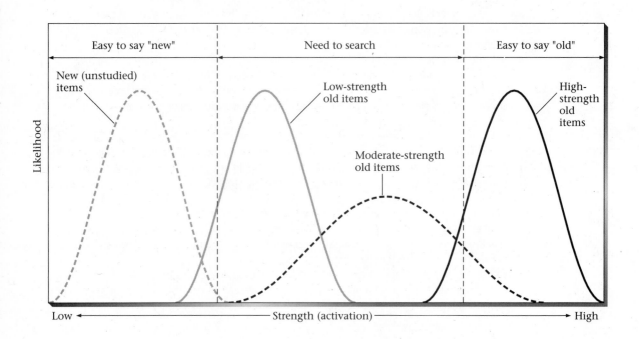

Section Summary: A History of Memory Distinctions

The development of ideas related to episodic memory as a form of memory in the long
term owes much, both methodologically and conceptually, to the initial work of Ebbinghaus. Ebbinghaus noted that general knowledge (eventually known as semantic memory
information) could influence the results of experiments examining new learning. Ultimately, this type of observation allowed for the development of the distinction between
episodic and semantic memory; the idea of encoding specificity; and the distinction
among item, associative, and order information. Distinctions among types of memory information raised questions about distinctions among types of memory processing. Types
of processing that have been proposed include levels of processing, as well as generation,
recognition, and search as component processes in retrieval.

IMPORTANT RELATIONS BETWEEN ENCODING
AND RETRIEVAL

In this chapter, we have been discussing episodic and semantic memory *information*. But
some psychologists maintain that *episodic* and *semantic* refer to distinct *types* of memory—
functionally distinct or even anatomically distinct. Evidence for an anatomically distinct
episodic memory has come from new and innovative methods of studying the relation-

ship between brain activity and cognition, such as the method described in Research Report 7.

On the basis of findings such as those in Research Report 7, Shallice and colleagues have proposed that episodic and semantic information are processed in different regions of the brain. In addition, they have suggested that encoding and retrieval processes may be isolated in different regions.

Transfer-Appropriate Processing

During the 1970s, Tulving and his associates were developing ideas about how the effectiveness of retrieval cues might depend on the nature of information already in memory. Their conclusion was that successful retrieval depends on the degree to which the properties of the information in memory, as they are determined at encoding, are similar to the properties of the retrieval cue. This is the encoding specificity principle discussed earlier in the chapter.

If you think about it, though, you can see that encoding involves much more than just the information available in the stimulus. It also involves the type of processing taking place. This is one of the important points made by the work on levels of processing. And, as we have noted, retrieval performance also depends on both the information itself and how it is processed. If this is the case, then perhaps the match between encoding processing and retrieval processing is important to consider. The notion that memory performance depends on the degree of match between the processing done at study and the processing done at test is referred to as **transfer-appropriate processing** (Bransford et al., 1979; Morris, Bransford & Franks, 1977).

To see the effects of transfer-appropriate processing, consider an experiment by Blaxton (Blaxton, 1989). In this experiment, subjects studied words either by reading them out loud or by generating them from word fragments. In addition, words were studied either with or without an accompanying (context) word. These conditions thus involved not only different types of information but also different types of processing.

Blaxton argued that the type of information processed at both study and test could be either specific to the study context (episodic information) or specific to the meaning of the item (semantic information). In addition, the type of processing at both study and test could depend on either the physical characteristics of the study cue (e.g., the length of the word fragment and the specific letters present) or the meaning of the item (a complete item studied alone or with a paired item). Blaxton referred to the first type of processing as "data driven," since this type of processing is driven by the observable characteristics of the stimulus. She referred to the second type of processing as "conceptually driven," since this type of processing is driven by the meaning of the stimulus (see also Jacoby 1983a, 1983b).

To thoroughly test the idea of transfer-appropriate processing, Blaxton had to come up with memory tests that use various combinations of the two types of information and the two types of processing. The specific tasks used by Blaxton and example retrieval cues for each task are presented in Figure 7.5.

We concentrate here on a small portion of Blaxton's results—specifically, on results from four tests following study conditions in which subjects either generated the target items or read them aloud, with no context words. The four tests used by Blaxton were (a) graphemic cued recall, where the cue was a word that physically resembled the target word (e.g., *bushel* for *bashful*); (b) word-fragment completion, where the target word was presented with some letters missing (e.g., B_SH_U_ for *bashful*); (c) semantic cued recall, where a synonym (e.g., *timid*) for the target word was the cue; and (d) a general knowledge

RESEARCH REPORT 7:   Evidence for an Anatomically Distinct Episodic Memory

An example of the creative ways in which newer brain-imaging technologies are being combined with standard experiments in cognitive psychology is a recent study by Shallice, Fletcher, Frith, Gasby, Frackowiak, and Dolan (1994). The researchers used positron emission tomography (PET) to observe the activity of regions of the brain while subjects performed a set of memory tasks. Shallice and colleagues were interested in the regions of the brain associated with acquisition and retrieval of episodic and semantic memory information.

To study acquisition, the researchers had subjects listen to short lists of paired words composed of a category name and an example from the category (e.g., furniture-table). The interesting twist was that the researchers had subjects perform one of two distractor tasks at the same time. One task was easy; and in this condition, the researchers proposed that subjects would be able to devote attention to encoding (or processing) episodic information. The other task was difficult, and in this condition, the researchers proposed that subjects would not be able to encode as many of the details of the learning episode (since they would be paying more attention to the distractor task). In this second condition, the researchers expected that mostly semantic information about the list items would be processed.

When Shallice and colleagues compared the data for the two groups, they noticed a striking difference. Figure 7A illustrates the critical areas of activation. The researchers concluded that these left frontal areas are associated with episodic processing at encoding.

test, where the "cue" was a question that probed knowledge about the object or concept referred to by the target word (e.g., *Which of the seven dwarfs comes first alphabetically?*). These data are also shown in Figure 7.5. We start by considering the difference between the level of performance in the condition in which subjects generated the words at study and the level of performance in the condition in which subjects read the words at study.

We can assume that the subjects who generated the words at study were focused on their knowledge of words and word meanings, since they would need this type of information to come up with a real word if given only a fragment (e.g., B_SH_U_ used to generate BASHFUL). We can also assume that the subjects who simply read the words out loud needed only to focus on each word as it was presented, since the presented string of letters contained all the information they needed to pronounce (read) the word out loud.

Now look at Figure 7.5 and compare the mean scores on the data-driven retrieval tasks. You will see that better performance was observed for the subjects who read the words at study than for the subjects who generated the words. That is, the subjects who did data-driven processing at study did better on the data-driven retrieval tasks. Now compare the mean scores for subjects who performed the conceptually driven retrieval tasks. You will see different results but come to a similar conclusion. On the conceptually driven retrieval tasks, performance was better for

FIGURE 7A   **Recorded Activity During Acquisition**   The images in the top row show brain regions that were active during encoding with the easy distractor task. These are the regions thought to be associated with episodic encoding. The images in the bottom row show brain regions that were active during encoding with the difficult distractor task. These are the regions thought to be associated with semantic encoding.

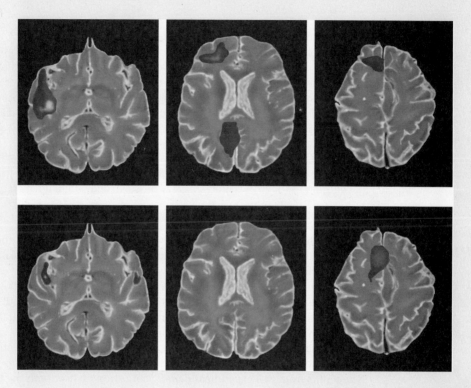

(Research Report 7 continued on p. 228)

subjects who focused on meaningful aspects of the words at study (the "generate" condition). Thus, for both the data-driven and the conceptually driven tasks, performance was best when the type of retrieval processing matched the type of study processing. This supports the basic prediction of transfer-appropriate processing.

But this is just part of the story. We have considered the type of processing, but what about the type of information? Can we conclude that semantic information has no effect on data-driven tasks or that episodic information has no effect on conceptually driven tasks? Let us consider first Blaxton's results from the data-driven tasks. Comparing the two means for graphemic cued recall with the two means for word-fragment completion shows

Research Report 7 (continued)

To study retrieval, Shallice and colleagues used two different tasks. The first was a recall task, which the researchers proposed would involve both episodic and semantic information. The second was a generation task, in which subjects were given the first item in each word pair (e.g., furniture) and were required to generate *any* relevant associated word (not necessarily the word that had been studied). The researchers proposed that this task would involve mostly semantic information. As with the encoding tasks, PET images were collected during the task.

To isolate the episodic processing areas, Shallice and colleagues noted the areas that were active during the recall task and those that were active during the generation task (see the areas of activation in Figure 7B). According to the logic of their experimental design, the regions that were active only during the recall task (i.e., those that were active during the processing of both episodic and semantic information, rather than those active during the processing of mainly semantic information) would be those involved in episodic retrieval. As you can see in Figure 7B, these regions were in the right frontal areas of the brain.

On the basis of these findings, Shallice and colleagues have proposed that episodic and semantic information are processed in different regions of the brain. In addition, they have suggested that encoding and retrieval processes may be isolated in different regions.

that, in both the generate and the read conditions, performance in the word-fragment completion test was better than performance in the graphemic cued recall test. This means that, for retrieval tasks that rely primarily on processing surface characteristics of the stimuli, semantic attributes of the information to be processed have important influences.

Now let us consider the results from the conceptually driven tasks. If we compare the two means for semantic cued recall with the two means for the general knowledge test, we see that semantic cued recall performance was better than general knowledge performance. This means that for retrieval tasks that rely primarily on conceptual aspects of the stimuli, episodic attributes of the information to be processed have important influences.

The results from this experiment demonstrate strongly how both the types of information available at study and test and the types of processing done at study and test determine performance on memory tasks. In particular, Blaxton's data show that if we focus only on the type of information being processed (episodic or semantic), we can miss important effects, such as the fact that data-driven processing can depend on semantic information.

Explicit and Implicit Memory

We generally think of memory retrieval as involving conscious or intentional recall of some information. Recently, however, researchers have become very interested in another aspect of memory performance, one that does not seem to involve conscious or intentional recollection. Schacter (1987a) notes that the distinction between a conscious, or explicit, use of memory and an unconscious, or implicit, use of memory goes back at least to Descartes in the seventeenth century. In the nineteenth century, a distinction was made between conscious and unconscious cerebration (thinking) (Carpenter, 1874); and in the

FIGURE 7B   **Recorded Activity During Retrieval**   The images in the top row show brain regions that were active during a retrieval task involving both episodic and semantic information. The images in the bottom row show brain regions that were active during a retrieval task involving mainly semantic information. The regions unique to the first task were proposed to be those principally involved in episodic retrieval.

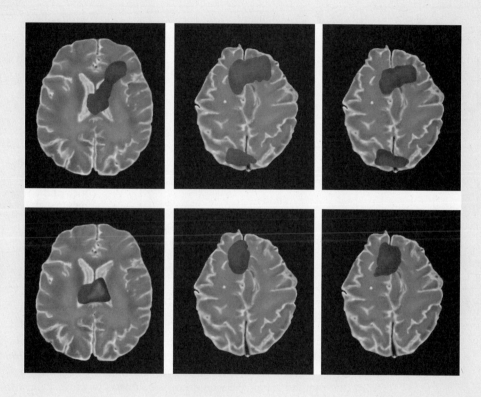

twentieth century, psychoanalytic psychologists proposed that one effect of hysteria could be to make memories inaccessible (Freud & Breuer, 1966). The debate involving explicit and implicit effects was at first framed in terms of two different types of memory, in the same way that short- and long-term memory or episodic and semantic memory were thought to be different types (or systems) of memory.

At present, **explicit memory** is commonly defined with respect to performance on a test that requires the intentional use of memory. An example of this type of test is a free recall test, in which subjects consciously attempt to recall things. In contrast, **implicit memory** is commonly defined with respect to performance on a test that does not require the subject to intentionally retrieve information from memory. For example, we could ob-

F I G U R E   7 . 5   **Tests of Transfer-Appropriate Processing**   The figure shows the types of memory tests used by Blaxton (1989), along with a subset of the data from Experiment 1. Note how each test involves a different combination of type of processing and type of information.

Memory Information

		Episodic	Semantic
Type of Processing — Data Driven	Test type	Graphemic cued recall	Word-fragment completion
	Cue	bushel	B_SH_U_
	Mean score: • Generate	.34	.46
	• Read	.45	.75
Conceptually Driven	Test type	Semantic cued recall	General knowledge
	Cue	timid	Which of the Seven Dwarfs comes first alphabetically?
	Mean score: • Generate	.76	.50
	• Read	.51	.33

Source: Based on Blaxton, 1989.

serve implicit memory if we had subjects study a list of words (without telling them we would be testing them) and then complete a word-fragment completion task. We would instruct our subjects to complete a set of word fragments (like B_SH_U_) with the first word that came to mind. We would not tell subjects to think about words from the list they had studied. Some of the words on the test (but not all) would be from the originally studied list. We would see that subjects were better at completing the fragments of previously studied words and that they could do this without necessarily intending to retrieve anything about the originally studied list.

One important reason that psychologists began to think that two different systems of memory support performance on these two types of tasks was that a great deal of evidence suggests *dissociations* between the two types of tasks. (Remember that a dissociation is observed when an independent variable affects one thing in one way and the other thing in a different way.) For example, study and test manipulations that emphasize surface, or episodic, aspects of items have large effects on implicit tests, whereas study manipulations that emphasize semantic aspects have large effects on explicit tests (Blaxton, 1989; Jacoby & Hayman, 1987).

Although the explicit/implicit distinction and the numerous dissociations observed generated much research, this distinction (like many others we have talked about) has not held up especially well. First, the distinction suffers from the same kind of logical difficulty associated with the distinction between short- and long-term memory: The fact that memory can have both explicit and implicit effects on performance does not mean there are two separate systems producing these effects (Church & Schacter, 1994). Second, the distinction confuses the type of task with the type of memory that is supposedly involved (Blaxton, 1989; Richardson-Klavehn & Bjork, 1988). Specifically, it is difficult, if not impossible, to observe implicit memory with anything except an indirect test task, or explicit memory with anything but a direct test task. Finally, the great volume of research generated by interest in the explicit/implicit distinction seems to have had the predictable effect of producing evidence suggesting that the distinction was not as clear as originally thought (Brown & Mitchell, 1994).

Perhaps the most parsimonious current view is that the dissociations related to these two types of memory effects represent another example of transfer-appropriate processing (Blaxton, 1989; Roediger & Blaxton, 1987; Roediger, Weldon & Challis, 1989). That is, implicit and explicit retrieval tasks most likely require different types of processing (e.g., data-driven and conceptually driven). Consequently, each type of retrieval task benefits from a different type of study processing, particularly the type of study processing similar to the specific type of retrieval processing involved. But the debate is far from settled.

Neuropsychological Aspects of Episodic Information

In Chapter 4, we reviewed evidence that multiple systems may be involved in visual perception. Similarly, memory researchers have asked whether distinct neural systems underlie different aspects of memory. In recent years, data identifying areas of the brain that may be critical to performance on episodic memory tasks have been accumulating (as we saw in Research Report 7). Although in general these data are suggestive rather than conclusive, some interesting patterns appear to be developing. In particular, it appears that the brain's frontal lobes and certain areas of the hippocampus are critical for memory specific to context or time (Moscovitch, 1989; Olton, 1989). And context and time are two critical aspects of episodic information. Think about how hard it would be to answer "where" or "when" questions without context or time information.

Pribram and Tubbs (1967; Schacter, 1987b) proposed one of the first theories addressing the role of the frontal lobes in memory for context. Essentially, their theory holds that one function of the frontal cortex is to segment experience into the units that are encoded into memory. Examples of tasks in which such chunking of experience is critical include remembering how frequently you eat Mexican food, the last time you ate Mexican food, and the name and location of your favorite Mexican restaurant.

The frontal lobes and hippocampus are closely related anatomically (See Figure 7.6). They also appear to have related roles in memory for information specific to place and time. A number of studies and reviews relate to the functions these two areas might play in encoding and retrieval of episodic information (Kolb, 1984; Olton, Becker & Handelmann, 1979).

Examples of such work are the studies conducted by David Olton and colleagues on the ability of rats to encode and retrieve temporal information (Meck, Church & Olton, 1984; Olton, Meck & Church, 1987). The logic of these studies is simple. If the frontal and hippocampal systems function in memory for temporally specific information, then selectively impairing either system or both systems by creating specifically localized lesions should produce an inability to respond to retrieval demands that reflect memory for time.

FIGURE 7.6   **Brain Structures Implicated in Memory for Context**

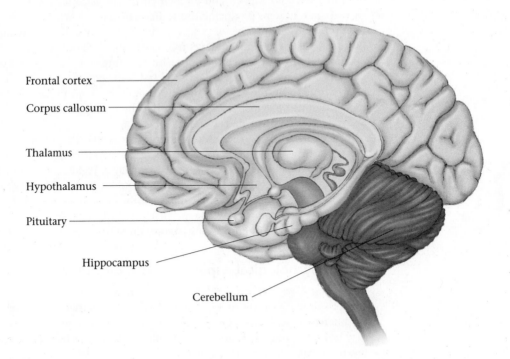

Frontal cortex

Corpus callosum

Thalamus

Hypothalamus

Pituitary

Hippocampus

Cerebellum

In addition, if the frontal lobes are important for the temporal segmentation of experience, lesions in this area should selectively impair performance that depends on memory for segments of time (i.e., durations of events).

One way in which animals can be trained to be sensitive to the duration of events is through use of a fixed-interval reinforcement schedule (Ferster & Skinner, 1957). In this type of reinforcement schedule, the experimenter defines a time period of fixed length and rewards the first desired response (such as pressing a bar in response to a light) that occurs after that interval elapses. Typically, after a number of trials on such schedules, animals adopt a pattern of responding in which they make very few responses *during* the interval and many responses *near the end* of the interval. Such a pattern of responding suggests that the animals have developed a memory for the duration of the interval.

Olton and his colleagues trained a group of animals on fixed-interval schedules and then created lesions in the animals' brains in one of two areas: the frontal cortex or the hippocampus. The animals were then tested again under the same fixed-interval reinforcement schedule. The results indicated that animals with lesions in the frontal cortex shifted the time at which they produced the greatest number of responses to a point later than the reinforcement time. In contrast, the animals with lesions in the hippocampus shifted the time at which they produced the greatest number of responses to a point earlier than the reinforcement time.

These data indicate that while the frontal lobes and the hippocampus are both involved in memory for temporal information, they are involved in different ways. In addition, these studies provide another demonstration of how behavioral and neurological methods can be creatively combined to investigate the relationship between psychological and neurological phenomena.

Section Summary: Important Relations Between Encoding and Retrieval

Some important ideas developed in current research on memory for episodic information focus on how retrieval of episodic information depends on the similarity of the demands for information and processing at encoding and retrieval. Research on transfer-appropriate processing shows how the older notion of encoding specificity (a hypothesis about information) has been extended to processing, including the manner in which it might account for the distinction between explicit and implicit memory. Building on this idea, neurophysiologists have successfully combined behavioral and neurophysiological techniques to define how specific brain areas might be involved in the processing of episodic information at both study and test.

THE IMPORTANCE OF CONTEXT IN EPISODIC RETRIEVAL

Earlier in the chapter, we introduced encoding specificity: the notion that, generally speaking, the best conditions for retrieval are the ones that are most similar to those at encoding. When we discussed this idea, we talked about experiments in which the match between study and test was manipulated by use of words and word cues. But if the idea of encoding specificity is correct, it should be possible to manipulate this match in other ways, including manipulation of the external world and a person's internal state.

In the 1970s and 1980s, a number of studies explored this possibility in interesting ways. For example, Godden and Baddeley (1975) had divers learn word lists in one of two settings (on the beach or underwater) and then tested them in either the same setting or the other setting. The divers who performed best at test were those who were tested in the same context in which they had learned the words. Other investigators achieved similar effects by manipulating the room used for study and test (Smith, Glenberg & Bjork, 1978). In addition, it has been shown that under specific conditions, a person who learns information while under the influence of alcohol or drugs will retrieve the information better when in an alcohol- or drug-induced state than when sober (Eich, 1989; Goodwin et al., 1969).

Intriguing as these results are, to understand the possible influences of contextual information on the use of other types of memory information, we first have to understand some of the basic characteristics of contextual information. This is the topic we take up next.

General Aspects of Context Effects

The idea that an activity or event has a *context* is probably familiar to you. But can you *define* context? For example, what is the context for the activity in which you are engaged right now? What is the boundary between the context and the activity (where does one leave off and the other begin)?

Since the earliest part of the twentieth century, psychologists have thought that context plays an important role in determining memory performance (Carr, 1917; Dulsky, 1935; Melton & Irwin, 1940). But they have not always had solid definitions of what context is. Currently, two very general definitions of context are used (Wickens, 1987).

The first type of context, called **context alpha,** refers to aspects of the surroundings or environment in which an activity or event takes place. Examples of features of context alpha that have been manipulated in experiments include features of the testing rooms, the background in pictures, and the sound of the voice used to present stimuli. Perhaps one of the most unusual manipulations of context alpha involved changing aspects of boxes that were placed over subjects' heads during an experiment (Dallett & Wilcox, 1968).

The second type of context is referred to as **context beta** (Wickens, 1987) and has also been called *interactive context* (Baddeley, 1982) and *integrated context* (Eich, 1985). Context beta includes things very close to the actual stimulus and functions by giving meaning to an otherwise ambiguous stimulus. For example, the word *bank* has a number of different meanings, but it has a very specific meaning when it occurs in the sentence, "I just witnessed a robbery at the *bank.*" In this case, the sentence provides context for the stimulus word *bank,* and the sentence information that restricts the meaning of *bank* is context beta. We are concerned here mainly with effects associated with context alpha.

Context Effects and Recall   Four basic types of phenomena are associated with context alpha effects in memory. To understand these effects, think about two distinctly different physical contexts—perhaps two distinctly different classrooms. We will call one context A and the other context B. Now let us add a third context, one that is different from both A and B and is generally neutral; we will call this context N.

Now imagine that we run different experiments in these different rooms (contexts) to see what types of effects either changing context or keeping context unchanged will have on memory performance. The basic experimental task is to learn lists of words in one context and recall them in another. The four effects generally obtained in these types of experimental situations are presented in Table 7.4 (from Bjork & Richardson-Klavehn, 1989).

The first of the effects listed in Table 7.4 you might have anticipated from our earlier discussion of transfer-appropriate processing: performance was better when learning and remembering took place in the same context. The second effect is one you might not have anticipated. That is, remembering in a new context was improved if the person *imagined* the original context.

Whereas these two effects show that context can have positive effects on memory performance, context can also have negative effects, as shown by the third and fourth effects. These two types of effects are obtained when more than one list must be learned. Essentially, the best performance is obtained when each of the lists is learned in a *different* context and the test context is neutral.

The sensitivity of memory to context might be easily interpreted as a weakness of our information processing systems. But think for a moment about the amount of information that you need to process on a daily basis—from getting ready to go to class to dealing with the work in each of your classes to talking to friends to relaxing in the evening. If each of these contexts were uniformly good at cueing retrieval of everything you know, your memory performance would probably be uniformly bad. For example, if watching a basketball game cued retrieval of calculus as well as it cued recall of the rules of basketball, you might have trouble deciding whether a player had blocked a shot or integrated an equation. Given the fact that humans seem to be able to store and retrieve an impressive amount of information (Landauer, 1986), this reliance on context might actually be a strength of our memory retrieval processes.

Context Effects and Recognition   The situation gets a little more complex (and ambiguous) when we consider recognition rather than recall. That is because, while the effects of context alpha seem to be fairly reliable in recall, they are much less reliable in recognition. Currently, three theories are used to explain this situation.

TABLE 7.4   **Context Effects**   A and B refer to two physically different contexts, and N refers to a context that is neutral relative to A and B. (IA) stands for "imagine A."

Manipulation	Experimental Conditions		Performance	
	Learn	Test	Best	Worst
Physically reinstate the learning context	A → A A → B		A→A	A→B
Reinstate the learning context by *imagining* it	A → B (IA) A → B		A→B (IA)	A→B
Learn two lists in two study sessions, then recall the first list	A, A → N A, B → N		A, B→N	A, A→N
Learn two lists in two study sessions, then recall both lists	A, A → N A, B → N		A, B→N	A, A→N

Source: Based on Bjork & Richardson-Klavehn, 1989.

The first of these is called the **outshining hypothesis** (Smith, 1986, 1994). To understand this hypothesis, think about what happens in the following recognition test. We present subjects with an item (like a word or a picture) and instruct them to answer "yes" only if they think the item was one they studied before the test; otherwise, they are to answer "no." On each trial, we present the item on a colored background (the context) on a computer screen. According to the outshining hypothesis, both the item and the context have a certain amount of strength as memory cues (Dalton, 1993; Murnane & Phelps, 1994, 1995). If the strength of the item is greater than the strength of the context, then the item will overpower the context, as a bright light outshines a weak light.

A second explanation recently offered as an alternative to the outshining hypothesis relies on an idea similar to the resonance metaphor discussed in Chapter 6. This second hypothesis holds that the item and the context *together* activate memory in a very general, or global, way. When an item and its context are the same at test as they were at study, then the global activation of memory will be higher than if the item is the same but the context is different.

Most versions of this global activation hypothesis assume that the item and context information are integrated in the test cue (Murnane & Phelps, 1994, 1995). In contrast, the outshining hypothesis holds that the item and context strengths are to some degree independent. By taking advantage of this difference between the outshining and global activation hypotheses, a number of experiments provide support for the global activation hypothesis and fail to support the outshining hypothesis (Murnane & Phelps, 1994, 1995).

There is, however, a third hypothesis, which says that a change in context does not change anything about memory. Instead, a change in context changes subjects' willingness to say "yes" to any item. Feenan and Snodgrass (1990) provided their own data along with a review of a number of other experiments to support this hypothesis. They documented that changing context has only a small (sometimes insignificantly small) effect on subjects' ability to tell studied and unstudied items apart. In essence, context has little if any effect on the discriminability of items. Instead, a change in context seems to make subjects less willing to say "yes." In more technical terms, a change in context produces a conservative response criterion. (Recall that discriminability and response criteria were discussed in the context of signal detection theory in Chapter 3.)

Mood as a Context for Memory

As we noted at the beginning of this section, during the late 1970s and early 1980s, memory researchers became very interested in whether memory performance might depend on external conditions or internal states. Two important studies (Bower, Monteiro & Gilligan, 1978; Weingartner, Miller & Murphy, 1977) appeared to demonstrate that, in both naturally occurring and experimentally induced depression, memory performance suffered. The effect was called "mood-dependent memory" (Bower, 1981). Yet by the mid 1980s, evidence had accumulated suggesting that what was taken to be dependence was actually something similar to transfer-appropriate processing. That is, memory performance as a function of emotional state may suffer when the emotional conditions at retrieval are different from the emotional conditions at encoding (Blaney, 1986). By the end of the 1980s, researchers investigating these effects had reviewed the available data and had seen no consistent patterns. Sometimes mood had an influence, and sometimes it did not (Bower & Mayer, 1989, pp. 165–166).

Since then, a small set of consistent facts has emerged. First, memory deficits in (for example) depression are very real. In fact, a set of basic cognitive mechanisms have been suggested to be those primarily affected by depression (Hertel & Hardin, 1990, 1991). Second, and more generally, mood-dependent memory effects can reliably be obtained under three conditions: subjects must (a) experience strong and stable states of the mood of interest, (b) be actively involved in generating the material to be remembered, and (c) be actively involved in producing the cues at retrieval (Eich, 1995).

Misinformation and False Memories

Can context—particularly retrieval context—negatively affect memory performance in the real world? Two effects that have drawn public attention recently suggest that it can. The **misinformation effect** occurs when a certain type of misleading information presented after the original event biases or disrupts memory. The **false memory effect** occurs when information that was not part of an event but that is related in some way to the original event is "recalled."

Both these effects have been tied to important real-world legal situations. The misinformation effect has come to be a model for the ways in which eyewitnesses can be convincingly misled about what they actually saw, and the false memory effect is a model for testing the possibility of "remembering" events that never occurred. For our purposes, the important things that are common to these two effects are that they demonstrate (a) the importance of retrieval context on memory performance and (b) the generally reconstructive nature of remembering.

To understand the importance of these two effects, we need to consider what people *believe* about how memory works. We are talking here about *pre-theoretical commitments:* beliefs we have about something (memory, in this case) that come into play *before* we start formulating and testing theories and hypotheses. To see how pre-theoretical commitments about memory can influence both science and society, read the following two statements. Which one best reflects *your* view of how memory works?

1. Everything we learn is permanently stored in the mind, although sometimes particular details are not accessible. With hypnosis or other special techniques, these inaccessible details can eventually be recovered.
2. Some details of what we learn may be permanently lost from memory. Such details can never be recovered by hypnosis or any other special technique because the details are simply no longer there.

Which one did you choose? If you chose the first statement, then you agree with the majority of both nonpsychologists and psychologists. In an informal survey, Loftus and Loftus (1980) found that 69 percent of nonpsychologists and 84 percent of psychologists agreed with the first statement. We have informally repeated this survey a number of times, in community seminars, graduate classes, and undergraduate classes (including introductory psychology classes) and have always obtained results consistent with those of Loftus and Loftus.

Now, if memory stores, perhaps permanently, the details of experience, and if we can figure out how to retrieve that information, then we should have a record of the original experience. Assuming that what was encoded was real and true (and, excepting dreams or fantasies, why would we assume anything else), then that record should be an accurate one, right?

This is all consistent with the beliefs of most people—psychologists included. The problem is that it is inconsistent with a large body of data (Lindsay & Read, 1994; Roediger, 1996; Schacter, 1995), some of it coming from the first part of the twentieth century (Bartlett, 1932), that suggests that memory can be quite malleable or fallible. With this in mind, let us consider the misinformation and false memory effects.

The Misinformation Effect   A classic example of the misinformation effect can be seen in an experiment conducted by Loftus and Palmer (1974). In this experiment (and many others based on it), subjects saw a film of an event. In this case, it was a traffic accident involving two cars. After watching the film, subjects were asked to estimate how fast the cars were going when they were involved in the accident. But in asking the question, experimenters varied the verbs they used. The results from this experiment are presented in Table 7.5. As you can see, the magnitude of the speed estimate was directly related to the form of the verb. If the verb was neutral (like *contacted*), the speed estimate was low. But if the verb implied something dramatic (like *smashed*), the speed estimates were appreciably higher.

The implication is that witnesses' memory for events can be affected by the ways in which they are questioned. But *how* is memory affected? Two prominent hypotheses deal with this effect. The **changed-trace hypothesis,** perhaps the earliest to deal explicitly with this effect, holds that the new information (in our example, the question asking for the estimate of speed) in some way alters or overwrites the original information in memory (Loftus, 1979a; Loftus & Loftus, 1980). Conversely, the **multiple trace hypothesis** holds that the original information is not lost from memory. Instead, the new information is added to memory and in some way interferes with the retrieval of old information (Bonto & Payne, 1991; Chandler, 1989, 1991; McCloskey & Zaragoza, 1985).

The changed-trace hypothesis generated a good deal of attention when it was first proposed, but the *methods* used to produce the evidence supporting this hypothesis also generated a good deal of scrutiny. A number of possible confounding factors were identified, including the types of alternatives used for responses in the memory test (McCloskey &

TABLE 7.5   **Effects of Context Alpha on Recall**   When subjects were asked to estimate the speed of two cars involved in a filmed traffic accident, the magnitude of their estimates was affected by the verb used in the question.

Verb	Average Speed Estimate (mph)
Smashed	40.8
Collided	39.3
Bumped	38.1
Hit	34.0
Contacted	31.8

Source: Ashcraft, 1989.

Zaragoza, 1985) and various social aspects of the testing situation (Ceci, Ross & Toglia, 1987). Identifying and controlling for these factors led to the proposal of the multiple trace hypothesis. Although the debate is far from settled, much of the evidence, particularly that dealing with various types of interference that can be observed in these experiments, suggests that the multiple trace hypothesis is closer than the changed-trace hypothesis to capturing what actually goes on in memory in the misinformation effect (Chandler, 1989; 1991).

The False Memory Effect   Whereas the misinformation effect shows that memory performance can be affected by the retrieval context and by information acquired after the target information, the false memory effect demonstrates that people can be led to believe that they remember something that actually never happened.

You should be aware of an important distinction concerning the false memory effect. The event that is supposedly being recalled never happened; so strictly speaking, it cannot be remembered. But as we will see, people *experience* this information as if it were a real memory. The false memory effect has gained a great deal of notoriety recently, with many people claiming (often as a result of psychotherapy) that they have somehow recovered painful memories hidden for years (Loftus & Ketcham, 1994; Pendergast, 1995). People's belief in the validity of these effects has had a pronounced impact on laws, as (at this writing) approximately half of the states have recently changed their statutes of limitations for filing charges based on "recovered" memories.

Although it is certainly true that painful or emotional experiences might change memory performance, perhaps a bigger question is the possibility that a person might report a memory for something that never occurred. Researchers have demonstrated that, under specific conditions, false *recognition* effects can be obtained (Anisfeld & Knapp, 1968; Hintzman, 1988; Underwood, 1965); but until recently, there have been few experimental reports of false *recall* effects.

Anecdotal examples from two prominent psychologists suggest the possibility of false recall. The memory researcher Ulrich Neisser (Neisser, 1982) reported that he had a vivid memory of what he was doing when he heard that the Japanese had attacked Pearl Harbor in December 1941. He remembered that he was listening to a baseball game on the radio

Elizabeth Loftus
Elizabeth Loftus was responsible for ground-breaking research into how eyewitnesses' memory can be misled. She continues to provide objective perspectives on topics such as repressed and traumatic memories.

when the broadcast was interrupted by the announcement of the attack. The problem is that this is impossible—no one was playing baseball in December. A second example comes from Jean Piaget (1945/1962), the developmental psychologist. Piaget remembered an incident from his childhood involving an attack on him and his caretaker. Piaget was able to remember details of the attack, including details about the injuries suffered by the caretaker. Later, though, the caretaker admitted to fabricating the entire event.

Much of the controversy around recovered memories concerns traumatic events, such as physical or sexual abuse, and many researchers have tried to create experimental analogs of these types of situations. For example, a vaccination can often be a traumatic event for a child. Bruck, Ceci, Francouer, and Barr (1995) took advantage of this possibility. They created a situation in which a child and his or her parents came to a physician's office. The physician (a male in this experiment) gave the child a simple physical exam, with witnesses present. The child then went into another room, where an assistant (a female) talked to the child about a number of simple things, including a poster on the wall. After five minutes, the physician returned and gave the child the vaccination.

Then, over a period of about 18 months after the vaccination, the researchers visited with the child three times. Each time, they included in their conversation a simple reminder about the event. For some of the children, the reminder was very general (*someone* gave you a shot and *someone* talked to you about a poster). For other children, the reminder was simple but inaccurate (the *assistant* gave you a shot and the *doctor* talked to you about a poster). It is important to note that the children were not *questioned* about the event. That is, these reminders were not suggested answers (e.g., "Who gave you the shot? It was the assistant, right?"). Instead, the reminders were simple statements made during the conversation.

Figure 7.7 shows the percent of children who incorrectly reported details about the doctor and the assistant by the third interview. By this time, nearly half the children were reporting that they remembered that someone who never actually touched them (the assistant) gave them the shot, some medicine, or even a physical exam. As well, more than half the children were reporting that they remembered that the person who *did* actually touch them did something else instead.

As you can tell from the description of the study by Bruck and her colleagues, obtaining an experimental analog to a real-world situation can be difficult. In fact, one of the major challenges facing psychologists interested in the false memory effect has been the ability to create an analog to the real world in the laboratory, where extraneous influences can be controlled. However, some recent efforts suggest that there may be a way to do this.

The work we will describe is based on a study reported by Deese (1959). In that study, subjects were presented with a list of related items, an example being the list *table, sit, legs, seat, soft, desk, arm, sofa, wood, cushion, rest,* and *stool.* These items are all related to each other, and they are also the words most usually associated with the word *chair* (Russell & Jenkins, 1954). When subjects were asked to recall lists like this, they quite often actually recalled the word *chair.* (If this study sounds familiar, don't worry, you are not experiencing a false memory. We presented a similar task in Experiment 1A.)

Deese's findings were apparently ignored for years, but they recently were "rediscovered" and replicated (Roediger & McDermott, 1995). You may be thinking that, although these findings are interesting, they do not have much to do with appearing to remember things that never really happened. For example, you might think that, even though people could conceivably mis-remember something from a list of words, they would not mis-remember specific details of an event, such as the identity of the person who read the list of words to them.

FIGURE 7.7   **A False Memory Effect**   As a consequence of three simple conversations about a non-traumatic visit to the doctor, a high proportion of children mis-remembered significant events about that visit.

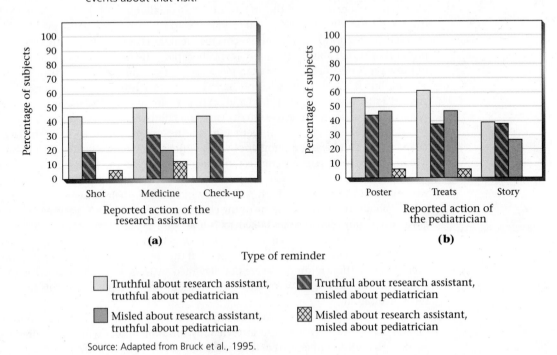

Source: Adapted from Bruck et al., 1995.

However, some recent work has shown that people not only mis-remember items but also mis-remember important episodic information about those items. Payne, Elie, Blackwell, and Nueschatz (1996) conducted a study similar to those of Roediger and McDermott and Deese, with an interesting twist. The lists of items were presented by means of a videotape in which two people (Jason and Carol) read the words out loud. After performing a recall test, subjects were asked to go back through the list of words and identify the person who had spoken each recalled word by placing a J or a C in front of the word. They were told that this was a difficult task and that if they were unsure about who had spoken the word, they should mark the word with a dash.

As in the earlier studies, subjects reliably recalled items that did not appear in the studied lists. But subjects were also very willing to identify someone as having spoken these unpresented items. Specifically, 94 percent of the studied items were labeled as having been spoken by either Jason or Carol, and 87 percent of the *unstudied* items were labeled as to the speaker, though in fact no one spoke those words. And this high percentage was obtained in a situation in which subjects had the option of not identifying a speaker.

Section Summary: The Importance of Context in Episodic Retrieval

The context of memory tasks, defined in terms of external conditions, internal states, or different types of information, can affect memory performance. A distinction can be made between two types of context, one corresponding to the surroundings (context alpha) and one corresponding to information that clarifies meaning (context beta). We concentrated on the effects of context alpha and discussed the fact that context effects in recognition are difficult to obtain. Context, particularly physical or environmental context (context alpha), can influence memory both positively and negatively in a number of ways. Two prominent recent examples of the effects of context on memory performance are the misinformation and false memory effects—effects that may be critically dependent on processing context. In addition to these external influences, internal states, such as mood, can also influence performance.

REVIEWING MEMORY IN THE LONG TERM: EPISODIC MEMORY

CONCEPT REVIEW

1. Summarize the distinction between episodic and semantic memory information using the questions that journalists ask when they cover an event. Does the distinction rely at all on a distinction between types of memory tasks? Is this a possible problem? *Hint:* Think about the problems associated with the distinction between short-term and long-term memory.

2. With what five issues is the distinction between episodic and semantic memory information concerned?

3. What is a dissociation? What would you have to do to observe dissociation in a memory experiment? *Hint:* Take a look at Table 7.1.

4. What are item, associative, and order information? How does the distinction among these three types of memory information differ from the distinction between episodic and semantic memory information or the distinction among types of stores in the Atkinson-Shiffrin model of memory?

5. What is the encoding specificity hypothesis? How does it relate to and how is it different from the transfer-appropriate processing hypothesis?

6. What is the levels-of-processing hypothesis? Why did research on this hypothesis pose problems for the total-time hypothesis? What are some logical problems with the levels-of-processing hypothesis?

7. What are generate-recognize theories of memory? What are some of the problems associated with these theories? Contrast generate-recognize theories with dual process theories.

8. Summarize the distinction between explicit and implicit memory information. How is the logic of this distinction similar to (or different from) the logic of the distinction between (a) short-term and long-term memory and (b) episodic and semantic memory?

9. How have neurobiological studies of animal memory helped us understand aspects of episodic memory?

10. What are context alpha and context beta? Which corresponds to the effects of your surroundings on your memory?

11. Compare and contrast the three theories used to explain why context effects are hard to obtain in recognition tasks.

12. What is the misinformation effect? What are two explanations for this effect?

13. What is the false memory effect? Is it possible for people to mis-remember not only information but also specific episodic aspects of that information? Discuss recent experiments investigating this question.

KEY TERMS

associative information (p. 216)
changed-trace hypothesis (p. 237)
context alpha (p. 233)
context beta (p. 234)
dissociation (p. 214)
dual process theory (p. 221)
encoding specificity hypothesis
   (p. 216)
episodic memory information (p. 210)

explicit memory (p. 229)
false memory effect (p. 236)
flashbulb memory (p. 213)
generate-recognize theory (p. 221)
heuristic (p. 214)
implicit memory (p. 229)
item information (p. 216)
levels-of-processing hypothesis (p. 218)
misinformation effect (p. 236)

multiple trace hypothesis (p. 237)
order information (p. 216)
outshining hypothesis (p. 235)
relearning task (p. 211)
savings score (p. 211)
semantic memory information (p. 210)
total-time hypothesis (p. 218)
transfer-appropriate processing (p. 225)

SUGGESTED READINGS

Volume 11, number 7 of the *Journal of Experimental Psychology: Learning, Memory, and Cognition* (1985) contains interesting perspectives on the contributions of Ebbinghaus written by some of the most influential psychologists currently working. D. L. Schacter's (1987) "Implicit memory: History and current status" is an excellent and readable review of the history of the distinction between implicit and explicit memory that also gives a sense for how research in the 1980s was approaching this issue (*Journal of Experimental Psychology: Learning, Memory, and Cognition, 13*, 501–518). Two provocative and accessible books dealing with false and repressed memories are E. Loftus and K. Ketcham's *The myth of repressed memory: False memories and accusations of sexual abuse* (New York: St. Martin's, 1994) and *Victims of memory: Incest accusations and shattered lives,* by M. Pendergast (Upper Access Books, 1995). In addition, D. L. Schacter (1995) provides a balanced comparison and commentary on both these books

in "Memory distortion: History and current status" (in D. L. Schacter, J. T. Coyle, M. M. Fishback, M. M. Mesulam, & L. E. Sullivan, eds., *Memory and distortion: How minds, brains, and societies reconstruct the past,* Cambridge, MA: Harvard University Press). The February 1996 issue of the *Journal of Memory and Language* contains a number of articles devoted to discussions of memory illusions. Finally, as we have discussed throughout this book, neuroscientists and cognitive psychologists are coming together in a number of ways to investigate interesting problems. One of these problems involves whether there are different memory systems. M.S. Weldon provides a thorough and balanced look at both the advantages and the potential problems of this type of work in "The memory chop-shop" (in Jonathan Foster and Marko Jelicic, eds., *Dissociations, dichotomies, and dissent: Unitary versus multiple systems accounts of memory* (New York: Oxford University Press, in press).

8 Memory in the Long Term: Semantic Memory

> *[W]e must speak* of meaningfulness as a composite of characteristics, each characteristic given an operational definition. . . . [W]e have no recourse but to define meaningfulness as the aggregate of these characteristics, if we are to use the term at all.—Benton Underwood (1966, p. 466)

IMAGINE A MEMORY EXPERIMENT in which we have a subject learn a short list that includes the words *bashful* and *cheetah*. Then we test the subject's memory using questions like "Which of the seven dwarfs comes first alphabetically?" (for *bashful*) and "What is the fastest animal on earth?" (for *cheetah*). As we discussed in Chapter 7, these probes of memory can be described as general knowledge questions. One reason they fit this description is that people can answer them by using their general knowledge of the world without having to think about the episode during which they learned the information.

In this chapter, we concentrate on semantic memory information, information that we can think of as comprising our general knowledge about the world. As the label suggests, semantic memory seems to be closely related to the understanding and use of language (which we discuss in detail in Chapters 9 and 10). In fact, when Tulving (1972, 1983) initially proposed the distinction between episodic and semantic memory, he defined semantic memory as "the memory necessary for the use of language for the manipulation of the symbols, concepts, and relations" (Tulving, 1972, p. 392).

SOME HISTORY OF THE STUDY OF MEANING

In each of the chapters so far, we have tried to give you a sense of some of the rich history involved in the study of various topics in cognitive psychology. Sometimes, this requires considering a rather long history. The history of the study of semantic memory closely parallels the history of scientific psychology, and so to review it we go back to around the beginning of the twentieth century.

Intellectual Predecessors

The study of semantic memory information is often traced to early work on how humans classify or associate things (Watt, 1905, as cited by Miller, 1951; we discuss categorization in detail in Chapter 13). Classification and association tasks are ideal for studying semantic memory information because, to perform these tasks, one has to know what something *means*. Furthermore, the methods of investigation being used early in the twentieth century were well suited to the use of these tasks to study semantic memory. Introspection was one of the principal methods for studying psychological phenomena, and the tasks used had to allow introspecters not only to perform the tasks but also to think about how they were performing and to remember everything that went on while they were performing. Determining what category something belongs in and producing a word related to another word appeared to meet these requirements.

But the apparent simplicity of these tasks may have been misleading. Mayer and Orth (1901, as cited by Miller, 1951) presented subjects with words and asked them to produce associated words. In addition, they asked subjects to introspect and report on how they arrived at the word they produced. When the researchers examined the process of going from the stimulus word to the production of the associated word, they identified four phases of the task: a preparatory period, reading or hearing the test word, searching for the associated word, and speaking or writing down the associated word. Subjects in these studies were able to give many details of three of these four phases but seemed unable to report anything about the process of searching for the associated word (which is, in many ways, the most interesting part of the task). Subjects were aware of doing something, but they could not seem to describe it.

Researchers began calling this part of the process *Bewusstseinslagen,* or "the lay of consciousness," where *lay* refers to the general shape, outline, or structure of consciousness (as in "the lay of the land"). This idea was related to a concept that, at the time, was being used by the first experimenters studying reaction time—a concept called *determining tendencies* (Selz, 1922, as cited by Miller, 1951). Broadly defined, determining tendencies are those aspects of processing that seem to push a task to some predetermined outcome. The problem was that although this notion appeared to *describe* what was happening, it really did not *explain* it.

Researchers were not blind to this problem. One solution was motivated by the suggestion that perhaps subjects had trouble introspecting on the search process because it occurred so quickly. In that case, a task that required more complicated processing could be used; the task would take longer, and subjects would be able to report on what was occurring. One task that was proposed for this endeavor was a **syllogistic reasoning task** (Storring, 1908, as cited by Miller, 1951), in which a subject was shown two premises, such as "All men are mortal" and "Socrates is a man," and asked to produce the logical conclusion or inference.

This task did slow subjects down, and it appeared to allow subjects to report on what they did. But experimenters found that no consistent method was used by subjects to complete the syllogism. Sometimes, subjects visualized the outcome, and sometimes they used logical rules. So researchers were no closer to answering the questions that really interested them. This continued to be the case through much of the middle part of the twentieth century. Studies of the use of knowledge consistently came up with less than the researchers desired. For example, an extensive study of the use of mathematical knowledge (Hadamard, 1945) pointed to processes that seemed to be just beyond the realm of examination, at least by way of introspection.

In the 1960s, researchers approached the questions of what semantic memory is and how it is processed using different tools: speeded-classification tasks and word (or object) naming. In a **speeded-classification task,** subjects are presented with a stimulus (for example, a word like *bashful* or *goofy*) and must quickly determine whether it names something that belongs in a particular class (for example, the seven dwarfs). Initially, studies of speeded classification examined specific relations among different types of stimuli (Pollack, 1963; Schaeffer & Wallace, 1969) rather than investigating the bigger questions of how semantic memory information might be organized or used. This quickly changed, however, and by the end of the 1960s, speeded classification was being used to address questions such as the organization and use of semantic memory information (Landauer & Freedman, 1968; Landauer & Meyer, 1972).

Other researchers asked these same types of questions using naming tasks. In a **naming task,** subjects are presented with a picture of something (such as a chair) and are asked to produce the name for it. Researchers reasoned that if the time to produce the name reflects the organization of semantic memory, then performance with various types of items might reveal important things about the organization of semantic memory.

Stop and think for a moment about all the things you know. If you start listing the classes of things you know (names of the 50 states, names of different foods, your relatives, arithmetic facts, etc.), you will quickly realize that there is a great deal of semantic memory information to be organized.

Researchers early on came to the same conclusion. For example, Oldfield (1963) estimated that an educated adult has an active vocabulary of about 75,000 words. Every time an adult speaks a sentence, he or she has to retrieve some of these 75,000 words from memory. Since people can speak reasonably quickly, the only way they can accomplish this is to have a memory for words that is organized efficiently.

Oldfield suggested that an efficient way of organizing memory would be to store words according to their frequency of occurrence in the language. In this case, the most frequently used words would be stored to allow for the quickest access, whereas the least frequently used words would be stored so that they would require more searching. If memory were organized this way, then objects with frequently used names (like *table*) would be named faster than objects with less frequently used names (like *pontoon*). In a series of studies, Oldfield and Wingfield (1964, 1965) found evidence suggesting that this was the case (see Figure 8.1).

Oldfield proposed that memory for words is organized in "bins," with each bin corresponding to a set of words that occur with similar frequency. According to this model, rather than having to search all of memory, subjects estimate the frequency of the word's occurrence and then search through the bin corresponding to that frequency. If semantic memory were partitioned into 10 bins, then subjects would need to search only one-tenth of memory—a substantial improvement in efficiency. This original proposal turned out to be a bit too simple (Lachman, Lachman & Butterfield, 1979), but the basic finding that ob-

FIGURE 8.1   **Naming Time Related to Frequency of Occurrence**   Data from some of the original studies of naming time indicate that the time required to name an object is a function of frequency of occurrence. The graph shows the mean response time (RT) as a function of the logarithm of the frequency of occurrence (plotted as filled circles), as well as the predictions from Oldfield's model (line).

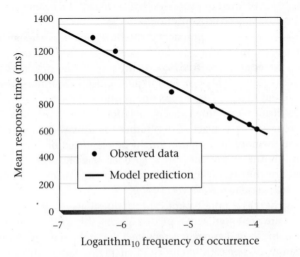

Source: Adapted from Lachman, Lachman, & Butterfield, 1979.

jects with frequently used names are named more quickly than objects with less frequently used names is quite reliable (Carroll & White, 1973; Lachman, 1973). In addition, recent research (Anderson, 1990; Anderson & Schooler, 1991; Schooler, 1997; Schooler & Anderson, 1997) suggests that, as Oldfield proposed, frequency of occurrence of items in the environment may provide one basis for the organization of semantic memory.

The work with speeded classification and object naming seemed to suggest that some important organizational characteristic was being used. Oldfield's model proposed one possibility; but for the most part, theorizing about possible structure was relatively limited during this period. A breakthrough occurred in the late 1960s, when two influential models of the representation of meaning were proposed. The first was Morton's (1969, 1970) *logogen model,* which we discuss in more detail in connection with language comprehension in Chapter 10. The second was Quillian's (1968) computational model for the organization of semantic memory.

Representing the Structure of Meaning

Quillian was working with Alan Newell and Herbert Simon, two scientists who were to be very influential in the development of **cognitive science,** a discipline that has combined psychological theorizing with computer technologies and applications (including artificial intelligence). Quillian's theory of the structure of semantic memory (the **Teachable Language Comprehender**) was itself a computer program intended to "extract and somehow retain meaning from natural language text" (Quillian, 1968, p. 459).

Quillian proposed that memory is organized as a data structure called a *network* composed of *nodes* and *links* among the nodes. The nodes represent concepts, and the links show the relations among concepts (see Figure 8.2a). In Quillian's computer model, at any node, the processing program had access both to the meaning of the concept represented by that node and to pointers (by way of links) to related concepts. This meant that by having access to the node for *bird,* the program had direct access to the concepts representing a bird's general characteristics (*wings, fly,* etc.).

Trying to Find the Structure   Consider this question. Given the structure presented in Figure 8.2a, if you started at any node in the network, what would determine how long it would take to get to any other node? Here is a hint: Think of the structure as a road map with the nodes being towns and the links being the only roads that connect those towns. You can think of traversing the network as being similar to taking a road trip through this mapped-out territory.

If you said that the number of links you would have to traverse (or the number of nodes you would have to go through) is the major factor, you are thinking in much the same way Collins and Quillian (1969) did when they conducted the first experimental test of Quillian's model. They presented subjects with statements like "A canary is a bird" and "A canary can fly" and then measured the time it took subjects to make a true/false response. From Figure 8.2, see if you can predict which of these two statements would take longer to verify.

The results of Collins and Quillian's study are presented in Figure 8.3. Here, you can see that the fastest response times (RTs) are those associated with statements that require accessing, or locating, only one node (e.g., "A canary is a canary"). This is equivalent to a road trip in which you do not leave the town you started in. In addition, statements that require moving across more nodes and links require more time to verify. In terms of the road-trip metaphor, the more highways you have to travel and the more towns you have to go through, the longer the trip will take.

FIGURE 8.2   **Quillian's Network Model**   (a) Quillian's data structure for semantic memory represents concepts such as *bird* and *animal* as nodes connected by links. (b) A modified version of a portion of the network shows that both *canary* and *chicken* are only one link away from *bird*, suggesting that there should be no difference in the response times required to verify statements relating canaries and chickens to birds. Unfortunately (at least for the model), this is not the case.

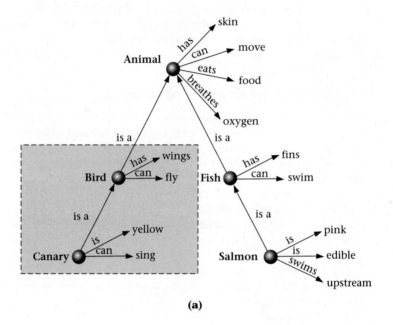

(a)

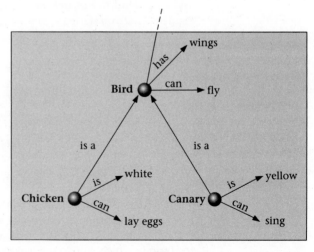

(b)

FIGURE 8.3   **A Test of Quillian's Model.**   The response time required to verify a sentence was found to be directly related to the structure proposed by Quillian. In particular, the graph shows that the mean response time required to verify sentences of the form "A *noun verb property*" (e.g., "A canary can sing") is a function of the number of links in the network separating the noun and the property.

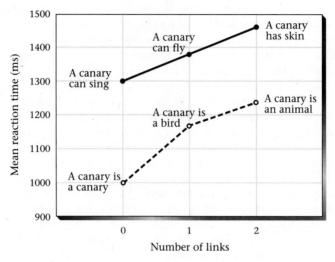

Source: Adapted from Lachman, Lachman, & Butterfield, 1979.

Complicating the Structure   Quillian's network seemed to be able to account for important aspects of the use of semantic memory information. But it was not long before researchers began to uncover aspects of performance that were difficult to explain using Quillian's basic structure.

Figure 8.2b shows a modification of the semantic network. Notice that we have added another link to the *bird* node: one representing the notion of a chicken. Based on this diagram and on the data we just discussed, which of the following two statements would take longer to respond to?

A canary is a bird.
A chicken is a bird.

If you answer this question using only what the network in Figure 8.2b tells you, you will have to say that the time required to verify these two statements is the same. This is because, for each statement, you only have to travel across one link to get from the first concept in the statement (*canary* or *chicken*) to the second concept (*bird*).

But suppose you answer the question using your intuition. You may say that the second sentence will take longer to verify than the first. If you do, your intuition is correct; the model is wrong. There actually is a difference in the time required to verify these two sentences (Rips, Shoben & Smith, 1973), with the second statement requiring more time than the first. Quillian's model could be modified to account for these results, but that would require things like links of variable length.

However, another model from the same period does not have difficulty with this difference in verification times. Instead of proposing that semantic memory information is organized in a network (as in Figure 8.2), the **feature list model** (Smith, 1978; Smith, Shoben & Rips, 1974) proposed that semantic memory information is organized into lists. Each concept in semantic memory (e.g., *bird, chicken, canary*) is represented by a list of features. Figure 8.4 shows what one of these lists for the concepts *bird, chicken,* and *canary* might look like.

Smith and colleagues (1974) suggested that two basic types of features go into these lists, and the lists are ordered according to these two basic types. The features that come first are called **defining features.** These features are in some basic way essential to the concept being represented. For example, *animate* is an essential feature of *canary, chicken,* and *bird*. Without the feature *animate,* each of these items is less like what it is supposed to be and more like something it should not be (like *dinner* or *road kill*).

Below the defining features in the list are features that are commonly or frequently associated with the concept but that are not essential to the meaning of the concept. These are called **characteristic features.** For example, chickens may or may not be raised for food (they may be kept for their eggs). But whether they are raised for food or to provide eggs, chickens can still be identified as chickens.

When we discussed retrieval of information in Quillian's model, we compared it to taking a trip. Retrieval in the feature list model is a very different type of process. For example, for a person verifying the statement "A chicken is a bird," retrieval in the feature list model involves randomly selecting a set of features from the list for *chicken* and a set of features from the list for *bird*. These subsets are then compared, and a feature overlap score (reflecting the number of features common to both lists) is computed. This score is an index of the similarity between the two concepts: the higher the overlap score, the greater the similarity.

If the overlap score is high enough, then subjects can produce fast verification responses. But if the overlap score is only moderately high, a second kind of comparison, involving *only* the defining features, has to be done. Thus, the feature comparison model is capable of predicting *ranges* of verification times where, according to network models like Quillian's, no such ranges should exist.

Nevertheless, research began to turn up cases that this model, too, had difficulty addressing (Ashcraft, 1976, 1978). We discuss some of these, along with related issues, when we discuss categorization in Chapter 13.

Priming and Spreading Activation   Quillian's theoretical structure, Collins and Quillian's data, and the feature list model proposed by Smith and colleagues provided the ba-

---

FIGURE 8.4   **A Feature List Model**   This example of a feature list model represents concepts from the network model presented in Figure 8.2b.

Bird	Chicken	Canary
• is animate	• is animate	• is animate
• has feathers	• has feathers	• has feathers
• can fly	• can lay eggs	• can sing
• etc.	• etc.	• etc.

sis for the development of two ideas that have profoundly affected the study of semantic memory—*priming* and *spreading activation*. We begin by discussing aspects of priming.

We discussed priming effects as they pertain to attention in Chapter 5. Generally speaking, **priming** refers to a change in a person's readiness to perform a task that results from the person's having advance information about the task. Priming that produces an improvement in performance is called **facilitation** (or *positive priming*), whereas priming that produces a decrement in performance is called **inhibition** (or *negative priming*). In the literature on priming, the items with which subjects work are referred to as *target items,* and the items that precede the target items are called the *primes*. It was the types of items that produce facilitation and inhibition that gave scientists clues about how semantic memory information might be structured and used.

One of the earliest studies of facilitation and inhibition in a semantic memory experiment (Meyer & Schvaneveldt, 1971) involved a **lexical decision task.** In a lexical decision task, subjects are presented with strings of letters. Their task is to decide whether or not the strings of letters are words. In the Meyer and Schvaneveldt study, target items were either words or pronounceable nonwords (like *manty*). These target items were presented with either related or unrelated primes (when the targets were words) or with other pronounceable nonwords.

Before we consider the results of this study, think about what kinds of evidence would suggest facilitation and inhibition. If you think about the definitions we gave for these terms, you will note that the idea of finding a benefit or a decrement in performance implies some starting point, or baseline. In the priming literature, this starting point, or baseline, is referred to as the *neutral,* or control, condition. The condition is called the neutral condition because experimenters assume that in this condition the relationship between the prime and the target item is neutral; the prime neither helps nor hinders the processing of the target. The Meyer and Schvaneveldt (1971) study used two neutral conditions: one in which the target was a word and the prime was an unrelated word and one in which the target was a nonword and the prime was also a nonword.

By comparing the data from the neutral conditions and the data from the other conditions, we can calculate *difference scores* to measure the amount of priming or inhibition. We calculate a difference score by subtracting the measure of performance (either RT or error percentage) for the experimental condition from the same measure of performance for the neutral condition. When the value for the experimental condition is less than that for the neutral condition (either shorter RT or fewer errors), we obtain a positive value, which indicates facilitation. When the value for the experimental condition is greater than that for the neutral condition (either longer RT or more errors), we obtain a negative value, which indicates inhibition. Table 8.1 presents some of the data from the Meyer and Schvaneveldt study. In this table, we have left spaces for you to calculate the difference scores for RTs and percent errors. Do these calculations now. Which of the conditions showed facilitation, and which showed inhibition?

If you calculated the difference scores correctly, you can see how these effects suggested that Quillian's ideas about the structure of memory had some validity. Providing a prime that was closely related to the target meant that subjects had access to all the nodes related to the prime. One of these nodes was the actual target, allowing subjects to respond to it quickly and accurately when it was presented. Providing a prime unrelated to the target meant that the target was not among the nodes to which subjects had access. So there was no benefit above and beyond the level of performance obtained when the target was presented with no associatively related word preceding it.

The data from priming experiments such as Meyer and Schvaneveldt's and many others

TABLE 8.1   **Results from a Priming Study by Meyer and Schvaneveldt**   Calculate the difference, or priming, scores for response times (RTs) and percentage of errors by subtracting the measure for the experimental condition from the measure for the neutral condition.

	Prime	Target	RT	Percentage of Errors
Words				
Neutral condition	bread	doctor	940	8.7
Experimental condition	nurse	doctor	855	6.3
Difference Score (subtract)			☐	☐
Pronounceable Nonwords				
Neutral condition	cabe	manty	884	2.6
Experimental condition	book	marb	1087	27.6
Difference Score (subtract)			☐	☐

Source: Data from Meyer and Schvaneveldt, 1971.

suggested that the structure of semantic memory might be based on meaningful relationships, just as Quillian had suggested. And this structure had implications for the type of processing that would be required. The term that psychologists applied to the processing implied by the network structure was called **spreading of activation.**

Collins and Quillian referred to the spreading of activation that occurred in the network as being something like the "harmless spreading of a plague" (1972, p. 326). Since it might be a bit difficult to think of a spreading plague as harmless, you could instead think of spreading activation as being like the ripples you see when you throw a rock into a lake. It seemed likely that the spread of the activation would take time, and so RT measures became the dependent variable of choice in studying spread of activation (Anderson, 1974, 1984).

Interactions with Episodic Memory   Even as ideas about the structure and processing of semantic memory information were developing, data began to accumulate documenting some of the ways in which semantic memory information interacted with episodic memory information. One of the most interesting demonstrations was that of Neely (1977). Neely used the lexical decision task, with an interesting modification: He told subjects what type of item they should expect to see after the prime. For example, sometimes subjects were told to expect a word from the same category as the prime; so if the prime was *bird*, the target might be *robin*. Sometimes, subjects were told to expect a word from a different category; so if the prime was *bird,* the target might be *arm*.

Neely set up his study so that these expectations were correct only part of the time. In addition, he varied the time that elapsed between the presentation of the prime and the presentation of the target, a timing pattern referred to as **stimulus onset asynchrony,** or **SOA.** This allowed Neely to examine a number of aspects of processing. First, as in other priming studies, the presence or absence of a meaningful relationship between the prime and the target could provide evidence about the structure of semantic memory informa-tion. Second, the time allowed to process the prime before presentation of the target (the SOA) could provide evidence about the relationship between processing time and the type and amount of information available in memory. This was important to ideas about spreading activation. Finally, subjects' expectations (and their responses to violations of those expectations) could provide evidence about how the information learned in the ex-periment (a type of episodic information) could be used intentionally to modify the out-comes of processing semantic information.

Some of the data from Neely's (1977) study are presented in Figure 8.5. On the left side of the figure are difference scores from conditions in which subjects expected that the prime and the target would be from the same category. You can see that when this expec-tation was met (e.g., when *robin* was primed by *bird*), facilitation was observed early and persisted to the longest SOA. But when this expectation was violated (when *arm* was primed by *bird*), inhibition was observed, and it increased as the length of the SOA in-creased.

On the right side of Figure 8.5 are data from the conditions in which subjects expected that the prime and target would be from different categories. When this expectation was met (e.g., when *door* was primed by *body*), subjects showed the effect of priming, although the effect appeared much later than when the target and prime were from the same cate-gory. Essentially, it was as if the knowledge obtained in the experiment allowed subjects to change how they accessed semantic memory information so that they could strategically gain access to the nodes for the unrelated category.

FIGURE 8.5 **Interaction of Semantic Memory Information and Subject Expectations** Data from Neely's (1977) study showed that even when subjects expected the target and the prime to be from different categories, priming occurred (at the shortest SOAs) when the target vio-lated the expectation and came from the same category as the prime.

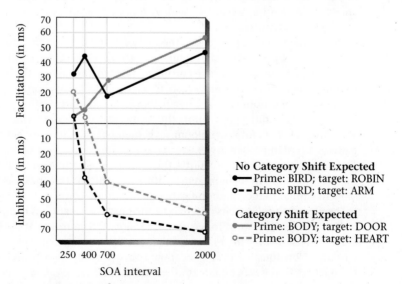

No Category Shift Expected
● Prime: BIRD; target: ROBIN
○- - Prime: BIRD; target: ARM

Category Shift Expected
● Prime: BODY; target: DOOR
○- - Prime: BODY; target: HEART

Source: Adapted from Ashcraft, 1989.

An intriguing finding was represented by data from the condition in which subjects expected the target and the prime to be from different categories and that expectation was violated (e.g., when *heart* was primed by *body*). In this case, when subjects had the least amount of time to process the prime before seeing the target, priming on the basis of the semantic relationship was observed, even though subjects *expected* that the target and prime would be unrelated. The inhibition that would be expected if subjects were completely unable to change how they accessed semantic memory information was not observed until subjects had been allowed quite a bit of processing time (700 milliseconds).

Although these data did suggest that information other than semantic information could influence performance, they also suggested that under some conditions semantic information had a strong and almost uncontrollable influence and that this influence was apparent quite soon after the target was presented. In fact, data such as these suggested that the semantic influence was beyond conscious control (Marcel, 1980, 1983a), though we should note that this conclusion is the focus of considerable controversy (Carr et al., 1982; Neely & Durgonoglu, 1985).

Chunks of Semantic Memory   Consider this string of letters:

FBIASAPPHDVCR

Now see what happens when we add some commas:

FBI, ASAP, PHD, VCR

By the early 1970s, a number of studies had documented what you probably noticed. If you can segment information into meaningful groups (chunks), the information is easier to comprehend and remember (Bower et al., 1969; Bower & Reitman, 1972; Tulving, 1962, 1968). This finding offered direct support for a highly influential idea from early research on human information processing: the notion of a "chunk" of information (Miller, 1956).

When Miller originally proposed this idea, it had a reasonably technical meaning and referred specifically to aspects of memory in the short term. But by the 1970s, the notion of a chunk of information had come to refer to aspects of the use of semantic memory at encoding. And using semantic memory information in this way came to be referred to (naturally) as **chunking.**

One of the first comprehensive theories of chunking and its importance in cognition was proposed by Newell and Rosenbloom (1981). They proposed that chunking involves combining information about recurring patterns in any task on the basis of their match to information in semantic memory. So, for example, you can chunk the string of letters presented above by noting that letter patterns in the string correspond to acronyms you know. But how did you acquire the knowledge needed to notice those meaningful acronyms? Newell and Rosenbloom suggested that each time we encounter a meaningful pattern, a certain probability exists that we will encode the pattern as a whole (a chunk). The more frequently we encounter the pattern, the more likely it is that we will have a number of chunks in memory representing the pattern. This makes it easier to chunk subsequent stimuli that contain the pattern.

The idea of chunking bits of semantic memory information is compatible with network models such as Quillian's. To see how, take a look at Figure 8.6. At the bottom of the figure are six letters. Assume for a moment that you have never seen these letters in this particular order. Now imagine that, over time, you repeatedly come into contact with the first three letters in the same context as the words *Federal Bureau of Investigation* and the last three letters in the same context as the words *Central Intelligence Agency.* With each en-

FIGURE 8.6   **Chunking**   Over time, you could use your repeated experience with these letters to form a network built of "chunks" of knowledge.

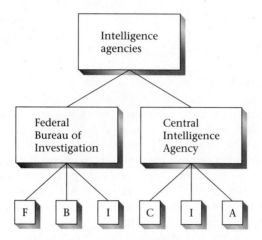

counter, you note these recurring patterns, and you use the associations to "build" nodes for the acronyms that tie the letter concepts and the associated names together. As you learn more, you may even build a node to tie the acronyms' nodes together under the concept *intelligence agencies*. Essentially, at each step in building this network, you take advantage of existing semantic memory information to organize new knowledge.

Knowledge as Productions   The notion of chunks of information has played an important role in the evolution of a comprehensive theory of memory and cognition developed by John R. Anderson (Anderson, 1993). The current version of the theory is called ACT-R (for "Adaptive Control of Thought—Rational"), and the theory has been through a number of evolutionary changes since it was initially proposed (Anderson, 1976).

Chunks, as we have been describing them so far, form the basis for one of two different types of memory information in ACT-R: declarative and procedural memory information. **Declarative memory information** is information that summarizes basic facts about the world, such as "A chicken can lay eggs." Declarative memory information can be reported verbally, and chunks are the basis for this type of information. **Procedural memory information** is information that allows the individual to perform a task, such as barbecuing a chicken. This type of memory information cannot always be reported verbally. Although there has been some controversy about the necessity or validity of this distinction, a fair amount of experimental data supports the distinction (Anderson, 1993).

Think for a moment about the act of riding a bike. If you were asked, you could probably report a number of facts (your declarative knowledge) about bicycles and riding them. But if you were asked, *while* you were riding a bike, what exactly you were doing (your procedural knowledge), you might have some problems reporting. You can probably see that, although there are differences in how you show evidence for these two types of information, they are closely related.

This is also the case in ACT-R, and the relation comes by way of something called a production. A **production** is a way of relating declarative knowledge to procedural knowledge, or a way of allowing general knowledge of the world to be translated into action. Roughly speaking, a production specifies a rule for taking some action based on some condition in the world (or the mind). For example, one extremely limited production could be stated like this: "If the item is a chicken, then barbecue it." Far more elegant uses have been made of productions and the distinctions between declarative and procedural memory (Anderson, 1993)—many more than we can cover here. But because translating knowledge into action is a critical part of skilled behavior, we return to this distinction and this model when we consider cognitive skill in Chapter 14.

Knowledge as Propositions   Another set of models of semantic memory that emerged in the 1970s were based on propositions (Anderson, 1976; Anderson & Bower, 1973; Kintsch, 1974; Rumelhart, Lindsay & Norman, 1972). In this context, a **proposition** is the smallest unit of knowledge that can be used to make a statement that can be judged to be true or false (Anderson, 1990b).

Whereas Quillian's model was concerned with representing the meaning of single concepts, such as *burrito,* models based on propositional representations were concerned with representing the meaning of statements about concepts, such as "Burritos are made from beans and tortillas." Propositions have two parts. The first is a *relation,* the part of the statement that relates all the other parts. In the statement "Burritos are made from beans and tortillas," the relation is the verb *make.* (Since we are concerned with representing the meaning of the statement, we are not concerned with the specific form of the verb; and the relation need not be a verb.) The second part of a proposition is the set of *arguments* that are joined by the relation. In our example, the arguments are the nouns *burritos, beans,* and *tortillas.* Thus, we can represent the sentence

Burritos are made from beans and tortillas

with the proposition

make, burritos, beans, tortillas

Although it may seem odd to think that the basic unit of semantic memory is an entire statement, there are data suggesting that this could be the case (e.g., Shiffrin et al., 1989). For example, Bransford and Franks (1971) had subjects study a set of 12 sentences, such as the following:

The ants ate the sweet jelly, which was on the table.
The ants in the kitchen ate the jelly.

These two sentences can be represented by the following propositions:

eat, ants, jelly
sweet, jelly
on, jelly, table, past
in, ants, kitchen, past

The set of sentences used in the study actually described two plausibly related situations. In the sentences given here, the situations are ants eating jelly on a table and ants eating jelly in the kitchen. But the details of the two situations were never explicitly related in the sentences—the sentences never stated that the table where the jelly was located was in the kitchen.

Bransford and Franks found that subjects were likely to say they had seen sentences composed of propositions they had encountered even if they had never seen the sentences. For example, subjects were equally likely to say they had read both "The ants in the kitchen ate the jelly," which they actually had read, and "The ants ate the sweet jelly in the kitchen," which they had not read. In fact, subjects were likely to say they recognized a sentence containing *all* of the propositions: "The ants in the kitchen ate the sweet jelly which was on the table." To get a sense for how powerful this effect can be, try the simple experiment described in Experiment 8.

Section Summary: Some History of the Study of Meaning

Modern research on semantic memory information can be traced back to work done around the beginning of the twentieth century on classification and association. Scientists who used introspection to understand the retrieval of semantic memory information consistently came up short in trying to discover the nature of this process, so they attempted to understand the process better by slowing it down through the use of syllogistic reasoning. Still, the nature of the structures of semantic memory and the processes that operate on those structures remained elusive. During the 1950s and 1960s, scientists found that semantic relations dominated performance on tasks like speeded classification and naming. A model that accounted for the effects of these types of semantic relations and that influenced most of the models and theories that followed was Quillian's network theory, which led to work on priming and spreading activation, two concepts related to the processing of structures such as Quillian's network. Alternative models, such as the feature list model, explained phenomena that were difficult to explain with the network model. Although semantic memory information seems to exert powerful influences, studies such as Neely's (1977) documented that it appears to interact in important ways with episodic information.

CURRENT KNOWLEDGE ABOUT THE FORM AND USE OF KNOWLEDGE

If you think about the tasks that rely on semantic memory information, you will probably realize that there are many—you need only consider the number of things you do every day that rely on your knowledge of basic facts. Consequently, it should not surprise you to learn that a wide range of experimental situations are currently of interest to psychologists studying various uses of semantic memory information.

Types of Information and Semantic Memory

The types of facts we have to remember, as just noted, are numerous and varied, as are the ways in which we store and process these facts. In this section, we discuss research on how different aspects of semantic memory information are stored and used.

Loss of Surface Information and Retention of Meaning Almost by definition, the types of details by which semantic memory information is specified are different from those for episodic memory information. For example, if you have taken a chemistry course, you might have reasonably detailed memory for the various entries in the periodic table of the elements, but you might have a poorly detailed memory for the room you were in the first time you studied those entries.

Besides this distinction, which is based on Tulving's (1972, 1983) original characterization, there is another distinction that helps characterize the types of semantic memory information. To understand this distinction, think about a task you might be doing right now: getting ready for a test in one of your courses. To prepare for this test, you are prob-

EXPERIMENT 8:   Abstracting Facts and the Power of Propositions

Instructions: Read each sentence in the following list individually. As soon as you have read a sentence, close your eyes and count to five. Then look at and answer the question that follows the sentence. Begin now.

The girl broke the window on the porch.	(Broke what?)
The tree in the front yard shaded the man who was smoking his pipe.	(Where?)
The hill was steep.	(What was?)
The cat, running from the barking dog, jumped on the table.	(From what?)
The tree was tall.	(Was what?)
The old car climbed the hill.	(What did?)
The cat running from the dog jumped on the table.	(Where?)
The girl who lives next door broke the window on the porch.	(Lives where?)
The car pulled the trailer.	(Did what?)
The scared cat was running from the barking dog.	(What was?)
The girl lives next door.	(Who does?)
The tree shaded the man who was smoking his pipe.	(What did?)
The scared cat jumped on the table.	(What did?)
The girl who lives next door broke the large window.	(Broke what?)
The man was smoking his pipe.	(Who was?)
The old car climbed the steep hill.	(The what?)
The large window was on the porch.	(Where?)
The tall tree was in the front yard.	(What was?)
The car pulling the trailer climbed the steep hill.	(Did what?)
The cat jumped on the table.	(Where?)
The tall tree in the front yard shaded the man.	(Did what?)
The car pulling the trailer climbed the hill.	(Which car?)
The dog was barking.	(Was what?)
The window was large.	(What was?)

Stop. Cover up the sentences. Now read each sentence below and decide if it is a sentence from the preceding list. If it is from that list, circle the word *Old;* otherwise, circle the word *New.*

1. The car climbed the hill.   Old? New?
2. The girl who lives next door broke the window.   Old? New?

ably relying on one of your textbooks. But are you concentrating on remembering the *specific wording* of passages of that text, or are you concentrating on remembering the *meaning* of what you are reading?

You are probably concentrating on the meaning, since instructors are generally more concerned that you retain the content of the information than its surface form. One of the most robust findings in studies of reading in situations like this is that people's memory

3. The old man who was smoking his pipe climbed the steep hill.   Old? New?
4. The tree was in the front yard.   Old? New?
5. The scared cat, running from the barking dog, jumped on the table.   Old? New?
6. The window was on the porch.   Old? New?
7. The barking dog jumped on the old car in the front yard.   Old? New?
8. The tree in the front yard shaded the man.   Old? New?
9. The cat was running from the dog.   Old? New?
10. The old car pulled the trailer.   Old? New?
11. The tall tree in the front yard shaded the old car.   Old? New?
12. The tall tree shaded the man who was smoking his pipe.   Old? New?
13. The scared cat was running from the dog.   Old? New?
14. The old car, pulling the trailer, climbed the hill.   Old? New?
15. The girl who lives next door broke the large window on the porch.   Old? New?
16. The tall tree shaded the man.   Old? New?
17. The cat was running from the barking dog.   Old? New?
18. The car was old.   Old? New?
19. The girl broke the large window.   Old? New?
20. The scared cat ran from the barking dog that jumped on the table.   Old? New?
21. The scared cat, running from the dog, jumped on the table.   Old? New?
22. The old car pulling the trailer climbed the steep hill.   Old? New?
23. The girl broke the large window on the porch.   Old? New?
24. The scared cat that broke the window on the porch climbed the tree.   Old? New?
25. The tree shaded the man.   Old? New?
26. The car climbed the steep hill.   Old? New?
27. The girl broke the window.   Old? New?
28. The man who lives next door broke the large window on the porch.   Old? New?
29. The tall tree in the front yard shaded the man who was smoking his pipe.   Old? New?
30. The cat was scared.   Old? New?

Stop. Count the number of sentences judged to be old.

How many test sentences did you judge to be old? Many people judge about 80 percent of the sentences old. A few assume that only 5 percent were experienced during acquisition. In fact, none of the test sentences occurred in the original list of sentences.

for the content of something they have read can be quite good, even with reasonably long retention intervals, whereas their memory for the specific way in which the information is presented (the way it is worded, for example) is fairly poor quite soon after they have read the information (Anderson & Paulson, 1977; Gernsbacher, 1985; Murphy & Shapiro, 1994; Sachs, 1967).

For example, Sachs (1967) had subjects read a paragraph of text and tested their memory for the sentences in the paragraph at different points while reading. She found that subjects could recognize the *exact* wording of a studied sentence if they were tested immediately after reading the sentence. However, if subjects were tested after reading an additional 80 syllables of text, their ability to recognize exact wording was fairly poor, whereas their memory for the meaning of the sentence was still quite good. To get a sense for how brief this period is, a normal adult reading a college textbook reads 80 syllables in less than 10 seconds.

Recently, Gernsbacher (1985, 1990) has proposed and tested two ways in which this *loss of surface information* might occur. The first concerns the manner in which individual words are encoded and the relationship between this new information and the information that was encoded just before it. According to Gernsbacher (1985), as each word is encoded, it is integrated into semantic memory structures representing the emerging meaning of the sentence. Thus, the specific word becomes part of a memory representation that is concerned with meaning on a level higher than that of the word.

This is something like the idea of chunking. However, there is an important difference. Whereas the idea of chunking implies that the lowest level of information stays around, Gernsbacher's notion of building structures suggests that the lowest level of information is lost. Essentially, what is retained is memory for the integrated meaning of the structure rather than memory for the specific words used to build the structure.

The second way in which surface information can be lost has to do with what happens when readers move from one structure to another. This can happen, for example, when readers move from one sentence to the next. In this case, Gernsbacher proposes that readers shift their attention from processing one structure to processing another *and* relating the two structures. So not only has the meaning been abstracted from the specific words of the first structure, but now attention is placed on the second structure and its semantic relationship to the *whole* of the first structure. In this way, the specific word (and memory for it) becomes unimportant.

Fuzzy Traces in Memory   The data we have just considered suggest that memory for the general semantic aspects of information is better at longer retention intervals than is memory for specific episodic aspects. But other data (Kolers, 1975a, 1976) suggest that surface features can be retained quite reliably, even with remarkably long retention intervals. Perhaps memory at any retention interval involves an interaction of semantic and episodic information, as suggested by some of Neely's (1977) findings.

One theoretical approach that considers the degree to which both general semantic and specific episodic information are represented and used in memory tasks is *fuzzy trace theory* (Brainerd et al., 1991). This theory starts with the assumption that memory is composed of two types of representations. The first is very similar to semantic memory structures we have been considering in this chapter—those, like the nodes in Quillian's network, that represent general meaning. Since these representations contain only the most general meaning information, they are called "fuzzy." The second type of representation is a set of episodic relationships that connect the fuzzy representations. These connections produce networks of relationships that are very rich, in that they contain both general semantic information and specific episodic information.

Relying on this rich network of relations, fuzzy trace theory makes some interesting predictions about how retrieval—free recall in particular—might operate. But to understand these predictions, you need to consider three additional concepts important to this theory: memory strength, output interference, and a process called "cognitive triage" (Brainerd et al., 1991).

Almost without exception, all the theories of memory that we have discussed assume that the probability of retrieving any type of information in memory is directly related to the strength of the representation of that information. As we have seen, memory strength can depend on the type of encoding activity or even the interaction of the types of information available at test with the types of information encoded during study. The intuitive assumption that memory performance will reflect memory strength dates back to some of the earliest theorizing about memory (Osgood, 1953). In fact, it was at one time even considered to be a "law" of cognitive processes (Marbe, 1901; Murdock, 1985; Thumb & Marbe, 1901, as cited by Brainerd et al., 1991).

Memory strength is associated with two types of activation. To understand them, let us return to the resonance metaphor that we have been using in our discussions of memory. Imagine that you have three bells of different sizes hanging very close to each other. Now imagine that you strike one of the bells at random. It responds to your strike by ringing and by knocking into one or both of the other bells.

If we think of the bells as entries in memory, and the act of striking a bell as the presentation of a retrieval cue to memory, we can see the two types of activation that are proposed in fuzzy trace theory.

1. The bell that was struck first knocks into the other bells: This corresponds to the first type of activation, the spreading episodic activation that ties the fuzzy traces together.
2. The bell that was struck first rings the loudest and makes it hard to hear the other bells. This second type of activation, called *output interference,* is produced when items are retrieved from memory. As its name suggests, output interference actually *interferes* with the retrieval of other items. Output interference has been noted to produce decrements in recall performance in a number of different experimental settings (Hasher & Zacks, 1988; Howe & Rabinowitz, 1989).

Fuzzy trace theory holds that at least two types of output interference can be produced. The first occurs because all of the component processes involved in retrieving and expressing a memory—finding all the information, ordering it, preparing the muscles to express the information (by speaking a word, for example)—generate outputs that must be dealt with in some way. This type of output interference is called *pre-response scheduling interference.*

The second type of interference has to do with the output from recall—or, more accurately, the expression of the recalled information. To understand this type of output interference, think about an experiment like this: Subjects hear a list of words, some time goes by, and they are asked to recall the words by speaking them out loud. In this situation, the target words are actually being heard *twice*—once during initial presentation and a second time when the subjects recall them. It would be unreasonable to think that when subjects hear themselves speak the words at recall they are not encoding any of that experience. So recalling an item can force another encoding operation. And the information being encoded this second time is not needed for recall of that item (since it was just recalled). It is possible that this encoding of unnecessary information might interfere with the recall of other, yet-to-be-recalled items. This type of output interference is called *post-response feedback interference.*

Thus, according to fuzzy trace theory, to control retrieval, the memory system has to deal with two types of influences: the strength of items and the output interference generated during retrieval and expression. The act of dealing with these influences so as to produce the optimal level of recall is called *cognitive triage,* taking its name from the practice of assigning priorities for medical treatment to casualties on a battlefield or victims of medical emergencies. Instead of prioritizing medical treatment according to the severity of patients' injuries, we are ordering the expression of memory information according to the strength of the traces and the amount of output interference.

To see how cognitive triage works, imagine that you have just started a new class with fifteen other people. Ten are friends from previous years at school and five are new to you. Imagine that someone asks you to recall the names of all the people in your class. You now have two things to deal with: the strength of the memory for each name and the interference produced by recalling each name. In what order (in terms of weak items and strong items) should you recall the names to produce the best level of recall?

You might think that your best bet is to recall the strongest items first, then work with the weaker items. But this strategy takes only the strength of the items into account—we still need to consider the output interference. According to fuzzy trace theory, one way of optimizing recall is to recall weak items, followed by strong items, followed by weak items. At the beginning of recall, output interference is low, so recall of weak items should not be impeded. But the act of recalling these items will produce some output interference, so the strong items will need to follow. Recalling these items will also generate output interference, so as recall progresses, you may slow down. This allows the output interference to subside, making it possible to recall weak items. Thus, fuzzy trace theory predicts an ordering in recall of weak → strong → weak—an ordering readily observed in actual recall performance (Brainerd et al., 1991). Fuzzy trace theory, then, demonstrates how different aspects of semantic memory information can interact and, as a result, makes an interesting prediction about recall performance.

Different Information at Different Times   The fact that, in some cases, surface information seems to be less available as time passes suggests interesting interactions among different types of information in semantic memory tasks as a function of time. Another type of research that has suggested similar conclusions has focused on the rate at which different types of information become available during memory retrieval. These are studies of **retrieval dynamics.**

One scientist who has contributed a great deal to our understanding of retrieval dynamics and our ability to explore aspects of retrieval dynamics experimentally is Barbara Dosher (1979, 1984; Dosher & Rosedale 1991; McElree & Dosher, 1993). Dosher has used a method developed in the 1970s (Wickelgren, 1977; Wickelgren & Corbett, 1977) called the *stop-signal paradigm,* in which subjects are allowed varying amounts of time to process a task and then are required to respond as soon as a signal (usually a tone) is presented, even if this means they need to guess.

The time allowed for processing in these experiments can range from a very short interval (less than 100 milliseconds) to a reasonably long one (around 3 seconds). If the accuracy of responses (usually measured using signal detection measures such as d', described in Chapter 3) is plotted against the total amount of time allowed for processing, a relationship between processing time and response accuracy called a *retrieval function* is produced.

Dosher and Rosedale (1991) used the stop-signal paradigm to explore the rate at which semantic information and episodic information become available. Subjects in this study learned pairs of words, some of which were semantically related (like *eating* and *drinking*) and some of which were not (like *burrito* and *hovercraft*). After studying lists of word pairs like these, subjects were shown test pairs from the following categories:

1. Test pairs could be both related and paired during study; these pairs possessed a semantic and an episodic relationship.

2. Test pairs could be semantically related and *not* paired during study; these pairs possessed a semantic relationship but not an episodic relationship.
3. Test pairs could be semantically unrelated and paired during study; these pairs possessed an episodic relationship but not a semantic relationship.
4. Test pairs could be semantically unrelated and *not* paired during study; these pairs possessed neither a semantic nor an episodic relationship.

Subjects were required to indicate, given different amounts of processing time, whether the words had been paired during study.

The results of this experiment are presented in Figure 8.7. When both semantic and episodic information were involved, the curve rose quickly and reached a high level (the dotted curve in the figure). When pairs were semantically related but not episodically related, semantic information influenced performance quite strongly early during processing, whereas episodic information became available only later (the solid curve in the figure). Dosher and Rosedale were able to estimate that episodic information became important in processing only after about 500 milliseconds of processing time was allowed. Until then, semantic information seemed to have the most dramatic influence on responding, even in a task in which subjects were required to judge the *episodic* relatedness of word pairs.

Types of Processes and Semantic Memory

Earlier in the chapter, we discussed how priming and lexical decision tasks have been used to explore ideas about the structure of semantic memory. As it turns out, priming and lex-

FIGURE 8.7 **Retrieval Functions** These retrieval functions from a study by Dosher and Rosedale plot the accuracy of responses as a function of the time allowed for processing. Note how semantic information exerts a powerful influence on responding early in retrieval, with episodic information becoming available later.

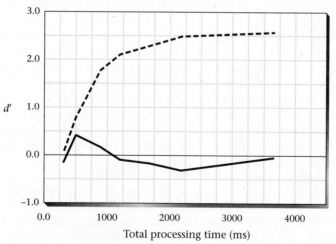

Source: Adapted from Dosher & Rosedale, 1991.

ical decision tasks continue to play important roles in the study of semantic memory. However, in recent years, they have been used to investigate the types of processes that operate on semantic memory information.

Perceptual and Conceptual Processes   Earlier, we presented the idea that the structure of semantic memory could be revealed by assessing the amount of time required to make the "road trip" across the relevant nodes in the network. But this ignores one serious issue: How do you get to the starting point for the road trip? More concretely (and psychologically), before the nodes and links can be traversed, the network has to be accessed. And this initial access involves processes of perception, encoding, and possibly even retrieval.

That perceptual processes could play a role in the processing of semantic memory information should not come as a complete surprise to you. For example, in Chapter 7, we presented a study by Blaxton (1989) that showed how episodic information could interact with semantic or conceptual processes. And earlier in this chapter, we presented work by Neely (1977) that demonstrated (among other things) that learning specific to the experimental episode could influence the processing of semantic information.

The specific contribution of perceptual processes and information in the processing of semantic memory information has become an issue of concern in part because of the large amount of work devoted to the distinction between explicit and implicit memory during the 1980s and early 1990s (see Chapter 7). Priming and word-fragment completion tasks were used in a number of these studies. One intriguing and consistent finding was that, whereas performance on memory tasks such as recognition and recall (explicit tasks) declines rapidly with time, priming on word-fragment completion tasks (implicit tasks) persists for quite some time (Roediger et al., 1992). Word-fragment completion can be seen as relying on the surface features of the stimulus. This fact suggests that things that affect subjects' ability to work with the surface features of the stimulus—such as the amount or quality of the *perceptual* information available from the stimulus—might influence the processing of *semantic* memory information.

The issue of the role of perceptual information in the processing of semantic information is important in at least two ways (Weldon, 1993). First, it raises the question of whether, on the one hand, distinct systems in memory are responsible for different types of remembering (Squire, 1992; Tulving & Schacter, 1990) or, on the other hand, a single memory system is used in different ways in response to different task demands (Roediger, Weldon & Challis, 1989). In the first case, contributions of perceptual processes would have important implications with respect to the connections among the perceptual and memory systems—connections that would of necessity exist in the nervous system (see Research Report 8). In the second case, contributions of perceptual processes would take the form of defining different types of retrieval cues on which memory processes could operate.

The second way in which the issue of perceptual contributions to the processing of semantic memory information is important has to do with ideas about the structure of memory. In particular, it raises the question of whether the structure of semantic memory can be abstracted in a way that makes it completely separate from the various types of episodic information available during the acquisition and repeated use of semantic memory information. For example, network models of semantic memory were not designed to deal with episodic information. Consequently, if perceptual information can influence the processing of semantic memory information, serious questions emerge about whether network models can provide accurate accounts of memory. In contrast, theoretical accounts such as the transfer-appropriate processing ideas introduced in Chapter 7, which emphasize the possible interactions among different types of retrieval processes and information, can deal with perceptual influences.

Weldon (1993) used a strategy similar to that used by Neely (1977) to ask questions about when perceptual and conceptual information might become available in processing—questions similar to those asked by Dosher in work discussed earlier. Subjects in Weldon's experiment were presented with a list of items either visually (as words or pictures corresponding to those words) or auditorily. Subjects did not know that their memory for these items would be tested later. After the entire list was presented, subjects were given a word-fragment completion test, in which they were presented (visually) with part of a target word and required to complete the word. In this task, half the items were repeated from the first part of the experiment, and half were new. In addition, the time each fragment was exposed was controlled; the times used were 500 milliseconds, 1 second, 5 seconds, and 12 seconds. The probability of correctly completing the fragment was calculated for each of the initial presentation conditions at each presentation duration for the previously presented and the new items. Then a difference score comparing the previously presented and new items was calculated, indicating the amount of priming. The results of this experiment are presented in Figure 8.8.

One of the first things you should notice in this figure is that facilitation on the word-fragment completion test (a positive difference score) was observed for all the presentation conditions. That is, subjects were better at completing word fragments for previously learned words even when those words had initially been learned in another form (either as pictures or from auditory presentation). However, this facilitation was not apparent until reasonably late in processing—after more than 5 seconds, in fact. This by itself suggests that perceptual aspects of the stimuli are reasonably unimportant in the processing of semantic memory information required in this task. However, the results for the condition in which the perceptual aspects of the stimuli at test *matched* those at study (the visual word presentation condition) lead to a different conclusion. In this condition, facilitation was robust across all exposure durations, including the earliest. In fact, the facilitation observed in this condition was more pronounced than that in either of the other conditions. This suggests that the perceptual aspects of the retrieval cue—particularly their match to those same aspects at study—can play a very important role in processing semantic memory information.

Repetition Priming   Up to this point, we have considered how performance in relation to a particular item can be improved by presentation of a related item. But presentation of a particular item more than once can also improve performance, an effect referred to as **repetition priming.**

You would probably predict that if an item is repeated, say in a lexical decision task, your response will be faster and more accurate on the second presentation than on the first. But stop for a moment and think about the semantic network representations we have been discussing. These networks can do a good job of capturing the psychological relationships among items (on the basis of their meanings). But what would you need to include in these networks to represent the benefit of repetition?

If you think for a moment about what the semantic networks represent, you will realize that, roughly speaking, they represent *what* we know. They cannot, generally, represent *how much* we know about any one thing at any one point in time. That is, the models are

RESEARCH REPORT 8:   Inferring Neural Systems from Behavioral Data

In recent years, interest in linking cognitive behaviors with structures and processes in the nervous system has grown dramatically. In previous chapters, we discussed how new technologies, such as PET and MRI, have been used in combination with typical cognitive tasks (such as memory tasks). These creative combinations have suggested how important cognitive processes might be localized in the nervous system. For example, Figure 8A shows brain areas that are active during the processing of semantic and perceptual information and during the repeated processing of semantic information.

Another approach, which has been somewhat controversial, has been to locate individuals who have suffered various types of damage to the nervous system and study in detail the types of abilities they do or do not have. This approach has been used to infer the existence of different types of memory systems, such as separate short-term and long-term systems or separate episodic and semantic systems. The approach has also been used to infer the presence of separate systems for the identification of different types of visual objects, such as printed words, everyday objects, and faces.

FIGURE 8A   **Brain Regions Active During Processing of Semantic Memory Information**   In recent years, creative combinations of new technologies and standard experimental tasks from cognitive psychology have made it possible to collect these types of data.

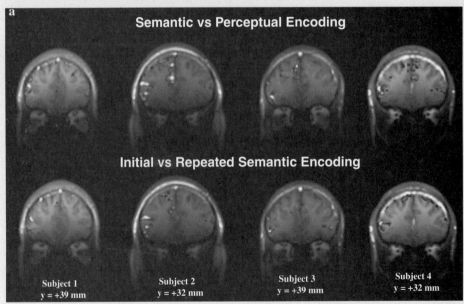

Source: Gabrieli et al., 1996.

One key type of evidence for this approach is called a *double dissociation*. To understand double dissociation, consider the question of whether, on the one hand, a single cognitive system is devoted to the identification of all types of objects or, on the other hand, separate systems exist for identifying common objects and faces (Farah, 1992). Individuals who, because of trauma to the nervous system, are unable to identify common objects (or pictures of them) have a deficit referred to as *agnosia*. People who, also because of trauma, are unable to identify faces have a deficit referred to as *prosopagnosia*.

There are documented cases in which people with prosopagnosia have little or no difficulty recognizing objects (DeRenzi, 1986). Thus, in these individuals, the ability to identify faces has been damaged while the ability to identify other types of objects has been unaffected. But is this evidence of separate perceptual and memory systems for faces and for other objects? Not necessarily, since we could argue that faces are more difficult to identify than other objects. However, in other cases, people with agnosia have no problems identifying faces (McCarthy & Warrington, 1986). Now it becomes more difficult to maintain that there is only one type of perceptual and memory system. This is because we have evidence that when we find damage to the object identification system, the face system may be unaffected. And we have evidence that when we find damage to the face identification system, the object identification system may be unaffected.

This is a double dissociation, and it seems to be strong evidence for two different systems, one for objects and one for faces. Farah (1992) reviewed many case studies of individuals with agnosia or prosopagnosia. She found numerous cases of double dissociations involving objects, faces, and printed words. This evidence led her to suggest that there are three different perceptual-memory systems: one for words, one for objects, and one for faces. But it is important to note (as did Farah) that this evidence is only suggestive. Creative experiments and creative combinations of new theories, new technologies, and standard cognitive tasks are needed to thoroughly test these suggestions.

static—they are unable to deal with change over time, such as might occur with item repetition.

As a number of researchers have observed, however, important changes in the way semantic memory information is processed occur as a function of repetition. In fact, repetition priming may provide clues about how information *changes* from something like episodic information to something like semantic information. The clues emerge from a comparison of the effects of repetition on words and nonwords in lexical decision and identification tasks.

We start by considering how repetition affects performance on these two types of items in a lexical decision task. Logan (1990) had subjects perform a lexical decision task in which items were repeated between 2 and 16 times. In other words, a subject would have to identify a particular item as a word or a nonword up to 16 times. The results from this experiment are presented in Figure 8.9.

Not surprisingly, performance on both types of items (words and nonwords) improved with increasing numbers of repetitions. Interestingly, repetition seemed to confer a greater benefit for the nonwords than for the words (i.e., the difference between the highest and

FIGURE 8.8   **Priming on a Word-Fragment Completion Test**   Although priming can be observed when target items were originally learned in a different form (either as pictures or from auditory presentation), this priming is observed only late in processing. In contrast, priming is observed early and throughout processing when the target items were learned in the same form (as printed words).

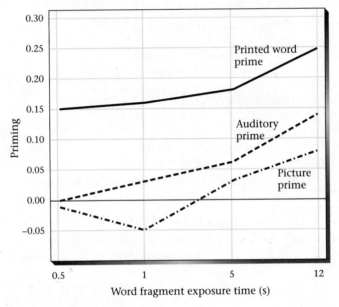

Source: Adapted from Weldon, 1993.

lowest points for the nonwords was slightly greater than the difference for the words). And by the time any particular nonword had been repeated 16 times, performance on that item was nearly as good as for a word that had been repeated an equal number of times and *better* than for a word that had been repeated up to 4 times!

We have already noted that any model of memory that restricts itself to a static set of relations (such as a traditional network model) has problems dealing with the effects of repetition on words, which are items represented in the network. But how could such models deal with the effects of repetition on nonwords—items that are *not* represented in the network?

One possible way would be to allow the learning that occurs with repetition to produce a new node in the network. In this way, repetition could allow for the transformation of episodic memory information into semantic memory information.

This idea was explored in some detail in a set of studies by Feustel, Shiffrin, and Salassoo (Feustel, Shiffrin & Salasoo, 1983; Salasoo, Shiffrin & Feustel, 1985). They used two tasks to study the effects of repetition on both the accuracy and the speed of word and nonword identification. To examine effects on the accuracy of identification, they used a task they called a *discrete threshold identification*. In this task, the item to be identified was presented *very* briefly and then covered up (masked). The duration of presentation was manipulated across a reasonably short range, and the presentation duration at which performance (accuracy) reached 50 percent defined the threshold.

FIGURE 8.9   **The Benefits of Repetition in a Lexical Decision Task**   Benefits can be observed for both words and nonwords, but the benefit for nonwords seems to be greater. In addition, by the time nonwords have been presented numerous times, performance for them is nearly as good as for words.

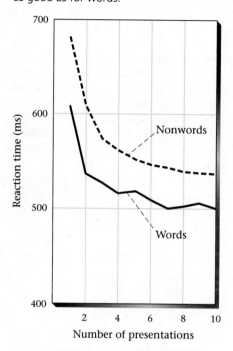

Number of presentations

Source: Adapted from Logan, 1990.

To examine the effects of repetition on the speed of identification (the processing time required), the researchers used a task called *continuous threshold identification*. In this task, the item to be identified was presented for *very* short durations (2 milliseconds) and then covered up. In addition, the item was presented repeatedly, with each repetition involving an increase in the exposure duration. To the subject, the display appeared to flicker, and the item seemed to emerge out of the flicker. Subjects stopped the display as soon as they could identify the item, and the exposure duration at which accuracy reached 50 percent defined the threshold.

In the first of these studies (Feustel, Shiffrin & Salasoo, 1983), the difference between words and nonwords (not considering repetition for the moment) was most pronounced on the discrete threshold task. The researchers suggested that this difference in accuracy was due to the fact that the words had representations in semantic memory and the nonwords did not, thus allowing for more accurate identification of the words.

The second study (Salasoo, Shiffrin & Feustel, 1985) explored this idea more fully and addressed the effects of repetition. The researchers hypothesized that repetition might serve the function of *unitizing*, or *codifying*, a representation of a nonword in semantic memory. Put in terms of the network model, repetition would allow for the creation of a new node in the network. If this occurred, then the difference between words and nonwords on the discrete threshold task should disappear with repetitions.

Figure 8.10 shows the results of part of this study. The most interesting aspect of these data, at least for our current discussion, is the curve that represents the change in threshold as a function of repetition on the discrete threshold task. As you can see, the difference between words and nonwords was pronounced for the initial presentations. But after about four repetitions, the difference nearly disappeared. This suggests that a reasonably small number of repetitions can produce, for nonwords, the type of memory information normally associated with words.

Priming by Repetition of Meaning   The type of priming we have been discussing so far is technically referred to as **direct priming**—priming in which subjects experience something (such as reading a word) and then, later, perform a task strictly related to that initial experience, usually an exact repetition of that initial experience (Cofer, 1967; Neely, 1991; Roediger & Challis, 1992). Direct priming occurs when the exact stimulus is repeated. However, in another type of repetition priming, **indirect priming,** the later phase of the experiment involves some event that has a semantic or associative relationship to the first event but is not the same event.

We are interested here in what the effects of indirect priming can tell us about how semantic memory information is processed in different tasks. In particular, we consider effects in lexical decision, word-fragment completion, and free recall tasks.

Consider first a study by Bainbridge, Lewandowsky, and Kirsner (1993). Their experi-

---

FIGURE 8.10   **The Effect of Repetition on Nonwords**   Repetition of nonwords produces learning that allows identification performance with nonwords to equal performance with words. This suggests that such learning may be an important part of the process of acquiring semantic memory information.

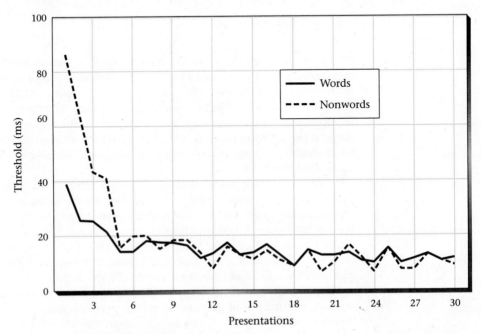

Source: Adapted from Salasoo, Shiffrin, & Feustel, 1985.

ment involved presentation of a target item (e.g., *token*) requiring a lexical decision response. The initial presentation of the target was preceded by presentation of a sentence in which the last word was the target item (e.g., "The man kicked the machine after it returned his. . . ."). The targets were repeated later in the experiment, and this repetition could be preceded by either the same sentence or a different sentence (e.g., "The young widow kept her husband's hair as a . . ."). Also presented were control sentences in which both the target and the preceding sentence were new. In addition, the target words were chosen to have either a number of different senses (such as *jam* in "traffic jam" and "bread and jam") or a single or limited sense (such as *marina*).

Some results from this study are presented in Table 8.2. Before reading further, use the data in the table to calculate difference scores to determine how much priming was observed in each of the conditions. Where was the greatest amount of facilitation observed?

What you should see is that, particularly for words with very few meanings or senses, facilitation was observed when the sentence preceding the target was different from the sentence used in the initial presentation. However, facilitation was also observed when the target item had multiple meanings. This suggests that whatever was done in the initial presentation of the sentence and target influenced processing in the second presentation, even when a number of different meanings were possible for the target item.

Now consider the two other tasks we mentioned: free recall and word-fragment completion. Roediger and Challis (1992) examined how either exact repetition of an item (e.g., *barbecue* followed by *barbecue*) or conceptual repetition, in which the second presentation involved a highly associated item (e.g., *barbecue* followed by *chicken*), affected later performance on either a word-fragment completion or a free recall task. In addition, they examined the degree to which the number of items intervening between repetitions affected the magnitude of any priming effects that might be obtained.

The results of one experiment from this study are presented in Figure 8.11. The first thing to note is that whereas exact repetition produced effects in both free recall and word-fragment completion, conceptual repetition produced effects only in free recall, and the magnitude of the effects appeared to diminish as the number of items between repetitions increased.

It appears, then, that indirect priming can be obtained in lexical decision and free recall tasks but its effects are minimal in word-fragment completion tasks. Why? Is it not true that in each of these tasks subjects are processing semantic memory information? Accord-

---

TABLE 8.2 **Results from a Priming Study by Bainbridge, Lewandowsky, and Kirsner** Calculate the difference, or priming, scores for response times by subtracting the measure for the "different context" condition from the measure for the neutral condition. "Many" and "few" refer to the number of senses for the target item.

Condition	Many	Few
Neutral	755	936
Different context	710	801
Difference score	☐	☐

Source: Data from Bainbridge, Lewandowsky & Kirsner, 1993.

FIGURE 8.11   **Effects of Exact Repetition and Conceptual Repetition**   Whereas exact repetition of an item had similar effects on free recall and word-fragment completion, conceptual repetition produced an effect only for free recall.

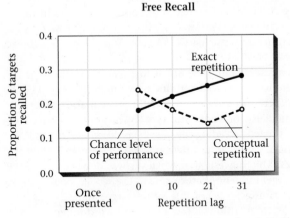
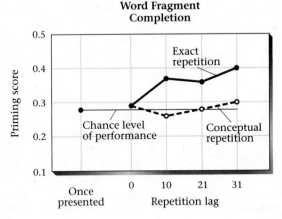

Source: Adapted from Roediger & Challis, 1992.

ing to Roediger and Challis (1992), it is the manner in which the semantic memory information is processed that makes the difference. For both free recall and lexical decision tasks, processing is essentially conceptually driven, in that these tasks are highly reliant on processing the meaningful aspects of the stimuli. In contrast, word-fragment completion is highly dependent on the surface features of the stimuli, making it a much more data-driven task. This is essentially the transfer-appropriate processing explanation (Blaxton, 1989) introduced in Chapter 7.

Costs of Semantic Memory Information

When you think about what memory information—short-term, long-term, episodic, or semantic—allows you to do, you probably think about how it helps you. But in a number of situations, semantic memory information can actually extract a cost in performance.

One example of how semantic memory information might actually impair performance is called the **fan effect**, which demonstrates that, in some cases, the more you know about something, the worse you do on a task that requires use of that knowledge (J. R. Anderson, 1974; Pirolli & Anderson, 1985). One of the first demonstrations of the fan effect (J. R. Anderson, 1974) involved a very simple manipulation. Subjects were required to study a set of sentences like these:

> The doctor is in the bank.
> The accountant is in the park.
> The lawyer is in the park.

In each set of sentences, a particular person (such as the doctor or the accountant) or a particular location (such as the bank or the park) could appear in either one or two sentences. Subjects studied these sentences a number of times and were then given a recognition test that involved two types of sentences: sentences that had appeared in the original list and distractor sentences formed by mispairing people and locations from the studied sentences.

This study was conducted not long after Quillian's model of semantic memory had been published and was motivated by a prediction that can be easily derived from the structure of that model. To see what this prediction is, get a blank piece of paper and draw five nodes, three on the left side of the paper and two on the right. Label the nodes on the left with the three participants mentioned in the sentences above and the nodes on the right with the two locations. Then draw links between the participants and the locations that occur together in these sentences.

Now imagine that we use these sentences as to-be-remembered (TBR) items in a memory experiment. Our subject reads the sentences then, a little later, we test the subject's memory by presenting the sentences again for a recognition decision. Consider the effects of presenting the first two sentences as probes. If you think of the amount of activation that results as being related to the number of nodes that can be activated by each probe, you will see that presenting *park* will activate both *lawyer* and *accountant*, whereas presenting *bank* will activate only *doctor*. In this case, then, the overall level of activation is higher when *park* is presented, but the system is also faced with the task of "selecting out" (in a rough sense) the specific sentence it has to work with. In contrast, although the overall level of activation may be a little lower when *bank* is presented, the system does not have to "select out" a specific sentence, so there may actually be *less* work to do.

The results from an experiment based on this idea are presented in Table 8.3. As you can see, response times increased with increases in the number of sentences in which a particular person appeared and the number of sentences in which a particular location appeared.

You might wonder whether fan effects are really very general. Learning a set of facts in a one-hour experiment does not seem to approximate the situations people face in the real world, where typically a piece of semantic knowledge is *highly* learned. However, two results suggest that the fan effect is quite general.

The first comes from a study (Pirolli & Anderson, 1985) similar to the one we just discussed. In this study, subjects repeated each of the individual sentences up to 600 times across the course of 25 days of practice. A number of different manipulations were used in this experiment; we will concentrate on a comparison between sentences that involved

TABLE 8.3 **An Example of the Fan Effect** Increasing the number of sentences in which either a particular person or a particular location was mentioned increased response time in a recognition test, demonstrating what is known as the fan effect.

Number of Sentences Using a Specific Locations	Number of Sentences About a Specific Person	
	1 Sentence	2 Sentences
1 sentence	1.11 sec	1.17 sec
2 sentences	1.17 sec	1.22 sec

Source: Anderson, 1974.

links to other sentences (fan sentences) and sentences that did not (no-fan sentences). The results of this experiment are presented in Figure 8.12.

You can see that although practice did appear to reduce the magnitude of the fan effect, it was still apparent even after an extensive amount of practice. Thus, even when information is highly learned, the costs of knowing more can be observed. More recent studies of the fan effect (Radvansky, Spieler & Zacks, 1993; Radvansky & Zacks, 1991) have demonstrated that one of the central components of this powerful effect is the way in which individual facts are organized. Specifically, in these studies, when the facts to be learned involved an object (such as a cola machine) located in a number of different places (such as a hotel and a library), a fan effect was observed. But when the facts involved a location (such as a hotel) where a number of different objects (such as a cola machine and a potted plant) were located, no fan effect was observed. Radavansky and colleagues (1993) suggested that the locations provided a way of organizing the facts about the objects, whereas the objects provided no such means of organization.

Perhaps even more telling evidence comes from studies involving training elderly adults to use classical mnemonic techniques (Belleza, 1981; Roediger, 1980b) to improve their memory for daily tasks (Kliegl, Smith & Baltes, 1989, 1990). These studies showed that while, in specific conditions, the memory performance of elderly adults could be just as good as the performance of college-aged students, the elderly adults had certain difficulties related to their levels of knowledge about the world. For example, the elderly adults had difficulty using the method of *loci,* in which a sequence of locations (such as the landmarks on your route from home to school) is used in remembering a list of items. It ap-

---

FIGURE 8.12   **Practice and the Fan Effect**   Although extensive practice on a set of fact sentences reduced the magnitude of the fan effect, it was still apparent after 25 days of practice and up to 600 repetitions.

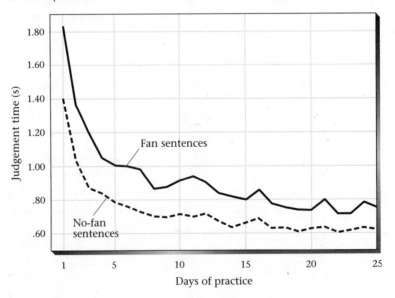

Source: Adapted from Pirolli and Anderson, 1985.

peared that the elderly individuals had so much knowledge about any particular path that they experienced difficulty selecting the specific associations to use.

Connectionism and the Future of Semantic Networks

Ideas about the representation of knowledge in Quillian's model inspired a great deal of important research on aspects of semantic memory information and the processes it involves. Although for the most part we have restricted ourselves to talking about current theories and models that share many of the characteristics of Quillian's semantic network, we close the chapter by briefly considering models that represent an evolution of the semantic-network idea and attempt to link theories of cognition with increasing knowledge of the structure and functioning of the nervous system (J. A. Anderson, 1995; Kohonen, 1989).

The specific models we refer to are the connectionist models first introduced in Chapter 1. The excitement generated by connectionist systems is due in part to their ability to show how learning can be incorporated into a semantic representation. Connectionist systems have also been used to explore ideas about how aspects of cognition, such as semantic memory information, can be represented in the nervous system.

To give you just a glimpse of this potential, we briefly consider a portion of a theory proposed by one of the most important and influential scientists working with connectionist systems, James McClelland (McClelland, McNaughton & O'Reilly, 1995; McClelland & Rumelhart, 1988). McClelland helped to draw attention to the potential of connectionist systems as models for cognition and has more recently been working to demonstrate how these models might be used to relate cognition to the structure of the nervous system.

In a very simple sense, the theory proposed by McClelland and his colleagues (McClelland, McNaughton & O'Reilly, 1995) focuses on two brain regions that seem critical in processing semantic and episodic memory information. These regions are the hippocampal system and the neocortex. As you can see in Figure 8.13, the hippocampal system is quite well connected, in that it receives inputs from all the sensory systems and sends outputs to all the major areas of the cortex. If you were trying to design a processing system that could deal with both episodic and semantic information, you would want something that does exactly the types of things the hippocampal system does.

The role of the hippocampal system in relating episodic and semantic information has been revealed in studies of humans and animals with damage to areas of the hippocampal system (Scoville & Milner, 1957; Squire, 1992). One of the most important findings is that individuals who have hippocampal damage often show a selective deficit in memory for information learned just before the damage was sustained. Memory for information learned longer ago seems to be spared, with the deficit *decreasing* with increases in the amount of time between learning and the injury.

In addition, researchers have documented how the hippocampal system can change in response to repeated exposure to a stimulus (McNaughton & Barnes, 1990). Essentially, it appears that the actual structure of the neural connections in the hippocampal system can change as a result of specific experience. These changes can be seen as representing storage of episodic types of information. The ability of the nervous system to change as a function of experience is not limited to the hippocampal system. In fact, it characterizes the nervous system in general. So it should not surprise you to learn that the changes that occur in the hippocampal system can lead to changes in the neocortical regions that receive its inputs.

FIGURE 8.13   **The Hippocampal System**   This schematic representation shows the hippocampal system and its multiple inputs and outputs. Note how "well connected" this system is in terms of its outputs to the cortical areas.

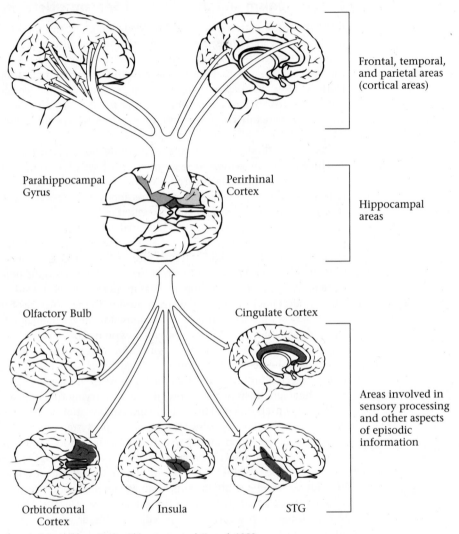

Source: Adapted from Squire, Shimamura, and Amaral, 1989.

McClelland and colleagues have taken advantage of this finding to suggest that experience-specific changes are stored first in the hippocampal system. Over time, and with similar repeated experiences, these changes themselves produce changes in the neocortex. In terms of the information being processed, this is referred to as *interleaved learning,* or the integrating of new knowledge into an existing structure of knowledge (Hinton, 1989; Rumelhart, 1990). Changes can occur quickly in the hippocampal system but take longer to be woven into the structure of the neocortex. This slower rate of change with learning guards against what can be disastrous levels of interference, which sometimes, in connectionist models, result from being forced to learn new associative structures quickly (McCloskey & Cohen, 1989).

In recent years, connectionist systems have been used to successfully model a wide range of cognitive processes, from aspects of attention (Cohen, Dunbar & McClelland, 1990) to word recognition (Rumelhart, Hinton & Williams, 1986) to categorization (Busemeyer, Forsyth & Nozawa, 1988; Kruschke, 1992, 1993). But some psychologists have some serious reservations about how this success has come about. For example, although learning is a central part of connectionist models, various aspects of the models (such as the number and types of layers of connections) are not open to experimental tests (Schweickert, Fisher & Goldstein, 1992).

Perhaps one of the most serious challenges to connectionist modeling is the idea that the relationship between any specific connectionist model and the theory that motivated it is tenuous. Essentially, a connectionist model can be built to do something that a human must do. Then the scientist has to infer the operation of the human processor from the operation of the connectionist model (McCloskey, 1991). However, for even moderately complex tasks, a connectionist model can quickly become quite complex, leading to what is called **Bonini's paradox,** in which the model is no easier to understand than the thing being modeled (Dutton & Starbuck, 1971; Lewandowsky, 1993).

Consequently, although connectionist models represent an important and intriguing evolution of many of the ideas originally represented in semantic network models, it remains to be seen whether their impact will be as significant as that of the semantic networks. It has been suggested (Estes, 1991) that combining some aspects of connectionist modeling with other forms of theorizing might lead to general advances. Another possibility is the development of more general ways of representing the ideas of connectionism (Schweickert, Fisher & Goldstein, 1992)—ways that would allow for more clearly defined relations between theory and models and greater possibilities for experimental tests.

Section Summary: Current Knowledge about the Form and Use of Knowledge

Contemporary research on semantic memory, which developed out of an initial concern with how semantic memory information is organized (or structured), boasts a wide range of studies that examine how semantic memory information changes across time and across tasks. As time passes, from initial learning to later use, detailed (episodic) information can be lost while general (semantic) information is retained. Studies of retrieval dynamics illustrate differences in the speed with which various types of memory information can be retrieved. Fuzzy trace theory illustrates how these different types of memory information may be important for retrieval in general. Studies of item repetition and repetition priming show how new information may become incorporated in existing knowledge. And studies of the fan effect illustrate how having large amounts of interrelated information may extract a cost in performance. Finally, models of the structure of semantic memory (specifically connectionists models) offer new insights into the relationships that might exist between memory information and neural structure.

REVIEWING MEMORY IN THE LONG TERM: SEMANTIC MEMORY

CONCEPT REVIEW

1. Give a simple definition of *semantic memory information* and contrast this type of memory information with episodic memory information. What two tasks were used in the initial experimental explorations of semantic memory information? Why were they good tasks to use?

2. Describe Quillian's network model. What task was it designed to perform? Did Quillian's theory focus on the structure of semantic memory or the processes involved? What type of evidence was used to support Quillian's model?

3. Contrast Quillian's network model with the feature list model. What finding that presented problems for the network model could the feature list model explain?

4. What is priming? What are the two types of priming effects? What evidence is used to infer these two types of priming effects? What task has been used most frequently to explore priming?

5. What types of evidence suggest important interactions between semantic and episodic memory information? Think about evidence from priming studies and from studies that have looked at how episodic information might be transformed into semantic information.

6. Describe how the process of chunking might transform simple patterns into meaningful semantic memory information.

7. What is a proposition—that is, what does a proposition represent?

8. Describe Gernsbacher's ideas about the loss of surface information in semantic memory. What types of evidence support these ideas? Compare and contrast these ideas with the ideas about chunking.

9. What two types of activation are important in fuzzy trace theory? What interesting prediction about the ordering of recall does fuzzy trace theory make? What is the theoretical basis for this prediction?

10. Describe how retrieval dynamics have been studied.

11. What evidence supports the idea that perceptual information might be important to the processing of semantic memory information? What questions are raised by the possible interaction between perceptual and semantic memory information?

12. What is repetition priming? Why is it important for the study of semantic memory information? What implication does repetition priming have for network models of semantic memory information?

13. Describe the fan effect and discuss its implications. Could this effect have been predicted by network models, such as Quillian's? By feature list models?

14. What is Bonini's paradox? Logically, is the potential for Bonini's paradox unique to connectionist models, or might this paradox exist with any type of cognitive model? Explain your answer.

KEY TERMS

Bonini's paradox (p. 277)
characteristic feature (p. 250)
chunking (p. 254)
cognitive science (p. 247)

declarative memory information (p. 255)
defining feature (p. 250)
direct priming (p. 270)

facilitation (p. 251)
fan effect (p. 272)
feature list model (p. 250)
indirect priming (p. 270)

KEY TERMS (*continued*)

inhibition (p. 251)

lexical decision task (p. 251)

naming task (p. 245)

priming (p. 251)

procedural memory information
(p. 255)

production (p. 255)

proposition (p. 256)

repetition priming (p. 265)

retrieval dynamics (p. 262)

speeded-classification task (p. 245)

spreading of activation (p. 252)

stimulus onset asynchrony (SOA)
(p. 252)

syllogistic reasoning task (p. 245)

Teachable Language Comprehender
(p. 247)

SUGGESTED READINGS

If you are interested in reading about how the idea of chunking has helped to form the basis for a large-scale theory of cognition, you will enjoy the first set of chapters in *Unified theories of cognition,* a text by A. Newell (Cambridge, MA: Harvard University Press, 1992). To gain an appreciation for how an important new theory is making use of interactions among semantic and episodic memory information, see "Fuzzy trace theory and cognitive triage in memory development" (*Developmental Psychology, 27,* 351–369) by C. J. Brainerd, V. F. Reyna, M. L. Howe, and J. Kevershan (1991), which provides a very readable introduction to this topic. The field of connectionist modeling is expanding rapidly and allowing for intriguing explorations of the relationship between aspects of cognition and neuropsychology. One perspective on this enterprise can be found in "Why there are complementary learning systems in the hippocampus and neocortex: Insights from the successes and failures of connectionist models of learning and memory" (*Psychological Review, 102,* 419–457), by J. L. McClelland, B. L. McNaughton, and R. C. O'Reilly (1995). Another perspective, one that includes some important cautions, can be found in S. Lewandowsky's (1993) paper, "The rewards and hazards of computer simulations" (*Psychological Science, 4,* 236–243).

The Production of Language

I F Y O U W E R E A S K E D to define *language*, you might say that it is a general term for the words we speak and hear. But language is much more than just the production and comprehension of words, in the same way that semantic memory is more than just memory for words. In this chapter, we consider language in terms of its structure and the ways in which we produce and process it. Considering both the structure and processing of language places us within the relatively young research field of **psycholinguistics.**

A young research area, like a young child, goes through many changes. This is certainly the case with psycholinguistics, as you will see when we review the history of this field. Perspectives on the "best" way to think about language have undergone, and continue to undergo, major changes. Our particular perspective is to view language as one important type of information to be processed, so we look at language in terms of its characteristics as a source of information and in terms of the general cognitive processes that work on that information. At times, as you will see, these general cognitive processes operate in very special ways with language. At other times, the general processes discussed in other chapters operate in similar ways with language.

Although psycholinguistics is a relatively new discipline, it has very deep roots; philosophers and scholars have been interested in language for thousands of years. In this chapter, we begin by putting the contemporary scientific study of psycholinguistics in a broader historical context. Then we consider various aspects of how we *produce* language. In Chapter 10, we use the historical context developed in this chapter to discuss research on how we *comprehend* (or process) language. Finally, in Chapter 11, on cognitive development, we discuss how people learn to produce and comprehend language.

The distinction between language production and language comprehension has important implications for the ways in which research on these two aspects of language processing is conducted. Scientists who are interested in spoken language production focus on how people coordinate the muscles in the vocal tract to utter a word, how they create new sentences out of familiar words, and how they adapt their language skills to new situations, as when learning a new language. Scientists interested in the comprehension of language focus on how people listen and attend to sounds and how they recognize words, process sentences, and obtain meaning from them. These different research strategies will be apparent in the studies we talk about in this chapter and the next.

THE DEEP ROOTS OF PSYCHOLINGUISTICS

The earliest experimental studies of language date to the nineteenth century (Paul, 1886; Wundt, 1900). But scholarly interest in language goes back much further. The Greek historian Herodotus (who lived approximately 2,500 years ago) relates a story about Psammetichus, an Egyptian pharaoh of the twenty-sixth dynasty (who lived approximately 2,600 years ago). The Egyptians believed that another group, the Phrygians, had a civilization older than theirs. Psammetichus wanted to be certain that no other civilization, except the Phrygians, was older than the Egyptian civilization. To gain evidence for his idea, Psammetichus chose two newborn babies from his kingdom and gave them to a shepherd to raise until they could talk. But there was one catch: No one could speak to or around these children until they uttered their first word. Psammetichus gave orders that as soon as the children uttered anything that was not meaningless babble, he was to be told what words they spoke. Psammetichus's logic was that, in the absence of any other influences, the first utterances of the babies would be in the original, or oldest, language of humans.

After supposedly spending two years in isolation, the children said the word *bekos* to the shepherd as he brought them their food and water. *Bekos* was a word from another language—Phrygian—and it meant "bread." When Psammetichus heard this, he concluded that Phrygian was the native language for all civilizations, including his own. Thus, Psammetichus believed he had solid experimental evidence to support his assertion that the Phrygians were the oldest civilized people.

With a little thought, you can probably identify quite a few problems with Psammetichus's approach to the experimental study of language. Nevertheless, the same experimental and logical approach has been used by others. James IV of Scotland (1473–1513) and Frederick II of Germany (1712–1786) both supposedly repeated Psammetichus's experiment. They did not replicate his findings, however; they concluded that Hebrew was the native language of all humans (Grene, 1987). The world would have to wait until the late nineteenth century before scientific studies of language were conducted.

The Wundtian Tradition

You may remember from Chapter 1 that Wilhelm Wundt (1832–1920) is known for, among other things, establishing the first laboratory in experimental psychology. He is also credited with being the father of psycholinguistics. Prior to Wundt's involvement in the study of language, psychologists and linguists shared similar views on language. Wundt and his contemporaries, however, may have set the stage for a theoretical split between these two fields.

Wundt developed a theory of language performance that considered both external phenomena, such as sound production and perception, and internal phenomena, such as the individual's "train of thought" (Blumenthal, 1974). This concern with internal thought should not surprise you, since you probably remember that *analytical introspection* was a primary tool of experimental psychologists at that time. One of Wundt's main interests was determining the basic units of speech and language. Wundt was convinced that the *sentence* was the basic element of language production and comprehension (Blumenthal, 1970, 1987). He believed that the production of speech involved transforming thought processes into sequentially organized speech segments and that comprehension involved the same process in reverse (Carroll, 1986).

Not all of Wundt's contemporaries agreed that sentences were the basic building blocks of language. For example, Hermann Paul, a linguist, saw the sentence as a chain of words that produces a distinct sound pattern. Thus, Paul saw *words* as the basic building blocks of language. Heated debates among Wundt, Paul, and others in the German scientific community continued for almost 40 years (Blumenthal, 1970). This disagreement, in fact, proved to be one of the reasons that, in the twentieth century, psychology and linguistics began to diverge as disciplines.

Early in the twentieth century, the split between the two areas widened, in part because behaviorism was pulling most psychologists away from introspective approaches. By the 1920s, Wundtian views on language had been abandoned, and behaviorism emerged as the dominant school of thought. During this same period, linguistic theory was influenced by linguistic structuralism, which emphasized the formal representation of language rather than the language user. Around the 1950s, however, psychological and linguistic theory began to emerge from their behavioral and structural approaches to begin a new and more interactive era in the study of language.

The Emergence of Modern Psycholinguistics

During the 1950s, linguistic and psychological theories began to come together, and the contemporary field of psycholinguistics was born. Maclay (1973) and Kess (1992) have identified four major periods in modern psycholinguistics: the formative period, the linguistic period, the cognitive period, and the contemporary period. Figure 9.1 illustrates these time periods, along with some influential researchers.

The Formative Period   The first of the modern periods—the formative period—began in the 1950s when groups of influential scientists concerned with the study of language met, first at Cornell University and later at Indiana University. These meetings are of historical importance in part because they mark the first documented use of the term *psycholinguistics* (Osgood & Sebeok, 1954).

During the latter part of the 1950s, psychologists and linguists began to consider the types of theoretical issues on which they agreed and disagreed. One of the major points of disagreement involved the nature of the theoretical constructs used to describe language

---

FIGURE 9.1   **History of the Study of Psycholinguistics**   This time line depicts the history of the study of psycholinguistics, starting with the European era (around the turn of the nineteenth century). The modern study of psycholinguistics is reflected in four periods of study in the United States, beginning in the 1950s.

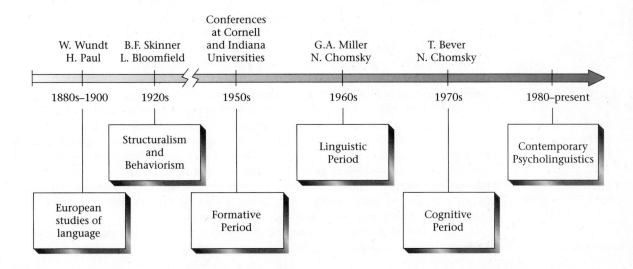

and the nature of the data used to support those constructs. Both groups believed that their theoretical ideas should be defined in terms of observable behaviors (Kess, 1992). In principle, these ideas seemed to agree with the ideas of behaviorist psychology. But some prominent behavioral psychologists had rather strong opposing opinions. In particular, they disagreed with those psychologists and linguists who dealt with language as something unique or distinct from other types of stimuli. For example, recall from Chapter 1 that B. F. Skinner (1957) held that the learning and use of language followed the same rules that governed other types of learning and behavior. Behaviorists believed that concepts such as reinforcement, extinction, and stimulus-response associations could be used to understand how humans learn and use language.

During this same period, information theory (an approach based in part on the technology of telephone and radio) influenced ideas about language (Kess, 1992). Within this theoretical framework, linguists and psychologists focused on various aspects of language as information. Whereas psychologists were concerned with the performance of the "transmitters and receivers" (the humans processing the signals), however, linguists were concerned with the content or form of the information (the signal itself).

The Linguistic Period   During the 1960s, the linguistic period, there was some unification of psychological and linguistic concerns. Grammar came to be seen as essential to language, and the sentence came to be held as the primary unit for understanding grammar.

One of the most influential scholars of this period was Noam Chomsky. Chomsky believed that a distinction had to be made between people's general level of competence with language and their performance at any specific time. **Competence** refers to knowledge of language in general and the rules that guide the use of language. **Performance** refers to the ability to follow those rules in the production and comprehension of language. Being a linguist, Chomsky preferred to study linguistic competence because it allowed him to focus on the nature of the language rather than aspects of the language user.

Chomsky's goal was to create a theoretical account of language that focused on sentence grammar, the rules needed to generate sentences in the correct form. A **generative grammar** is the system of rules by which the ideas the speaker wants to convey are transformed into the final grammatical form. The ideas or thoughts that are transformed are called the **deep structure** of the sentence, and the final grammatical form, or the output of the transformation, is called the **surface structure** of the sentence. Chomsky developed several versions of his theory (Greene, 1972): we will focus here on two of these, one described in 1957, and one in 1965. The changes in the theory from 1957 to 1966 illustrate how linguistics and psychology came to share a more common focus.

The 1957 version was very much a linguistic theory in that it was concerned with aspects of information. This version of the theory defined the aspects of grammar according to the rules from which strings of symbols (or sentences) are formed. There are *phrase-structure rules, transformational rules,* and *morphophonemic rules.* Phrase-structure rules are applied to the individual symbols in the sentence. These symbols are analyzed according to a hierarchical plan, referred to as a *phrase-structure tree.* Figure 9.2 shows a sentence and its corresponding phrase-structure tree. Transformational rules are applied to strings of symbols, and morphophonemic rules turn the symbols in strings into the form they take on when spoken. Morphophonemic rules primary work on **morphemes,** the smallest meaningful units of words, such as *cat* and *-s* in the word *cats.*

The 1965 version of Chomsky's theory concerned itself with both linguistic and psychological aspects of language. In this version of the theory, Chomsky emphasized the

Noam Chomsky
Noam Chomsky may have been one of the most influential linguists of the 1960s and 1970s. The evolution of his theoretical perspective during this period reflected and motivated the efforts of psychologists and linguists.

FIGURE 9.2   **A Phrase-Structure Tree**   Represented in the phrase-structure tree for the sentence "The politician ate the potato," are the grammatical symbols for sentence (S), noun phrase (NP), verb phrase (VP), noun (N), verb (V), and determiner (Det).

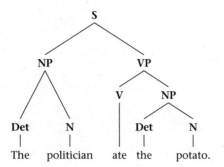

syntactic, phonological, and *semantic* components of grammar. These labels are probably more familiar to you than those used in the 1957 version of the theory. Greene (1972), however, points out that the syntactic component corresponds to the phrase-structure and transformational rules, and the phonological component corresponds to morphophonemic rules. Table 9.1 depicts the relationship between the two versions of the theory.

Basically, while Chomsky's 1957 theory described language in linguistic terms, his 1965 theory incorporated more philosophical and psychological terms (Greene, 1972). For example, consider the sentence, "The shooting of the hunters was awful." The 1957 version would state that different interpretations of this sentence are transformationally derived from different underlying kernel strings (a kernel is the simplest, active-voice, affirmative, declarative sentence possible). The 1965 version, however, would claim that the sentence has one surface structure (the final grammatical form) but two or more deep structures (the meaning to be conveyed; Greene, 1972).

It is interesting to note that Chomsky and Wundt, working in very different contexts at very different times, shared some similar ideas about language. Although Wundt was a psychologist and Chomsky is a linguist, their starting point for the consideration of language was actually the same—the sentence. However, Chomsky's detailed theoretical work may actually have been more similar to that of Wundt's contemporaries (such as Paul), in that Chomsky believed that a sentence could be analyzed into constituent aspects, while Wundt considered the sentence to be a basic or elemental psychological form.

Remember that we described the linguistic period as one during which linguists and psychologists were working in a rather unified way. As we move to the cognitive period of the 1970s, we will see that the relationship between psychologists and linguists grows apart once again.

What happened? The philosopher of science Robert McCauley (1987) suggests that while Chomsky claimed to be looking for a way to combine linguistic and psychological ideas, he tended to rely primarily on linguistic theories. According to McCauley, "Chomsky has rather consistently ignored the experimental work not only of cognitive psychology generally but even of the psycholinguistics that his theoretical work has inspired" (p. 346). This rather uncharitable characterization of Chomsky's approach, however, was in

TABLE 9.1   **Chomsky's Theory of Generative Grammar**   In this comparison of the major components of the 1957 and 1965 versions of the theory, note how the later version concentrates
more on psychological aspects than the earlier version.

	Version	
Component	**1957**	**1965**
Meaning	None	Semantic component
Syntax	Phrase-structure rules	Base rules
	Transformational rules	Transformational rules

some sense true of psychologists as well. That is, psychologists were equally guilty of ignoring many of the advances made by their colleagues in linguistics. So it should come as
no surprise to learn that psychology and linguistics went their separate ways.

The Cognitive Period   The cognitive period is most closely identified with the research
of Thomas Bever, Jerry Fodor, and their colleagues. During this period, emphasis was
placed on the dependence of language use on cognitive processes. The importance and independence of grammar were rejected, and language performance rather than language
competence was studied. For example, Bever (1970) and Slobin (1973) searched for cognitive bases for linguistic structures (Kess, 1992). This concern with the dependence of language on general cognitive abilities was an important assumption for the study of
language acquisition, which began to receive more attention (see Chapter 11).

Contemporary Psycholinguistics   No single label describes the contemporary period
in psycholinguistics, and the theories and findings being produced are not limited to one
or two leaders in the area. Instead, prominent scientists are researching language perception (e.g., Connine, Blasko, & Titone, 1993; Massaro, 1987; Pisoni & Luce, 1986; Strange,
1989), language production (e.g., Dell, 1986, 1988; Fromkin, 1993; Garrett, 1988; Spoehr,
1981), language acquisition (e.g., Gleitman et al., 1988; Pinker, 1984, 1991), language
comprehension (e.g., Caplan & Waters, 1990; Gernsbacher, 1990; Kintsch, 1988), and biological aspects of language (e.g., Dingwall, 1988; Kimura, 1992). But the rift between psychology and linguistics, in terms of theoretical focus and research methods, remains large.

Because the distinction between linguistics and psychology has become such a broad
one, and because this is a text written by a pair of psychologists, the view of language presented here is different from the view that you would get from a pair of linguists. The research we have selected and the way we present it are based on our concern with human
information processing. As we mentioned earlier, we consider language to be a particular
type of information that is processed, sometimes in very specific ways, by some of the
same cognitive processes and abilities that operate on other types of information. However, you should be aware that in your future studies you may encounter other, equally
useful perspectives on language.

Section Summary: The Deep Roots of Psycholinguistics

One of the earliest "studies" of language was described by Herodotus, who described an Egyptian pharaoh's attempt to discover the native language of all humans. The study of language began to be approached in scientific ways in the late nineteenth century. Wilhelm Wundt, an early and major contributor, emphasized the individual using the language. Other scientists, such as Paul, disagreed with Wundt on the fundamental characteristics of language. These disagreements, as well as the emergence of new theoretical views, such as behaviorism, changed the study of language. During the 1950s, in the so-called formative period of psycholinguistic research, linguistic and psychological theories began to come together. The term *psycholinguistics* was coined to describe the integration of psychological and linguistic interests. Research during the 1960s, the linguistic period, focused on linguistic structure and language competence. Noam Chomsky's theory of generative grammar was an important theoretical contribution of this period. The cognitive period of the 1970s marked a shift in research emphasis from language competence to language performance. Finally, the current period of contemporary psycholinguistics is marked by research diversity and a wide gap between psychology and linguistics.

LANGUAGE AS AN INFORMATION SOURCE

One of the points we made in our discussion of memory (Chapters 6–8) was that, to understand how memory "works," we need to consider both the types of information to be processed and the types of processes involved. Since we are considering language as a specific type of information to be processed, it is important for us to start by considering the types of physical and linguistic information involved. The reason we include both of these types of information is that the physical characteristics of language (spoken, written, gestural, etc.) play an important part in our abilities to produce and comprehend language. Typically, four levels of analysis have been used to examine language and its use: phonology, syntax, semantics, and pragmatics. These aspects are important in various ways for both the production and comprehension of language.

Throughout this chapter and the next, we talk a great deal about spoken and written language. But there is a more general way of looking at communication. The study of **discourse** is the general study of communicative interactions between two or more individuals, with the interaction being independent of the medium. For example, discourse can refer to a conversation between two people, the lyrics of a song, the story line of a film, or even the content of this book. The study of discourse as a general topic goes well beyond the domains of psycholinguistics and cognitive psychology and can include aspects of social psychology and the creative arts. Consequently, we will not spend much time talking about discourse in general.

Phonology

The study of the sound system of language is referred to as **phonology.** With respect to studying language production, phonology is concerned with the sound that results from a specific coordination of muscle movements in the face, mouth, and throat. With respect to the perception of language, phonology is concerned with the physical make-up of the sound itself and the way the sensory mechanisms in our ears deal with the sound. This latter aspect of the study of phonology is often referred to as the study of *acoustics*.

In terms of phonology, the basic units of language are small units of distinct sounds referred to as **phonemes.** When scientists write about phonemes, they sometimes represent them as letters inside slashes (e.g., /b/) to distinguish them from the printed letters of the alphabet. Phonemes are **contrastive,** in that a change from one phoneme to another can change the meaning of a word (e.g., changing /b/ to /d/ results in a change from *bad* to *dad*) or change a legitimate word into a nonword (e.g., *burrito* to *durrito*). Many languages sound different from one another because of the phonemes used. As you will see in Chapter 11, phonemes are very important for language acquisition, since children rely in important ways on phonemic distinctions to learn words.

One way to study the production of phonemes is to study where and how they are made. Distinct speech sounds can be made at various points along the vocal tract. Figure 9.3 shows some of the important parts of the vocal tract and gives an example of the type of consonant sound produced at each location. Before continuing with your reading, try saying each of the example words in the figure. Note how your tongue, lips, and teeth are used to produce the initial consonant sound in each word (for example, the /b/ in *bin*). Doing this should help you make sense of the names for the different types of consonant sounds.

FIGURE 9.3   **The Vocal Tract**   This representation of the human vocal tract includes some of the consonant sounds and their location and manner of production. Articulate each of the example words and note the approximate location of your tongue, teeth, and lips. Doing this should help you make sense of the labels for each of these consonant sounds.

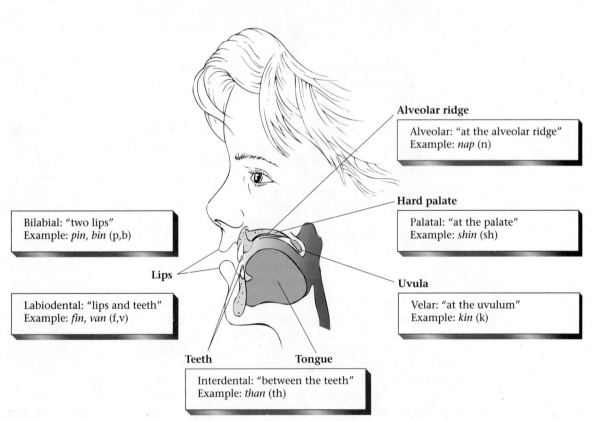

Alveolar ridge
Alveolar: "at the alveolar ridge"
Example: *nap* (n)

Hard palate
Palatal: "at the palate"
Example: *shin* (sh)

Bilabial: "two lips"
Example: *pin, bin* (p,b)

Uvula
Velar: "at the uvulum"
Example: *kin* (k)

Lips

Labiodental: "lips and teeth"
Example: *fin, van* (f,v)

Teeth   Tongue
Interdental: "between the teeth"
Example: *than* (th)

An important distinction regarding consonants has to do with whether the vocal chords vibrate when the consonant sound is produced. When the air from the lungs vibrates the vocal chords, the sound is said to be **voiced. Voiceless** sounds are produced without this vibration. To feel these vibrations, place your finger lightly on the middle of your throat. You should feel the vibrations when making voiced sounds, like /n/ in *nap,* but the vibrations should be absent when you make sounds that are voiceless, like /s/ in *sin.*

Syntax

Syntax refers to how words are put together to form phrases, clauses, and sentences. With respect to the production of language, syntax concerns how we use rules about word order (among other things) to form sentences. With respect to the comprehension of language, syntax concerns how we are able to determine if a particular sentence we read or hear is grammatical and logical. A major concern in the study of syntax is the manner in which we, as language producers and comprehenders, place words in their respective syntactic categories. This process—the process of assigning words to particular syntactic categories (e.g., identifying *dog* as a noun)—is referred to as **parsing.**

Word order is one important aspect of syntax. Word ordering relies on the functions of specific types of words, such as subjects and verbs, to provide cues that determine the meaning of a sentence. Rearranging the word order of a sentence can produce an entirely new sentence, in part because two words that work as, say, subject and object might not work if their roles were reversed. For example, the sentence "My dogs ate burritos" certainly does not mean the same thing as "Burritos ate my dogs." The first sentence sounds plausible, but the second sentence sounds like the title of a bad movie. Yet the only difference between these two sentences is word order.

In English, we usually expect the first noun in a simple sentence to be the subject of the sentence and the next noun to be the object. In our example, "My dogs ate burritos," *dogs* is the subject and *burritos* is the object. Between these two nouns, we expect the appearance of a verb, like *ate.* The example sentence follows the subject-verb-object (S-V-O) word order and is known as an active sentence in the English language. Approximately 75 percent of the world's languages use the S-V-O word order (Bernstein Ratner & Berko Gleason, 1993). Japanese, however, uses an S-O-V order, and Welsh and Arabic use a V-S-O order (Bernstein Ratner & Berko Gleason, 1993). But in each of these languages, it is the syntactic properties of the words that allow word order to act as an important cue for successful production and comprehension.

Many rules dictate how sentences should be formed. One of these rules is based on the notion of phrase structure. We introduced the idea of phrase-structure grammar and phrase-structure trees when we discussed Chomsky's (1957, 1965) theories. From the phrase-structure grammar, we can specify several phrase-structure rules. The parts of the phrase-structure grammar can be combined in a hierarchical manner to represent and derive the relationships among key phrases in the sentence.

To illustrate how a sentence can be represented by phrase-structure grammar, look at Figure 9.4, a representation of the sentence "Confident Dan spelled the word *potato.*" We start with the sentence level representation (S). Then we can rewrite the sentence in terms of a noun phrase (NP) and a verb phrase (VP). Next, we can rewrite the noun phrase as an adjective (*Confident*) and a noun (*Dan*) and can rewrite the verb phrase as a verb and another noun phrase (NP). Once we have specified the components of this second noun phrase, the sentence has been specified at the single-word level.

Earlier in the chapter, we briefly introduced Chomsky's notion of transformational rules. These rules enabled Chomsky to explain how a sentence can be modified to form new versions of the same sentence. For example, we can change an active sentence into a passive sentence, change a declarative sentence into a question, and change a positive sentence into a negative sentence while still perceiving the meaning of the original sentence. Thus, we can change the active sentence "Dan spelled the word *potato*" to the passive sentence "The word *potato* was spelled by Dan," though to do so, we need to add a few words to make the passive sentence grammatically correct.

In the decades that followed Chomsky's original work on transformational rules, a number of limitations were found with Chomsky's theory. Most of the limitations concerned the ways in which the grammar could deal with ambiguities in the meanings of sentences. For example, the transformations that Chomsky specified can change a sentence that makes sense, such as "Dan left Indiana for Arizona," into a sentence that is grammatically correct but does not make sense, "Indiana left Arizona for Dan." Chomsky (1981) devised a new theory modifying his transformational grammar theory to deal with some of these problems. This later theory, called *government and binding theory,* assigns more importance to individual words than did the earlier theory and provides only one transformation rule, "move *x*." The one rule for transformation is intended to provide a general approach for transformation that allows for many functions with only a few changes.

Semantics

Although syntax of language is important for both production and comprehension, considering syntax alone would not give us a very complete understanding of how language is produced and processed. For example, the sentence "The hovercraft denied the dog's neighborhood" is syntactically correct but does not have much meaning. This is where the study of **semantics**—the processing of the meaning of language information—comes in. The study of semantics in language production has focused in part on the situation in which individuals have difficulty producing meaningful statements, as in the case of individuals with damage to the language centers in the brain (e.g., Broca's area, Wernicke's

---

FIGURE 9.4   **Using Phrase-Structure Grammar**   In this phrase-structure tree for the sentence "Confident Dan spelled the word *potato,*" note how the assignment of individual words to syntactic categories is captured at the lowest level of the tree. These syntactic assignments are combined into larger units, the noun and verb phrases.

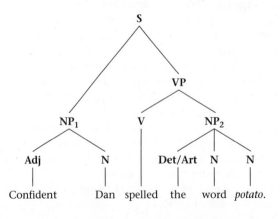

S = Sentence
NP = Noun phrase
VP = Verb phrase
V = Verb
Det = Determiner
N = Noun
Art = Article
Adj = Adjective

area). The study of semantics in language comprehension involves research on the selection of word meanings and the comprehension of written and spoken language.

Word meanings are often complex, and the same word can be used in a variety of ways. To give you an example cf the many facets of meaning, and thus of semantics, we next consider five characteristics of language that are important in the study of semantics (Bierwisch, 1970). The first is ambiguity. When a word has more than one meaning, it can be *ambiguous*. For example, in the sentence, "The fishermen were trying to get a measurement on the scale," does the word *scale* refer to a weighing instrument, or are these fishermen trying to get the size or weight of a piece of a fish's skin? The word *scale* is the ambiguous word. The fact that we can easily come up with examples of ambiguity suggests that deriving meaning from words is not a simple task.

Words can also be used in sentences in which the syntactic structure is correct but the meaning does not make sense logically. This occurrence is called an *anomaly* in meaning. In the sentence, "Crayons make for very poor eggplants," the sentence is syntactically correct but would not make sense to most listeners or readers. Anomalies suggest that both syntax and meaning are important to the use and understanding of language.

Sometimes, words represent more meaning than they appear to at first glance. In the sentence, "Chris is my sister," the implication is that Chris is female. This is often referred to as *entailment* and allows language users to communicate complex information using relatively simple means.

To add to their complexities, the meanings of words in a sentence can actually contradict one another. In the sentence, "My couch is not a piece of furniture," the words *couch* and *furniture* appear to contradict each other (because of the negation *not*) but the implied meaning may be that the couch is more than just a piece of furniture: Perhaps it is also a cherished possession of the speaker. These *conflicting meanings* are often key elements in sarcasm.

Finally, the meaning of a sentence can also imply a similar meaning not directly stated in the sentence. The sentence, "The chair is too hard," could mean "This chair is not soft enough" or "Capital punishment is too harsh." This type of *implication* allows language users to communicate complex information in a variety of ways.

One structure of language essential to the study of meaning is the morpheme. Morphemes, as noted earlier, are the smallest meaningful units in a language. **Morphology** is the study of how words are formed. The typical English speaker knows and uses approximately 50,000 morphemes. In both spoken and written language, roots of words are morphemes; and suffixes, like -s, and prefixes, like *un-*, are also morphemes. For example, the word *trees* is made up of two morphemes, *tree,* a semantic concept and physical object, and *s,* a suffix that tells us we are talking about more than one of these objects. Some morphemes, such as *s,* cannot stand alone and still be meaningful. These morphemes are said to be *bound*. Those that can stand alone as meaningful, such as *tree,* are said to be *free*.

A unique approach to studying semantics, the **case grammar approach,** suggests that our knowledge of certain words and their relationship to other words influences how we derive meaning from sentences. Proponents of this approach (Bresnan & Kaplan, 1982; Filmore, 1968; Mitchell & Holmes, 1985) claim that when we parse sentences, the parsing is based on the *semantic* role the word plays in the sentence, not the *syntactic* role. These roles are called *semantic cases*. For example, the following series of sentences describes a girl named Devren, accompanied by her dog, throwing a ball in a park.

Devren threw the ball in the park.
The dog caught the ball.

Devren threw the ball to the dog.
The dog was in the park.

If we were to analyze these sentences using the phrase-structure grammar introduced earlier, we would develop structures (one for each sentence) like those in Figure 9.4. By doing this, we would certainly gain a thorough understanding of how the sentences were built, in terms of the roles the words and phrases were playing. But we might not have a thorough understanding of all the meaningful ideas represented in the sentences. For example, a phrase-structure analysis would not reveal anything about the possible entailments and implications of the words in the sentences.

In contrast, if we used the case grammar approach, we would analyze these sentences based on the individual language user's semantic and lexical knowledge about words, including knowledge about the types of things that can be thrown or caught and who can throw or catch. Some of the assumptions made by this approach include the notion that readers and listeners process each sentence immediately, as soon as they perceive the words. As the words are being processed, each one is assigned a semantic case (or role); this in turn allows the reader or listener to comprehend the sentence. This process is similar to the parsing already discussed; but according to the case grammar approach, instead of placing the words of sentences in syntactic roles, we place them in semantic roles.

Pragmatics

Knowledge of the social rules for how to use language when interacting with others is called **pragmatics.** These rules help us to determine which words to use and when to use them in a conversation, which is the focus of research concerning the pragmatic aspects of the production of language. These rules also indicate how to interpret words in different social contexts, which is the focus of research on the pragmatic aspects of the comprehension of language.

Whereas syntax refers to the rules of language organization, pragmatics refers to the rules of the group or society within which language is used. Consider a situation like this: You are taking a class that you detest from an instructor you really dislike. Unfortunately, it is a required class for your major and (even worse) you need to maintain a good relationship with the professor, from whom you know you will be taking additional classes. Now consider how you would answer the question "How do you feel about the fact that the semester is nearly over?" in two different situations: when asked by the professor for this class and when asked by your closest friend.

Each of these situations would place different pragmatic constraints on your reply. Two possible responses to the question would be, "My, whole new worlds of knowledge have opened up to me!" and, "Yes! Only two more weeks of this punishment!" Your choice of which response to use in each situation would (we hope) be guided by your knowledge of the pragmatics of the situation.

If you told your professor that you would be relieved to see the punishment end, your interpretation of the context of the conversation (one between student and professor) might not have been appropriate. Interpretation of the social context is facilitated when the people involved in the conversation share similar background knowledge and experiences. This allows for mutual understanding about particular topics of conversation and particular ways of conversing. Your professor might not understand why you think the class is punishing, for example; but your friend, who we will assume has taken a class from this professor, will definitely understand your anticipated relief.

Individuals engaged in communication with one another, even when that communication occurs by way of printed text, follow various rules and guidelines. Haviland and Clark (1974) suggested that sentences are often organized—and are best processed—according to a **given-new strategy.** When individuals are trying to present new information to a listener, they usually try to relate it to information the listener already knows. According to Haviland and Clark's ideas, the listener then combines the new information with the old information. Haviland and Clark found that people are faster to comprehend sentences that maintain this given-new organization. For example, we would process the sentence "Devren's dog is a shepherd mix" quickly if we had been told in advance that Devren owns a dog. If we did not know that, it would take us a little longer to make sense of the new information.

Another aspect of pragmatics concerns how communication is coordinated. For example, in a conversation, two people need to take turns speaking and listening (Goodwin, 1981; M. L. McLaughlin, 1984). To make the conversation work, the two people must have some things in common, such as similar experiences or backgrounds. These shared experiences and backgrounds help each speaker understand what the other is saying. And they help the speakers know when it is appropriate to switch from listener to speaker. For example, a typical "fast-talking" New Yorker and a "slow-talking" southerner might have some difficulty coordinating the roles of speaker and listener at various points in a conversation.

One analysis of the pragmatics of conversation is that of Grice (1975), who proposed a set of **conversational maxims,** or rules of conduct. According to these maxims, effective discourse depends on the participants' being informative, truthful, relevant, and clear. But the need to closely adhere to these maxims depends on the individuals involved. For example, a conversation between you and your best friend may allow more flexible interpretations of the conversational rules than a conversation between you and one of your professors.

Some studies of conversational rules have concerned types of statements made during conversation and expected responses to these statements. Searle (1979) and others (e.g., Ervin-Tripp, 1993), for example, have studied specific statements and responses. An *assertive* is an utterance or spoken statement in which a speaker asserts an opinion or belief about some matter ("I am a student"). Assertives do not require a response from the listener. A *commissive* is a statement that commits the speaker to complete an action ("I will carry the laundry to the car"). The listener may respond to this statement in a number of ways to acknowledge the commitment ("Thanks," "Oh, sure," or perhaps, "I would appreciate it"). A *declaration* is a statement of fact ("You won the lottery!"). The listener may not have a specific response to such a statement. A *directive* is an instruction to the listener from the speaker ("Take out the trash"). The listener is supposed to comply with the request, perhaps without a verbal response. Finally, an *expressive* describes the mental state of the speaker ("I am grateful for your hospitality"). Again, the listener may respond in a variety of ways. Your job as a listener is to identify the statements and respond accordingly.

General Properties, Specific Effects

The study of pragmatics leads us to an interesting observation about the similarities among languages used by people in different countries and cultures. Many linguists believe that all languages have certain aspects in common. These aspects are called **language universals.** For example, all individuals need some way of referring to people and things, so all languages have nouns. People and things are often moving or doing something, and consequently all languages use verbs to express action and states of being. But languages have characteristics even more general than grammatical categories, like nouns and verbs. For example, according to Hockett (1960a, 1960b, 1966), 13 general properties are common to all human languages. Hockett's list of linguistic universals is shown in Table 9.2.

One interesting thing that you might see in this list of linguistic universals is that each of them refers to some characteristic of language that allows us, as users of language, to do something. For example, the characteristic of displacement allows us to use language to convey an idea, description, request, or the like with a message that is not specific to a particular instant in time. In this sense, language can be thought of as a tool for the human information processor, just as a handsaw is a tool for a craftsperson.

Think for a minute about the effect that a tool, like a handsaw, has on the task it performs. A saw is intended to cut wood, but it has different effects on different types of

---

TABLE 9.2   **Language Universals**   Hockett identified 13 linguistic universals—characteristics common to all human languages.

Universal	Description
Arbitrariness	There is no inherent connection between symbols and the objects they refer to
Broadcast transmission	Messages are transmitted in all directions and can be received by any hearer
Cultural transmission	Language is acquired through exposure to a culture
Discreteness	A distinct range of possible speech sounds exists in language
Displacement	Messages are not tied to a certain time
Duality of structure	A small set of phonemes can be combined and recombined into an infinitely large set of meanings
Interchangeability	Humans are both message perceivers and message producers
Productivity	Novel messages can be produced according to the rules of the language
Semanticity	Meaning is conveyed by the symbols of language
Specialization	Sounds of a language are specialized to convey meaning (as compared with nonlanguage sounds)
Total feedback	The speaker of a language has auditory feedback that occurs at the same time the listener receives the message
Transitoriness	Linguistic messages fade rapidly
Vocal-auditory channel	Means of transmission of the language is vocal-auditory

wood. One type of saw may produce very fine cuts on hardwoods but large rough cuts on softwoods, for example. Just as it is possible for the saw to influence how the task is performed, it has been hypothesized that language influences the way humans process information.

This idea has taken the form of the **linguistic relativity hypothesis.** Benjamin Lee Whorf (1956), one of the most famous theorists associated with linguistic relativity, claimed that language shapes the way people perceive and organize their world. An object represented by a particular word is perceived differently by individuals using different languages. Put simply, the hypothesis states that language determines what thoughts we have about objects and events in our world. If we do not have a word in our language to describe a perception or thought, we will have difficulty perceiving or thinking it.

A widely cited example of the linguistic relativity hypothesis is the suggestion that the Eskimo language has many words describing snow. In reality, Martin (1986) found that Eskimos have no more words describing snow than individuals who live in warmer, drier climates. This example suggests that, in fact, our particular language may not structure the way we perceive and organize the world. Experimental evidence seems to support this conclusion as well. For example, research on color names and categories, first collected by Berlin and Kay (1969) and further explored by Eleanor Rosch (1987), suggests that our experience with color and how we perceive it influences how we group certain colors into named categories. Thus, the research implies that our experience with the world shapes our linguistic categories.

Section Summary: Language as an Information Source

Language has several characteristics as a source of information. A physical characteristic of language, particularly spoken language, is its phonology—its structure as sound. A logical characteristic of language is its syntax—the way words can be put together to form phrases, clauses, and sentences. Word order is one part of syntax. The meaningful characteristics of language are the focus of semantics. Although the semantics of language can be complex, it is possible to identify basic units of meaning, called morphemes. The social characteristics of language are considered in the study of pragmatics. The study of pragmatics has led to the suggestion that certain characteristics are common to all languages. The idea that language influences perception, an idea that has been widely discussed, has been discredited by recent research.

PROBLEMS IN LANGUAGE PRODUCTION

Scientists interested in language production study not only the correct use of language but also the ways in which people make errors in language use (Dell, 1986, 1988; Dell, Burger & Svec, 1997; Fromkin, 1988). These so-called "slips of the tongue" occur when the rules of language are misapplied or when the timing of speech is off, such as when a person talks too fast. The important thing to note is that, while the actual output (the language that is produced) may contain errors, those errors have important regularities. That is because they are based in part on the rules for correct (error-free) language. Thus, these errors can give us important information about error-free language production.

Although speech errors can occur at the phonological level, as would be the case if you said "boster poard" instead of "poster board," they can also occur at the phrase level. You would make this kind of error if you said "The house ran inside the dog" instead of "The dog ran inside the house." To restate a point we just made, we bring up these errors not for the sake of cheap comedy but instead to emphasize how the errors can tell us something about the processes and information that support error-free language production. All these errors follow the rules of the language discussed previously. We do not violate the rules of syntax, for example, when we make an error in our production of a sentence. Nouns may be exchanged with nouns, but not with verbs, which would violate the rules of word order.

So what do speech errors tell us? Speech errors seem to indicate that we plan what we are going to say well before we actually say it. It appears that the content of a spoken message is planned, and as the rules of language are being followed to produce that message, errors occur. For example, speech errors are typically mistimings or misapplications of words or parts of words. Speech errors follow the rules of grammar. We do not place a word in a location that is not grammatically correct, but instead, we may exchange words within a phrase, such as when "I love to dance" comes out as "I dance to love."

Both consonants and vowels can be transposed, but consonant transposition is more common. Some of the most famous examples of this type of speech error come from Reverend William A. Spooner, the head of New College in Oxford from 1903 to 1924. Spooner gained fame by producing speech errors, which have been referred to as "spoonerisms." For example, "noble sons of toil" became "noble tons of soil" and "the dear old queen" became "the queer old dean." Word substitutions rarely cross clause boundaries. Word error data show that we sometimes leave the pluralization in the same place in the sentence but exchange the words, as in "rules of word formation" to "words of rule formation." A number of other types of common speech errors are summarized in Table 9.3.

Models Accounting for Language Errors

Several theories of speech production have taken into account data on normal speech errors. Fromkin's (1971) Utterance Generator includes several stages of representations of an utterance and considers when and how speech errors can be produced. According to a model by Levelt (1989), a message begins with a conceptualization of what we plan to say (Fromkin, 1993). Between this plan and the actual behavior of producing the message, a number of important opportunities to generate speech errors arise.

Gary Dell (1988) has proposed a connectionist model of word selection that actually makes speech errors. He suggests that we form sentences word by word. As the sentence is planned, these words are connected with their respective sound representations. You can think of these networks of connections as being similar to the semantic networks described in Chapter 8. Recall that the idea of *activation* was important to making these networks "work." Similarly, activation is an important part of Dell's model—it is the "fuel" for the network's "engine."

According to Dell's model, activation can spread from words to sounds, sounds to words, words to words, and sounds to sounds. When the words and their sounds are activated together, sometimes other, similar sounds, or sounds previously activated by other words, are activated as well. So the correct sounds and the incorrect sounds, at least for the target word, are all activated at the same level. To give you a better idea for how Dell's model can predict speech errors, consider the phrase "dear old queen." Figure 9.5 illustrates what Dell's model (in greatly simplified form) would predict for the processing of this phrase.

To begin, the phrase would be planned at the word level. These words would then be connected to the nodes representing their constituent sounds. In Figure 9.5, we have represented the activation between the words *dear* and *queen* and their initial sounds (/d/ and /kw/) with the variable α. We have represented the activation between each word and the second sound it contains with the variable β. But the activation connects more than just

Gary Dell
Gary Dell is a prominent contemporary psycholinguist who has created connectionist models of speech production capable of predicting speech errors.

TABLE 9.3   **Some Common Speech Errors**

1. *Errors at phonemic segments*

   Consonant anticipation: a reading list → a leading list

   Consonant deletion: speech error → peach error

   Vowel exchange: fill the pool → fool the pill

2. *Errors at phonetic features*

   Voicing reversal: big and fat → pig and vat

   Nasality reversal: cedars of Lebanon → cedars of Lemadon

3. *Errors at syllables*

   Syllable deletion: unanimity of opinion → unamity of opinion

   Syllable reversal: Stockwell and Schacter → Schachwell and Stockter

4. *Errors of stress* (with the stressed syllable given in capital letters)

   apples of the Origin → apples of the oRIgin

   eCONomists → ecoNOMists, I mean, eCONomists

5. *Errors of word selection*

   Word exchange: tend to turn out → turn to tend out

   Word movement: I really must go → I must really go

6. *Errors at morphemes*

   Inflectional morpheme error: cow tracks → track cows

   Derivational morpheme error: easily enough → easy enoughly

7. *Errors at phrases*

   A hummingbird was attracted by the red color of the feeder → the red color was attracted by a hummingbird of the feeder

   My sister went to the Grand Canyon → the Grand Canyon went to my sister

8. *Semantic and phonological word errors*

   Semantic substitution: too many irons in the fire → too many irons in the smoke

   Phonological substitution: white Anglo-Saxon Protestant → white Anglo-Saxon prostitute

9. *Errors at morphologically complex words*

   Lexical selection error: it spread like wild fire → it spread like wild flower

   Exchange error: ministers in our church → churches in our minister

Source: Fromkin, 1993.

the words and sounds; the sounds are also connected to one another. We have represented the connection between the first and second sounds in each word with the variable γ.

Now let us assume that the sound actually produced is a function of the total (or summed) activation for that sound. In Figure 9.5, you can see that the total (summed) activation for /d/ is as follows:

$$/d/ = \alpha + \beta + \gamma$$

We will call this quantity $\Sigma(/d/)$ (the Σ stands for a summation). You can also see that the total (summed) activation for /kw/ is:

$$/kw/ = \alpha + \beta + \gamma$$

We will call this quantity $\Sigma(/kw/)$. From this simple version of Dell's model, you can see the following relationship:

$$\Sigma(/d/) = \Sigma(/kw/) = \alpha + \beta + \gamma$$

That is, the initial activations for /d/ and /kw/ are equal, and it is possible for the model to predict that both the error ("queer old dean") and the correct phrase ("dear old queen") will be produced.

FIGURE 9.5   **A Prediction Based on Dell's Connectionist Model**   The figure presents a simplified version of how Dell's (1988) connectionist model of speech production would be capable of predicting the spoonerism "queer old dean" when the planned phrase is "dear old queen." The phrase is initially planned, and the words and their sound representations are connected. The strength of activation is represented here by the three variables α, β, and γ.

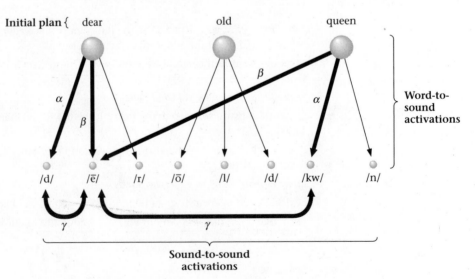

Total activation for /d/ and /ē/ $= \alpha + \beta + \gamma = \Sigma(/d/)$
Total activation for /kw/ and /ē/ $= \alpha + \beta + \gamma = \Sigma(/kw/)$

Disorders in Language Production

As we have emphasized, errors in language production can tell us about normal language production. Similarly, our knowledge about the normal processing of language and its relationship to the brain has benefited from the study of people who have suffered brain injuries resulting in impaired language abilities. Before we can talk about specific language disorders and the brain, however, we must first consider some general points about the relationship between the brain and language abilities.

Chapter 2 explained that certain cognitive abilities appear to be controlled or determined by specific areas in the brain. Generally, it has been thought that speech and language abilities are controlled and determined by areas in the left hemisphere of the brain. (If one side, or hemisphere, of the brain appears to control a certain function, that function is said to be *lateralized.*) Cases in which speech and language are located in the right hemisphere have been identified, but these cases are rare. There has been some speculation that lateralization of language is related to handedness, but the lateralization of language may also be related to age, gender, race (Tsunoda, 1985) and perhaps even educational background (Bogen et al., 1972).

Historically, our knowledge about the language areas of the brain has come from studies of individuals with damage to certain areas of the brain. As you may recall, these types of studies are called clinical case studies, as they focus on a single medical patient's case and examine in detail that individual's injury or disorder and its relation to the ability of interest. For example, a number of clinical case studies have examined various types of aphasia. **Aphasia** is a language deficit or difficulty that results from physical damage to the brain, infections or tumors in the brain, and even birth defects. Research Report 9 presents a few examples of how the relationship between brain damage and language abilities has been studied. Included in this discussion are details of two classic case studies that we mentioned briefly in Chapter 1, those of Broca and Wernicke, and modern-day alternatives to studying the brain-language relationship.

As described in Research Report 9, Broca's patient Tan, as well as other patients Broca studied, had difficulty producing fluent, grammatical speech. Individuals identified as having *Broca's aphasia* have deficits in their use of syntax and their speech patterns are not fluent compared with individuals who have no brain damage. The deficits in language ability can be observed in either speech or writing. This type of language production disorder is sometimes called *expressive aphasia,* and it is also known as *cortical motor aphasia* because the disorder occurs in the speech planning center along the motor pathway of the brain.

Another type of disorder of language production is called *transcortical motor aphasia.* This disorder is similar to Broca's aphasia, although individuals with the disorder can repeat what is said to them in a fluent manner. *Subcortical motor aphasia,* also known as *pure word mutism,* occurs when Broca's area is disconnected from the facial area. Individuals with this disorder cannot control motor movements in the vocal tract and are unable to speak voluntarily or repeat words.

Agraphia, the inability to write, is also associated with speech disorders. This language-use impairment, however, is not necessarily caused by damage to one specific area of the brain. It is more likely caused by damage to connections between language centers in the brain and motor function centers as well.

Although each of these disorders is interesting in its own right, what each tells us about the connection between normal language production and the brain is more important (at least for our purposes). And one message that seems to consistently come from studies of

RESEARCH REPORT 9:   Language Processing in the Brain

The first known written record of language impairment caused by brain damage came from a papyrus scroll said to have been dated to around 5000 years ago. In this scroll, approximately 48 brain-injury cases were described. One case detailed the loss of speech skills following head trauma. This may be the first mention of aphasia on record (Dingwall, 1993). Many reports of brain damage and language impairments have appeared since then, including one from Johann Schenk Von Grafenberg in the sixteenth century, who distinguished between language impairment caused by brain damage (aphasia) and impairment caused by paralysis of the tongue, now called *dysarthria,* or an impairment in the ability to articulate speech sounds (Dingwall, 1993).

In the nineteenth century, a surgeon and a neurologist discovered two important language centers in the brain. The French surgeon Pierre Paul Broca (1824–1880) studied patients' behaviors and, when they died, performed autopsies. In the brains of most of his cases, Broca discovered a lesion in the posterior section in the left frontal lobe. A German neurologist, Carl Wernicke (1848–1904), also examined and recorded patients' behavior and discovered on autopsy that these patients had damage to the posterior section of the left temporal lobe.

The primary behaviors associated with Broca's patients were the ability to understand language along with an impaired ability to speak coherently. Broca's most famous patient, Leborgne, also known as "Tan," was a patient living in a Paris nursing home. Leborgne was admitted at the age of 31 because he had lost his ability to speak. Leborgne had been at the nursing home for 21 years when Broca became interested in his case. Broca soon discovered that Leborgne understood what was said to him but answered all questions and statements with the single syllable "tan" followed by gestures. Leborgne was also capable of producing a few curses (Dingwall, 1993). The lesions later discovered in Leborgne's brain are in an area now known as Broca's area.

Wernicke's patients were able to speak but could not understand language. Their language comprehension skills were impaired, and although they could speak fluently, their choice of words often did not make sense to listeners. Individuals with damage to Wernicke's area, as it is now known, do not understand their own speech, which is why their word choices do not make sense to others.

Modern studies of language impairment in the brain involve the relatively new methods described in Chapter 2. CAT, MRI, and PET technologies have all been used to examine patients with damage to the language regions of the brain. Figure 9A shows PET scan images of an individual generating words (verbs), listening to words, speaking words, and passively viewing words. The four PET scan images in the figure show different areas of activation in the brain for the four tasks. The first image (a) shows that the generation of verbs activates Broca's area on the cerebral cortex but also involves other areas, such as the cerebellum. The second image (b) shows activation in Wernicke's area while the subject is listening to words. The third image (c) shows activation in the motor cortex while the subject is speaking words. The fourth image (d) shows that passively viewing words primarily activates the occipital lobe, although the inner surface of the left hemisphere is also activated.

FIGURE 9A **PET Scan Images of Brain Activity** The images show activated portions of the brain during the tasks of (a) generating words (verbs), (b) listening to words, (c) speaking words, and (d) passively viewing words.

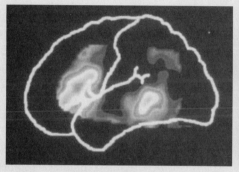

Passively viewing words

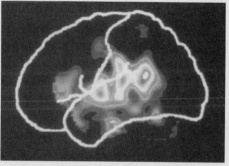

Listening to words

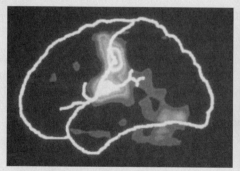

Speaking words

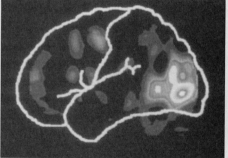

Generating verbs

Source: Posner & Raichle, 1994.

this relationship is that the structure of the brain, with respect to the functions of language, is much more complicated than was previously thought. The simple notion of one "spot in the brain" for language is being replaced by ideas (such as those in Dell's model) that emphasize connections among numerous important areas in the brain.

Section Summary: Problems in Language Production

Our knowledge about the normal production of language and the relationship between normal language production and the brain has come in part from what might seem like two unlikely sources: errors in speech production and damage or injury to the brain that results in language difficulties. Speech errors contain important regularities and are based in part on the rules for generating error-free speech. Dell's connectionist model illustrates how a model of normal speech production can naturally predict and produce speech errors. Clinical case studies of individuals with damage or injury to various brain areas have been used to explore the possible localization of language abilities in the brain. These clinical case studies have a long and important history, and they continue to provide important data on the relationship between brain function and language abilities.

UNDERSTANDING OTHER FORMS OF LANGUAGE

Up to this point, our discussion has been limited to the types of language you are probably most familiar with: spoken and written language. But other important types of language (including alternative ways of speaking and writing) share the general properties we have been discussing. We consider these next.

Gestures and Language

While talking to a friend, have you ever become aware that you were moving your hands and fingers while speaking? Perhaps you were trying communicate something about the size of an object or the speed or direction in which it was moving. In either case, you were using gestures to add to the information you were trying to communicate.

Many scientists believe that the first forms of language were based on gestures (Corballis, 1991). Prior to the development of tools such as hammers and knives, the hands were used as the primary "tools" for communication. The referential gesture—pointing to refer to an object or person—may have been the most common and universal gesture. Corballis (1991) suggests that pointing may be unique to humans. Infants understand the importance of pointing by 12 to 14 months (Schaffer, 1984), but a chimpanzee will point only after being taught to do so (Woodruff & Premack, 1979).

Can we communicate entire thoughts and ideas through the use of gestures? Experiment 9 asks you to try to communicate your thoughts through the use of gestures by participating in a demonstration of this ability.

Languages exist today that are based entirely on gestures, such as American Sign Language (ASL). Research in the past few decades has revealed that languages based entirely on gestures have many of the basic characteristics that underlie spoken languages. Gesture-based languages are rule-based, arbitrary systems of communication capable of supporting the creation of new phrases. They are spontaneously acquired by infants who are exposed to them, just as infants appear to spontaneously acquire spoken language. The rate at which gestures and speech are produced are very similar. Gesture-based languages have syntactic rules for the formation of signed phrases and follow certain social rules, just as spoken language has syntactic and pragmatic aspects. Some gestures are more formal than others and are not used in casual conversation, just as certain spoken phrases and terms are more or less formal. Some gestures signal a question, some symbolize time, and others represent one word or one letter.

Some words, then, are spelled out with signs for letters of the alphabet, and some are represented entirely by one sign. In fact, just as people create new words in spoken and written language to deal with new things and situations (e.g., *Internet*), people also create new signs to represent new things and situations. This ability to generate new signs has the added benefit of improving the efficiency of gestural communication, since having a single sign for something is much more efficient than spelling out the label for that thing.

The acquisition of gestural language and the acquisition of oral language follow similar paths (we will have more to say about the development of language abilities in Chapter 11). For example, infants with normal hearing begin to babble around the age of 7 to 10 months. Deaf infants use partial gestures and elements of gestures in their babbling at about the same age.

Communication with Other Species

We know that animals can communicate with other animals, particularly within their own species. But can animals and humans communicate, using one form of communication that both species understand? The communication abilities of various animals, such as dogs, bees, and monkeys, have been studied; but most of the research on communication across species has focused on the ability of apes to use gestural languages in interactions with humans.

Several researchers have confirmed that apes cannot vocalize language as humans do (Hayes, 1951; Kellogg & Kellogg, 1933). Essentially, they cannot speak in a form that humans would recognize as language because they do not have the vocal machinery required to produce recognizable speech. Thus, several researchers have attempted to teach apes gestural languages, such as ASL. Allen and Beatrix Gardner (1969) taught ASL to a chimpanzee named Washoe. After four years of training, Washoe knew 132 signs to name objects and characteristics of objects. She could also generalize signs to different objects, such as using the sign for open to refer to the car door and the refrigerator. Washoe also taught another chimpanzee, Loulis, to use approximately 50 signs. Washoe's and Loulis's trainers did not sign in the presence of Loulis, so they knew that Washoe taught her these signs.

Other chimpanzees and apes have been taught to use signs from ASL to communicate with their trainers. Herbert Terrace taught a chimpanzee named Nim Chimpsky sign language, and Francine Patterson taught a gorilla named Koko over 300 signs. Ann and David Premack taught a chimpanzee named Sarah to use language by teaching her to use plastic chips of various shapes and colors to represent certain words (Premack, 1971). Sarah could form sentences by arranging the chips in a particular order. Duane Rumbaugh taught Lana, a chimpanzee, to use a computer-based sign board to create sentences. Large keys featuring different geometric shapes represent particular words on the sign board. Lana formed sentences by pressing the keys in a certain order (Rumbaugh, Gill & von Glasersfeld, 1973).

Other mammals besides apes have been taught to use gestural language. Recent research on dolphins (Herman, Kuczaj & Holder, 1993; Herman, Richards & Wolz, 1984) and sea lions (Gisiner & Schusterman, 1992) has documented attempts to teach these animals gestural language. Although researchers have had some difficulty teaching the sea lions to use gestural language, research with dolphins has been more successful. In one study, for example, an artificial gestural language similar to human sign language was created. For

EXPERIMENT 9:   A Demonstration of Gesture Use in Language

You have probably watched active and dynamic speakers give presentations. They may use bold gestures to enhance what they are trying to communicate. If you were trying to communicate the same information, would you use the same gestures? To test this idea, we would like you to perform a demonstration with two of your classmates or friends.

The first thing we would like you to do is watch a cartoon or television sitcom with one of your friends or classmates. Do not discuss with each other what you are watching. Then, one at a time, each person is to describe the cartoon or sitcom to the third person. This third person should record the types of gestures each of you makes as you describe the program. After you have both described the program to the third person, compare the types of gestures that you and the other person made when describing the program. Did you make similar gestures to describe particular actions of characters in the program, such as climbing a tree, or were the gestures different?

This demonstration is based on an experiment conducted by David McNeill (1985). He had five participants watch a cartoon show and then describe it to a listener. The listener recorded the gestures made by the five participants while they described the show. McNeill found that the five participants verbally described the cartoon in very similar ways, using similar words and phrases. He found that the gestures used to describe scenes from the show were also very similar across the participants in the experiment. For example, when one of the characters in the cartoon tried to go up a drainpipe, the participants in the experiment made the gesture of raising their hands and pointing upward.

McNeill (1985) has suggested that when we plan our speech, we also plan our gestures. He believes that gestures and speech are formed together early in production and that both are essential for verbal communication.

some dolphins, the artificial gestural language was made up of visual gestures; and for others, auditory whistle-like sounds. The gestures and sounds were used to form hundreds of different sequences, each with a unique meaning. Louis Herman and his colleagues found that dolphins can discriminate between properly formed language sequences and sequences that violate the semantic and syntactic rules of the artificial language (Herman et al., 1993).

All of these findings are impressive, but are these animals really learning language in the same way humans learn language? Can the animals create new sentences that they have never used before? Some critics claim that the animals are merely being conditioned to respond by signing or by pressing computer keys to obtain rewards. Critics also claim that spontaneous gestures by animals—those made to human trainers when the trainers have not signed first—are just responses to subtle cues given unintentionally by trainers.

There are, however, data that seem to strongly suggest that animals can use language in the human sense. For example, Koko, Patterson's gorilla, creates new sequences of words to describe objects, such as calling a zebra a "white tiger." Additional evidence comes from research conducted by Duane Rumbaugh and Sue Savage-Rumbaugh and their chimpanzees, Austin and Sherman (Savage-Rumbaugh et al., 1980). Austin and Sherman can categorize words based on their semantic categories (e.g., as edible or inedible) and can request objects from one another. Such abilities seem to go beyond what we might expect on the basis of conditioning. Instead, they suggest that these animals may have learned to use language as a tool, just as humans do.

Bilingualism

Our discussion of gestural language and communication with other species brings up an interesting point. That is, the general characteristics and utilities of language do not seem to be tied to any particular language. If you know how to program a computer (or know people who do), then you may already be familiar with this general idea. For example, many people know how to work with a computer in more than one way, such as by programming with C and Pascal. People who have this ability (and there are many) have essentially gained the ability to use more than one language to communicate with the computer. They can accomplish a number of programming goals in any of the languages that they know.

The ability to use more than one language seems to be almost universal among humans, and it is an ability often revealed fairly early in childhood (Beebe, 1988; B. McLaughlin, 1984). Historically, diplomats and traders have benefited from being able to use more than one language and have sometimes played critical roles in historical events because they possessed this ability. A prominent example from the last part of the twentieth century is Pope John Paul II, who has the ability to communicate effectively in more than a dozen different languages. However, we can also find examples of problems (sometimes minor, sometimes not) that arise when people can only *approximate* the ability to use a nonnative language. For example, U.S. President John Kennedy, on a visit to Germany, once announced "Ich bin ein Berliner," which was intended to be a statement about the closeness of the United States and Germany but which could be roughly translated as "I am a cream-filled pastry."

This raises the question of what it means to be bilingual. Historically, this question has been answered in terms of two extreme views (B. McLaughlin, 1984). At one extreme is the view that knowing some words in another language is sufficient to classify a person as bilingual. At the other extreme is the view that a person must be able to use a second language with the same facility as the native language in order to be considered bilingual (Bloomfield, 1935). More recent definitions characterize bilingualism in terms of *degrees* of ability to use a nonnative language (De Avila & Duncan, 1980; Jakobovits, 1970) and focus on the degree to which complete, meaningful statements can be produced in that nonnative language (Haugen, 1956; B. McLaughlin, 1984).

The ability to competently use two distinct languages (like English and Spanish) must be distinguished from the ability to use different forms of the same language. For example, in the late 1990s, a debate emerged regarding the use of something called *Ebonics* (from the words *ebony* and *phonics*), a form of American English used in the African American community. African Americans who can communicate in both Ebonics and standard American English exhibit **diglossia**—the ability to use two different versions, varieties, or dialects of one language (Ferguson, 1959; Fishman, 1964, 1966; Gumperz, 1962). Diglossia has functional importance (e.g., the ability to use both Ebonics and American English allows many

African Americans to succeed in very different social settings), but it is quite different from bilingualism. And since bilingualism has received much more attention from researchers than has diglossia, we concentrate on bilingualism here.

A number of distinctions have been made regarding the types of bilingualism a person might exhibit. For example, in the 1950s, a distinction was made between *compound* and *coordinate* bilingualism. Compound bilingualism refers to a type of language use in which people attribute identical meanings to corresponding words and expressions in two languages. For example, we can attribute identical meanings to *gato* (in Spanish) and *cat* (in English). Coordinate bilingualism, in contrast, refers to a type of language use in which people derive partially or totally different meanings from words in two languages. For example, *corazon* and *heart* could be given two very different meanings in Spanish and English, with the Spanish word implying something much more spiritual and emotional and the English word signifying something much more biological and anatomical. Although the distinction has some historical importance, its usefulness has declined, primarily because careful experimental studies have failed to find critical and consistent differences in language use that correspond to these ideas (B. McLaughlin, 1984).

One common distinction that does appear to have a body of experimental support identifies three types of bilingualism, which can be characterized in terms of the level of competence the individual possesses in the two languages. This idea, originally proposed by Cummins (1979), is based on the idea of a *threshold* of language ability or skill (Lambert, 1990). Figure 9.6 illustrates this idea. Imagine that, for each of two languages a person might use, there is some level of skill or ability (a threshold) above which that person can be considered to have a high degree of skill and below which that person can be considered to have a low degree of skill.

A person who is above the threshold in the ability to use both languages is said to exhibit *additive bilingualism.* Individuals who exhibit additive bilingualism tend to experience positive consequences, both cognitively and socially, as a result of these abilities. A person who is above the threshold in only one of the two languages is said to exhibit *dominant bilingualism.* Individuals who show dominant bilingualism do not appear to experience any positive consequences as a result of their bilingual abilities, but they do not appear to experience any negative consequences (cognitively or socially) either. Finally, a person who is below the threshold for both languages is said to exhibit *subtractive bilingualism.* In this case, the person can actually experience negative consequences (cognitively and socially) from the use of two languages.

A great deal of research on bilingualism is currently being conducted, with the interest being motivated (at least in the United States) by the fact that increasing numbers of people speak English and at least one other language (Spanish, for example). This research is revealing problems with a number of long-standing generalizations about bilingualism, and we close this section by considering some of those misconceptions.

Throughout this book, we have tried to stress how adaptable, flexible, and redundant the brain is with respect to various cognitive abilities. This emphasis contrasts with a number of earlier views about the localization of abilities in particular brain regions (recall the localism/holism debate we discussed in Chapter 2). With respect to bilingualism, it was once thought that the left hemisphere was specialized for the acquisition of a first language and the right hemisphere was specialized for the learning of a second language (Vildomec, 1963). However, beginning in the late 1980s research began to reveal that this distinction was far too strong and that multiple brain regions across both hemispheres are involved in first- and second-language learning and use (Genesee, 1988).

It has been widely assumed that, because children are somehow biologically "primed"

FIGURE 9.6 **Three Types of Bilingualism** Three types of bilingualism have been proposed; the particular type is a function of the individual's abilities in each of the languages.

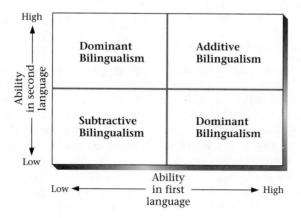

for learning language, they can learn a second language more easily than can adults (Fodor, Bever & Garrett, 1974). It appears, however, that number of methodological and conceptual problems characterized research that supposedly supported this idea. More recent work suggests that when the same criteria for learning are used for both children and adults, and when the experiments carefully control for a number of important confounding factors (such as social influences), children actually may do *worse* than adults in language-learning tasks. This suggests some critical problems with the idea of differences in biological readiness (B. McLaughlin, 1984).

It has also been assumed that the learning of a second language is quite different from the learning of a first language. This idea has its roots in some of the influential ideas of Noam Chomsky, who argued that there is a certain ability, or faculty, for the learning of a first language, and this ability declines with age, meaning that the learning of a second language has to rely on other abilities (Chomsky, 1968). However, research beginning in the 1970s revealed that the developmental sequence of second-language learning in many ways recapitulates (copies) the sequence of first-language learning (Dato, 1971; B. McLaughlin, 1984; Milon, 1974; Ravem, 1974).

Finally, it has commonly been assumed that the early learning of a second language has consistently positive (or consistently negative) effects on language development and cognitive and intellectual functioning in general. In some ways, this assumption is similar to an idea about learning in general that was promoted early in this century—namely, that learning something like Latin would lead to general improvements in cognitive and intellectual abilities. This was known as the *doctrine of formal discipline* (Angell, 1908; Pillsbury, 1908; Woodrow, 1927), and we will have more to day about it in Chapter 14. With regard to bilingualism, the idea that second-language learning can have consistent consequences (positive or negative) has received a great deal of attention, again largely because of changes (in the United States in particular) in the ethnic composition of the population. Unfortunately, many of the findings that support this idea (in either of its forms) have been contaminated by lack of careful experimental control. A review of the available research that employed careful control suggests that there is no consistent advantage or disadvantage—at least cognitively—to the learning of a second language (B. McLaughlin, 1984). Instead, it appears that the likelihood of positive or negative consequences (cognitive or social) is directly related to the degree of skill the person possesses in the two languages (Mohanty, 1992; Ricciardelli, 1992), as we emphasized in the discussion of additive, dominant, and subtractive bilingualism.

Cognitive Aspects of Writing

A great deal of our knowledge about language production has come from research on speech; however, the processes that support writing have recently begun to enjoy more attention from researchers (see Kellogg, 1990). Part of this interest has been motivated by the importance of designing written information that can effectively support other tasks (e.g., training and reference manuals; see Spyridakis & Wenger, 1992). Attention is also being paid to the ways in which new technologies like the World Wide Web and hypertext (see Wenger & Payne, 1996) can take advantage of basic cognitive processes.

Spoken and written language do share some similarities, and yet they differ in important ways. You may have heard of a distinction made between speaking vocabulary and written vocabulary. Typically, a person's written language is more complex and grammatically correct; in speaking, the person is more likely to use vernacular (the everyday language typical in the surroundings) and to adjust the language used to the person being spoken to (Chafe & Danielewicz, 1987). Furthermore, unless you are speaking into a tape recorder, speech tends to be a less permanent form of communication (Ellis & Beattie, 1986).

As people write, they go through three general phases of composing: prewriting, preparing a first draft, and rewriting (Kellogg, 1987; Sommers, 1979). Within each of these phases, four processes occur (Hayes & Flower, 1986): collecting information, planning (creating and organizing ideas), translating (actual language production), and reviewing (correcting errors). Here, we consider the process of planning in detail, since you probably have been exposed to a systematic approach to this step in writing.

It is likely that you have been encouraged, or even required, to produce an outline for a class paper. Your instructor may have told you that creating an outline would help make your writing more clear and effective. Research on the processes of writing offers some support for this suggestion. By creating an outline, you reduce some of the attentional demands placed on you during writing, and you can speed up the writing process. The resulting piece of written material will be more fluent and higher in quality than if you did not complete any prewriting or planning (Kellogg, 1987, 1990). Studies have also shown that individual differences in prewriting techniques are quite large (Hayes, 1989). Students vary in how they form outlines, how they translate information into written material in their own words, and how they revise their written work. Some students write completely new versions of their essays, whereas others make very few changes (e.g., changes in spelling and grammar).

Do expert writers differ from college students in how they approach writing? Typically, the answer to this question is yes. Research comparing revision techniques of expert writers with those of first-year college students reveals that expert writers tend to focus on the organization of the written passage and the transition between ideas more than do students. Expert writers also tend to identify problem sentences correctly and to identify the source of the problem, whereas students tend to miss complex mistakes and brush over explanations of why sentences present problems (Hayes et al., 1987). Experts in a particular field do have a problem, however, identifying when writing may be unclear to readers who lack background knowledge about the material being presented. Hayes (1989) suggested

Ronald T. Kellogg
Ronald T. Kellogg is a pioneer in the study of the cognitive processes involved in producing written communication.

that writers who are knowledgeable about their writing topics are much less likely to identify material as unclearly written. This is actually a major problem for working scientists (such as cognitive psychologists) who write textbooks for undergraduates.

With new and powerful developments in information technologies, new forms of written communication are becoming important, particularly electronic mail (e-mail). Since this type of written language use is reasonably new, not many careful studies of it have been conducted. Those that have been completed, however, have revealed some interesting facts. E-mail letters tend to be short, to consist of grammatically incorrect or incomplete sentences, and even to contain a different type of language. In addition, the language used tends to be informal and imaginative (Harris, 1994).

Section Summary: Understanding Other Forms of Language

Other forms of language share general properties with spoken and written language. Gestures can be important components of standard spoken language, and gestural languages share many general properties with spoken language. Studies in which other species have been trained to use a language system that can also be used by humans have demonstrated that many of the cognitive abilities once thought to be unique to humans can be observed in other species. Research on bilingualism has led to refinements in early conceptions and assumptions about the ability to use another language, and the associated costs and benefits, with recent work suggesting that bilingualism reflects important general characteristics of language processing. Finally, research on the cognitive aspects of writing are revealing important characteristics of the processes that support the successful production of this form of language.

REVIEWING THE PRODUCTION OF LANGUAGE

CONCEPT REVIEW

1. Describe Wundt's conception of how speech is produced. What did Wundt believe to be the basic element of language production and comprehension? In what ways were Wundt's views on language similar to or different from those of Noam Chomsky?

2. Define and describe the four major periods in modern psycholinguistics.

3. When and where do we find the first documented use of the term *psycholinguistics?*

4. Define and describe Chomsky's distinction between language competence and language performance.

5. What are phonemes? What are morphemes? Are they related? If so, in what way? What places in the vocal tract are important in the production of various phonemes?

6. What does it mean for a language to depend on word order for successful production and comprehension?

7. What is the difference between semantics and syntax? What are five characteristics of language that are important in the study of semantics? Provide examples for each.

8. What is meant by *pragmatics,* and why is it important to distinguish among syntax, semantics, and pragmatics?

9. Why is the case grammar approach unique in its approach to the study of semantics?

10. What are language universals? What is the linguistic relativity hypothesis?

11. What aspects of gestural languages provide evidence relative to language universals and the linguistic relativity hypothesis?

12. What is aphasia? What appears to underlie the presence of aphasia?

13. In what ways have studies of speech errors and the relationship between brain trauma and language difficulties been informative for our general understanding of language and its relationship to brain function?

14. Using a simple version of Dell's model, such as the one presented in Figure 9.5, see if you can predict the possibility of producing the spoonerism "noble tons of soil" for the intended phrase "noble sons of toil."

15. Define and describe subtractive, dominant, and additive bilingualism.

16. What three broad phases appear to be involved in composing text?

KEY TERMS

aphasia (p. 299)
case grammar approach (p. 291)
competence (p. 284)
contrastive (p. 288)
conversational maxim (p. 293)
deep structure (p. 284)
diglossia (p. 305)
discourse (p. 287)
generative grammar (p. 284)

given-new strategy (p. 293)
language universal (p. 293)
linguistic relativity hypothesis (p. 295)
morpheme (p. 284)
morphology (p. 291)
parsing (p. 289)
performance (p. 284)
phoneme (p. 287)

phonology (p. 287)
pragmatics (p. 292)
psycholinguistics (p. 281)
semantics (p. 290)
surface structure (p. 284)
syntax (p. 289)
voiced (p. 289)
voiceless (p. 289)

SUGGESTED READINGS

The first four chapters in *The speech chain: The physics and biology of spoken language* (New York: Freeman), by P. B. Denes and E. N. Pinson (1993), provide a good introduction to the logical structures of language and the physical aspects of spoken language production. A thorough and thoughtful review of the linguistic relativity hypothesis is provided by E. Hunt and F. Agnoli (1991) in "The Whorfian hypothesis: A cognitive psychology perspective" (*Psychological Review, 98,* 377–389). This article presents a balanced consideration of the evidence for and against the hypothesis and pro-

vides a modern cognitive interpretation of the hypothesis. We think you will find the presentation interesting, and you may be intrigued by the authors' conclusions. A number of common misconceptions persist about the nature of bilingualism and the learning of a second language. The final chapter in the first volume of *Second language acquisition in childhood,* 2nd ed. (Hillsdale, NJ: Erlbaum), by B. McLaughlin (1984), provides a very readable summary of the misconceptions and the data clarifying these misconceptions.

10 Language Comprehension

Language is a poor thing. You fill your lungs with wind and shake a little slit in your throat, and make mouths, and that shakes the air; and the air shakes a pair of little drums in my head—a very complicated arrangement, with lots of bones behind—and my brain seizes your meaning in the rough. What a round-about way, and what a waste of time!—Daphne du Maurier, as cited by George Miller (1951, p. 10)

CHAPTER 9 INTRODUCED you to psycholinguistics and the history of the psychological study of language, along with some of the basic aspects of language production. This chapter focuses on how we process and comprehend language.

The chapter is a little different in its organization from the other chapters in this book, because we have not included a separate section on the history of the study of language comprehension. We have done this partly because we covered a good bit of the general history in Chapter 9. But there is also a more pragmatic reason. As noted by Crowder (1982), the 1960s and 1970s saw a "virtual stampede of experimental psychologists" into areas of research concerned with language comprehension, particularly reading. That stampede produced a huge body of research findings as well as a large number of theoretical perspectives. Our goal here, as in the preceding chapter, is to focus on language as a specific type of information to be processed. To reach that goal, and to do so without creating an extremely long chapter, we focus on current and influential research and include historical perspectives whenever we can.

The chapter contains two main sections: one on processing spoken language and one on processing written language. Each section begins by considering the basic information to be processed. We then consider the important processes that operate on that information.

PROCESSING SPOKEN LANGUAGE

Spoken language, from the standpoint of the listener, is an auditory signal, the same as any other sound pattern (such as music). One of the important things that distinguishes spoken language from written language is the fact that speech is a **continuous signal.** Basically, the sounds that result from the shaking of the little slit that du Maurier mentioned in the opening quote are combined in a single, unbroken, complex sound pattern. It is the job of the person listening to that sound pattern to break that single auditory pattern into pieces—into the component parts of an understandable communication, such as the words in a sentence. In contrast, in written language, the components of the visual signal language (the words on this page) are separated by blank spaces and punctuation.

Since speech is a continuous pattern of sounds, we can begin our consideration of speech by examining it in terms of general characteristics of sounds. Two fundamental characteristics of sounds are their frequency and their amplitude. When a sound is made, it causes changes in the pressure of the air. These pressure changes are regular and can have, in some cases, very regular cycles. The measure of the number of cycles in a unit of time characterizes the *frequency* of sound. The magnitude of the pressure changes characterize the *amplitude* of sound.

Speech sounds can, like most other sounds, be analyzed in terms of their frequency and their amplitude. However, unlike simple sounds, speech sounds change across the course of an utterance. That is, a speaker may generate an /o/ sound, but if that were the only sound she made each time she spoke, she would probably have very few and very brief conversations. To analyze the sound characteristics of speech, then, we need to consider frequency and amplitude at each point in a segment of speech.

Figure 10.1 shows two representations of the sentence "I owe you a yo-yo." The written representation at the top of the figure is easy to understand. Each word is isolated by empty space before its first and after its last letter. The graphic in the figure is a digitally generated **spectrogram** of the spoken sentence. Frequency is displayed on the *y*-axis, time is displayed on the *x*-axis, and the intensity (the darkness) of the markings represents the amplitude of the various frequencies. Put simply, a spectrogram is a visual summary of the physical characteristics of the speech signal, and we will frequently use spectrograms to illustrate the physical energy present in a segment of speech.

This visual representation of speech sounds illustrates the challenge that we as processors of auditory information face with speech. If you asked everyone in your class to separate out the words in the *printed* form of the sentence by drawing lines between the words, everyone would draw the lines in the same places. But if you asked these same people to find the breaks between the words in the spectrogram, you would have a far lower level of agreement.

If you looked long and hard at the spectrogram, you might think you saw blank spaces between the words represented there. But you would be mistaken; these spaces actually

---

FIGURE 10.1   **Representations of Sound**   Read the sentence at the top of this figure. Did you have any problem segmenting the sentence into words that you could understand? The bottom part of the figure shows what this same sentence "looks" like as a sound pattern, plotted with frequency on the *y*-axis and time on the *x*-axis. Although the "clumps" of frequencies represent different words, you can see that the signal is fairly continuous, without sharp breaks.

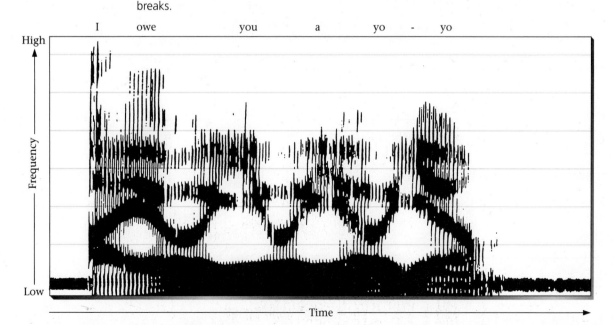

Source: Goldinger, Pisoni & Luce, 1990.

represent parts of the speech signal that are weaker than the other parts. Vowels and consonants have very different patterns in the speech signal. The vowels represent the strongest part of the signal, whereas some of the consonants are only visible at the highest and lowest frequencies. So one cannot segment a spectrogram by looking for blank spaces as indicators of breaks between words. Instead, the words form a continuous signal that the listener must parse using segment cues that are far different from the cues available in written language (Yeni-Komshian, 1993).

As we just discussed, one way in which speech sounds are studied is by analysis of their **acoustical properties**—their physical characteristics. Vowel sounds are determined by the resonant characteristics of the vocal tract; these sounds change when aspects of the vocal tract change during the production of speech. Bands of resonant frequencies, or **formants,** are numbered (when shown on a spectrogram) from the lowest to highest frequency. The first formant (F1) is associated with the lowest frequency; the second for-

FIGURE 10.2 **Spectrograms for Vowels and Diphthongs** The figure shows frequency spectrograms for (a) some of the vowels and (b) some of the diphthongs in American English.

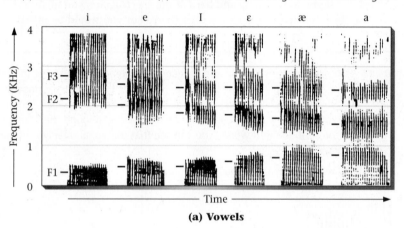

(a) Vowels

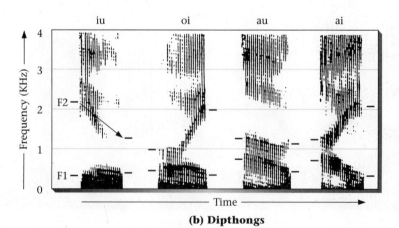

(b) Dipthongs

Source: Pickett, 1980.

mant (F2), with the next frequency; and this pattern continues up to five or more frequencies (Yeni-Komshian, 1993). Each vowel is characterized by at least three formants.

Figure 10.2a shows spectrograms for some of the vowel sounds of American English. The small, dark bars next to each vowel spectrogram (labeled F1, F2, etc.) indicate the formants. Vowels are distinguished according to the relative positions of the first two formants. If you compare the spectrograms for the vowels /i/ and /a/ (the leftmost and rightmost vowel sounds in Figure 10.2a), you can see that the first two formants for the vowel /i/ are relatively far apart, whereas those for the vowel /a/ are close together.

Another type of vowel sound is a **diphthong,** which is made up of two vowel sounds produced in a smooth gliding transition from the first to the second sound. For example, the diphthong /iu/ is produced by gliding from /i/ to /u/. The spectrogram for this diphthong is presented in the leftmost portion of Figure 10.2b. Look at what happens to the second formant (F2) as you go from the beginning of the sound to the end. You can see how this formant moves from a high frequency to a low frequency. Compare this spectrogram to the spectrogram for the vowel sound /i/ in Figure 10.2a. You can see that in the spectrogram for /i/, the second formant (F2) does not change in frequency.

Figure 10.3 shows the spectrogram for the sentence "She sells sea shells." First, take a look at the segment that corresponds to the vowel sound /i/ in the word *sea* (a phonetic representation of the sounds appears below the spectrogram). Compare this portion of the spectrogram with the spectrogram for /i/ in Figure 10.2a. You should be able to locate the first and second formants in Figure 10.3 by finding them in Figure 10.2a. This clear patterning of energy is generally what makes the sound signals for vowels easy to analyze.

FIGURE 10.3   A Spectrogram for the Sentence "She Sells Sea Shells"   The words of the sentence appear below the spectrogram, and phonetic representations are located just above the words and below the spectrogram. Compare the segment of this spectrogram that contains the vowel sound /i/ in *sea* to the spectrogram for the vowel sound /i/ in Figure 10.2.

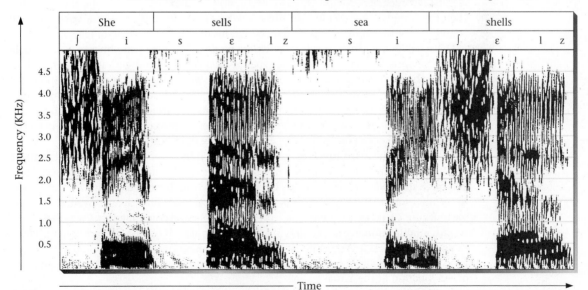

Source: Yeni-Komshian, 1993.

Now look at the segments of the spectrogram corresponding to the consonant sounds. In particular, consider the patterns for the consonant /l/ in *shells* and the consonant /s/ in *sells* or *sea*. You can see that the consonant /l/ projects energy through most of the frequency range but that /s/ has only a small amount of energy, which is concentrated at the high and low frequencies. So while the vowels we have looked at have reasonably clear and easy to identify patterns of energies, the energy patterns for consonants seem to be much more complex and difficult to analyze. For consonants, sound patterns are analyzed in terms of places of articulation—where in the vocal apparatus the sounds are made, the manner of articulation, and the range of frequencies contained in the pattern. Refer back to Figure 9.3, page 288, to review some of these basic properties.

Processing the Auditory Signal

Having briefly described the basic acoustical properties of vowels and consonants, we next consider how we humans process these basic aspects of the speech signal. As you will see, it appears that many of the basic cognitive abilities described throughout this book are put to use in the complex task of speech comprehension.

Processing Vowels   One way to study the perception of vowels in the auditory signal is to compare the processing of vowels in isolation with the processing of vowels in the context of other sounds (Chapter 4 describes context effects in *visual* perception). The first situation yields information about how the basic sound might be processed, and the second yields information about how processing the specific sound might interact with the processing of sounds that precede and follow it.

Winifred Strange and her colleagues (Jenkins, Strange & Edman, 1983; Strange, 1989a, 1989b) have created an interesting way to make this comparison. They use consonant-vowel-consonant (CVC) syllables that begin and end with /b/ but have different vowel sounds in between—for example, *beb* and *bab*. With specialized equipment, the syllables are first recorded on a computer. The vowel sounds are next modified in specific ways, and then the sounds are presented to subjects, who are asked to identify the vowel in each sound. Figure 10.4 shows simplified spectrograms of some of these modified sounds.

The syllables used in Strange's research are made up of three components. Figure 10.4a shows the spectrograms for two basic types of syllables—one using a short vowel, such as /ĕ/, and the other using a long vowel, such as /ē/—with labels on the three components. The first component is the transition from the initial consonant to the vowel, the second is the central vowel portion, and the third is the transition from the vowel to the final consonant. The two spectrograms in Figure 10.4a represent the control syllables, which contain all three components as they appear before any modifications.

The first modification involves removing the middle vowel portion from the syllable and replacing it with a silent period of exactly the same duration as the vowel (see Figure 10.4b). In these *silent-center* syllables, the transitions from the initial consonants and those to the final consonants are preserved, but the actual vowel sounds are removed. As you can see in Figure 10.4b, no frequencies are present in the vowel component of the syllable. The second modification involves removing the initial and final consonant components while preserving the middle vowel portion in its actual duration (see Figure 10.4c). These are *variable-center* syllables, since the duration of the central vowel is variable and a function of the duration of the actual vowel.

The third modification is similar to the variable-center modification, but here, the duration of the vowel is fixed at the duration of the shortest of the vowels being compared (see

FIGURE 10.4 **Spectrograms of CVC Syllables** These schematic spectrograms show the types of CVC syllables used in the work of Winifred Strange and her colleagues.

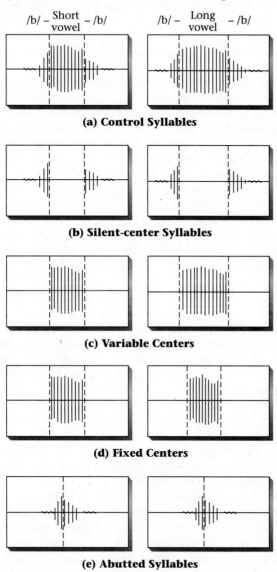

(a) Control Syllables

(b) Silent-center Syllables

(c) Variable Centers

(d) Fixed Centers

(e) Abutted Syllables

Source: Jenkins, Strange & Erdman, 1983.

Figure 10.4d). Thus, if the actual vowel had a duration *longer* than the fixed value, its duration in the modified syllable would be truncated. These are called *fixed-center* syllables, since the duration of the central vowel is fixed at a specific value, independent of the duration of the actual vowel in the syllable. The last modification involves removing the central vowel component so that the transition from the first consonant goes directly to the last consonant, without anything in between (see Figure 10.4e). These types of syllables are called *abutted syllables*.

Strange and her colleagues presented subjects with these various types of syllables and asked them to identify the vowel sound in each. Before reading any further, see if you can predict which type of syllable produced the fewest errors and which produced the most errors in vowel identification. What did you base your predictions on?

The researchers found that subjects were most accurate at identifying the vowels in the *silent-center* condition—the condition in which the vowel was not even present! Subjects made the most errors in the fixed-center condition, where the vowel was present and had a fixed duration. The researchers concluded that perception of vowels is based on the movement into and out of the vowel sound—the transition. The fixed-center sounds contain only steady-state information (information about the stable characteristics of sound, without information about changes like transitions to and from consonants). In contrast, the silent-center sounds contain the transitions into and out of the vowel, even though the vowel itself is missing.

Given that transitions seem so important to accurate identification of vowels, Strange and her colleagues came to the larger conclusion that the perception of isolated sounds and the perception of continuous speech differ. That is, different cues are important to performance in these different situations. Probably the strongest evidence in support of this conclusion was the finding that performance in the silent-center condition was superior even to performance in the variable-center condition.

Processing Consonants   Stop consonants (a consonant produced by first stopping the air flow in the throat and then releasing the built up pressure suddenly; see Chapter 9) have received most of the attention in speech perception research on consonants. In English, the voiced stop consonants are /b/, /d/, and /g/, and the voiceless stop consonants are /p/, /t/, and /k/. To get a better appreciation for the difference between the voiced and voiceless stop consonants, put your finger on the front of your throat and say these stop consonants, one at a time: /b/ and /p/; /d/ and /t/; /g/ and /k/. You should feel vibrations in your throat only for the first member of each pair.

We have just discussed some of the problems humans have in identifying vowels in isolation. The same is true for consonants; they are also difficult to identify in isolation from other phonemes. For example, /b/ cannot be identified well when it is isolated from /a/ in the syllable /ba/. If it is to be identified correctly, the stop consonant must contain part of the transition to the vowel in the syllable.

But if the transition to the vowel is so critical, what happens when we change the vowel but keep the *consonant* constant? Actually, stop consonants paired with different vowels are identified as the same consonant despite a change in vowel transitions. Take, for example, the two syllables /di/ and /du/, shown as simplified spectrograms in Figure 10.5. The dark bars represent the formants that could be observed in an actual spectrogram. Notice that the second formant in /di/ has a higher frequency than the second formant in /du/. Also notice that the transition in the second formant in /di/ goes from low to high, while the second formant in /du/ goes from high to low. In spite of these important differences—differences that are critical to the perception of vowels—people perceive the /d/ to be the same in both syllables (Liberman, 1970).

Earlier, we noted that the basic sound patterns of consonants are more complex than those of vowels. The findings of Liberman (1970) suggest that this increased complexity might extend to the ways in which consonants interact with other sounds. In order to bet-

FIGURE 10.5 **Simplified Spectrograms of the Syllables /di/ and /du/**   The syllables /di/ and /du/ begin with the same stop consonant but have very different vowel transitions. Nevertheless, subjects can accurately identify the consonant.

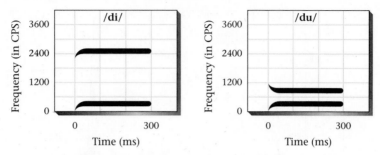

Source: Yeni-Komshian, 1993.

ter understand these potentially complex interactions, psychologists have used specific, fine-grained details characteristic of consonant sound patterns.

For example, **voice-onset time (VOT)** is a measure frequently used to define the difference between voiced and voiceless stop consonants. VOT is the time between the release of air in the production of the consonant and the onset of the vocal-cord vibrations associated with the voicing of the following vowel. In a spectrogram, the VOT is the time between a sharp onset of energy and the onset of the vowel's first formant. Figure 10.6 shows spectrograms for the syllables /di/ and /ti/. Both /d/ and /t/ are stop consonants, but /d/ is voiced and /t/ is voiceless.

Since /d/ involves voicing while /t/ does not, you might expect that the time between the initial burst of energy and the beginning of vibrations in the vocal cords would be shortest for /d/. And indeed, that is what we see in the spectrograms for these two syllables. The spectrograms show a VOT of approximately 10 milliseconds for /di/ and a VOT of approximately 60 milliseconds for /ti/.

But VOT measures can be ambiguous in defining differences among consonants. In fact, VOT varies greatly within the sets of voiced and voiceless stop consonants. It turns out, however, that listeners cannot perceive variations involving a single stop consonant; they can only perceive differences *between* stop consonants. This general pattern is often referred to as an example of **categorical perception** (Liberman et al., 1957). Generally, when subjects have trouble distinguishing among things that are of the same type while easily distinguishing among things of different types, it is taken as evidence for categorical perception. For example, you might have trouble perceiving differences among examples of Manx cats while having no trouble perceiving differences between examples of Manx and Maine Coon cats.

Given this description, what do you think would be required for an experiment designed to investigate whether categorical perception is occurring? You would have to be able to identify the potential categories, and you would have to be able to generate different examples of stimuli within each category. In our case, the categories are the various stop consonants. Now let us see if you can predict what type of evidence would be needed to support an inference of categorical perception.

Imagine that we are conducting an experiment in which we vary some aspect of the

FIGURE 10.6   **Spectrograms of the Syllables /di/ and /ti/**   Notice that the VOT in /di/ is 10 milliseconds while the VOT in /ti/ is 60 milliseconds.

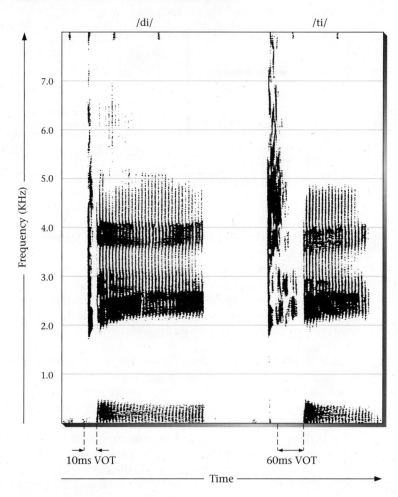

Source: Yeni-Komshian, 1993.

speech signal and measure the frequency with which subjects respond in a certain way. For example, imagine that we manipulate VOT in the presentation of the syllable /di/ and measure the frequency with which subjects identify the presented syllable as /di/. On a piece of paper, draw a graph. Label the x-axis as VOT, and let its range be from 0 to 100 milliseconds. Label the y-axis as percent of syllables identified as /di/. Now draw a vertical line on the x-axis at about 40 milliseconds. We will use this as the "boundary" between categories, with /di/ on one side of the boundary and /ti/ on the other. Note how this corresponds to the psychophysical notion of an absolute threshold, discussed in Chapter 3. Now, use the data we have talked about so far (for example, in Figure 10.6) and the definition of categorical perception to predict what the data would look like if categorical perception is occurring. Do this before you continue reading.

You probably produced a line that stayed at or about 1.0 until you got to the category break, then dropped to almost 0. This translates to identifying all stimuli that have a VOT of less than 40 milliseconds as /di/, while identifying none of the stimuli that have a longer VOT as /di/. Stated a little differently, if 40 milliseconds can be taken as the boundary separating the categories of /di/ and /ti/, then subjects will have difficulty discriminating between stimuli within the category (i.e., all the stimuli will be identified as /di/), but they will find it easy to discriminate between stimuli from different categories (i.e., none of the stimuli on the /ti/ side of the category boundary will be mislabeled as /di/).

Now let us see how well our predictions hold up. The thought experiment we have been performing has actually been done with a variety of vowel sounds (Eimas & Corbit, 1973; Yeni-Komshian, 1993). Figure 10.7 shows the results from an experiment in which the two categories were the syllables /da/ and /ta/ and the primary experimental manipulation was a variation of VOT. As you can see, the actual data look exactly like what we would expect if we were looking for evidence of categorical perception. That is, the percentage of /da/ responses remains at 100 percent right up to the boundary, after which it quickly drops to near 0 percent.

More than a generation ago, when these findings first appeared, they suggested to a number of researchers that the perception of speech sounds was somehow different from the perception of other sounds. At the time, there was little evidence that similar patterns could be observed for other types of stimuli or in other species. However, in the past two decades, numerous demonstrations of categorical auditory perception have been provided for nonspeech stimuli, such as buzzes and tones (Miller et al., 1976; Pisoni, 1977). This suggests that categorical auditory perception may not be unique to speech stimuli. And examples of performance strongly suggestive of categorical perception have been found in monkeys, chinchillas, and quail (Kluender, Diehl & Killeen, 1987; Kuhl, 1986, 1989), suggesting that categorical perception may not be unique to humans.

Some Simplifying Assumptions   The data we have considered so far indicate that, in spite of the amazing complexities of the auditory signal, there are important regularities as well. And it appears that these regularities can and do function as important cues for processing the signal. Some of these cues include formants, transitions, and voice-onset time. But being able to describe the cues used to process the speech signal does not constitute a theory of speech perception. Given the complexity of the signal, it is not surprising that scientists have had to make some simple but important assumptions about aspects of the speech signal and how it is perceived in order to develop theoretical accounts of how we process the signal. We focus here on three common and important assumptions.

The first is the assumption of **linearity,** a one-to-one mapping between a perceived phoneme and a segment of the physical speech signal (Chomsky & Miller, 1963). The assumption of linearity implies that the order of perceived phonemes corresponds exactly to the order of segments in the speech signal; we should emphasize that linearity primarily refers to the one-to-one relation between the perceived phoneme and the speech signal, and secondarily to the ordering of the perceived phonemes.

The second assumption, that of **invariance,** has to do with an assumed lack of variability in the speech signal. It is commonly assumed that each phoneme has acoustical properties that occur in all contexts. Recognition of a phoneme is based on the occurrence of these properties.

The final assumption, the assumption of **separability,** has to do with the segmentation of the signal. Just as we are able to separate out words in reading, we should be able to parse the components of the auditory signal to determine what is being said.

Patricia Kuhl
Patricia Kuhl has explored the perception of auditory stimuli, such as speech sounds. Some of her work has been important in challenging the idea that speech is a special type of stimulus.

FIGURE 10.7   **Categorical Perception as a Function of VOT**   In this example of categorical perception of consonant sounds as a function of VOT, note how the percentage of syllables identified as /da/ stays near 100 percent until a "boundary" is reached between 40 and 50 milliseconds of VOT, after which the percentage drops quickly to 0.

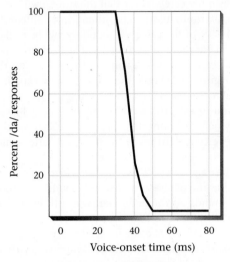

Source: Based on data from Eimas & Corbit, 1973.

How well do actual speech signals match these assumptions? Linearity is not always guaranteed, as the *McGurk effect* demonstrates (MacDonald & McGurk, 1978). Briefly, the McGurk effect occurs when a subject *sees* a speaker repeating a simple syllable but *hears* a signal that corresponds to a different syllable. The syllable the subject *reports* is different from both the visual cue (what the speaker's mouth is forming) and the auditory cue. This effect is a profound violation of the linearity assumption, because nothing in the auditory signal corresponds to what is perceived. Experiment 10 shows how you can reproduce the McGurk effect.

What about the invariance assumption? In natural speech, the way in which a particular phrase is produced can vary significantly from person to person or from situation to situation. The sources of this variability include differences in background noise, differences in frequencies (such as the differences between male and female voices), differences in speaking rates, differences due to regional accents, and even differences due to hearing a particular voice for the first time (Nygaard, Sommers, & Pisoni, 1994).

Finally, what about the separability assumption? We know that segmentation of a continuous auditory signal *can* be difficult—much more complicated than the segmentation of written language. Figure 10.1 provides a demonstration. No clear segments seem to be available in the auditory signal, yet listeners rarely have difficulty separating this phrase into its parts (Goldinger, Pisoni & Luce, 1990). So the continuous auditory signal can be perceived as being segmented, even though no immediately apparent acoustical properties in the physical signal support this segmentation.

Although we can find violations of the three simplifying assumptions commonly made about the speech signal, these assumptions are nevertheless extremely helpful in the con-

EXPERIMENT 10:   The McGurk Effect

The McGurk effect is formally known as *cross-modal cue integration,* because the cues from two different modalities (visual and auditory) are integrated to produce the perceived effect. In the research in which the effect was originally documented, McGurk and his colleagues (MacDonald & McGurk, 1978; McGurk & MacDonald, 1976) showed subjects a videotape of a person speaking a simple vowel-consonant syllable, such as /ga/. The volume on the videotape was turned down. At the same time, a separate audiotape of a spoken syllable, such as /ba/, was played. The sound on the audiotape was synchronized with the speaker's lip movements on the videotape. Subjects did not report hearing either the syllable mouthed on the videotape or the syllable pronounced on the audiotape. Rather, they reported hearing something in between: /da/. This is the McGurk effect.

In the text, we noted that this effect violates one of the basic simplifying assumptions made about the speech signal, the assumption of linearity. This is because the perceived signal has no correspondence to the actual physical signal being processed. To get a sense for how powerful this effect is, try this simple demonstration. You and a friend will act as experimenters, and another friend will act as a subject. Try to recruit someone who does not know about this effect or about what you are trying to demonstrate.

You and your fellow experimenter will take on the roles of the videotape and the audiotape in McGurk's experiments. One of you will make the mouth movements that go along with the syllable /ga/ but will not make any sound. The other will say the syllable /ba/. You should practice together so that the one speaking can be synchronized with the one doing the mouthing.

The ideal place for conducting this demonstration is a place where the experimenter doing the mouth movements can be separated from the subject by something like a clear glass. The subject should be able to see the experimenter who is making the mouth movements and should be able to hear the experimenter who is speaking but should not be able to see this second experimenter. After you have practiced and are sure that you can be synchronized, bring in your subject. Tell the subject that you will be presenting a simple syllable a number of times and that his or her job is to identify the syllable. Then begin, and present the stimulus (mouth movements and speech) about ten times. Then ask your subject to identify the sound. We think you will be impressed with how powerful this effect is.

After you have demonstrated the effect, repeat the experiment by mouthing the word *garb* and saying the word *barb.* What does your subject report hearing? Then try other visual and vocal combinations in which the syllable is actually a word (Easton & Basala, 1982). Does the effect still occur? How do you interpret the fact that it does (or does not) occur?

struction of theories of speech processing. However, scientists must always be mindful that the basic assumptions that support their theories are simplifications. If a theory makes absolutely no sense without a basic assumption, then a violation of that assumption can be devastating. If a theory can easily accommodate violations of an assumption, or can be easily modified to take account of exceptions, then a violation is not so critical.

Comprehending Spoken Language

A point implicit in the preceding discussion should be made explicit: Although we have been referring to assumptions scientists make about the auditory signal, what we have really been talking about are assumptions regarding our *processing* of the auditory signal. As just explained, actual, physical auditory signals may sometimes fail to correspond with simplifying assumptions. But human performance with the auditory signal can be described reasonably well by use of these assumptions. Cognitive psychologists hold on to the assumptions, in spite of the violations, because they communicate important details about the cognitive processing of speech. With these assumptions in mind, let us now consider three general theoretical accounts of speech comprehension.

Motor Theory   The primary claim of the **motor theory** is that our ability to process speech is guided by what we know about producing speech. That is, we interpret auditory signals by making reference to the way in which we create speech sounds through the movement of mouth and throat (Liberman, 1970; Liberman et al., 1967).

For example, consider the two syllables /di/ and /du/. The actual acoustic patterns associated with these two syllables are very different, yet listeners can correctly identify the initial consonant /d/ in both syllables. The motor theory was motivated in part by the need to account for how this could be so. A simple experiment may help you understand the appeal of motor theory. Pronounce the two syllables /di/ and /du/ out loud a number of times. Concentrate on where your tongue is placed. Notice that your tongue is placed at very similar locations when you pronounce these two syllables.

Motor theory proposes that listeners, when faced with the task of identifying a particular sound in speech, make use of what they know about how to produce that speech sound. Knowing that two sounds are formed in similar ways makes it easy to identify particular parts of those sounds as being the same. A strong prediction of motor theory is that in order to successfully process speech, it is necessary to have some knowledge of how speech is produced. In addition, since speech processing is seen as dependent on knowledge of speech production, motor theory seems to suggest that speech is a different or special type of auditory stimulus. In contrast, for example, you could successfully process a piece of music without understanding how to play an instrument.

In fact, over the past few decades, evidence has been collected suggesting flaws in both of these suggestions (Yeni-Komshian, 1993). Before moving on, though, let us consider some of the evidence that led to the suggestions, particularly the suggestion that speech represents a special type of stimulus, since this proposal has proved to be very controversial.

What evidence would have led Liberman and his colleagues (Liberman, 1970; Liberman et al., 1957; Liberman & Mattingly, 1985) to propose that the speech signal is very different from other auditory stimuli that people process? We have already introduced one type of evidence: categorical perception. An early (1957) study of categorical perception by Liberman and his colleagues revealed that individuals are very good at distinguishing among different phonemic categories, such as /b/, /p/, and /d/, but are not very good at identifying different sounds within the same phonemic category, such as /ba/, /bi/, and /be/. This result was initially found only with speech sounds, not with nonspeech sounds, such as pure tones. Evidence for categorical perception of speech sounds was also found in young infants, suggesting that a specialized speech processor is present at birth and that an individual's ability to perceive speech signals is innate (Eimas et al., 1971).

A second type of evidence supporting the idea of a specialized speech processor is a phenomenon called **duplex perception.** In duplex perception studies (Liberman, 1982), two sounds are presented simultaneously, one in each ear. In one ear is the base syllable, consisting of the first two formants with their transitions and the third formant without its transition (i.e., the vowel in the syllable is not complete). Presented in the other ear is the isolated third formant transition, which sounds like a nonspeechlike chirp.

Interestingly, when these two sounds are presented together, the sound perceived by the subject is rather different from what is presented. Specifically, the subject perceives the complete vowel along with a distinct and separate chirp. What appears to be happening is that when the components of a speech signal are presented simultaneously, they are transformed into a speech component and a nonspeech component, heard at the same time. It is the perceptual system's apparent preference for creating distinct speech and nonspeech components that suggests some perceptual mechanism specialized for the processing of speech.

Other data were also used to suggest perceptual processes specialized to speech. Many of these studies used stimuli composed of speech and nonspeech components and demonstrated categorical perception effects for the speech components, while showing noncategorical effects for the nonspeech components (Liberman, 1982). Other studies appeared to demonstrate that the perception of speech and nonspeech components could be affected independently (Bentin & Mann, 1990; Nygaard & Eimas, 1990).

Recall that the idea of perceptual processes specialized for the auditory signal has proved controversial. That controversy sparked a good deal of experimentation aimed at investigating whether the effects observed in speech could be observed for auditory nonspeech stimuli. The research results suggest that effects observed with speech can also be observed with other types of auditory signals.

For example, we mentioned earlier that in several studies researchers have reported observing categorical perception using nonspeech sounds as stimuli and other (nonverbal) species as subjects. In other studies, experimenters have been able to bias subjects, so that they thought a particular sound was a speech sound when it really was not (Neath, Surprenant & Crowder, 1993; Remez et al., 1981). Duplex perception, another major source of evidence for specialized speech processors, can be demonstrated in the perception of musical chords (Pastore et al., 1983) and of sounds from normal events in the environment, such as the slamming of a door (Fowler & Rosenblum, 1990).

Direct Perception   A theoretical approach that is very similar to the motor theory is the recent proposal by Fowler (1986; Fowler & Rosenblum, 1990; Fowler & Rosenblum, 1991) for a direct-realist approach to speech processing. According to this perspective, speech is an event rather than just an object (a signal). Speech consists of auditory waveforms structured by **articulatory gestures,** such as the coordination of the muscles in the vocal tract. This is similar to the idea that visual waveforms are structured by events in the world, such as being reflected off the surfaces of objects (Gibson, 1966, 1979; see Chapter 4). Our auditory perceptual systems come into direct contact with the structured auditory waveforms, which themselves have been given structure by the articulatory gestures. Consequently, from this perspective, we perceive speech directly, without the need for any additional processing.

You can see that direct perception shares some important characteristics with motor theory. Probably most apparent is that both theories rely on aspects of speech production to guide speech perception. But there is a critical difference on this point. Motor theory claims that knowledge of how speech is formed must be retrieved from memory in order for the speech signal to be processed. The direct-realist approach, in contrast, says that the motor activities that produce speech give structure to the auditory waveforms received by the listener. The listener need not retrieve *anything* related to speech production but need only perceive the structured, organized signal.

Given the fact that the direct-realist approach has a starting point similar to that of motor theory, it is not surprising that much of the data that can be explained by motor theory can also be explained by the direct-realist approach. But there have been difficulties with and numerous criticisms of direct-realist theory (Diehl, 1986; Massaro, 1986; Remez, 1986), primarily with respect to the logic of its approach. Another problem is that only limited experimental tests of this approach have been conducted (Goldinger, Pisoni & Luce, 1990). Still, its basic ideas offer intriguing challenges to more standard approaches to speech processing.

Information Processing Models   Both the motor theory and the theory of direct perception refer to the specific mechanisms of speech production to understand speech comprehension. In this sense, they concern themselves with cognitive abilities that are in some way particular to the processing of a single type of information (speech), although they differ in how strongly they assume that speech is a special type of stimulus for humans. Contrasting with these approaches are information processing models of speech processing, which propose that the processing of speech is accomplished through general cognitive mechanisms.

An important idea behind information processing models is that the basic cognitive structures used in other cognitive tasks are used in the processing of speech. Consequently, these models must elaborate on how relatively general models of the cognitive system can accommodate special purposes. For example, take a look at the schematic representation of an early example of this approach (Pisoni & Sawusch, 1975) presented in Figure 10.8. Compare this model with the modal model of memory presented in Figure 6.5. You will notice important similarities in the structures of these two models. In particular, note the way in which the general approach to a cognitive process (memory) can be applied to a specific problem (speech processing).

Think for a moment about how you perform any of a number of different language processing tasks, from perceiving the elements of the auditory signal, to recognizing a particular word, to comprehending a sentence. Usually, when we study performance on tasks like these, we set up the experiments so that only a small number of experimental factors can affect the outcome. This is good science, but it is a bit different from what we do in the world outside the laboratory. When we perceive speech in everyday life, we often use a number of different cues to help us process the auditory signal.

For example, think about having a conversation with a friend in a noisy environment, such as at a basketball game, at a party, or perhaps in one of your classes just before the lecture begins. In such a situation, you often need more than just the cues in the auditory signal to help you process that signal. For example, you might watch your friend's mouth, or the expression on his face, or something he is pointing at. In each instance, you are combining, or integrating, information from different sources to process the spoken information.

One successful information processing model of speech processing is Massaro's fuzzy logical model of perception, or FLMP (Massaro, 1987; Massaro & Friedman, 1990). A central insight of the FLMP is that speech processing, and most other cognitive tasks, are **multiply determined** (Anderson, 1981, 1991; Massaro, 1987; Massaro & Friedman, 1990). That is, the information we use to perform these tasks comes from different sources. The

FIGURE 10.8   **An Information Processing Model of Speech Perception and Recognition**   Compare this early model of speech processing to the general model of memory presented in Figure 6.5. Note how the general approach is used to model a more specific process. It is this sort of reliance on general cognitive abilities that sets information processing models apart from other theoretical approaches.

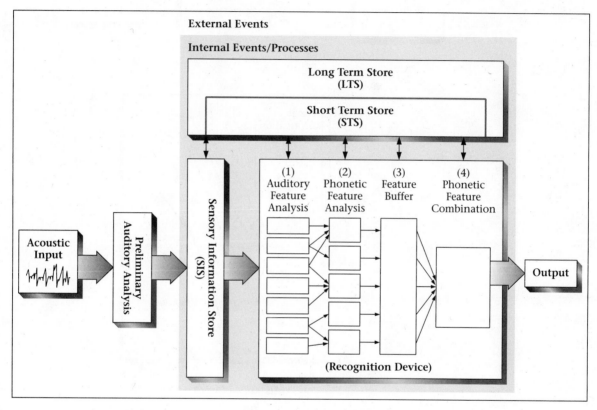

Source: Pisoni & Sawusch, 1975.

importance of considering that cognitive performance may be multiply determined has been demonstrated in a number of areas (Anderson & Cuneo, 1978; Busemeyer, 1991; Cuneo, 1980; Massaro, Weldon & Kitzis, 1991; Wenger & Payne, 1997). And the finding that speech processing might be multiply determined has major implications. To appreciate these implications, we need to understand the basic aspects of the theory.

According to the FLMP, three general operations are logically required in any information processing task that relies on multiple sources of information: *evaluation* of the input, *integration* of the results of that evaluation, and *decision* based on the results of the integration. A schematic representation of these processes is presented in Figure 10.9a. To see how the processes apply to speech processing, consider a situation in which you are trying to understand something a friend is saying at a noisy party.

Imagine that you have arrived at this party and you know your friend is hungry. She tells

FIGURE 10.9   **The Fuzzy Logical Model of Perception**   The figure illustrates how the FLMP would explain the use of two different types of information (auditory and visual) in speech perception.

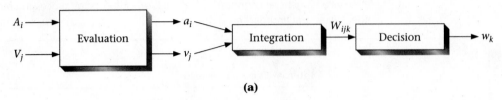

(a)

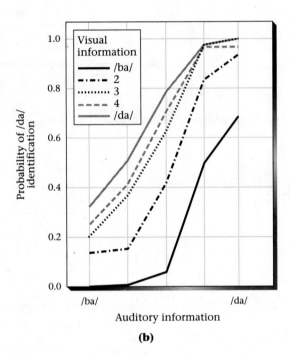

(b)

Source: Part b from Massaro, 1992.

you that she wants to go over to get a particular item to eat. Because it is noisy, you watch her mouth to help you understand what she is saying. You now have two sources of information. The first is the auditory signal of your friend's speech. That signal can exist in any one of several levels of noise (owing to changes in the level of the music, conversation, etc.); we will let A_i represent the level of the auditory signal at some level i of noise. For example, imagine that the music is particularly loud and all you can hear your friend say is something that sounds like ". . . /r/ . . /to/." The second source of information is the visual cues you get by watching your friend's mouth. These cues can be more or less difficult to see (owing to changes in level of lighting, etc.); we will let V_j represent the level of the visual information at some level j of visibility. Imagine that lights are flashing when your friend is speaking, and all you can see is that it looks like the word begins with a /b/ sound.

According to the FLMP, the first thing you do is evaluate the two sources of information, A_i and V_j. Essentially, you perceive and encode these two sources of information and transform the signals from the external world into a psychological representation. To distinguish the results of evaluation from the information that is evaluated, we will let a_i refer to the results of evaluating the auditory information and let v_j refer to the results of evaluating the visual information. These two psychological quantities are then combined, or integrated.

The result of this integration is a measure of preference or support for a particular word. We will let W_{ijk} represent the level of support that the auditory (A_i) and visual (V_j) information provide, when combined, for a particular word W_k. For example, imagine that when the auditory information "... /r/ ... /to/" and the visual information /b/ are combined, the result is a high degree of support for the word *burrito*. This value W_{ijk} is then input to a decision process, which compares the level of support for *burrito* against the level of support for alternative words or phrases (like *burnt toast*). The output of the decision process is the probability that word W_k will be selected. In this case, it is the probability that you will interpret what your friend said as the word *burrito*.

Although this description might seem logically appealing, the true test of the FLMP, as of any model or theory, is an experiment. Massaro (1992) describes an experiment very similar to the situation just described. In that experiment, subjects watched an animated computer-generated face while listening to that face speak a certain syllable. Then subjects were asked to identify the syllable as either /ba/ or /da/. The experimenters varied the auditory signal by altering the first 80 milliseconds of the syllable. They varied the visual information by making stepwise changes in the animated face.

The results of this experiment are presented in Figure 10.9b. The various lines on the graph represent different levels of visual information, ranging from information supporting /da/ to information supporting /ba/. The points on the *x*-axis represent different levels of auditory information, ranging as well from information supporting /da/ to information supporting /ba/. As you might expect, when both sources of information supported /ba/, subjects were nearly perfect at identifying the syllable as /ba/. And when both sources of information supported /da/, subjects were nearly perfect at identifying the syllable as /da/.

But note how the lines move smoothly *between* these two endpoints. Do you see any evidence of a strong break between the two categories, such as you would expect in categorical perception? What the data seem to suggest is that increasing the level of combined support for one of the syllables continuously increases the probability of identifying that syllable.

This type of finding, and the basic assumptions of the FLMP, mean that this theory offers a strong challenge to the idea of a specialized speech processor, for two reasons. First, it emphasizes the influence of *multiple* sources of information in speech processing. If there were a specialized speech processor, it should respond only to auditory information and should not be affected by visual information. But data such as those we just described suggest that speech processing can be strongly influenced by visual information (Massaro, 1995). Second, since the basic approach can be used with any type of information, it can be extended to tasks other than speech processing, such as letter and word recognition (Massaro, 1979; Oden, 1984), syllable and word recognition in speech perception (Massaro, 1989; Oden & Massaro, 1978), categorization of visual codes (Oden, 1981; Thompson & Massaro, 1989), and certain aspects of memory retrieval (Massaro, Weldon & Kitzis, 1991; Wenger & Payne, 1997).

Section Summary: Processing Spoken Language

Spoken language differs from written language in that written language can be easily segmented into parts (like words or letters), whereas spoken language is, physically, a continuous signal. Nevertheless, the cognitive system is able to parse the continuous auditory signal and operate on it in complex ways. Cues that aid in this processing include formants, the transitions between vowels and consonants, and the acoustical patterns that result from various ways of articulating consonants. The processing of consonants is more complex than the processing of vowels. Some early and influential data from studies manipulating voice-onset time (VOT) in the processing of consonants appeared to suggest that this complex processing is unique (or special) to the processing of human speech. However, more recent evidence from studies using nonspeech sounds as stimuli and nonhuman species as subjects suggests a different conclusion. Owing to the complexities involved in processing spoken language, researchers have found it necessary to make a number of simplifying assumptions about the nature of that processing. Three common assumptions are linearity, invariance, and separability. Although the physical signal may violate these assumptions, it has been possible to talk about the processing of the auditory signal while making these assumptions. Three theoretical perspectives that have made use, to varying degrees, of these assumptions are motor theory, the direction perception approach, and information processing models (such as the FLMP).

PROCESSING WRITTEN LANGUAGE

As a species, we humans have had vast experience working with an *auditory* signal for communication. Although no one knows for sure when spoken language evolved, the ability to produce and use a patterned auditory stimulus to communicate seems to have appeared at least 100,000 years ago, probably as a result of some important evolutionary change to the brain (Rayner & Pollatsek, 1989). In comparison, we as a species have far less experience working with patterned *visual* signals, or written communication. Perhaps the earliest pieces of evidence for written communication are records of business transactions, from an area of the world that is now Iraq, dating to more than 5,000 years ago (Gelb, 1963).

The first evidence of what we might think of as *sentences* can be found in artifacts from Sumeria that date to about the same period. These records show symbols used to represent objects and ideas (see Figure 10.10). But over a relatively short period of time after that, the symbols used in writing became increasingly abstract, and writing developed from concrete representations to stylized and abstract representations. By 4,000 years ago, a number of writing systems incorporated representations of syllables; and within another 1,500 to 2,000 years, the basics of the major writing systems of the world were present in the Greek alphabet and Aramaic and Hebrew scripts.

In this part of the chapter, we consider the ways in which we process complex visual signals in order to perform what might seem to be an effortless and almost automatic process: reading. Just as we began our study of spoken language processing by considering the nature of the speech signal, we begin our study of written language processing by considering the nature of the visual signal.

In discussing written language, as in discussing spoken language, we emphasize the complexity of the tasks involved in language processing. Many of the advances in our understanding of the normal ways of accomplishing these tasks, along with advances in technology that are allowing us to explore the workings of the nervous system, are being used

FIGURE 10.10 **The Evolution of Writing Systems** Writing systems evolved from symbols that closely corresponded to the objects and ideas they were intended to represent to highly stylized and abstract symbols, as these examples show.

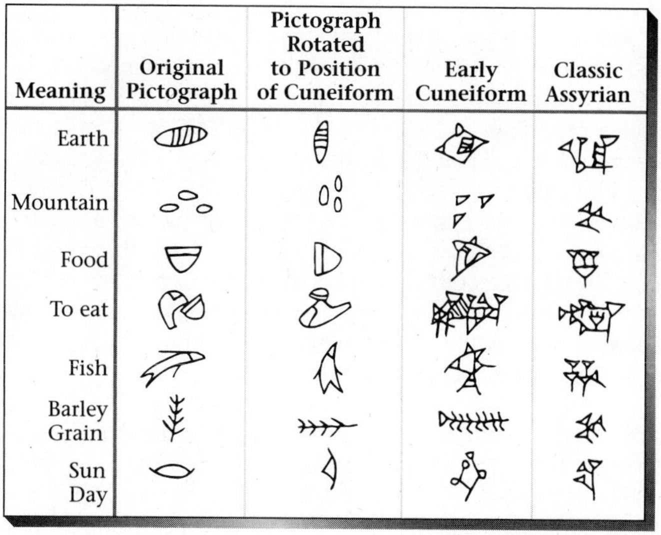

Meaning	Original Pictograph	Pictograph Rotated to Position of Cuneiform	Early Cuneiform	Classic Assyrian
Earth				
Mountain				
Food				
To eat				
Fish				
Barley Grain				
Sun Day				

Source: Rayner & Pollatsek, 1989.

to increase our understanding of problems in processing language. Research Report 10 shows how knowledge from traditional experimental approaches and newer neuroscientific approaches are being combined to yield a better understanding of the reading disorder known as dyslexia.

Some Characteristics of the Visual Signal

Although there are numerous forms of writing and visual representations of language—such as Chinese pictographs and ideographs, Japanese Kanji and Kana, and Korean Hangul—we are concerned with the processing of alphabetic systems such as written English. The basic elements of alphabetic systems are letters, such as those you are reading now. So let us start by considering the aspects of printed letters that affect our ability to process written language.

Scientific interest in the processing of written language goes back to the latter part of the nineteenth century and the early part of the twentieth century (Erdmann & Dodge, 1898; Pillsbury, 1897). But perhaps the most extensive studies of the physical characteristics of the visual signal in reading were performed by Miles Tinker and his colleagues between 1927 and 1965 (Morrison & Inhoff, 1981; Tinker, 1963, 1965). Tinker collected data from more than 30,000 subjects in his experiments. He used careful comparisons and even photographed the movements of his subjects' eyes to determine what was actually happening as a function of various changes in aspects of printed letters.

One interesting thing that Tinker's research revealed is that the factors that make it easier to process a single letter are not always the factors that make it easier to read printed text. In fact, some such factors actually make it *harder* to read text, if you measure perfor-

RESEARCH REPORT 10:   Understanding the Deficits in Dyslexia

Between 4 and 10 percent of all children in the United States reportedly show some evidence of dyslexia, a pronounced difference between actual and potential reading abilities (Eden & Zeffiro, 1996). Over the past few decades, a number of researchers have tried to determine what the actual processing problems in dyslexia might be. Some researchers have, on the basis of this work, concluded that the deficits in dyslexia are purely linguistic or in some way isolated to cognitive processes that operate only on linguistic stimuli (Liberman, 1989; Vellutino, 1987). However, others have concluded that the deficit in dyslexia is more general. Tallal (1984; Tallal & Curtis, 1990) has suggested that individuals with dyslexia have a *phonemic* deficit and that the source of this deficit is a more general problem in processing the temporal (time-based) aspects of stimuli. Farmer and Klein (1996) recently reviewed a wide range of studies relative to this hypothesis and found evidence supporting the more general notion of a deficit in processing temporal aspects of stimuli.

In general, four dimensions characterize the processing of temporal characteristics of stimuli (Hirsh & Sherrick, 1961). The first is the ability to identify or detect a single, briefly presented stimulus. On tasks involving this ability, individuals with dyslexia appear to perform at levels no different from those of individuals without dyslexia. The second dimension is the ability to distinguish two stimuli presented rapidly and sequentially. On tasks involving this ability, people with dyslexia appear to be impaired relative to people without dyslexia, and this impairment can be shown with auditory stimuli such as clicks and tones and visual stimuli such as lines and patterns. The third dimension is the ability to judge which of a set of stimuli came first in a sequence. Here again, individuals with dyslexia do worse than those without dyslexia, and the difficulties can be demonstrated with both linguistic and nonlinguistic stimuli. The fourth dimension is the ability to tell whether two temporal patterns are the same or different. Again, people with dyslexia appear to perform at lower levels than people without dyslexia, and the impairment can be demonstrated with linguistic and nonlinguistic stimuli, including tones, dots, symbols, and flashes.

Farmer and Klein present a wealth of evidence that contradicts the assertion that dyslexia is specific to linguistic stimuli. And as we might expect in light of the general debate over whether speech represents a special type of stimulus, the evidence presented by Farmer and Klein has generated intense argument (Martin, 1996; Rayner, Pollatsek & Bilsky, 1996; Studdert-Kennedy & Mody, 1996).

But in addition to the evidence summarized by Farmer and Klein, additional evidence from a different source may provide a challenge to the idea that the difficulties in dyslexia are restricted to language processes. Eden and Zeffiro (1996) investigated the possibility that at least one component of the deficits in dyslexia is a set of brain abnormalities that affect areas responsible for the processing of visual motion. Figure 10A shows the results of a study using functional magnetic resonance imaging (fMRI) to observe the responses of brain regions to the presentation of visual motion. The image on the left shows the active regions of a normal

FIGURE 10A **Brain Areas Active in the Perception of Motion** These functional magnetic resonance images (fMRI) show brain areas active in the perception of motion in a person with dyslexia (right) and a person without dyslexia (left).

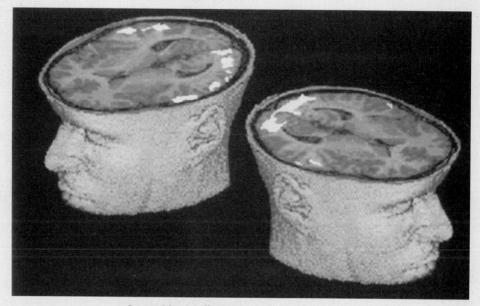

Source: Eden & Zeffiro, 1996.

individual when processing visual motion, and the image on the right shows the active regions of an individual with dyslexia. The differences, as you can see, are dramatic.

It is tempting, as suggested, to conclude that this finding provides additional evidence for Farmer and Klein's assertions, since motion seems so closely related to sequences in time, but the evidence for that link is very preliminary. As we have noted in previous chapters, new technologies such as fMRI are currently suggesting many new sources of evidence for cognitive scientists. It may be through creative combinations of typical cognitive methods and the newer approaches that we gain important insights into problems such as those associated with dyslexia.

mance in terms of aspects of reading speed. For example, capital letters, by themselves, are easier to see at longer distances than are lower-case letters. But when people read something printed in capital letters, their reading speed actually *decreases*. Another factor is the size of the type. Large letters are easier to see at a greater distance than are smaller letters, but they slow down reading speed.

The effects of many other factors on reading speed were studied by Tinker and his colleagues. These included the effects of changes in line lengths for type of different sizes, the effects of spacing between and within lines of text, the brightness contrast between the page and the print, and the effects of color. Tinker found, for example, that simple use of color did not affect reading speed much at all. Tinker also noted that light level had much less effect on reading speed than you might expect. For example, when Tinker was doing his research, suggested light levels were based on data from tasks that measured things like the ability to see very small objects. Tinker documented that the best light levels for reading were actually *much* lower than what these data suggested. In fact, Tinker found that light levels that are too high can actually impair reading performance (Tinker, 1963, 1965).

Processing the Visual Signal

Over the past few decades, cognitive scientists have acquired an immense amount of information on what people's eyes do while they read. The foundation for this progress was laid down more than a century ago.

As you read this textbook, you probably have the sense that your eyes are moving smoothly across and down the page. In reality, however—as we pointed out in Chapter 1—your eyes are making all sorts of jumps and stops in the process of your taking in this printed information. The fact that the eyes move in a series of small jumps was first noted by the French scientist Emile Javal (1878), who referred to the jumps as **saccades** (the French word for "jumps"). In between saccades, the eye moves to bring a small region of text into the fovea for a detailed analysis. This is called a **fixation.** Reading, from the standpoint of the work your eyes are doing, is basically a series of fixations inserted between saccades.

Each saccade that occurs during reading involves a movement of about seven to nine character spaces, and a typical saccade requires 20 to 35 milliseconds to be completed, with the duration directly related to the distance the eyes travel during the saccade (Rayner & Pollatsek, 1989; Young, 1963). Saccades are considered to be ballistic movements, which means that once they have started, they cannot be halted. For readers of English (and similar languages), most saccades involve moving the eyes to the right. However, saccades can also go backward or to the left; these saccades are called **regressions.** Typically, we make four to five saccades per second and one regression every two seconds while we are reading.

Fixations can last anywhere from 15 to 500 milliseconds, and they appear to be where the major information processing occurs during reading. This was originally noted late in the nineteenth century (Erdmann & Dodge, 1898; Pillsbury, 1897). These early studies found that the perception of a visual stimulus appeared to take place during the fixations, with little if any perception occurring during saccades, though evidence collected in this part of the century has suggested that it is possible to perceive and recognize simple stimuli during saccades (Uttal & Smith, 1968). Thus, the actual process of reading is a lot like watching a series of slides (Rayner & Pollatsek, 1989). Each fixation is like a slide in the series, and the saccades are like the changing of the slides.

Scientists interested in reading use eye movements as indications of what information people are collecting as they read. Some of the earliest studies involved taking photographs of the eyes during reading. Today, the technology used to track the eyes during reading is much more advanced and allows for very fine measurements of the location of the eyes during the reading of a sentence, word, and even letter (Raney & Rayner, 1993; Rayner, 1993). Such detailed measurements allow psychologists to get a precise picture of what the eyes fixate on during reading, and these fixations give important clues about the types of information that are important in reading.

This research has shown us that, during a single fixation, a person may encode information that lies up to 15 character spaces to the right of the fixation point. The exact time at which information is extracted during a fixation remains unclear (Rayner & Pollatsek, 1989). But some evidence suggests that during saccades, the information that is extracted during one fixation is integrated with the information that was extracted during earlier fixations (Balota, Pollatsek & Rayner, 1985; Balota & Rayner, 1983). Regressions reveal when a reader has encountered a confusing or ambiguous situation and is returning to a previous point in the sentence to resolve the confusion.

Given these basic facts about what is happening as a reader's eyes move through a text, let us take a look at some data from an experiment in which the movements of the eyes were tracked. Figure 10.11a shows a passage of text, with the fixation sequence and fixation durations given below each word that was fixated. As you can see, some words are read faster than others, some are completely passed over, and some are read out of their written sequence. In fact, different types of text produce very different patterns of eye movements. Figure 10.11b gives a more complete listing of how reading times vary for different types of text.

Controlling the Eyes   The eyes do a lot of work while reading, much of it complex and fast. How do we control these fast, accurate, and complex movements to produce the experience of smooth, effortless reading?

One of the earliest contemporary models of eye-movement control in reading, and one that is very intuitively appealing, was originally proposed by McConkie (1979). That model made use of the metaphor of a spotlight. In McConkie's model, the spotlight of attention moves across the page until the reader encounters some type of difficulty. This difficulty can be something as simple as a bit of text that is hard to see or read (e.g., perhaps there is a coffee stain on the page) or something as complex as a long and complicated sentence.

When this point of difficulty is reached, an eye-movement control system directs the attention spotlight to focus back on the location of the difficulty. So you can see that this model seems to correspond to what we might think we are doing when we read: We read until we encounter something difficult to process. When we find this point of difficulty, we move our eyes there.

McConkie's model in this basic form is able to predict some basic features of eye movements during reading (Rayner & Pollatsek, 1989). But the model has trouble with various aspects of the point of difficulty. First, it seems to equate difficulties associated with visual factors (picking out a word under a coffee stain) with difficulties associated with comprehension (a complex sentence). This is probably an unreasonable simplification. Second, the model does not specify how the system is able to decide when it is having difficulty. Finally, the model seems to predict that fixations—particularly those at points of difficulty—should be much longer than those that are actually observed in reading.

Problems with McConkie's model led to the development of what may be the most widely cited model of eye-movement control, one proposed by Morrison (1984). In Morrison's model, eye-movement control works from *successful* processing of the visual information rather than from difficulties. Basically, when a word is correctly identified, attention, and then the eyes, move to a point farther along in the text.

An important distinction must be made here between attention and the location of the eyes—that is, where the eyes are fixated. In Morrison's model, attention and eye fixation can be moved *separately*. In fact, that distinction is one of the reasons that Morrison's model can predict important aspects of eye movements.

Keith Rayner and Alexander Pollatsek
Keith Rayner (right) and Alexander Pollatsek (left) are responsible for work analyzing the movements of the eyes in reading—work that has given us very precise pictures of how reading is accomplished.

FIGURE 10.11   **Eye Movements in Reading**   These data come from an experiment in which the movements of the eyes were tracked. The first number below each word in the chart (top) indicates which fixation involved that word. The second number indicates the duration of the fixation (in milliseconds). The table (bottom) indicates how reading times varied for different types of text.

Roadside joggers endure sweat, pain and angry drivers in the name of

Fixation sequence
| 1 | 2 | 3 | 4 | 5 | 6 | 7 | 8 |

Fixation duration (ms)
| 286 | 221 | 246 | 277 | 256 | 233 | 216 | 188 |

fitness. A healthy body may seem reward enough for most people. However,

| 9 | 10 | 12 | 13 | 11 | 14 | 15 | 16 | 17 | 18 | 19 |
| 301 | 177 | 196 | 175 | 244 | 302 | 112 | 177 | 266 | 188 | 199 |

for all those who question the payoff, some recent research on physical

| 21 | 20 | 22 | 23 | 24 | 25 | 26 | 27 |
| 216 | 212 | 179 | 109 | 266 | 245 | 188 | 205 |

activity and creativity has provided some surprisingly good news.

| 29 | 28 | 30 | 31 | 32 | 33 | 34 | 35 |
| 201 | 66 | 201 | 188 | 203 | 220 | 217 | 288 |

Topic	WPM[a]	Fixation Duration[b]	Saccade Length[c]	Regressions (%)[d]
Light fiction	365	202	9.2	3
Newspaper article	321	209	8.3	6
History	313	222	8.3	4
Psychology	308	216	8.1	11
English literature	305	220	7.9	10
Economics	268	233	7.0	11
Mathematics	243	254	7.3	18
Physics	238	261	6.9	17
Biology	233	264	6.8	18
M	288	231	7.8	11

[a]Words per minute, reading speed.

[b]In milliseconds.

[c]In character spaces.

[d]Percentage of total fixations that were regressions.

Source: Rayner & Pollatsek, 1989.

To see the implications of the idea that attention can be directed to areas of the visual field other than the area of fixation, let us walk through Morrison's model, presented in Figure 10.12. Suppose we are reading the sentence "My dog ate my burrito!" We begin when the eyes fixate on the word *My.* This word is encoded, and as soon as it is identified, *attention* moves to the word *dog,* and the eyes follow. Once *dog* is successfully encoded and identified, attention moves to *ate,* and the eyes follow. Essentially, attention goes ahead of the eyes and, in fact, can move ahead even while the currently fixated word is being processed.

According to Morrison's model, each time attention moves ahead, a command to move the eyes is issued. And this command is issued regardless of whether previous commands to move the eyes have been carried out. This means that more than one order to move the eyes can be waiting to be executed at any one time. The rules for following these orders become complicated; but one thing Morrison's model predicts is that an order that is waiting to be executed can be canceled, if the lag between orders being issued is short enough.

When would this happen? First, it could happen when attention needs to spend only a very short time on a word in advance of the eyes, as with words that are short, common, and easily identified. Essentially, Morrison's model predicts that the eyes will skip these types of words. And that, in fact is exactly what can be observed in normal reading. In addition, Morrison's model predicts certain other aspects of fixation times that are associated with words that follow skipped words (Hogaboam, 1983; Pollatsek, Rayner & Balota, 1986). Morrison's model has also been extended to include skipping, refixations (i.e., when the eyes go back to a previously fixated word), and regressions (Rayner & Pollatsek, 1989).

FIGURE 10.12   **Morrison's Model of Eye-Movement Control**   According to the model proposed by Morrison (1984), attention precedes eye movement. Each time attention moves ahead, a command to move the eyes is issued.

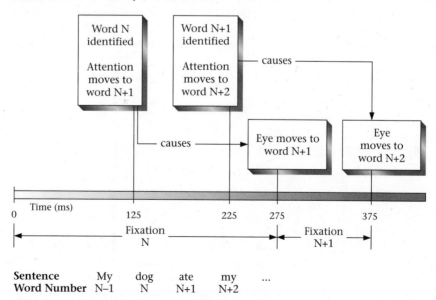

Source: Adapted from Figure 5-3, Rayner & Pollatsek, 1989, p. 169.

Identifying and Comprehending Words A critical determinant of performance in Morrison's model is the identification of words during reading. Being able to identify a string of letters as a particular word is what allows attention to direct the eyes through the text.

In Chapter 4 we briefly described a classic study on word identification that was conducted in the early 1960s by Tulving and Gold (1963), who asked subjects to identify a word that was presented *very* briefly. Tulving and Gold asked the question: Will increasing the amount of semantically related information that is available *before* the target word appears affect the minimum amount of time that subjects need to identify that word?

Tulving and Gold asked their subjects to identify the last word in a sentence. What they varied was how many words of the sentence were presented before the target word was presented. For example, for the target word *performer,* subjects were presented with 0, 1, 2, 4, or 8 words from the sentence "The actress received praise for being an outstanding. . . ." To make sure that it was the meaningfulness of the sentence, relative to the target word, that was at work, Tulving and Gold used other sentences that had no relationship to the target word, such as "The dog retrieved the burrito from the neighborhood's. . . ."

Tulving and Gold measured the minimum time required for subjects to correctly identify the word *performer.* Figure 10.13 shows some of the results from this study. As you can see, increasing the number of *related* words in the preceding sentence reduced the amount of time required to identify the target word. In contrast, increasing the number of *unrelated* words increased the amount of time required to identify the target word. As we noted in Chapter 4, this shows that context can both aid and hinder visual perception. Finally, before going on, think about whether these results "make sense" in the context of McConkie's model for eye-movement control. The conclusion: This model predicts these effects. Why is this true?

FIGURE 10.13 **Effect of Semantically Related Information on Word Identification** Results from a study by Tulving and Gold (1963) show that increasing the number of words presented in a relevant sentence reduced the amount of time needed for identifying the final word. Increasing the number of words in an irrelevant sentence had the opposite effect.

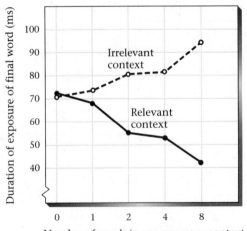

Source: Solso, 1995.

As you would expect from McConkie's model, the meaningful context of the early words in a sentence can have an important impact on how long it takes to process the later words. This is because the meaningful relationships among the early words and the later words reduces the likelihood that the later words will present challenges to processing. Since McConkie's model predicts that any processing challenge will slow reading, anything that reduces the likelihood of such a challenge will reduce the likelihood of slowing reading down (or, conversely, increase the likelihood of fast and efficient reading).

Another factor that can affect the ease with which words are processed is the frequency with which the words appear in written and spoken communication. We discussed in Chapter 8 that the frequency with which words appear in the environment can have important effects on the way in which memory is used (Anderson & Schooler, 1991). And since memory is essential for working with words in a sentence (e.g., we must be able to retrieve knowledge of their meaning), it is logical that word frequency would affect performance on word identification tasks. For example, high-frequency words are responded to more quickly in lexical decision tasks (Rubenstein, Garfield & Millikan, 1970) and naming tasks (Forster & Chambers, 1973) than are low-frequency words. And data from the 1950s (Howes & Solomon, 1951) shows that word frequency has a major impact on the minimum time required to identify the word. In addition, factors such as the degree to which a word allows a subject to generate images can affect the processing of words (Paivio, 1969), as can a word's phonological characteristics (Yeni-Komshian, 1993).

But the data on these types of effects are not completely consistent (see Gernsbacher, 1984). For example, Balota and Chumbley (1984) failed to find frequency effects in naming tasks and found only minimal effects in semantic verification tasks. So something else may be going on. It is certainly true that characteristics of the words that act as context for the target words can affect the processing of the target word on measures such as naming time and fixation time (Rayner & Pollatsek, 1989; Stanovich & West, 1983). But evidence is accumulating that the benefit for target words is due to a kind of "spillover" from the processing of words other than the target words.

Let us think about this in concrete terms. In most of these studies, the target words are the words that subjects are asked to focus their eyes and attention on. These items are assumed to be *foveated,* or viewed in such a way that their image is projected onto the fovea of the eye. The other items (e.g., subsequent targets) are presented *parafoveally,* or outside the direct focus of the eyes. It appears that information processing in the parafovea is aided by contextual information such as that provided by the foveated information (Balota, Pollatsek & Rayner, 1985). With the parafoveal information being processed better because of the information from the foveated word, there may be less need for processing the parafoveal information when it becomes foveated (i.e., when the eyes move to it). This translates into predictions for a higher likelihood of skipping these parafoveal words in reading and shorter processing times in reading tasks in general. And, in fact, this is what is observed (Rayner & Pollatsek, 1989).

Word Identification: The Logogen Model Word identification is clearly an important, basic aspect of reading, and a huge body of research on word identification has been amassed. A large number of theoretical perspectives on word identification also have been developed (Jacobs & Grainger, 1994). One of the first of these models, and one of the most influential, is the logogen model, originally proposed by Morton (1970) and given additional development by Treisman (1978).

A critical component of the logogen model, as well as many other models of language use, is something that, in the various research literatures dealing with language processing, is called the **lexicon.** The lexicon is that aspect of memory that is specialized for the storage and processing of information about words. In this sense, the idea of a lexicon is very similar to the idea of semantic memory information (see Chapter 8). Indeed, it is probably acceptable to think of the lexicon as being roughly the same thing as semantic memory information; but in general, models that use the idea of a lexicon conceive of it as a specialized and separate type of memory.

According to the logogen model, the items stored in the lexicon are abstract units of word information called **logogens.** The word logogen is derived from *logos,* meaning "word," and *genus,* meaning "birth." Logogens can contain a variety of sensory and linguistic properties of a word, such as its appearance, its sound, and its meaning. What is important to note is that the *word* is not stored in the logogen. Instead, all the information necessary to retrieve (or "give birth") to the word is stored in the logogen. When a stimulus word is input to the cognitive system for identification, the features of the input are compared with the features of all of the stored logogens. If the features of the input and one of the logogens match in some way, the activation of that logogen is increased. Any logogen whose activation reaches a predetermined threshold is accessed; and if more than one logogen is accessed, the one with the highest activation value is retrieved.

Let us consider a simplified version of how word identification works according to the logogen model. Imagine that the lexicon is represented by three logogens, corresponding to the words *dog, dig,* and *burrito.* And imagine that the human possessing this somewhat limited lexicon is the subject in a word identification experiment. Before the word to be identified is presented, the activation of all three logogens is at or around some resting level. Once the target word, *dog,* is presented, the activation of the *dog* and *dig* logogens increases, according to the match between the features of the presented word and the information stored in each of the logogens. After a brief period of time spent viewing the target word, the activation levels for both the *dog* and *dig* logogens may exceed the threshold, but the final level for the *dog* logogen will be higher than the final level for the *dig* logogen, because of the greater number of featural matches between *dog* and the target word. So it is the *dog* logogen that supports the identification response.

Word Identification: A Connectionist Model   Another important and influential model of word identification is the interactive activation model proposed by McClelland and Rumelhart (1981, 1986), a model we discussed in Chapter 4. In this model, implemented as a neural network, simulation activation of the cognitive system by a presented stimulus can be considered at three levels.

The first is called the *feature* level. For example, we could think of the letter F in the word at the beginning of this sentence as comprising three features: one vertical segment and two horizontal segments. Presenting any stimulus word containing an uppercase F would activate these features and then pass that activation to the second, higher level.

This second level of activation is the *letter* level. In the McClelland and Rumelhart model, each letter in each position in a stimulus word has a node. Each of the basic feature detectors can feed activation to each of these nodes. In addition, all of the nodes are connected. So they can pass activation among each other, and they also can pass activation to the third and highest level.

This highest level is the *word* level. The nodes at this level correspond to entries in the lexicon, or items in memory. It is the relative levels of activation at this level that support word identification.

So far in this brief description, we have been talking about activation in a positive sense—as something that increases. But, as you might remember from our discussion of this model in Chapter 4, the McClelland and Rumelhart model actually proposes two types of activation: excitatory and inhibitory. Excitatory activation serves to increase the activation level of a node at any of the three levels, while inhibitory activation serves to decrease levels of node activation. In addition, in the McClelland and Rumelhart model, these two types of activation can flow among nodes at any one level and from the nodes at one level to nodes at a higher level. And the nodes at the word level can also pass activation (excitatory and inhibitory) back down to the nodes at the letter level.

Including both excitatory and inhibitory connections in the model is motivated in part by the fact that both types of connections exist in the nervous system. In addition, the three structural levels of the McClelland and Rumelhart model have been indirectly supported by evidence from neurocognitive studies of word processing (Peterson et al., 1988; Posner et al., 1988).

Word Identification: A Comprehensive Model   The final model of word identification that we will consider is a comprehensive model proposed by Carr and Pollatsek (1985). An important aspect of this model is that, unlike the logogen and connectionist models just reviewed, it attempts to consider all possible processes involved and their possible interactions. As such, it can almost be seen as a theory about theories of language processes (a *metatheory*).

Carr and Pollatsek derived their model from an extensive review of available knowledge about word identification. As just noted, it proposes to account for all aspects of word identification, beginning with the perceptual processes that occur when the image of the word is registered on the retina and running to the cognitive processes that occur when the response indicating word recognition (naming, lexical decision, etc.) is made. A schematic representation of this model is presented in Figure 10.14.

In Figure 10.14, we have numbered each of the processes considered by Carr and Pollatsek. Before reading further, look back at the discussions of the logogen and McClelland and Rumelhart models. Which of the processes in Figure 10.14 are explicitly considered in each of the other models? Are there any processes in the logogen and McClelland and Rumelhart models that are *not* considered in the Carr and Pollatsek model?

You should be able to find that the processes considered in both the logogen model and the McClelland and Rumelhart model are represented in the Carr and Pollatsek account. In addition, you should see that the Carr and Pollatsek model does not overlook or miss processes described in the other models. It is the comprehensiveness and completeness of this model that have made it the benchmark: the point of comparison for all contemporary accounts of word identification (Jacob & Grainger, 1994).

The sheer number of processes represented in Figure 10.14 should convince you that in considering word identification, we are not dealing with something that is simple or straightforward. Yet we are still dealing with only the basic level of processing involved in the more complex processes of reading and understanding the simplest sentence!

Comprehending Written Language

We have just seen that even an apparently simple task, such as identifying a single word, is remarkably complicated. In the face of this complexity, a number of scientists have concluded that we are still a long way from completely understanding how people comprehend entire word sequences, such as sentences, paragraphs, and books (Rayner & Pollatsek, 1989, p. 266). In this section, we consider research that is bringing us closer to that goal.

FIGURE 10.14   **A Comprehensive Model of Word Recognition**   As shown in this schematic drawing, the comprehensive model of word recognition proposed by Carr and Pollatsek (1985) traces the processing of a word from the registration of the image of the word on the retina to the response made to identify the word.

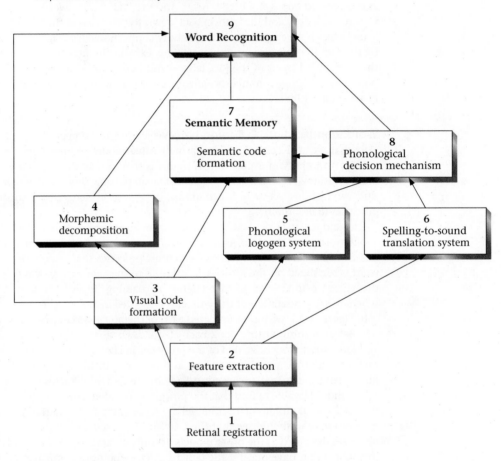

Source: Jacobs & Grainger, 1994.

One of the most important distinctions made in research on the comprehension of written language involves macrostructure and microstructure. We encountered these terms in a different context earlier in Chapter 4 when we discussed McClelland and Rumelhart's (1981) interactive activation model. With regard to written language, **macrostructure** refers to the overall, global meaning of the information being read, while **microstructure** refers to more restricted, local levels of meaning, such as the meaning of a word. This distinction, originally made in the context of a specific theory of language comprehension (Kintsch & van Dijk, 1978), captures two important tasks that readers must perform. The first is to derive the meaning of the text while moving through it. This corresponds to perception and abstraction of the microstructure of the text. The second task is to derive the overall meaning of the material. This corresponds to perception and abstraction of the macrostructure of the text. For both these tasks, the ability of readers to make connections among various elements in the text seems to be critical.

Anaphora: Connections Based on Pronouns   Consider these two sentences (Rayner & Pollatsek, 1989):

1. John lent his car to Bill because he needed it.
2. John lent his car to Bill because he was generous.

Did you have any problem understanding which person the pronoun *he* refers to in each sentence? You probably did not, in spite of the fact that the pronoun refers to different people in the two sentences. Understanding which antecedent word a pronoun is referring to is perhaps the simplest example of **anaphora,** the use of one word or concept to refer to a previously named word or concept.

An effect related to understanding anaphora is the **distance effect.** This effect is demonstrated when the reading time for a sentence containing a pronoun increases as the distance (e.g., the number of words) from a noun to the pronoun that refers to it increases (Clark & Sengul, 1979). The distance effect is pronounced; and although it probably seems intuitively obvious to you, the details of the process are surprisingly complex.

Ehrlich and Rayner (1983) studied the patterns of eye movements in processing pronouns. The researchers used three experimental conditions, defined by the distance between the pronoun and the noun it referred to. In the *near* condition, the noun and the pronoun were next to each other. In the *intermediate* condition, the noun and the pronoun were separated by about a line of text. In the *far* condition, the noun and the pronoun were separated by at least three lines of text. The dependent measure—the duration of the encoding fixation—was the amount of time the eyes spent on the pronoun.

Ehrlich and Rayner observed that the duration of the encoding fixation increased relative to the fixation just before it, and it increased in all three distance conditions. This suggests that some processing going on when readers got to the pronoun slowed down the movement of the eyes. But Ehrlich and Rayner noted something very interesting about the two fixations that followed the encoding fixation. In the near and intermediate conditions, these two fixations were of normal and short duration. But in the far condition, these two fixations actually got longer. It seems as though the processing required by the pronoun continued to slow the eyes down, even after they had moved past the pronoun, meaning that the distance effect could influence more than just the processing of the pronoun.

Some data suggest that the distance effect may be due to factors other than just distance. For example, Clifton and Ferreira (1987) found that varying whether or not the noun being referred to was still the topic of the text had a much more pronounced effect on reading times than did distance. In fact, this and other studies have shown that it is possible to manipulate distance *without* producing a distance effect (Anderson, Garrod & Sanford, 1983; Garrod & Sanford, 1985). What seems more important are factors affecting how text information is represented and manipulated in memory. We discuss how these factors have formed the basis for theoretical developments later.

Inferences: Connections Based on Assumptions   Anaphoric references represent simple inferences that readers use to construct the meaning of text. Connections based on three other types of inferences have received attention from reading researchers: instrumental, elaborative, and causal inferences.

Consider the sentence, "The man swept the floor." If, after you read this, you assumed that the man used a broom, then you made an inference about the *thing* (the instrument) that was used to perform the action—this is an **instrumental inference.** Some early work in reading comprehension concluded that readers generally make instrumental inferences while reading. But ask yourself this question: As you read the sentence, did you immediately and explicitly draw a conclusion about the item being used to sweep the floor, or did you make the inference only after we pointed out the connection?

You probably answered that you were able to make the inference but that you did not explicitly do so immediately on reading the sentence. In fact, a series of experiments documented that although subjects *can* make instrumental inferences while reading, it is not something that *has* to happen (Corbett & Dosher, 1978). In addition, the earlier conclusion that instrumental inferences are generally made by readers may be questionable because of methodological problems in the procedure used in many of the studies (McKoon & Ratcliff, 1981, 1986).

Another type of inference thought to be important to reading comprehension involves inferring a general concept from a specific one (e.g., inferring *food* from *burrito*), or vice versa. This is known as an **elaborative inference.** According to some evidence, readers can make but need not make elaborative inferences when reading one or two sentences; however, the picture is more interesting when longer text segments are used.

For example, O'Brien, Shank, Myers, and Rayner (1988) examined the eye movements of readers when presented with paragraphs such as this one:

> All the mugger wanted was to steal the woman's money. But when she screamed, he stabbed her with his (weapon/knife) in an attempt to quiet her. He looked to see if anyone had seen him. He threw the knife into the bushes, took her money, and ran away.

Of interest here was the time the eyes spent on the word *knife* in the last sentence as a function of whether *weapon* or *knife* was used in the second sentence. Before continuing, consider how we have defined *elaborative inference*. Then see if you can predict what would happen if readers were making an elaborative inference about the word *weapon*.

What O'Brien and colleagues observed was that the time taken to read the last sentence was no different when *weapon* was used than when *knife* was used in the second sentence. This is what you would expect if readers had made the elaborative inference of *knife* from *weapon*. But they also noted something interesting in a condition in which they replaced *stabbed* (in the second sentence) with *assaulted* and kept *knife* in the last sentence. In that case, the eyes remained on *knife* quite a bit longer when *weapon* rather than *knife* was used in the second sentence (i.e., "assaulted her with his weapon"). This seems to indicate that whether elaborative inferences are made may depend on the context.

The third type of inference of interest in reading may also be the most complicated: **causal inference,** the inference that something will cause something else. For example, consider the following paragraph (Rayner & Pollatsek, 1989, p. 282):

> John was eating in the dining car of a train. The waiter brought him a bowl of soup. Suddenly, the train screeched to a stop. The soup spilled in John's lap.

Although the first three sentences in this paragraph seem to be heading toward a conclusion in which soup will be dumped in John's lap, this conclusion is not a logical necessity. Thus, although it is possible that making the causal inference when reading the third sentence will speed or improve the processing of the last sentence, it may not be necessary to make the causal inference in order for reading to proceed at a normal, rapid, rate. Instead, it may be that readers can make but do not necessarily need to make causal inferences, in the same way that they can but need not make instrumental and elaborative inferences.

How are causal inferences made? Three possibilities seem likely (Duffy, 1986; Myers & Duffy, 1990; Seifert, 1990). First, readers could wait for the description of the event before searching back (through memory) for the cause of the event. Second, readers could be generating inferences and hypotheses about what is going to happen as they read, which are then supported or contradicted by what follows. Third, readers could be mentally focusing on specific, salient types of information that they believe are critical to the meaning of the text.

Duffy (1986) tested these possibilities using paragraphs like the one you just read. She found that subjects' performance reflected a complex use of text information in the making of causal inferences. Although it was not possible to strictly rule out the first two possibilities, the data did appear to be most consistent with the third possibility. That is, readers seem to highlight important information for later use. In a more general sense, this pattern seems consistent with data for other types of inferences. That is, as with instrumental and elaborative inferences, readers can make causal inferences when they need to, but it appears that they do not always need to make causal inferences while reading.

Theoretical Accounts: Modeling the Connections   Our discussion of pronoun processing (anaphora) indicates that understanding of how and when memory information and processes are used is critical to understanding how language comprehension works. Our consideration of the various types of inferences also suggests that readers can perceive and hold various types of information in memory, with the specific task determining when and if that memory information is expressed (e.g., in making a particular type of inference). In this section, we consider two influential approaches to accounting for how, when, and why various types of memory information and processes are used to comprehend text.

Walter Kintsch developed one of the best-known models of text processing and comprehension. Kintsch (1974) proposed that information in memory is represented by **propositions,** logical structures that consist of a *predicate* (verb, adjective, or conjunction) and one or more *arguments* (nouns). The argument describes the proposition, and the predicate is the assertion in the argument (Carroll, 1986). For example, the sentence "The Egyptian king prepared an impressive pyramid" contains three propositions:

> Proposition 1: Egyptian (predicate), king (argument)
> Proposition 2: Prepare (predicate), king, pyramid (arguments)
> Proposition 3: impressive (predicate), pyramid (argument)

Represented in this way, propositions can be defined reasonably precisely, the meaning of each sentence can be easily and reliably determined, and the relationships among the propositions can be mapped out. This last point is very important to Kintsch's approach (Kintsch, 1974; Kintsch & van Dijk, 1978). That is because propositions are related to one another if they share common arguments. In our example, Propositions 1 and 2 are related because they share the *king* argument, and Propositions 2 and 3 are related because they share the *pyramid* argument. This repetition of arguments sets up a hierarchical organization in that it allows later propositions to be subordinated to previous propositions. In our example, Proposition 2 is subordinate to Proposition 1, and Proposition 3 is subordinate to Proposition 2, with the hierarchical relationship developing from the order of the propositions in the sentence. Figure 10.15 illustrates how this hierarchy develops for this example.

Kintsch and his colleagues (Kintsch, 1988; Kintsch & van Dijk, 1978; Kintsch & Welsch, 1991) have expanded this approach into a theory of text comprehension called construction-integration theory. *Construction* refers to the building of a mental representation of the text and a mental model of the situation described in the text. *Integration* refers to pulling together the information provided by the text and any previous information about the situation. Comprehension involves both information from the situation, or text, and the personal knowledge of the reader.

Various levels of representation of the text meaning are considered during the construction process. For example, at the local level (microstructure), the words that make up the text are represented. At the semantic level (macrostructure), propositions, like those described above, are represented. The integration process involves spreading activation among the propositions, linking together the levels of representation from the construction process by keeping the critical information available in working memory.

Construction-integration theory has been successfully applied to a wide variety of comprehension tasks (Kintsch & Welsch, 1991), but situations exist that the model has difficulty explaining. For example, Albrecht and Myers (1995) document situations in which previously read text information, which can be assumed not to be the focus of immediate processing, can be accessed if it overlaps sufficiently with the information being read. The previously read information can be assumed to be unavailable in working memory, yet it still can influence performance during what would be considered the integration process. Such a situation can be handled by a model (Albrecht & Myers, 1995; Albrecht & O'Brien, 1993; Myers et al., 1994) based on a general conception of memory similar to the resonance ideas mentioned in Chapters 7 and 8 (Ratcliff, 1978).

FIGURE 10.15   **Hierarchical Relations in Construction-Integration Theory**   The hierarchical relations among propositions in construction-integration theory develop according to shared arguments and the order of the propositions in the sentence.

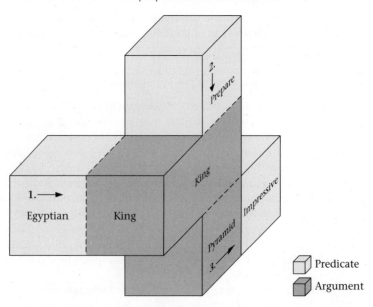

A second influential approach that explicitly takes into account memory processes is Gernsbacher's (1990, 1991) structure-building framework. We mentioned Gernsbacher's work in Chapter 8, when we discussed how surface information from a sentence might be preserved or lost in memory. The structure-building framework relies on the idea of abstract structures that serve as mental representations of sentences. One structure may represent an entire sentence; or where the sentence has multiple clauses, each clause may be represented by a structure.

Three memory processes operate on these structures: building the foundation, mapping new structures onto the foundation, and shifting processing among structures. According to the structure-building framework, when readers encounter a sentence, they begin by abstracting an initial structure, representing, for example, the first clause of the sentence. This first structure serves as the foundation for the representation of the rest of the sentence. As readers continue through the sentence, new structures are built and mapped onto the existing foundation. Put simply, this involves finding the ways in which the new structures "fit" the existing foundation. As the overall sentence-level structure is being formed, shifting can occur among structures in order to form one representation for the entire sentence.

Gernsbacher and her colleagues (Gernsbacher & Hargreaves, 1988; Gernsbacher, Hargreaves & Beeman, 1989) tested this framework by presenting subjects with two-clause sentences, such as, "Ann gathered the kindling, and Pam set up the tent." Subjects' memory for the participants in the sentence was tested by presenting a proper name (Ann, Pam) and probing for subjects' recognition of that name.

If the name probe appeared immediately after the end of the sentence, subjects were faster to say that the second-mentioned participant (Pam) had appeared in the sentence than the first-mentioned participant (Ann). This supports the idea that the second clause was being worked on, getting it ready to be integrated into the larger structure of the sentence. But if some time passed between the end of the sentence and the name probe, then subjects were faster to say that the first-mentioned participant had appeared in the sentence. This second finding supports the idea that the clauses had been integrated into a single structure, with the beginning of the sentence representing the "entry point" to the structure.

In addition to the basic processes involved in building memory structures, Gernsbacher (1990, 1991) has proposed two mechanisms important in comprehension: *enhancement* and *suppression*. These mechanisms are very similar in principle to the two types of priming (facilitation and inhibition) discussed in Chapter 8. **Enhancement** increases the activation of memory information about the sentence, and **suppression** decreases activation of this information.

When a word in a sentence has more than one meaning, enhancement allows for the correct meaning to remain activated, while suppression works to deactivate meanings that are not correct. For example, in the sentence, "Pam was diagnosed by a quack," where *quack* is the ambiguous word (meaning an unqualified doctor or a duck sound), both meanings of the word *quack* are activated at first. The mechanism of suppression works to decrease the activation of the inappropriate meaning (the duck sound), which allows for the appropriate meaning to remain activated and incorporated into the comprehended message.

Like the construction-integration model, Gernsbacher's structure-building framework has been successful in accounting for performance in a number of different contexts. In addition, Gernsbacher's approach takes advantage of knowledge about basic characteris-

Morton Ann Gernsbacher
Morton Ann Gernsbacher's work explores the roles of basic cognitive processes in the comprehension of written language.

tics of memory to explain the complex task of comprehending text. But Gernsbacher's model cannot directly address certain issues. One of these is the basic issue of the capacity of memory processes (Shiffrin, 1975, 1976; see also Chapter 7). An alternative approach, one based on the notion of processing capacity (Just & Carpenter, 1992), has been developed to address this issue. This alternative model is sparking some interesting debate (Just, Carpenter & Keller, 1996; Waters & Caplan, 1996), and the possibilities for its development remain to be seen.

Section Summary: Processing Written Language

Our species has a long history of processing spoken language, but our history of processing written language is much shorter. Careful examination of the effects of physical characteristics of printed language on language processing can be traced to the work of Tinker, who focused on reading speed as a measure of performance. Scientists have increasingly used finer and more detailed measures of the movements of the eyes (saccades and fixations) to assess the processing of written language. As data have become available on the movement of the eyes during reading, scientists (such as McConkie and Morrison) have begun to develop models to describe this eye control. A critical component of these models is the process of word identification. The logogen model and the connectionist model of McClelland and Rumelhart detail the important ways in which various types of information, from perception information to memory information, interact in the apparently "easy" process of identifying a word. Carr and Pollatsek's model provides a comprehensive view of the wide variety of cognitive processes involved in word identification. Anaphora-based and knowledge-based (or assumption-based) inferences reveal the abilities and the flexibility of the cognitive system during reading. Kintsch's model and Gernsbacher's approach build on knowledge of these abilities and this flexibility to provide theoretical accounts for how written language is eventually comprehended.

REVIEWING LANGUAGE COMPREHENSION

CONCEPT REVIEW

1. Describe the acoustical properties of vowels. Compare and contrast the acoustical properties of vowels with those of consonants (e.g., in terms of their relative complexity).

2. What are silent-center, variable-center, fixed-center, and abutted syllables? Which of these types of syllables proved easiest to identify in the work of Strange and colleagues? What does this finding imply about the types of acoustical information important in the perception of vowels?

3. What is voice-onset time? What type of evidence obtained through a manipulation of voice-onset time suggested categorical perception of the speech signal? Why was evidence of categorical perception used to support the idea that speech might be a special type of stimulus? What types of evidence contradict this conclusion?

4. Define three common simplifying assumptions that have been used to account for the processing of the speech signal. Describe evidence supporting *and* violating each of these assumptions.

CONCEPT REVIEW *(continued)*

5. What is the McGurk effect? What simplifying assumption regarding the processing of the speech
   signal does it violate?

6. Describe, compare, and contrast the motor theory,
   the direct perception theory, and information processing models of speech perception. Which of
   these models is closely related to the idea that
   speech is a special type of stimulus?

7. Summarize the evidence for and against the idea
   that speech is a special type of stimulus. What do
   you conclude, and why?

8. Based on the evidence in this chapter, prepare a
   presentation either supporting or refuting the idea
   that the processing of both spoken and written language is multiply determined.

9. Define and describe saccades, fixations, and regressions. During which of these does it appear that
   most information processing is occurring?

10. Describe Morrison's model of eye-movement con-
    trol. How does Morrison's model predict that words
    can be skipped while reading? How does it differ
    from and/or improve upon McConkie's model?

11. What does it mean for a stimulus to be foveated?
    To be presented parafoveally?

12. Describe the logogen and the McClelland and
    Rumelhart models of word identification. How are
    they similar to or different from the semantic net-
    work models of memory discussed in Chapter 8?

13. Define macrostructure and microstructure relative
    to text comprehension.

14. What is the distance effect? What did the data of
    Ehrlich and Rayner (1983) imply about the distance
    effect? Is it possible to manipulate distance without
    getting a distance effect?

15. What are the three types of inferences thought to
    be important in reading comprehension? Do read-
    ers always make these types of inferences? Explain.

16. What are propositions? How are they used in
    Kintsch's model of discourse processing?

17. Describe the major aspects of Gernsbacher's
    structure-building framework, and contrast it
    with Kintsch's construction-integration model.

KEY TERMS

acoustical property (p. 314)
anaphora (p. 343)
articulatory gesture (p. 325)
categorical perception (p. 319)
causal inference (p. 344)
continuous signal (p. 312)
diphthong (p. 315)
distance effect (p. 343)
duplex perception (p. 325)
elaborative inference (p. 344)

enhancement (p. 347)
fixation (p. 334)
formant (p. 314)
instrumental inference (p. 344)
invariance (p. 321)
lexicon (p. 340)
linearity (p. 321)
logogen (p. 340)
macrostructure (p. 342)
microstructure (p. 342)

motor theory (p. 324)
multiply determined (p. 326)
proposition (p. 345)
regression (p. 334)
saccade (p. 334)
separability (p. 321)
spectrogram (p. 313)
suppression (p. 347)
voice-onset time (VOT) (p. 319)

SUGGESTED READINGS

Two sources provide a general introduction to issues relating to the processing of the auditory speech signal. One, by G. H. Yeni-Komishan (1993), is a chapter (Speech perception) in *Psycholinguistics,* a text edited by J. Berko Gleason and N. Bernstein Ratner (Fort Worth: Holt, Rinehart and Winston). The second is *The speech chain: The physics and biology of spoken language* (New York: Freeman), by P. B. Denes and E. N. Pinson (1993), recommended as well in Chapter 9. The first two chapters of *The psychology of reading* (Englewood Cliffs, NJ: Prentice Hall), by K. Rayner and A. Pollatsek (1989), provide a thorough and readable introduction to the study of reading. In addition, a 1993 paper by G. E. Raney and K. Rayner (Event-related brain potentials, eye movements, and reading, *Psychological Science, 4,* 283–286) provides a brief introduction to some important technologies that have been used in recent years to study reading. Finally, a 1981 article by R. E. Morrison and A. W. Inhoff (Visual factors and eye movements in reading, *Visible Language, 15,* 129–146) may make you think twice about getting carried away with the font choices on your word processor. Its capable summary of Tinker's research on aspects of typography that influence reading actually *illustrates,* through its own formatting, the effect that different type styles, sizes, and so forth can have on readers.

11

Cognitive Development

COGNITIVE PSYCHOLOGISTS traditionally focus their research efforts on identifying and describing the cognitive processes of adults between the ages of, say, 18 and 40. But how did those cognitive abilities develop? How different are the cognitive processes of infants or children? Are they different at all? Do babies have the same memory abilities as adults when they are born, or do those abilities emerge over time? Infants do not produce adult-like speech, but they do have ways of communicating. Is that still language? And what about older adults? Do college students and older adults remember telephone numbers using the same strategies?

In this chapter, we focus on how cognitive abilities develop across the lifespan, from infancy through late adulthood. We discuss how some of the cognitive processes presented in the previous chapters evolve. Rather than considering the development of all cognitive processes, we look at a few representative areas of cognition and discuss how abilities in these areas develop and change across the lifespan.

A LITTLE HISTORY

In Chapter 9, we introduced you to Psammetichus and his search for the language native to all civilizations. This Egyptian pharaoh thought that by raising two children in silence and isolation, and waiting until they could talk, he could observe their first words and from those words infer the native language of all people. You may have concluded that one critical problem with Psammetichus's logic was that he was trying to infer something about our species from the development of a few individual members. This is the "flip side" of another notion—one with a rather long history. This notion holds that the course of an individual's development, or **ontogeny,** recapitulates (or repeats) the course of the development of the species, or **phylogeny.**

Ontogeny and Phylogeny

In the nineteenth century, the embryologist Karl Ernst Von Baer (1792–1876) observed that the embryos of humans and some animals were very similar. Von Baer and some of his colleagues believed that the evolutionary path of humans over thousands of years was expressed (recapitulated) in an abbreviated version in each developing embryo. This belief became known as *Von Baer's law*—the notion that embryonic development documented the history of human development (Teeter, 1987).

Faulty logic and problematic proposals relating the development of an individual to the development of the species turn up even today. The hypothesis that ontogeny recapitulates phylogeny has been applied and extended in a number of areas, including cognition and mental activities. For example, Jaynes (1976) discussed Von Baer's hypothesis as a way of explaining the origin of consciousness by suggesting that inner experiences—hopes, fears, and pleasures—evolved over the course of our species' history. More specifically, Jaynes suggested that consciousness emerged from the evolution of the physical structures of the central nervous system.

Generally, Von Baer's hypothesis is not followed in its strict form by most developmental researchers and is considered by some to be false (Giegerich, 1975; Lickliter & Berry, 1990; Skinner, 1984). To be sure, the idea of looking to phylogenetic development for useful information about ontogenetic development has been important for some researchers and theorists (Greenfield, 1991; Terrace, 1993). Most theories in developmental psychology, however, focus on individual development, not the historical development of the species.

Theories of Cognitive Development

Interest in the development of cognitive abilities is a relatively recent phenomenon among cognitive psychologists. When cognitive psychology itself was an infant and young child (in the late 1950s and 1960s), learning and development were topics that did not receive much attention, as they seemed so tightly connected to the behaviorism of the then-recent past. Still, scientists have been concerned with the development of cognitive abilities throughout the twentieth century, though they may not have considered themselves to be cognitive psychologists.

Piagetian Theory   One of the most famous scientists associated with cognitive development is Jean Piaget (1896–1980), who was born in Switzerland and trained in the natural sciences. At one point in his career, in attempting to standardize Binet's reasoning tests with children, he became interested in children's logical abilities. By asking children what they thought about their own correct and incorrect responses to the questions in Binet's tests, Piaget thought that he might learn more about cognitive processes in children in general.

Piaget referred to his research as *genetic epistemology,* the study of developmental changes in the processes of knowing and the organization of knowledge (Miller, 1993). Piaget considered children's development of the ability to differentiate themselves from objects in the world as a central part of these changes. Children first deal with the world through external actions and later develop the ability to experience the world through internal actions. Piaget suggested that all thought is organized in a logical manner and that this organization helps people to reason. Logic, however, comes in different forms, with the particular form determined in part by the logical abilities of the developing mind. These forms of logic define the cognitive stages through which children develop: the sensorimotor, preoperational, concrete operational, and formal operational stages. Piaget's proposals regarding these cognitive stages are summarized in Table 11.1.

According to Piaget, cognitive abilities develop through organization and adaptation. We organize our experiences to make sense of things in the world around us and adapt our thinking to include new ideas and gain further understanding about these ideas. Piaget (1954) suggested that we adapt in two ways: assimilation and accommodation. *Assimilation* is the process of incorporating new information into existing knowledge. *Accommodation* is the process of changing existing knowledge in light of new information that has been assimilated.

Piaget assumed that infants do not know much about the world at the beginning of the sensorimotor stage. As infants develop through this stage, they begin to generate hypotheses about the world based on knowledge obtained through assimilation and accommodation. Piaget's assumption that infants do not know much about the world reflected a

TABLE 11.1   **Piaget's Four Stages of Cognitive Development**

Stage	Age Group	What Develops
Sensorimotor	Birth to 2 years	An infant progresses from reflexive, instinctual action at birth to the beginning of symbolic thought. The infant constructs an understanding of the world by coordinating sensory experiences with physical (motor) actions.
Preoperational	2 to 7 years	The child begins to represent the world with words and images; these words and images reflect increased symbolic thinking and go beyond the connection of sensory information and physical action.
Concrete operational	7 to 11 years	The child can now reason logically about concrete events and classify objects into different sets.
Formal operational	11 to 18 years	The adolescent reasons in more abstract and sophisticated ways. Thought is more idealistic.

viewpoint common during the early and middle parts of the twentieth century. For example, Freud's stages of psychosexual development (Freud, 1905/1953) and Erikson's stages of psychosocial development (Erikson, 1959) both assumed that infants possess very little knowledge.

Along with this assumption, Piaget's theory illustrates another characteristic of this period in the history of developmental psychology: the popularity of **stage theories.** Stage theories of development propose that as humans develop, they move through an orderly and predictable series of changes. Freud and Piaget have been regarded as the most prominent stage theorists of developmental psychology (Miller, 1993). Freud's psychosexual stages were dominant in clinical psychology through much of the twentieth century. Erikson, who was heavily influenced by Freud, used the idea of stages to specify biological and social development. Piaget was a contemporary of both these influential psychologists. Through the influence of theorists like Freud, Erikson, and Piaget, the general notion of stages of development has had a pronounced impact on developmental psychology. However, as we will soon see, powerful conceptions of development that are very different from stage theories have recently been proposed and are currently being developed.

Piaget deserves credit for his unique way of studying how children think. His observations led to the identification of important developmental concepts, such as object permanence—the awareness that objects continue to exist after they disappear from view—and conservation—the concept that the physical properties of an object, such as its volume, remain the same despite superficial changes in the object's permanence. Piaget believed that children are active thinkers and experimenters. Piaget's theory, however, has been challenged in many ways.

Piaget has been criticized for his tendency to underestimate the cognitive abilities of children. Today, most researchers believe that children acquire some of the cognitive skills Piaget specified much earlier than he first indicated. Piaget also believed that certain cognitive skills, such as conservation and classification, develop at the same time. This, however, does not appear to be true of most children. Finally, Piaget often only observed a few children, usually his own children. Today, large, diverse samples are used to provide evidence of cognitive development. Because of such weaknesses, some psychologists have argued that developmentalists should acknowledge Piaget's historical importance but move forward in their thinking and theorizing (Cohen, 1983).

In contrast, prominent counterarguments have been offered suggesting that Piaget has been misrepresented and unfairly criticized (Lourenco & Machado, 1996). This view acknowledges a number of problems with Piaget's work that go beyond those we have just discussed, including a disregard for accurate communication of research and a concern with abstract and often ill-defined constructs. The strengths of Piaget's approach, according to these arguments, can be found in the emphasis on comprehensiveness and synthesis of knowledge about the developmental aspects of cognition.

This strength of Piaget's approach, according to Lourenco and Machado (1996), contrasts with a number of other theoretical perspectives, including the information processing perspective that has dominated much of cognitive psychology. Whereas Piaget emphasized a comprehensive view, information processing emphasizes "fragmentation and local knowledge" (Lourenco & Machado, 1996, p. 158). (This criticism may itself be an unfair one, but we will leave that for you to decide.)

Information Processing Theory   The emergence of the information processing approach in scientific psychology (beginning in the late 1950s), which we have documented in other chapters, began to have an impact on developmental psychology, displacing the stage theories that had dominated until then. Theorists in developmental psychology accepted information processing after expressing doubts about the value of behavioristic learning theories, such as those exemplified by Skinner, and Piaget's account of cognitive stages. With respect to development, the information processing approach emphasizes that thinking can be seen as information processing, stresses the processes involved in thinking (such as remembering and problem solving), and focuses on the precise analysis of change or developmental mechanisms.

One of the greatest impacts of the information processing approach on developmental psychology has been the discovery that children possess certain cognitive abilities at a very early age, usually much earlier than prior theorists had observed or assumed. One example concerns the ability of children to think in relative terms. The **transitive inference task** is used to test this ability. In a transitive inference task, a child is asked to infer a third relation from two other relations. The child might be told that a blue line is longer than a green line and that a green line is longer than a yellow line. From this information, it is possible to infer that the blue line is longer than the yellow line. But to make this inference requires specific logical abilities. According to Piaget, preschoolers should not be able to perform this task because they lack these critical logical skills.

Examples of materials typically used in a transitive inference task are shown at the top of Figure 11.1. Researchers usually present these stimuli a limited number of times. Then, using questions such as those in the bottom of Figure 11.1, they ask children to make inferences about a relationship involving the stimuli. This might suggest to you that one reason children might make mistakes on this task is that they forget the items that were presented. Thus, the inability to perform the transitive inference task might reveal a failure of memory rather than a lack of logical abilities.

Bryant and Trabasso (1971) tested this possibility in an experiment with preschoolers. They presented premise statements, like those in the middle of Figure 11.1, to preschoolers until the preschoolers remembered all the statements perfectly. The children never saw colored lines; they only heard verbal descriptions. When the children were tested with the inference questions (bottom of Figure 11.1), they were able to perform the task rather well, suggesting that if memory limitations are removed, the logical abilities of children are revealed at a much earlier age than assumed by Piaget.

As a result of findings such as those of Bryant and Trabasso, researchers have come to realize that young children, infants, newborns, and even fetal organisms possess many cognitive abilities (Smotherman & Robinson, 1991). Studies using ideas from the information processing approach show that young infants have memory for objects (Rovee-Collier, 1989) and can recognize their mothers' faces shortly after birth (Walton, Bower & Bower, 1992). Studies examining learning and memory in rats reveal that rat fetuses can associate events based on senses, such as touch and smell (Smotherman & Robinson, 1991), showing evidence for memory abilities that exist even before birth.

Based on a variety of findings, then, we now know that young humans and animals possess many more cognitive abilities than previously assumed. Why did earlier scientists underestimate the abilities of the young as they did? One reason for the earlier assumptions is that the methods scientists used to assess cognition were inappropriate in a fundamental way. Essentially, many research techniques were not matched to the ability of young orga-

---

FIGURE 11.1　　**A Transitive Inference Task**　Bryant and Trabasso (1971) demonstrated that when memory limitations were alleviated, children could show the logical abilities needed to perform the transitive inference task. Children never saw the colored lines but were given the premise relations to memorize.

Stimuli normally shown to children	 Yellow　Green　Red　Blue　Orange
Examples of statements used by Bryant and Trabasso (1971)	1. Yellow is shorter than green.　Green is longer than yellow. 2. Green is shorter than red.　Red is longer than green. 3. Red is shorter than blue.　Blue is longer than red.
Examples of the possible inference questions	1. Which is shorter, yellow or red? 2. Which is longer, green or blue?

nisms to *express* their abilities. When more age-appropriate methods are used, we often find that infants (and even younger organisms) possess surprisingly complex cognitive skills.

For example, infants do not possess the verbal ability to express what they remember (or do not remember) about something. They cannot tell researchers that one object had green circles, and a second object had red squares. A technique that has been used to allow infants to express their memory for objects is called **habituation.** This procedure involves repeatedly presenting the same stimulus or object to an infant. After several presentations the infant habituates and the amount of time the infant looks at and pays attention to the object decreases. This is sometimes known as the "bore the babies" technique (Santrock, 1996). When a new object is presented, the infant will look at it longer if he or she sees it as different from the first object. The assumption, then, is that an infant who looks longer at the second object remembers the first object and sees it as different from the second object. The renewed interest created by presentation of the new object is called **dishabituation.**

The phenomena of habituation and dishabituation suggest one way we might test an infant's memory. We could present the infant with two types of objects: one to which the infant has habituated (the "old" object) and one that has not been shown before (the "new" object). We could then measure the time the infant spends looking at each. If the time spent looking at the new object is short (and roughly equivalent to the time spent looking at the habituated object, after all its presentations), the infant is "saying" that the new object seems "old" to them. If the time spent looking at the new object is much longer, the infant is "saying" that the object appears to be "new."

The insight that the experimental task must be matched to the abilities of the subject has also helped us discover that as humans age, their cognitive abilities do not inevitably decline. A variety of cognitive tasks have been modified to better examine the development of cognitive processes in older adults. We consider changes in cognition associated with aging later in this chapter, along with explanations that have been advanced to account for the presence and absence of changes in cognitive abilities with age. For example, several theories have been advanced to explain why memory changes with age.

Section Summary: A Little History

The hypothesis that ontogeny recapitulates phylogeny may have seemed like an intuitive way to describe development, but it was substantively inaccurate and did not address practical issues of how to study development. Piaget contributed greatly to the study of cognitive development through his proposal for cognitive stages. Owing to the influence of the information processing perspective and the use of developmentally appropriate tasks, however, scientists now believe that Piaget's stages underestimate cognitive development in infants and young children. The information processing perspective and the use of sophisticated research techniques have been the driving forces behind discoveries that the very young have cognitive abilities they once were thought not to possess and that cognitive abilities do not inevitably decline in aging adults.

PHYSICAL ASPECTS OF COGNITIVE DEVELOPMENT

Knowledge obtained through perceptual and motor activity affects how infants react and what they subsequently learn about the world (Bushnell & Boudreau, 1993). In this section, we focus on physical aspects of development and why these aspects are important for cognitive development.

Brain Development

Much of what we know about human brain development has been guided by what we know about animal brain development (Diamond, 1988). In both humans and rats, the brain changes continuously between infancy and adulthood. The rat brain does not take as long to become adultlike as does the human brain, but development in the rat brain is a useful model for development in the human brain. As the human brain grows, its size and complexity, including interconnections among neurons and myelinization, are important contributors to development, just as they are in the rat brain (see Spear & Riccio, 1994).

Myelin is a fatty substance found in the brain. It surrounds and insulates neurons and aids in the rapid conduction of neural impulses. The degree of myelinization, or myelin formation, is a good index of brain growth and maturity of neural activity and conduction in the brain. Figure 11.2 shows what a myelinated neuron looks like. In general, the more myelinated the neurons in the brain, the more mature the brain is. Myelinization occurs in different parts of the brain at different points in development. For example, the neurons in the hippocampus, which influences many memory processes, are not fully myelinated until the individual is approximately 10 years old.

The number of neurons and the complexity of their interconnections also change during development (Spear & Riccio, 1994). Most of the neurons we possess are formed before birth. Maturation of the neurons takes place in different areas of the brain at different points in development. The synaptic connections among neurons also increase in number. Much of the chemical activity responsible for the storage of information occurs at the

FIGURE 11.2   **A Myelinated Neuron**   The myelin sheath aids in the transmission of electrochemical signals in the nervous system. The degree of myelinization is related to the maturity of the nervous system, and different areas in the nervous system undergo myelinization at different times in development.

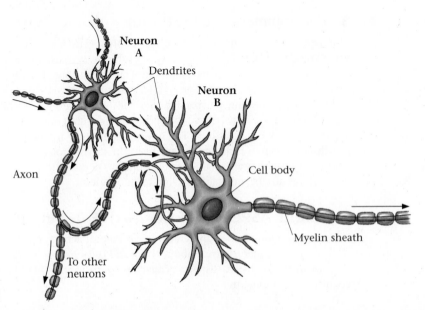

synapses. Figure 11.3 shows how synapses in the rat brain increase in number over the first 90 days of life.

As we continue to develop across our lifetimes, the number of neurons in our brains continues to change, as does the complexity of their interconnections. Connections that are not "correct" or that are incomplete may be lost, whereas reliable connections remain. So at any point in time, it is difficult to get a complete picture of the complexity of the brain's structures—whether for a human brain or a rat brain.

The human brain in late adulthood, however, is smaller and slower in its functioning than the brain in early adulthood. This reduction is thought to be caused by the death of neurons, which do not regenerate. Neurons die at an increasing rate after age 60. The proportion of neurons that die varies across different parts of the brain. In the visual area, the death rate is about 50 percent. In the motor areas, the death rate varies from 20 to 50 percent. In the memory and reasoning areas, the death rate is less than 20 percent (Whitbourne, 1985). The production of certain neurotransmitters also declines with age. Dendritic connections (connections made from the dendrites of one cell to portions of other cells), however, continue to form throughout the lifespan (Buell & Coleman, 1980).

These changes in the brain provide a useful explanation for why certain cognitive processes develop when they do. The sensory and motor cortexes are two primary areas of the brain that complete myelinization early in development. Perceptual development, in turn, affects later cognitive development.

Perceptual Development

The development of the visual system affects how infants view people and objects around them. Typically, newborn infants have poor *visual acuity* (Maurer, 1985). That is, they have difficulty detecting details in complex figures. One way to measure visual acuity is to use

FIGURE 11.3   **Increase in the Number of Synapses with Development**   The graph shows the number of synapses in the neocortex of a rat at several ages during development.

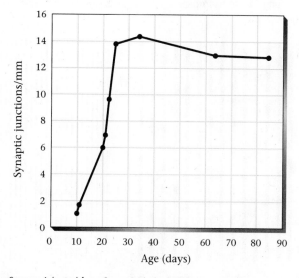

Source: Adapted from Spear & Riccio, 1994.

patterns of alternating white and black lines that are of equal length and width. The narrower the lines, the higher the spatial frequency; and as spatial frequency increases, the pattern begins to look uniformly gray. If you are able to detect the lines in a high-spatial-frequency pattern, then your visual acuity is very good. Figure 11.4 gives some examples of spatial frequency patterns. Infants' ability to detect these patterns appears to be only ⅟₃₀ as good as normal adult ability (Banks & Salapatek, 1983).

As physiological maturation proceeds, visual acuity in infants improves rapidly. Acuity at six months of age is much improved, but it is still not as good as that of a normal adult. As the infant grows older, eye movements, such as saccades and fixations (discussed in the context of reading in Chapter 10), become more stable. Older infants are able to focus better. More stable eye movements and improved focusing ability allow infants to more consistently foveate (project the object's image on the center of the retina), and this improves acuity (Banks, 1980).

Contrast sensitivity, the ability to discriminate differences between light and dark, is also poor in newborn infants. As we noted in Chapters 3 and 4, the ability to discriminate between light and dark areas is important with respect to finding the edges of objects and object parts. Contrast sensitivity improves with age, up to a point. As individuals get older, however, both acuity and contrast sensitivity decline. Many young adults need corrective lenses for nearsightedness. As they grow older, however, they become more farsighted, making bifocal lenses necessary (Berger, 1994).

While acuity and contrast sensitivity are improving during development, other visual abilities are also taking shape. For example, depth perception is important for developing knowledge about where objects are and for maneuvering in the environment. Several cues to depth are available to the infant. *Monocular cues,* using information from one eye, can be *static,* such as pictorial cues, or *kinetic,* based on movement. *Binocular cues,* using information from both eyes, are also available.

FIGURE 11.4   **Spatial Frequency Patterns**   Spatial frequency patterns are used to test visual acuity and contrast sensitivity. These examples show patterns of (a) low spatial frequency and (b) high spatial frequency.

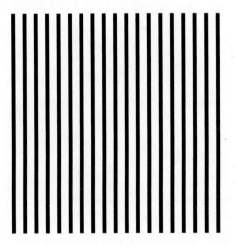
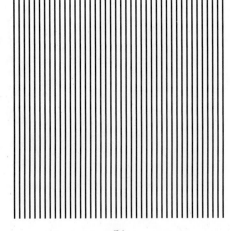

(a)   (b)

But at what age can infants utilize these cues? One method that has been used to explore this question is called the *looming* technique. In this procedure, patterned stimuli surround the infant and quickly approach the infant's location. Researchers have found that infants as young as one to two months of age use kinetic cues and make backward head movements to avoid the objects (Yonus et al., 1977). Infants show the ability to perceive depth on the basis of kinetic monocular cues at approximately three months of age (Kellman, 1984; Owsley, 1983). Sensitivity to binocular cues occurs at around four months of age (Birch, Gwiazda & Held, 1982, 1983), and sensitivity to static monocular cues occurs after seven months of age (Granrud & Yonus, 1984). In general, depth perception improves during childhood and begins to decline during middle adulthood.

One interesting way of studying depth perception in infants was developed by Eleanor J. Gibson and R. Walk (1960; Walk & Gibson, 1961). They devised an apparatus called the **visual cliff,** which is basically a table divided into halves (see Figure 11.5). On one half, a patterned surface can be seen directly underneath a sheet of glass. This glass extends to the other half of the table, but this second half (a patterned surface like the first half) is placed several feet below the glass. The infant is placed on the half of the table where the patterned surface is just below the glass, and the infant's mother stands at the other end of the table, where the patterned surface is well below the glass. The mother then coaxes the infant to move across the table. Gibson and Walk found that at around six to nine months of age, infants begin to avoid the end of the table where the patterned surface is well be-

---

FIGURE 11.5   **A Visual Cliff**   An identical pattern lines the shallow and deep sides of the table. Clear plastic or glass creates a level surface on the top of the table so the infant can crawl on the deep side.

low the glass. They concluded that when infants begin to exhibit avoidance of the "deep" end, it is because they can perceive depth.

As creative as the visual cliff technique is, we now know that it gives a conservative estimate of the onset of the ability to perceive depth, probably because the visual cliff requires that the infant be able to crawl. Later research findings have shown that infants can perceive depth before six to nine months of age. Using heart-rate and looking measures, Campos and his colleagues (Campos & Langer, 1971; Campos, Langer & Krowitz, 1970) found that infants between one and one-half and three months of age could discriminate between the deep and shallow ends of the table. Infants were placed on the table oriented to either the deep or shallow half. Campos and his colleagues observed a change in heart rate when infants looked toward the deep rather than the shallow side. The researchers interpreted these findings as evidence that infants can perceive depth, as shown by their discrimination between the deep and shallow sides of the table.

Motor Development

Having developed sensitivity to cues for depth, especially kinetic cues, the infant has the necessary tools for perceiving objects in the world and gaining knowledge about those objects through observation and physical manipulation. As suggested by Gibson and Walk, the ability of infants to explore their world and the importance of crawling to depth perception are important processes in cognitive development.

One of the pioneers of research in motor development was Arnold Gesell. Gesell identified seven categories of behaviors in the infant, and three of them—posture, locomotion, and prehension—are critical to motor development. *Posture* is the general position of the body while sitting or standing. *Locomotion* is the ability to move from one place to another, either by crawling or by walking. And *prehension* is the ability to grasp objects with the hands. From each of these categories, developmental norms and milestones pertaining to things such as the state of neurological development and the ability to coordinate muscles and joints were inferred. Some of these norms and milestones are outdated now, owing mainly to increased attention to motor development in controlled studies.

Much of current locomotion research focuses on the coordinated movements infants make when learning to crawl or walk. An example is Esther Thelen's well-known work on precursors to locomotion in the form of spontaneous leg kicking. In experiments conducted by Thelen and her colleagues (Thelen & Fisher, 1982, 1983; Thelen & Ulrich, 1991), infants are held upright on treadmills (see Figure 11.6), and their steplike movements are observed. Thelen and her colleagues have observed stepping movements in young infants that are typical of mature walking movements. But the development of these steplike movements follows an interesting course.

Several researchers (Bower, 1976; Strauss, 1982; Thelen & Fisher, 1982) have observed that when newborns are held erect on treadmills, they perform coordinated, steplike movements. This ability disappears at about two months of age and reappears around eight to ten months of age. Some researchers have called this **regressive development:** the infant seems to possess a skill and then lose it, only to show it again later. Such regressive development in walking is explained in part by the fact that, in infants, the legs gain mass before they gain strength (Thelen, Fisher & Ridley-Johnson, 1984). Infants' heavy heads and short legs also make it difficult for them to balance, postponing independent walking until around the first birthday.

Although newborn infants do appear to be able to execute the motor behaviors required for walking, they have very little control over fine-motor movements, such as those involved in reaching and grasping. Newborns show a sort of reflexive reach and grasp, but

FIGURE 11.6   **Treadmill Procedure**   Thelen and her colleagues used this treadmill procedure to elicit steplike movements in young infants.

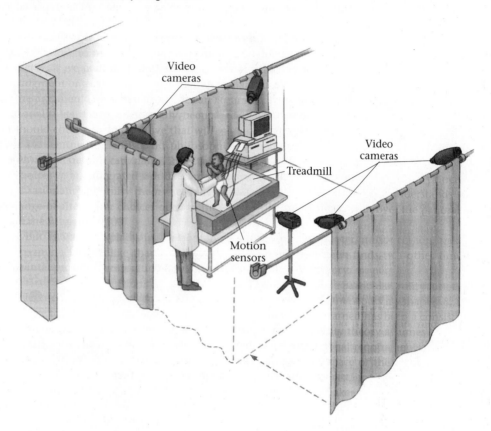

Video cameras

Video cameras

Treadmill

Motion sensors

Esther Thelen
Esther Thelen is a leader in the study of infants' motor abilities and is at the forefront in exploring the use of dynamic systems theory in the study of development.

this is often distinguished from a type of motor behavior called **visually guided reaching**—the action of reaching and grasping in response to seeing something, such as a stuffed animal. Visually guided reaching demonstrates the coordination of the visual system with the motor system. For this type of reaching and grasping to be successful, infants must have good visual abilities (Clifton et al., 1991). Posture is also important for infants to reach and grab with one or two hands (Rochat, Elliot, & Hoffmeyer, 1989). And limb coordination, like that learned during crawling and walking, is essential for successful reaching and grasping.

Development and Dynamic Systems Theory

The regressive development documented for motor skills, as well as some of the shortcomings of Piaget's theory, provided, in part, the motivation for a powerful new perspective on development. This perspective makes use of the tools of dynamic systems theory, tools designed to deal with systems that change over time. The basic approach has a long history in the physical sciences and engineering. In psychology, important initial applications have involved motor development, with newer work involving topics in cognitive development (Smith & Thelen, 1993; Thelen, 1992; Thelen & Smith, 1994).

A good general description of a dynamic system comes from Arnold Gesell, whose work we mentioned earlier in relation to motor development. He conceives of motor development as a "waxing and waning of components combining in multiple ways in a spiral course. At each stage components emerge, merge, and are replaced, creating new maturational transformations" (von Hofsten, 1989, p. 950). This metaphorical description captures the essence of **dynamic systems theory,** as it has been applied in developmental research (see Chapter 12 for an application to judgment and decision making).

The approach here is very different from that in stage theories, such as Piaget's. Stage theories propose that development occurs in a step-by-step manner, always progressing forward and upward to a new level. The dynamic systems approach suggests that development involves both progressive and regressive movement. At one time, an infant can produce grasping movements, but later, the infant cannot grasp an object. Still later, the infant can grasp and hold objects. Development, then, does not always progress forward and upward. Instead, a skill or behavior may remain stable for a time, then move forward, then move backward, and then move forward again.

The notion of dynamic systems is very appealing in developmental applications because it is consistent with some long-standing ideas and observations about development. For example, we know that novel behaviors come from already existing capabilities, much as new species arise from already existing species. Dynamic systems thinking emphasizes a shift away from static, structured, time-independent processes (e.g., cognitive operations within a stage in stage theories) to a focus on more complex, self-organizing, time-dependent systems (Thelen, 1992).

Dynamic systems theory suggests that developmental change occurs in a series of states of stability, instability, and shifts to new levels of development. Change in a behavioral or cognitive system is predicted by a loss of stability; and during this change, other behavioral or cognitive systems might also become unstable. For example, as we have seen, stable steplike leg movement patterns observed before two months of age become unstable and disappear after two months of age and then reappear after seven months of age.

Thelen and Smith (1994) propose that higher-order mental functions, such as concept formation and language, arise through processes similar to the dynamic processes that underlie the development of motor and perceptual abilities (Thelen, 1995). Fine-motor movements are discovered by young infants through varying attempts at matching the hand to an object. According to the dynamic systems view, cognitive abilities emerge in similar ways, by considering context, history, and activity occurring at that moment in time (Thelen, 1995). As mentioned, work on the application of dynamic systems theory to cognitive development is just beginning. But we expect that this theory will significantly change the way we think about developmental processes in the years ahead.

Section Summary: Physical Aspects of Cognitive Development

Supporting all the changes that occur in cognitive abilities across development are the changes that occur in the nervous system across development. Our knowledge of these changes is critically dependent on research on the developing nervous systems of animals. From this work, we know of the relationship between neural maturity and level of myelinization and the changes in neural and synaptic density over time. Accompanying the development of the nervous system are changes in perceptual abilities, such as the ability to make use of static and kinetic monocular and binocular cues in depth perception. Research on perceptual and motor abilities have documented that very young infants have abilities that go beyond what was previously thought. The early appearance of such abilities, followed by their disappearance and later reappearance, has provided some of the motivation for new and important perspectives on development based on dynamic systems theory.

COGNITIVE DEVELOPMENT ACROSS THE LIFESPAN

Up to this point, we have focused on changes that occur during the earliest periods of life. But changes in physical and mental abilities continue across the lifespan. In this section, we consider some of these changes in the areas of memory, language, and conceptual abilities.

Memory Abilities in Infants

Earlier, we discussed how infants are initially limited in their vision and movements. Because of these limitations, it was once assumed that infants do not have good memory abilities—that they cannot remember much for any extended period of time. But this assumption may have been based on measurements that inherently underestimated the abilities of infants, in that they did not match the ability of infants to express what they remembered. Infants are simply not able to make the same types of responses as older children. Some creative developmental research has been exploring the memory capabilities of infants and revealing abilities that go well beyond earlier assumptions.

One of the measurement techniques is designed to test an infant's memory for objects. The technique is based on the observation that, by connecting an infant's ankle with a ribbon to a mobile hanging in the crib, one can easily train the infant to kick to move the mobile (see Figure 11.7). Carolyn Rovee-Collier and her colleagues (Davis & Rovee-Collier, 1983; Rovee-Collier & Sullivan, 1980; Sullivan, Rovee-Collier & Tynes, 1979) have used this kicking response to develop a measure of memory. They train two- to three-month-old infants to kick one foot to move the mobile. Later, they reintroduce the infants to the mobile to see if they will perform the previously learned response (kicking).

Think for a moment about the tests of memory considered in Chapters 6–8. Many of these tests take advantage of a response ability that normal adults possess: verbalizing something (e.g., "yes" or "no" on a recognition test or the name of something on a recall test). Infants do not possess this ability, but they do show the ability to kick in particular situations. Rovee-Collier and her colleagues took advantage of this ability to obtain a measure of an infant's ability to remember—in this case, the ability to remember the action required to make the mobile move. Using this technique, Rovee-Collier has shown evidence for memory in the short term and long term for very young infants, two to three months of age. This contradicts a previously held idea that memory for the long term does not emerge until the eighth or ninth month of life (Rovee-Collier, 1989).

Other researchers have also developed clever nonverbal measures of memory capabilities in infants and young children. Patricia Bauer and her colleagues (Bauer, 1996; Bauer & Hertsgaard, 1993; Bauer & Wewerka, 1995) have used imitation of action sequences to demonstrate that very young children have impressive memory capabilities. Props, such as a blanket, a teddy bear, and a bed, are used by an experimenter to enact an event, such as putting a teddy bear to bed. After the child has been repeatedly exposed to the event, the props are given to the child with instructions such as "Now you put the teddy bear to bed, just like I did" (Bauer, 1996).

By use of this technique, measures of memory can be taken immediately after the child has observed and recreated the event or following a delay. The memory test involves giv-

FIGURE 11.7   **Kicking Behavior**   Rovee-Collier used a mobile tied loosely to an infant's leg to elicit kicking behavior. The mobile moved when the infant kicked, and the infant's later responses to the mobile gave evidence for the infant's memory.

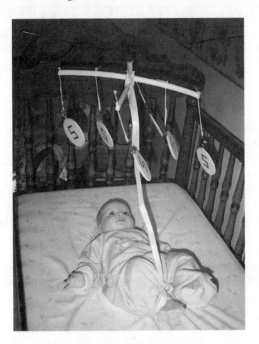

Carolyn Rovee-Collier
Carolyn Rovee-Collier is responsible for the development of a test of infant memory that takes advantage of infants' ability to express memory.

ing the children the props *without* giving them any instructions. To the extent that the children recreate the original event, the experimenters infer evidence of memory for the event. Children as young as one and two years old are able to demonstrate memory over both the short term and the long term in tests using this technique. Figure 11.8 illustrates memory performance for 21-, 24-, and 29-month-old children after an 8-month delay. Children who had previous experience with the event performed more event sequences correctly than did nonexperienced control subjects.

It appears, then, that matching the test requirements to the response abilities of the infant or young child yields quantitative evidence of substantial memory abilities. But does this mean that these abilities are the same qualitatively as those of older children or adults? Perhaps not, as indicated by something called infantile amnesia. There is some indication that as our memory abilities develop, we lose the ability to retrieve very early memories, a phenomenon known as **infantile amnesia.** In fact, both humans and animals have difficulty remembering events from their infancy (Spear & Riccio, 1994). For example, a 40-year-old can remember a great deal of her life at 21, but a 20-year-old cannot remember details from her life as a 1-year-old. Some researchers believe that memories from infancy do not survive the transition from infancy to childhood (Nelson, 1993a). Others suggest that memories formed during infancy are inaccessible later because of changes in the brain (increases in the number of synapses, organization of neurons, etc.). Experiment 11 discusses infantile amnesia and recent investigations into the mechanisms responsible for this apparent memory loss.

FIGURE 11.8   **Results from a Memory Test**   The study examined children's ability to recreate events after an eight-month delay. The experienced group had seen the events, while the naive group (the controls) had not.

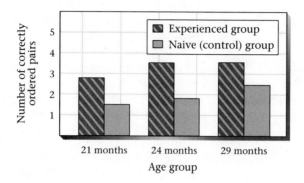

Memory Abilities in Children and Adolescents

Research on memory development is typically subdivided into its different aspects, such as capacity, knowledge base, strategies, and metacognition. Although these aspects are related and interact with one another, researchers have attempted to isolate them and study each independently. We discuss memory development in terms of each of these aspects for children and adolescents and return to these aspects of memory when we consider memory abilities in adulthood later in this section.

Capacity   Developmental studies of memory capacity are more concerned with how memory capacity changes with time than with how much capacity we ultimately possess. In such studies, the *capacity* of memory refers to the total amount of information that can be retained. The general assumption is that with more capacity, we can perform more complex cognitive tasks. One measure of memory capacity in a complex task is the memory span task. Several researchers (e.g., Dempster, 1981) have found that memory span increases with age: The older you are, the more items you will be able to correctly recall in a memory span task. There has been some debate, however, concerning what aspects of memory allow for this improvement (Pressley & Van Meter, 1994). For example, is the change in capacity due to maturation and improvement of memory skills, or is it due to some other factor that also affects memory performance and, in turn, memory capacity?

One prominent position in this debate argues that what develops is the speed of processing involved in the task. **Speed of processing** refers to the rate at which a cognitive process can be executed and is measured in terms of the amount of time required to execute a cognitive process (Kail, 1991a). When children are able to recognize objects faster or rehearse more quickly, less overall demand is placed on the capacity of the cognitive system, and additional time and processes can be reserved for processing other information. If we are able to process more information, then, it is likely that our memory performance will improve. Therefore, the result of greater speed of processing is an increase in memory performance, which appears to be due to an increase in memory capacity.

Children vary according to age in their processing speed when attempting to retrieve names of items, rotate mental images, search visual displays, and perform other tasks that

EXPERIMENT 11:   Infantile Amnesia

When you turned two years old, what happened at your birthday party? What kind of cake did you have? Do you remember the people who were there? If you find it difficult to remember this event, you are not alone. Most people have a difficult time remembering any events that occurred in their lives before they were three years old, although some research suggests that remembering may depend on the event (Usher & Neisser, 1993). It cannot be the case that you had no memory abilities when you were two years old. As noted in the chapter text, infants, even before they are born, have the ability to remember things. The inability of people to re-member events in their lives that occurred before they were three years old is called infantile, or childhood, amnesia.

Here is an experiment that you can use to test this phenomenon. Ask a group of 20-year-old friends or classmates to try to remember details about what happened on their first birthday, 19 years ago. They should try to distinguish between their true memories and memories of what people have told them about their first birthday party or what they have seen in pho-tographs. This will probably be very difficult. They are then to write down the details that they remember.

Then ask a group of 40-year-olds to remember and write down details of a particular event, such as a birthday party, in which they were personally involved 19 years ago, when they were 21. The point is to make the retention interval the same for both groups of participants in your experiment.

require quick (or speeded) responses (Kail, 1986, 1988, 1991a; Kail & Park, 1992). Older children are typically faster at these speeded tasks than younger children, and the older children are in turn slower than adults (Hale, 1990; Kail, 1991b). Robert Kail (1991a) has shown that processing speed increases quickly and then levels off as a function of age. That is, the differences in performance for different age groups gets smaller as the groups define older individuals. This increase in speed of processing occurs across many tasks, such as moving pegs from one row to another and naming pictures. Kail and Hall (1994) found that as children get older, they are better able to name familiar objects more rapidly. Late in adolescence and in early adulthood, individuals start to slow down and continue to do so as they age. We will return to this observation later in the chapter.

Knowledge Base   In our discussions of capacity and speed of processing, we said that once children can process information more efficiently, as shown in faster rates of pro-cessing, they can process more information. Improvement in the speed of processing also allows for growth in the amount of information children have. And this improvement in speed of processing with age may reflect an improvement in the organization of informa-tion. The amount and organization of information defines a child's knowledge base.

Scientists have suggested that when children are one or two years of age, their knowl-edge base is made up of information about people and objects. After the age of two years, children begin to fill their knowledge base with information about events. Nelson and her

Once you have collected these remembered details from both groups of participants, compare the amount of detail remembered by the two groups. If the phenomenon of infantile amnesia is real, then the amount of detail remembered by the 40-year-olds should be far greater than the amount of detail remembered by the 20-year-olds. Did you find this to be the case?

What happens during development that causes us to have such difficulty remembering early events? Freud (1916/1963) believed that only negative emotions can be remembered from infancy and that, even then, the memories will be distorted. Another explanation focuses on the use of language. Children younger than three are just beginning to learn and use language regularly. Before language is used, however, information is encoded differently, in a nonverbal code. If you attempt to remember an event using words you did not know when you experienced the event, you cannot retrieve the memory of the event, because you are not using the same code to describe it (Spear & Riccio, 1994). A similar explanation comes from Nelson (1992, 1993b), who suggests that when children are comfortable using language and compare their experiences with the experiences of others, then they form memories that are specific to themselves.

A final explanation uses a neuropsychological perspective. During development, many changes are occurring in the central nervous system. In particular, the number of synapses in the brain increases and their organization becomes more complex. The receptor sites for and the chemical make-up of some neurotransmitters may also change. These neurological changes may create a situation in which memories formed during infancy are inaccessible later (Spear & Riccio, 1994).

colleagues (Nelson, 1986; Nelson & Gruendel, 1981) have described event knowledge, such as what happens when we bake cookies, as scripts, or *generalized event representations*.

Most of the research examining people's knowledge base has been conducted using adults with varying degrees of knowledge about a specific topic, such as chess (e.g., Chase & Simon, 1973). We know from these studies that people differ in both their level of knowledge and their organization of that knowledge. Such studies have also been conducted with 10-year-old chess experts and adult chess novices. In these studies, when chess boards were arranged with legal and meaningful positions, the expert children were able to remember more about those positions than were the novice adults (Chi, 1978; Horgan & Morgan, 1990).

The point to be made is that memory performance was, in this case, more a function of knowledge than a function of age. Other experiments have demonstrated that knowledge is a critical determiner of memory performance in children. Chi and Koeske (1983) conducted a case study involving a child of four and one-half years with extensive knowledge of dinosaurs. They found that when the child was presented with familiar and unfamiliar dinosaur names and asked to recall them later, he recalled more familiar names than unfamiliar names. From this, Chi and Koeske argued that the reason children perform poorly on many memory tasks is that they lack knowledge for the items on the memory tasks.

With time and experience, we assume that the knowledge base is growing larger. And with time and experience, we can see improvements in a child's performance on memory tasks. It seems logical, then, that if children knew everything that adults know, memory performance for the two groups might be equivalent. But the content of the knowledge base is not the only consideration (Peverly, 1991). Being able to efficiently obtain information from the knowledge base also affects memory. The ability to efficiently obtain information is the concern of research on strategies.

Strategies   **Strategies** are systematic approaches to the efficient management of processing demands in a task. Strategies can demonstrate how the knowledge base is organized and can also show that a child understands how he or she can obtain information from memory. Young children are able to use strategies to improve their memory performance. What distinguishes strategy use in older children from that in younger children is the spontaneous use of the strategy. Younger children are less likely to spontaneously use an appropriate or effective rehearsal strategy. This observation has been termed a **production deficiency** (Keeney, Cannizzo & Flavell, 1967). Some researchers (Howe & O'Sullivan, 1990) have argued that for younger children, strategies are more effortful, and the effort put forth to perform the strategy does not always result in an improved memory outcome.

Ornstein, Naus, and Liberty (1975) found that strategies become more systematic and organized with age. Third-graders tend to rehearse the words in a list separately. For example, if the list contained the words *dog, burrito,* and *hovercraft,* the third-grader would rehearse, *dog, dog, dog,* and then *burrito, burrito, burrito,* and then *hovercraft, hovercraft, hovercraft.* Eighth-graders, however, would rehearse in a cumulative fashion—*dog, burrito, hovercraft, dog, burrito, hovercraft,* and so on. Older children are also able to select strategies that fit the task better than younger children (Pressley, 1982). In addition, older children are more likely than younger children to select the relevant information needed for the task (Miller, 1990).

Yet, just as growth in the knowledge base cannot explain why children's memory improves with age, strategies alone cannot explain this improvement (Hall & Tinzmann, 1989). In the next section, we consider whether knowing things about how memory works can account for improvement in children's memory performance.

Metacognition   As you might expect, older children have more knowledge about their own abilities than younger children, in that they have a better sense than do younger children of how well and how fast they can perform certain cognitive tasks. **Metacognition** refers to a person's ability to monitor and evaluate his or her own current cognitive capabilities (Flavell, 1985). **Metamemory** involves the same type of monitoring and evaluation, but it focuses exclusively on memory processes.

Let us consider some data to illustrate how these abilities change across time. Flavell, Friedrichs, and Hoyt (1970) presented items to preschool and elementary-school students and asked them to study the items until they thought they would be able to remember them. The elementary-school students were better able to judge when they had studied the items enough and to predict how many of the items they would be able to remember than were the preschool children. O'Sullivan (1993), however, found that four-year-olds have well-established knowledge about how recall performance will change with increased effort and incentives. She found that four-year-olds understand that recall performance will improve with more effort and the offering of higher incentives.

Just as younger children are less likely than older children to use strategies spontaneously, they are less likely to spontaneously monitor their cognitive performance. They are able to do so when asked to, however (Markman & Gorin, 1981). Monitoring cognitive performance allows children to change their behavior according to the task demands. Older children are more likely to benefit from knowing how they are doing on a task because they are more likely to change their strategies if the ones they are using are not working. Younger children often do not realize when it would be beneficial to change their behavior.

Metacognitive knowledge affects memory performance in an indirect way, aiding in the selection of strategies and the organization of information. This, in turn, may increase memory performance through the implementation of better rehearsal strategies or an increase in processing speed. Although researchers tend to study capacity, knowledge base, strategies, and metacognition independently, these aspects of memory performance are not functionally independent in the developing child. For example, if we equate children and adults on the basis of their knowledge of a certain topic, such as chess, who will show the better performance? If speed of processing underlies the difference in memory performance between children and adults, we should still see a difference in memory performance between the children and adults, since they both know the same amount of information about chess. The difference in performance comes from the fact that the adults are processing the information faster.

Memory Abilities in Adulthood

You may have noticed that individuals in late adulthood tend to complain more about their memory abilities than individuals in early adulthood (see Light, 1991). The most common complaint from older adults is that they believe their memory, in general, is declining. Older adults do tend to perform worse on memory tasks such as free recall, cued recall, and recognition (Burke & Light, 1981; Craik, 1977; Guttentag, 1985; Hultsch & Dixon, 1990). Older adults, however, appear to retain their ability to accurately predict their levels of memory performance (metamemory). Researchers investigating the memory abilities of older adults, like those investigating memory in children, tend to focus on one aspect of memory performance and examine how that aspect changes with age. We consider some of the research pertinent to these different aspects next.

Speed of Processing   On many speeded tasks, such as naming, reading prose, and mentally rotating visual images, older adults are slower than younger adults (Geary & Wiley, 1991; Hartley et al., 1994; Salthouse, 1993; Salthouse & Coon, 1993; Sliwinski et al., 1994). This slowing has led some researchers to believe that a general cognitive mechanism or ability is declining with age (Cerella, 1991; Kail, 1986; Kail & Salthouse, 1994). In other words, an aspect of cognition contributes to performance in the speeded tasks and so affects all the tasks in a similar way.

Figure 11.9a, b, and c plot the response times of younger and older subjects in three different speeded tasks—mental rotation, visual search, and abstract matching. In each of these tasks, you can see that older adults appear to be both slower and more affected by task difficulty (which increases as we move from left to right on the x-axis of each panel) than younger adults. Figure 11.9d, called a Brinley plot, plots the response times of the older adults against those of the younger adults. For example, the two data points circled in Figure 11.9a show a response time of just over 1.0 second for the older adults and a response time of around 0.6 second for the younger adults. The combination is plotted as the single point (the square) at (0.6, 1.0) in Figure 11.9d. The remaining points in the Brinley plot were obtained in the same way from all the pairs of data points in the other parts of the figure.

FIGURE 11.9 **Performance of Older and Younger Adults on Speeded Tasks** In parts a, b, and c, performance of older adults is represented by the unfilled symbols, and performance of younger adults is represented by the filled symbols. These data are combined in part d, which displays performance of older adults as a function of performance of younger adults.

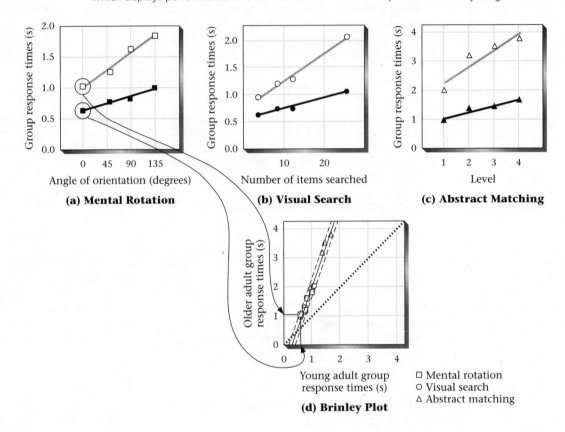

(a) Mental Rotation

(b) Visual Search

(c) Abstract Matching

(d) Brinley Plot

□ Mental rotation
○ Visual search
△ Abstract matching

Now, if task difficulty (the *x*-axis in parts a, b, and c of the figure) affects older adults and younger adults to the same degree, the points in part d should fall along the dotted diagonal line. But you can see that the data actually follow a line with a much steeper slope. This suggests that task difficulty affects older adults much more than it affects younger adults.

Some researchers, however, believe that plotting the processing speeds of older adults as a function of those of younger adults hides patterns of task-specific slowing (Fisher, Fisk & Duffy, 1995; Fisk & Fisher, 1994; Fisk, Fisher & Rogers, 1992). These researchers differ in their explanation for the differences in processing performance exhibited by younger and older adults. Fisk and Fisher and their colleagues suggest that what might be at work is slowing in *specific* cognitive components of the actual task. For example, if a naming task requires encoding, selection, and retrieval of information, the slowing might occur in any one of these components. By encompassing encoding, selection, and retrieval in the global mechanism of "memory," researchers may be masking the effects of these individual components. Fisk and Fisher suggest that the slowing occurs at the level of an individual component and that researchers should attempt to identify where slowing occurs at this level (Fisher and Glaser, 1996).

Although clarifying this issue is important for our understanding of the processes responsible for slowing with age, this debate does not deny that cognitive slowing exists. The debate concerns whether it is due to a decline in general cognitive mechanisms or a decline in performance of specific cognitive tasks.

Strategy Use   Interestingly, observations made for young children with regard to strategy use are also made for older adults. The age-related changes in strategy use that we discussed with respect to children involve knowing when to use a strategy. In this regard, older adults have the same difficulty as younger children—a production deficiency, or a failure to spontaneously use a strategy (Hasher & Zacks, 1979; Reese, 1976). Older adults tend to rehearse single words rather than sets of words, similar to the rehearsal strategies of young children (Ornstein & Naus, 1978; Sanders et al., 1981), although they are able to rehearse in a cumulative manner if asked to do so (Sanders et al., 1981). Older adults also tend not to use organization as a strategy, as in failing to spontaneously cluster semantically related words (Denney, 1974; Zivian & Darjes, 1983).

Metacognition   One hypothesis for the source of memory decline with age suggests that older adults do not remember as well because they hold incorrect beliefs about memory and strategies appropriate for memory tasks. However, few studies have found evidence supporting this hypothesis. Bruce, Coyne, and Botwinick (1982) found that older adults overestimate their memory spans, but other studies have found that older adults underestimate their memory abilities (Smyer, Zarit, & Qualls, 1990). A majority of the studies investigating metamemory have found no difference between young and old adults in ability to predict memory performance (Chaffin & Herrmann, 1983; Hultsch, Hertzog & Dixon, 1987; Lachman, Lachman & Thronesbery, 1979; Rabinowitz et al., 1982).

Task-Related Declines in Memory   In Chapter 7, we discussed direct and indirect memory tasks with respect to the distinction between explicit and implicit expressions of memory. Studies of performance of older adults on direct and indirect memory tasks show results that are intriguingly similar to results obtained with amnesics. Specifically, just as there are differences between normal and amnesic subjects on direct memory tasks, there are reliable differences between younger and older adults on these types of memory tasks (Light, 1991). But just as amnesics' performance on indirect tasks can be almost indistinguishable from the performance of normal subjects, the differences between older and younger adults on indirect memory tasks are minimal and unreliable.

An explanation for these results focuses on the mechanisms involved in direct and indirect tasks (Light, 1991). Remember from Chapter 7 that indirect tasks are tasks that show evidence for memory without the intentional use of memory. These tasks can be performed simply because the information that exists in memory has in some way been activated. Direct tasks, in contrast, require the intentional use of memory and so may require more elaborate processing of the information to be remembered and the context for that information. And this could be the source of the differences between younger and older adults on direct tests.

Older adults do recall less information about context than younger adults. The context may be the voice in which the information was presented (Kausler & Puckett, 1981a), the color of the information (Park & Puglisi, 1985), or whether the information was presented visually or auditorally (Kausler & Puckett, 1981b; Lehman & Mellinger, 1984, 1986). How-

RESEARCH REPORT 11:   Alzheimer's Disease

Jack loved to shop in the mall. Although he was in an early stage of Alzheimer's disease, his family did not suspect anything was wrong until the wild shopping sprees began. He would buy television sets, refrigerators, and other expensive items with his credit card. Then he would come home relaxed and happy. The next day, having forgotten what he had bought the previous day, he would return to the mall and start over. Meanwhile, back home, trucks arrived regularly to deliver television sets, refrigerators, and other items. The items were all returned; and after several shopping sprees, Jack's family had his credit card canceled (Danna, 1995).

This example illustrates the changes in behavior exhibited by an individual with Alzheimer's disease, a form of dementia. *Dementia* is a pathological loss of intellectual functioning involving severe impairments of thinking, memory, and problem-solving abilities (Berger, 1949). Dementia is not an inevitable result of old age. Less than half of the population of people over 90 years of age have dementia.

Alzheimer's disease is a degenerative, irreversible brain disorder that impairs memory and social behavior and results in the progressive loss of intelligence and awareness, as well as a decline in motor skills. More than 4 million individuals in the United States over the age of 65 have been diagnosed with Alzheimer's disease (Danna, 1995). Scientists project that this figure may reach 14 million by the year 2050. The incidence of Alzheimer's disease in the 65-to-74 age group is about 3 percent of this population. In the 75-to-84 age group, the incidence rises to about 19 percent. And in the 85-and-over age group, the rate of occurrence has been estimated at anywhere from 33 to 50 percent (Danna, 1995; Heston & White, 1983; Holden, 1987). Neurological tests are the most reliable way to diagnose Alzheimer's disease. Figure 11A shows a PET scan image of an Alzheimer's patient with severe memory loss.

Several hypotheses have been proposed about the causes of Alzheimer's disease. When the disease is diagnosed in a middle-aged patient (40 to 65 years old), then a genetic disorder is

ever, some studies have shown that memory for target information as well as context information is impaired in older adults (Denney et al., 1991).

It is easy to see how difficult it is to isolate the source of the decline in memory abilities with age. The decline may be due to a decline in a general cognitive mechanism, which in turn affects all aspects of memory. Or it may be due to changes in how older adults approach different memory tasks and the particular information they retrieve to perform those tasks. Either way, elderly adults' complaints about "poor memory" involve something more complicated than simple forgetting.

In spite of the general impression that age affects memory in a negative way, close examination of research findings suggests that memory abilities may *change* with age but do not inevitably *decline*. For example, access to general knowledge and historical personal information does not decline with age. Bahrick, Bahrick, and Wittlinger (1975) found that older adults were able to recognize, from photographs, 70 to 80 percent of their high

thought to be the source. For the more common form of Alzheimer's disease, that which affects individuals over the age of 65, possible causes are immune system deficiencies, concentrations of aluminum in the brain (Cohen, 1988), brain infections, and plaques and tangles in the brain tissue. No way to slow down or stop the progression of Alzheimer's disease is currently known; but early diagnosis will help the patient and the family plan for the future and cope with the inevitable deterioration.

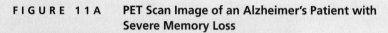

FIGURE 11A   **PET Scan Image of an Alzheimer's Patient with Severe Memory Loss**

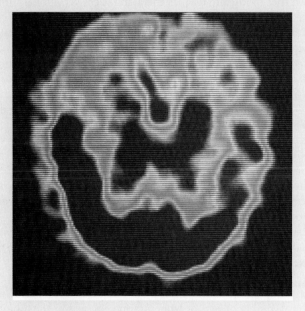

school classmates 50 years after graduation. As research on memory and aging continues, accumulation of evidence regarding the changes that occur will help us to understand more clearly how aging affects the functioning of memory processes. Research Report 11 discusses a dramatic example of an age-related decline in memory—Alzheimer's disease.

Language Development

In general, early in the course of development, humans learn how to speak, how to form grammatically correct sentences, how to attach labels to meaningful things, and how to communicate with others. It may seem remarkable that we learn to do all this before we begin our formal education. Linguists like Noam Chomsky argue that we are born with the capacity to learn the essential aspects of language. Learning the specifics of language comes easily, then, because our cognitive systems are set up to work with language. Other theorists suggest that the ability to produce language relies on the *maturation* of the sensory, motor, and cognitive systems (Lenneberg, 1967; Newport, 1990). Motor abilities must be in place for the infant to explore and perceive the world and give meaning to the environment. And until other cognitive abilities, such as memory, are available to the child, language will not develop.

Precursors to Language Use   In order for children to begin to talk, they must be able to coordinate muscle movements to articulate sounds. While children are "waiting" for this muscle coordination to develop, they are learning speech sounds and developing the ability to discriminate sounds. An infant's first exposure to speech is usually "motherese," or **child-directed speech,** which is characterized by slower pronunciation, exaggerated intonation, a higher-than-normal frequency, repetition, and use of simple syntax and vocabulary. Kemler-Nelson and colleagues (1989) have suggested that infants prefer to listen to motherese and that motherese teaches them about conversational turn-taking, grammar, and syntax.

While infants are listening to child-directed speech, they are learning valuable information about speech sounds specific to their language. Infants of English-speaking parents, for example, prefer the stress patterns of English and are able to discriminate between strong and weak syllables (Jusczyk, Cutler & Redanz, 1993). Young infants, around six to eight months of age, can discriminate speech sounds and exhibit what has been called categorical perception for syllables spoken in their native language (Eimas et al., 1971; Jusczyk et al., 1980; Werker & Lalonde, 1988).

There is some indication that up to about eight months of age, infants can hear differences in phonemes from languages other than their native language (Werker, 1984, 1991). Werker and her colleagues measured the ability of infants of English-speaking parents to discriminate differences among Hindi phonemes. Infants younger than eight months of age in this study could discriminate among the Hindi phonemes just as well as they could discriminate among the English phonemes. But in infants older than eight months of age, the ability to discriminate phonemes from the nonnative language diminished. Werker has suggested that infants begin life with the ability to discriminate a wide range of sounds but that they lose the ability to discriminate sounds not used in their native language.

The Path of Language Acquisition   Have you ever overheard a person making speech-like noises when examining objects or when no one else was in the room? If this person was an adult, you might have found the behavior a little disconcerting. But if the person was an infant, you undoubtedly found the behavior perfectly normal. What are infants doing when they behave in this way? Infants between the ages of about three and seven months are *babbling* when they make such sounds. Some babbling appears to be sound play, engaged in simply because infants like the sounds of their voices. However, babbling sometimes resembles certain pitch patterns similar to those found in spoken language.

During the babbling period, infants engage in preverbal forms of speech that are truly communicative actions. They may make requests by reaching with their hands and opening and closing their fingers. If the object they want is out of reach, this grasping action becomes insistent and may be accompanied by whining and sad expressions. Infants also make assertions about objects. They point to objects in a nonurgent manner as if to make a declarative statement, such as "This is a ball," or to ask a question, such as "What is this?"

Around 10 to 13 months of age, infants begin to produce their first words. In these one-word utterances, called **holophrases,** a single word represents an entire sentence of meaning. The words are usually concrete and often end in a vowel. The words may be negations, such as *no;* requests for recurrence, such as *more;* statements of nonexistence, such as *gone;* or statements of notice, such as *hi.*

Infants using holophrases usually understand more than they can verbalize. One clever study showed action sequences on video involving familiar characters (e.g., Big Bird and Cookie Monster) to infants (Golinkoff et al., 1987). The infants were read a sentence that correctly or incorrectly described an action sequence (e.g., Big Bird is tickling Cookie Monster). Infants tended to look longer at the video that matched the sentence they were given than at a video that depicted a different action sequence (e.g., Cookie Monster tickling Big Bird). This study shows that infants are able to use the syntactic order in a sentence to construct the meaning of the situation.

During this period, the one-word labels used for objects tend to be overextended (Clark, 1973). An **overextension** involves extending one word's meaning to include an inappropriately broad range of objects. *Doggie* may be used as the label for dogs, for example, but it may also be applied to cats, rabbits, stuffed animals, and other small furry things. (We consider the development of categories and concepts in more detail in Chapter 13.) **Underextension** also occurs; here, children use a particular word to refer to only one event or object rather than applying it more broadly to other, similar events or objects. It is not altogether clear why young children do this.

At about 18 to 24 months of age, children begin to produce very brief sentences that include no function words (e.g., *the*). These utterances are often referred to as **telegraphic speech** because of their similarity to telegrams, which use minimal numbers of words. By this age, children have learned about 50 words, and they begin to put them together in meaningful ways. They can express several different relationships even in sentences consisting of only two words. Table 11.2 lists 12 relations, specified by Brown (1973), that can be expressed with two-word utterances.

T A B L E   1 1 . 2   **Brown's Classification of Relations in Two-Word Utterances**

Relation	Example Utterance
Agent—Action	Mommy kiss
Action—Object	Hit ball
Agent—Object	Mommy doll
Action—Locative	Sit chair
Entity—Locative	Cup table
Possessor—Possession	Daddy car
Entity—Attributive	Big car
Demonstrative—Entity	That car
Negation	No bath
Recurrence	More juice
Nonexistence	Allgone cookie
Notice	Hi, Mommy

After approximately 18 months of age, the rate of learning new words increases rapidly. Between 18 months and 6 years of age, children learn approximately 14,000 words. Carey (1978) has pointed out that this rate of language acquisition amounts to learning about nine new words a day!

As children learn new words, they also learn to organize and categorize these words. They try to identify regularities in meaning that will help them to organize the words within their growing knowledge base. They also begin to use function words, such as *the.* In light of these advances, the appearance of **overregularization errors** during this period may seem surprising. Overregularization errors are rule-based errors involving word and syntactic formations. Children at this age may say *mouses* instead of *mice* and *breaked* instead of *broke,* for example. The surprising fact about these errors is that these same children, before this period of development, produced these formations without error.

This type of misapplication of grammar rules shows that children are actively experimenting to learn new rules about language. Children sometimes produce grammatically incorrect sentences and look to their parents for feedback. Parents, however, do not usually correct grammatical mistakes. Instead, they usually make corrections based on meaning (Brown & Hanlon, 1970). What happens to the grammatically incorrect sentence in this case? Is it incorporated into the child's knowledge base of grammar? Because grammar was not corrected by the parent, the child now has negative evidence to deal with (see Pinker, 1990). This negative evidence may contradict grammar rules the child already possesses. Because children are able to learn grammar rules, they eventually resolve this conflict of negative evidence with positive evidence to produce the correct form of grammar appropriate to the language.

Cognitive Development and Approaches to Reading   Listening to words, processing how they sound, and being able to discriminate among different sounds are important aspects of language learning and use. These skills are emphasized in one well-known approach to reading instruction, which focuses on basic skills and phonetics. This approach is based on the idea that reading instruction should stress phonetics and the basic rules for translating written symbols into sounds (Santrock, 1996). Instruction emphasizing phonetics also involves the use of simplified materials for early reading. Under this approach, children learn strategies for decoding and pronouncing words they have never seen before. Because this instruction involves monotonous repetition of phonological rules, it can be tedious for both children and teachers. Additionally, children may not be able to comprehend large passages of text because they have not learned how to connect the meanings of the words they are reading.

A second approach to reading instruction, called the whole-language approach, stresses that reading instruction should parallel the child's natural language learning and reading materials should be whole and meaningful (Santrock, 1996). Children learning to read with this method are given stories and poems in their complete forms. The goal is for the children to learn how to integrate meaning and increase overall understanding. Critics, however, claim that children often ignore words they do not know and therefore fail to learn them. Additionally, critics claim that children taught using the whole-language approach never learn to decode the alphabet.

Which instruction technique is best? Recently, many states have been debating this issue (Hancock & Wingert, 1996). One solution appears to be a combination of the two approaches. A third approach, which also combines the phonics and whole-language approaches, emphasizes a developmental information processing approach to reading

(Spear-Swerling & Sternberg, 1994). This new approach involves use of a sequence that allows reading instruction to change with changes in development. For example, preschoolers and kindergartners are taught how to recognize words through the use of salient visual cues, such as the golden arches at MacDonald's restaurants. Kindergartners and first-graders are taught how to use their knowledge of sounds to recognize words, such as by sounding out the word *dog* by saying /d/ and /g/. Between first and second grade, children begin to recognize words automatically and can devote more of their cognitive abilities to comprehension rather than recognition. At this time, strategies to improve reading comprehension can be taught. This instruction is heavily emphasized with students in the middle to late grades of elementary school. In these final stages of the sequence, the whole-language approach is implemented.

Conceptual Development

When we discussed the content of an individual's knowledge base, we described how organization can aid in the retrieval of information from memory. The organization of the knowledge base reflects how a child thinks about concepts. Usually, children have very elaborate theories about how the world works, but they often cannot verbalize these theories (Carey & Gelman, 1991; Wellman & Gelman, 1992). Infants are also thought to have implicit theories about the world. Most of their theories concern objects that are physical in nature, have boundaries, and continue to exist even when they are out of view (Spelke et al., 1992).

The development of knowledge regarding biological concepts occurs relatively early in life. Infants and children appear to be very interested in things that move, both living and inanimate. Infants can distinguish between motion that comes from objects that are alive and motion that is created by nonliving objects (Bertenthal, 1993). Young children three to four years of age often have elaborate biological concepts. They understand that plants and animals grow and that other objects do not. And they understand that living things not only grow but also consume food and maintain their identity, despite sometimes great changes in appearance, as when a caterpillar changes into a butterfly.

An interesting and essential area of conceptual development concerns physical concepts. Infants appear to understand key properties of physical objects. For example, contrary to what Piaget believed, infants do seem to understand that objects continue to exist when they are out of sight. Children must also understand and develop knowledge of space. Infants have a rudimentary understanding of space, usually concentrated in the area around them. Children tend to form three types of representations of space. *Egocentric* representations concern the relation between the child's location and that of other people or objects. This sort of representation best describes an infant's understanding of space. Movement is very important in developing an understanding outside of this egocentric space. The second type of representation, classifying space based on *landmarks,* develops during the first year after birth and improves dramatically over the next several years of life. Finally, *allocentric* representations involve an understanding of relations among all the entities within the space. Such representations usually first appear around four to six years of age.

Most of the interesting and revealing research concerning the development of concepts involves infants and young children. In adolescents and adults, the development of conceptual understanding itself is usually not the focus of investigation. Instead, research in this area focuses on how adolescents and adults use concepts in their daily lives, such as in problem solving.

Section Summary: Cognitive Development Across the Lifespan

At one time, the cognitive abilities of infants were believed to be rather limited, but contemporary research has documented that infants possess impressive cognitive abilities. These findings have come from studies in which experimental tests, such as Rovee-Collier's use of the kicking response and Bauer's use of imitation, are adapted to infants' abilities to express their skills. As infants develop into children and children develop into adults, their memory capacity increases. One prominent explanation for this increase is that what is changing is the speed of processing. Yet the organization and amount of information in memory—the knowledge base—also changes across this period of development. Another prominent change that occurs during this period involves the information processing strategies used, with evidence suggesting that strategies become more systematic and efficient with increasing maturity. In addition, individuals' metacognitive abilities increase during this time. It is commonly assumed that, as adults age, their cognitive abilities (particularly their memory abilities) inevitably decline. Yet evidence suggests that these abilities may remain intact. Although some scientists have argued that a generalized slowing underlies the apparent decline, others have suggested that task-specific slowing may be mistaken for a more global slowing of cognitive processes. Older adults do appear to change the strategies they use in cognitive tasks, showing strategy use more similar to that of young children than that of younger adults. It has been suggested that the metacognitive abilities of older adults may be at fault in apparent memory declines, but research has failed to support this hypothesis. The development of the ability to produce and process language builds on the sensory, motor, and cognitive abilities that develop in infancy. The path of language acquisition—beginning with babbling and the use of gestures and continuing through the development of holophrases, telegraphic speech, and explosive vocabulary growth—suggests increasing complexity in abilities and knowledge. Along with the ability to use language comes the development of knowledge about the concrete and abstract aspects of the world, beginning with knowledge of physical concepts.

REVIEWING COGNITIVE DEVELOPMENT

CONCEPT REVIEW

1. What is Von Baer's law? Give examples of implicit or explicit uses of Von Baer's law in the study of cognitive abilities.

2. Contrast the basic assumptions of Piaget's theory with the basic assumptions of dynamic systems theory. What are some of the limitations of Piaget's theory, and what are some ways in which Piaget's theory may have been misrepresented or unfairly criticized?

3. Identify a major contribution of the information processing approach to the study of the development of cognitive abilities, and discuss Bryant and Trabasso's use of the transitive inference task as an example of this contribution.

4. Describe some of the techniques (experimental methodologies and tasks) that have been used to show that infants' cognitive abilities are much more highly developed than earlier theories (such as Piaget's) predicted.

CONCEPT REVIEW *(continued)*

5. Summarize the important aspects of brain development that support cognitive development.

6. Describe the visual cliff and explain how it has been used to explore the development of perceptual abilities.

7. What is regressive development? Give an example of regressive development, and discuss why it presents problems for stage theories and why it suggests the need for an approach like dynamic systems theory.

8. Describe Rovee-Collier's and Bauer's tests of infant memory. What are the important similarities between these two tests?

9. Define *infantile amnesia,* and identify some of the possible sources of this phenomenon.

10. Identify and define four components of memory and cognitive ability that are examined across development.

11. How can the speed of processing hypothesis account for the changes in cognitive abilities that are observed across the lifespan? What are some deficiencies in this account?

12. Compare and contrast the cognitive and memory strategies used by children, young adults, and older adults. What deficiency appears to be operating for both children and older adults?

13. How does the Brinley plot in Figure 11.9 suggest that older adults exhibit some generalized cognitive slowing? What are some of the arguments against this conclusion?

14. What parallel can be drawn between older adults and amnesics in terms of performance on specific types of memory tasks? What are some possible sources for this parallel?

15. Summarize the path of language development. Note and define the various communicative behaviors used as language develops.

16. Define and contrast errors of overextension and underextension in language development.

17. Define and contrast the basic-skills-and-phonetics approach and the whole-language approach to reading instruction.

18. Identify and define the three types of representations thought to be important in the development of physical concepts.

KEY TERMS

child-directed speech (p. 376)
dishabituation (p. 357)
dynamic systems theory (p. 364)
habituation (p. 357)
holophrase (p. 376)
infantile amnesia (p. 366)
metacognition (p. 370)
metamemory (p. 370)

ontogeny (p. 352)
overextension (p. 377)
overregularization error (p. 378)
phylogeny (p. 352)
production deficiency (p. 370)
regressive development (p. 362)
speed of processing (p. 367)
stage theory (p. 354)

strategy (p. 370)
telegraphic speech (p. 377)
transitive inference task (p. 355)
underextension (p. 377)
visual cliff (p. 361)
visually guided reaching (p. 363)

SUGGESTED READINGS

You can read about major theories and topics of research in cognitive development in *Child development: A thematic approach,* a 1998 text by D. Bukatko and M. W. Daehler (Boston: Houghton Mifflin Company). Several current reviews of information on cognition and aging have been written by major researchers in this area. F. I. M. Craik's (1994) article, "Memory changes in normal aging" describes what types of memory changes might occur during the normal course of aging (*Current Directions in Psychological Science, 3,* 155–158). L. L. Light (1991) provides a review of four hypotheses that have directed much of the work in memory and aging in "Memory and aging: Four hypotheses in search of data" (*Annual Review of Psychology, 42,* 333–376). A 1996 article by Salthouse, "The processing-speed theory of adult age differences in cognition," provides a current and complete account of changes in the speed of processing with age. J. E. Birren and K. W. Schaie's (1996) *Handbook of the psychology of aging* (San Diego: Academic Press) includes several chapters on cognition and aging and describes research in other areas of psychology as well. As a complete package, this text provides a current and interesting look at the factors involved in the study of aging.

12 Judgment and Decision Making

I N T H I S C H A P T E R , we begin to explore thinking—those higher-level cognitive activities that depend on and take advantage of the abilities, skills, and limitations that we have explored in the preceding chapters. Judgment and decision making, topics covered in this chapter, are products of complex interactions among perception, attention, memory, and the ability to use language. Studying human judgment and decision making also helps us to address fundamental questions about human behavior—questions such as "Why?" and the more philosophical "Do we have choices?"

Economics provides both simple and complex examples that help to illustrate the study of choice. Consider this simple choice: You need to buy a pair of jeans. This sounds pretty straightforward, right? But think about it: Where we are living as we write this, at least twenty stores sell jeans, and we could choose from at least that many brands. You probably enjoy the same abundance of choices. With this many options available to you, how do you make your decision?

There are a number of reasons to be interested in this question. For example, in the jeans business, a great many people with a great deal of money at stake are interested in how they can *influence* your decision. If a company that manufactures jeans determines that a specific shade of denim can be easily distinguished from other shades, perhaps it can use that shade to suggest something unique about the person who wears its brand. Or perhaps the manufacturer can associate its brand with an important or desirable celebrity. Perhaps the brand name has been chosen to imply some desirable characteristic or simply to be outlandish or unique. The point is that the processes and information that go into making decisions can and do have important applications and implications.

Our interest in judgment and decision making is more basic. We are interested in understanding judgment and decision making as information processing rather than as activities carried out for specific purposes (though certainly these goals are not mutually exclusive). We begin by reviewing some of the important contributions made by scientists trying to understand fundamental aspects of judgment and decision making and then discuss contemporary issues in this field.

WHY DID YOU DO THAT? A LITTLE HISTORY

Let us return to the example of deciding which type of jeans to buy. We noted that most of us have many stores and brands from which to choose. But what do we mean when we say we can *choose* among these alternatives? Put yourself in the manufacturers' or vendors' shoes (*not* their jeans) for a moment.

You might be tempted to think that if you knew all the different variables that contribute to consumers' choices, then you could design your products and your advertising to address each of these variables and virtually *guarantee* that people would buy your jeans. In fact, this is the logic that drives a great deal of marketing and manufacturing. But if you follow this logic, then what do you conclude about your customers' freedom to make choices?

In the extreme, what we are talking about here is a view of human behavior that is **deterministic.** This view says that if we simply know enough, we can both predict and control human behavior precisely. Put in other terms, if we know what the input to the human information processing "system" is, we can predict exactly what the output will be. This type of determinism is actually referred to as *hard determinism* (Beck, 1990, pp. 8–9) and represents an ideal but unattainable situation. A weaker form, *soft determinism,* basically holds that while some behaviors can be predicted and determined (given the appropriate and necessary knowledge), other behaviors cannot. This is probably the least attractive view of determinism from a scientific standpoint, since it generally specifies no rules for deciding which behaviors fall into which category.

A third type of determinism is referred to as *probabilistic determinism* and approaches predictions about behavior in the same way insurance companies do. According to this view, behavior can be predicted with a certain probability, given a certain level of knowledge. More precisely, for any defined set of outcomes (e.g., judgments or decisions), probabilistic models say that there is some probability function that assigns each of those outcomes a value between 0 and 1, inclusive (Busemeyer & Townsend, 1993).

We can classify approaches to studying judgment and decision making in part by the type of determinism that is assumed. The type of determinism assumed by a model or theory of judgment and decision making specifies the relationship between the environment and behavior. This relationship is often called the **preference relation** (or probability function, for probabilistic models) of the model or theory.

Another way of classifying approaches to studying judgment and decision making involves how the model or theory proposes that the preference relation (or probability function) changes over time (Busemeyer & Townsend, 1993; Townsend & Busemeyer, 1989). **Static theories** hold that the preference relation or probability function does not depend in any way on the amount of time involved in making the judgment or decision. **Dynamic theories,** in contrast, hold that the preference relation or probability function changes according to the amount of time spent in making the judgment or decision.

Motivation and Cognition

One of the most basic questions in judgment and decision-making research is "Why?" Why did a particular person make a particular decision? Why did you buy a particular brand of jeans? These types of questions have to do with the motivation for a particular judgment or decision.

Some scientists (e.g., Arkes & Hammond, 1986, p. 3) contend that the systematic study of judgment and decision making did not begin in earnest until the 1960s, with the decline of behaviorism as the dominant viewpoint in psychology and the development of the digital computer as both a tool and a metaphor for the emerging discipline of cognitive psychology. But, as we hope we have convinced you in the preceding chapters, much important psychological research was done before the 1960s, including work done in the behaviorist tradition. This is as true for the study of judgment and decision making as for the areas discussed previously and is particularly true for work on **motivation,** internal and external information and processes that energize and direct behavior.

The Role of Motivation in Judgment and Decision Making   One of the most basic questions you can ask about any behavior or action—"Why?"—is a question about motivation. You may be most familiar with the notion of motivation from crime stories or popular conceptions of Freudian psychology, where motivation is often attributed to un-conscious, primeval energies. However, motivation has been an area of interest for a broad range of psychologists throughout the century. And currently, scientific interest in motivation seems to be particularly high (Deci, 1992; Dweck, 1992; Locke & Latham, 1990).

Motivation has traditionally been viewed from one of two perspectives. The first, which we will call the **regulatory view,** describes motivations for behavior in terms of their regulatory functions. For example, a regulatory view of behavior would look for the ways in which some action (such as eating) might help manage or control physiological or psychological systems. Regulatory views date back at least to Darwin's evolutionary theory and were associated with the functionalist psychology of William James and John Dewey early in this century (Beck, 1990). But perhaps the most famous examples of regulatory views of behavior are Pavlov's and Sherrington's work on reflexes and unconditioned responses to certain types of stimuli (such as the salivation response made by a food-deprived animal when presented with food).

In terms of judgment and decision making, the regulatory approach gained an important concept with Woodworth's (1918) introduction of the notion of a **drive,** something that energizes behavior. Woodworth argued that two mechanisms were important to understanding motivation. The first is a *driving* mechanism, and the second is a *steering* mechanism, which directs the energized behavior toward some goal that aids in the regulation of some physical or psychological state.

We can easily apply these concepts to our example of buying jeans. The driving mechanism for buying jeans might be physical, such as wanting something warm for the cooler fall weather; or it might be social or psychological, such as wanting something stylish to wear. The steering mechanism might be the influences of advertising, your friends (what they think is stylish, for example), or the specific stores to which you have access.

In contrast to the regulatory approach, the **purposive approach** focuses on why one of a set of alternatives is chosen over the others. According to the purposive approach, we can imagine the future. When we have to choose among a set of alternatives, we can imagine what the future would be like if we chose any one of those alternatives. Our final choice will be the one associated with the imagined outcomes that are the most valued or desirable to us. In the purposive view, there is no need for something like a driving mechanism. Instead, there is a need for something like an internal *will* (James, 1890) that is exercised in making the choice among the relevant and available alternatives.

Freud's view of motivation—perhaps the most influential with respect to everyday conceptions of motivation—actually blends the regulatory and purposive perspectives. For example, Freud (1938) held that all behavior is in some way determined by the need to regulate (for example) sexual and aggressive drives. In addition, according to Freud, psychic forces exert what might be thought of as willful influences in directing expression of these drives toward different outcomes.

Activation and Arousal   All the ideas we have discussed so far are rather abstract psychological notions. But motivation—the underlying reasons for particular decisions and choices—has been examined from a neurophysiological perspective as well.

Woodworth's notion of drives gained a neurophysiological basis during the middle part of the century. During this time, a number of theorists interested in the physiological basis of emotional states suggested that aspects of autonomic nervous system functioning formed the basis for drives. For example, Elizabeth Duffy (1934) proposed that drives are based on the mobilization of neuropsychological energy. A number of scientists (Hebb,

1955; Lindsley, 1950; Malmo, 1959) suggested that the source of this energy is the *reticular activating system (RAS)* of the midbrain (see Figure 12.1).

A number of characteristics of the RAS make it a likely candidate as the source of drives. First, it receives input from all of the sensory systems, with the exception of smell. Second, these inputs are widely distributed to areas of the association cortex via the ascending pathways of the RAS. In fact, the distribution of sensory inputs for the RAS is so diffuse that the specific *type* of sensory input is lost in the distribution to the associative areas of the brain. Finally, the descending pathways of the RAS send projections to the muscles and actually serve to maintain muscle tone and preparedness (Beck, 1990).

These types of connections would allow the RAS to play a direct role in regulatory behaviors, such as eating. And the RAS also seemed to have a role in what appeared to be the physiological basis for drives. For example, systematic investigations of the RAS provided evidence for its role in psychological activation. Some of this evidence was based on patterns of electrical activity as recorded in electroencephalograms (EEGs), and these findings have relevance for our understanding of cognitive processes.

For example, as we discussed in Chapter 3, much of the information we process comes from visual input. Now consider EEGs associated with visual stimuli. These EEGs are recorded from the occipital lobe. Imagine that we are recording these EEGs from a subject

FIGURE 12.1 **The Reticular Activating System (RAS)** Around the middle of the twentieth century, some scientists proposed that the reticular activating system of the midbrain was the source of the neuropsychological energy that formed the basis of drives and activation.

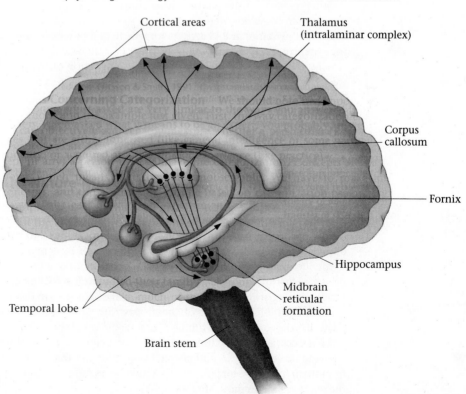

who is resting in a darkened room. In this case, we would see a high-voltage, low-frequency pattern (an alpha pattern) that is synchronized with EEGs recorded near the front of the brain. Now imagine that we turn the light on. The alpha pattern would be immediately replaced by a low-voltage, high-frequency beta pattern that is not synchronized with other recordings. This desynchronization occurs as the effects of visual stimulation are passed from the receptors of the eyes through the RAS to the occipital lobe.

This desynchronization can be produced by direct electrical stimulation of the RAS (Moruzzi & Magoun, 1949). That is, we can observe the effect we obtained through external stimulation by directly stimulating a portion of the nervous system. In addition, if the RAS is destroyed in a laboratory animal, the animal is left comatose and unresponsive to any type of external stimulation. Finally, stimulants like amphetamines increase RAS activity and psychological alertness, while depressants like barbiturates decrease RAS activity and psychological alertness. All this evidence suggests that the RAS could be the center, or source, of the psychological energy underlying drives.

Various explorations of activation raised the question of whether there might be an *optimal* level of activation (Hebb, 1955; Malmo, 1959). Evidence suggesting some type of optimal level came from studies in which stimulation was reduced to a low, constant level (Bexton, Heron & Scott, 1954; Pritchard, 1961). These studies showed that, after extended time in unchanging or low-variability environments, subjects began to report abnormalities in perception (such as "seeing" the walls of the room bow). It was argued that sustained exposure to an unchanging environment leads to reduced activity in the RAS. This reduced activity was thought to represent a condition exactly opposite the conditions under which additional learning and responding take place (Reisen, 1961).

Other research suggested that either consistently high or consistently low levels of nervous system activation were detrimental. At least one theorist (Hebb, 1955) suggested that consistent extremes of RAS activity impede neural functioning by interrupting or disrupting synchronies such as those just discussed for the visual system. Over time, this research was integrated with research that examined the notion of an optimal level of arousal. This work became important in examining the effects of stress on task performance (Hockey, 1986; Kennedy & Coulter, 1975; Yerkes & Dodson, 1908).

Approach and Avoidance   If you think about the various types of things you do in a typical week, and the ways in which motivation might be important in these situations, you will quickly come to realize that there are things you are highly motivated to do (like spend time with friends) and things you are highly motivated not to do (like spend time with a textbook). This simple observation is associated with a research tradition that dates to the early part of this century. It also relates to important considerations about the positive and negative aspects of goals, events, and objects. And it relates to notions about how behavior changes across time with respect to both positive and negative goals, events, and objects (Busemeyer & Townsend, 1993; Townsend & Busemeyer, 1989).

The idea that certain goals, events, or objects can have both positive and negative aspects was first studied in connection with **approach-avoidance behaviors.** One of the first psychologists to study approach-avoidance behaviors in detail, and offer a reasonably detailed theoretical account of them, was Kurt Lewin (1935; Townsend & Busemeyer, 1989). Lewin conceived of humans as actors in a psychological and physical space. This space is occupied by psychological (unobservable) and physical (observable) objects that have the power either to pull people toward them (attractive forces) or push people away from them (repulsive forces). The attractive forces motivate *approach* to the object, whereas the repulsive forces motivate *avoidance.*

While Lewin was developing his notions of approach and avoidance for concepts such as social interaction (Bower & Hilgard, 1981; Estes, 1954b), Clark Hull was developing concepts of approach and avoidance at the level of individual behavior (Koch, 1954). Whereas Lewin used metaphors to describe approach and avoidance (Estes, 1954b), Hull used simple mathematics to describe his theoretical ideas. Hull's approach was much more precise than Lewin's and also far more complex, as illustrated in Figure 12.2. In fact, one criticism of Hull's work was its occasionally overwhelming (and possibly unnecessary) complexity (Koch, 1954).

FIGURE 12.2 **Hull's Conceptualization of Behavior** Hull's model included components corresponding to both motivating (approach) and inhibitory (avoidance) aspects of a situation. A drawback of the approach was the occasionally overwhelming level of detail.

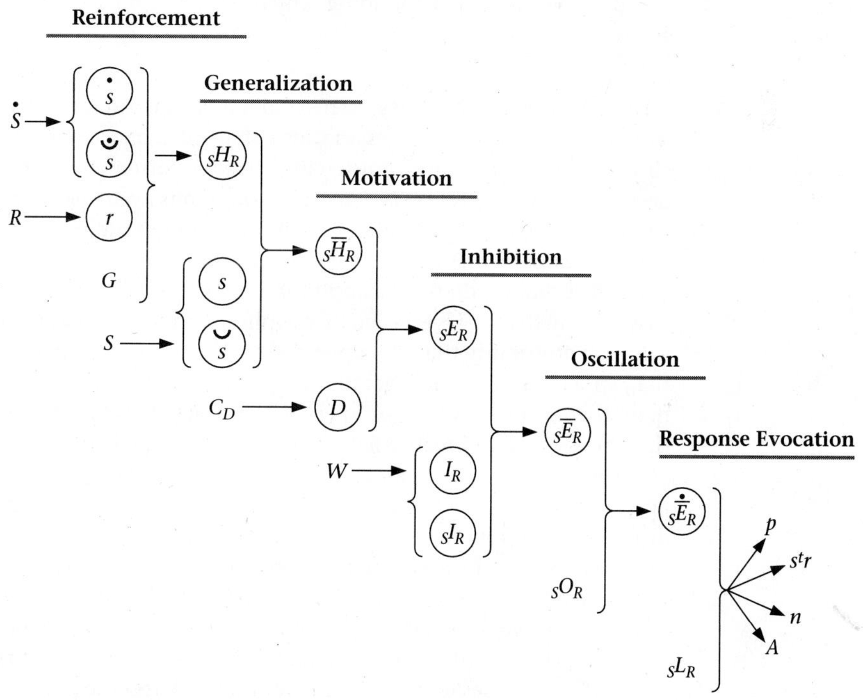

Source: Hull, 1943.

In this diagram $\dot{S}$ represents the physical stimulus energy involved in learning; R, the organism's reaction; $\dot{s}$, the neural result of the stimulus; $\breve{s}$, the neural interaction arising from the impact of two or more stimulus components; r, the efferent impulse leading to reaction; G, the occurrence of a reinforcing state of affairs; $_sH_R$, habit strength; S, evocation stimulus on the same stimulus continuum as $\dot{S}$; $_s\bar{H}_R$, the generalized habit strength; C_D, the objectively observable phenomena determining the drive; D, the physiological strength of the drive to motivate action; $_sE_R$, the reaction potential; W, work involved in an evoked reaction; I_R, reactive inhibition; $_sI_R$, conditioned inhibition; $_s\bar{E}_R$, effective reaction potential; $_sO_R$, oscillation; $_s\dot{E}_R$, momentary effective reaction potential; $_sL_R$, reaction threshold; p, probability of reaction evocation; $_sL_R$, latency of reaction evocation; n, number of unreinforced reactions to produce experimental extinction; and A, amplitude of reaction. Above the symbols the lines beneath the words *reinforcement, generalization, motivation, inhibition, oscillation* and *response evocation* indicate roughly the segments of the chain of symbolic constructs with which each process is especially concerned.

Approach and *avoidance* are terms that, in contemporary psychology, seem to have become associated more with the study of abnormal phenomena (such as fears and phobias) than with the study of cognition. This is due, at least in part, to the efforts of one of Hull's students, Neal Miller. Miller (1959; Dollard & Miller, 1950) extended Hull's notions in the areas of psychotherapy and social psychology but seems to have abandoned the study of approach and avoidance around 1960 (Townsend & Busemeyer, 1989). As you will see later in the chapter, ideas about approach and avoidance are again receiving attention from cognitive psychologists.

Choice, Uncertainty, and Heuristics

Conflicts between approach and avoidance arise in situations that have both positive and negative aspects. However, we often deal with situations in which we have to choose among alternatives that are either all positive or all negative. For example, when faced with the choice of which jeans to buy, we must decide which one of several possible brands is best as well as deciding which brands should be sought and which should be avoided.

Choice Under Uncertainty   The study of choice—or, more specifically, **choice under uncertainty**—acknowledges the idea that, in many cases, we are faced with making choices and decisions without having all the information we want or need. In addition, even when a great deal of objective information is available, additional uncertainty arises, because we seem to process objective information in subjective ways, leading to outcomes that could not be predicted on the basis of the objective information.

The fact that we do this has been of interest for a very long time. It was noted and discussed more than 250 years ago by the philosopher-scientists who were responsible for developing probability theory (Puppe, 1991). The phenomenon of which they took note was that, in games of chance (gambling), people seem to base their behavior on something more than just the known prospects of winning. This behavior was described in 1728 by the philosopher and mathematician Nicholas Bernoulli and came to be known as the St. Petersburg paradox (Jorland, 1987). The paradox is that, if the odds of winning are known, people should behave according to those odds; but behavior in fact is not completely predicted by this knowledge.

The resolution of the paradox was proposed independently by two theoreticians, one of whom was Daniel Bernoulli, Nicholas Bernoulli's cousin. His argument was this: In any game (or gamble) that has some defined set of outcomes, a set of possible payoffs, or benefits, is associated with those outcomes. We will let b_i represent the payoff, or benefit, for one of the outcomes. Each of the outcomes also has some probability of occurring; we will let p_i represent the probability of one of the outcomes. These are the known probabilities that, along with the benefits, should guide behavior.

But each individual places some *subjective* value on a specific benefit. For example, one person might find winning a free scratch-and-win card in a state lottery to be very desirable, while another person might find this benefit less than thrilling. Some psychological function must evaluate the benefit to produce a subjective value; we will let $u(b_i)$ represent this function.

The various outcomes of a game are evaluated in light of both the probability of the outcome (p_i) and the subjective evaluation of the benefit $[u(b_i)]$; this is represented by the multiplication of the probability of the outcome by the subjective evaluation of the benefit: $p_i u(b_i)$. To evaluate the total situation, we add up these individual evaluations:

$$\sum_i p_i u(b_i)$$

This general formulation was used with some success for 200 years and was developed into a more formal and rigorous theory around the middle of the twentieth century (von Neumann & Morganstern, 1947). It came to be known as the *expected utility hypothesis* or **subjective expected utility hypothesis.** The hypothesis was of great interest to scientists studying economics and economic models of human interaction (Jorland, 1987; Suppes & Atkinson, 1960).

Interestingly, at about the same time that the more formalized theory of subjective expected utility was being developed, similar notions were being explored by psychologists working in the behavioral tradition of verbal learning. Of interest to these scientists was the observation that knowledge of and sensitivity to the probability, amount, and *expectation* of reinforcement dramatically influenced the types of learning and forgetting that could be observed (Grant, Hake & Hornseth, 1951; Humphreys, 1939). In the mid-1950s, the work in verbal learning and the work on economic models of behavior came together to form the basis of the modern study of judgment and decision making (Atkinson, 1961; 1962). A small set of important achievements was involved.

First, the expected utility hypothesis was developed formally in a variety of ways (Edwards, 1962; Fishburn, 1988; Savage, 1954). Second, theories of learning had begun to evolve into more formal accounts, particularly in the theoretical work of William K. Estes (1950; Estes & Burke, 1953). This work allowed an account of basic learning and memory to be easily adapted to the problem of making choices based on prior learning about a situation (Estes, 1954a). Third, general and systematic models of choice were proposed and developed.

Possibly the most influential of these general and systematic models of choice has come to be known as *Luce's choice axiom* (Luce, 1959, Axiom 1). Although Luce is generally and accurately credited with some of the fundamental developments of this approach, a two-alternative version had been proposed by other authors (Bradley & Terry, 1952) almost a decade before Luce's work appeared. Luce's model rigorously related the probability of observing one of a set of responses to the strength of association between the situation and that response, relative to the strengths all the other relevant responses. To show this relationship in a somewhat more precise form, we can let R represent a set of possible response choices in any situation and let $v(x)$ represent the associative strength of any one of the responses in that set. Then, according to the choice axiom, the probability (P) of observing response a is

$$P_R(a) = \frac{v(a)}{\sum_{b \in R} v(b)}$$

R. Duncan Luce
R. Duncan Luce is responsible for one of the most widely applied formalizations of a decision rule and has also made important contributions to the application of mathematical models to psychological processes.

For example, let us assume that we can choose among three brands of jeans. Because of a variety of factors (what our friends wear, what brand fits us best, etc.), a particular "strength" is associated with our preference for each brand. We can call these strengths $v(1)$, $v(2)$, and $v(3)$. Now, if we specify these strengths, we can predict the probability of choosing a particular brand. For example, the probability of choosing Brand 2 is:

$$P_R(2) = \frac{v(2)}{v(1) + v(2) + v(3)}$$

This formulation and some related ideas have seen extensive application in an impressive number of areas in psychology (Luce, 1977). These include studies of confusability of response alternatives (Townsend & Landon, 1982; Yellott & Curnow, 1967), studies of response biases (Luce, 1963), models of learning and choice in animals (Fantino & Navarick, 1974), and models of perception and memory in humans (Massaro, 1987).

Heuristics   As suggested earlier, the coming together of the expected utility hypothesis, learning theory, and models of choice laid the foundation for the modern study of decision making. It also laid the foundation for exploration of a wide variety of intriguing and related concepts, such as the study of making risky choices (Myers & Katz, 1962; Myers & Sadler, 1960; Myers, Suydam & Gambino, 1965) and theoretical accounts of regret (Loomes & Sugden, 1982, 1987). In addition, the flowering of research in decision making began to reveal the systematic ways in which people make incorrect decisions.

Possibly the most influential work done in this area was done by Kahneman and Tversky (Kahneman & Tversky, 1973; Tversky & Kahneman, 1974), who drew attention to the most general ways in which we make decisions. These "rules of thumb," or **heuristics,** are reasonably efficient and intuitive. They also can and frequently do lead to errors.

The first of the heuristics described by Kahneman and Tversky is the **representativeness heuristic.** Consider this question: Is Bob a member of a fraternity? People are using the representativeness heuristic when their answer to this question is influenced by the degree to which the item (Bob, in this case) has characteristics that are generally representative of the class (fraternities, in this case). For example, if we are told that Bob likes group activities, owns a nice sports car, has great hair and clothes, and drinks to excess on weekends, we might (depending on where we go to school) be more likely to say that Bob is a member of a fraternity than to say that he is president of the math club.

Use of the representativeness heuristic can lead to rather predictable errors of several types. First, the degree to which Bob represents the stereotypic fraternity member is not at all dependent on the relative frequency (or base rate) of fraternity members in the community. This is referred to as an *insensitivity to base rates.* Suppose we decide that Bob is a fraternity member because he "fits the mold" for fraternity members. What if, in fact, there are very few fraternity members on our campus? Our decision has not taken account of this fact, even though having fewer fraternity members on campus should lower the likelihood of any one person's being a fraternity member.

Second, Bob's representativeness as a fraternity member is not at all dependent on the size of the sample from which Bob is drawn (e.g., whether Bob's school is large or small), even though objective probability is dependent on sample size. This is referred to as an *insensitivity to sample size.*

The third way in which the representativeness heuristic can lead to errors involves a *misconception of chance* (or probability). We make this error when we decide Bob is more likely to belong to a particular class (fraternity member) than someone else—say, Bif—because Bob has more of the characteristics associated with that class than Bif, even though Bob and Bif have the same objective probability of being fraternity members.

The fourth way in which the representativeness heuristic can lead to errors has to do with the reliability of the source of the information about the item. Basically, the error occurs when it does not matter if information (for example, a description of Bob as having characteristics representative of fraternity members) comes from a reliable source or an unreliable source. This is referred to as the *illusion of validity.*

The second heuristic considered by Kahneman and Tversky concerns the ease of remembering related information about the class. This ease of remembering is referred to as availability. The **availability heuristic** captures the idea that information that is easily remembered appears to be more available for use than information that is difficult to re-

Daniel Kahneman and Amos Tversky
Daniel Kahneman (top) and Amos Tversky may be best known for their study of errors in judgment that result from the use of heuristics. Their work has seen application in a wide number of areas outside of traditional cognitive psychology.

EXPERIMENT 12:   The Power of Familiarity and Availability

This experiment is similar to one reported by Tversky and Kahneman (1973). The experiment is quite simple. Get together a group of about 10 friends to act as subjects. Give each a blank slip of paper and a pen or pencil. Tell the subjects that you are going to read a list of names to them and that, after you have read the list, you are going to ask them to do some simple math. Do not tell them that you will be testing their memory for any aspect of the list or that you will be asking them to make judgments based on the list. (These types of instructions could affect the types of results you get. Can you say why?)

After you have given the instructions, read the following list of names, at a rate of about one name every two to three seconds. (You may want to practice pacing yourself ahead of time.)

Harriet Beecher Stowe	Edith Wharton	Claude Elie
Whoopi Goldberg	Jeffrey Anastasi	Jane Austen
John Dickson Carr	Julie Andrews	Steve Luenberger
Hillary Clinton	Agatha Christie	Henry Bugl
Thomas Fikes	David Rowland	Emily Brontë
Cybil Shepherd	Maxine Hong Kingston	Michael Smithson
Jason Blackwell	Virginia Woolf	Eric Reichle
Edward Lytton	Randy Marshall	Alice Walker
Martha Stewart	Judy Blume	Brian Hooker
Michael Drayton	Aaron Houston	

After you have finished reading the list, ask your subjects to estimate whether the list included more women or more men. If it is possible to test your subjects individually or in small groups, ask half of the subjects "Did the list include more women or more men?" and ask the other half "Did the list include more men or more women?" (Why would you want to do this?) Do not allow your subjects to answer "about the same." When you have finished, determine the percentage for each response.

What were your results? If fame can lead to greater familiarity, and your subjects were using the availability heuristic, what would you have predicted the results would be?

member. People use this heuristic when their judgment about something is influenced by the ease with which they can remember information about it.

The problem with the availability heuristic becomes apparent with a little thought (and possibly a look back to Chapters 6–8, on memory). Although it is true that the frequency of seeing something affects the ability to remember it, it is also true that a number of other factors (e.g., the time spent studying an item and the distinctiveness or imageability of an item) that have nothing to do with frequency can also make the item easier to remember. Experiment 12 demonstrates the power of and problems with the availability heuristic.

The third heuristic considered by Kahneman and Tversky has to do with the task of making a numerical estimate of something, such as estimating a probability. For example, instead of asking you *if* Bob is a member of a fraternity, we might ask you to estimate the *probability* that Bob is a member of a fraternity. If we were to provide some prior estimate of that probability, we would find that your estimate would be highly biased toward that initial estimate, even if it was wrong. In essence, you would show very little tendency to adjust the initial estimate toward a more correct one. This is referred to as **anchoring,** since the initial value we provided serves as an anchor value holding you in place as an anchor holds a boat. The difficulty people experience in moving away from the anchor is referred to as a *difficulty in adjustment.*

Kahneman and Tverksy's analysis of representativeness, availability, and anchoring has proved to be very influential, in psychology and in other fields. Indeed, it is sometimes seen as the prototypical work in judgment and decision making. Part of this may be due to the fact that their effort was based on solid logic, scholarship, and experimental data. However, part may be due to use of the availability heuristic! Specifically, Kahneman and Tversky's work is among the most often cited in its domain and shows up in most textbooks. However, a great deal of research occurred before and has occurred since, including much by Kahneman and Tversky.

Section Summary: A Little History

Although some scientists have suggested that the scientific study of judgment and decision making began with the emergence of cognitive psychology, a great deal of important research on concepts critical to the understanding of judgment and decision making was done in the early and middle parts of the twentieth century. This work, like the research that followed, can be understood in terms of the type of determinism (hard, soft, or probabilistic) that is assumed and whether the theory is static or dynamic. Some of the earliest work related to judgment and decision making investigated aspects of motivation. This work led to investigations into the physiological source of motivation, with the RAS once thought to be a likely candidate. It also led to investigations of approach and avoidance as expressions of different aspects of motivation. With the emergence of cognitive psychology as a discipline, scientists began to ask questions about judgment and decision making in terms of information and the processes that operate on that information. Kahneman and Tversky's research on heuristics is a prominent example of work describing how such processes can operate on information incorrectly.

CONTEMPORARY ISSUES IN JUDGMENT AND DECISION MAKING

Current research on judgment and decision making is both intriguing and influential. As we review it, keep in mind the concepts of subjective expected utility and the use of decision rules, discussed in the previous section, for they continue to play important roles in modern theories.

Utility Theory and the Principle of Rationality

Let us return to a question we asked at the beginning of the chapter—the question "Why?" One way to answer this question is to apply basic logic to the situation being considered and define what, objectively, would be the best outcome. If we were able to do that, then our answer to the question "Why?" could make reference to the logic of the analysis. A particular choice should or will be made because, logically, it is the best or optimal choice.

Another way of saying this is that the choice indicated by the logical analysis is the rational choice.

Rationality and Cognition

Logical analysis and rationality are at the heart of utility theory (Savage, 1954). Underlying utility theory is the basic assumption that if we can ascertain the probabilities and subjective values people relate to various choices, we can predict those choices. This is called the **principle of rationality** (Anderson, 1990; Newell, 1982): If we understand the objective and subjective knowledge that is used to make a judgment or a decision, and we know the particular goals or desires of the person making the judgment or decision, then we can accurately predict the outcome. The principle of rationality as it has traditionally been used in utility theory says that a decision maker should choose the alternative that will maximize the expected value of the outcome.

The eminent scientist and philosopher Herbert Simon called this basic approach an *Olympian view* of rationality, one that pictures a "heroic man making comprehensive choices in an integrated world" (Simon, 1986, p. 112). According to Simon, the principle of rationality in utility theory sees the decision maker as someone who "understands the range of alternative choices open to him, not only at the moment but over the panorama of the future" (p. 100).

But as Simon explains in the quotation that opens this chapter, most decision makers are much less godlike than required by this description. Simon finds two other fundamental problems with rationality as it is defined by utility theory.

First, many applications of utility theory fail to explain how a particular utility function is learned. However, as we noted in the discussion of semantic networks in Chapter 8, the failure to address how important concepts or knowledge are learned has been a consistent problem for many theories of cognition. Second, because utility theory assumes the ability to evaluate all alternative choices, the human computational requirements are enormous. In practice, this problem is solved by restricting the space of the problem under consideration to something small and clearly delimited. But as Simon notes, this is far from what each of us must normally deal with as a decision maker.

An alternative to this Olympian view of rationality is one that Simon formally proposed (Simon, 1956; 1972) not long after the touchstone work on utility theory was published (Savage, 1954). This view is called **bounded rationality.** The idea here is that the world includes a multitude of variables that *might* be important with respect to a particular decision or judgment but that some of the variables can be disregarded. For example, your decision about where to buy your jeans could conceivably be influenced by the world supply of crude oil (particularly as it might affect the cost of a gallon of gas), but most of the time you can disregard this information.

An obvious implication of the idea that the environment for decision making can be analyzed in terms of such simplified systems is that human computational requirements can be drastically reduced. If some things can be disregarded or ignored, then the computational problems associated with the ideal view of utility theory (specifically, the need to consider all possible alternatives) are quickly solved.

Applying the Notion of Bounded Rationality

One issue raised by the consideration of bounded rationality is the distinction between **globally optimal solutions** and **locally optimal solutions.** A globally optimal solution is the best of all possible solutions. A locally optimal solution is the best of a small set of possible solutions defined by (for example) excluding solutions based on dimensions that can be ignored. For example, the globally optimal solution to the problem of needing to buy a pair of jeans might fac-

Herbert Simon
Herbert Simon is one of the most influential thinkers in cognitive psychology, and his theoretical and empirical work has influenced numerous disciplines.

tor in the cost of the gas required to get to the store, while a locally optimal solution might not.

The distinction between globally and locally optimal solutions has been of some importance in work on evolution; many scientists have come to view evolution as providing locally optimal solutions (Dupre, 1987). Similarly, a recent account of cognition by Anderson (1990) presents a view of rationality that views cognition as providing locally optimal solutions. This view has been applied to a range of cognitive tasks. As it applies to judgment and decision making, it relies on an analysis of the decision-making task in terms of the probability that a particular action will lead to an intended or desired outcome or goal. Each possible action, and each step required by that action, is associated with a cost, such as the time, energy, or money required. Finally, reaching the intended or desired outcome is associated with a certain gain.

According to Anderson's theory, the alternatives in a decision-making task should be ordered according to the ratio P_i/C_i, where P_i indicates the probability of reaching the desired outcome using alternative i and C_i indicates the cost of using alternative i. Rationality in this view is defined by choosing the alternative that has the *highest* probability of achieving the desired outcome with the *lowest* cost. Since the value, or gain, associated with the desired outcome, G, must be evaluated with respect to the probability that an action will lead to that outcome, no action decision should be made in which the cost is greater than the gain multiplied by the probability of that gain, or $C_i > P_i G$.

The specific applications and tests of Anderson's theory have been reasonably limited, but the general approach has been successful and has received a good deal of attention (J. R. Anderson, 1991). In addition, this approach has the enviable quality of being a *general* theory of cognition that has been applied to *specific* problems in judgment and decision making. In contrast, all of the approaches we present later in this chapter are theories specific to judgment and decision making, though they may have some implications for other aspects of cognition.

Decision Analyses

Let us go back again to the example we started with: buying jeans. Suppose one of your friends has just bought some jeans and you want to discover how he came to choose the particular brand and store. To do this, you could try to analyze the relationships between your observations (the specific outcome of the jeans-buying episode) and the unobservable events you are interested in (such as your friend's preferences for different jeans and stores). Alternatively, suppose your friend is planning to buy some jeans, and you want to know what kind he will buy and where he will buy them. In this case, you could come up with an analysis of the set of choices that your friend will have to make.

These two scenarios characterize two broad approaches that have been taken in the contemporary study of judgment and decision making. The first of these is referred to as an *a posteriori* approach, since it relies on an analysis done after the fact. It has been applied with some success to understanding social judgments (Hammond et al., 1986), but it has had much less impact in cognitive psychology. Consequently, we do not discuss it here.

The second approach is referred to as an *a priori* approach, since it is done ahead of the event as an attempt to predict the outcome. This approach has been used with great success in analyzing and understanding basic aspects of decision making, and variants of the approach have been used to understand a variety of other issues in cognition, such as aspects of memory retrieval (Batchelder & Riefer, 1990; Riefer & Batchelder, 1988; Schweickert, 1993).

An *a Priori* Analysis   To show how this approach works, and how it makes use of ideas from utility theory, we will simplify the jeans-buying situation and perform an *a priori* analysis to see if we can predict the outcome. For this simple situation, we will assume that your friend is faced simply with making the decision whether or not to buy jeans. Whether he decides to buy the jeans or not, some probability exists that his level of social approval will not change. If he does decide to buy the jeans, his social approval may go up. If he decides not to buy the jeans, however, his social approval may go down (e.g., people may start to judge him to be a slob).

In deciding how this decision will be made, we can use a tool that is used often in decision analyses: a **decision tree.** The decision tree offers a way of analyzing a situation that considers the possible outcomes and the paths that lead to those outcomes. The decision tree for the situation we are considering is presented in Figure 12.3. In analyzing the decision tree, we work from left to right. At the beginning is the basic decision: to buy jeans or

FIGURE 12.3   **A Decision Tree**   This decision tree shows an analysis of the decision whether or not to buy a pair of jeans (represented by the letter *b*). The term *p* indicates the objective probability of an outcome, and *v* represents the subjective value of that outcome.

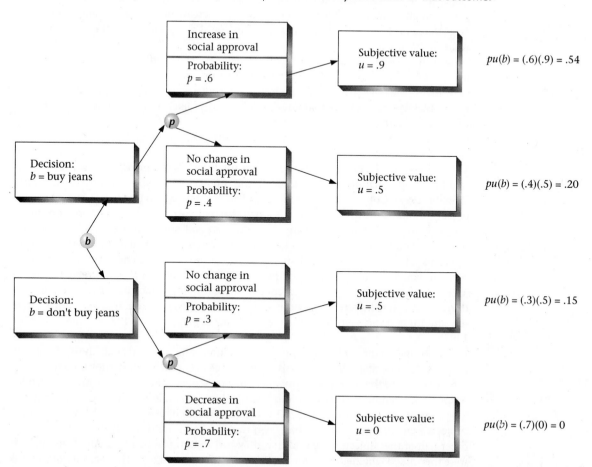

not to buy jeans. Each of these outcomes represents one of the two initial branches of the tree. The node from which these branches emanate is called a *decision node,* referring to the fact that this is the point of decision.

At the end of each of the two initial branches are two possible outcomes. These are represented as additional branches emanating from what are called *probability nodes,* since they summarize the probabilities of the possible outcomes. For example, the decision to buy jeans leads to a probability node that branches to the outcomes "increase in social acceptance" and "no change in social acceptance." The probabilities associated with these outcomes are .6 and .4, respectively. (These values are arbitrary, and we include them only as examples of how the approach is used.)

As you may recall from earlier in the chapter, more than 250 years ago, philosophers noted that decision making does not always follow objective probabilities. Something else was needed to understand how decisions are made. That something was the notion of subjective utility, and it is usually represented in decision trees by the addition of what are called *subjective values* to the outcomes—usually, but not always, given on a scale running from 0 to 1. In our simple situation, we assign the outcome "increase in social acceptance" a subjective value of .9, the outcome "no change in social acceptance" a subjective value of .5, and the outcome "decrease in social acceptance" a subjective value of 0. (Again, these values are for illustration only.) Roughly speaking, what this means is that your friend places a high subjective value on experiencing an increase in social acceptance, only an average value on experiencing no change in his social acceptance, and the lowest possible value on having his social acceptance drop.

With these probabilities and subjective values, we can predict the subjective expected utilities of the outcomes. As discussed earlier in the chapter, this is commonly done by multiplying the objective probability by the subjective value. We have done this for you in Figure 12.3. We can now see that your friend will most likely decide to buy the jeans, since the total subjective expected utility for that decision (.54 + .20 = .74) is much greater than the total subjective expected utility for the alternative (.15 + 0 = .15).

The Sure-Thing Principle   Scientists have used the basic approach of decision analysis to understand violations of what is called the sure-thing principle (Savage, 1954; Tversky & Shafir, 1992). Consider a choice like this: You must choose to buy or not buy a new pair of jeans tomorrow, since that is the last day they will be on sale. In addition, your financial aid check should be arriving any day, which is good, since you are running a little low on cash. If you know that your check will arrive tomorrow, you will definitely prefer to buy the jeans rather than not buy them. But if you know that your check will not arrive tomorrow, you will still prefer to buy the jeans. So, logically, you should prefer to buy the jeans whether you know that your check will be arriving tomorrow or not. It is a "sure thing" that you will prefer to buy the jeans. Interestingly, however, frequent violations of the sure-thing principle can be observed (Tversky & Kahnemann, 1986; Tversky & Shafir, 1992).

Tversky and Shafir (1992) have presented an interesting theoretical analysis of these violations. To understand their analysis, consider the experimental task they used to explore the violations of the sure-thing principle. They presented their subjects with a written description of a gambling situation (coin tossing). In this gamble, subjects were told they had a 50 percent chance of winning $200 and a 50 percent chance of losing $100. Half of the subjects were told that the coin had been tossed a first time and that they had won. The other half of the subjects were told that they had lost on this first toss. All of the subjects were then asked whether they would go ahead with a second toss. The majority of subjects in both conditions (69 percent of the subjects who "won" on the first toss and 59 percent of the subjects who "lost") chose to go ahead with the second toss.

Tversky and Shafir then ran the experiment in a slightly different way. They told this same group of subjects about the coin toss, with the same odds and same gains and losses as before. However, they now asked these subjects to imagine that the result of the first coin toss would not be revealed to them *until* they made a decision about going ahead with a second coin toss. In the earlier version, remember, the majority of these subjects had preferred to go ahead with the second toss, whether they had won or lost. So according to the sure-thing principle, lacking knowledge of the result of the first coin toss should not change the preferred choice of these subjects; they should still prefer to go ahead with the second gamble.

The results, however, showed a rather clear violation of the sure-thing principle. The majority of subjects (64 percent) preferred to *not* go ahead with the second gamble. Tversky and Shafir explained this violation using what they call a *value function*, or $v(x)$ (see Figure 12.4). The value function relates the objective gain or loss to the subjective gain or loss using a nonlinear function (a power function) that is different for gains and losses: Specifically, $v(x) = x^{.65}$ when $x \geq 0$, and $v(x) = x^{.75}$ when $x < 0$. The difference in the function for gains and losses corresponds to the empirical observation that the subjective value of larger gains grows faster than the subjective value of larger losses. The value function is used in the same way as subjective values: the objective probability is multiplied by the value function.

To understand why we observe violations of the sure-thing principle, we can use this value function to analyze the decisions of the subjects when they knew the outcome of the first toss and when (later) they did not. We start with the situation in which the subjects

---

FIGURE 12.4   **A Value Function for a Simple Gambling Situation**   Tversky and Shafir (1992) used the two-part power function $v(x) = x^{65}$, $x \geq 0$ and $v(x) = -(-x)^{.75}$, $x < 0$ to relate the subjective value of a gain or loss (the y-axis) to the actual value of the gain or loss (the x-axis).

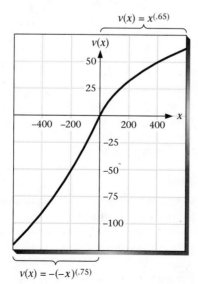

knew that they had won the first toss. In this case, they had already won $200 and were now faced with the possibility of either not taking the second toss and walking away with $200 or taking the second toss and ending up with a total of either $400 (if they won on the second toss) or $100 (if they lost). According to the gain portion of the value function, the value of stopping and keeping the $200 from the first toss would be:

$$P(x)v(x) = (1.00)\left(200^{(.65)} \right) = 31.31$$

$P(x)$ is 1.00 in this case because the $200 is guaranteed. In contrast, the value of going ahead with the second toss would be:

$$\Sigma P(x)v(x) = (.50)\left(100^{(.65)} \right) + (.50)\left(400^{(.65)} \right) = 69.08$$

This is because the probability of each outcome is .50 (assuming the coin is fair).

So the value of taking the second toss is much higher than the value of sticking with the outcome of the first toss for subjects who won the first toss. How about the subjects who lost on the first toss? These subjects were faced with choosing between a sure loss of $100 (the results of the first toss) and the possibility of either winning $100 or losing $200. Using the value function, we see that the value of sticking with the results of the first toss would be:

$$P(x)v(x) = (1.00)\left[-\left(100^{(.75)} \right) \right] = -31.62$$

And the value of going ahead with the second toss would be:

$$\Sigma P(x)v(x) = (.50)\left[\left(100^{(.75)} \right) \right] + (.50)\left[-\left(200^{(.75)} \right) \right] = -10.78$$

So again the value of going with the second toss is higher than the value of sticking with the outcome of the first toss.

What about the subjects who did not know the outcome of the first toss? According to Tversky and Shafir, subjects use what they know: That is, in this condition, subjects simply assume that they have not gained or lost anything yet. It is as if the first toss really has not happened. So for the first toss, the subjective value is 0, while for the second toss the subjective value is:

$$SP(x)v(x) = (.50)\left(200^{(.65)} \right) + (.50)\left[-\left(100^{(.75)} \right) \right] = -.16$$

Although the value is small, it is negative (less than 0), meaning that subjects should prefer to *not* take the second toss. In essence, then, by specifying the function that translates the actual gains and losses into subjective values, then using these subjective values with the objective probabilities (by way of the decision-tree approach), Tversky and Shafir demonstrated that observed violations of a logical principle can be predicted.

Decision Making and Expertise

As convenient as it is to discuss decision making in simple situations, most important decisions are more complex than the decision whether or not to buy jeans. Some of the most important decisions that affect your life are made by people who have a great deal of *expertise*—specific knowledge or highly developed and specific skills—people like your doctor, your dentist, and your mechanic. Each of these individuals has both training and experience that are specific to one area (medicine, dentistry, your car), and each is faced with making decisions that can and do have major effects on your life and the lives of others.

The study of decision making by experts has relied on some of the tools that have been used to explore the processes involved in decision making by nonexperts, such as the decision trees discussed in the previous section (Kleinmuntz, 1968). This work pointed out that one of the greatest challenges facing an expert in making a decision is the need to organize information, including the need to exclude potentially irrelevant information from consideration (Gaeth & Shanteau, 1984).

Experts organize and relate all the details they are able to consider about a task in ways that are generally consistent, that show a high degree of relationship to the critical aspects of the task, and that show a general insensitivity to the types of heuristic errors, or biases, that we talked about earlier. These three characteristics of task organization are often referred to as inter- and intra-expert reliability, construct or task validity, and insensitivity to judgmental bias (Einhorn, 1974), respectively.

Once the information is organized, the expert is faced with the challenge of finding an appropriate way to combine the organized information in order to yield the best outcome (Sawyer, 1966; Slovic & Lichtenstein, 1971). This is often referred to as a challenge of weighting and combining different sources of information about a task (Einhorn, 1974; Slovic & Lichtenstein, 1971). Much of the study of these aspects of decision making by experts has used physicians or clinicians (e.g., clinical psychologists) as expert subjects (Joseph & Patel, 1990; Kleinmuntz, 1984; Patel & Groen, 1991).

One way of describing how expert decision makers weight and combine the information involves a distinction between *forward and backward reasoning.* To understand this distinction, consider a situation in which you might need to relate a set of observations and come up with a plan of action on the basis of those observations. This is something like what a physician needs to do when making a diagnosis. In this situation, a number of possible observations can be made, such as the patient's blood pressure, body temperature, and so on. A number of hypotheses about the patient's condition are also possible; for example, the patient might be suffering from a heart condition or simply be experiencing pain from intestinal gas.

In Figure 12.5, we show two possible ways to work with these observations and hypotheses. Figure 12.5a shows how we can move from the observations (the symptoms) to the hypotheses (the diagnosis). This type of reasoning is called **forward reasoning,** and it is generally related to inductive reasoning, which moves from the specific to the general. In contrast, we can begin with a plausible hypothesis and move toward the specific observations, as in Figure 12.5b. This is referred to as **backward reasoning,** and it is generally related to deductive reasoning, which moves from the general to the specific.

Which type of reasoning do you think experts rely on, and which type do you think novices rely on? To answer this question, Patel, Groen, and Arocha (1990; Patel & Groen, 1991) presented cardiologists and endocrinologists (experts in two different areas of medicine) with case descriptions of individuals showing signs of either cardiac or endocrine problems. After having each subject read one of the two case descriptions, the researchers then asked the subjects to think aloud and describe the information they used and the manner in which they used that information to arrive at a diagnosis.

One interesting observation was that the cardiologists and endocrinologists were equally able to *recall* the information about the two types of cases. That is, there was no apparent advantage in recall for the endocrinologists when working with the endocrine case study or for the cardiologists when working with the cardiology case study. But there was a difference in terms of how that information was processed.

FIGURE 12.5   **Reasoning with Observations and Hypotheses**   For a given situation (e.g., a situation in which a physician needs to make a diagnosis), it is possible to come up with a set of observations and a set of hypotheses relating to those observations. (a) Forward reasoning works by moving from the observations to the hypotheses (e.g., from the symptoms to the diagnosis). (b) Backward reasoning works by moving from the possible hypotheses to the observations (e.g., from a possible diagnosis to the supporting symptoms).

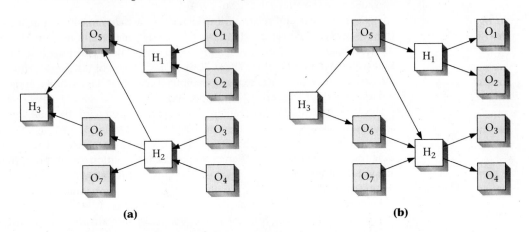

(a)   (b)

In particular, all of the physicians who made accurate diagnoses used forward reasoning, while none of the physicians who made inaccurate diagnoses used this form of reasoning. And in terms of accuracy of diagnosis, there was an effect of expertise, with the endocrinologists providing more accurate diagnoses on the endocrine case and the cardiologists providing more accurate diagnoses on the cardiology problem.

An example of how forward reasoning is used in this task is presented in Figure 12.6, which traces the path that an endocrinologist took to arrive at the accurate diagnosis of an endocrinological problem. One of the striking things about this representation is that the expert appears to move quickly from a situation in which a great deal of information needs to be organized and related to a much simpler situation involving the need to relate a much smaller number of more general observations and hypotheses. This corresponds to Patel and Groen's (1991) observation that experts quickly arrive at a reasonably accurate diagnosis and then spend time evaluating the evidence to confirm the hypothesis and relate additional observations about the patient's condition.

In contrast to those who made accurate diagnoses, those who made inaccurate diagnoses relied on backward reasoning. An example of how backward reasoning was used by an endocrinologist working with a cardiological problem is presented in Figure 12.7. This figure provides a stark contrast to Figure 12.6. Instead of rapid simplification, here we see an actual *increase* in the information that the physician has to consider (moving from left to right in the figure)—an increase in complexity rather than an increase in simplicity. This is consistent with Patel and Groen's (1991) observation that, for the nonexperts, the task seemed to increase in difficulty as time progressed, with subjects gradually becoming *less able* to discriminate among and eliminate competing hypotheses.

Another way in which expertise can influence judgments and decisions has to do with how judgment and decision-making performance change under stress. The ways in which people respond to different levels of stress in critical environments is of great importance.

An Example of Forward Reasoning   This schematic representation shows how forward reasoning was used by an expert (an endocrinologist) to arrive at an accurate diagnosis in a case of an endocrinological disorder.

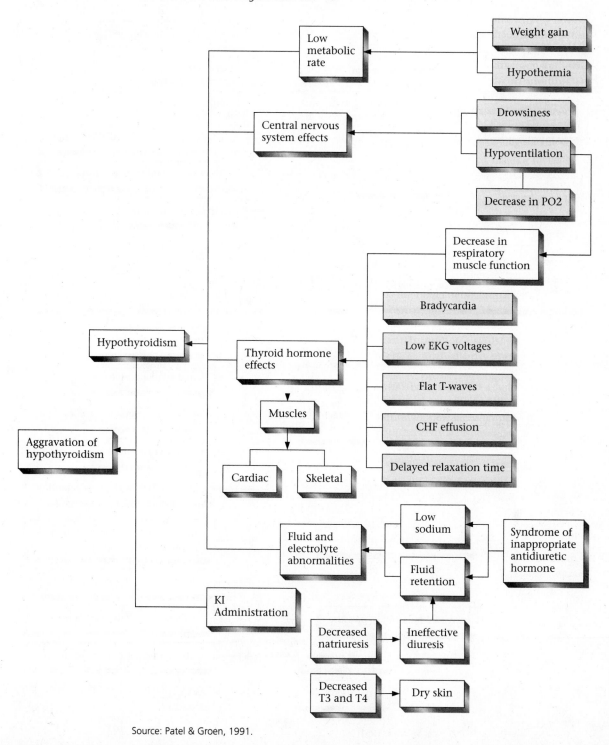

Source: Patel & Groen, 1991.

FIGURE 12.7 **An Example of Backward Reasoning** This schematic representation shows how backward reasoning was used by a nonexpert (an endocrinologist) to arrive at an inaccurate diagnosis in a case of a cardiological disorder.

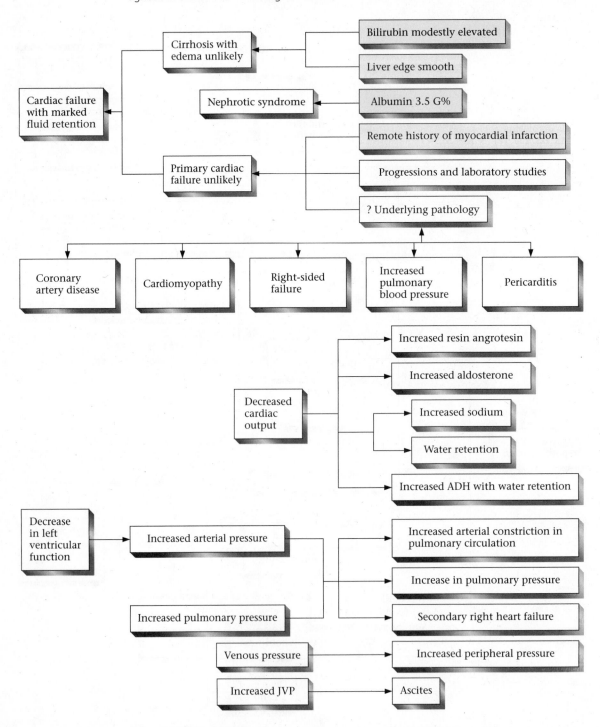

Source: Patel & Groen, 1991.

Consider, for example, the types of decisions that an airline pilot might have to make in bad weather or when engine problems arise. In addition, as we noted in our earlier discussion of the RAS and motivation, investigation of the influence of stress on performance has a long history. Research Report 12 describes some interesting current work aimed at finding out how decision-making performance can be improved in high-stress situations.

Cognitive Algebra

Take a look back at Figure 12.3, the decision tree representing how your friend might arrive at the decision to buy a pair of jeans. In that example, and in the work we described relating to subjective expected utility, we evaluated the possible outcomes and paths to those outcomes by multiplying the probability that a particular outcome would occur by the subjective value of that outcome. In a general sense, we tried to capture the cognitive processes in an algebraic formula.

This is similar in a sense to relating the mileage (m) we get from a car to our normal or average speed (s) on the freeway. We could express the mileage as a *function* of our speed in this way:

$$m = f(s)$$

For our purposes, f is some unspecified function. In the same general way, we can say that a decision (d) is some function of the subjective probability (p) and the subjective value (v):

$$d = f(p, v)$$

In the examples we presented earlier, the specific function involved multiplication, but that is unimportant for the moment. The idea is that this is basically algebra: We are using concepts like variables, functions, and basic mathematical operations (such as multiplication) to describe what we believe to be going on in some cognitive process.

As noted in preceding chapters, the use of mathematics to describe phenomena in psychology has a fairly long history (Townsend & Kadlec, 1990). And as our discussion of subjective expected utility points out, mathematical descriptions have been crucial in understanding judgment and decision making. One approach to studying aspects of judgment and decision making that makes explicit use of ideas from algebra is an approach, developed by Norman H. Anderson (1981, 1991), called *cognitive algebra*.

Multiple Determinants of Judgment and Decision Making   The cognitive algebra approach relies on four basic assumptions. First, it assumes that any reasonably complicated cognitive process is determined by a number of variables. Although this might seem obvious to you, it is important to understand that *stating* that cognitive processes are multiply determined is tantamount to saying that we cannot capture the important aspects of cognition by focusing only on one thing. For example, we cannot capture the way people make decisions by focusing only on the probabilities of certain kinds of outcomes—we must also consider the value people place on those outcomes.

Since cognitive processes are assumed to be determined by multiple variables, then (by assumption) cognitive processes like decision making must involve the combination (or integration) of information represented by variables. To demonstrate, we will again simplify the situation for the moment. Let us assume that we want to understand what influences people when they make decisions about buying jeans. We will assume that two factors, or sources of information, are important: the brand of jeans and the store where the jeans are bought. Let us now assume that we can represent this situation as a matrix in

RESEARCH REPORT 12:   Aiding Decision Making in High-Stress Situations

Deciding when, if, and where to buy a pair of jeans is not terribly stressful, even at the worst mall. Some of the most challenging situations for decision making are environments in which critical aspects are changing, sometimes very quickly. In these types of situations, people—even experts—tend to rely on simple pattern-recognition strategies, or heuristics (Hammond, 1988; Kirlik, Miller & Jagacinski, 1993). Yet these strategies do not always support optimal performance. In fact, people can actually focus on the *wrong* type of information (Fisk & Jones, 1992).

If people tend to focus on simpler information, including simpler rules for performance, when the stress of a situation increases, and if people are likely to focus on the wrong type of information when that happens, then perhaps performance in high-stress situations can be improved by strategically "highlighting" the right type of information. Kirlik, Walker, Fisk, and Nagel (1996) examined this possibility by simulating a particularly stressful situation: decision making on a battlefield.

Kirlik and colleagues presented subjects with a simulated task called the extended joint surveillance and target attack radar system (EJSTARS). In this task, subjects monitor a map (presented on a video screen) on which positions of friendly and potentially threatening vehicles are plotted. The map is dynamic in that it changes moment by moment, with vehicles changing position and new vehicles appearing at different rates. Subjects need to gain information about each of the vehicles; and if an enemy vehicle gets too close to a friendly location, subjects must take some kind of offensive or defensive action. Subjects are awarded points for keeping their locations and vehicles safe and lose points if an enemy vehicle destroys one of their vehicles or locations.

One source of stress in this task is the rate at which new vehicles appear on the map. When this happens, the amount of information that subjects have to keep track of increases, along with potential risk if subjects do not have complete information about the new vehicles. Kirlik and colleagues analyzed this situation and came up with a way to highlight critical information by adding four types of graphical elements to the map. For example, constantly changing colors were used to indicate the directions in which vehicles could and could not move, a circle indicating the range of each vehicle's weapons was added and updated as the vehicle moved, and bar graphs indicating the relative importance of various locations and vehicles were added.

One group of subjects worked with the system containing this new information, and one group worked with the system without the additions. Subjects became expert users of the system across 16 days of practice. On the seventeenth day, the researchers increased the stress by *doubling* the number of vehicles on the map. Then, to make things even more interesting, on the nineteenth day, the group that had been working with the system containing the new information was required to work with the system with the new information *removed*. The results of this study are presented in Figure 12A.

FIGURE 12A   **Performance on EJSTARS**   The graph tracks performance on a simulated battlefield decision-making task across 20 days of practice.
Adding specific types of simple visual information improved performance and helped subjects perform in high-stress situations (when the
number of vehicles was doubled).

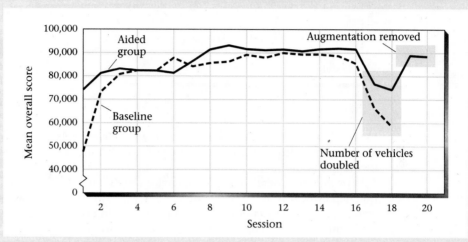

Source: Kirlik et al., 1996.

Three findings seem to be important. First, adding the visual information improved the learning of the task. Second, when the stress was increased, subjects with the additional information did not suffer as many losses. Finally, the performance of those subjects who became task
experts using the additional information did not suffer when it was taken away after they had
become experts. What this seems to indicate is that cues selected to be strategically informative in high-stress situations can have numerous benefits. The key is to be able to identify what
those cues are, and that is the focus of ongoing research (Kirlik, 1995).

which the rows (Factor A) represent the possible brands of jeans and the columns (Factor
B) represent the possible stores where those jeans can be purchased. Figure 12.8 shows
what this matrix would look like for an arbitrary set of brands and an arbitrary set of stores.

Now assume that we recruit a group of subjects and ask each of them to decide whether
they would buy a particular brand of jeans at a particular store. For each of the subjects,
the test stimulus is a pair of stimulus values (representing a specific jeans-store combination) from the matrix in Figure 12.8. One member of that pair of values is the particular
brand of jeans; this corresponds to one of the rows in the matrix, and we can refer to it as
S_{Ai}, for the specific stimulus derived for Factor A at level i. For example, in the matrix in
Figure 12.8, Brand 3 is stimulus S_{A3}.

The other member of the pair of values is the particular store where the jeans can be purchased. This corresponds to one of the columns in the matrix, and we can refer to it as S_{Bj},

A Matrix for Two Factors   We can represent the two sources of information for the simplified jeans-buying decision as a matrix in which the rows represent brands (Factor A) and the columns represent stores (Factor B).

Factor B

	Store 1	Store 2	Store 3
Brand 1	(S_{A1}, S_{B1})	(S_{A1}, S_{B2})	(S_{A1}, S_{B3})
Brand 2	(S_{A2}, S_{B1})	(S_{A2}, S_{B2})	(S_{A2}, S_{B3})
Brand 3	(S_{A3}, S_{B1})	(S_{A3}, S_{B2})	(S_{A3}, S_{B3})

Factor A

for the stimulus derived for Factor B at level j. In our example matrix, Store 2 is stimulus S_{B2}. Thus, if we were to ask one of our subjects whether they would buy Brand 3 at Store 2, the stimulus pair that we would be considering would be (S_{A3}, S_{B2}).

As we said, the cognitive algebra approach assumes that these two sources of information, represented in our example by the pair (S_{A3}, S_{B2}), are somehow combined or integrated when the subject processes the information in making a decision. More precisely, the cognitive algebra approach assumes that the observable values of these stimuli (the specific brands and stores) are transformed into unobservable (internal) psychological values, which are then combined to allow for the selection or determination of some response choice. This response choice is also an unobservable (internal) psychological representation, and it leads to an observable behavior (e.g., buying a particular brand of jeans at one of the stores). This is the approach used in the fuzzy logical model of perception discussed in Chapter 10.

Figure 12.9 schematically represents these aspects of the cognitive algebra approach. The box in this figure separates what is observable (things outside the box) from what is unobservable (things inside the box). Each observable stimulus (S) is transformed into an internal value (s); these values are then combined in some algebraic way to lead to some internal response (r) to guide some external, observable response (R).

Valuation and Cognitive Algebra   Figure 12.9 also points to the second and third assumptions made by the cognitive algebra approach. The second assumption is called the assumption of *valuation*. This assumption captures the notion of subjective utility, in that it refers to the fact that observable aspects of the stimuli are transformed into internal psychological values. It is important to realize that by making this assumption, the cognitive algebra approach explicitly acknowledges that behavior may not be guided in a straightforward way by the objective, observable aspects of the situation; the subjective, internal values for those aspects must also be considered.

The third assumption of the cognitive algebra approach is represented in Figure 12.9 by the combining of the internal values in the selection of a response. This is where we get to the "algebra" in cognitive algebra. According to this approach, response selection is made by use of some algebraic combination of the internal values. For example, the values could be combined by addition or multiplication (such as in Figure 12.3) or put into some kind

FIGURE 12.9 **Transformation of Observable Stimuli into Unobservable Values** Approaches based on cognitive algebra assume that an internal transformation links observable stimuli with observable responses. Each observable stimulus (S) is transformed into an internal value (s); these values are then combined in some algebraic way to lead to some internal response (r), which guides some observable response (R).

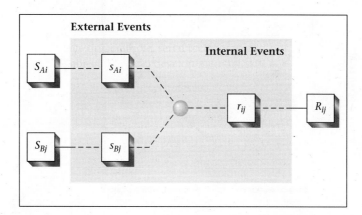

of ratio, as in Luce's choice rule, introduced in the first part of this chapter. A critical issue for researchers using the cognitive algebra approach is to discover the particular algebraic combination that subjects use to guide response selection.

Functional Measurement In order to do this, the cognitive algebra approach makes one final, critical assumption. It assumes that by examining the various observable choices made in response to the possible combinations of observable stimulus pairs, we can make inferences directly about the internal values and the ways in which those values were acted on. This is called the assumption of *functional measurement.*

According to the assumption of functional measurement, then, the observed patterns of responses suggest the algebraic form of the integration rule. For example, suppose the observable responses to certain combinations of stimuli (such as the combinations in Figure 12.8) result in a graph in which parallel lines relate the dependent variable of interest to the manipulated aspects of the stimuli; in that case, we can infer that the algebraic combination of the internal values follows some kind of additive rule. Essentially, parallel lines indicate that the internal values are added together to guide response selection.

One example of this additive combination can be found in studies of "person" perception, or attributions made about individuals. For example, in an early application of this approach (Anderson, 1962), subjects were asked to rate the likableness of a described individual. Two sets of characteristics of this individual's personality were presented. One set of characteristics referred to whether the person was level-headed, unsophisticated, or ungrateful, while the other referred to whether the person was good-natured, bold, or humorless. These two sets of characteristics were combined in a matrix (like that in Figure 12.8), producing nine possible combinations of characteristics. The degree to which the described individual was rated as being likable, as a function of specific combinations of characteristics, is presented in Figure 12.10.

FIGURE 12.10   **Addition of Values**   The data are from two subjects asked to rate the likablity of a described person as a function of combinations of characteristics. The parallel lines, according to the cognitive algebra approach, suggest that the subjective values for the characteristics were added together to guide the ratings.

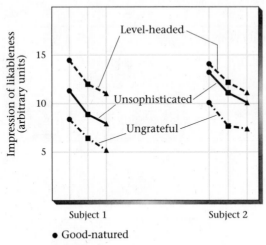

Source: Anderson, 1962.

As you can see, the lines in this figure are roughly parallel, suggesting (according to the cognitive algebra approach) that the subjective values are added together to guide the ratings given. This basic pattern has been found in further studies of person perception (Anderson, 1974) and in studies of judgments about quantity (Anderson & Cuneo, 1978; Cuneo, 1980).

An alternative pattern that might be observed is a set of lines that fan out in some way. This type of pattern suggests some sort of multiplication of internal values. For example, Lopes (1976) had subjects participate in a simulated game of poker in which they were asked to make their bets according to whether they thought they could beat two opponents. The strength of each of these opponents' hands (the relative value of the specific combination of cards the opponent held) was manipulated, with each opponent's hand being low, medium, or high in strength. The average bets of subjects in response to the combination of strengths is presented in Figure 12.11.

As you can see, the lines in this figure appear to fan out from the point representing the combination of a low hand for both opponents. According to the cognitive algebra approach, this indicates that some type of multiplication operation was used to combine the information. Similar results have been found in semantic judgments (Oden, 1977). More complex variations have been found to suggest averaging rules (Busemeyer, 1991; Schlottmann & Anderson, 1993) and ratio rules (Massaro & Cohen, 1977) for information combination. And as suggested earlier, the influential fuzzy logical model of perception for the processing of spoken language—a model that has been extended to a number of other cognitive processes—is based in part on the cognitive algebra approach.

FIGURE 12.11   **Multiplication of Values**   The figure shows average bets of subjects in a simulated poker game. Subjects were asked to bet according to whether they thought they could beat two simulated opponents, whose hands (the sets of cards they held) were low, medium, or high in strength (these lines represent the strengths of the first opponent's hand, while the values on the x-axis represent the strengths of the second opponent's hand). The fan-shaped pattern suggests that some sort of multiplication was used.

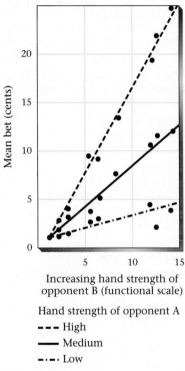

Increasing hand strength of
opponent B (functional scale)

Hand strength of opponent A

- - - High
——— Medium
-·-· Low

Source: Anderson, 1962.

Decisions in Real Time

All the models and theories we have discussed in this chapter deal with one aspect of judgment and decision making: the likelihood of making a particular judgment or decision. Each of the models tries in some way to relate that likelihood to an inference about the processes used to arrive at that judgment or decision. But the *probability* of a particular response is only one of two standard dependent variables that we can use in experimental explorations of cognition. The other, as we have suggested in other contexts, is the *time* required to make the response. In addition—as noted at the beginning of the chapter—we can consider how the probability of a response might change as processing goes on. Specifically, we can consider the *dynamics* of making a judgment or decision.

For most of the history of the study of judgment and decision making, theorists have focused on the likelihood, or probability, of a response and have neglected the time it takes and how it might change over time. That is, most models have been *static* rather than *dy-*

namic. However, recent work has begun to focus on time variables and in particular has attempted to simultaneously account for the probability of a response, the time required to arrive at that response, and the way the probability of the response changes over time (Busemeyer & Townsend, 1993; Heath, 1992; Townsend & Busemeyer, 1989). This contemporary interest in the dynamics of decision making complements contemporary interest in the dynamic aspects of development (see Chapter 11).

An example of this work is the theoretical model of Busemeyer and Townsend (1993) called *decision-field theory.* Two aspects of this account make it interesting for our purposes. First, it explicitly relates the likelihood of a response to the time required to arrive at that response, and it does so in a way that incorporates many ideas that have been used to account for more basic phenomena in cognition (Busemeyer, Forsyth & Nozawa, 1988; Link, 1992; Ratcliff, 1978; Townsend & Ashby, 1983). Second, it explicitly takes into account some basic ideas about motivation that form part of the historical basis for the study of judgment and decision making—notions, such as approach and avoidance, that we discussed early in this chapter.

Although a complete understanding of decision-field theory requires dealing with complex math (Busemeyer & Townsend, 1992), the central ideas of the theory are accessible through intuition. Once again, consider a simple choice you might face on any weeknight: the choice of studying for an upcoming exam or socializing with your friends. Each choice involves some gains (e.g., being better prepared for your exam versus having an enjoyable evening with your friends) and some losses (e.g., being behind in your studying versus not getting to spend time with your friends).

Decision-field theory models this situation by proposing that three cognitive systems are involved in going from a situation to an action (see Figure 12.12). The first, the *valence system,* assesses the gains and losses for each alternative and outputs this assessment to the second system. This system, the *decision system,* translates the assessments into a preference value, which in turn is used to guide the expression of the preference by way of the third system, the *motor system.* Let us consider each of these systems in a little more detail.

Assume that you face the decision just described: choosing between studying for an exam and socializing with friends. Each of these alternatives provides positive and negative emotional (affective) input to the system. The positive input is acted on by what is called the *approach subsystem,* while the negative input is acted on by what is called the *avoidance subsystem.* In Figure 12.12, being better prepared for the exam has a positive input valued at +200, while spending time with friends has a positive input of +500. (As in our earlier examples, these values are completely arbitrary.) In contrast, falling behind in studying has a negative input of –500, while losing a night with friends has a negative input of –200.

These inputs are weighted and combined to arrive at a valence for each of the alternatives. The term *valence* comes from the Latin word for vigor; and in this context, it refers to the general "strength" of each alternative in a positive (approach) or negative (avoidance) direction. The weighting factor represents the contribution of aspects of attention and memory to assessment of gains and losses for each alternative, and this weighting is allowed to change over time. The change over time corresponds to aspects of the gains or losses attended to or associations retrieved as a function of time spent considering (deliberating on) the alternatives.

The product of the dynamic, weighted combination associated with each alternative is, as noted, a valence (a positive or negative value). The valence summarizes aspects of approach and avoidance with respect to the alternative. The valences are used in real time to compute a *preference state.* This preference state can be thought of as a collection of values

FIGURE 12.12 **Decision-Field Theory** Decision-field theory uses three systems to model the process of going from a situation to an action. The first, the valence system, provides assessments based on aspects of avoidance and approach. The second, the decision system, uses the output of the valence system to arrive at a preference state. The third, the motor system, translates that preference state into observable behavior. W_1 and W_2 indicate the weights for each of the alternatives and V_E and V_S represent the values for the exam and socializing, respectively.

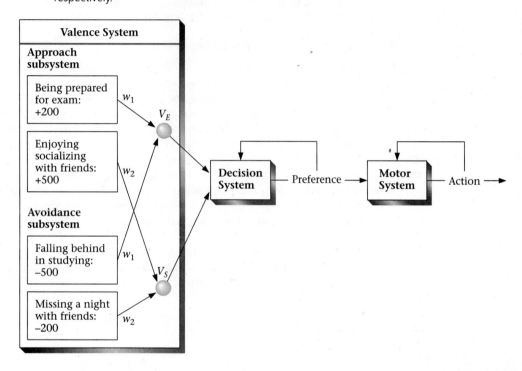

that is compared against some threshold for action. This comparison is performed in the decision system. The results of the comparison operation are used by the motor system to inhibit overt responding until the threshold is reached.

A critical point to note about these subsystems is that information processing is going on continuously, in real time. What this means is that, at every instant in time, information is "flowing" through all of the systems. This dynamic conception is very different from traditional static flowchart models of cognition, in which the processing represented by one box often must be completed before the processing represented by the next box can begin. The dynamic conception of decision making represented in decision-field theory corresponds to the sense you might have, as you consider some important choice, of "leaning" in one direction at one time, "leaning" in another direction later, and then committing to one of the choices after you've spent some time thinking about it.

Decision-field theory has been applied to understanding a variety of decision-making phenomena (Hogarth & Einhorn, 1990; Lopes, 1987). In addition, because it incorporates both approach and avoidance aspects of a situation, it can be used to address issues such as regret and conflict in decision making (Houston, 1991; Myers, Suydam, & Gambino, 1965). And it can, in a precise and principled way, relate a specific choice or judgment to the time required to make that choice or judgment. Although the mathematics of this relationship go beyond what we can consider here, it is important to note that the way in which choice and time are related in decision-field theory explicitly takes into account variability, or randomness. In this sense, decision-field theory is both dynamic and non-deterministic and so may be well equipped to deal with a complex range of cognitive processes related to judgment and decision making.

Section Summary: Contemporary Issues

The principle of rationality has played an important role throughout the history of the study of judgment and decision making. Modern theories continue to be influenced by this principle, in many cases adopting the principle of bounded rationality. Decision analyses, such as those using decision trees, provide ways of understanding how bounded rationality and utility theory might apply in a given situation. Tversky and Shafir used this type of approach, along with a value function, to explain how the sure-thing principle can be violated. How information supporting judgments and decisions is organized varies according to the level of expertise of the person processing that information. An important difference between experts and novices has to do with the degree to which forward and backward reasoning are used. The cognitive algebra approach provides a way of relating aspects of observable external factors (such as the information involved in a judgment or decision) to aspects of unobservable internal factors by way of a set of assumptions that allow different models of processing to be tested. Finally, decision-field theory represents a unique perspective on judgment and decision making that takes into account traditional concepts (such as approach and avoidance) while modeling processing in a dynamic fashion.

REVIEWING   JUDGMENT AND DECISION MAKING

CONCEPT REVIEW

1. Describe hard, soft, and probabilistic determinism. What specific relationship do these types of determinism refer to?

2. Explain the difference between a static and a dynamic theory.

3. Compare and contrast regulatory and purposive approaches to motivation. Why do *you* think it would be important to consider motivation in studying judgment and decision making?

4. What is the reticular activating system, and what role has it been thought to play in arousal and motivation?

5. What are approach-avoidance behaviors? Why is it important to consider both positive and negative aspects of decision-making situations?

6. Describe the idea of subjective expected utility. Why is it important to consider subjective as well as objective sources of information in judgment and decision making?

CONCEPT REVIEW *(continued)*

7. What is Luce's choice axiom?

8. What is a heuristic? Describe the representativeness heuristic, the availability heuristic, and anchoring.

9. Identify the assumption underlying the principle of rationality. How does the idea of bounded rationality modify this principle?

10. Describe how a decision tree can be used to construct a model that takes subjective expected utilities into consideration.

11. Compare and contrast forward and backward reasoning. Which type seems to be the one most commonly used by experts in a field?

12. Identify the basic assumptions of the cognitive algebra approach.

13. What is decision-field theory? What topics that have been important at other times in the history of psychology does it explicitly consider?

KEY TERMS

anchoring (p. 394)
approach-avoidance behavior (p. 388)
availability heuristic (p. 392)
backward reasoning (p. 401)
bounded rationality (p. 395)
choice under uncertainty (p. 390)
decision tree (p. 397)
deterministic (p. 385)

drive (p. 386)
dynamic theory (p. 385)
forward reasoning (p. 401)
globally optimal solution (p. 395)
heuristic (p. 392)
locally optimal solution (p. 395)
motivation (p. 385)
preference relation (p. 385)

principle of rationality (p. 395)
purposive approach (p. 386)
regulatory view (p. 386)
representativeness heuristic (p. 392)
static theory (p. 385)
subjective expected utility hypothesis
   (p. 391)

SUGGESTED READINGS

The editors of *Judgment and decision-making: An interdisciplinary reader,* H. R. Arkes and K. R. Hammond (1986), have included a number of important articles representing the range of research activities in judgment and decision making (Cambridge: Cambridge University Press). Although some of the articles may seem dated, they will give you a sense of the breadth of this area of cognitive psychology. In its early chapters, R. C. Beck's (1990) *Motivation: Theories and principles* (3rd ed.) provides a solid discussion of the relevance of motivation to judgment and decision making (Englewood Cliffs: NJ: Prentice-Hall). J. Busemeyer and J. T. Townsend (1993) discuss the basic aspects of decision-field theory and illustrate how dynamic conceptions of cognition can be applied to judgment and decision making in "Decision-field theory: A dynamic-cognitive approach to decision-making in an uncertain environment" (*Psychological Review, 100,* 432–459).

13 Categorization and Concept Formation

> *To categorize is to render* discriminably different things equivalent, to group the objects and events and people around us into classes, and to respond to them in terms of their class membership rather than their uniqueness.—Jerome S. Bruner, Jacqueline J. Goodnow, and George A. Austin, 1956.

N THIS SECOND CHAPTER ON THINKING, we focus on the mental processes that allow us to classify or categorize objects or events into groups that we call categories or concepts. What good does it do us to categorize the objects and events we encounter? Why do we learn to use concepts and categories?

It turns out that the ability to use concepts and to categorize items has many benefits, including the fact that we never experience the same object or event in exactly the same way on two occasions. Even though you can easily identify friends or family members each time you see them, they are in fact always different—their hair, clothing, voices, and other features are never exactly the same. This raises an interesting question: How do we identify a person as being the same individual even though she may look very different on different occasions? Similarly, how are we able to group different objects (e.g., flowers in a field) into common groups (e.g., daisies, roses)?

To solve the problem of classifying different objects and events into common groups, humans and other animals have developed the ability to ignore some differences among objects and events and classify these objects and events into groups based on common features or attributes. Even though no two apples look exactly the same, then, we can easily identify a specific piece of fruit as an apple and also distinguish it from a pear.

One reason psychologists study categorization and concept formation is that the processes we use to classify items are in many regards fundamental processes that are used in almost all cognitive tasks. For example, imagine that you witnessed a crime and were later asked to look at a police lineup that included the person who committed the crime along with several innocent people. The actual criminal would not look exactly the same as he did at the time of the crime, and yet if you are to identify this person, you need to somehow match this person with your memory of the crime scene. In essence, all of our knowledge of the world around us is an abstraction based on our experiences, and we are constantly comparing the objects and events we encounter to what we have learned from the world. Classification, then, is at the heart of almost all that we know and all of our behaviors (Estes, 1994).

ORGANIZING THE WORLD AROUND US

Our study of concept formation and categorization begins with an interesting observation. People have an incredibly powerful ability to discriminate among objects. For example, we are able to perceive some 7 million different values in the color spectrum (Goldstein, 1984). If you were shown two *extremely* similar shades of blue, you would most likely be able to tell that they were not identical.

What may be more interesting than our ability to discriminate among so many color variations, however, is that we almost never use this ability. Colors are generally grouped into a much smaller number for which we have learned color names. Thus, you might say that two books in your bookcase both have blue covers, yet you can easily discriminate the differences in the two shades of blue. Consider the alternative to such a grouping—we would need a name for each of those 7 million colors! A witness at a crime scene, for example, would need to identify the *exact* color of the shirt worn by a bank robber—saying that the person wore a "blue" shirt wouldn't be adequate to identify the shirt.

Psychologists have been studying categorization and concept formation for many years. Bruner, Goodnow, and Austin (1956) wrote an influential text (*A Study of Thinking*) that reported many important experiments on categorization. In addition to their empirical work, Bruner and his colleagues described some of the motivations an organism would have for categorizing events and objects in the world, and they identified five advantages that can be achieved through categorizing. These five benefits are described below. For each benefit, see if you can come up with an alternative to categorization that would achieve the same goal. In other words, ask yourself "How would an organism that could not categorize behave and survive under these conditions?"

> *Benefit 1:* The complexity of the environment is greatly reduced. Remember, for example, that we can discriminate among about 7 million colors. If we had to treat each and every color we experienced as unique, our lives would be incredibly complicated. Think of trying to decide whether some berry is poisonous. You can remember becoming sick after eating a berry that was a specific shade of red, but the shade of the berry in your hand is just barely different. Do you classify this berry as the same as the one that made you sick, or do you treat it as a completely new berry, since its color is slightly different from that of the other?

> *Benefit 2:* The second benefit, strongly related to the first, is that categorization allows us to *identify* objects. For example, if you come across the type of berry that previously made you sick, you can say to your friend, "That is a poisonous berry—don't eat it." From now on, you will be able to identify that kind of berry by its category.

> *Benefit 3:* The organism that categorizes is not faced with the need to learn about every "novel" object. Instead of having to taste every single berry, you can simply categorize the berry and then move on to learn about things you have not yet learned to categorize. Similarly, you do not have to relearn how to use a hammer when you get a new hammer that differs from the old one.

> *Benefit 4:* Knowing the category to which an item belongs provides a cue for your behavior. If you know that a berry is poisonous, you know you should avoid it. If you know that Larry is a liar, you know you should not believe everything Larry says.

> *Benefit 5:* Being able to categorize items allows us to learn the relationships between classes of objects and events. One sort of relationship we can learn is cause and effect. If we know the category *matches* and the category *fires,* then we can relate the two categories in a cause-and-effect relationship—matches cause fires. If we were not able to categorize, we would have to treat each new match as a completely novel object and each new fire as a novel event. We would have no way to form the idea that a match can cause a fire.

The advantages described by Bruner and colleagues are not merely convenient to possess—they are necessary for survival. An organism who could not categorize would be unable to perceive patterns in its environment since each new event would have to be treated as completely novel, and it would not be able to behave appropriately in the presence of those patterns.

Basic Terminology in Categorization Research

One difficulty faced by cognitive psychologists is that many of the terms we use are also used in everyday language. The word *concept,* for example has a meaning to native speakers of English who have never formally studied cognition. We have already used terms like *concept, concept formation,* and *categorization* in this text, and you probably understood what we meant when we used those terms. In some situations, terms like *categorization* and *concept formation* are interchangeable—if two people were talking to one another on a bus, the speaker could substitute one term for the other, and the listener would not bat an eyelash. However, the terms have very different meanings for cognitive psychologists.

Categorization In some ways, the simpler term that we will be using is **categorization.** All we mean when we use this term is that a set of objects or events are divided into at least two groups. Consider a case in which we give a person a deck of playing cards and ask her to divide the cards into four piles. When she is finished with the task, we find that the deck of cards is separated into four stacks. We can conclude that our subject has categorized the cards. We could also say that the subject has *classified* the cards. Note that we have not looked at the cards, and hence we do not know which cards were put into which piles. Also, we have not asked the subject how she classified the cards. We do know, however, that the subject did classify them. In other words, categorization is observable—it is measurable behavior.

Concepts The use of the term *concept* carries with it a great deal more theoretical baggage. You can think of a **concept** as a mental representation that groups together sets of objects or events. Consider the card example again. Our subject has categorized the cards, and we can now ask, "What concept did she use to categorize them?" One way we might try to answer this question is to look at the piles of cards. Imagine that all the hearts are in one pile, all the diamonds are in a second, and so forth. If this were the arrangement, we would probably say that the subject used the concept of *suit* to make the categorization. Another way that we might attempt to determine the concept would be to ask the subject how she categorized the cards. In this example, the subject would probably tell us, "I put each suit into a separate stack."

Caveats Concerning Categorization We should note two important points about the definitions and the example just given. First, the way categorization is defined means that we can objectively and reliably measure whether a person has categorized a set of items, because we can directly observe this behavior. But we can never know for sure what concept (if any) a person used to make the categorization. Concepts are mental representations, which means that they are unobservable. We have to make inferences about concepts, and those inferences can be based on categorization performance. In the card example, we used a behavioral measure (categorization performance) to make an inference about the mental representation (the concept of suit) used by the subject.

A second point to note is that the card example is only slightly similar to the categorization tasks given to subjects in real experiments. Subjects in experiments are generally not allowed to create their own categories and then assign items to those categories. Instead, the experimenter creates the categories and then asks the subjects to classify the stimuli into those categories. In some sense, the concept is in the mind of the experimenter—the subjects' task is to categorize the items so that their performance matches the experimenter's concept.

In an experiment, we might give our subjects a deck of cards and ask them to divide the cards into four stacks, which we label A, B, C, and D. The subject might place the first card, the Jack of diamonds, into stack D. We tell the subject, "No, the Jack of diamonds belongs in stack B." The Jack is then placed back into the deck, and the next card is drawn. The subject makes another decision and is given more feedback (i.e., is told that the categorization was correct or incorrect). Eventually, the subject will be able to categorize the items correctly—putting hearts into the A pile, diamonds into the B pile, clubs into the C pile, and spades into the D pile. Once performance is perfect, we can conclude that the subject understands the concept of suit and has used it to categorize the items.

When we discuss tests of the theories we describe, they will almost always be framed in terms of categorization performance. The behavioral measures used to study categorization and concept formation include proportion of correct responses (for each item, for each block of trials, etc.), speed of learning (the number of blocks of trials before learning is complete), and reaction time (the speed with which an individual item is categorized). The theories make different assumptions about the internal representation of categorical structure, and those assumptions lead to predictions about these measures. But remember—we *observe* categorization behavior, and from that we make inferences about the person's knowledge of things like concepts and category structure.

Stimuli Used in Concept Formation Studies

All models and theories of concept formation and categorization were created to predict the classification of some sort of stimuli. We can refer to a stimulus that belongs to a category as an **exemplar,** or example, of the category. Consider a simple, real-world example. Suppose we describe to you a particular animal that you have never seen before by saying that this specific animal (an exemplar) has four legs, fur, a tail, and retractable claws and makes a meowing sound. You will be able to decide pretty quickly what type of animal it is. Very few people (over a certain age) would think that the animal was a dog rather than a cat. Notice, though, that although you are able to categorize this specific exemplar, the description of the animal is lacking in several details; the color of the fur is not specified, and no information is given about the length of the tail or the animal's size, for example.

The immense variability among the exemplars of real-world categories can make it difficult to study the basic processes involved in categorization. Therefore, real-world stimuli are rarely used in experimental studies of categorization. Instead, researchers typically use artificial categories involving fairly simple stimuli. In this context, *artificial* means that subjects in the experiments have had no experience with the categories.

Researchers often use simple artificial stimuli such as those presented in Figure 13.1. A basic term used in categorization research to describe stimuli, or sets of stimuli, is *attribute*. **Attributes** are qualities that can vary across a set of stimuli. The example in Figure 13.1 features three attributes of the stimuli: shape (square, circle, rectangle, or triangle), size (small, medium, large, or extra-large), and pattern (white, black, or shaded).

By using very simple stimuli, researchers can limit and simplify the number of attributes—something that would be much more difficult if they used, for example, the attributes of actual animals. As we will see later, naming the attributes of animals or other natural categories is no simple feat. As a thought experiment, examine Figure 13.1 and try to determine which of the attributes determines category membership. In other words, why would a stimulus belong to Category A instead of Category B? If you were presented with a large, shaded triangle, to which category would you assign it? What would you infer about how you were performing the categorization task from this response?

In trying to figure out how you would classify a large, shaded triangle in terms of the categories presented in Figure 13.1, you probably considered which features seem to be associated with Categories A and B. This is similar to the situation children are in as they try to learn to discriminate cars, trucks, buses, and other vehicles. What do people learn about

FIGURE 13.1 **Sample Stimuli for a Categorization Study** The stimuli on the left belong to Category A, and those on the right belong to Category B.

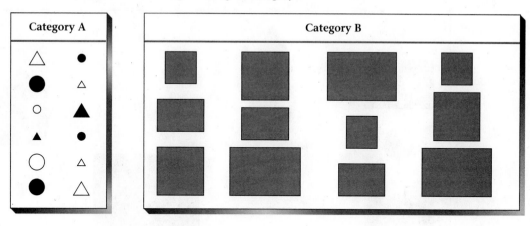

the exemplars they experience, and how do they use that information to categorize new items? These questions are at the heart of the theories we consider in this chapter.

The Categorization Task

The fact that a subject has learned to correctly classify a set of stimuli does not necessarily mean that she has attained the concept. One possibility is that the subject has simply associated each item with the correct category label. The critical test involves presenting novel stimuli—stimuli that have no prior association with a category.

Imagine that the stimuli shown in Figure 13.1 have all been presented to our subject, and she has learned to provide the correct response for each of the items in the set. We cannot conclude, just from these data, that she has learned to use the correct concept. It is possible that she has simply memorized each of the items in the set and its associated label.

Now suppose that we test our subject by presenting the stimuli shown in Figure 13.2 and measuring her accuracy. If she places the black and white items in Category A and the shaded items in Category B, can we conclude that she has learned the correct concept? What if she places all small and medium-sized stimuli in Category A and all large, extra-large, and extra-extra-large stimuli in Category B? Would that show that she had learned the correct concept? What about the ∞ stimulus—which category does that belong to? In fact, Category B is defined as any stimuli that do have an even number of sides. As you can see, even with very simple stimuli, concept formation can be rather difficult, and knowing what concept a person is using requires careful selection of materials.

Section Summary: Organizing the World Around Us

Categorizing objects and events has many benefits. Bruner and his colleagues pointed out five advantages of categorizing: It reduces the complexity of the environment, allows us to identify objects as members of a class, reduces our need to learn about new objects that are members of a group, allows us to respond to objects and events on the basis of knowledge of the category, and allows us to learn relationships between classes of objects and events. Cognitive psychologists use the term *categorization* to refer to the behavior of dividing ob-

FIGURE 13.2   **Sample Stimuli to Categorize**   To which of the two categories presented in Figure 13.1 do these stimuli belong? On what basis are you making your decisions?

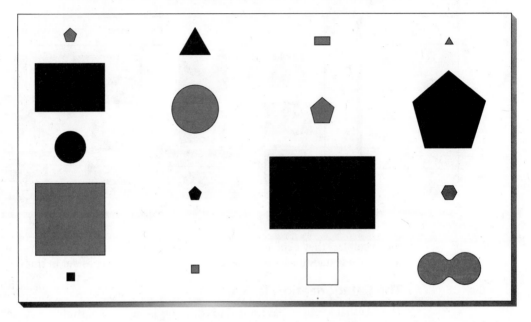

jects and events into groups and the term *concept* to refer to a mental representation in which objects and events are grouped together. Because we can observe categorization but not concepts, we must be careful when drawing inferences involving concepts based on categorization. In laboratory research, simple stimuli are often used to examine categorization and the formation of concepts. Even when simple stimuli are used, however, researchers must take care in trying to determine what a person has learned in categorizing stimuli into groups.

EARLY RESEARCH ON CLASSIFICATION

Although scholars have long debated issues relevant to categorization and concept formation, empirical investigations of how people learn concepts and categorize objects and events began fairly recently. The approach taken in early research on classification was to try to create concept-formation tasks that reflected how people learn concepts and categories in the real world.

Consider for a moment how a child learns the concept *car*. The child might see a Honda Civic and ask his parent what it is. Mom tells him that it is a car. Then he might see a pickup truck and call it a car. Mom tells him, "No, that is not a car; it is a truck." This might convey to the child that not all large objects that carry people and have four wheels are cars. He might next come across a school bus and ask if that is a car. "No," Mom replies, "That is a bus. Buses carry a lot of people." This conveys a bit more information about cars, but it might also lead the child to believe that large vehicles that carry a lot people are not cars. If the next vehicle the parent and child come across is a "stretch" limousine, the child might call it a bus, since it is closer in size to the bus he saw than to the Honda Civic. In learning the concept *car,* then, children are exposed to many instances and types of vehicles and are told what those vehicles are called. Somehow, this experience allows them to correctly label various vehicles as cars, buses, and so forth.

In order to study the formation of concepts in controlled experiments, early researchers created artificial categories using stimuli with which the subjects were not familiar. Doing so has several advantages: subjects have no prior experience with the items to be categorized, experimenters are free to assign the items to whatever category they choose, and the stimuli themselves can easily be manipulated so that theories can be tested.

Hull's Categorization Research

In a classic early study of categorization, Clark Hull (1920) used the stimuli presented in Figure 13.3, which are Chinese logographs. Hull used these stimuli because it seemed quite likely that his English-speaking subjects would not know the meaning of the logographs.

Each concept in Hull's experiment was defined (or identified) by a specific *radical,* a common element that is present in each of the logographs representative of that concept. All the logographs in a given row of Figure 13.3 contain a common radical. Hull used a pronounceable label (e.g., Oo, Yer, Li) to name each of the concepts.

Columns 1–6 represent the *original learning lists* that Hull used in his experiments. During the first trial of the learning phase, subjects were presented with the logographs from List 1, and the experimenter pronounced the name (e.g., Yer) of that concept. On subsequent trials, the subjects' task was to name the appropriate concept as each logograph ap-

FIGURE 13.3 **Original Learning Lists for Hull's Study** These six lists were used in the original learning phase of Hull's (1920) study. Each row represents a category of items, which is defined by the radical in that row.

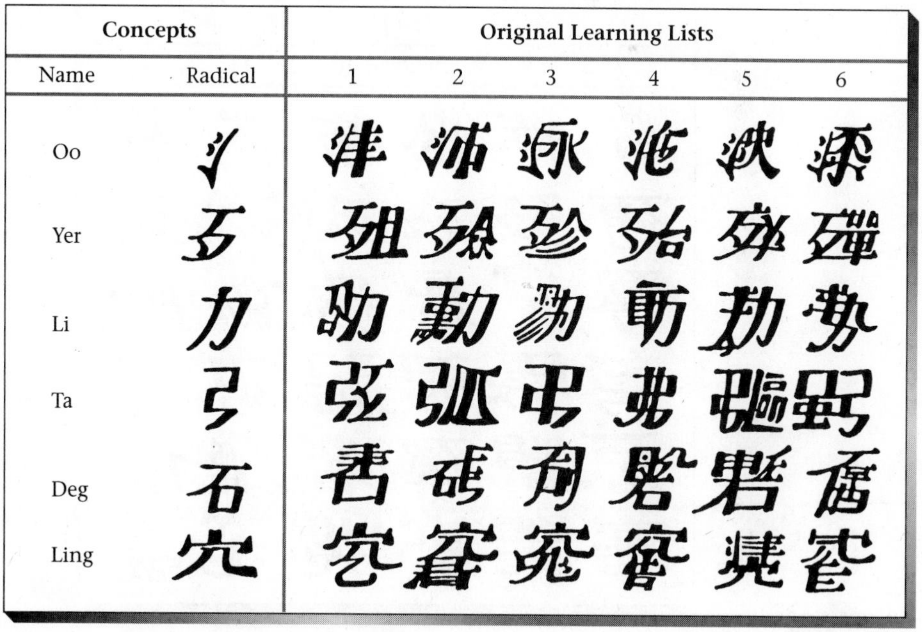

Source: Hull, 1920.

peared. If the subject could not name the concept correctly, then the experimenter provided the name.

After the subject could name all the concepts in List 1, the learning process was repeated with Lists 2–6. This original learning phase is somewhat similar to the situation in which a child and parent see a series of different vehicles and the parent teaches the child to label (i.e., categorize) each of these specific vehicles as car, truck, bus, or the like.

The original learning trials in Hull's experiment ensured that the subjects could name the logographs presented in Lists 1–6. The question of interest in this study was whether the subjects had learned anything beyond the labels for the specific stimuli used in those lists. This is analogous to a child's learning the names of all the drawings of vehicles in a favorite book and then being given a new book with different pictures of vehicles. Will the child be able to label the new drawings correctly?

To test whether the subjects in his experiment had learned the concepts defined by the radicals, Hull next presented subjects with the logographs in Figure 13.4 and asked them to name the concept that each stimulus represented. Subjects responded correctly to 67 percent of the new logographs in these *test lists*. This **positive transfer** from the training lists to the test lists showed that the subjects had learned more than a simple association between the logographs presented in the training lists and the associated concepts; rather, they had learned something about what made an item a member of a particular category. Something similar takes place when the child with the new picture book can correctly label most of the vehicles in the new book.

FIGURE 13.4 **Test Lists for Hull's Study**   These six lists were used by Hull (1920) to test what people who had memorized the lists in Figure 13.3 had learned. Subjects were presented with the items and asked to name the category to which each item belonged.

Source: Hull, 1920.

Theoretical Accounts of the Early Concept-Formation Experiments

The fact that Hull's subjects showed positive transfer does not tell us exactly *what* the subjects learned during the training trials—it tells us only that they learned something that allowed them to correctly classify about two-thirds of the test stimuli. Remember, the only observable information is the subjects' categorization of the items; we must draw an inference about whether subjects were using some concept. The issue of how to determine exactly what subjects learn in a concept-formation task has not yet been fully resolved. We return to this issue later in the chapter. In this section, we review two general interpretations of how people (as well as other animals) perform tasks like those used by Hull. Before you read these accounts, read Experiment 13A to get a feel for what it is like to participate in one of these experiments and to gain an appreciation for the two theoretical accounts we discuss next.

Continuity Theory   According to **continuity theory,** the learning that took place in Hull's (1920) experiment is simple stimulus-response association learning. Continuity theory assumes that these stimulus-response associations form gradually over the course of learning—there are no sudden "insights" that lead subjects to the correct answer. If you can imagine a smooth learning curve where performance begins at a very low level and gradually increases to better and better performance, you have the basic prediction of continuity theory.

Continuity theory would account for Hull's results by assuming that subjects formed associations between the specific stimuli used in the original learning phase of the experiment and the concept labels. During the test phase, when the new stimuli were presented, subjects mentally compared these test stimuli to the stimuli from the original learning lists and labeled each test stimulus according to which of the six sets of training stimuli it was most similar to.

Because the stimuli used by Hull were rather complex, it is difficult to appreciate how similarity between the original and test stimuli might have been determined. Furthermore, the six radicals were what defined the six concepts, and it might seem that subjects would have noticed this and categorized the test stimuli accordingly. However, in many concept-formation experiments, no single feature determines category membership.

Continuity theory provides a reasonable theoretical account of the learning that may have occurred in Hull's study. In general, this theory has several admirable features. One is its specification of a simple learning mechanism, the formation of stimulus-response associations. Another is the fact that it can be tested on nonhuman subjects. For example, we could reinforce animals for making certain responses to items from an original list and then present them with stimuli from a test list to see how they responded.

Noncontinuity Theory   According to an alternative view, **noncontinuity theory,** the learning that takes place in concept-formation tasks does not involve a gradual development of stimulus-response associations. Rather, it involves a discontinuous process of forming and then testing hypotheses about what specifies membership in a given category or concept. Noncontinuity theory assumes that people try to learn concepts by actively formulating hypotheses—rules that determine category membership. For example, after looking at the stimuli in Figure 13.1 and being told that a small shaded triangle is not a member of Category B, you might form the hypothesis that only large and extra-large objects are members of Category B. When then presented with a small red circle, you will say that this stimulus is not a member of Category B, because it does not conform to your hy-

EXPERIMENT 13A: Concept Identification

Take a sheet of paper and cover the columns marked "correct response" in Figure 13A before you read any further. Your task is to attempt to identify a concept that we have created for this exercise. You will complete a series of trials in which you will try to decide whether each stimulus is or is not a member of the category defined by our concept.

Each of the stimuli has four attributes: shape (circle, square, cross), pattern (cross-hatched, black, white), number of shapes (1, 2, 3), and number of borders (1, 2, 3). The concept we have selected is a value of one of the attributes (i.e., either circle, square, or cross; cross-hatched, black, or white; one, two, or three shapes; one, two, or three borders).

For the first stimulus, you will have to simply take a guess at whether the item is a member of the category or a nonmember. After you have made your choice, slide the sheet of paper down to reveal the correct response. After that, continue on to the next stimulus. Continue with the exercise until you have either completed all the stimuli or predicted the correct response five times in a row. Good luck!

pothesis. But when told that this stimulus is, indeed, a member of Category B, you will have to revise your hypothesis to account for this new information.

According to noncontinuity theory, then, learning a concept involves actively formulating hypotheses for what determines category membership and then testing these hypotheses against other stimuli. If your hypothesis works, then you can correctly categorize new stimuli; if not, then you must devise a new hypothesis in light of this new, disconfirming evidence. This approach to hypothesis testing is called a **win/stay, lose/switch strategy.** Does this approximate what you were doing as you were trying to learn the concept in Experiment 13A? Note that whereas continuity theory views learning a concept as a gradual process, noncontinuity theory proposes that finding the correct rule (or rules) for category membership is an all-or-none process. Either you have identified the correct rule, or you have not. Did you identify the correct concept rule (a double border) for Experiment 13A?

Testing Continuity and Noncontinuity Theories   Let us consider two sets of predictions that can be derived from continuity and noncontinuity theories. The first concerns how the percentage of correct responses should change across trials. Continuity theory holds that subjects are gradually learning associations between the individual stimulus attributes and the category labels; so over trials, we should see a gradual increase in the percentage of correct responses. In contrast, noncontinuity theory holds that, until subjects identify the correct rule for making category assignments, their performance will basically be the same as if they were guessing.

Bower and Trabasso (1963, 1964; Trabasso & Bower, 1964, 1968) reported a series of experiments designed to test the predictions of continuity and noncontinuity accounts of

FIGURE 13A   Concept-Formation Stimuli

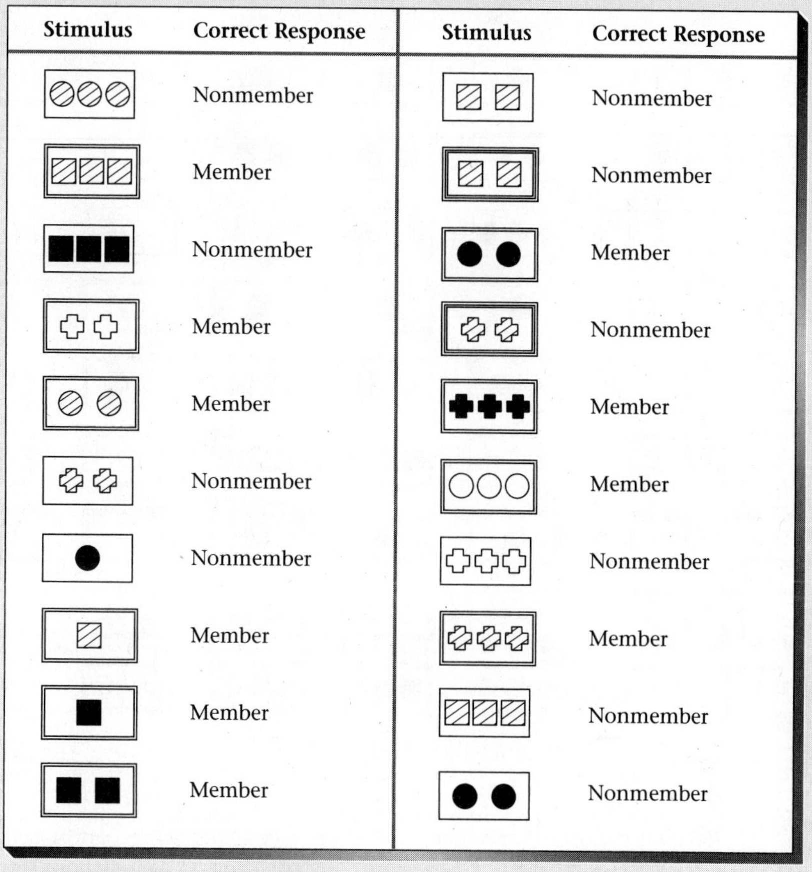

Stimulus	Correct Response	Stimulus	Correct Response
	Nonmember		Nonmember
	Member		Nonmember
	Nonmember		Member
	Member		Nonmember
	Member		Member
	Nonmember		Member
	Nonmember		Nonmember
	Member		Member
	Member		Nonmember
	Member		Nonmember

Source: Adapted from Bruner, Goodnow & Austin, 1956.

concept formation. They presented college-age subjects with a concept-identification task using stimuli with six attributes, each of which had two possible values: shape (square, hexagon), color (red, blue), size (large, small), number of figures (three, four), position (right, left), and shaded area (upper right and lower left, upper left and lower right). A similar way of defining stimuli according to attributes is used for the stimuli shown in Figure 13.5, from which the stimuli used in Experiment 13A were selected.

In the Bower and Trabasso study, subjects were presented with one stimulus at a time and asked to decide which of two categories each stimulus belonged to. After the subject made a decision, the experimenter identified the correct answer (this is similar to the way you completed Experiment 13A). This procedure continued across many stimuli, and the researchers carefully analyzed the pattern of correct and incorrect responses across trials. They found that across trials, subjects' performance remained at about chance accuracy

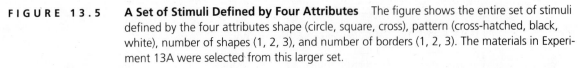

FIGURE 13.5   **A Set of Stimuli Defined by Four Attributes**   The figure shows the entire set of stimuli defined by the four attributes shape (circle, square, cross), pattern (cross-hatched, black, white), number of shapes (1, 2, 3), and number of borders (1, 2, 3). The materials in Experiment 13A were selected from this larger set.

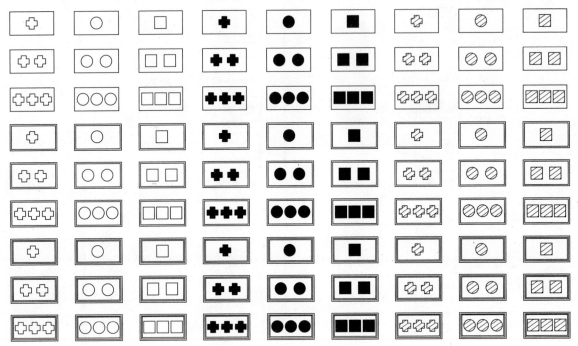

Source: Bruner, Goodnow & Austin, 1956.

(50 percent correct) and then suddenly moved to perfect responding (100 percent correct). Clearly, this pattern of data is more consistent with the predictions of noncontinuity theory than with those of continuity theory.

Bower and Trabasso also tested a second prediction from these two theories. Imagine that subjects are gradually learning associations between stimulus attributes and category labels. In this case, switching the rule used to determine category membership before performance becomes perfect should hurt subsequent performance. In contrast, noncontinuity theory would predict that this switch should have no effect on performance, because subjects have not yet identified the classification rule. Results from Bower and Trabasso's research showed that when the classification rule was changed for a group of subjects before their performance had become perfect, their learning was not slowed relative to that of a control group in which the same rule was used throughout the entire set of trials. This finding provides further evidence for noncontinuity theory and against continuity theory.

Bower and Trabasso's studies, as well as other studies (e.g., Kendler & Kendler, 1962a, 1962b, 1975), indicate that noncontinuity theory generally provides a better explanation of concept formation than does continuity theory. It is important to note, however, that fairly wide ranges of individual differences in response patterns are observed in individuals who differ in age, IQ, and other factors (Mayer, 1992).

Section Summary: Early Research on Classification

People can be said to have learned to categorize items based on a concept when they can classify novel stimuli based on previous experience with other stimuli. We can describe stimuli as being constituted by attributes (e.g., color and shape) that can vary in their values (e.g., red or green, circle or square). Early research on classification employed simple artificial stimuli with a small number of attributes and values. The basic categorization task consists of presenting items to subjects for classification and then presenting feedback for each response. After subjects have been presented with members of various categories, they are then given novel stimuli and asked to categorize these items. Continuity theory assumes that category learning involves a continuous process of associating items with categories. Noncontinuity theory argues that people actively generate hypotheses and test these against the items they are given. Overall, noncontinuity theory provides a better explanation of concept formation than does continuity theory.

THE CLASSICAL APPROACH: RULE-BASED CATEGORIZATION

In the early work on categorization just discussed, noncontinuity theory is an example of a rule-based approach to categorization. This classical, **rule-based approach** to categorization assumed that learning to categorize items involves learning what rules determine category membership and then applying these rules to new instances. According to the rule-based approach, concept learning is a function of the stimuli we encounter and the rules that define categories.

An important aspect of the early research on the cognitive processes and representations used for categorization (e.g., Bruner et al., 1956) is that it made certain assumptions that determined the types of categories, the nature of the stimuli, and the characteristics of the tasks the researchers used. For example, noncontinuity theory assumes that humans act like hypothesis testers when they are presented with a new task or a problem to solve. To be more specific, it assumes that people approach a categorization task as a problem-solving task. This view assumes that people attempt to solve these problems by noticing features of stimuli, creating hypotheses or guesses regarding these features, and then testing the hypotheses, rejecting those that fail to provide adequate solutions and keeping those that do provide an adequate solution.

Assumptions such as these affected the type of stimuli and the tasks used to study concept formation. Unfortunately, some of these decisions lead the researchers into drawing invalid conclusions. One such decision involves the use of deterministic categories to study categorization, which we discuss next.

The Task and Stimuli

The categorization scheme used in early categorization studies involved **deterministic categories;** that is, certain stimulus features *always* belonged to one and only one of the categories involved. (These can be contrasted with **probabilistic categories,** in which stimuli features *usually* belong to one category but may sometimes belong to another category.) In early studies, the categories were constructed by the experimenter so that a rule regarding stimulus features could be used to classify all stimuli. Hull's (1920) and Bruner, Goodnow, and Austin's (1956) experiments are examples of this type of research and theorizing.

Remember that, in regard to the stimuli in Figures 13.1 and 13.2, a subject who responded by placing stimuli with an even number of sides in one category and other stim-

430 Chapter 13 Categorization and Concept Formation

uli in the second category would always be correct. Supporters of the rule-based view would claim that the subject who responded correctly to all the items had learned the rule, "If an item has an even number of sides, it belongs to Category B; otherwise, it belongs to Category A." In other words, the memory representations of the categories amount to a rule, and the only process necessary to categorize a new item is to compare the relevant attribute of the item (here, the shape) to the antecedent of the rule (the "if" part) and then draw a conclusion based on the rule. For example, if the item is a large, shaded triangle, the subject can effectively ignore the shading and the size. Once shape is recognized as the critical attribute, the shape of a stimulus is simply compared with the internal representation—the rule.

For this example, we can say that having an even number of sides is both *necessary* and *sufficient* for membership in Category B. In order for a certain quality to be *necessary* for category membership, no members of that category can *lack* the quality. Thus, no member of Category B can be, for example, circular or triangular. For a quality to be *sufficient* for category membership, no member of the alternative category can have that quality. If having an even number of sides is a sufficient condition for membership in Category B, then no member of Category A can have an even number of sides.

To give these terms a little more meaning, consider a real-world example. What conditions are necessary or sufficient for a person to be a bachelor? There are two relevant attributes here: gender (male or female) and marital status (married or single). Is being single necessary for being a bachelor? To answer that, you should ask whether anyone who is a bachelor is married. If the answer is no, then being single is a necessary condition of bachelorhood. If the answer is yes, then being single is not a necessary condition. Of course, being single is a necessary condition. Now, what about sufficiency? Here you must ask, "Are any nonbachelors single?" If yes, then being single is not a sufficient condition for being a bachelor. If no, then it is a sufficient condition. Well, a large class of people who are not bachelors are single: unmarried women. So being single is *necessary* but not *sufficient* for being a bachelor.

According to the classical, rule-based view, part of the task of the categorizer is to determine which rules work and which rules do not. Imagine that you are just learning the English language. During a conversation, someone mentions that John Smith is a bachelor, but you have never heard the word *bachelor* before. Short of asking the speaker, how can you determine what the word means? John has an infinite number of qualities that might make him a bachelor (e.g., his hair color, the length of his nose, his taste in clothing). According to the classical view, you will start with a hypothesis about some attribute or set of attributes: for example, "Anyone with brown hair is a bachelor." You will probably soon abandon that simple rule—you may find a person with red hair who is a bachelor or someone with brown hair who is not. In the classical view, once you determine that the rule does not work, you will pick another one and test it.

Problems for the Rule-Based Approach

A number of studies found that people could learn to categorize stimuli, even when the rules were quite complex (e.g., Bruner et al., 1956; Shepard, Hovland & Jenkins, 1961). Also, subjects in these experiments were sometimes able to articulate the rules that had been used to create the categories (if they could, they were said to have learned the concept). The rule-based view also has intuitive appeal because many people have had the introspective experience of testing and rejecting hypotheses—is this what you experienced when you completed Experiment 13A?

There are, however, several problems with the approach, which eventually led to its demise as the dominant theory of categorization. Many of the problems stem from the use of deterministic categories created with simple stimuli. In basic research, using simple tasks involving simple stimuli is often quite desirable, but that did not prove to be so in this case. Note that *simple,* here, is a relative term—Hull's (1920) stimuli do not look at all simple, but their structure is simple when compared with stimuli we encounter every day.

Logical and Empirical Problems   The end of the classical view's dominance was the result of an attack on two fronts: logical and empirical. We consider some logical problems first.

One such problem is that few of the categories we encounter in the real world closely resemble the ones used in the laboratory. How many categories can you think of that can be described by simple rules? Take a seemingly simple category like *game*. What rule can we use to determine whether an activity or object qualifies as a game? That it is fun? Well, some games are fun, but not all (e.g., Russian roulette) are. And some things that are fun, like watching a young child visit a petting zoo for the first time, are not games. That there is a winner? Some games, like tag, do not have winners. If you think about it, there are few categories (outside of mathematics) for which necessary and sufficient conditions can be listed.

Another problem is that, although subjects were sometimes able to articulate the rule used to create a category, they could have done so without actually having used it to perform the categorization. Unfortunately, a person's subjective report about his or her cognitive processes is often not useful and can even sometimes be misleading.

As already mentioned, the deterministic category structures that were almost always used in the early experiments posed problems as well. If an item belonged to a category, it would always belong to that category—the boundaries between the categories were fixed. Such is not the case for many natural categories—under some circumstances, for example, we might call being in love a game, whereas it would not be a game at all under other circumstances.

In addition to these logical problems, several empirical findings also cast doubt on the rule-based view. One simple criticism is that people are unable to list necessary and sufficient conditions of many natural categories. For example, what makes a bird a bird? When we ask people to name the necessary and sufficient conditions of many natural categories, the responses we get differ across subjects and even within subjects across time (Rosch & Mervis, 1975). This criticism is relatively weak, however, since people may use rules without having conscious access to them or without being able to verbalize them (Dienes & Berry, 1997; Reber, 1989; Whittlesea & Wright, 1997).

A second, more serious, empirical problem for the rule-based view has to do with the structure of natural categories. According to the rule-based view, all members of a category have equal status as category members. That is, if an item fulfills the rule, then it typifies the category no more and no less than any other item that fulfills the same rule. As several researchers demonstrated, however, this assumption is not always borne out by what we observe.

In an influential study, Rosch and Mervis (1975) asked subjects to list all members of specified categories. Because, according to the classical view, each member of the category has an equal probability of being recalled, for the category *bird*, *chicken* should be written as often as *canary*. As you can probably guess, however, large differences appeared in the frequencies with which certain exemplars were listed by Rosch and Mervis's subjects. Certain category members seem to have a privileged status—they are recalled more quickly and by more subjects than are other items. We see the same type of effect with a **sentence verification task** using sentences like, "A canary is a bird" and, "A chicken is a bird." (This procedure is discussed in Chapter 8.) Responses are much faster for the former question, indicating that *canary* somehow represents the bird category better than does *chicken*. The effect whereby certain category members are better representatives of the category than others is called the **typicality effect.**

A Test of the Rule-Based Approach   The criticisms just described are, in some sense, indirect attacks on the rule-based view. Nosofsky (1991) used a simple categorization task to test directly the assumptions about representations and processes made by the rule-based approach. Nosofsky used a very simple set of stimuli and a deterministic category structure, thereby allowing the rule-based model its best opportunity to succeed.

Examples of the stimuli used by Nosofsky are presented in Figure 13.6. The stimuli are circles consisting of two varying attributes: size and the angle of a radial line. The rows of stimuli are numbered so that the smallest items are in Row 1 and the largest items are in Row 5. Size is the relevant dimension for categorization—items in Rows 1 and 2 (the smaller circles) belong to one category, while items in Rows 3, 4, and 5 (the larger circles) belong to the other category. The angle of the line within the circle is irrelevant.

During training, subjects were presented with items from Rows 1–4 only. Subjects were shown one circle at a time, guessed at the category, and were told if their answers were correct or incorrect. Subjects were never explicitly told what stimulus attribute determined category membership. Once subjects had achieved a high level of accuracy in classifying the training stimuli, testing began. Test stimuli included items from all five rows. The question of most interest was: How would subjects respond to the new stimuli from Row 5? Specifically, would subjects be faster at categorizing stimuli closer to the boundary between the two categories (Row 3), items at an intermediate distance (Row 4), or those furthest from the boundary (Row 5)?

Before we describe the actual results, think about what the classical rule-based view would predict. If subjects were using the rule, "Large stimuli belong to Category A, and small stimuli belong to Category B," would they be faster working with intermediate values of size or extreme values?

Nosofsky used the rule-based view to predict that stimuli of extreme size would be categorized faster than stimuli of intermediate size. That is, according to the rule-based approach, responses to the largest items, those in Row 5, should be faster than responses to items in Row 4, which should in turn be faster than responses to items from Row 3. Nosofsky's reasoning was that a large stimulus would fulfill the rule better than a medium-sized stimulus. Alternatively, one could predict that the size of the stimulus would have no effect on the speed of response, since all category members would be treated equally (i.e., they would either fulfill the rule or not). The important point is that—if the subjects were indeed responding on the basis of a rule—one would not predict that they would respond faster to stimuli *closer* to the category boundary. Interestingly (and unfortunately for the rule-based view), Nosofsky found that subjects responded faster to items in Row 4 than to items in Row 5.

Section Summary: Ruled-Based Categorization

The classical, rule-based approach assumes that humans are hypothesis testers. We can generate rules that may or may not account for the organization of stimuli and can use strategies to test those rules (e.g., looking for violations of our hypotheses). The evidence

FIGURE 13.6   **The Stimuli Used by Nosofsky**   Nosofsky used these stimuli to test predictions concerning mental representations and processes made by the classical, rule-based approach to categorization.

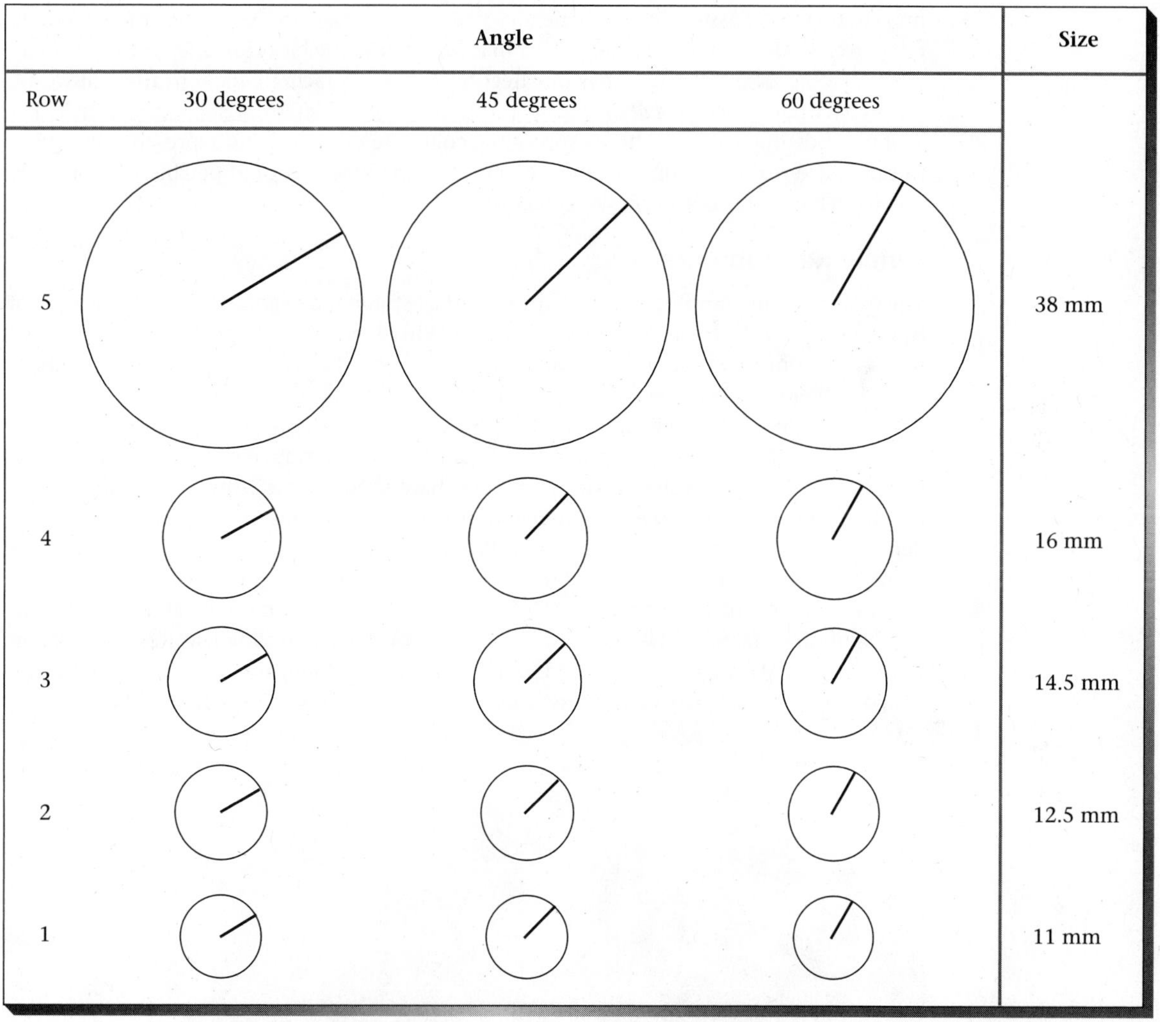

	Angle			Size
Row	30 degrees	45 degrees	60 degrees	
5				38 mm
4				16 mm
3				14.5 mm
2				12.5 mm
1				11 mm

Source: Adapted from Nosofsky, 1991.

supporting this approach came from studies using deterministic category structures and stimuli with reasonably simple attributes. The problems associated with the approach are serious, however, and outweigh its advantages. In the real world, most categories are probabilistic, not deterministic. Thus the rule-based view is logically untenable as an account of many real-world phenomena. The rule-based approach is also unable to predict or account for certain empirical phenomena observed in the laboratory (e.g., the typicality effect).

INFORMATION PROCESSING ALTERNATIVES TO RULE-BASED MODELS

Not surprisingly, some of the empirical failings of the rule-based approach have become the strong points of several alternative models that take an information processing approach. Instead of assuming rigid category structures that can be described by logical rules, the newer models make the assumption that *similarity* is the basis for categorization. In an attempt to approximate the types of categorization tasks facing people in the real world, researchers have used *probabilistic* categories along with deterministic categories. If the goal of modeling is to somehow capture the cognitive processes and representations used to categorize real-world objects and events, then the model should be able to accurately predict behavior for both types of categories.

Family Resemblance

The basis for some developments in the empirical study of categorization was the work of the philosopher Wittgenstein (1958). Much of Wittgenstein's work dealt with natural categories, or concepts that we deal with on a daily basis. In fact, the game example mentioned earlier was developed by Wittgenstein.

Wittgenstein considered categories to be similar in some respects to human families. If you look at a group of people from a single family, you will notice many physical similarities. Rarely, though, do two or more people share all the same features. Looking across family members, we will see a good deal of featural overlap, but no single feature will be defining—that is, necessary or sufficient. Wittgenstein called this overlapping of features **family resemblance** and applied it to the idea of natural categories.

Think again of the category *game*. Although this category has no one defining feature or combination of features, we can find a good deal of overlap among features. *Most* games have winners. *Many* games are played for fun. Even if a certain game lacks a central feature (i.e., one that is shared by many other category members), it probably has many other fea-

Tiger Woods and Family
The golfer Tiger Woods shares some of the facial features of both his parents. In other words, he has a family resemblance to both parents.

tures in common with other category members. Presumably, when presented with a novel item, we attempt to categorize it based on its featural overlap with—or family resemblance to—the other members of the category. The more shared features, the more likely is a correct response. In other words, the family resemblance view predicts the typicality effect.

Consider the difference in strategy between the classical view and the family resemblance view. The classical view starts with assumptions about how results from studies using deterministic categories will generalize to the real world and about how humans approach any learning situation. The family resemblance view, in contrast, starts by noting how categories in the world are actually constructed. Models based on this view thus looked at category structures for real-world categories rather than making assumptions about the types of stimuli and categories that should be used to study categorization.

Prototype Models

Rosch and Mervis (1975) incorporated Wittgenstein's ideas into a new information processing model of categorization, the **prototype model.** In this section, we provide an overview of the assumptions of a basic prototype model.

In a prototype model, similarity among items determines category membership—that is, items that are similar are grouped together in categories. When a new item is presented for categorization, its similarity to each of the alternative categories is determined, and the category with the highest similarity is chosen. To appreciate how this model works, we need to answer two questions: "To what, exactly, is the novel item compared?" and, "How is similarity computed?" The first of these questions concerns the issue of the *memory representations* stored during concept formation, and the second concerns the *cognitive processes* used in categorization.

First, what information about category members is retained in memory? In the rule-based view, the only information retained is the rule or hypothesis developed to determine category membership. A prototype model, in contrast, assumes that a summary representation of the category is preserved, similar to an average, or central tendency, of the category. That is, a memory trace is not created for each new item. Instead, a "running average" of the presented exemplars of a category is stored. That "average" item is called the *prototype*.

Second, what cognitive processes are used to categorize stimuli? According to the rule-based approach, the person examines the stimulus for the features that determine category membership (e.g., even number of sides). According to prototype models, the stimulus is compared with the prototype stored in memory, and the stimulus is categorized as being a member of whichever category prototype it is most similar to.

Prototype models have been shown to be good predictors of categorization performance for both artificial and natural categories (e.g., Estes, 1986a, 1986b; Medin & Schaffer, 1978; Rosch & Mervis, 1975). Thus, if we test a group of people on a categorization task and compare their performance to the predictions of a prototype model, the predictions are fairly accurate. So prototype models seem to have captured a good deal of the representations and processes used by people when they classify items.

But is there any direct evidence for the existence of prototypes? Two types of data have been used to provide such evidence: Categorization performance and tests of memory for individual items. Specifically, if prototypes are formed and used to categorize items, we should see evidence that prototypes are learned faster (or are easier to categorize) than other items. We should also find that information about prototypes is remembered better than information about other items. Before we describe two studies that address these questions, try Experiments 13B and 13C.

EXPERIMENT 13B: Prototype Formation

Presented below are nine cartoon faces. Study each face for a few seconds and try to remember both the face and the name of the cartoon character. After you have studied the faces, turn to Experiment 13C and follow the instructions there.

FIGURE 13B   **Study These Faces and Names**

Categorization Performance as Evidence for Prototypes   Posner and Keele (1968, 1970) performed several prototype studies using dot patterns, examples of which are shown in Figure 13.7. Each dot pattern consists of nine dots, and Posner and Keele chose four random dot patterns as the prototypes for four categories. You can think of the location of each dot as an attribute of a stimulus, where the location can vary both vertically and horizontally.

FIGURE 13.7 **Sample Stimuli from the Posner and Keele Study** Posner and Keele used stimuli with dot patterns to study prototype formation.

Three random
dot prototypes

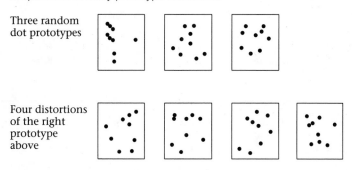

Four distortions
of the right
prototype
above

Source: Posner, 1973.

To create a stimulus set, the researchers modified each prototype according to certain rules. The exact rules for modifying, or distorting, the prototype are not important; the main point is that if you average the location of each dot from all the patterns of a category, that location is equivalent to the location of that dot in the prototype. You can appreciate how these distortions appeared by looking at Figure 13.8, which shows a prototype and its distortions.

Subjects were presented with 16 stimuli, 4 from each category, until they were able to categorize them all perfectly. It is important to note that the prototypes were *not* presented during study. Once subjects had learned to categorize the study items, the test phase started. During the test phase, the 16 studied items were presented, along with 3 new stimuli from each category—the prototype and 2 new distortions of the prototype. The subjects' accuracy on the old and new items was measured. This is similar to the recognition test you took in Experiment 13C.

Posner and Keele found that for *old* items, those presented during the study phase, accuracy was quite high—around 80 percent. Note that if subjects had been guessing at the items, then their accuracy would have been only about 25 percent (since there are four categories, the probability of choosing correctly just by guessing is one in four). Subjects were correct on about 50 percent of the new *non-prototype* items, still better than guessing. This shows that they did learn something about the categories during the study phase—they did not just memorize the labels for the old items.

A final important question is: How did subjects perform with the *prototypes?* If they developed or learned the prototypes during training, then they should have done better with the prototypes than with the new non-prototype items. In fact, subjects' accuracy was close to 70 percent on the prototypes. That is, performance on the prototypes was closer to performance on studied items than to performance on nonstudied items. This finding was taken as evidence supporting the prototype model.

Did you show any evidence of learning a prototype when you studied the faces in Experiment 13B? Here are the correct answers for the test in Experiment 13C: Faces 1, 2, 4, and 5 are old faces, and Faces 3 and 6 are new faces. How did you do overall? More importantly, did you identify Face 3 as a new face? If not, you were responding to the prototype of the faces presented in Experiment 13B, since Face 3 is the prototype face. Figure 13.9 illustrates how the faces in Experiment 13B were constructed from the prototype face.

EXPERIMENT 13C: Memory for Faces

Presented below are six faces. Decide whether each face was presented in Figure 13B. Then specify how confident you are of your decision, using a scale of 1 (not at all confident) to 5 (very confident). After you have made your decisions and rated your confidence, continue reading in the text.

FIGURE 13C   **Test Your Memory for Faces**

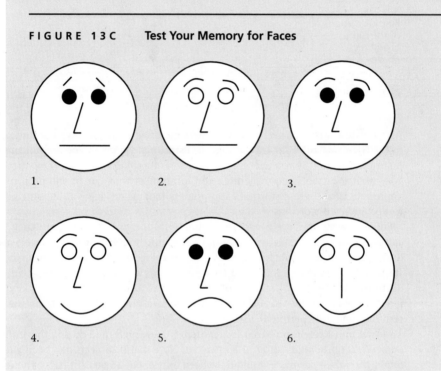

1.   2.   3.

4.   5.   6.

Memory Performance as Evidence for Prototypes   A second piece of evidence that supports prototype models comes from a different type of data: recognition performance. During the study phase of experiments that look at recognition performance, subjects are first provided with a set of items to learn and then given a recognition test. The test amounts to a list of items, some of which were actually present on the test (targets) and some of which were not (distracters). Subjects are asked to indicate whether they recognize each item from the study period. Often, *confidence ratings* are also requested. A confidence rating is simply subjects' judgment of their confidence about the accuracy of their recognition decision (usually on a numeric scale). For example, subjects could be asked to indicate if they were highly confident that they had seen an item, fairly confident that they had seen it, fairly confident that they had not seen it, or highly confident that they had not seen it.

Franks and Bransford (1971) used a recognition test procedure in a study in which geometric forms were presented to subjects. Like Posner and Keele, Franks and Bransford be-

FIGURE 13.8   **Distortions of a Prototype**   The stimulus on the left is the prototype, and the degree of distortion in the other five stimuli increases from left to right.

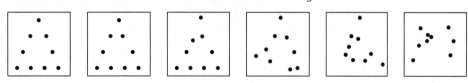

Source: Posner, Goldsmith & Welton, 1967.

gan with prototypes and created distortions of the prototypes for study items. That is, subjects were presented only with distortions of the prototypes during the study phase. The subjects were told to look at and try to remember these items. Once the distortions had been presented, subjects participated in a recognition test. For the recognition test, both prototypes and prototype distortions were presented. Subjects were asked to decide if they recognized the items and then to rate their confidence in their decisions on a three-point scale, with higher confidence being represented by higher numbers.

Figure 13.10 shows the results of the experiment for nonstudied items. The *x*-axis shows the number of distortions from the prototype. An item with four distortions was more different from the prototype than an item with only three distortions. The average of subjects' confidence in their answers is plotted on the *y*-axis. Notice that any point that falls on the upper half of the graph is an *error,* since subjects had not actually seen any of the items during the study phase. The higher a point is above zero, the more confident subjects were about an *incorrect* recognition.

Franks and Bransford's results showed that subjects were actually quite confident that they *had* seen the prototype despite the fact that it had never been presented. As the similarity to the prototype decreased, subjects became more accurate. This result is consistent with the idea that a prototype is formed in memory (in this case, even when subjects did not have to actively classify the items).

Processes Involved in the Formation of Prototypes   If people do create prototypes, is it a "conscious," intentional process, or does it occur merely as a result of exposure to stimuli? Do people have to learn how to create prototypes? An experiment performed by Walton and Bower (1993) addresses this question. The subjects of the experiment were 16 newborns (all less than four days old). The infants were presented with computer-generated pictures of faces.

The researchers created the stimuli by taking pictures of eight adult female faces. The eight faces were divided into two sets of four, and a computer program was used to create the prototype of each set. The four faces were blended together by the computer so that each face had an equal impact on the composite.

The infants were presented with six stimuli. The first four were the faces from one of the sets. Next, the two prototypes of the categories were presented. For half the infants, the first prototype belonged to the set that had been presented to them; for the other half, the first prototype came from the other set. Walton and Bower measured the amount of time the infants spent looking at the prototypes. On average, the infants looked for 9.6 seconds at the prototype of the category they had actually seen but looked for only 5.3 seconds at the other prototype. In other words, the infants looked at the prototype of the category with which they had had experience nearly twice as long as they looked at the prototype of the other category.

FIGURE 13.9   **Construction of Faces from a Prototype**   The face is the prototype, and it has the four features shown in the left-hand column of the box. The faces in Figures 13B and 13C were made up of various combinations of these features.

Prototype

Feature	Prototype	Alternatives	
		1	2
Eyebrows			
Eyes			
Nose			
Mouth			

What do these differences in gaze durations mean? Walton and Bower (1993) took them to mean that the infants had developed some sort of prototype by merely viewing the stimuli. If no prototype had been developed, the infants should have spent an equal amount of time looking at the two prototypes.

Prototype models are supported by the results of these and many other studies. These models certainly seem to do a better job than rule-based models, so if we were forced to choose one or the other, the obvious choice would be a prototype model. However, think for a moment about your own experience in learning about the rule-based view and the prototype view. Which of these two views seems more intuitive? If you had to explain the two models to someone who had never taken a psychology course, which do you think would require more explanation? The rule-based model makes intuitive sense—the processes and representations seem like what we experience when we categorize items. The prototype view may seem alien—trying to describe an "average car" to someone would be difficult. Simply put, the prototype view is much more complex and less intuitive than the rule-based view. However, the prototype view can make better predictions (in terms of specificity and accuracy) than the rule-based view.

Exemplar Models   Prototype models are not the only categorization models based on similarity. The alternative type of similarity-based model that has attracted the greatest attention is the exemplar model (e.g., Medin & Schaffer, 1978). **Exemplar models** assume that people store in memory a representation of each episode in which they encounter a stimulus. You read about an exemplar model in Chapter 5, where we discussed Logan's instance theory of attention; that theory is an exemplar model because it assumes subjects store a representation of each stimulus they encounter. (This also represents a common occurrence in cognitive psychology: Concepts and ideas used to explain one set of phe-

FIGURE 13.10 **Franks and Bransford's Results** As the number of changes to the prototype increased, subjects were more and more confident that they had not seen the item. In fact, none of the items had appeared before, and yet when the prototype was presented, subjects were quite confident that they had seen it.

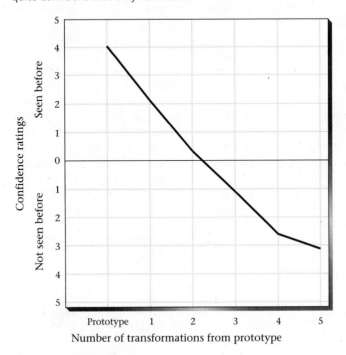

Source: Data from Franks & Bransford, 1971.

nomena [e.g., categorization] are often employed to account for other phenomena [e.g., attention].) The storage of stimuli is not perfect—some information may be lost (e.g., through interference), but we will assume for now that memory is perfect, just to keep things simple.

You may recall that prototype models assume that a person retains only information about the prototype after learning to categorize; no item-specific information is stored. If you take a moment to question that assumption, you will see that it doesn't make much sense. If we asked you to categorize a group of animals as dogs or cats, for example, you would probably call upon some memories about individual animals—a particularly cute puppy, for example.

It would be possible, of course, to account for such memories simply by modifying the prototype model to include storage of both prototypes and information about individual exemplars. But is it necessary to do this? Or could we instead account for both item-specific memory and observed prototype effects (e.g., typicality effects and faster learning of prototypes) *without* assuming that a prototype is stored in memory? Exemplar models attempt to do this.

As mentioned, both prototype models and exemplar models are based on similarity, but they differ in the way in which similarity is computed. For prototype models, what is stored in memory is the prototype, and the items to be categorized are compared with the prototypes stored. For exemplar models, all the exemplars encountered, along with the categories to which they belong, are stored; and items to be categorized are compared with all these items. The differences between prototype and exemplar models are summarized in Figure 13.11.

How might we test the prototype and exemplar models against each other? One way would be to use a measure such as recognition of items. Both models, though, make very similar predictions about recognition, although for different reasons. For the prototype model, recognition involves comparisons of items to prototypes. If an item is similar enough to a prototype, it may be "confused" with the prototype (which is the only item preserved in memory) and "recognized" even if it was not presented earlier. In terms of the exemplar model, however, this same item may be recognized because of its overall similarity to other items in memory, since an item similar to a "prototype" will of necessity be one that shares many features with other items in memory.

Deciding which model is the "right" or "best" model, then, is not simple. Most of the research performed in categorization today deals with exemplar models, even when a prototype model would produce similar results. Part of the reason researchers seem to prefer exemplar models is that they do not have to assume the creation of a prototype in order to use them. Thus, exemplar models may be more parsimonious—that is, may make fewer assumptions—than prototype models.

A possible criticism of exemplar models involves the assumptions they make about memory storage. Do we continue storing each exemplar, even those we have already seen

FIGURE 13.11   **Prototype and Exemplar Models Compared**   The prototype and exemplar models make very different assumptions about memory representations and cognitive processes yet arrive at quite similar predictions.

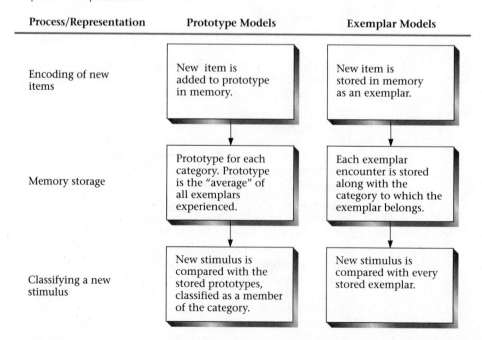

Process/Representation	Prototype Models	Exemplar Models
Encoding of new items	New item is added to prototype in memory.	New item is stored in memory as an exemplar.
Memory storage	Prototype for each category. Prototype is the "average" of all exemplars experienced.	Each exemplar encounter is stored along with the category to which the exemplar belongs.
Classifying a new stimulus	New stimulus is compared with the stored prototypes, classified as a member of the category.	New stimulus is compared with every stored exemplar.

hundreds of times? Is there a limit on memory capacity that would prevent such a thing? None has been found, but it is difficult for some researchers to accept the assumption that we can store a near-infinite amount of information in memory.

The issue of what is retained in memory has recently begun to be examined in studies using subjects with specific types of cognitive deficits, and this approach offers promise in helping to resolve some of these theoretical issues. These studies also highlight the importance of the types of materials used in these tasks. Kolodny (1994) examined the role of conscious recollection in category learning by comparing amnesic and normal subjects. In most categorization experiments, after the learning phase, subjects are given the test items and are simply asked to indicate which category these items belong to. It is thus possible that this task does not require explicit memory but relies on implicit memory (Schacter, 1987). If so, then amnesic patients may be able to learn to categorize simple items such as the random dots used by Posner and Keele. In contrast, some stimuli are more complex, and subjects may need to retrieve previous exemplars in order to classify them.

Kolodny presented his amnesic and normal subjects with two types of stimuli and asked them to learn to classify them. The simple materials used in this study were random dot patterns similar to those used by Posner and his colleagues (see Figure 13.7). The complex materials were Renaissance-style paintings by three artists. Kolodny took special care to make sure that the learning procedures were adequate for his amnesic subjects to learn the items. After subjects had learned to classify the dot patterns or paintings into groups, Kolodny presented them with stimuli from the study set as well as new exemplars. The main question of interest was whether the subjects would correctly categorize the new exemplars.

Results showed that for the dot patterns, the amnesic subjects performed about as well as normal subjects. This shows that for some types of materials, conscious recollection of prior exemplars may not be required. Knowlton, Ramus, and Squire (1992) have shown a similar result with amnesics using a different task. In contrast, the amnesic subjects in Kolodny's study were severely impaired in learning to classify the complex paintings according to artist. Some materials, then, make much larger memory demands than others. Furthermore, some people may find specific types of materials difficult to categorize.

Support for this latter point comes from research that has shown that people with various forms of visual agnosia may find certain classes of stimuli difficult to recognize or categorize. For example, as we mentioned in Chapter 4, people with prosopagnosia have a selective impairment in the ability to recognize faces. Similarly, Farah, Meyer, and McMullen (1996) reported on two brain-damaged people with deficits in naming living objects. Some theorists (e.g., Konorski, 1967) have argued that multiple systems in the nervous system support various types of visual classification. The important point for our purposes here is that these clinical cases show we can use converging evidence from different sources to examine the assumptions of theories of categorization.

Section Summary: Information Processing Alternatives

Prototype and exemplar models are information processing models based on the idea that the degree of similarity of an item to one or more internal representations determines the classification of the item. Prototype and exemplar models differ in their assumptions about memory representations and the cognitive processes used in categorization. Prototype models assume that a prototype is created for each category. As learning progresses, the prototype develops from the features of the studied items. When an item is presented for categorization, it is compared with the prototypes of the alternative categories, and one that is most similar is chosen. Exemplar models assume that information about every instance is stored in memory, along with information about its category membership. When a new item is presented for categorization, it is compared, on the basis of similarity, with the memory representations of all of the items in all categories. The category with which it shares the greatest overall similarity is chosen. In general, exemplar models are now looked on somewhat more favorably than are prototype models. The notion of similarity comes from Wittgenstein's (1958) concept of family resemblance, which refers to the overlap of features of related items.

CONNECTIONIST MODELS

Connectionist models of categorization have also attracted attention recently. Connectionist models offer an interesting alternative to information processing models such as exemplar and prototype models. Exemplar and prototype models assume the existence of internal representations. Connectionist models make very different assumptions about what is stored in the system and how the system processes items in a categorization task. In this section, we briefly review some of the main aspects of connectionist models and describe one model that has been applied to categorization. In describing the model, we summarize its architecture, how it represents information, how it responds to stimuli, and how it accounts for learning.

Connectionist Architecture

As you may recall from Chapter 1, a connectionist model is made up of simple computing units, or *nodes,* linked in a hierarchical network, with each node in one layer connected to all of the nodes in the next layer. Figure 13.12 presents an example of a very simple network.

Let us work through the architecture of the model to see how it functions. We will assume that a series of stimuli will be presented to the system and these stimuli will be categorized into two categories, A and B. Let us see how the system is organized (i.e., its architecture), how it represents information about the stimuli it encounters, how these stimuli are classified, and how learning progresses as more and more stimuli are presented.

FIGURE 13.12   A Connectionist Network   This simple, two-layer network can be used to categorize simple stimuli.

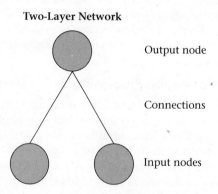

Two-Layer Network

Output node

Connections

Input nodes

The network in Figure 13.12 has two layers of nodes: an *input layer* and an *output layer*. We can think of the input layer as a set of feature detectors, with each node coding for a different feature (recall that we discussed feature detectors in Chapter 4). In this case, the stimuli that can be processed can have two attributes (since there are two input nodes), but of course we could add more nodes to accommodate more features.

Each node takes a different value based on the level, or "quality," of the attribute presented. For example, the first node might code for shape, taking a value of 1 for circle and a value of –1 for square. The second node might code for color, taking a value of 1 for red and –1 for blue. These values are called levels of *activation*.

If no stimulus is present, all nodes are inactive, and they have a value of 0. Once a stimulus is presented, the nodes are activated. For example, if we present a red square, the first node (which codes for shape) takes the value –1, and the second node (which codes for color) takes the value 1.

Figure 13.12 shows connections linking the input nodes to the output layer. We say that the activation of the input nodes is *propagated* to the output layer via the connections. Those connections are the key parts of connectionist models; and they, too, can be weighted with different values. The activation of an input node is multiplied by the weight of its connection to the output node. Suppose, for example, that the weight on the connection between the first input node and the output node is 0.75, and the stimulus presented is a square. An activation of –0.75 would be received at the output node. This activation is simply the weight (.75) times the activation of the node for square (–1). In general, the larger the weight on a connection, the greater the impact of the node on the output.

The output node is what we measure to know what the system's decision is for a given stimulus. In this case, we could define the output as +1 if Category A is chosen and –1 if Category B is chosen. The output of the node is the sum of the weighted activations of the input nodes. To calculate the activation of the output node in response to a given stimulus, then, we multiply the activation of each node by the associated weight and add the products together. This general process is given by the following equation:

$$\text{Output} = w_1 a_1 + w_2 a_2$$

Let us say for our simple example that the weight on the first connection is 0.75 and the weight on the second connection is 0.2. Substituting these values into the equation yields:

$$\text{Output} = (0.75)(-1) + (0.2)(1) = -0.55$$

Learning in a Connectionist Model

Now that we know the architecture of the system, how it represents features, and how it responds to stimuli, we can ask the next question: "How does the model learn to categorize items?" The only parts of the system that can change are the weights on the connections. Over time, the weights come to take values that will produce the desired output. The manner in which this occurs is called the **back-propagation of error.** Because of this, such networks are sometimes called *back-propagation networks* or simply *backprops*.

How does a back-propagation system work? What the system requires is a rule that determines how the weights are changed when errors are made. These changes should be made in such a way that the changes are commensurate with the degree of error. In this way, larger changes will be made when errors are large (e.g., producing a +5 at output

William K. Estes
William K. Estes is a Harvard University professor of psychology who created a number of influential theories of various cognitive phenomena, including categorization and concept formation. In 1997, Professor Estes was awarded the National Medal of Science, the United States' highest scientific commendation. This award was given in recognition of the tremendous impact that Professor Estes's work has had on the field of psychology.

when a −1 was expected). For the model to function, it must be given feedback about its decisions that is similar to the feedback given to humans who are categorizing items.

The mathematical rule used to update the weights is called a **delta rule.** In mathematical equations, the Greek symbol delta (∆) is used to mean a change in some value—in this case, a change in the weights. If we let w_i denote the weight on connection i (here, there only two connections), O_e represent the expected output of the output node, and a_i represent the activation of input node i, then we can write an equation representing a delta rule for this system:

$$\Delta w_i = (O_e - O)a_i$$

This equation is applied to all of the weights after a response is made. That is, the delta value is added to each weight. For the next presentation of a stimulus, the new weights will be used to compute the output. The delta rule allows the network to come closer and closer to the correct response with each additional iteration through the stimuli. Because connectionist models specify a learning rule, researchers can compare the performance of the model with that of subjects across trials in an experiment.

Support for a Simple Connectionist Model

Although connectionist models have been used to predict a variety of behaviors, we are concerned here with categorization. The question we are interested in is, "How well does the model predict human categorization behavior?" The answer is that connectionist models do remarkably well, even when the model is a very simple one.

Gluck and Bower (1988) constructed a model to "diagnose" diseases. In the experiment, two bogus diseases were described to subjects. Subjects were given lists of symptoms and were asked to choose which disease the hypothetical patient had. One pattern of symptoms might be runny nose, high fever, and clammy skin. Another patient might have only a runny nose, while another might have clammy skin, a high fever, and an accelerated pulse. Gluck and Bower used an arrangement of four possible symptoms that were either present or absent—thus, the network tested had four input nodes and one output node. The model performed impressively at capturing subjects' classificatory behavior. Estes, Campbell, Hatsopoulos, and Hurwitz (1989; see also Nosofsky, Kruschke & McKinley, 1992) demonstrated that the simple network model outperforms both the prototype and exemplar models on predictions of categorization performance.

Problems with the Connectionist Approach

One serious problem with connectionist models is that it is extremely difficult to use them to derive predictions about behavior other than categorization. For example, since there is no record in the system of what items have been presented, how can one predict recognition performance? Estes and colleagues (1989) did use the Gluck and Bower (1988) model to predict probability estimates produced by subjects (e.g., "How likely is it that a patient with a runny nose has Disease 1?"), but the approach assumed that subjects had access to the weights outside of using them for categorization. The predictions were consistent with subjects' responses, but there is no clear reason to assume that subjects had access to the weights.

A second problem for the connectionist models concerns the types of categories the models can learn. For connectionist models, the categories must be linearly separable. In other words, if the assignment of stimuli to categories does not permit the separation of the categories by a "straight line," the network will never be able to learn the categorization. However, it is possible to solve this problem by adding a middle layer to the network. In other words, a model that is a bit more complex can account for learning for which the simpler, two-layer model cannot account.

You might be surprised to learn that exemplar models have not been abandoned with the advent of connectionist models, even though connectionist models sometimes produce better predictions. It is ironic that a major strength of connectionist modeling—its flexibility—is also a weakness. Since a connectionist model can be altered quite simply so that it produces radically different results (e.g., by addition of nodes or use of a different learning rule), it is difficult to provide a direct test of these models. In other words, it is difficult to assess connectionist models' testability (or falsifiability) or parsimony. For example, if adding a single node to a connectionist model will allow it to predict categorization behavior that it was previously unable to predict, was the original model proved wrong? Is the new model really a new model? Is the new model, with one additional node, less parsimonious than the older model? These questions become much more complex as the complexity of the network increases.

Section Summary: Connectionist Models   Connectionist models offer an interesting alternative to information processing models such as exemplar and prototype models. Connectionist models assume that information is processed through a collection of simple computing units, or nodes, that are arranged in a specific architecture. One strength of connectionist models is that they incorporate a specific learning rule that allows the researcher to examine how the performance of the model compares with the performance of subjects across trials. Several studies have demonstrated that these models can account for human performance. However, problems with connectionist models have arisen as well. The models cannot be easily used to derive predictions about performance in tasks other than categorization; and presently, not enough is known about connectionist models to allow theorists to choose between alternative versions. It is also difficult to contrast connectionist models with information processing models.

REVIEWING CATEGORIZATION AND CONCEPT FORMATION

CONCEPT REVIEW

1. What is the difference between categorization and concept formation?

2. Identify the five advantages conferred by the ability to categorize objects and events.

3. Why did early researchers often use artificial stimuli in studying categorization and concept formation? What implications do the types of materials used have on the types of theoretical accounts offered?

4. Describe the main assumptions of continuity and noncontinuity theories.

5. What two methods did Bower and Trabasso use to test between continuity and noncontinuity theories? Which theory did the results support?

6. What basic assumptions underlie the classical, rule-based approach to categorization?

CONCEPT REVIEW *(continued)*

7. Explain the difference between deterministic and probabilistic categories.

8. What is family resemblance? Why is this concept important to prototype models?

9. Describe the main differences between prototype and exemplar models of categorization.

10. What is meant by *back-propagation of error?* Why is this concept important to connectionist models?

KEY TERMS

attribute (p. 420)
back-propagation of error (p. 445)
categorization (p. 419)
concept (p. 419)
continuity theory (p. 425)
delta rule (p. 446)

deterministic category (p. 429)
exemplar (p. 420)
exemplar model (p. 440)
family resemblance (p. 434)
noncontinuity theory (p. 425)
positive transfer (p. 424)

probabilistic category (p. 429)
prototype model (p. 435)
rule-based approach (p. 429)
sentence verification task (p. 432)
typicality effect (p. 432)
win/stay, lose/switch strategy (p. 426)

SUGGESTED READINGS

William K. Estes's (1994) book *Classification and cognition* (New York: Oxford University Press) is one of the best comprehensive reviews of work on categorization and concept formation. *Categories and concepts* (Cambridge, MA: Harvard University Press, 1981), by Edward Smith and Douglas Medin, gives an outstanding review of the empirical work on categorization and concept formation as well as discussing some of the important theoretical and philosophical issues in this field. Philip T. Quinlan's (1991) book on connectionist models, *Connectionism and psychology: A psychological perspective on new connectionist research* (Chicago: University of Chicago Press) offers an interesting discussion of the application of connectionist models to categorization.

Mental Expertise and Problem Solving

In nearly all human endeavors there always appear to be some people who perform at a higher level than others, people who for some reason stand out from the majority. Depending on the historical period and the particular activity involved, such individuals have been labeled exceptional, superior, gifted, talented, specialist, expert, or even lucky.—K. A. Ericsson and J. Smith (1991, p. 2)

I N T H I S   C L O S I N G   C H A P T E R, we narrow our focus from the general characteristics of cognition to concentrate on specific and exceptional aspects of cognition—expertise and problem solving. Although it might be tempting to think that the basic processes of cognition differ greatly between average and skilled individuals, we will see that what sets skilled individuals (experts) apart from others are the ways in which they have learned to use the capacities and capabilities of normal cognition to accomplish exceptional ends.

People can be skilled at a variety of tasks; here, we concern ourselves with exceptional performance on tasks that are primarily cognitive. In particular, we explore tasks in which exceptional performance is in some way linked to particular aspects of mental processes or capacities (such as memory or the use of knowledge) rather than physical processes or capabilities (such as muscular strength or coordination). This is not to imply that there are not important similarities and relationships between these two types of skill (see Masson, 1990). But our focus is how some of the processes and abilities discussed in preceding chapters are used to produce exceptional outcomes.

DEFINITIONS AND CHALLENGES: A LITTLE HISTORY ON RESEARCH IN EXPERTISE

What does it mean to be an expert? How do you know if someone is skilled at something? If you wanted to use the basic tools of the scientific method to investigate questions like these, what would be the biggest challenges? Before going on, take a moment to write down your answers to these questions and to list the ways you might go about studying skill and expertise.

Experimental psychologists have struggled with questions like these for as long as they have studied expertise and skill. For example, Irion, in his review of the history of the study of motor skill, commented that "the lack of a serviceable basic concept [of skill] is . . . a significant deficiency" (1966, p.2). Twenty-five years later, Ericsson and Smith (1991), writing about the study of cognitive skill and expertise, argued that basic problems of defining what skill is and where it comes from (such as defining skill with respect to stable aspects of the environment rather than important aspects of the skilled individual) continue to affect research in this area.

To show you what we mean by basic problems in defining skill and its source, consider Table 14.1. Here, we list what generally have been thought to be the sources of exceptional performance, the types of theoretical constructs that have been used to represent these sources, and the general research approaches that have been taken to measuring or investigating these constructs.

How do these methods of studying skill and expertise listed in Table 14.1 compare with the ways you listed? More than likely, the ways in which scientists have answered the

TABLE 14.1   **Approaches to Accounting for and Studying Exceptional Performance**

Expertise/Skill Attributed to:	Theoretical Construct	Research Approach
Inherited Abilities (Nature)		
General abilities	Intelligence, personality	Correlations (statistical relationships) of aspects of exceptional performance with general measures of intelligence (e.g., IQ) or personality (e.g., MMPI)
Specific abilities	Musical or artistic talent, athletic or mathematical ability	Correlations among measures relevant to the specific skill
Acquired Abilities (Nurture)		
General learning and experience	General knowledge and cognitive strategies or capacities	Measurement of basic or common abilities (e.g., digit or word memory)
Domain-specific	Domain- or task-specific knowledge	Detailed and analytic study of specific task performance (e.g., chess)

Source: Adapted from Ericsson & Smith, 1991.

questions we just asked are very similar to the ways you answered those same questions. That is, when asked what it means to be an expert, you probably answered in terms of abilities that are either inherited (like general intelligence or some particular aspects of personality) or acquired as a function of experience (like practice).

The Nature-Nurture Issue

Some of the earliest work on expertise and skill was based on the assumption that exceptional performance was largely due to inherited or inherent abilities (i.e., due to nature). For example, well over one hundred years ago, Galton (1869) argued that exceptional achievement was the product of inherent intellectual ability and some aspect of individual motivation. Galton identified highly accomplished individuals in a variety of areas and then studied their family backgrounds (including aspects of their genetic origins). Galton's work, like much of the research being done at that time, was concerned with identifying individual differences that could be correlated (statistically related) with exceptional performance.

It is interesting that Galton's work and much of the initial work on individual differences in intelligence was being done in the context of what was then a new and somewhat controversial theory, Darwin's (1896) evolutionary theory on the differentiation of species. The important coincidence here is that, in psychology and the social sciences, one impact of evolutionary theory was to direct scientific attention to questions of individual differences in abilities to adapt or excel.

Much of the work that followed Galton's used the same general approach: identify exceptional performers (by way of, for example, social evaluations) and then see if their expertise or skill can be correlated with some general measures, such as intelligence or personality traits. For example, de Groot (1946) and Doll and Mayr (1987) examined the relationship between high levels of skill at chess and global, or general, measures of basic cognitive and perceptual abilities. In spite of some methodological problems (see Cooper & Regan, 1982), these studies, like many of those that have attempted to find links between specific skills and general individual characteristics, basically came to the same conclusion: They found that experts did not differ from normal, average adults on these general measures (Cattell, 1963; Hunt, 1980; Kelley, 1964).

Other researchers have approached the question of skill and expertise by examining performance on specific measures of abilities and performance. For example, researchers interested in athletic ability have examined individual differences in physiology (Ericsson & Crutcher, 1990). It is appealing to think that certain innate aspects of a person's physiology, such as height, weight, and general musculature, might determine whether or not he or she can attain a high level of skill in sport. Research indicates, however, that many of the important aspects of physiology that are associated with accomplished athletes (such as larger hearts and different proportions of specific types of muscle fibers) are *developed,* or acquired, over years of practice (i.e., they are nurtured; Ericsson & Crutcher, 1990).

So what can we conclude about what expertise is and what its source is? Although the answers to these questions are not simple, it does seem that expertise emerges from the basic abilities and capabilities that humans in general possess. That is, it is due to both nature and nurture. For example, a great deal of research indicates that specific and intensive practice across an extended period may be one of the most important factors in attaining exceptional levels of performance (Ericsson, 1990; Ericsson & Crutcher, 1990; Ericsson, Krampe & Tesch-Römer, 1993; Simon & Chase, 1973), perhaps a more important factor than characteristics of the individual that might be independent of the effects of practice (such as IQ).

We return to this idea frequently in this chapter. But before we discuss some of the evidence that supports it, we should place the study of skill within a historical context.

Development of the Study of Skill and Expertise

Now that we have described some general problems that face researchers interested in skill and expertise, we can briefly examine some of the history of this research and see how scientists at different times have addressed these problems. We discuss this history in terms of four general periods of research, each with its own reasonably distinct character. It is the work from the last, and current, period that is of central importance to us. But, as we hope to have convinced you in the preceding chapters, this modern work is highly influenced by data and ideas from the decades that came before.

The First Period: Exploration and Speculation   One of the best examples from the first period of research may be the first: Bryan and Harter's (1897, 1899) study of the acquisition of skill in Morse code. This work was basically descriptive, and one of its most important observations concerned **plateaus** in learning—points at which improvement levels off for a while before continuing. You can see such points in the practice curves shown in Figure 14.1. Bryan and Harter (1897, 1899) thought that during plateaus impor-

FIGURE 14.1   Practice Curves for the Acquisition of Morse Code Skill from One of the Earliest Studies of Skill Acquisition

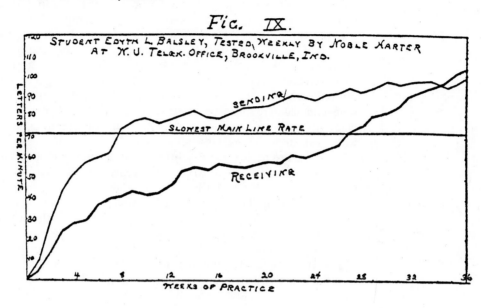

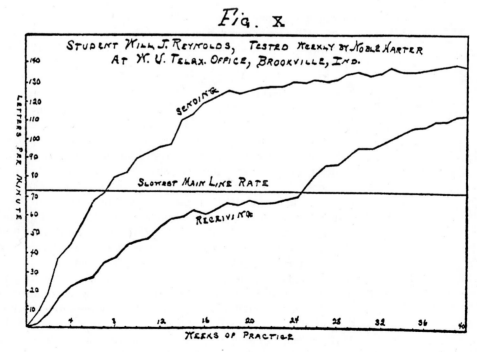

Source: Bryan & Harter, 1897.

tant psychological and physical changes were occurring. The idea of plateaus corresponds to the notion of a *stage* in the development of skill (see the discussion of stage theories in Chapter 11).

A great deal of effort was invested during the first period in describing the types of activities that produced practice curves such as those documented by Bryan and Harter. For example, two issues of great interest during this period were (1) differences in the effectiveness of spaced and distributed practice and (2) the importance of rest periods during practice (Jost, 1897; Pyle, 1913, 1914; Starch, 1912). We will see how these same issues have been the focus of more modern research later in the chapter.

Few theories of skill acquisition were proposed during this initial period, and those that were proposed were somewhat sketchy and speculative. Prominent examples of this speculative thinking can be found in general writings on education, including works dealing with the doctrine of formal discipline and the theory of identical elements.

The **doctrine of formal discipline** (Angell, 1908; Pillsbury, 1908; Woodrow, 1927) held that the mind is composed of a set of general abilities. Training in these general abilities would, it was believed, lead to increases in performance in specific areas. The basic idea was that, if children are trained in areas such as Latin (a language thought to use general cognitive abilities), their performance in other areas (math, for example) will improve.

The doctrine of formal discipline was challenged on logical and empirical grounds by the work of Thorndike (1906; Thorndike & Woodworth, 1901), who proposed the **theory of identical elements.** Thorndike suggested that skill learning depends on the degree to which the training activity and the target skill share stimulus-response elements. The idea was that if you want to increase children's ability to do geometry, then you should train them on geometry problems very similar, if not identical, to the ones they will have to do later on, rather than having them learn Latin.

One of the first thorough reviews of the literature of skill and skill acquisition was published by McGeogh in 1927. We can look at this landmark as the end of the first period.

The Second Period: Theoretical and Technical Refinement   During the second period, which extended to around 1949, a number of refinements were made in theories of skill learning. Researchers moved from descriptive research such as Bryan and Harter's to attempts to unify and explain what had been learned during the first period.

Probably the greatest impact on theories of skill acquisition was made by Hull in the theoretical work presented in his *Principles of Behavior* (1943). Earlier, we saw how Hull's views influenced the study of judgment and decision making and categorization and concept formation. Ideas from Hull's theory, such as those dealing with the influences of learning occurring before and after a skill is initially learned, played central roles in research on topics such as transfer of skill (Bruce, 1933; Buxton & Grant, 1939; Buxton & Henry, 1939). Hull's ideas were also important in basic research on verbal learning (Britt, 1935). In addition, variations of Hull's theory were important in directing work in a new area of research that emerged during this period—work on retention and forgetting of skill. And one of the most profound influences of theories such as Hull's was to motivate researchers interested in skill to move from descriptive and exploratory work to research testing hypotheses in support of the development of theories specific to skill. For example, Ammons (1947a, 1947b) attempted to apply Hull's ideas to specific motor skills.

While Hull's work had a theoretical influence on researchers during this period, the resources of the U. S. Air Force had a much more practical influence. Much of World War II was fought in the air, and the Air Force spent vast sums of money on research aimed at developing ways to test and train air crews (see Irion, 1966). In fact, much of the research on skills conducted during and after World War II was performed with equipment designed for selecting and training air crews. In addition, scientists began to use more elaborate and sophisticated statistical techniques, including the analysis of variance techniques that were developed decades earlier and are now common in experimental research (Fisher, 1918; Fisher, 1956; see also Cowles, 1989).

The Third Period: Increasing Research   The end of World War II set the stage for a great increase in skills research (particularly motor skills research). Irion (1966) notes four factors that were important in producing this increase.

1. During the second period, substantial theoretical work had been done, and psychologists interested in skill had both general (Hull, 1943) and specific (e.g., Ammons, 1947a, 1947b) theories to guide and inform their work.
2. Experimental techniques, tools, and equipment, along with the tools and techniques for data analysis, had become much more refined and generally available.
3. The Air Force had trained a large group of psychologists, all with similar experience and research interests, who were interested in developing active research careers.
4. Plentiful money had become available, primarily from the military, to fund research on skills.

The combination of these factors resulted in, according to one estimate (Irion, 1966), a *tripling* of the number of research publications produced on skill.

A major focus of research during this period was the conditions of practice: those that help and those that do not. Early research in this area had not distinguished the effects of practice from the effects of rest. During the third period, researchers began to see practice and rest during practice as contributing separately to learning and performance (Kientzle, 1946, 1949). Researchers at this time began to accept an argument offered earlier (Dore & Hilgard, 1938), that **distribution of practice** (having periods of rest in between periods of practice) is a factor that influences *performance* of a skill rather than learning of the skill.

Transfer of skill (application of an ability learned on one task to another) received a good deal of emphasis during this period as well, with major theoretical and conceptual papers published by Gagné, Foster, and Crowley (1948) and Osgood (1949). Another area of research involved standardized tests that could be used to predict psychomotor skill after training. This work, like some work we mentioned earlier, was originally done to help in the selection of air crews to meet the wartime needs of the Air Force. But the end of the war allowed the work to become much more general and to consider a wider range of tasks (Reynolds, 1952).

The Fourth Period: Cognitive Skills   The third period came to a close in the early 1970s. A number of occurrences during the third period had set the stage for psychologists to begin to ask questions about cognitive skill and expertise.

1. Researchers in the motor skills area had begun to take notice of theoretical advances in verbal learning (Underwood, 1957; Underwood & Postman, 1960).
2. Studies on problem solving by psychologists from the Gestalt tradition (Luchins, 1942) had demonstrated that factors much more cognitive in nature than those previously examined had significant effects on both learning and performance.
3. Some of the ideas about learning from the behaviorist tradition had come up against logical and empirical challenges. For example, Lashley (1951) had provided a number

of arguments that discredited the behaviorist view on the acquisition of the ordered or sequential aspects of skilled performance (Crowder, 1976).

4. Chomsky (1959) had published an influential general challenge to the theoretical and explanatory methods of behaviorist psychology.

But perhaps the most important achievement from the standpoint of the study of mental expertise had been the influential work of de Groot (1946) on expertise in chess. This work, which provided the model for a substantial amount of research on mental expertise, also served as the model for methodological refinements. We will see an example of this influence in the work on skilled memory discussed in the next section. As Ericsson and Smith (1991) have pointed out, however, much of this research has been—almost by necessity—descriptive and exploratory. Only recently has theoretical development begun to advance (Anderson, 1982), though some of the most recent advances have gone far beyond what existed previously (Anderson, 1993) in terms of coherence and generality. In some respects, research on mental expertise has only progressed past the point where general research on skills was during the first quarter of the century.

Section Summary: Definitions and Challenges

One of the most persistent sets of challenges faced by researchers interested in expertise and its origins has been to provide a solid definition of what expertise is and what its origins might be. Historically, various researchers have tended to emphasize either nature *or* nurture as the source, with contemporary work emphasizing the interacting contributions of nature and nurture. During the twentieth century, four periods have marked the study of skill and expertise. The first period, one of exploration and speculation, began with Bryan and Harter's study of the acquisition of telegraphic skills and ended in 1927 with the publication of one of the first thorough reviews of the literature on skill and skill acquisition. The second period extended to 1949, just after the end of World War II. It was a time of advances in technology and experimental methods as well as the emergence and influence of theoretical views, particularly Hull's. The third period, which extended to the early 1970s, saw a wealth of research on motor skills and the publication of initial work on cognitive influences in skilled performance, as well as influential work on chess skill by de Groot. The final period includes the present and is marked by the emergence of research on cognitive skills as an area of research separate and distinct from motor skills.

CURRENT PERSPECTIVES ON COGNITIVE SKILL AND EXPERTISE

With a general sense for how research in skill and expertise has evolved, we can begin to examine current thinking about skill and expertise. We begin by reviewing a general theory of memory skill. Although the theory does not provide a complete explanation for every aspect of skill and expertise, its general principles do offer a useful way of organizing what we know about a variety of aspects of cognitive skill.

Skilled Memory Theory

Skilled memory theory (Chase & Ericsson, 1981, 1982) was developed from extensive studies of two normal college undergraduates, SF and DD. These two people were studied over long time periods (DD was studied for more than four years). The starting point for the research was an interest in the development of high levels of serial recall performance on a *digit-span task,* in which subjects are presented with a sequence of digits and asked to recall the digits in the order they were presented. This might sound like a simple task; but before you jump to that conclusion—and before you continue reading—begin the small experiment described in Experiment 14.

Now that you have tried the task, think about this: SF was eventually able to serially recall more than 80 digits that had been presented at rate of 1 per second (Chase & Ericsson, 1981, 1982), while DD, who had been trained to use the mnemonic strategy developed by SF, eventually achieved serial recall of more than 100 digits (Staszewski, 1993).

But do you consider this a *skill?* Chase and Ericsson (1982) argued that digit-recall ability provides a general model for the performance of cognitive skills. Essentially, they argued that the general abilities involved in this task are the same general cognitive abilities involved in the skilled performance of any complex task.

To understand how Chase and Ericsson came to this conclusion, let us analyze the nature of the ability SF and DD developed. SF was a competitive long-distance runner who had extensive knowledge of record running times. (DD was a long-distance runner as well.) At a relatively early point in practice, SF noticed that certain portions of the strings of digits he was being asked to memorize corresponded to record running times. This made them easier to remember. He later began to notice that other strings of digits corresponded to important dates, making them easier to remember as well. Although SF was able to tell Chase and Ericsson *how* he was remembering the digits, Chase and Ericsson were faced with the challenge of accounting for *why* his strategies worked.

To do this, Chase and Ericsson (1981, 1982) proposed skilled memory theory. They developed the theory based on data from a number of tasks designed to capture the critical aspects of SF's memory skill. The data on which Chase and Ericsson relied included recall data from the digit-span task, SF's and DD's own descriptions (verbal protocols) of their study and recall strategies, and a set of experiments that tested hypotheses about SF's and DD's developing skills.

Skilled memory theory includes three basic principles and two related notions that follow directly from these principles. The three principles are (1) mnemonic encoding, (2) structured retrieval, and (3) speed-up of both encoding and retrieval as a function of experience. The first of the two related ideas is that high levels of memory performance reflect a change in the ways in which long-term memory is used, rather than a change in aspects of short-term memory. The second is that, with increasing skill, memory experts become better able to detect and use chance occurrences of meaningful patterns to help them remember.

The Mnemonic Encoding Principle   The first principle of skilled memory theory is the **mnemonic encoding principle.** This principle holds that high levels of memory performance (serial recall, in the case of SF and DD) rely on the use of existing knowledge. In particular, existing knowledge is used to organize the items that need to be remembered and make them more meaningful at encoding. Remember that SF and DD were long-distance runners and had extensive existing knowledge of running statistics (e.g., record times for specific distances). They used this knowledge to organize the random strings of digits they studied and make them meaningful at encoding. This is similar to the notion of chunking described in Chapter 8. For example, if presented with the digit string 349, SF or DD could encode the digits as a single item (a near-record mile time) rather than three unrelated digits. They could then remember the single items and find meaningful relationships among all of the items they were studying. An example of how SF could use his knowledge of running times to organize the digits he had to memorize is presented in Figure 14.2.

EXPERIMENT 14:   The Skill of Remembering Digits

As you read our description of SF and DD and their memory skill, you might have wondered whether what they were doing (remembering lists of random numbers) was much of a skill. But think back to our discussion of the Brown-Peterson task in Chapter 6. In that task, subjects have to remember simple three-letter stimuli: Not very challenging, but performance declines rapidly over reasonably short intervals. Perhaps learning how to manage the use of your memory, even for very simple materials, is a skill.

This experiment should convince you that there is more to the task that SF and DD mastered than you might have thought. You will need to ask someone to help you in this experiment. That person will act as the experimenter, and you will be the subject. Your task is simple. Below is a set of lists of random digits. The lists increase in length, starting with seven digits. (Why do you think we chose this list length to start?) The experimenter should read the list to you at a rate of one digit per second. As soon as the experimenter finishes the list, you should recall the digits, in the order in which they were read. The experimenter should keep track of how many digits you recall in correct order.

A note about scoring: The experimenter should count only those digits that were recalled in correct order. Suppose, for example, that you recall (in this order) the first, second, fourth, and fifth digits; these are all scored as correctly recalled, since they were recalled in order (even though the third digit was not recalled). If you recall (in this order) the first, fourth, second, and fifth digits, you can only score three digits as being correctly recalled.

Conducting the whole experiment will take you four days. Do not try to do more than what we have suggested each day (think back to Chapter 6 to figure out why we recommend this). When you are done, calculate and graph the mean number of digits recalled in serial order for each list length. Good luck!

Day 1	*Day 2*
List 1 (7 digits): 2 4 8 1 9 3 0	List 1 (9 digits): 0 2 6 3 7 1 5 8 2
List 2 (7 digits): 9 7 0 5 3 8 3	List 2 (9 digits): 9 4 7 1 9 4 3 5 6
List 3 (7 digits): 0 8 7 4 5 3 4	List 3 (9 digits): 7 0 2 3 4 4 8 2 7
List 4 (9 digits): 1 5 6 9 8 2 9 1 0	List 4 (11 digits): 0 7 9 7 2 7 1 7 5 2 9
List 5 (9 digits): 3 2 6 7 7 4 5 7 0	List 5 (11 digits): 5 8 5 2 1 6 4 8 7 2 6
List 6 (9 digits): 3 5 1 3 2 4 5 1 2	List 6 (11 digits): 3 2 5 8 0 4 5 2 0 2 2
List 7 (11 digits): 0 9 4 0 1 7 5 4 0 7 2	List 7 (13 digits): 8 8 7 9 6 3 0 8 2 9 3 5 9
List 8 (11 digits): 7 3 4 2 4 3 1 7 1 1 6	List 8 (13 digits): 3 1 5 2 5 8 2 7 4 6 9 3 5
List 9 (11 digits): 3 7 0 7 5 8 1 3 7 8 5	List 9 (13 digits): 0 2 7 4 7 3 5 9 8 0 7 1 3

Day 3

List 1 (13 digits): 7 4 0 2 8 4 2 1 6 4 4 6 7

List 2 (13 digits): 3 0 1 7 4 2 6 7 2 7 3 9 3

List 3 (13 digits): 7 2 9 4 1 8 5 6 1 3 8 6 9

List 4 (15 digits): 9 3 2 5 2 8 9 0 4 5 2 5 1 4 1

List 5 (15 digits): 4 1 2 7 2 9 4 0 4 1 9 8 5 3 1

List 6 (15 digits): 7 0 9 2 7 1 8 6 3 5 6 1 5 2 3

List 7 (17 digits): 0 4 5 9 5 7 6 9 2 6 1 1 0 0 7 6 7

List 8 (17 digits): 7 1 1 6 5 4 7 0 3 2 8 5 0 2 1 6 5

List 9 (17 digits): 2 1 3 6 0 4 1 6 7 3 7 1 1 9 2 8 5

Day 4

List 1 (15 digits): 8 1 3 1 2 8 1 2 1 5 9 9 8 5 8

List 2 (15 digits): 8 6 4 6 6 1 3 2 2 9 7 6 2 6 4

List 3 (15 digits): 2 7 3 3 4 3 3 8 0 4 9 3 5 9 2

List 4 (17 digits): 0 5 0 7 4 8 3 9 4 1 2 5 0 3 4 3 6

List 5 (17 digits): 9 7 5 1 3 2 7 5 2 9 6 6 4 1 9 3 5

List 6 (17 digits): 2 7 7 9 1 8 2 5 0 4 3 3 5 2 3 2 7

List 7 (19 digits): 3 3 1 4 7 4 6 0 5 8 9 2 3 7 8 1 0 1 5

List 8 (19 digits): 6 7 2 4 3 1 0 4 5 4 4 0 2 6 9 4 6 0 1

List 9 (19 digits): 7 8 1 7 6 7 0 3 6 8 9 5 5 2 3 0 9 1 3

Over the time that he practiced the digit-span task, SF's ability to memorize and recall the digits became quite dependent on the presence of strings of digits that could be meaningfully coded. For example, when Chase and Ericsson provided SF with lists of digits that could not possibly be organized as running times, his performance dropped to near baseline levels. In addition, when the lists were composed of digit strings *all* of which could be organized as running times, SF's performance improved substantially.

The Structured Retrieval Principle   The second principle of skilled memory theory, the **structured retrieval principle,** holds that experts develop abstract and reusable organizational structures in memory (referred to as *retrieval structures*) that are derived from the mnemonic encoding system. What this means is that experts develop ways of organizing the material they need to remember, and these organizational strategies do not depend on the specific items with which they are working.

For example, SF could use his knowledge of digit patterns to organize the digits with which he was presented, and his performance did not depend on the *specific* digits that

FIGURE 14.2   **Mnemonic Encoding**   The diagram represents an example of how SF used his knowledge of running times and digit patterns to organize random digit strings.

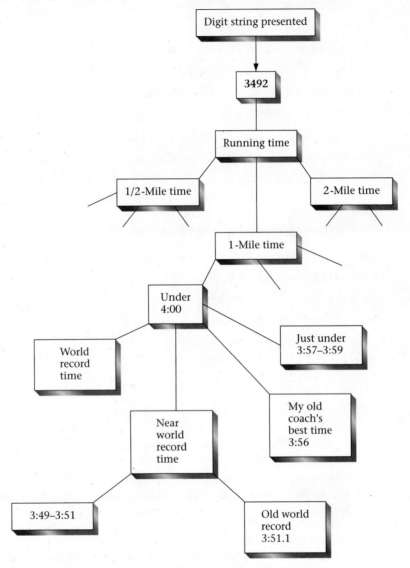

Source: Adapted from Chase & Ericcson, 1981.

were presented, as long as the digits could be organized based on his background knowledge. Essentially, all the expert has to do is remember the organized patterns and then use them to guide retrieval of the specific items.

The Speed-up Principle   The third principle of skilled memory theory is the **speed-up principle,** which holds that both encoding and retrieval processes become faster with practice. Increased speed of processing is a common characteristic of skill acquisition (Logan, 1988; Newell & Rosenbloom, 1981; Staszewski, 1988), and, as we mentioned in Chapter 11, memory development (Kail, 1988, 1991).

Chase and Ericsson (1981) documented the speed-up at encoding and retrieval for SF in a number of ways. First, they noted that in self-paced study sessions, SF's study time per item dropped significantly across practice. Second, they examined SF's performance on a particular memory task (Luria, 1968) and contrasted this performance with that of the memory experts S (Luria, 1968) and VP (Hunt & Love, 1972) and subject AB (an expert mental calculator who was also involved in Chase and Ericcson's research). At first, SF showed study times that were roughly equivalent to those of S, slightly shorter than those of AB, and dramatically shorter than those of VP. After 100 additional days of practice on the digit-span task, SF was able to further reduce his study time. Basically, SF's performance showed dramatic evidence for speed-up. In addition, SF showed a level of performance that was much higher than that of the memory experts. Remember, SF was a normal college undergraduate!

Two Related Notions Having described the three principles of skilled memory theory, we can consider the two related ideas mentioned earlier. The first of these—that skilled memory is a phenomenon related to the use of memory in the long term rather than changes in memory in the short term—follows from the mnemonic encoding and structured retrieval principles. These two principles hold that what changes with practice is how experts use their existing knowledge to organize the material to be learned, rather than their ability to maintain or rehearse that information for recall.

Evidence for the involvement of memory in the long term (rather than short term) in the skilled memory of SF and DD comes from data from an end-of-session recall task. SF and DD were periodically asked to recall all of the digit sequences presented across all of the trials in a session. By the end of the period described in Chase and Ericsson (1982), both SF and DD were able to recall more than 90 percent of all the digit sequences presented during an experimental session. This indicates that SF and DD were able to retain and use information over a period much longer than that implied by the notion of short-term memory.

The second of the two related notions, called *context coding* (Staszewski, 1990; Wenger & Payne, 1995), involves the ability to detect and use patterns in the target list that add to the meaningfulness (and hence the memorability) of items or groups of items. These patterns differ from the patterns used in mnemonic encoding because they do not rely on specific background knowledge, as mnemonic encoding does. Both ideas, though, are related to the notion of chunking. For example, Staszewski (1990) reports that DD, after three years of practice with the digit-span task using SF's mnemonic system, began to use a variety of relations among groups of items to better organize recall; in one such relation, three digits form a group DD referred to as an "add-em-up" (e.g., 426, where the third digit in the group is the sum of the first and second digits).

Acquiring Skill and Expertise

In our discussion of the history of research on skill, we summarized one of the earliest studies of skill and its acquisition: Bryan and Harter's (1897, 1899) study of the skill of telegraph operators. According to these researchers, the acquisition of this skill involved increases in ability followed by plateaus during which psychological and physical changes occurred that allowed further increases in ability.

Bryan and Harter's account can be seen as one that implicitly relies on the notion of *stages* in skill development. Roughly speaking, we can see the plateaus as stages and the rapid changes that lead from one plateau to the next as periods of transition between stages. In this section, we consider a contemporary account of skill acquisition that is explicitly based on the notion of stages. To illustrate these stages, we use a simple task—writing a short computer program to compute and print the sum of two variables.

```
main( )
{
    int a = 4, b = 2;
    a += b;
    printf("%d", a);
}
```

The specific theory we describe, originally proposed by Fitts and Posner (1967), has had enormous impact on how modern scientists look at questions of skill and expertise (Proctor & Dutta, 1995). In the course of our discussion, we also consider one of the most influential bodies of modern research on cognitive skill—that of John Anderson (1982, 1987, 1993). We will see that many of Anderson's ideas have formed much of the foundation for basic theorizing on cognitive skill.

Fitts and Posner (1967) described three general stages in the acquisition of a skill. The first stage is referred to as the **cognitive stage.** The type of information processed at this stage is often referred to as **declarative knowledge** or information: basic facts about the task. At this stage, people spend a great deal of time memorizing and rehearsing basic facts about the task. They also use very general procedures to apply those facts to performance of the task. In our programming example, individuals at the cognitive stage would approach the task by consciously retrieving facts such as, "variables need to be declared and initialized," "statements need to end with a semicolon," and "the addition (or incrementing) operator is +=." They would then use these retrieved facts to write the program, possibly rehearsing individual facts out loud as they worked through the program.

The second stage of skill acquisition is the **associative stage.** At this stage, people find and eliminate errors in task performance and strengthen the connections (or associations) among elements of task knowledge. The type of information processed during this stage differs from that processed during the cognitive stage. In the associative stage, procedural knowledge becomes important. **Procedural knowledge** refers to information about *how* to perform a task. During the associative stage, individuals come to use procedures that are specific to the task they are performing, in contrast to the general methods they used during the cognitive stage. In our programming task, individuals at the associative stage would retrieve the specific order of operations (declare a variable, increment, print) rather than the general facts they retrieved in the cognitive stage.

The switch from declarative to procedural information in the associative stage is an important one for some theories of skill acquisition. For example, Anderson (1982) suggests a computer programming metaphor to illustrate the possible nature of this change. You probably know that computer programs use words or strings of letters that look much like words, along with familiar mathematical operators (like + and =), to give the computer a set of instructions for performing a task. We can consider each line of the computer program to be equivalent to a declarative fact committed to memory during the cognitive stage.

Although these lines of program code give the human an easy way of providing the computer with instructions, the language that the human uses is not the language that the computer can process fastest. In particular, if the computer has to perform the task by reading the program line by line (interpreting the code, in computer science terms), performance is going to be relatively slow. This is similar to how individuals might process task information at the cognitive stage. They apply very general procedures (reading the code line by line) to sets of facts (the lines of code).

Now, the computer could work much faster if the instructions it had to process were written in a language it was better at using: digital codes that quickly direct the operations of the computer's central processor (referred to as machine language). And in fact, many programs are translated (compiled) from a form that can be more easily read by humans to a form that can be easily processed by the computer. In the same way, declarative knowledge is thought to be transformed to procedural knowledge, and this knowledge is very specific but can be used very efficiently. Anderson (1982, 1983) refers to this transformation as *knowledge compilation*.

The third stage of skill acquisition is referred to as the **autonomous stage.** At this stage, people speed up their task performance to the point at which performance can seem almost "automatic." A person at the autonomous stage would approach the programming task by quickly generating the necessary code, possibly without appearing to think about it much. In fact, the person could probably do the task while actually concentrating on something else (like TV or music).

Earlier, we suggested that skilled memory theory provides a general way of thinking about how skills are learned and performed. If this is so, then we should be able to find some important points of contact between skilled memory theory and Fitts and Posner's approach.

If we consider the data on Chase and Ericcson's subject SF, we can see that the cognitive stage of skill acquisition corresponds to the time before SF discovered that he could use his knowledge of running times to make the digits more meaningful. At this point, SF's performance can be characterized as relying on very general procedures, such as rote memorization. SF's later use of existing knowledge to guide encoding and retrieval represents a use of task-specific procedures. So we can see that the development and refinement of mnemonic encoding strategies and structured retrieval corresponds roughly to the types of changes described for the associative stage of skill development. Finally, the increased speed and fluency of SF's performance corresponds to the autonomous stage of skill development.

The Way You Practice Makes a Difference

Here is a problem you will face more than once during your time in college. You have an exam coming up, and you have a limited amount of time to study for it. You know that the exam will require you not only to remember specific facts but also to relate those facts. For example, you know the exam will include both true/false and essay questions. So you have some decisions to make. First, how do you distribute your studying across the time you have: a little each day or one long study session the night before? Second, should you study by rehearsing facts separately or by relating them in ways you think will be covered on the test?

For the most part, the research on practice has focused on these two general issues: massed versus distributed practice and part- versus whole-task training. These issues, and in particular the issue of massed versus distributed practice, have dominated not only the motor skills literature (see Irion, 1966) but the cognitive skills literature as well (Bruce & Bahrick, 1992; Payne & Wenger, 1992, 1996).

Massed Versus Distributed Practice If you have taken more than one psychology course, you have probably been subjected to a sermon about keeping up with your reading and assignments that goes something like this: "Don't cram." This advice reflects the results of research on a number of tasks indicating that **distributed practice,** which is spaced over a set of sessions, produces better performance than **massed practice,** which is "crammed" into a single session.

Originally, the issues of massed versus distributed practice and part- versus whole-task training were studied together, perhaps unintentionally. (Remember that the initial period of research on skills involved primarily descriptive and exploratory work that was not guided by specific theories.) For example, one of the earliest studies of the relationship between task length and task difficulty (Lyon, 1914) actually studied this relationship in the context of conditions of massed and distributed practice. The results from the study indicated that the longer or more difficult the material or skill to be learned, the greater the benefit of conditions in which practice was distributed across time. Lyon's (1914) conclusion, in rough paraphrase, was "Don't cram."

If the superiority of distributed over massed practice is so reliable and so general, you would think that people would pick up on it naturally over time. But that is not the case. Zechmeister and Shaughnessy (1980) looked at the effects of spacing practice on later performance in a memory task. Being memory researchers, Zechmeister and Shaughnessy had their subjects perform a free recall task. And being creative memory researchers, they also asked subjects to give estimates of how well they thought they would recall items after either massed or distributed practice. Some of the words in the lists to be learned appeared only once, and others appeared multiple times, either grouped together (massed) or spaced throughout the list (distributed).

Performance on the recall test showed some predictable results. Words that had been repeated were recalled better than words that had been presented once (a predictable effect of practice). And repeated words that were spaced were recalled better than were repeated words that were grouped (a predictable effect of spacing). The interesting finding was that subjects' estimates of how likely they would be to recall the repeated items was *opposite* the actual results: Subjects thought that they would be better at recalling the words that were grouped than the words that were spaced.

The belief that massed practice is better than spaced practice (in spite of the data that suggest otherwise) is also reflected in the ways in which subjects rehearse items. Modigliani and Hodges (1987) asked subjects to learn lists of 20 words and had some of the subjects rehearse the words out loud. These rehearsals were tape-recorded, and the recordings were analyzed with respect to the types of rehearsal patterns used. The data indicated that the majority of the items (65 percent in one experiment and 75 percent in another) were rehearsed or repeated together and then never repeated again. Basically, when subjects are given control over how they rehearse a list, they cram. In spite of their subjects' preference, Modigliani and Hodges (1987) found that recall was better for the items that had been rehearsed in a distributed manner than for the items that had been rehearsed in a massed fashion.

An effect related to the use of massed versus distributed practice is the **spacing effect,** the finding that increasing the interval (the space) between successive rehearsals of information leads to improvements in memory performance. The spacing effect is one of the most robust findings in studies of cognitive skill. It has been demonstrated in the learning of new words (Dempster, 1987), sentences (Rothkopf & Coke, 1963), paragraphs (Glover & Corkill, 1987), text passages (Reder & Anderson, 1982), and even portions of entire lectures (Di Vesta & Smith, 1979; Smith & Rothkopf, 1984). It has been demonstrated when spacing occurs over days and even over a week (Bloom & Shuell, 1981; Glenberg &

Lehman, 1980). Finally, it has been shown with subjects of different ages (Kausler, Wiley & Phillips, 1990), including five- and six-month-old infants (Cornell, 1980).

What we have been talking about up to this point is the effect of spacing *rehearsal*. What about the effect of spacing *retrieval?* Landauer and Bjork (1978) combined spacing in encoding and retrieval to produce a simple and effective memory-improvement technique. Of interest was the type of situation in which we have to, for example, remember the name of a newly introduced person, such as a person we have just met at a party. Landauer and Bjork noted that people tend to rehearse the name by repeating it over and over. This is essentially massed practice; and based on the research presented so far, we would predict that such a rehearsal strategy would not be very effective.

The technique that Landauer and Bjork developed is called *expanding rehearsal*. In this procedure, learners begin by attempting to recall the target items soon after the first presentation, in order to ensure that they can indeed retrieve them. Retrieving the items soon after the first presentation also makes forgetting less likely. However, retrieving the information really serves as another presentation of the items, and in order for these later presentations to be maximally effective, they should be spaced out in time. So following the initial short interval between first presentation and retrieval, the time between successive retrieval attempts is increased.

The initial work with expanding rehearsal (Landauer & Bjork, 1978) produced some very encouraging results. Later research has also demonstrated the effectiveness of expanding rehearsal, particularly for individuals with memory difficulties. For example, Camp and McKittrick (1992) reported some success with a modified version of the procedure to train face-name and object-location associations in individuals with Alzheimer's disease. Schacter, Rick, and Stamp (1985) reported that the procedure can also be effectively used with individuals with a variety of clinical memory disorders. Finally, the expanding rehearsal procedure even works for memory researchers. Linton (1988) used the procedure to learn the common and scientific names for more than 1,600 varieties of flowers. And one of the authors of this book has used the procedure to quickly and reliably learn the names of the players on his tennis teams.

Part- Versus Whole-Task Training   The question of **part-task training** versus **whole-task training** concerns whether it is better to practice the complete task or just parts of it. Although this question has received much less attention than the question concerning massed and distributed practice, it has continued to be the focus of a great deal of work (Whaley & Fisk, 1993).

One of the first theoretical accounts of the differences between part- and whole-task training was offered by Annett and Kay (1956). Annett and Kay suggested that if a task consists of a series of independent or recurring events, then it is best trained using the whole-task method. In contrast, if the performer's responses can in some way change the series of events (if the task events are somehow interdependent), then training using the part-task method will produce the best results.

To illustrate these ideas, consider two tasks: playing a piece of music on the piano and shifting gears in a car with a manual transmission. In the first case (playing the piano), the task can be seen as being composed of somewhat independent events. Basically, the notes you play with your left hand do not change the notes you play with your right. In the second case (shifting gears), responses to some of the events do change the ways in which the other events occur. For example, what you do with the clutch can affect what you do with the shifter. In this case, the events can be seen as being dependent on one another. So, according to Annett and Kay, the piano piece should be practiced as a whole, whereas shifting should be broken down into components for practice (Wightman & Lintern, 1985).

Whaley and Fisk (1993) examined the question of part- versus whole-task training in a task that involved searching for exemplars of a category within a set of rapidly presented items. Some subjects were trained with two or three of the categories separately before being exposed to all the categories, and others were trained from the outset with all the categories. Whaley and Fisk examined two aspects of subjects' performance: their acquisition of the task and their retention of the task over a period of 30 days. Their results showed few differences between the two training methods in terms of acquisition, although the whole-task subjects showed a slight superiority in acquisition. However, the part-task training produced better retention.

On the surface, these results might appear to contradict the conclusions of Annett and Kay (1956). But if we distinguish between acquisition and retention as important aspects of skill, then the results seem a bit less contradictory. Learning Whaley and Fisk's task can be seen as involving essentially independent responses, in that responding to an exemplar of one category should not affect responses to another category. In this case, Annett and Kay would predict better performance with whole-task training. And in fact, the patterns in Whaley and Fisk's data are generally consistent with this prediction. Retention of Whaley and Fisk's task, on the other hand, can be seen as involving a degree of dependency, in that performance after the 30-day retention interval was highly dependent on how well the categories had been learned initially. In this case, Annett and Kay would predict that part-task training would produce the best results. And indeed, this is exactly what Whaley and Fisk found.

Our own research on memory skills (Wenger & Payne, 1995) is also consistent with Annett and Kay's (1956) conclusions and shows how skilled memory theory can accommodate these findings. This work involved training a normal college undergraduate to remember long lists of random words in serial order, based on the encoding and retrieval strategies of another normal college undergraduate. This subject (whom we will refer to as Subject A) had, over the course of a single semester, developed the ability to serially recall a list of almost 80 words. Her skill involved quickly and reliably generating meaningful associations among groups of five to seven words in order to form sentences. These sentences were then linked into a story.

In the terminology of skilled memory theory, the generation of the sentences was evidence for mnemonic encoding, since it was the subject's knowledge of the language that allowed her to link the words. The thematic linking of the sentences was also evidence for mnemonic encoding and for structured retrieval, since the story structure could be used to guide both encoding and later retrieval. And the use of structured retrieval implies dependence between how the words were studied and how they were later recalled. Thus, according to the conclusions of Annett and Kay (1956), part-task training should be the most effective.

The training we designed (Wenger & Payne, 1995) was based on the sentence generation strategy used by Subject A. Essentially, the subject to be trained (whom we will call Subject B) was exposed to a series of trials involving the presentation of a list of words, one word at a time, at a three-second rate. Subject B's task was to quickly generate a sentence that used the presented words. As Subject B got quicker at generating the sentences and more reliably generated sentences containing all of the presented words in their correct serial positions, the length of the list was increased. Eventually, Subject B was working with lists that were 17 to 21 words long.

The important thing to note is that this training emphasized the generation of the sentences, not the recall of the list. After 201 trials of generating sentences, Subject B was transferred to a situation that demanded accurately recalling increasingly longer lists of words.

The effects of the training were observable in a number of aspects of Subject B's performance. First, she became quite quick at generating sentences and came to require very little time studying each item in the list. In fact, she spent less time studying each item than had the subject whose skill formed the basis for the training (Subject A)! In addition, the practice generating the sentences allowed Subject B to reach levels of memory performance that were equal to those of the most highly skilled subjects studied in our other work (Wenger & Payne, 1995). Basically, practice on the part of the task that involved generating associations among words (mnemonic encoding) produced benefits for the whole task (learning and recalling increasingly longer lists of words).

The Effects of Variability During Practice In discussing part- and whole-task training, we noted that we could look at effects of the different types of practice on both acquisition and retention. Another manipulation of different types of practice shows another difference between acquisition and retention of a skill. The effect is this: If you increase the similarity among the items to be learned or vary the processing requirements from trial to trial, you will interfere with acquisition but improve retention. This effect has been referred to as the **contextual interference effect** (Battig, 1966; Schmidt & Bjork, 1992; Shea, Kohl & Indermill, 1990).

As with much of the research we have discussed so far, interest in this effect in the context of cognitive skills (e.g., Carlson & Schneider, 1989) can be traced to similar work done with motor skills. A consistent finding in the research on motor skills is that if subjects randomly practice component movements, they take longer to learn the entire set of movements but retain the learning longer and show more ability to transfer what they have learned to a new situation (Shea & Morgan, 1979).

Carlson and Yaure (1990) investigated the contextual interference effect in a task involving the evaluation of four Boolean logic functions. Boolean logic functions take two input values, each of which can be either 0 or 1, and specify a resulting value, also either 0 or 1. Subjects practiced evaluating the logic functions in one of two ways. In the first— referred to as a *blocked schedule*—subjects practiced with only one of the functions for a block (set) of trials. They then moved on to another function, practicing it alone. In the second type of practice schedule—a *random schedule*—any of the different types of logic functions could appear at random during a single block of trials. After training, all subjects were transferred to a task in which a *series* of functions had to be evaluated, with the results of one step dependent on the results of preceding steps. An example set of functions and a sample problem are presented in Figure 14.3.

The results of this study were consistent with results from studies of motor skills. During acquisition, subjects who had practiced in the random condition took longer to respond than did subjects who had practiced in the blocked condition (see Figure 14.4). But when subjects were transferred to the task in which the steps were interdependent, the subjects who had practiced in the random condition responded faster than the subjects who had practiced in the blocked condition (see Figure 14.5).

Feedback During Practice Another finding that is general to both motor and cognitive skills is that subjects learn a task faster if they get feedback about whether or not their responses are correct (Anderson, 1990; Irion, 1966). In fact, the generality and robustness of this finding prompted one researcher to conclude that feedback "is the single most im-

FIGURE 14.3   **Example Boolean Logic Functions and Problem**   Carlson and Yaure used Boolean logic
functions and problems to examine the effects of variability during practice.

Boolean Logic Functions	Sample Problem

AND (#): X will be 1 if and only if A AND B are 1
    X = #(A,B)
 	
OR ($): X will be 1 if and only if A OR B is 1
    X = $(A,B)
 	
NAND (*): X will be 0 if and only if A AND B are 1
    X = *(A,B)
 	
NOR (^): X will be 0 if and only if A OR B is 1
    X = ^(A,B)
	A = #(0,1) ⎧ These statements ⎫
	B = ^(A,C) ⎪ need to be used ⎪
	C = $(1,1) ⎬ together to
	D = *(0,1) ⎩ evaluate ────▸ ⎬ X = #(B,D)
	                                    ⎭

Source: Adapted from Carlson & Yaure, 1990.

FIGURE 14.4   **Response Times During Acquisition of a Boolean Logic Task**

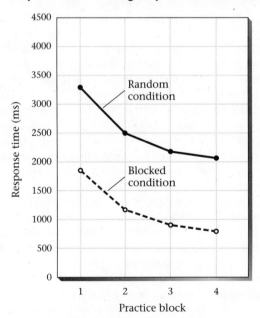

Source: Adapted from Carlson & Yaure, 1990.

FIGURE 14.5　　**Response Times After Transfer to a Task with Interdependent Steps**

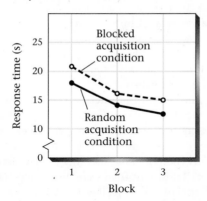

Source: Adapted from Carlson and Yaure, 1990.

portant variable governing the acquisition of skillful habits" (Irion, 1966, p. 34). The earliest work on this issue was interpreted in the context of early work by Thorndike (see Thorndike, 1931, 1932). Later work was influenced by animal research on reinforcement and was influenced in particular by the theoretical work of Hull (1943).

Although the general finding that feedback improves learning is quite robust, it is possible to change the *specific* effects of feedback by manipulating different aspects of it (Lewis & Anderson, 1985). Delaying feedback has little impact on whether the feedback itself has an effect, with feedback producing an effect even after a delay of one week or more (Bilodeau, Sulzer & Levy, 1962; Ryan & Bilodeau, 1962). And although the amount of feedback may have an effect on learning, some evidence suggests that this effect may not be a general one (Bilodeau & Bilodeau, 1958; Schmidt et al., 1989).

How Your Performance Changes During Practice

In the preceding section, we discussed some important ways in which aspects of practice can affect the learning of a skill. In terms of skilled memory theory, this involved issues relating to the ability to learn and use mnemonic encoding and retrieval structures. In this section, we discuss the general ways in which performance changes as practice proceeds. In terms of skilled memory theory, an important consideration will be how performance speeds up. And we will see that other important and general changes occur during practice as well.

Changes in Strategy and the Use of Available Information   Imagine a chess board. Imagine that the pieces are arranged to represent their positions following a couple of moves by two master players. And imagine that seated alongside the two master players are two novices—two individuals who know next to nothing about the game. Now ask yourself this question: Does the information available from the board differ depending on who is looking at it? It should be obvious that the sensory information is basically the same for both the experts and the novices. What separates the experts from the novices is the uses to which the experts put that information.

We introduced you to this idea when we discussed expertise and decision making in

Chapter 12. With respect to the study of expertise, some of the best illustrations of these differences come from studies of chess expertise, such as those by Chase and Simon (1973)—studies that initiated the contemporary period of research on cognitive skills. Chase and Simon (1973) began their work by following up on research originally reported by de Groot (1946/1978). De Groot had observed that chess masters appeared to have exceptional memory for chess positions. Whereas de Groot relied mainly on a descriptive, observational approach, Chase and Simon (1973) used an experimental approach to compare and contrast chess masters and novices.

Two findings from Chase and Simon's research are critical. First, the chess masters showed exceptional levels of recall for the positions of pieces. This finding replicated the finding of de Groot in a situation with a much higher degree of experimental control. Second, the exceptional memory of the chess experts was limited to *legal* chess positions. When presented with positions composed of randomly placed pieces, the chess masters were not any better able to recall positions than were the novices. Essentially, when they were presented with arrangements that did not allow them to use their knowledge of chess to mnemonically encode and structure the retrieval of the chess pieces, chess masters did not perform at superior levels. So the practice that had allowed the chess masters to become chess masters changed how they were able to use their memory in a specific task. It did not produce an overall change in memory ability.

But what is the nature of this change? Some scientists have suggested that, as a result of gaining experience with a task, experts shift from relying on surface features to relying on deep, or semantic, features (Anderson, 1990). While novices rely on the surface features of a problem, experts rely on semantic relationships derived from knowledge of the domain. For example, when novices are asked to classify or group various physics problems, they do so on the basis of surface features of the problems, such as whether the problems deal with rotations or angular movement. In contrast, when experts (individuals with a high degree of physics knowledge) are asked to perform the same task, they categorize or group problems according to basic principles, such as the principle of the conservation of energy (Anzai, 1991; Chi, Feltovich & Glaser, 1981). These types of differences have been documented in a number of domains, including mathematics (Schoenfeld & Herrmann, 1982), medical diagnosis (Patel & Groen, 1991), musical performance (Halpern & Bower, 1982; Sloboda, 1991), and writing abilities (Bereiter, Burtis & Scardamalia, 1988).

Changes in the Speed of Performance   When you think of expert or skilled performance, you probably think of performance that is fast. In fact, one of the basic ways in which Western cultures recognize experts or skilled performers is by the speed of their performance. But, as noted by Sternberg and Frensch (1992), "the emphasis on quickness that pervades our notions of intelligence is not shared by most cultures in the world" (p. 191; see also Sternberg, 1985; Sternberg et al., 1981). Still, one of the most basic changes that takes place during practice on both motor and cognitive tasks is that performance speeds up.

In fact, the manner in which performance speeds up is incredibly regular across tasks. The mathematical relationship between reaction time *(RT)* on a task and the number of trials *(N)* is summarized by the following equation:

$$RT = bN^{-c}$$

Here, b is a parameter that allows the relationship to be specific to the range of *RT*s observed for the task, and c is a parameter that determines the rate of change across trials.

This might appear somewhat complicated, but we can quickly simplify things. If we take the logarithm of both sides of this equation, then the relationship becomes:

$$\log(RT) = \log(b) - c\log(N)$$

If we graph the first function, we can see that RT decreases rapidly for the initial trials and then bottoms out (see Figure 14.6a). And if we graph the second function, we get a straight-line, or linear, relationship between RT and the amount of practice (see Figure 14.6b). Remember, these two panels show the same data—the second panel is just a transformation of the first.

The regularity of this reduction has been documented for a number of tasks (see Table 14.2), including cigar rolling (Crossman, 1959), visual search (Neisser, Novick & Lazar, 1963), simple decision making (Seibel, 1963), mental addition, the generation of geometry proofs (Neves & Anderson, 1981), sentence recognition (Anderson, 1983), alphabet arithmetic (Logan, 1988, 1992), determining the number of dots in simple displays of dot patterns (Lassaline & Logan, 1993), and reading (Kolers, 1976). In fact, some authors (Logan, 1992) have argued that, because of this regularity, any theory of skilled performance must be able to predict this relationship.

Changes in the Variability of Performance   With motor skills, such as those required in sports or piano playing, it seems reasonable to assume that there is some physical limit on how fast a particular task can be performed. With cognitive skills, too, it seems reasonable to assume basic limitations on how fast we can process information.

Assume that such limits exist. As you continue to practice, and continue to speed up, not only will you come closer to the lower limit, but your performance will also become less

---

FIGURE 14.6   **The Power Function Relationship Between Practice and Response Time**   (a) The relationship between the amount of practice and response time across a number of tasks is summarized by a power function. (b) When this same relationship is transformed via logarithms, response time becomes a linear decreasing function of the amount of practice.

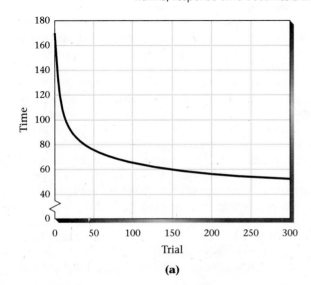

(a)

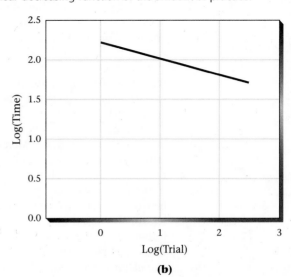

(b)

TABLE 14.2   **Response Time Improves as a Power Function of Practice**

Task	Source
1. Mirror tracing	Snoddy (1926)
2. Machine production	Hirsch (1952)
3. Cigar manufacturing	Crossman (1959)
4. Visual search	Neisser, Novick & Lazar (1963)
5. Simple choice task	Seibel (1963)
6. Reading transformed text	Kolers (1975)
7. Using a mouse or joystick	Card, English & Burr (1978)
8. Sentence recognition	Anderson (1980)
9. Text editing (on computer)	Moran (1980)
10. Geometry proofs	Neves & Anderson (1980)
11. Simple card game	Newell & Rosenbloom (1981)
12. Lexical decision	Logan (1990)
13. Alphabet arithmetic	Logan & Klapp (1991)
14. Dot counting	Lassaline & Logan (1992)

Source: Adapted from Newell & Rosenbloom.

variable, for two reasons. First, you will not be able to go any lower than the lower limit, so the range of possible response times will be bounded on the low side. And second, practice has made you faster, so the range of response times will be bounded on the upper side.

Data from a number of tasks have produced evidence consistent with what we would predict based on this logic. A decrease in variability with increasing practice has been documented for both motor skills (e.g., Adams, 1957) and cognitive skills (e.g., Logan, 1988, 1992). For cognitive skills, in fact, the decrease is regular and in many cases is systematically related to the change in response time (see in particular Logan, 1992). The interesting thing to note about this general finding is that most theories of skill acquisition do not directly address changes in variability, since variability is rarely, if ever, a dependent measure of interest. (Variability has been the focus of some recent work by researchers interested in development; see Wenger & McKinzie, 1996.) It has been suggested (Logan, 1992) that an important test for any theory of skill acquisition is whether it can predict not only decreases in response time but also decreases in variability of response time as a function of practice.

Another fairly general pattern of changes related to variability concerns the correlations between performance on trials as practice proceeds. Imagine a task in which subjects practice for 10 trials. If we calculate the correlations between performance on Trial 1 and performance on each of the succeeding trials (e.g., between Trials 1 and 2, Trials 1 and 3, Trials 1 and 4, and so on) we will find that the correlations *decrease*. However, if we calculate the correlations between pairs of successive trials (e.g., between Trials 2 and 3, 3 and 4, 4 and

5, and so on), we will find that the correlations *increase*. What this means is that initial performance is a poor indicator of the eventual level of performance. In a broader sense, it seems to mean that practice is more important than initial performance when it comes to knowing how skilled someone may be become.

These patterns and the conclusions they imply were first noted in motor skills by Woodrow (1938a, 1938b, 1938c). Evidence for their generality in both motor and cognitive skills has been noted in recent work as well (Ericsson, 1990; Ericsson & Faivre, 1988). For example, in our own research looking at the development of exceptional memory for word lists (Wenger & Payne, 1995), we found that a number of measures of initial memory performance (for example, serial recall of words, nonwords, or digits) failed to distinguish between subjects who did develop memory skill and those who did not.

How Long You Practice Is Critical: The 10-Year Rule

Thorndike (1921) originally noted that most adults perform at levels well below what they are capable of: "It is that we have too many other improvements to make, or do not know how to direct our practice, or do not care about improving, or some mixture of these three conditions" (Thorndike, 1921, p. 178, quoted in Ericsson, Krampe & Tesch-Römer, 1993). Yet considerable amounts of data suggest that even skilled individuals can show additional improvements in performance with consistent and deliberate practice in tasks such as Morse code telegraphy (Keller, 1958) and typing (Dvorak et al., 1936). How long does a person need to practice to achieve truly *exceptional* levels of performance?

Ericsson and his colleagues (1993) have suggested that, in general, a minimum of 10 years of consistent and intensive practice is required to reach truly exceptional levels of performance. In chess, for example, few people reach the level of grand master with fewer than 10 years of practice (Chase & Simon, 1973); individuals who learn the rules of the game after age 11 require 11.7 years, and those who learn the rules before age 11 require 16.5 years (Krogious, 1976). Even the prodigies of the chess world need nearly 10 years of preparation to reach the grand-master level.

The same appears to hold in skills other than chess. Exceptional composers (Hayes, 1981), musicians (Sosniak, 1985), mathematicians (Gustin, 1985), tennis players (Monsaas, 1986), swimmers (Kalinowski, 1985), long-distance runners (Wallingford, 1975), and medical diagnosticians (Lesgold, 1984; Patel & Groen, 1991) all appear to require about 10 years of practice before reaching exceptional levels of performance.

The same may hold true for scientists as well. Raskin's (1936) examination of 120 scientists from the nineteenth century indicated that the average age at which most scientists of this period published their first paper was 25.2 years and the average age at which these same scientists published their most important work was 35.4 years. So on average, these scientists required about 10 years of active work to reach an exceptional level of performance.

In a world of "overnight sensations" and "one-hit wonders," this might seem daunting. But it should also reinforce the idea that practice is a much more critical aspect of exceptional achievement than are initial levels of performance. Many truly exceptional performers have begun practice in their life's work at an early age and continued with periods of intense practice throughout their lives (Ericsson et al., 1993). For example, Mozart, one of the most prolific and gifted musicians in Western history, began composing and performing well before he was 10 years old. While Mozart died when he was still reasonably young, in the period before his death, he practiced his craft consistently and for intense periods.

The message in all of this is that, even though achieving exceptional levels of ability may require a good deal of time and energy, it appears that skill can be achieved by individuals with apparently normal abilities given extended periods of consistent practice. Our own work with normal college undergraduates who have acquired high levels of memory ability for word lists (Wenger & Payne, 1995) suggests to us that high levels (although not world-class levels) of skill can be achieved under conditions of consistent and well-designed practice in far shorter periods of time.

For athletes, a number of external changes result from extended practice—well-developed musculature, for example. Individuals with exceptional cognitive skills experience no analogous *external* changes. But recent innovative work with neuroimaging technology has demonstrated that some important *internal* changes may occur. Evidence suggests that portions of the nervous system critical to some skills may actually change over the course of extended periods of practice. In Research Report 14, we describe some of this new and intriguing work.

Transfer of Skill

Early in the chapter, we discussed the doctrine of formal discipline—the idea that general exercise of the mind could lead to specific improvements. We noted that this idea was challenged by Thorndike, who offered instead the theory of identical elements—the notion that training on one task would benefit performance on another only to the degree that the two tasks shared identical component behaviors. These two views represent interesting and extreme perspectives on the question of transfer of learning.

In general, the notion of **transfer of skill** refers to a shift in which skill on one type of task is used on another task. The literature on transfer of both motor and cognitive skill seems to suggest a middle ground between the two extremes of the doctrine of formal discipline and the theory of identical elements. Perhaps the most famous example of this middle ground is the theoretical analysis of the conditions of transfer by Osgood (1949). Osgood's conceptualization was heavily influenced by behaviorist psychology.

Osgood represented the probability of observing transfer between two tasks as the interaction of two continuous variables: the degree of stimulus similarity and the degree of response similarity. Osgood's *transfer surface* is shown in Figure 14.7. The height of the figure represents the degree of transfer between the two tasks, both positive and negative, with zero representing no transfer. The dimension that runs along the width of the figure represents stimulus similarity, ranging from an identical relationship (S_I) to a completely neutral relationship (S_N). The dimension that runs along the length of the figure represents response similarity, ranging from an identical relationship (R_I) to a completely antagonistic relationship (R_A). Osgood's representation suggests that the degree of task transfer that can be expected is a function of a range of compatibility between different aspects of what was originally learned and the novel task (Kornblum, Hasbroucq & Osman, 1990).

A great deal of research has been conducted on the conditions of transfer of motor skills (an issue that was and continues to be important for training pilots and others who deal with complex or high-risk situations), but much less research on transfer of cognitive skills has been done (Singley & Anderson, 1989). Research that has addressed the transfer of cognitive skill has been based to a great extent on research on the transfer of motor skills. Another major (though indirect) influence on contemporary cognitive research on skill transfer comes from the work of Gestalt psychologists.

A notion that came out of the Gestalt tradition was that of **functional fixedness** (Duncker, 1945), the tendency of people to perceive objects in terms of their common or familiar uses. This tendency can create difficulties when those objects must be used in novel or unfamiliar ways. For example, Glucksberg and Danks (1968) demonstrated that

FIGURE 14.7   **The Osgood Transfer Surface**

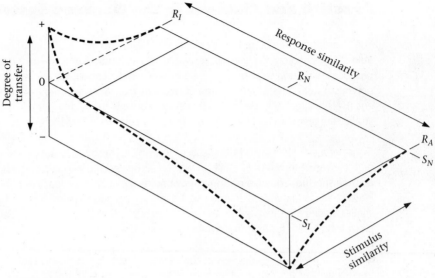

Source: Osgood, 1949.

the manner in which an object was labeled (in terms of familiar or unfamiliar relations) could either facilitate or impede later work with that object.

Another concept from the Gestalt tradition that is pertinent to the conditions of transfer is that of **_Einstellung,_** or "set." The idea here is that experience working with certain types of tasks can bias individuals to prefer a particular response strategy. The original work on _Einstellung_ effects (Luchins, 1942; Luchins & Luchins, 1959) was based on a task in which subjects must measure out different amounts of water using three jugs that hold known amounts. It is possible to solve all the problems by adding and subtracting the capacities of the three jugs. Subjects who were given a series of problems that required one specific strategy performed quite well when given new problems that relied on that same strategy but performed worse than untrained control subjects when given new problems that required a different strategy. In essence, these subjects had developed a problem-solving "set."

Some Truly Exceptional Individuals

Although we think it is important to emphasize that normal people are capable of high levels of performance, you should also know that some individuals have skills and abilities that go well beyond those of an "average" expert. In this section, we consider two types of exceptional individuals: professional mnemonists and savants.

Professional **mnemonists** are individuals who have made it their job, in one way or another, to be exceptionally skilled at remembering some specific type of information. These people have attracted attention from both scientists and nonscientists. At least a dozen published scientific descriptions of mnemonists can be found in the literature (e.g., Brown & Deffenbacher, 1975, 1988; Thompson et al., 1991). Many of these are detailed descriptions of the skill of a mnemonist, while others involve extensive analysis of the skill. We

RESEARCH REPORT 14:   Pumping Up Your Brain—Practice and Changes in the Nervous System

You know that practicing a physical skill (like lifting weights or running) can produce noticeable changes in your body. Now, research is revealing that practice in some other skills can produce changes in your nervous system. It has been known for some time that the brain and nervous system have a high degree of plasticity (i.e., they can change as a function of experience). Newer technologies are revealing how quickly these changes can take place. These studies are also showing how the brain may change to reflect the effects of practice.

Consider a skill like playing the piano or the violin. These tasks require the development of a high degree of motor skill, much of which can be specific to one particular piece. For example, the specific sequence of finger movements a pianist must learn in order to perform a Beethoven sonata will be of little use when she needs to perform a piece by Bach. But once she learns the Beethoven, she will be able to retain that skill, even after being away from the piece for a while (for example, while she learns the Bach).

Recently, a group of researchers at the National Institutes of Health examined changes in brain activity as a function of learning these types of skills (Karni et al., 1995). They used two sequences of finger movements in which the fingers of the subject's nondominant hand touched the thumb of that hand. The two sequences are shown in Figure 14A. Subjects were instructed to practice one of the sequences for 10 to 20 minutes each day for 4 to 6 weeks. The other sequence served as a control sequence.

Once each week, subjects performed the practice and the control sequence while having their brains scanned by a functional magnetic resonance imaging (fMRI) device. Neural activity in the motor cortex was the dependent measure. When the patterns of activity for the two sequences were compared, the researchers found that during the practiced sequence, a much larger area of the motor cortex was active, as shown in Figure 14A. In related work, these researchers and others have found that changes in the area of the brain devoted to the task persist for as long as a year!

concentrate here on one detailed examination, the description by Thompson and colleagues (1991) of the memory abilities of an individual named Rajan (see also Hunt & Love, 1972; Gordon, Valentine & Wilding, 1984).

Rajan Srinivasan Mahadevan, whom we introduced in Chapter 1, showed an exceptional ability to remember sequences of digits early in life. His most impressive performance occurred on July 5, 1981, when he recited the first 31,811 digits of π from memory in approximately 150 minutes (that translates to a rate of about 3.5 digits per second!).

Later in life, Rajan became acquainted with Charles Thompson and his colleagues and agreed to work on a project intended to analyze this mnemonic skill. After a series of experiments, Thompson and his colleagues concluded that two of the principles of skilled memory theory—structured retrieval and speed-up—applied to Rajan's abilities. However,

---

FIGURE 14A   **Changes in Brain Activity with Skill Learning**   (a) Two motor sequences were trained. (b) Different areas of the motor cortex were active for unpracticed and practiced sequences.

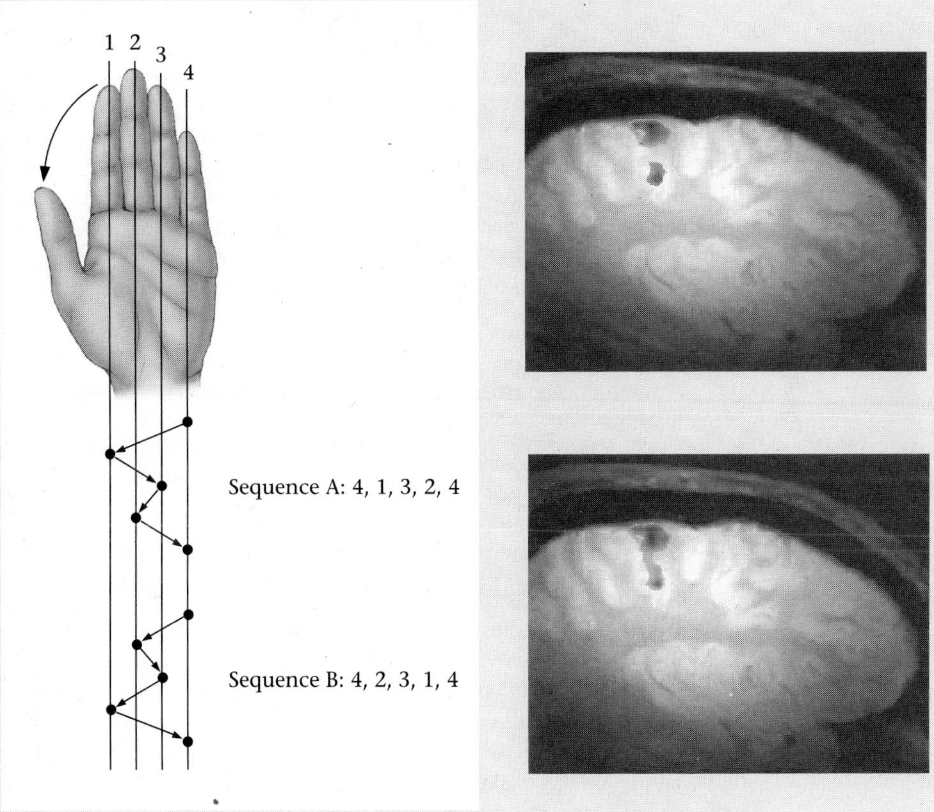

Sequence A: 4, 1, 3, 2, 4

Sequence B: 4, 2, 3, 1, 4

(a)   **(b)**

Source: Karni et al. 1995.

they were unable to define any type of mnemonic encoding strategy that Rajan might be using and concluded that Rajan's skill was something unique and innate.

From early childhood on, Rajan invested a great deal of time in practicing his memory skill. Consistent with the suggestions of Ericsson and colleagues (1993), this extended period of consistent practice resulted in an exceptional skill for remembering digits. Essentially, Rajan was able to refine a unique and innate ability over the course of a number of years. But in most other respects, Rajan's other cognitive abilities were no different from those of other normal, educated adults (Thompson et al., 1991).

Another type of exceptionally skilled individual is one who is extremely skilled at a particular type of task but who appears to be *below* normal on other measures of mental abilities. Such individuals are referred to as **savants,** from the French word for "knowledge."

A number of savants have been described in the scientific literature. These include "Blind Tom," a man with apparently below-normal intellectual abilities and a variety of language deficits who nonetheless possessed exceptional skills in memorizing, performing, and improvising music (Southall, 1979, 1983); the "Genius of Earlswood Asylum," who possessed exceptional mechanical abilities and was reportedly able to construct intricate scale models of machines and buildings (Tredgold & Tredgold, 1982); and "calendar savants" who show a remarkable ability to calculate future or past dates (Sacks, 1985).

One very detailed analysis of the skills of a savant is presented by Miller (1989). Miller analyzed the skills of Eddie, a musical savant. At the time of the study, Eddie was a five-year-old with a number of developmental disabilities who was enrolled at a center for retarded children. Eddie's mother had had rubella during her pregnancy, and when Eddie was born, it was discovered that he had a congenital heart defect. Over the next few years, Eddie showed a general failure to thrive or develop in the same way as other children. He was generally unresponsive to external stimuli and at one point was thought to be both deaf and blind. But Eddie did seem to have an exceptional talent for music. Miller (1989) provides this description of his first meeting with Eddie, in which he played a simple melody and had Eddie repeat it:

> I played (on the piano) the simple melody line of "Twinkle Twinkle Little Star" without harmonic accompaniment. . . . Eddie's playing reflected transposition to a new key with no hesitation. . . . The final trial was probably the most instructive of the series, however. Upon hearing "Twinkle Twinkle" again presented in the key of C, Eddie's response changed in several respects. First, he was no longer content to play the simple melody, instead adding several left-hand chords. Second, he transposed the piece to a minor key with several unexpected modulations in the harmonic structure. . . . He had already demonstrated that he could copy me if he wished, so these could not be considered errors. . . . Eddie was generating a new version of the piece. (p. 3)

Miller went on to conduct a number of small experiments with Eddie designed to explore the nature of Eddie's skill. Eddie's abilities seemed to be limited to music and also seemed to reflect the effects of periods of intense practice, as Eddie would spend long periods of time at the piano. Similar exceptional and specific abilities have been documented for other savants (Hill & Black, 1978; Spitz & La Fontaine, 1973). Although these cases demonstrate aspects of skilled performance that are consistent with the general characteristics we have been describing throughout this chapter, they also seem to indicate important contributions of specific unique and innate abilities.

Section Summary: Current Perspectives on Cognitive Skill and Expertise

Skilled memory theory provides a way of organizing current research on cognitive skill and expertise. Skilled memory theory includes three principles—mnemonic encoding, structured retrieval, and speed-up—which have been shown to apply to a range of cognitive skills. And the principles of skilled memory theory are consistent with both earlier stage theories of skill acquisition (such as that of Fitts and Posner) and more contemporary computational models (such as that of Anderson). Contemporary research has shown that various aspects of practice influence the rate at which a skill is learned and the amount of time it can be retained. Many of these factors are common to both motor skills and cognitive skills. They include the benefits of distributed over massed practice, the task-specific effects of part- and whole-task training, the effects of variability of practice on acquisition and retention of skill, and the positive effects of feedback during practice. Performance changes in regular and intriguing ways as practice continues. For example, as people become increasingly skilled, they shift from using surface characteristics of the task to using semantic aspects. Speed and variability of performance also change in very regular ways. Although practice does produce consistently positive effects, exceptional performance seems to require extended periods of consistent practice. In both physical and cognitive skills, it appears that at least 10 years of consistent practice is required to reach exceptional levels. Once a skill is acquired, the ability to transfer that skill to a new domain seems to be a function of both general and specific relationships between the original and the new task. The skills of mnemonists and savants in performing particular tasks seem consistent in some respects with knowledge of expertise in general, but these individuals also appear to have unique, innate abilities.

PROBLEM-SOLVING SKILL

Our discussion of *Einstellung* effects provides a good introduction to an important area of skill—skill in problem solving. Problem-solving skill may be one of the most general types of skills we possess. Think about the things you do every day. The situations you face differ from day to day but at the same time represent problems to be solved that are similar to problems you have solved before. For example, if you drive to campus or to the mall, you have to solve the problem of finding a parking space. After you have done this a number of times, you find ways of accomplishing the task quickly and efficiently, even though the specific characteristics of the situation (e.g., the specific arrangement of the other cars in the parking lot) change from day to day.

Problems and Problem Spaces

Typically, psychologists use two types of problems in their studies of problem solving (Proctor & Dutta, 1995). The first type is the **knowledge-lean problem.** Knowledge-lean problems are usually simple problems that are well defined and that can be successfully (though not always skillfully!) solved by use of the instructions for the task and general approaches to problem solving. An example of a knowledge-lean problem is finding a place to park in a parking lot. You can solve this problem by simply following the "instructions" for the task: Find an open space, and put your car in it.

One of the most widely used tasks in problem-solving research is known as the Tower of Hanoi problem (see Figure 14.8). In this task, a subject has three pegs. On the left-most peg are some disks. The subject must move the disks from the left-most peg to the right-most peg, following some rather simple rules in the process. Before continuing, read the instructions in Figure 14.8 and try the task yourself.

A number of things about this problem are attractive from an experimenter's point of view. Primary among these is that the problem is *well defined:* Subjects know exactly where they are starting from, what their goal is, and what the rules are for getting them from the starting point to the goal. But being well defined does not make the problem uninteresting. As you probably noticed when you tried the task, the rules can make it more challenging than it might at first appear to be. This combination of characteristics has made the Tower of Hanoi problem an important tool in experimental investigations of problem solving (see Newell, 1980).

The second general type of problem used in studies of problem solving is the **knowledge-rich problem.** Solving knowledge-rich problems requires specific knowledge or

FIGURE 14.8   **A Simple Tower of Hanoi Problem**

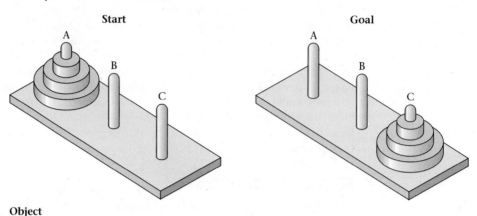

Object

To transfer all the disks on peg A to peg C by moving one disk at a
time and never placing a larger disk on top of a smaller disk at any
time during the moving process.

skill. An example of such a problem is programming a computer to perform some particularly complex task. In contrast to the problem of finding a parking space, this task requires
very specialized knowledge.

One very prominent approach to the study of problem solving proposes that, whether
the problem to be solved is knowledge-lean or knowledge-rich, the situation can be analyzed in terms of a problem space (Newell & Simon, 1972). A **problem space** is a general
and abstract analysis of a problem-solving situation. The problem space includes two elements: (1) a description of all possible states of the task and problem solver and (2) a list
of the ways of moving among those states. For example, in the task of parking your car, the
states include "car outside parking lot," "car in parking lot without any open spots in
sight," and "car in empty spot," among others. The ways of moving among the states include "driving into the parking lot," "driving slowly through the parking lot," and "turning into an available spot."

Basically, the problem space is a mental representation of the task to be solved. In order
to solve a problem, then, a person must mentally generate the appropriate set of states as
well as the steps he or she could take to move among those states. But note that the ability to generate and work with a problem space implies two things. First, the problem solver
must have enough knowledge of the task to be able to generate the set of possible states
and the ways of moving among the states. And second, he or she must consider all the
ways of moving successfully through the states to complete the task.

With respect to the first point, the processes and experiences that allow a person to derive a problem space for the task are referred to as *understanding* (Van Lehn, 1989). Numerous changes in the individual's understanding can occur as experience with the task
increases, particularly for problems that are complex or difficult.

The second process involves *search* (Van Lehn, 1989). It may be helpful to think of
search as a kind of planning. A search of the problem space involves starting at some state,
choosing a way of moving to some other state, and evaluating the potential result to see if

the problem is any closer to solution. This general process is repeated until the problem is solved. Table 14.3 lists some of the most common methods of searching a problem space. As an exercise, see if you can apply each of these methods to the problem of finding a parking space in a crowded parking lot.

Problem-Solving Abilities Across the Lifespan

As you might remember from Chapter 11, cognitive abilities (including problem-solving) change in important ways as we go through life. During infancy, problem solving begins with imitation—watching a more knowledgeable person attempt to solve the problem and then repeating (or trying to repeat) that person's actions. As development progresses, problem-solving abilities change in ways consistent with developmental changes in information processing, discussed in Chapter 11.

Problem-solving abilities can change rapidly in young children. Deloache (1989) demonstrated this fact in research involving a scale model of a laboratory room. A small toy was hidden in the scale model, and a larger version of the toy was hidden in the corresponding location in the laboratory room itself. A child of 2½, when shown the small toy and told that a bigger version of the toy is hidden in the laboratory room, will have difficulty retrieving the bigger version of the toy. A 3-year-old, however, can go into the laboratory room and find the bigger toy.

Older children's problem solving demonstrates the ability to examine the problem they need to solve, set a goal, and plan a procedure to get from the current situation to the goal. Younger children can evaluate the current situation but may have difficulty setting the

---

TABLE 14.3 **Some General Methods for Searching a Problem Space**

Method	Description
Generate and test	Generate a sequence of steps to go from present state to goal state. At each step, check to see if the now current step is equivalent to the goal state.
Heuristic search	Use a "rule of thumb" or some general approach (a heuristic) to define the way of getting from the present to the goal state. Maintain a memory for which states you have been in and which steps you have taken.
Hill climbing	Use a set of operations on the present state. Compare the outcomes from each operation and select the one that gets you closest to the goal state. Repeat as needed until the goal state is reached.
Means-ends analysis	Compare the present state to the goal state and take a step that gets you as close as possible to the goal state.

Source: Proctor & Dutta, 1995.

goal and the plan to reach the goal. That is, they may have some difficulty understanding the problem space. The more steps involved in reaching the goal, the more difficulty a younger child will have. That is, younger children may also have problems searching the problem space.

A significant portion of the research on the abilities of older adults to problem-solve focuses on everyday problem solving (Willis, 1996). Problem solving in everyday life is less impaired with age than problem solving in an experimental situation (Cavenaugh et al., 1985; Reese & Rodeheaver, 1985). Everyday problems might include what do to if you are caught in a blizzard or if your eight-year-old daughter is not home from school when you expect her (Denney & Palmer, 1981). Older adults solve these everyday problems correctly as often as or only slightly less often than younger adults.

An older adult's approach to a problem to be solved may be different from the approach of a younger adult, however. Older adults' problem-solving procedures resemble those of expert problem solvers. They tend to consider fewer alternatives, use smaller pieces of information, emphasize personal knowledge, and use a top-down processing strategy (Willis, 1996). This allows an older adult to make a decision and reach a solution faster and earlier in the problem-solving processes, compared to a younger adult.

Although older adults may use different strategies to solve problems, they have to contend with factors that make any type of cognitive processing more difficult. A general conclusion based on everyday problem solving and other research on cognitive abilities is that information-processing abilities slow down with age, and this appears to negatively affect memory and abstract problem solving. Everyday problem solving, however, appears to involve other factors, such as expertise, that may help an older adult overcome other cognitive shortcomings.

Section Summary: Problem-Solving Skill

One important area of research on cognitive skill focuses on the skill of solving problems. Understanding this skill requires understanding the problem space and the processes that operate on this problem space (understanding and search). Problem-solving abilities change across the lifespan, and these changes are consistent with the developmental changes in information processing discussed in Chapter 11.

REVIEWING MENTAL EXPERTISE AND PROBLEM SOLVING

CONCEPT REVIEW

1. Summarize the differences between the nature and nurture approaches to understanding skill and expertise.

2. Describe the four historical periods of study of skill and expertise. What current topics of study of skill and expertise have their roots in the work done in these four periods?

3. What is the doctrine of formal discipline? The theory of identical elements? Compare and contrast these two perspectives.

4. What are the three principles of skilled memory theory? What are two related ideas? Describe some data that support each of these principles and ideas.

CONCEPT REVIEW *(continued)*

5. Summarize the stage theory of skill acquisition of Fitts and Posner. How does this theory relate to the work by Bryan and Harter? How does it relate to skilled memory theory?

6. What is knowledge compilation, and why is it important for understanding skill acquisition? How does knowledge compilation relate to Posner and Fitts's theory?

7. Describe the differences between massed and distributed practice. What effects do these two types of practice have on the acquisition and retention of a skill?

8. What is the spacing effect? With respect to what aspect of memory (encoding, storage, or retrieval) has the spacing effect typically been studied? Relate the spacing effect to the expanding rehearsal technique.

9. Define part-task and whole-task training. What types of tasks benefit from each of these types of training?

10. What is the contextual interference effect? How does variability during practice affect acquisition and retention of a skill?

11. Describe the techniques that Chase and Simon used to provide experimental confirmation of results originally reported by de Groot.

12. Summarize the important and regular changes that occur in the speed and variability of performance with increasing practice.

13. What is the 10-year rule?

14. Describe Osgood's transfer surface. How does contemporary work on the transfer of skill relate to the doctrine of formal discipline and the theory of identical elements?

15. What distinguishes a mnemonist, a savant, and a skilled individual?

16. What is a problem space? What is the difference between knowledge-rich and knowledge-lean problems?

17. What two processes are thought to be required to operate on a problem space? Define and describe each of these processes.

18. How do problem-solving approaches change across the lifespan?

KEY TERMS

associative stage (p. 462)
autonomous stage (p. 463)
cognitive stage (p. 462)
contextual interference effect (p. 467)
declarative knowledge (p. 462)
distributed practice (p. 464)
distribution of practice (p. 455)
doctrine of formal discipline (p. 454)
Einstellung (p. 475)

functional fixedness (p. 474)
knowledge-lean problem (p. 479)
knowledge-rich problem (p. 479)
massed practice (p. 464)
mnemonic encoding principle (p. 457)
mnemonist (p. 475)
part-task training (p. 465)
plateau (p. 452)
problem space (p. 480)

procedural knowledge (p. 462)
savant (p. 472)
spacing effect (p. 464)
speed-up principle (p. 460)
structured retrieval principle (p. 459)
theory of identical elements (p. 454)
transfer of skill (p. 474)
whole-task training (p. 465)

SUGGESTED READINGS

The introductory chapters from two books provide more on the background of the issues we have been discussing. The first chapter in *Skill acquisition and human performance* (Thousand Oaks, CA: Sage), by R. W. Proctor and A. Dutta (1995), lays out some of the basic issues in the study of skill. And the first chapter in K. A. Ericsson and J. Smith's (1991) book entitled *Toward a general theory of expertise* (Cambridge: Cambridge University Press) provides an interesting and different perspective on many of these same issues. The review by Ericsson et al. (1993) of data on the acquisition of exceptional levels of skill provides an interesting discussion of how extended practice is required in a wide range of skills.

Glossary

absolute threshold The lowest level of physical stimulation that a person can detect; a psychophysical concept.

acoustical property A physical characteristic of the sounds in an auditory stimulus, such as the speech signal.

acquisition The process of putting information into memory. *Acquisition* is sometimes used as a synonym for *learning* and is also called *encoding*.

action potential The rapid change in cell membrane potential from −65 mV to +50 mV and then back to slightly more than −70 mV. The action potential results in the release of neurotransmitters, which allow neurons to communicate.

analytical introspection Wilhelm Wundt's method of having trained observers report on the contents of their conscious, moment-to-moment experience as they perceive an object or event.

anaphora The use of one word or concept to refer to a previously named word or concept.

anchoring An effect in which a person's numerical estimate of something (such as the probability of an event) is based on some previous estimate, which serves as an anchor. *See also* **representativeness heuristic; availability heuristic.**

aphasia A language deficit or difficulty that results from physical damage to the brain, infections or tumors in the brain, or birth defects.

approach-avoidance behavior Behavior resulting from a condition in which an organism is both attracted toward and repelled away from a particular goal, event, or object.

architecture In regard to a model of memory, the types and arrangements of structures that make up memory.

articulatory gesture In the direct-realist approach to speech perception, an action that gives structure to the auditory waveforms directly perceived by listeners; the coordinated movements of the muscles in the vocal tract are articulatory gestures.

associative information Memory information that is associated with the item but that is not the item's identity. *See also* **item information; order information.**

associative stage The second stage in Fitts and Posner's stage model of skill acquisition. At this stage, people find and eliminate errors in their performance of the task and strengthen the associations among elements of task knowledge. *See also* **cognitive stage; autonomous stage.**

attenuation model An early selection model of selective attention proposed by Anne Treisman. The model assumes that attended-to messages are processed completely and unattended messages are processed in an attenuated, or weakened, form.

attribute A quality that can vary across a set of stimuli. Categorization researchers often identify attributes (e.g., size) and then select several different values of these attributes (e.g., small, medium, large) to create stimuli for experiments.

automatic task A well-learned task that does not require attention and that involves processes that may require little if any capacity for their execution.

autonomous stage The third stage in Fitts and Posner's stage model of skill acquisition. At this stage, people speed up in their performance of the task, and performance sometimes seems "automatic." *See also* **cognitive stage; associative stage.**

availability heuristic A heuristic in which a person's judgment about something is influenced by the ease with which he or she can remember information about that object or event. *See also* **representativeness heuristic; anchoring.**

average evoked potential (AEP) The overall electrical activity in the brain as measured by electrodes placed on the scalp. *See also* **electroencephalogram; event-related potential.**

axon A projection from the cell body of a neuron. The axon carries the action potential, which results in the release of neurotransmitters from the synaptic boutton.

back-propagation of error A learning method used with connectionist models. The method changes the weights of connections between nodes when errors are made so that the changes are commensurate with the degree of error.

backward reasoning Reasoning by moving from hypotheses to observations; backward reasoning is related to deductive reasoning, which moves from the general to the specific. *See also* **forward reasoning.**

behaviorism A school of psychology that takes the theoretical position that psychology should focus on observable events, including stimuli, responses, and reinforcers. Behaviorism rejects the study of the mind as unscientific because the mind is not directly observable.

ß (beta) In signal detection theory, the measure of response bias, or the response criterion the subject sets in order to respond that a signal is present.

blind spot The point on the retina at which the optic nerve leaves the retina. There are no photoreceptors in this area.

blob A shape identified by the visual system but not yet classified.

Bonini's paradox The situation in which a theoretical model is no easier to understand than the phenomenon being modeled.

bottom-up theory A theory that assumes that the processing of information begins with low-level information, which is passed along to higher cognitive processes.

bounded rationality In the context of judgment and decision making, rationality based on the assumption that, although many variables may be important with respect to a particular judgment or decision, some of these variables can be disregarded.

Brown-Peterson distractor task A memory task that was central in developing the notion of short-term memory. The experimenter presents subjects with items to study. Immediately after the last item is presented, the experimenter gives subjects a number and tells them to quickly count backward by threes. The subjects' task is to remember as many studied items as they can after the counting period.

capacity (1) Attentional resources. Capacity is a hypothetical construct that serves an energizing function for the perceptual and cognitive system. In order for a perceptual or cognitive process to operate, it must be supplied with adequate capacity. (2) Memory. The amount of information that can be retained in memory (or processed in some other way) in a given unit of time.

case grammar approach An approach to the study of semantics that holds that people's parsing of sentences is based on the semantic role the word plays in the sentence, not the syntactic role.

categorical perception Perception characterized by the situation in which subjects have trouble distinguishing among things from the same category while easily distinguishing among things from different categories.

categorization Behavior whereby a person divides a set of objects or events into at least two groups. Based on how people divide these objects or events, inferences are made about the types of knowledge or rules being used. *See also* **concept.**

causal inference With respect to the comprehension of written language, an inference that something being discussed in a text will cause something else to happen. *See also* **elaborative inference; instrumental inference.**

cerebral cortex The layer of neural tissue that surrounds the cerebral hemispheres. The cerebral cortex is highly convoluted, which allows for a much larger surface area than would be possible with a smooth cortex of comparable dimensions.

changed-trace hypothesis An explanation for the misinformation effect that holds that new information can overwrite (or change) old information in memory. *See also* **misinformation effect; multiple trace hypothesis.**

characteristic feature In a *feature list model,* an aspect of a concept that is commonly or frequently associated with the concept but not essential to its meaning. *See also* **defining feature.**

child-directed speech The speech mothers and other adults often use in talking to babies (hence sometimes called "motherese"); it is characterized by slower pronunciation, exaggerated intonation, a higher-than-normal frequency, repetition, and use of simple syntax and vocabulary.

choice under uncertainty Choice in situations in which one does not have all the information one wants or needs.

chunking The use of semantic memory information to organize stimulus information when it is being encoded.

clinical neurological case study Detailed investigation of the brain and cognitive functioning of an individual or individuals who have suffered damage to the nervous system either as a result of accident (e.g., stroke) or through surgical interventions designed to deal with neurological problems.

cocktail party phenomenon A phenomenon in which people attend to one among many simultaneous conversations. While they seem to be ignoring other conversations, they nevertheless sometimes notice things such as their names being mentioned in an "ignored" conversation.

coevolutionary research approach An interdisciplinary research approach in which behavioral analyses of cognitive processes are conducted along with analyses of the physiological functioning of the nervous system.

cognitive map Edward Tolman's term for the internal representation of the environment that is developed as organisms explore the environment.

cognitive neuropsychology The interdisciplinary study of the physiological underpinnings of cognitive processes.

cognitive psychology The empirical research science that has as its primary goal understanding the processes that underlie the workings of the human mind.

cognitive science A discipline that combines psychological theorizing and experimentation with computer models, technologies, and applications (including artificial intelligence).

cognitive stage The first stage in Fitts and Posner's stage model of skill acquisition. At this stage, people spend a great deal of time memorizing and rehearsing basic facts and use very general procedures to apply those facts to the task. *See also* **associative stage; autonomous stage.**

cognitive workload A measure of the extent to which the information processing system is involved in performing a task.

competence In terms of language, a person's knowledge of language in general and the rules that guide the use of language.

complementary relations Relations among research activities in which the study of a phenomenon in one discipline is supplemented by the analysis of a similar phenomenon in another discipline.

complex cell Cell in the visual system that is most responsive to edges at a particular orientation, regardless of where it occurs in the receptive field.

computational theory A theory that specifies the mathematical functions that underlie perceptual and/or cognitive processes.

computerized axial tomography (CAT) A computerized x-ray procedure that produces a two-dimensional picture of the structure of the human brain.

concept A mental representation that a person uses to group sets of objects or events together. The mental representation is inferred from how the person categorizes items. *See also* **categorization.**

configural superiority effect A phenomenon in which observers are able to perceive a difference among stimuli that are integrated more readily than they are able to perceive the same difference among simple stimuli.

connectionist model A theoretical model that represents the mind as simple computing units linked in a network architecture. Such models are also sometimes called *parallel distributed processing models.*

conservative response criterion In a signal detection experiment, a decision criterion that results in few false alarms but few hits.

consistent mapping condition An experimental condition in which the same stimulus is always mapped onto the same response. This type of mapping helps in the development of automatic processing. *See also* **varied mapping condition.**

consolidation hypothesis The idea that encoding an external event causes neural activity that persists for some time, leading to physical changes (perhaps permanent) in the nervous system.

context alpha Contextual information involving aspects of the surroundings or environment of an activity or event.

context beta Contextual information that functions to give meaning to an otherwise ambiguous stimulus.

contextual interference effect Effect whereby increasing the similarity among the items to be learned or varying the processing requirements from trial to trial interferes with acquisition but improves retention.

continuity theory Theory of concept formation that assumes that people learn concepts by forming stimulus-response associations between the items and events they encounter and the category labels given to those items. Continuity theory assumes that these stimulus-response associations form gradually over learning. *See also* **noncontinuity theory.**

continuous signal A single, unbroken signal. Speech is described as a continuous signal because the sounds that result from the vibrations of the vocal apparatus form a single, unbroken, and complicated sound pattern.

contrastive A property of *phonemes* describing the fact that a change from one phoneme (e.g., /b/) to another (e.g., /d/) can change the meaning of a word (e.g., changing *bog* to *dog*).

controlled processing task A task that involves processes that are slow, that are limited by the available capacity, and that require conscious attention.

control process One of the operations in a model of memory that work on the *architecture* of the model.

convergent relations Situations in which research efforts in two or more disciplines are coordinated so as to investigate a particular issue or phenomenon with the tools and ideas of all of the disciplines. Convergent relations represent a truly interdisciplinary enterprise. *See also* **complementary relations.**

converging operations Situations in which the manipulation of two or more independent variables converge upon, or provide support for, a specific hypothesis or theory. Converging operations involve the evaluation of hypotheses and theories on the basis of multiple, independent lines of evidence. *See also* **independent variable.**

conversational maxim One of four principles of effective discourse proposed by H. P. Grice; in this view, effective discourse depends on the participants' being informative, truthful, relevant, and clear.

corpus callosum The largest of the commisures between the two hemispheres of the brain. The corpus callosum plays an important role in transmitting information from one cerebral hemisphere to the other.

correct rejection In a signal detection experiment, the situation in which the subject responds that no signal was present when in fact there was no signal present.

d' (d-prime) In signal detection theory, the measure of how sensitive a person is when discriminating between Signal + Noise trials and Noise Alone trials.

decision tree A tool for analyzing a decision-making situation that depicts possible outcomes and the paths that lead to those outcomes.

declarative memory information Information that summarizes basic facts about the world, such as "a chicken can lay eggs." Declarative memory information can be reported verbally, and "chunks" are hypothesized to be the basis for this type of information. *See also* **procedural memory information; production.**

deep structure In the context of *generative grammar,* the ideas or thoughts that are transformed into the *surface structure* of spoken or written language.

defining feature In a *feature list model,* an aspect of a concept that is basic and essential to the concept. *See also* **characteristic feature.**

delta rule A mathematical rule used in some connectionist models to update weights during learning. *See also* **back-propagation of error.**

dendrite Branching filament from the cell body of a neuron that collects information from adjacent neurons.

dependent variable A variable that is observed, or measured, in an experiment. *See also* **independent variable.**

deterministic Characterized by determinism, the idea that decisions, acts, and events occur outside the influence of the human will. The deterministic view of human behavior holds that if we know enough, we can predict and control human behavior precisely.

deterministic category Category in which specific stimulus features unambiguously determine whether a stimulus is or is not a member of the category. *See also* **probabilistic category.**

dichotic listening task A task involving the presentation of different auditory stimuli to subjects' left and right ears through stereo headphones.

diglossia The ability to use two different versions, varieties, or dialects of one language.

diphthong A phoneme that consists of a smooth glide between two vowel sounds, such as /iu/.

direct perception approach A theoretical view that holds that much of what we perceive about the world is directly available in the stimulus information that strikes the sensory systems.

direct priming A change in performance (*facilitation* or *inhibition*) observed when subjects experience something (such as reading a word) and then later perform a task that is directly related to that initial experience (such as reading that same word again). *See also* **indirect priming.**

discourse Communicative interactions between two or more individuals, with the interaction being independent of the medium.

discrimination ratio The ratio of the time between item presentations (within a list, the inter-presentation interval) and the time that elapses between the presentation of the last item and the administration of the memory test (the retention interval); thought to be a determinant of the discriminability of items in memory. *See also* **inter-presentation interval; retention interval.**

dishabituation Condition in which renewed interest is shown in response to a stimulus seen as different from the stimulus to which the subject has been habituated.

dissociation A phenomenon observed when an experimental variable has certain effects on the processing of one type of memory information and distinct and different effects on another type.

distance effect An effect in which the reading time for a sentence containing a pronoun increases as the distance (e.g., the number of words) between a noun and the pronoun referring to it increases.

distributed practice Practice in which the total practice time is spread out over a set of practice sessions. Having periods of rest between periods of practice, rather than having a single long period of practice. *See also* **massed practice.**

divided attention An attentional condition that exists when a person is attempting to perform more than one task at the same time.

doctrine of formal discipline An account of skill learning from the early part of the twentieth century based on the idea that the mind is composed of a set of general abilities and training in these general abilities leads to improvements in specific areas. *See also* **theory of identical elements.**

drive Something that energizes behavior; drives are important in *regulatory views* of motivation.

dual process theory The proposal that memory retrieval involves a familiarity, or activation-based, process and a search process.

dual-task methodology A research procedure in which subjects are required to perform two tasks either singly or at the same time.

dual trace hypothesis Hebb's hypothesis that the formation of memories requires two processes, a short-term process that keeps information active in the nervous system and a long-term process that results in the storage of a permanent memory trace.

duplex perception The situation in which two speech sounds, presented to different ears, are perceived as a single speech sound in one ear and a non-speech sound in the other. In a duplex perception experiment, two sounds are presented simultaneously, one in each ear. In one ear is the base syllable, consisting of the first two formants with transitions and the third formant without a transition. Presented in the other ear is the isolated third formant transition, which sounds like a non-speechlike chirp. What the subject reports hearing is the complete syllable in one ear and an isolated chirp in the other.

dynamic systems theory Theory stating that developmental change occurs in a series of states of stability, instability, and shifts to new levels of development.

dynamic theory In the context of judgment and decision making, a theory that holds that the preference relation or probability function depends on the time involved in making the judgment or decision. *See also* **static theory.**

early selection model One of a class of selective attention models that assume that selective attention operates before perceptual analysis of messages.

echoic store Ulric Neisser's (1967) term for the brief sensory memory store for audition. Echoic store maintains a representation of the physical stimulus for a short time. *See also* **iconic store.**

ecological validity The extent to which a process studied in the laboratory captures the important aspects of a real-world task of interest. If a study has high ecological validity, then the results from the laboratory can be generalized to make predictions about the real world.

Einstellung Effect whereby experience in working with certain types of tasks biases people to prefer a particular response strategy; also known as "set."

elaborative inference With respect to the comprehension of written language, inference of a general concept from a specific one or vice versa. *See also* **causal inference; instrumental inference.**

electroencephalogram (EEG) A recording of the overall electrical activity of the brain as detected by small electrodes placed on a person's scalp. *See also* **event-related potential (ERP).**

encoding The process of putting information into memory. *Encoding* is sometimes used as a synonym for *learning* and is also called *acquisition*.

encoding specificity hypothesis A hypothesis stating, in its simplest form, that the best conditions at retrieval are those that are most similar to the conditions at encoding. It was originally proposed by Tulving and colleagues and later extended to the idea of *transfer-appropriate processing*.

engram The record left in memory by an experience. You can think of an engram as a track laid down in memory, similar to the tracks on musical recordings. *Engram* is often synonymous with *memory trace*.

enhancement With respect to Gernsbacher's model of reading comprehension, a mechanism that increases the activation of memory information about the sentence.

episodic memory information Information specific to some particular event. *See also* **semantic memory information.**

event-related potential (ERP) An EEG in which brain waves are measured when a subject is presented with a stimulus at a specific time. The ERP measures the brain's responses to stimuli as a person completes a task.

exemplar An example or instance of a category.

exemplar model One of a class of information processing models that assume that people store in memory a representation of each episode in which they encounter a stimulus. *See also* **protype model.**

experience error The mistake of assuming that one's perceptual experience in viewing a stimulus is directly available in, or given by, the stimulus itself.

explicit memory Memory evidenced by a test requiring the intentional use of memory, such as recognition or free recall. *See also* **implicit memory.**

facilitation A type of priming in which the advance information produces an improvement in task performance.

false alarm In a signal detection experiment, the situation in which the subject responds that a signal was present when in fact there was no signal.

false memory A memory for an event that did not occur. Some researchers have suggested that some "recovered memories" may be false memories.

false memory effect The phenomenon in which people recall or recognize information that was not part of an event but that is in some way related to the event.

family resemblance Sharing of features among the members of a given family (or concept). This notion has been used in familiarity-based models of categorization.

fan effect An effect in which, when subjects learn a set of facts containing overlapping or shared information (e.g., similar people or objects), the subsequent time required to verify or recognize statements increases with the amount of overlapping or shared information.

feature analysis model A theoretical model that assumes that the perceptual system analyzes the extent to which basic features are present in a target stimulus.

feature comparison theory A perceptual model that assumes that the perceptual system tests for the presence of basic visual features in stimuli and uses this information to attempt to identify stimulus patterns.

feature detection model A model that assumes that the perceptual system detects the presence or absence of specific features and uses this information to determine what stimulus is being perceived.

feature list model A model for the organization of semantic memory information that proposes that this information is partitioned into lists; a list is ordered according to the relative ability of the items in the list to characterize the concept represented by the list.

figure The portion of the visual field that is segregated into a distinct shape in the foreground of the visual field. *See also* **ground.**

filter theory An early selection model of selective attention proposed by Donald Broadbent. The model assumes that a filter selects a message from all those available in sensory stores based on the physical properties of the message; the message can then be processed completely.

fixation An event in reading when, between *saccades*, the eye brings a small region of text into the fovea for detailed analysis.

flashbulb memory A memory that has distinct meaningful and situational components.

formant A band of resonant frequencies in the speech signal.

forward reasoning Reasoning by moving from observations to hypotheses; forward reasoning is related to inductive reasoning, which moves from the specific to the general. *See also* **backward reasoning.**

fovea The area of the retina that supports the best visual acuity. If we look directly at an object, the light reflected from that object falls on the fovea.

functional fixedness In Gestalt psychology, the tendency to perceive objects in terms of their common or familiar uses.

generate-recognize theory A theory of memory retrieval that proposes two processes: the generation of a set of possible responses and the recognition (or selection) of the best response.

generative grammar The system of rules by which the ideas a speaker wants to convey (the *deep structure*) are transformed into their final grammatical form (the *surface structure*).

geon A basic shape identified by the visual system on the basis of, among other things, the nonaccidental properties of lines in the retinal image. Geons (from *geo*metrical i*ons*) are essentially three-dimensional volumes such as cones, cylinders, and wedges.

Gestalt principles of organization Principles identified by the Gestalt psychologists that specify how the perceptual system organizes patterns and objects into stimuli and groups of stimuli.

Gestalt psychology A school of psychology that emphasizes the importance of whole patterns in perception as opposed to the reduction of perception into constituent parts. *See also* **structuralism.**

given-new strategy A strategy by which individuals who are trying to present new information to a reader try to relate it to information the reader already knows. The reader then integrates the new information and the old information into memory.

globally optimal solution The best possible solution to a problem. *See also* **locally optimal solution.**

ground The portion of the visual field that is behind the figure. *See also* **figure.**

habituation Condition in which attention to a stimulus declines as a result of repeated presentation of the stimulus.

hemispheric specialization The concept that the right and left halves of the brain are differentially involved in performing certain types of tasks.

heuristic A guiding principle or rule of thumb used in decision making and judgment.

hit In a signal detection experiment, the situation in which a subject responds that a signal was present when in fact there was a signal.

holophrase An early form of speech consisting of a single word carrying the meaning of a complete sentence.

human factors field A discipline that deals with the interaction of people and machines. Human factors researchers come from various academic backgrounds,

including psychology, engineering, and computer science.

human information processing approach The theoretical view that perception and cognition involve stages of information processing that transform various types of information used to perceive and think.

hypercomplex cell Cell in the visual system that is sensitive to the length of stimuli and their angular orientation. These cells respond most vigorously to fairly specific stimuli.

hypothetical construct A concept describing an unobservable factor or variable that accounts for existing data (or knowledge) as well as providing implications for new observations. *See also* **intervening variable.**

iconic store Ulric Neisser's (1967) term for the brief sensory memory store for the visual modality. Iconic store maintains a representation of the physical stimulus for a short time. *See also* **echoic store.**

identification/recognition The final stage in the information processing model of the perceptual system, in which meaning is assigned to percepts.

implicit memory Memory evidenced by a test that does not require the intentional use of memory, such as word-fragment completion. *See also* **explicit memory.**

independent variable A variable that is manipulated in an experiment. Independent variables are under the control of the experimenter. *See also* **dependent variable.**

indirect priming A change in performance (*facilitation* or *inhibition*) observed when subjects experience something (such as reading a word) and then later experience something that is semantically or associatively related to the initial experience (such as in a word-fragment completion task). *See also* **direct priming.**

infantile amnesia Condition marked by great difficulty remembering the events of infancy.

information processing model A theoretical model that proposes that information is processed through a series of stages, with each stage performing unique operations on the information. *See also* **human information processing approach.**

inhibition A type of priming in which the advance information hurts task performance.

instance theory A theory of automaticity proposed by Gordon Logan. According to the theory, controlled processes rely on the application of an algorithm, or set of rules, while automatic processes reflect the retrieval of memories of prior instances in which the task was performed.

instrumental inference With respect to the comprehension of written language, an inference about what was used to perform the action in a sentence. *See also* **causal inference; elaborative inference.**

interactive activation model A connectionist model of word recognition proposed by McClelland and Rumelhart and including both bottom-up, or data-driven, processes and top-down, or conceptually driven, processes.

interference An impairment of memory performance as a function of information learned before or after target information. *See also* **proactive interference; retroactive interference.**

inter-presentation interval (IPI) The time between the presentations of any two adjacent items in a study list. *See also* **discrimination ratio.**

intervening variable A variable used to conveniently summarize several related concepts with a single term. *See also* **hypothetical construct.**

invariance With respect to the processing of spoken language, the occurrence of certain acoustical properties with particular phonemes in all contexts. *See also* **separability; linearity.**

item information Memory information that is specific to the identity of the item (e.g., the name of the item). *See also* **associative information; order information.**

knowledge-lean problem Simple problem that is well defined and that can be successfully solved by use of the instructions for the task and general approaches to solving problems. *See also* **knowledge-rich problem.**

knowledge-rich problem Problem whose solution requires specific knowledge or skill. *See also* **knowledge-lean problem.**

language universal A characteristic common to all languages.

late selection model One of a class of selective attention models that assume that all stimuli undergo perceptual analysis and selection occurs after this perceptual analysis.

levels-of-processing hypothesis Hypothesis proposing that the quality of rehearsal activity is just as important as or more important than the quantity. An emphasis on meaningful (deep) characteristics of a stimulus produces richer or stronger representations in memory than an emphasis on surface (shallow) characteristics.

lexical decision task A task, used in studies of priming, in which subjects must decide whether a string of letters is or is not a word.

lexicon The portion of memory specialized to the storage and processing of information about words. *See also* **semantic memory.**

liberal response criterion In a signal detection experiment, a decision criterion that results in many hits but also many false alarms.

linearity With respect to the processing of spoken language, the one-to-one mapping between a perceived phoneme and a segment of the physical speech signal. *See also* **invariance; separability.**

linear perspective A monocular depth cue in which lines that are parallel in the real world appear to come closer together as objects recede into the distance.

linguistic relativity hypothesis A hypothesis that holds that language can determine the thoughts people have about objects and events.

localization of function The principle that certain areas of the brain are more closely involved with one kind of function (e.g., memory, strategic planning) than with other kinds of functions.

locally optimal solution The best of a small or restricted set of possible solutions. *See also* **globally optimal solution.**

logogen The unit of mental representation in the model proposed by J. Morton (1970); the logogen stores a variety of sensory and linguistic properties of a word, such as its appearance, its sound, and its meaning.

macrostructure With respect to the comprehension of written language, the overall, global meaning of the information being read. *See also* **microstructure.**

magnetic resonance imaging (MRI) A brain-imaging procedure that uses powerful magnetic fields to produce an image of the brain that has high spatial resolution.

massed practice Practice conducted in a single practice session. *See also* **distributed practice.**

memory trace The record left in memory by an experience; the change in the nervous system that results from experience. You can think of a memory trace as a track laid down in memory, similar to the tracks on musical recordings. *Memory trace* is often synonymous with *engram.*

metacognition Ability to monitor and evaluate one's current cognitive capabilities.

metamemory Ability to monitor and evaluate one's current memory capabilities.

metatheoretical assumption A theoretical assumption that goes beyond the specifics of any individual theory. Metatheoretical assumptions are shared by investigators operating within a given theoretical orientation, even if these researchers do not state them explicitly in their theories.

microstructure With regard to the comprehension of written language, a restricted, local level of meaning, such as the meaning of a word. *See also* **macrostructure.**

misinformation effect An effect by which certain types of misleading information presented after an event bias or disrupt memory for the event.

miss In a signal detection experiment, the situation in which the subject responds that no signal was present when in fact there was a signal present.

mnemonic encoding principle One of the principles of skilled memory theory. This principle holds that high levels of memory performance depend on the use of existing knowledge to organize the material that needs to be remembered and make it more meaningful at encoding. *See also* **structured retrieval principle; speed-up principle.**

mnemonist One who is exceptionally skilled at remembering some specific type of information.

modality effect The phenomenon in which the last few items in a list are recalled better when the list is presented auditorally rather than when the list is presented visually.

model A description or analogy that is used to account for a limited set of phenomena. Models generally account for a rather small range of observations.

morpheme The smallest meaningful unit of language; *cat* and *-s* in the word *cats* are morphemes.

morphology The study of how words are formed from *morphemes*.

motivation Internal and external information and processes that energize and direct behavior.

motor theory Theory holding that people's ability to perceive speech is guided by what they know about producing speech.

multiple resource model A model of attention that assumes that separate pools of perceptual and cognitive resources can be applied to different processes. *See also* **single capacity model.**

multiple trace hypothesis An explanation for the misinformation effect that holds that new information interferes with, rather than changes, old information. *See also* **changed-trace hypothesis.**

multiply determined With respect to speech perception and other cognitive processes, the quality by which information we use to perform a task is derived from different sources.

naming task A task in which subjects are presented with a picture of something (like a chair) and are asked to produce (say out loud) the name for it. The time to produce the name has been thought to reflect important characteristics of semantic memory.

negative priming An experimental effect in which an item ignored on one trial is slower to be processed as an attended-to item on the next trial, relative to a control condition.

neuron The basic building block of the nervous system. These specialized cells can communicate with each other, store information, and, in certain arrangements, "compute" decisions.

neurotransmitter Chemical involved in communication between cells. Neurotransmitters released into the synapse increase or decrease the membrane potential of adjacent neurons.

nonaccidental property A property of stimuli that is only rarely produced by accidental alignments of viewpoints and object features in the real world. Nonaccidental properties play an important role in Biederman's recognition by components theory of object recognition.

noncontinuity theory Theory of concept formation that assumes that learning involves a discontinuous process of forming and then testing hypotheses about what specifies membership in a given category or concept.

ontogeny The course of an individual's development.

optical flow pattern The dynamic changes in the retinal image that occur as an observer moves through the world or as objects move past the observer.

order information Memory information about an item's place in a series or sequence of items. *See also* **associative information; item information.**

output interference The phenomenon in which people are less likely to recall additional items after they have recalled the initial items. The items that have already been recalled interfere with the person's ability to recall other items.

outshining hypothesis A hypothesis proposed to explain why context effects are not reliably obtained in recognition tasks. If an item is a strong enough cue, it will overpower the context cue in the same way that a bright light outshines a weak light.

overextension An early language error involving extending one word's meaning to include an inappropriately broad range of objects. *See also* **underextension.**

overregularization error A type of rule-based error involving word and syntactic formations that occurs in early language development; rules are generalized to cases to which they do not apply.

pandemonium model A model of pattern recognition proposed by Selfridge in which "demons" perform various information processing tasks. The pandemonium model is a feature analysis model that assesses the degree to which various features are present in a stimulus and uses this information to determine the nature of target stimuli.

parsing The process used to assign words in a sentence to their syntactic categories, a process that many scientists assume is critical to understanding a sentence.

partial report The technique introduced by George Sperling to estimate the amount of information a person can take in from a briefly presented stimulus. On partial report trials, subjects are given cues as to which subsets of the items displayed they are to report. *See also* **whole report.**

part-task training Practicing part of a task rather than the complete task. *See also* **whole-task training.**

percept The internal representation of an external object that arises from perceptual processes. Percepts are the observer's working descriptions of the nature of objects around them.

perception The processes that create internal representations of objects and events in the environment.

perceptron A device created by Frank Rosenblatt consisting of photocells and a simple logical device. The perceptron was able to recognize letters and other visual patterns. Rosenblatt's work on the perceptron laid the groundwork for the later development of connectionist models.

performance In terms of language, an individual's ability to follow certain rules in the production and comprehension of language.

pertinence value In Donald Norman's late selection model, a quality related to the personal relevance of a stimulus. Such stimuli have additional "weight," so that a weak stimulus with a high pertinence value can attract attention.

phoneme The smallest units of distinct sound in a language.

phonology The study of the sound system of language.

phrenology The attempt to identify human mental abilities by measuring the bumps on a person's head.

phylogeny The course of the development of a species.

plateau In skill learning, a time in training during which improvement in performance levels off for a while before continuing. Early researchers believed that important psychological and physical changes necessary for further improvement occurred during plateaus.

positive priming An experimental effect in which an item presented on one trial facilitates processing of an item presented on the next trial. Positive priming is reflected in faster reaction times, relative to a control condition.

positive transfer The phenomenon whereby participation in one task benefits performance in a second task. The learning from the first task is said to transfer to the second task.

positron emission tomography (PET) A brain-imaging technique that measures the activity levels of various regions in the brain. In the PET scan procedure, the patient is injected with a radioactive substance similar to glucose, and the subatomic particles given off by this substance (positrons) are measured by detectors in the PET scanner.

pragmatics The social rules governing how people use language when they interact with others.

precategorical sensory store Memory store that maintains a relatively accurate representation of the physical characteristics of stimuli encoded by the sensory systems. *See also* **iconic store; echoic store.**

preference relation The specific way in which any model or theory of judgment and decision making relates the environment to behavior.

primacy effect The effect by which, in a recall or recognition test, performance is better for early items than for middle items. *See also* **serial position effect; recency effect.**

primal sketch The first representation formed in Marr's (1982) computational theory of object recognition. The primal sketch is a two-dimensional representation of the changes in the patterns of light intensity across the retina.

primary visual cortex The portion of the cerebral cortex at the occipital lobe that receives projections from the visual system. This area of the cortex is involved in sensing and perceiving visual stimuli.

priming A change in performance (facilitation or inhibition) observed when subjects receive advance information about the task. Priming can be either positive (facilitation), in which case the prime makes the target easier to process, or negative (inhibition), in which case the prime makes the target more difficult to process. *See also* **direct priming; indirect priming.**

principle of rationality In the context of judgment and decision making, a principle stating that if we understand the objective and subjective knowledge used to make a judgment or decision, and we know the particular goal or desires of the person making the judgment or decision, then we can accurately predict the outcome of the judgment or decision.

proactive interference An impairment of memory performance as a function of information learned before the target information. *See also* **retroactive interference.**

probabilistic category Category in which stimulus features *usually* belong to one category but may sometimes belong to an alternative category. *See also* **deterministic category.**

problem space A general and abstract analysis of a problem-solving situation; its elements are (1) a description of all the possible states of the task and problem solver and (2) a list of the ways of moving among those states.

procedural knowledge Information about how to perform a task. *See also* **declarative knowledge.**

procedural memory information Information that allows an individual to perform a task, such as barbecuing a chicken or riding a bike. This type of memory information often cannot be reported verbally. *See also* **declarative memory information; production.**

production A way of relating declarative knowledge to procedural knowledge, or a way of allowing general knowledge of the world to be translated into action. Roughly speaking, a production specifies a rule for taking some action based on some condition.

production deficiency A tendency not to produce the appropriate strategy for a given task.

proposition (1) The smallest unit of knowledge that can be used to make a statement that can be judged to be true or false. (2) In Walter Kintsch's model of text processing and comprehension, a logical structure that consists of a predicate (verb, adjective, or conjunction) and one or more arguments (nouns).

prototype model An information processing model of category learning that assumes that as exemplars of categories are encountered, the cognitive system creates a running "average," or prototype, of the members of the category. When a new item is presented for categorization, its similarity to alternative categories is determined, and the category to which it is most similar is chosen.

psycholinguistics The subdiscipline of psychology concerned with the structure and processing of language. Psycholinguistics as an area of study emerged from psychology and linguistics.

psychophysics The subdiscipline of psychology that examines how changes in physical stimulation from the environment are translated into psychological experiences.

purposive view View of motivation that holds that people can imagine the future in terms of various available alternatives; the alternative chosen is the one whose anticipated outcomes are most desirable.

reaction time The time between the presentation of a stimulus and a subject's response. Reaction times are used extensively by cognitive psychologists in their efforts to specify how cognitive processes operate.

recency effect The effect by which, in a recall or recognition test, recall is better for late items than middle items. *See also* **serial position effect; primacy effect.**

receptive field In the visual system, that portion of the retina which, when stimulated, causes a change in the activity level of neurons in the optic nerve and visual cortex.

recognition by components (RBC) theory An object recognition theory proposed by Biederman that assumes that people recognize objects by identifying the basic shapes, known as *geons,* that make up the objects, as well as how the geons are arranged.

redintegration The process of reconstructing or refreshing degraded memory information during retrieval.

regression A "backward" saccade in which the eye moves from right to left rather than left to right.

regressive development A course of development in which an infant seems to possess a skill, then lose it, and then show it again later.

regulatory view View of motivation that focuses on the ways in which some action (such as eating) helps manage or control physiological or psychological systems.

relative size A monocular cue given by the fact that objects closer to the observer tend to cast larger retinal images than objects farther away.

relearning task An experimental task developed by Ebbinghaus in which items are initially learned to a specific criterion. After a specified amount of time has elapsed, the information is relearned to the same criterion. *See also* **savings score.**

release from proactive interference In the Brown-Peterson task, an effect by which switching from one type (or category) of item to another prevents interference and thus prevents forgetting.

repetition priming The improvement in performance that is observed when an item is presented a second time (for example, in a lexical decision task).

representativeness heuristic A heuristic in which judgment about something is influenced by the degree to which that thing has characteristics representative of some class of things. *See also* **availability heuristic; anchoring.**

repressed memory A memory that a person has but cannot bring into conscious awareness. Proponents of repressed memories argue that under the right conditions a person can retrieve such memories and that the memories provide a clear representation of the event that gave rise to them.

resting potential The relatively constant electrical charge of a neuron's cell membrane when the neuron is not being stimulated. Various neurotransmitters can increase or decrease this electrical potential. The increases and decreases are related to the chance that the neuron will fire an action potential.

retention The process of holding onto information once it has been stored in memory.

retention interval (RI) The time that elapses between presentation of the last item in a list and administration of the test of memory. *See also* **discrimination ratio.**

retrieval The actions or processes required to get information out of memory.

retrieval dynamics Patterns of differences in the rates at which different types of memory information become available to support responding.

retroactive interference An impairment of memory performance as a function of information learned after target information. *See also* **proactive interference.**

rule-based approach A classical approach to categorization that assumes that people learn the rules of category membership and apply these rules when categorizing objects and events.

saccade A jump that the eyes make while reading, from the French term for "jump."

savant An individual who is extremely skilled at a particular type of task but who appears to be below normal on other measures of mental ability.

savings score Dependent measure in the relearning task developed by Ebbinghaus; the difference between the number of trials needed to originally learn the information and the number of trials needed to relearn the information, expressed as a percentage, reflecting the amount of original learning that was saved in memory.

selective attention The ability to attend to one among several possible streams of information.

selective interference A condition in which performance of one task interferes with performance of another task that is similar in nature to the first task.

semantic memory information Information that has general meaning and is not specific to any particular event. *See also* **episodic memory information.**

semantics The study of the meaning of language.

sensation The processes whereby physical energy from the environment is transduced into neural responses that code, or represent, basic information about the stimulation received by the sensory receptors.

sentence verification task A task in which a sentence is presented and the subjects decide whether the sentence is true (e.g., "A tulip is a flower") or false (e.g., "A potato is a flower"). The reaction times are used to make inferences about how the facts described in the sentences are stored in memory.

separability With respect to the processing of spoken language, the ability of the speech signal to be divided into segments. *See also* **invariance; linearity.**

serial position effect Effect describing differences in subjects' ability to remember items in lists as a function of the positions of the items in the lists. *See also* **primacy effect; recency effect.**

simple cell Cell in the visual system containing oblong receptive fields with *on* and *off* areas arranged in parallel along the axis of the oblong. Simple cells are quite specific in terms of the types of stimuli to which they will respond.

single capacity model A model of attention that assumes a single pool of capacity, which may be allocated among any processes that require capacity. *See also* **multiple resource model.**

spacing effect Effect whereby increasing the interval (the space) between successive rehearsals of information leads to improvements in memory performance.

span of apprehension The number of items subjects can report when presented with a brief display. The span of apprehension was once thought to measure how much information a person could apprehend, or take in.

spectrogram A visual display of an auditory signal showing frequency on the y-axis and time on the x-axis; the intensity (darkness) of the markings represents the amplitude of the signal.

speech-shadowing task A dichotic listening task in which a person attends to one message and repeats, or shadows, what is said in the attended message.

speeded-classification task A task in which subjects are presented with a word and required to quickly determine if it names something that belongs to a particular class of things.

speed of processing The time required to execute a cognitive process.

speed-up principle One of the principles of skilled memory theory. This principle holds that both encoding and retrieval processes become faster with increasing amounts of practice. *See also* **mnemonic encoding principle; structured retrieval principle.**

split-span task A dichotic listening task in which two pairs of items are presented, with one item presented to each ear. The listener's task is to report all the items that were presented to the two ears.

spreading of activation The increase in activation thought to occur in semantic network models as a result of accessing one of the nodes; activation spread from the node that was accessed to all the connected nodes.

stage theory One of the theories that propose that all humans move through an orderly and predictable series of changes in their development.

static theory In the context of judgment and decision making, a theory that holds that the preference relation or probability function does not depend in any way on the time involved in making the judgment or decision. *See also* **dynamic theory.**

stimulus onset asynchrony (SOA) In a priming experiment, the variable time interval between when the prime is presented and when the target item is presented.

strategy Systematic approach to the efficient management of processing demands in a task.

structuralism A school of psychology, founded by Wilhelm Wundt, that holds that the primary goal of psychology is to specify the nature of conscious experience through the use of introspection.

structured retrieval principle One of the principles of skilled memory theory. This principle holds that experts develop ways of organizing the material they need to remember and these ways of organizing do not depend on the specific items with which they are working. *See also* **mnemonic encoding principle; speed-up principle.**

subjective expected utility hypothesis Hypothesis that holds that a situation (such as a gamble) cannot be described by objective information alone; the probability of each event and the subjective value of the objective outcome also must be considered. Also known as the expected utility hypothesis.

subjective organization The process by which people organize lists of randomly ordered items. Subjective organization is one form of evidence that humans are active processors of information.

suffix effect The finding in memory experiments that recall of the last few items in a list is worse when a suffix, or extra item, is included at the end of the list.

suppression With respect to Gernsbacher's model of reading comprehension, a mechanism that decreases the activation of memory information about the sentence.

surface structure In the context of *generative grammar,* the output of the transformations that act on the *deep structure.*

syllogistic reasoning task A task in which subjects are shown two premises and asked to produce the logical conclusion or inference.

synapse Region where communication between neurons takes place.

syntax The system by which words are put together to form phrases, clauses, and sentences.

tachistoscope (T-scope) A device used to present visual stimuli to people with very close control over the timing of the presentations.

Teachable Language Comprehender A computer program intended to extract meaning from natural language text; it was an early and influential model for the organization and use of semantic memory information.

telegraphic speech Early speech consisting of short (often two-word) sentences from which function words are omitted.

template matching theory A pattern recognition theory that assumes that people identify patterns by comparing the patterns of neural excitation caused by stimuli to patterns, or *templates,* stored in memory.

texture segregation task A task in which subjects are presented with displays containing many elements and asked to identify which part of the display is different from the rest. These tasks are used to identify the types of basic features to which the visual system responds.

theory A set of related statements proposed to explain phenomena of interest. Theories may be stated as verbal descriptions, systems of mathematical equations, or computer programs. Theories are used to organize findings and to make predictions that are tested in further research.

theory of identical elements Theory that proposes that skill acquisition depends on the degree to which the training activity and the target task share stimulus-response elements. *See also* **doctrine of formal discipline.**

thought experiment Mental exercise in which one considers what might happen in a specific hypothetical situation. Thought experiments can be used to develop a better understanding of a phenomenon or theory or to see how well a theory can account for actual data.

3-D sketch In Marr's (1982) computational theory of object recognition, the final representation, which contains a description of the shapes of objects and the relative positions of these objects in the visual field.

top-down theory A theory that assumes that information and knowledge from higher cognitive processes is used to guide lower-level perceptual processes.

total-time hypothesis Hypothesis proposing that the more time is spent rehearsing an item, the better will be the memory for the item. This idea was refuted, in part, by the *levels-of-processing hypothesis.*

transduction The process by which the physical energy from the stimulus that strikes the sensory receptors is translated into a change in activity in the nervous system.

transfer-appropriate processing Condition in which the processing done at study matches the processing done at test; memory performance depends on the degree of transfer-appropriate processing. *See also* **levels-of-processing hypothesis.**

transfer of skill A shift in which a skill on one type of task is used on another type of task.

transitive inference task A task in which a child is asked to infer a third relation from two other relations.

2½-D sketch In Marr's (1982) computational theory of object recognition, the second representation, which contains information about the depth and orientation of the surfaces of objects.

typicality effect Effect wherein certain members of a category are better representatives of the category than are other members. Typicality effects are obtained in memory tasks and speeded-decision tasks such as sentence verification tasks.

unconscious inference Helmholtz's term for the processes whereby observers use knowledge to perceive. These processes are thought to be outside of awareness and to have been learned through experience.

underextension An early language error in which children use a particular word to refer to only one event or object rather than applying it more broadly to other, similar events or objects. *See also* **overextension.**

varied mapping condition An experimental condition in which the targets and distracters in a visual search task are mixed across trials, so that an item that is a distracter on one trial may be a target on another trial. *See also* **consistent mapping condition.**

verbal learning theory A subdiscipline of behaviorism concerned with how people learn to respond to verbal stimuli. Verbal learning theory focuses on the acquisition and retention of learned associations.

visual cliff A device for assessing depth perception in infants; it consists of a clear surface that extends over an apparently deep side and an apparently shallow side.

visually guided reaching The action of reaching and grasping in response to seeing an object; this action demonstrates the coordination of the visual system with the motor system.

visual search task A task in which subjects are asked to detect the presence of one or more target items among a set of distracter items. These tasks are used in studies of perceptual processes to identify the types of basic features to which the visual system responds.

voiced A property of *phonemes;* a phoneme produced by vibration of the vocal chords is said to be voiced (e.g., /n/). *See also* **voiceless.**

voiceless A property of *phonemes;* a phoneme produced without vibrations of the vocal cords is said to be voiceless (e.g., /s/). *See also* **voiced.**

voice-onset time (VOT) The time between the release of air in the production of the consonant and the onset of the vocal cord vibrations associated with the voicing of the following vowel.

whole report A technique used in span of apprehension studies in which the subject is asked to report all of the items from a display. *See also* **partial report.**

whole-task training Practicing a complete task rather than a single part. *See also* **part-task training.**

win/stay, lose/switch strategy An approach to hypothesis testing; if one's hypothesis about what constitutes a category member works when one encounters a new stimulus, one stays with that hypothesis; if not, one de-

vises a new hypothesis in light of the disconfirming evidence.

word superiority effect The effect whereby people can more easily identify letters when they are presented in words than when they are presented individually.

working memory A model of memory, originally proposed by Baddeley and Hitch and described in detail by Baddeley, that emphasizes both processing and storage aspects of memory.

References

Adams, J. A. (1957). The relationship between certain measures of ability and the acquisition of a psychomotor criterion response. *Journal of General Psychology, 56,* 121–134.

Albrecht, J. E., & Myers, J. L. (1995). Role of context in accessing distant information during reading. *Journal of Experimental Psychology: Learning, Memory, and Cognition, 21,* 1459–1468.

Albrecht, J. E., & O'Brien, E. J. (1993). Updating a mental model: Maintaining both local and global coherence. *Journal of Experimental Psychology: Learning, Memory, and Cognition, 19,* 1061–1070.

Allen, F. (1926). The persistence of vision. *American Journal of Physiological Optics, 7,* 439–457.

Allport, D. A., Antonis, B., & Reynolds, P. (1972). On the division of attention: A disproof of the single channel hypothesis. *Quarterly Journal of Experimental Psychology, 24,* 225–235.

Ammons, R. B. (1947a). Acquisition of motor skill: I. Quantitative analysis and theoretical formulation. *Psychological Review, 54,* 263–281.

Ammons, R. B. (1947b). Acquisition of motor skill: II. Rotary pursuit performance with continuous practice before and after a single rest. *Journal of Experimental Psychology, 37,* 393–411.

Anderson, A., Garrod, S., & Sanford, A. J. (1983). The accessibility of pronomial antecedents as a function of episodic shifts in narrative text. *Quarterly Journal of Experimental Psychology, 35A,* 427–440.

Anderson, J. A. (1995). *An introduction to neural networks.* Cambridge, MA: Bradford.

Anderson, J. R. (1974). Retrieval of propositional information from long term memory. *Cognitive Psychology, 5,* 451–474.

Anderson, J. R. (1976). *Language, memory, and thought.* Hillsdale, NJ: Erlbaum.

Anderson, J. R. (1980). *Cognitive psychology and its implications.* San Francisco: W. H. Freeman.

Anderson, J. R. (1981). *Cognitive skills and their acquisition.* Hillsdale, NJ: Erlbaum.

Anderson, J. R. (1982). Acquisition of cognitive skill. *Psychological Review, 89,* 369–406.

Anderson, J. R. (1983). *The architecture of cognition.* Cambridge, MA: Harvard University Press.

Anderson, J. R. (1984). Spreading activation. In J. R. Anderson and M. S. Kosslyn (Eds.), *Essays in learning and memory.* New York: W. H. Freeman.

Anderson, J. R. (1987). Skill acquisition: Compilation of weak-method problem solutions. *Psychological Review, 94,* 192–210.

Anderson, J. R. (1990a). *Cognitive psychology and its implications* (3rd ed.). New York: W. H. Freeman.

Anderson, J. R. (1990b). *The adaptive character of thought.* Hillsdale, NJ: Erlbaum.

Anderson, J. R. (1991). Is human cognition adaptive? *Behavioral and Brain Sciences, 14,* 471–517.

Anderson, J. R. (1993). *Rules of the mind.* Hillsdale, NJ: Erlbaum.

Anderson, J. R. (1995). *Cognitive psychology and its implications* (4th ed.). New York: W. H. Freeman.

Anderson, J. R., & Bower, G. H. (1972a). Configural properties in sentence memory. *Journal of Verbal Learning and Verbal Behavior, 11,* 594–605.

Anderson, J. R., & Bower, G. H. (1972b). Recognition and retrieval processes in free recall. *Psychological Review, 79,* 97–123.

Anderson, J. R., & Bower, G. H. (1973). *Human associative memory.* New York: Wiley.

Anderson, J. R., & Paulson, R. (1977). Representation and retention of verbatim information. *Journal of Verbal Learning and Verbal Behavior, 16,* 439–452.

Anderson, J. R., & Pirolli, P. L. (1984). Spread of activation. *Journal of Experimental Psychology: Learning, Memory, and Cognition, 10,* 791–798.

Anderson, J. R., & Schooler, L. J. (1991). Reflections of the environment in memory. *Psychological Science, 2,* 396–408.

Anderson, N. H. (1962). Application of an additive model to impression formation. *Science, 138,* 817–818.

Anderson, N. H. (1974). Information integration theory: A brief survey. In D. H. Krantz, R. C. Atkinson, R. D. Luce, & P. Suppes (Eds.), *Contemporary developments in mathematical psychology* (Vol. 2, pp. 215–298). San Francisco: Freeman.

Anderson, N. H. (1981). *Foundations of information integration theory.* San Diego: Academic Press.

Anderson, N. H. (Ed.). (1991). *Contributions to information integration theory.* Hillsdale, NJ: Erlbaum.

Anderson, N. H., & Cuneo, D. O. (1978). The height + width rule in children's judgment of quantity. *Journal of Experimental Psychology: General, 107,* 335–378.

Angell, J. R. (1908). The doctrine of formal discipline in the light of the principles of general psychology. *Educational Review, 36,* 1–14.

Anisfeld, M., & Knapp, M. (1968). Association, synonymity, and directionality in false recognition. *Journal of Experimental Psychology, 77,* 171–179.

Annett, J., & Kay, H. (1956). Skilled performance. *Occupational Psychology, 31,* 69–79.

Anzai, Y. (1991). Learning and use of representations for physics expertise. In K. A. Ericsson & J. Smith (Eds.), *Toward a general theory of expertise: Prospects and limits* (pp. 64–92). Cambridge: Cambridge University Press.

Arkes, H. R., & Hammond, K. R. (Eds.). (1986). *Judgment and decision-making: An interdisciplinary reader.* Cambridge: Cambridge University Press.

Ashcraft, M. H. (1976). Priming and property dominance effects in semantic memory. *Memory & Cognition, 4,* 490–500.

Ashcraft, M. H. (1978). Property dominance and typicality effects in property statement verification. *Journal of Verbal Learning and Verbal Behavior, 17,* 155–164.

Ashcraft, M. H. (1989). *Human memory and cognition.* New York: Harper Collins.

Aslin, R. N. (1989). Discrimination of frequency transitions by human infants. *Journal of the Acoustical Society of America, 86,* 582–590.

Atkinson, R. C. (1961). A generalization of stimulus sampling theory. *Psychometrika, 26,* 281–290.

Atkinson, R. C. (1962). Choice behavior and monetary payoff: Strong and weak conditioning. In J. H. Criswell, H. Solomon, & P. Suppes (Eds.), *Mathematical models in small group processes* (pp. 23–34). Stanford, CA: Stanford University Press.

Atkinson, R. C., Herrmann, D. J., & Westcourt, K. T. (1974). Search processes in recognition memory. In R. L. Solso (Ed.), *Theories in cognitive psychology: The Loyola Symposium* (pp. 101–146). Hillsdale, NJ: Erlbaum.

Atkinson, R. C., & Juola, J. F. (1973). Factors influencing speed and accuracy of word recognition. In S. Kornblum (Ed.), *Attention and performance IV* (pp. 583–612). New York: Academic Press.

Atkinson, R. C., & Juola, J. F. (1974). Search and decision processes in recognition memory. In D. H. Krantz, R. C. Atkinson, & R. D. Luce (Eds.), *Contemporary developments in mathematical psychology. Volume 1: Learning, memory, and thinking* (pp. 243–293). San Francisco: Freeman.

Atkinson, R. C., & Shiffrin, R. M. (1968). Human memory: A proposed system and its control processes. In K. W. Spence & J. T. Spence (Eds.), *Advances in the psychology of learning and motivation: Research and theory* (Vol. 2). New York: Academic Press.

Averbach, E., & Sperling, G. (1960). Short-term storage of information in vision. In C. Cherry (Ed.), *Information theory.* London: Butterworth.

Averbach, E., & Coriell, A. S. (1961). Short-term memory in vision. *Bell System Technical Journal, 40,* 309–328.

Ayres, T. J., Jonides, J., Reitman, J. S., Egan, J. C., & Howard, D. A. (1979). Differing suffix effects for the same physical suffix. *Journal of Experimental Psychology: Human Learning and Memory, 5,* 315–321.

Baddeley, A. D. (1978). The trouble with levels: A re-examination of Craik and Lockhart's framework for memory research. *Psychological Review, 85,* 139–152.

Baddeley, A. D. (1982). Domains of recollection. *Psychological Review, 89,* 708–729.

Baddeley, A. D. (1986). *Working memory.* Oxford: Clarendon Press.

Baddeley, A. D., & Hitch, G. J. (1974). Working memory. In G. Bower (Ed.), *The psychology of learning and motivation* (Vol. 8, pp. 47–89). New York: Academic Press.

Baddeley, A. D., & Hitch, G. (1977). Recency re-examined. In S. Dornic (Ed.), *Attention and performance VI* (pp. 647–667). Hillsdale, NJ: Erlbaum.

Baddeley, A. D., & Hitch, G. (1993). The recency effect: Implicit learning with explicit retrieval? *Memory & Cognition, 21,* 146–155.

Baddeley, A. D., & Lieberman, K. (1980). Spatial working memory. In R. Nickerson (Ed.), *Attention and performance VIII* (pp. 52–539). Hillsdale, NJ: Erlbaum.

Baddeley, A. D., Papagano, C., & Vallar, G. (1988). When long-term learning depends on short-term storage. *Journal of Memory & Language, 27,* 586–595.

Baddeley, A. D., & Scott, D. (1971). Short-term forgetting in the absence of proactive interference. *Quarterly Journal of Experimental Psychology, 23,* 275–283.

Baddeley, A. D., Thomson, N., & Buchanan, M. (1975). Word length and the structure of short-term memory. *Journal of Verbal Learning and Verbal Behavior, 14,* 576–589.

Baddeley, A. D., & Warrington, E. K. (1970). Amnesia and the dissociation between long- and short-term memory. *Journal of Verbal Learning and Verbal Behavior, 9,* 176–189.

Bahrick, H. P. (1970). Two-phase model for prompted recall. *Psychological Review, 77,* 215–222.

Bahrick, H. P., Bahrick, P. O., & Wittlinger, R. P. (1975). Fifty years of memory for names and faces: A cross-sectional approach. *Journal of Experimental Psychology: General, 104,* 54–75.

Bainbridge, J. V., Lewandowsky, S., & Kirsner, K. (1993). Context effects in repetition priming are sense effects. *Memory & Cognition, 21,* 619–626.

Balota, D. A. (1983). Automatic semantic activation and episodic memory encoding. *Journal of Verbal Learning and Verbal Behavior, 22,* 88–104.

Balota, D. A., & Chumbley, J. I. (1984). Are lexical decisions a good measure of lexical access? The role of word frequency in the neglected decision stage. *Journal of Experimental Psychology, 10,* 340–357.

Balota, D. A., Pollatsek, A., & Rayner, K. (1985). The interaction of contextual constraints and parafoveal visual information in reading. *Cognitive Psychology, 17,* 364–390.

Balota, D. A., & Rayner, K. (1983). Parafoveal visual information and semantic contextual constraints. *Journal of Experimental Psychology: Human Perception and Performance, 9,* 726–738.

Banks, M. S. (1980). The development of visual accommodation during early infancy. *Child Development, 51,* 646–666.

Banks, M. S., & Salapatek, P. (1983). Infant visual perception. In M. M. Haith & J. J. Campos (Eds.), *Handbook of child psychology: Infancy and developmental biology* (Vol. 2). New York: Wiley.

Banks, W. P. (1983). On the decay of the icon. *The Behavioral and Brain Sciences, 6,* 14.

Bartlett, F. C. (1932). *Remembering: A study in experimental and social psychology.* Cambridge: Cambridge University Press.

Bass, E., & Davis, L. (1988). *The courage to heal: A guide for woman survivors of child sexual abuse.* New York: Harper & Row.

Batchelder, W. H., & Riefer, D. M. (1990). Multinomial processing models of source monitoring. *Psychological Review, 97,* 548–564.

Battig, W. F. (1966). Facilitation and interference. In E. A. Bilodeau (Ed.), *Acquisition of skill* (pp. 215–244). New York: Academic.

Bauer, P. J. (1996). What do infants recall of their lives? Memory for specific events by one- to two-year-olds. *American Psychologist, 51,* 29–41.

Bauer, P. J., & Hertsgaard, L. A. (1993). Increasing steps in recall of events: Factors facilitating immediate and long-term memory in 13.5- and 16.5-month-old children. *Child Development, 64,* 1204–1223.

Bauer, P. J., & Wewerka, S. S. (1995). One- to two-year-olds' recall of events: The more expressed, the more impressed. *Journal of Experimental Child Psychology, 59,* 475–496.

Beck, A. T., & Emery, G. (1979). *Cognitive therapy of anxiety and phobic disorders*. Philadelphia: Center for Cognitive Therapy.

Beck, R. C. (1990). *Motivation: Theories and principles* (3rd ed.). Englewood Cliffs, NJ: Prentice-Hall.

Beebe, L. M. (Ed.). (1988). *Issues in second language acquisition: Multiple perspectives*. New York: Newbury.

Behrmann, M., Moscovitch, M., & Winocur, G. (1994). Intact visual imagery and impaired visual perception in a patient with visual agnosia. *Journal of Experimental Psychology: Human Perception & Performance, 20*, 1068–1087.

Belleza, F. S. (1981). Mnemonic devices: Classification, characteristics, and criteria. *Review of Educational Research, 51*, 247–275.

Belli, R. F., Lindsay, D. S., Gales, M. S., & McCarthy, T. T. (1994). Memory impairment and source misattribution in postevent misinformation experiments with short retention intervals. *Memory and Cognition, 22*, 40–54.

Benson, D. F., & Greenberg, J. P. (1969). Visual form agnosia. *Archives of Neurology, 20*, 82–89.

Bentin, S., & Mann, V. (1990). Masking and stimulus intensity effects on duplex perception: A confirmation of the dissociation between speech and non-speech modes. *Journal of the Acoustical Society of America, 88*, 64–74.

Bereiter, C., Burtis, P. J., & Scardamalia, M. (1988). Cognitive operations in constructing main points in written composition. *Journal of Memory & Language, 27*, 261–278.

Berger, K. S. (1994). *The developing person through the life span* (3rd ed.). New York: Worth.

Berlin, B., & Kay, P. (1969). *Basic color terms: Their universality and evolution*. Berkeley: University of California Press.

Bernstein Ratner, N., & Berko Gleason, J. (1993). Introduction to psycholinguistics: What do language users know? In J. Berko Gleason & N. Bernstein Ratner (Eds.), *Psycholinguistics* (pp. 1–40). Forth Worth: Holt, Rinehart and Winston.

Bertenthal, B. I. (1993). Infants' perception of biomechanical motions: Intrinsic image and knowledge-based constraints. In C. E. Granrud (Ed.), *Visual perception and cognition in infancy*. Hillsdale, NJ: Erlbaum.

Besner, D., & Davelaar, D. (1982). Basic processes in reading: Two phonological codes. *Canadian Journal of Psychology, 36*, 701–711.

Bever, T. G. (1970). The cognitive basis for linguistic structures (pp. 279–362). In J. R. Hayes (Ed.) *Cognition and the development of language*. New York: Wiley.

Bexton, W. H., Heron, W., & Scott, T. H. (1954). Effects of decreased variation in the sensory environment. *Canadian Journal of Psychology, 8*, 70–76.

Biederman, I. (1985). Human image understanding: Recent research and a theory. *Computer Vision, Graphics and Image Processing, 32*, 29–73.

Biederman, I. (1987). Recognition-by-components: A theory of human image understanding. *Psychological Review, 94*, 115–147.

Biederman, I., Glass, A. L., & Stacy, E. W. (1973). Searching for objects in real world scenes. *Journal of Experimental Psychology, 97*, 22–27.

Biederman, I., Rabinowitz, J. C., Glass, A. L., & Stacy, E. W. (1974). On the information extracted from a glance at a scene. *Journal of Experimental Psychology, 103*, 597–600.

Bierwisch, M. (1970). Semantics. In J. Lyons (Ed.), *New horizons in linguistics* (pp. 166–184). Baltimore: Penguin Books.

Bilodeau, E. A., & Bilodeau, I. M. (1958). Variation of temporal intervals among critical events in five studies of knowledge of results. *Journal of Experimental Psychology, 55*, 603–612.

Bilodeau, E. A., Sulzer, J. L., & Levy, C. M. (1962). Theory and data on the interrelationships of three factors of memory. *Psychological Monographs, 76*.

Birch, E. E., Gwiazda, J., & Held, R. (1982). Stereoacuity development for crossed and uncrossed disparities in human infants. *Vision Research, 22*, 507–513.

Birch, E. E., Gwiazda, J., & Held, R. (1983). The development of vergence does not account for the onset of stereopsis. *Perception, 12*, 331–336.

Birren, J. E., & Schaie, K. W. (1996). *Handbook of the psychology of aging*. San Diego: Academic Press.

Bjork, R. A., & Richardson-Klavehn, A. (1989). On the puzzling relationship between environmental context and human memory. In C. Izawa (Ed.), *Current issues in cognitive processes: The Tulane Floweree Symposium on Cognition*. Hillsdale, NJ: Erlbaum.

Blaney, P. H. (1986). Affect and memory: A review. *Psychological Bulletin, 99*, 229–246.

Blaxton, T. A. (1989). Investigating dissociations among memory measures: Support for a transfer-appropriate processing framework. *Journal of Experimental Psychology: Learning, Memory, and Cognition, 15*, 657–668.

Bloom, K. C., & Shuell, T. J. (1981). Effects of massed and distributed practice on the learning and retention of second language vocabulary. *Journal of Educational Research, 74*, 245–248.

Bloomfield, L. (1933). *Language*. New York: Henry Holt.

Bloomfield, L. (1935). *Language*. London: Allen and Unwin.

Blumenthal, A. L. (1970). *Language and psychology: Historical aspects of psycholinguistics*. New York: Wiley.

Blumenthal, A. L. (1974). An historical view of psycholinguistics (pp. 1105–1135). In T. A. Sebeok (Ed.), *Current trends in linguistics, Vol. 12*. The Hague: Mouton.

Blumenthal, A. L. (1987). The emergence of psycholinguistics. *Synthese, 72*, 313–323.

Bogen, J., Dezure, R., Tenhouten, W. D., & Marsh, J. (1972). The other side of the brain IV: The A/P ratio. *Bulletin of the Los Angeles Neurological Societies, 37*, 49–61.

Bonto, M. A., & Payne, D. G. (1991). Role of environmental context in eyewitness memory. *American Journal of Psychology, 104*, 117–134.

Boring, E. G. (1950). *A history of experimental psychology*. New York: Appleton-Century-Crofts.

Bower, G. H. (1981). Mood and memory. *American Psychologist, 36*, 129–148.

Bower, G. H., Clark, M. C., Lesgold, A. M., & Winzenz, D. (1969). Hierarchical retrieval schemes in recall of categorized word lists. *Journal of Verbal Learning and Verbal Behavior, 8*, 323–343.

Bower, G. H., & Hilgard, E. R. (1981). *Theories of learning* (5th ed.). Englewood Cliffs, NJ: Prentice-Hall.

Bower, G. H., & Mayer, J. D. (1989). In search of mood-dependent retrieval. *Journal of Social Behavior and Personality, 4*, 133–168.

Bower, G. H., Monteiro, K. P., & Gilligan, S. G. (1978). Emotional mood as a context for learning and recall. *Journal of Verbal Learning and Verbal Behavior, 17*, 573–578.

Bower, G. H., & Reitman, J. S. (1972). Mnemonic elaboration in multilist learning. *Journal of Verbal Learning and Verbal Behavior, 11*, 477–485.

Bower, G. H. & Trabasso, T. R. (1963). Reversals prior to solution in concept identification. *Journal of Experimental Psychology, 66,* 409–418.

Bower, G. H., & Trabasso, T. R. (1964). Concept identification. In R. C. Atkinson (Ed.), *Studies in Mathematical Psychology.* Stanford, CA: Stanford University Press.

Bower, T. G. (1976). Repetitive processes in child development. *Scientific American, 235* (November), 38–47.

Bradley, R. A., & Terry, M. E. (1952). Rank analysis of incomplete block designs. I. The method of paired comparisons. *Biometrika, 39,* 324–345.

Brainerd, C. J., Reyna, V. F., Howe, M. L., & Kevershan, J. (1991). Fuzzy trace theory and cognitive triage in memory development. *Developmental Psychology, 27,* 351–369.

Brandimonte, M. A., Hitch, G. J., & Bishop, D. V. M. (1992). Influence of short-term memory codes on visual image processing: Evidence from image transformation tasks. *Journal of Experimental Psychology: Learning, Memory, and Cognition, 18,* 157–165.

Bransford, J. D., & Franks, J. J. (1971). The abstraction of linguistic ideas. *Cognitive Psychology, 2,* 331–350.

Bransford, J. D., Franks, J. J., Morris, C. D., & Stein, B. S. (1979). Some general constraints on learning and memory research. In L. S. Cermak & F. I. M. Craik (Eds.), *Levels of processing in human memory* (pp. 331–354). Hillsdale, NJ: Erlbaum.

Bregman, A. S. (1990). *Auditory scene analysis: The perceptual organization of sound.* Cambridge, MA: MIT Press.

Bresnan, J., & Kaplan, R. M. (1982). Introduction: Grammars as mental representations of language. In J. Bresnan (Ed.), *The mental representation of grammatical relations* (pp. xvii–lii). Cambridge, MA: MIT Press.

Britt, S. H. (1935). Retroactive inhibition: A review of the literature. *Psychological Bulletin, 32,* 381–440.

Britton, B. K., Glynn, S. M., Meyer, B. J., & Penland, M. J. (1982). Effects of text structure on use of cognitive capacity during reading. *Journal of Educational Psychology, 74,* 51–61.

Britton, B. K., & Tessler, A. (1982). Effects of prior knowledge on use of cognitive capacity in three complex cognitive tasks. *Journal of Verbal Learning and Verbal Behavior, 21,* 421–436.

Broadbent, D. E. (1954). The role of auditory localization in attention and memory span. *Journal of Experimental Psychology, 47,* 191–196.

Broadbent, D. E. (1958). *Perception and communication.* London: Pergamon Press.

Brodie, D. A., & Prytulak, L. S. (1975). Free recall curves: Nothing but rehearsing some items more or recalling them sooner? *Journal of Verbal Learning and Verbal Behavior, 14,* 549–563.

Brooks, L. R. (1968). Spatial and verbal components in the act of recall. *Canadian Journal of Psychology, 22,* 349–368.

Brown, A. S., & Mitchell, D. B. (1994). A reevaluation of semantic versus nonsemantic processing in implicit memory. *Memory & Cognition, 22,* 533–541.

Brown, E., & Deffenbacher, K. (1975). Forgotten mnemonists. *Journal of the History of the Behavioral Sciences, 11,* 342–349.

Brown, E., & Deffenbacher, K. (1988). Superior memory performance and mnemonic encoding. In L. K. Obler & D. Fein (Eds.), *The exceptional brain: Neuropsychology of talent and special abilities* (pp. 191–211). New York: Guilford Press.

Brown, J. (1958). Some tests of the decay theory of immediate memory. *Quarterly Journal of Experimental Psychology, 10,* 12–21.

Brown, M. W., Wilson, F. A. W., & Riches, I. P. (1987). Neuronal evidence that inferomedial temporal cortex is more important than hippocampus in certain processes underlying recognition memory. *Brain Research, 409,* 158–162.

Brown, R. (1973). *A first language: The early stages.* Cambridge, MA: Harvard University Press.

Brown, R., & Hanlon, C. (1970). Derivational complexity and order of acquisition in child speech. In J. R. Hayes (Ed.), *Cognition and the development of language* (pp. 11–53). New York: Wiley.

Brown, R., & Kulik, J. (1977). Flashbulb memories. *Cognition, 5,* 73–99.

Bruce, C. J., & Goldberg, M. E. (1985). Primate frontal eye fields: I. Single neurons discharging before saccades. *Journal of Neurophysiology, 53,* 603–635.

Bruce, D., & Bahrick, H. P. (1992). Perceptions of past research. *American Psychologist, 47,* 319–328.

Bruce, P. R., Coyne, A. C., & Botwinick, J. (1982). Adult age differences in metamemory. *Journal of Gerontology, 37,* 354–357.

Bruce, R. W. (1933). Conditions of transfer of training. *Journal of Experimental Psychology, 13,* 343–361.

Bruck, M., Ceci, S. J., Francouer, E., & Barr, R. (1995). "I hardly cried when I got my shot!" Influencing children's reports about a visit to their pediatrician. *Child Development, 66,* 193–208.

Bruner, J. S., Goodnow, J. J., & Austin, G. A. (1956). *A study of thinking.* New York: Wiley.

Bryan, W. L., & Harter, N. (1897). Studies in the physiology and psychology of the telegraphic language. *Psychological Review, 4,* 27–53.

Bryan, W. L., & Harter, N. (1899). Studies on the telegraphic language. The acquisition of a hierarchy of habits. *Psychological Review, 6,* 345–375.

Bryant, P. E., & Trabasso, T. (1971). Transitive inferences and memory in young children. *Nature, 232,* 456–458.

Buckhout, R. (1974). Eyewitness testimony. *Scientific American, 231,* 23–31.

Buell, S. J., & Coleman, P. D. (1980). Individual differences in dendritic growth in human aging and senile dementia. In D. G. Stein (Ed.), *The psychobiology of aging: Problems and perspectives.* New York: Elsevier North Holland.

Bugelski, B. R. (1962). Presentation time, total time, and mediation in paired-associate learning. *Journal of Experimental Psychology, 63,* 409–412.

Burke, D. M., & Light, L. L. (1981). Memory and aging: The role of retrieval processes. *Psychological Bulletin, 90,* 513–546.

Busemeyer, J. R. (1991). Intuitive statistical estimation. In N. H. Anderson (Ed.), *Contributions to Information Integration Theory, Volume 1: Cognition* (pp. 187–215). Hillsdale, NJ: Erlbaum.

Busemeyer, J. R., Forsyth, B., & Nozawa, G. (1988). Comparisons of elimination by aspects and suppression of aspects choice models based on choice response time. *Journal of Mathematical Psychology, 32,* 341–349.

Busemeyer, J. R., & Townsend, J. T. (1992). Fundamental derivations for decision field theory. *Mathematical Social Sciences, 23,* 255–282.

Busemeyer, J. R., & Townsend, J. T. (1993). Decision-field theory: A dynamic-cognitive approach to decision-making in an uncertain environment. *Psychological Review, 100,* 432–459.

Bushnell, E. W., & Boudreau, J. P. (1993). Motor development and the mind: The potential role of motor abilities as a determinant of aspects of perceptual development. *Child Development, 64,* 1005–1021.

Buswell, G. T. (1937). *How adults read.* Chicago: University of Chicago Press.

Butter, M. A., Glisky, E. L., & Schacter, D. L. (1993). Transfer of new learning in memory-impaired patients. *Journal of Clinical & Experimental Neuropsychology, 15,* 219–230.

Butterworth, B., Campbell, R., & Howard, D. (1986). The uses of short-term memory: A case study. *Quarterly Journal of Experimental Psychology, 37A,* 435–475.

Buxton, C. E., & Grant, D. A. (1939). Retroaction and gains in motor learning: II. Sex differences and a further analysis of gains. *Journal of Experimental Psychology, 25,* 198–208.

Buxton, C. E., & Henry, C. E. (1939). Retroaction and gains in motor learning: II. Similarity of interpolated task as a factor in gains. *Journal of Experimental Psychology, 25,* 1–17.

Camp, C. J., & McKittrick, L. A. (1992). Memory interventions in Alzheimer's-type dementia populations: Methodological and theoretical issues. In R. L. West & J. D. Sinnott (Eds.), *Everyday memory and aging: Current research and methodology* (pp. 155–172). New York: Springer-Verlag.

Campos, J. J., & Langer, A. (1971). The visual cliff: Discriminative cardiac orienting responses with retinal size held constant. *Psychophysiology, 8,* 264–265.

Campos, J. J., Langer, A., & Krowitz, A. (1970). Cardiac responses on the visual cliff in prelocomotor human infants. *Science, 170,* 196–197.

Caplan, D., & Waters, G. (1990). Short-term memory and language comprehension: A critical review of the neuropsychological literature. In G. Vallar & T. Shallice (Eds.), *Neuropsychological impairments of short-term memory.* Cambridge: Cambridge University Press.

Caramazza, A., Basili, A. G., Koller, J., & Berndt, R. S. (1981). An investigation of repetition and language processing in a case of conduction aphasia. *Brain and Language, 14,* 236–271.

Card, S. K., English, W. K., & Burr, B. (1978). Evaluation of mouse, rate controlled isometric joystick, step keys, and text keys for text selection on a CRT. *Ergonomics, 21,* 601–613.

Carey, S. (1978). The child as word learner. In M. Halle, J. Bresnan, & G. A. Miller (Eds.), *Linguistic theory and psychological reality.* Cambridge, MA: MIT Press.

Carey, S., & Gelman, R. (1991). *The epigenesis of mind.* Hillsdale, NJ: Erlbaum.

Carlson, N. R. (1994). *Physiology of behavior.* Needham Heights, MA: Allyn and Bacon.

Carlson, R. A., & Schneider, W. (1989). Acquisition context and the use of causal rules. *Memory & Cognition, 17,* 240–248.

Carlson, R. A., & Yaure, R. G. (1990). Practice schedules and the use of component skills in problem solving. *Journal of Experimental Psychology: Learning, Memory, and Cognition, 10,* 484–496.

Carpenter, W. B. (1874). *Principles of mental physiology.* London: John Churchill.

Carr, H. R. (1917). Maze studies with the white rat: I. Normal animals. *Journal of Animal Behavior, 7,* 259–275.

Carr, T. H., McCauley, C., Sperber, R. D., & Parmalee, C. M. (1982). Words, pictures, and priming: On semantic activation, conscious identification, and the automaticity of information processing. *Journal of Experimental Psychology: Human Perception and Performance, 8,* 755–777.

Carr, T. H., & Pollatsek, A. (1985). Recognizing printed words: A look at current models. In D. Besner, T. G. Waller, & G. E.

MacKinnon (Eds.), *Reading research: Advances in theory and practice 5* (pp. 1–82). San Diego: Academic Press.

Carroll, D. W. (1986). *The psychology of language.* Monterey, CA: Brooks/Cole.

Carroll, J. B., & White, M. N. (1973). Word frequency and age of acquisition as determiners of picture-naming latency. *Quarterly Journal of Experimental Psychology, 25,* 85–95.

Cattell, J. M. (1886). The influence of the intensity of the stimulus on the length of the reaction time. *Brain, 9,* 512–514.

Cattell, J. M. (1883). Uber die Tragheit der Netzhaut und des Sehcentrums. *Phil. Stud., 3,* 94–127.

Cattell, R. B. (1963). The personality and motivation of the researcher from measurements of contemporaries and from bibliography. In C. W. Taylor & F. Barron (Eds.), *Scientific creativity: Its recognition and development* (pp. 119–131). New York: Wiley.

Cavanagh, P. (1988). Pathways in early vision. In Z. Pylyshyn (Ed.), *Computational processes in human vision* (pp. 239–261). Norwood, NJ: Ablex.

Cavanaugh, J. L., Kramer, D. A., Sinnott, J. C., Camp, C. J., & Markley, R. P. (1985). On missing links and such: Interfaces between cognitive research and everyday problem-solving. *Human Development, 28,* 146–148.

Ceci, S. J., Ross, D. F., & Toglia, M. P. (1987). Suggestibility of children's memory: Psychlegal implications. *Journal of Experimental Psychology: General, 116,* 38–49.

Cerella, J. (1991). Age effects may be global not local: Comment on Fisk and Rogers (1991). *Journal of Experimental Psychology: General, 120,* 215–223.

Chafe, W., & Danielewicz, J. (1987). Properties of spoken and written language. In R. Horowitz & S. J. Samuels (Eds.), *Comprehending oral and written language* (pp. 83–113). San Diego: Academic Press.

Chaffin, R., & Herrmann, D. J. (1983). Self reports of memory abilities by old and young adults. *Human Learning Journal of Practical Research and Application, 2,* 17–28.

Chandler, C. C. (1989). Specific retroactive interference in modified recognition tests: Evidence for an unknown cause of interference. *Journal of Experimental Psychology: Learning, Memory, and Cognition, 15,* 256–265.

Chandler, C. C. (1991). How memory for an event is influenced by related events: Interference in modified recognition tests. *Journal of Experimental Psychology: Learning, Memory, and Cognition, 17,* 115–125.

Chase, W. G., & Ericsson, K. A. (1981). Skilled memory. In J. R. Anderson (Ed.), *Cognitive skills and their acquisition* (pp. 141–189). Hillsdale, NJ: Erlbaum.

Chase, W. G., & Ericsson, K. A. (1982). Skill and working memory. In G. H. Bower (Ed.), *The psychology of learning and motivation* (Vol. 16, pp. 1–58). New York: Academic Press.

Chase, W. G., & Simon, H. A. (1973). Perception in chess. *Cognitive Psychology, 4,* 55–81.

Cheng, P. W. (1985). Restructuring versus automaticity: Alternative accounts of skill acquisition. *Psychological Review, 92,* 414–423.

Cherry, E. C. (1953). Some experiments on the recognition of speech with one and two ears. *Journal of the Acoustical Society of America, 25,* 975–979.

Chi, M. T. H. (1978). Knowledge structure and memory development. In R. S. Siegler (Ed.), *Children's thinking: What develops?* (pp. 73–96). Hillsdale, NJ: Erlbaum.

Chi, M. T. H., Feltovich, P. J., & Glaser, R. (1981). Categorization and representation of physics problems by experts and novices. *Cognitive Science, 5,* 121–152.

Chi, M. T. H., & Koeske, R. D. (1983). Network representation of a child's dinosaur knowledge. *Developmental Psychology, 19,* 29–39.

Chomsky, N. (1957). *Syntactic structures.* The Hague: Mouton.

Chomsky, N. (1959). A review of Skinner's "Verbal Behavior." *Language, 35,* 26–58.

Chomsky, N. (1965). *Aspects of the theory of syntax.* Cambridge, MA: MIT Press..

Chomsky, N. (1968). Noam Chomsky and Stuart Hampshire discuss the study of language. *The Listener, 79,* No. 2044.

Chomsky, N. (1981). *Lectures of government and binding.* Bordrecht, Netherlands: Foris.

Chomsky, N., & Miller, G. A. (1963). Introduction to the formal analysis of natural language. In R. D. Luce, R. Bush, & G. Glanter (Eds.), *Handbook of mathematical psychology: Volume II* (pp. 269–321). New York: Wiley.

Chow, S. L. (1991). Partial report: Iconic store or two buffers? *Journal of General Psychology, 118,* 147–169.

Church, B. A., & Schacter, D. L. (1994). Perceptual specificity and auditory priming: Implicit memory for voice intonation and fundamental frequency. *Journal of Experimental Psychology: Learning, Memory, and Cognition, 20,* 521–533.

Churchland, P. S., & Sejnowski, T. J. (1989). *The computational brain.* Cambridge, MA: MIT Press.

Churchland, P. S., & Sejnowski, T. J. (1991). Perspectives on cognitive neuroscience. In R. G. Lister & H. J. Weingartner (Eds.), *Perspectives on cognitive neuroscience.* New York: Oxford University Press.

Clark, E. (1973). What's in a word? On the child's acquisition of semantics in his first language. In T. Moore (Ed.), *Cognitive development and the acquisition of language.* New York: Academic Press.

Clark, H. H., & Sengul, C. J. (1979). In search of referents for nouns and pronouns. *Memory & Cognition, 7,* 36–41.

Clark, S. E. (1969). Retrieval of color information from perceptual memory. *Journal of Experimental Psychology, 82,* 236–266.

Clifton, C., & Ferreira, F. (1987). Discourse structure and anaphora: Some experimental results. In M. Coltheart (Ed.), *Attention and performance XII.* London: Erlbaum.

Clifton, R. K., Rochat, P., Litovsky, R. Y., & Perris, E. E. (1991). Object representation guides infants' reaching in the dark. *Journal of Experimental Psychology: Human Perception and Performance, 17,* 323–329.

Cofer, C. N. (1967). Conditions for the use of verbal associations. *Psychological Bulletin, 68,* 1–12.

Cohen, D. (1983). *Piaget: Critique and assessment.* London: Croom Helm.

Cohen, G. D. (1988). *The brain in human aging.* New York: Springer.

Cohen, J. D., Dunbar, K. O., Barch, D. M., & Braver, T. S. (1997). Issues concerning relative speed of processing hypotheses, schizophrenic performance deficits, and prefrontal function: Comment on Schooler et al. (1997). *Journal of Experimental Psychology: General, 126,* 37–41.

Cohen, J. D., Dunbar, K., & McClelland, J. L. (1990). On the control of automatic processes: A parallel distributed processing account of the Stroop effect. *Psychological Review, 97,* 332–361.

Cohen, J. D., Noll, D. C., & Schneider, W. (1993). Functional magnetic resonance imaging: Overview and methods for psychological research. *Behavior Research Methods, Instruments and Computers, 25,* 101–113.

Collins, A. M., & Quillian, M. R. (1969). Retrieval time from semantic memory. *Journal of Verbal Learning and Verbal Behavior, 8,* 240–247.

Collins, A. M., & Quillian, M. R. (1972). How to make a language user. In E. Tulving & W. Donaldson (Eds.), *Organization of memory* (pp. 309–351). New York: Academic Press.

Coltheart, M., Lea, C. D., & Thompson, K. (1974). In defense of iconic memory. *Quarterly Journal of Experimental Psychology, 26,* 633–641.

Connine, C. M., Blasko, D. G., & Titone, D. (1993). Do the beginnings of spoken words have a special status in auditory word recognition? *Journal of Memory & Language, 32,* 193–210.

Conrad, R. (1964). Acoustic confusions in immediate memory. *British Journal of Psychology, 55,* 75–84.

Conrad, R. (1967). Interference or decay over short retention intervals? *Journal of Verbal Learning and Verbal Behavior, 6,* 49–54.

Conrad, R., & Hull, A. J. (1968). Input modality and the serial position curve in short-term memory. *Psychonomic Science, 10,* 135–136.

Cooper, L. A., & Regan, D. T. (1982). Attention, perception and intelligence. In R. J. Sternberg (Ed.), *Handbook of human intelligence* (pp. 123–169). Cambridge: Cambridge University Press.

Corballis, M. C. (1991). *The lopsided ape: Evolution of the generative mind.* New York: Oxford University Press.

Corbett, A. T., & Dosher, B. A. (1978). Instrumental inferences in sentence encoding. *Journal of Verbal Learning and Verbal Behavior, 17,* 479–491.

Coren, S., & Ward, L. M. (1989). *Sensation and perception.* New York: Harcourt, Brace.

Coren, S., Ward, L. M., & Enns, J. T. (1994). *Sensation and perception* (4th ed.). New York: Harcourt Brace.

Cornell, E. H. (1980). Distributed study facilitates infants' delayed recognition memory. *Memory & Cognition, 8,* 539–542.

Corteen, R. S., & Dunn, P. (1974). Shock-associated words in a nonattended message: A test for momentary awareness. *Journal of Experimental Psychology, 102,* 1143–1144.

Corteen, R. S., & Wood, B. (1972). Autonomic responses to shock-associated words in an unattended channel. *Journal of Experimental Psychology, 94,* 308–313.

Cowan, N. (1984). On short and long auditory stores. *Psychological Bulletin, 96,* 341–370.

Cowan, N. (1988). Evolving conceptions of memory storage, selective attention, and their mutual constraints within the human information processing system. *Psychological Bulletin, 104,* 163–191.

Cowan, N. (1993). Activation, attention, and short-term memory. *Memory & Cognition, 21,* 162–167.

Cowan, N. (1995). *Attention and memory: An integrated framework.* New York: Oxford University Press.

Cowan, N., & Morse, P. A. (1986). The use of auditory and phonetic memory in vowel discrimination. *Journal of the Acoustical Society of America, 79,* 500–507.

Cowles, M. (1989). *Statistics in psychology: An historical perspective.* Hillsdale, NJ: Erlbaum.

Craik, F. I. M. (1977). Age differences in human memory. In J. E. Birren & K. W. Schaie (Eds.), *Handbook of the psychology of aging* (pp. 384–420). New York: Van Nostrand Reinhold.

Craik, F. I. M. (1994). Memory changes in normal aging. *Current Directions in Psychological Science, 3,* 155–158.

Craik, F. I. M., & Lockhart, R. S. (1972). Levels of processing: A framework for memory research. *Journal of Verbal Learning and Verbal Behavior, 12,* 599–607.

Craik, F. I. M., & Tulving, E. (1975). Depth of processing and the retention of words in episodic memory. *Journal of Experimental Psychology, 104,* 268–294.

Crease, R. P. (1993). Biomedicine in the age of imaging. *Science, 261.*

Crossman, E. R. F. W. (1959). A theory of the acquisition of speed-skill. *Ergonomics, 2,* 153–166.

Crowder, R. G. (1976). *Principles of learning and memory.* Hillsdale, NJ: Erlbaum.

Crowder, R. G. (1982a). The demise of short-term memory. *Acta Psychologica, 50,* 291–323.

Crowder, R. G. (1982b). *The psychology of reading: An introduction.* New York: Oxford University Press.

Crowder, R. G. (1986). Auditory and temporal factors in the modality effect. *Journal of Experimental Psychology: Learning, Memory, & Cognition, 12,* 266–278.

Crowder, R. G. (1993). Short-term memory: Where do we stand? *Memory & Cognition, 21,* 142–145.

Crowder, R. G., & Neath, I. (1991). The microscope metaphor in human memory. In W. E. Hockley & S. Lewandowsky (Eds.), *Relating theory and data: Essays on human memory in honor of Bennet B. Murdock* (pp. 111–125). Hillsdale, NJ: Erlbaum.

Crutcher, R. J. (1994) Telling what we know: The use of verbal report methodologies in psychological research. *Psychological Science, 5,* 241–244.

Cummins, J. (1979). Linguistic independence and the educational development of bilingual children. *Review of Educational Research, 49,* 222–251.

Cuneo, D. O. (1980). A general strategy for judgments of quantity: The height + width rule. *Child Development, 51,* 299–301.

Dallett, K., & Wilcox, S. G. (1968). Contextual stimuli and proactive inhibition. *Journal of Experimental Psychology, 78,* 475–480.

Dalton, P. (1993). The role of stimulus familiarity in context-dependent recognition. *Memory & Cognition, 21,* 223–234.

Damasio, H., Grabowski, T., Frank, R., Galaburda, A. M., & Damasio, A. R. (1994). The return of Phineas Gage: Clues about the brain from the skull of a famous patient. *Science, 264,* 1102–1105.

Danna, J. (1995). *When Alzheimer's hits home.* New York: Palomino Press.

Darwin, C. (1896). *The origin of species by means of natural selection; or, The preservation of favored races in the struggle for life, with additions and corrections from sixth and last English edition.* New York: Appleton.

Darwin, C. J., Turvey, M. T., & Crowder, R. G. (1972). An auditory analogue of the Sperling partial report procedure: Evidence for brief auditory storage. *Cognitive Psychology, 3,* 255–267.

Dato, D. P. (1971). The development of the Spanish verb phrase in children's second language learning. In P. Pinsleur & T. Quinn (Eds.), *The psychology of second language learning.* Cambridge: Cambridge University Press.

Davis, J. M., & Rovee-Collier, C. K. (1983). Alleviated forgetting of a learned contingency in 8-week-old infants. *Developmental Psychology, 19,* 353–365.

Dawson, M. E., & Schell, A. M. (1982). Electrodermal responses to attended and nonattended significant stimuli during dichotic listening. *Journal of Experimental Psychology: Human Perception and Performance, 8,* 315–324.

De Avila, E. A., & Duncan, S. E. (1980). *Definition and measurement of bilingual students.* Paper presented at Bilingual Program, Policy, and Assessment Issues, Sacramento, CA.

DeCasper, A. J., & Fifer, W. P. (1980). Of human bonding: Newborns prefer their mothers' voices. *Science, 208,* 1174–1176.

DeCasper, A. J., & Spence, M. J. (1986). Prenatal maternal speech influences newborn's perception of speech sounds. *Infant Behavior and Development, 9,* 133–150.

Deci, E. L. (1992). On the nature and functions of motivation theories. *Psychological Science, 3,* 167–171.

Deese, J. (1959). On the prediction of occurrence of particular verbal intrusions in immediate recall. *Journal of Experimental Psychology, 58,* 17–22.

de Groot, A. (1946). *Thought and choice in chess.* The Hague: Mouton.

Dell, G. S. (1986). A spreading activation theory of retrieval in sentence production. *Psychological Review, 93,* 283–321.

Dell, G. S. (1988). The retrieval of phonological forms in production: Tests of predictions from a connectionist model. *Journal of Memory and Language, 27,* 124–142.

Dell, G. S., Burger, L. K., Svec, W. R. (1997). Language production and serial order: A functional analysis and a model. *Psychological Review 104* (1), 123–147.

DeLoache, J. S. (1989). Young children's understanding of the correspondence between a scale model and a larger space. *Cognitive Development, 4,* 121–139.

Dempster, F. N. (1981). Memory span: Sources of individual and developmental differences. *Psychological Bulletin, 89,* 63–100.

Dempster, F. N. (1987). Effects of variable encoding and the spaced presentations on vocabulary learning. *Journal of Educational Psychology, 79,* 162–170.

Denes, P. B., & Pinson, E. N. (1993). *The speech chain: The physics and biology of spoken language.* New York: Freeman.

Denney, N. W. (1974). Clustering in middle and old age. *Developmental Psychology, 10,* 471–475.

Denney, N. W., Miller, B. V., Dew, J. R., & Lavav, A. L. (1991). An adult developmental study of contextual memory. *Journals of Gerontology, 46,* P44–P50.

Denny, N. W., & Palmer, A. M. (1981). Adult age differences on traditional and practical problem-solving measures. *Journal of Gerontology, 36,* 323–328.

DeRenzi, E. (1986). Current issues in prosopagnosia. In H. D. Ellis, M. A. Jeeves, F. Newcome, & A. Young (Eds.), *Aspects of face processing.* Dordrecht, Netherlands: Martinus Nijhoff.

Desimone, R., & Ungerleider, L. G. (1989). Neural mechanisms of visual processing in monkeys. In F. B. Grafman &. J. Grafman (Eds.), *Handbook of neuropsychology* (pp. 267–299). New York: Elsevier Science Publishers.

Deutsch, F. A., & Deutsch, D. (1963). Attention: Some theoretical considerations. *Psychological Review, 70,* 80–90.

Diamond, M. C. (1988). *Enriching heredity.* New York: Free Press.

Diehl, R. L. (1986). Coproduction and direct perception of phonetic segments: A critique. *Journal of Phonetics, 14,* 61–66.

Dienes, Z., & Berry, D. (1997). Implicit learning: Below the subjective threshold. *Psychonomic Bulletin & Review, 4,* 3–23.

Dingwall, W. (1988). The evolution of human communicative behavior. In F. Newmeyer (Ed.), *Linguistics: The Cambridge Sur-*

vey. Volume III. Language: Psychological and biological aspects. Cambridge: Cambridge University Press.

Diringer, D. (1962). Writing. London: Thames & Hudson.

Di Vesta, F. J., & Smith, P. A. (1979). The pausing principle: Increasing the efficiency of memory for ongoing events. Contemporary Educational Psychology, 4, 288–296.

Doll, J., & Mayr, U. (1987). Intelligence and achievement in chess—a study of chess masters. Psychologische Beitrage, 29, 270–289.

Dollard, J., & Miller, N. E. (1950). Personality and psychotherapy: An analysis in terms of learning, thinking, and culture. New York: McGraw-Hill.

Dore, L. R., & Hilgard, E. R. (1938). Spaced practice as a test of Snoddy's two processes in mental growth. Journal of Experimental Psychology, 34, 359–374.

Dosher, B. A. (1979). Empirical approaches to information processing: Speed-accuracy tradeoff or reaction time. Acta Psychologica, 43, 347–359.

Dosher, B. A. (1984). Degree of learning and retrieval speed: Study time and multiple exposures. Journal of Experimental Psychology: Learning, Memory, and Cognition, 8, 173–207.

Dosher, B. A., & Rosedale, G. (1991). Judgments of semantic and episodic relatedness: Common time-course and failure of segregation. Journal of Memory and Language, 30, 125–160.

Duffy, E. (1934). Emotion: An example of the need for reorientation in psychology. Psychological Review, 41, 184–198.

Duffy, S. A. (1986). Role of expectations in sentence integration. Journal of Experimental Psychology: Learning, Memory, and Cognition, 12, 208–219.

Duis, S., Dean, R. S., & Derks, P. (1994). The modality effect: A result of methodology? International Journal of Neuroscience, 78, 1–7.

Dulsky, S. G. (1935). The effect of a change of background on recall and relearning. Journal of Experimental Psychology, 18, 725–740.

Dunbar, K., & MacLeod, C. M. (1984). A horse race of a different color: Stroop interference patterns with transformed words. Journal of Experimental Psychology: Human Perception and Performance, 10, 622–639.

Duncker, K. (1945). On problem-solving. Psychological Monographs, 58 (270).

Dupre, J. (1987). The latest on the best. Cambridge, MA: MIT Press.

Dutta, A., Schweickert, R., Choi, S., & Proctor, R. W. (1995). Cross-task cross talk in memory and perception. Acta Psychologica, 90, 49–62.

Dutton, J. M., & Starbuck, W. H. (Eds.). (1971). Computer simulation of human behavior. New York: Wiley.

Dvorak, A., Merrick, N. L., Dealy, W. L., & Ford, G. C. (1936). Typewriting behavior. New York: American Book Co.

Dweck, C. S. (1992). The study of goals in psychology. Psychological Science, 3, 165–167.

Easton, R. D., & Basala, M. (1982). Perceptual dominance during lip-reading. Perception & Psychophysics, 32, 562–570.

Ebbinghaus, H. (1885/1913). Memory: A contribution to experimental psychology (H. A. Ruger & C. E. Bussenius, Trans.). New York: Columbia University Teacher's College.

Eden, G. F., & Zeffiro, T. A. (1996). Looking beyond the reading difficulties in dyslexia, a vision deficit. The Journal of NIH Research, 8, 31–35.

Edwards, W. (1962). Subjective probabilities inferred from decisions. Psychological Review, 69, 109–135.

Egan, J. P., Carterette, E. C., & Thwing, E. J. (1954). Some factors affecting multi-channel listening. Journal of the Acoustical Society of America, 26, 774–782.

Ehrlich, S. F., & Rayner, K. (1983). Pronoun assignment and semantic integration during reading: Eye movements and immediacy of processing. Journal of Verbal Learning and Verbal Behavior, 22, 75–87.

Eich, E. (1984). Memory for unattended events: Remembering with and without awareness. Memory & Cognition, 12, 105–111.

Eich, E. (1985). Context, memory, and integrated item/context imagery. Journal of Experimental Psychology: Learning, Memory, and Cognition, 11, 764–770.

Eich, E. (1989). Theoretical issues in state-dependent memory. In H. L. Roediger & F. I. M. Craik (Eds.), Varieties of memory and consciousness: Essays in honour of Endel Tulving. Hillsdale, NJ: Erlbaum.

Eich, E. (1995). Searching for mood-dependent memory. Psychological Science, 6, 67–75.

Eimas, P. D., & Corbit, J. D. (1973). Selective adaptation of linguistic feature detectors. Cognitive Psychology, 4, 99–109.

Eimas, P. D., Siqueland, E. R., Jusczyk, P. W., & Vigorito, J. (1971). Speech perception in infants. Science, 171, 303–306.

Einhorn, H. J. (1974). Expert judgment: Some necessary conditions and an example. Journal of Applied Psychology, 59, 562–571.

Ellis, A., & Beattie, G. (1986). The psychology of language and communication. New York: Guilford.

Ellison, K. W., & Buckhout, R. (1981). Psychology and criminal justice. New York: Harper & Row.

Erdelyi, M. H., & Becker, J. (1974). Hypermnesia for pictures: Incremental memory for pictures but not for words in multiple recall trials. Cognitive Psychology, 6, 159–171.

Erdmann, B., & Dodge, R. (1898). Psychologische untersuchungen uber das lesen auf experimenteller Grundlage. Halle: Niemeyer. [Cited in Sperling, G. (1960). The information available in brief visual presentations. Psychological Monographs, 74 (Whole no. 498).]

Ericsson, K. A. (1990). Peak performance and age: An examination of peak performance in sports. In P. B. Baltes & M. M. Baltes (Eds.), Successful aging: Perspectives from the behavioral sciences (pp. 164–195). Cambridge: Cambridge University Press.

Ericsson, K. A., & Crutcher, R. J. (1990). The nature of exceptional performance. In P. B. Baltes, D. L. Featherman, & R. M. Lerner (Eds.), Life-span development and behavior (Vol. 10, pp. 187–217): Hillsdale, NJ: Erlbaum.

Ericsson, K. A., & Faivre, I. A. (1988). What's exceptional about exceptional abilities? In L. K. Obler & D. Fein (Eds.), The exceptional brain: Neuropsychology of talent and special abilities (pp. 436–473). New York: Guilford Press.

Ericsson, K. A., Krampe, R. T., & Tesch-Römer, C. (1993). The role of deliberate practice in the acquisition of expert performance. Psychological Review, 100, 363–406.

Ericsson, K. A., & Simon, H. A. (1984). Protocol analysis: Verbal reports as data. Cambridge, MA: MIT Press.

Ericsson, K. A., & Smith, J. (1991). Toward a general theory of expertise. Cambridge: Cambridge University Press.

Erikson, E. H. (1959). Identity and the life cycle. Psychological Issues, Monograph 1. New York: International Universities Press.

Ervin-Tripp, S. (1993). Conversational discourse. In J. Berko Gleason & N. Bernstein Ratner (Eds.), *Psycholinguistics* (pp. 238–271). Forth Worth: Holt, Rinehart and Winston.

Estes, W. K. (1950). Toward a statistical theory of learning. *Psychological Review, 57,* 94–107.

Estes, W. K. (1954a). Individual behavior in uncertain situations: An interpretation in terms of statistical association theory. In R. M. Thrall, C. H. Coombs, & R. L. Davis (Eds.), *Decision processes* (pp. 127–137). New York: Wiley.

Estes, W. K. (1954b). Kurt Lewin. In A. T. Poffenberger (Ed.), *Modern learning theory: A critical analysis of five examples* (pp. 317–343). New York: Appleton-Century-Crofts.

Estes, W. K. (1972). An associative basis for coding and organization in memory. In A. W. Melton & E. Martin (Eds.), *Coding processes in human memory* (pp. 161–190). Washington, DC: Winston.

Estes, W. K. (1986a). Array models for category learning. *Cognitive Psychology, 18,* 500–549.

Estes, W. K. (1986b). Memory storage and retrieval processes in category learning. *Journal of Experimental Psychology: General, 115,* 155–174.

Estes, W. K. (1991). Cognitive architectures from the standpoint of an experimental psychologist. *Annual Review of Psychology, 42,* 1–28.

Estes, W. K. (1994). *Classification and cognition.* New York: Oxford University Press.

Estes, W. K., & Burke, C. J. (1953). Theory of stimulus variability in learning. *Psychological Review, 60,* 276–286.

Estes, W. K., Campbell, J. A., Hatsopoulos, N., & Hurwitz, J. B. (1989). Base-rate effects in category learning: A comparison of parallel network and memory storage-retrieval models. *Journal of Experimental Psychology: Learning, Memory, and Cognition, 15,* 556–571.

Fantino, E., & Navarick, D. (1974). Recent developments in choice. In G. H. Bower (Ed.), *The psychology of learning and motivation* (Vol. 8, pp. 147–185). New York: Academic Press.

Farah, M. J. (1992). Is an object an object an object? Cognitive and neuropsychological investigations of domain-specificity in visual object recognition. *Current Directions in Psychological Science, 1,* 164–169.

Farah, M. J. (1994). Neuropsychological inference with an interactive brain: A critique of the "locality" assumption. *Brain and Behavioral Sciences, 17,* 43–104.

Farah, M. J., Meyer, M. M., & McMullen, P. A. (1996). The living/nonliving dissociation is not an artifact: Giving an a priori implausible hypothesis a strong test. *Cognitive Neuropsychology, 13,* 137–154.

Farmer, M. E., & Klein, R. M. (1996). The evidence for temporal processing deficit linked to dyslexia: A review. *Psychonomic Bulletin and Review, 2,* 460–493.

Feenan, K., & Snodgrass, J. G. (1990). The effect of context on discrimination and bias in recognition memory for pictures and words. *Memory & Cognition, 18,* 515–527.

Feinberg, T. E., & Farah, M. J. (1997). *Behavioral neurology and neuropsychology.* New York: McGraw-Hill.

Ferguson, C. A. (1959). Diglossia. *Word, 15,* 325–340.

Ferster, C. B., & Skinner, B. F. (1957). *Schedules of reinforcement.* New York: Appleton-Century-Crofts.

Feustel, T. C., Shiffrin, R. M., & Salasoo, A. (1983). Episodic and lexical contributions to the repetition effect in word identification. *Journal of Experimental Psychology: General, 112,* 309–346.

Filmore, C. J. (1968). Toward a modern theory of case. In D. A. Reibel & S. A. Schane (Eds.), *Modern studies in English* (pp. 361–375). Englewood Cliffs, NJ: Prentice-Hall.

Fishburn, P. C. (1988). Expected utility: An anniversary and a new era. *Journal of Risk and Uncertainty, 1,* 267–284.

Fisher, D. L., Fisk, A. D., & Duffy, S. A. (1995). Why latent models are needed to test hypotheses about the slowing of word and language processes in older adults. In P. A. Allen & T. R. Bashore (Eds.), *Age differences in word and language processing. Advances in psychology* (pp. 1–29). Amsterdam: Holland/Elsevier Science Publishers.

Fisher, D. L., & Glaser, R. A. (1996). Molar and latent models of cognitive slowing: Implications for aging, dementia, depression, development, and intelligence. *Psychonomic Bulletin and Review, 3,* 458–480.

Fishman, J. A. (1964). Language maintenance and language shift as fields of inquiry. *Linguistics, 9,* 32–70.

Fishman, J. A. (1966). *Language loyalty in the United States.* The Hague: Mouton.

Fisk, A. D., & Fisher, D. L. (1994). Brinley plots and theories of aging: The explicit, muddled, and implicit debates. *Journal of Gerontology: Psychological Sciences, 49,* 81–89.

Fisk, A. D., Fisher, D. L., & Rogers, W. A. (1992). General slowing alone cannot explain age-related search effects: A reply to Cerella. *Journal of Experimental Psychology: General, 121,* 73–78.

Fisk, A. D., & Hodge, K. A. (1992). Retention of trained performance in consistent mapping search after extended delay. *Human Factors, 34,* 147–164.

Fisk, A. D., & Jones, C. D. (1992). Global versus local consistency: Effects of degree of within-category consistency on performance and learning. *Human Factors, 34,* 693–705.

Fisk, A. D., & Schneider, W. (1981). Control and automatic processing during tasks requiring sustained attention: A new approach to vigilance. *Human Factors, 23,* 737–750.

Fitts, P. M., & Posner, M. I. (1967). *Human performance.* Belmont, CA: Brooks/Cole.

Flavell, J. H. (1985). *Cognitive development.* Englewood Cliffs, NJ: Prentice-Hall.

Flavell, J. H., Friedrichs, A. G., & Hoyt, J. D. (1970). Developmental changes in memorization processes. *Cognitive Psychology, 1,* 324–340.

Fodor, J. A. (1983). *Modularity of mind.* Cambridge, MA: Bradford Books.

Fodor, J. A., Bever, T. G., & Garrett, M. F. (1974). *The psychology of language.* New York: McGraw-Hill.

Forster, K. I., & Chambers, S. M. (1973). Lexical access and naming time. *Journal of Verbal Learning and Verbal Behavior, 12,* 627–635.

Fowler, C. A. (1986). An event approach to the study of speech perception from a direct-realist perspective. *Journal of Phonetics, 14,* 328.

Fowler, C. A., & Rosenblum, L. D. (1990). Duplex perception: A comparison of monosyllables and slamming of doors. *Journal of Experimental Psychology: Human Perception and Performance, 16,* 742–754.

Fowler, C. A., & Rosenblum, L. D. (1991). The perception of phonetic gestures. In I. G. Mattingly & M. Studdert-Kennedy (Eds.), *Modularity and the motor theory of speech perception* (pp. 33–59). Hillsdale, NJ: Erlbaum.

Frankfurter, F. (1927). *The case of Sacco and Vanzetti.* Boston: Little, Brown and Company.

Franks, J. J., & Bransford, J. D. (1971). Abstraction of visual patterns. *Journal of Experimental Psychology, 90,* 65–74.

Freud, S. (1905/1953). Three essays on the theory of sexuality. In J. Strachey (Ed. and Trans.), *The standard edition of the complete psychological works of Sigmund Freud* (Vol. 7, pp. 135–243). London: Hogarth Press.

Freud, S. (1916/1963). Introductory lectures on psycho-analysis. In J. Strachey (Ed. and Trans.), *The standard edition of the complete psychological works of Sigmund Freud* (Vol. 15, pp. 199–201). London: Hogarth Press.

Freud, S. (1938). *The basic writings of Sigmund Freud.* New York: Random House.

Freud, S., & Breuer, J. (1966). *Studies on hysteria* (J. Strachey, Trans.). New York: Avon.

Freyd, J. J., & Gleaves, D. H. (1996). "Remembering" words not presented in lists: Relevance to the current recovered/false memory controversy. *Journal of Experimental Psychology: Learning, Memory, and Cognition, 22,* 811–813.

Fromkin, V. A. (1971). The nonanomalous nature of anomalous utterances. *Language, 47,* 27–52.

Fromkin, V. A. (1988). The grammatical aspects of speech errors. In F. J. Newmeyer (Ed.), *Linguistics: The Cambridge survey, Vol. 11* (pp. 117–138). Cambridge: Cambridge University Press.

Fromkin, V. A. (1993). Speech production. In J. Berko Gleason & N. Bernstein Ratner (Eds.), *Psycholinguistics* (pp. 271–300). Forth Worth: Holt, Rinehart and Winston.

Funahashi, S., Bruce, C. J., & Goldman-Rakic, P. S. (1989). Mnemonic coding of visual space in the monkey's dorsolateral prefrontal cortex. *Journal of Neurophysiology, 61,* 331–349.

Gabrieli, J. D. E., Desmond, J. E., Demb, J. B., Wagner, A. D., Stone, M. V., Vaidya, C. J., & Glover, G. H. (1996). Functional magnetic resonance imaging of semantic memory processes in the frontal lobes. *Psychological Science, 7,* 278–283.

Gaeth, G. J., & Shanteau, J. (1984). Reducing the influence of irrelevant information on experienced decision makers. *Organizational Behavior and Human Performance, 33,* 263–282.

Gagné, R. M., Foster, H., & Crowley, M. E. (1948). The measurement of the transfer of training. *Psychological Bulletin, 45,* 97–130.

Galanter, E. (1962). Contemporary psychophysics. In R. Brown, E. Galanter, E. Hess, & G. Mandler (Eds.), *New directions in psychology* (pp. 87–157). New York: Holt, Rinehart & Winston.

Galton, F. (1869). *Hereditary genius.* New York: Macmillan.

Gardner, R. A., & Gardner, B. T. (1969). Teaching sign language to a chimpanzee. *Science, 165,* 664–672.

Garner, W. R., Hake, H. W., & Eriksen, C. W. (1956). Operationism and the concept of perception. *Psychological Review, 63,* 149–159.

Garrett, M. F. (1988). Processes in language production. In F. Newmeyer (Ed.), *Linguistics: The Cambridge Survey. Volume III. Language: Psychological and biological aspects* (pp. 69–96). Cambridge: Cambridge University Press.

Garrod, S., & Sanford, A. J. (1985). On the real-time character of interpretation during reading. *Language and Cognitive Processes, 1,* 43–59.

Geary, D. C., & Wiley, J. G. (1991). Cognitive addition: Strategy choice and speed-of-processing differences in young and elderly adults. *Psychology and Aging, 6,* 474–483.

Gelb, I. J. (1963). *A study of writing* (2nd ed.). Chicago: University of Chicago Press.

Genesee, F. (1988). Neuropsychology and second language acquisition. In L. M. Beebe (Ed.), *Issues in second language acquisition: Multiple perspectives.* New York: Newbury House.

Gernsbacher, M. A. (1984). Resolving 20 years of inconsistent interactions between lexical familiarity and orthography, concreteness and polysemy. *Journal of Experimental Psychology, General, 113,* 256–281.

Gernsbacher, M. A. (1985). Surface information loss in comprehension. *Cognitive Psychology, 17,* 324–363.

Gernsbacher, M. A. (1990). *Language comprehension as structure building.* Hillsdale, NJ: Erlbaum.

Gernsbacher, M. A. (1991). Cognitive processes and mechanisms in language comprehension: The structure building framework. In G. H. Bower (Ed.), *The psychology of learning and motivation, Vol. 27* (pp. 217–263). New York: Academic Press.

Gernsbacher, M. A., & Hargreaves, D. J. (1988). Accessing sentence participants: The advantage of first mention. *Journal of Memory and Language, 27,* 699–717.

Gernsbacher, M. A., Hargreaves, D. J., & Beeman, M. (1989). Building and accessing clausal representations: The advantage of first mention versus the advantage of clause recency. *Journal of Memory and Language, 28,* 735–755.

Gevins, A. S., Le, J., Martin, N., & Reutter, B. (1994). High resolution EEG: 124 channel recording, spatial deblurring and MRI integration methods. *Electroencephalograhic Clinical Neuropsychology, 90,* 337–358.

Gibson, E. J. (1969). *Principles of perceptual learning and development.* Englewood Cliffs, NJ: Prentice-Hall.

Gibson, E. J., & Walk, R. D. (1960). The visual cliff. *Scientific American, 202,* 64–71.

Gibson, J. J. (1966). *The senses considered as perceptual systems.* Boston: Houghton Mifflin.

Gibson, J. J. (1979). *The ecological approach to visual perception.* Boston: Houghton Mifflin.

Giegerich, W. (1975). Ontogeny = phylogeny? A fundamental critique of Erich Neumann's analytical psychology. *Spring,* 110–129.

Gillund, G., & Shiffrin, R. M. (1984). A retrieval model for both recognition and recall. *Psychological Review, 91,* 1–67.

Gisiner, R., & Schusterman, R. J. (1992). Sequence, syntax, and semantics: Responses of a language-trained sea lion (Zalophus californianus) to novel sign combinations. *Journal of Comparative Psychology, 106,* 78–91.

Glanzer, M. (1972). Storage mechanisms in recall. In G. H. Bower & J. T. Spence (Eds.), *The psychology of learning and motivation, Vol. 5.* New York: Academic Press.

Glanzer, M., & Cunitz, A. R. (1966). Two storage mechanisms in free recall. *Journal of Verbal Learning and Verbal Behavior, 5,* 351–360.

Gleitman, L., Gleitman, H., Landau, B., & Wanner, E. (1988). Where learning begins: Initial representations for language learning. In F. Newmeyer (Ed.), *Linguistics: The Cambridge Survey. Volume III. Language: Psychological and biological aspects.* Cambridge: Cambridge University Press.

Glenberg, A. M., & Lehman, T. S. (1980). Spacing over 1 week. *Memory & Cognition, 8,* 528–538.

Glenberg, A. M., Bradley, M., Gretz, A. L., Fish, J. H., & Turpin, B. M. (1980). A two-process account of long-term serial position effects. *Journal of Experimental Psychology: Human Learning and Memory, 6,* 356–369.

Glenberg, A. M., Bradley, M. M., Kraus, T. A., & Renzaglia, G. J. (1983). Studies of the long-term recency effect: Support for a contextually guided retrieval hypothesis. *Journal of Experimental Psychology: Learning, Memory, and Cognition, 9,* 231–255.

Glisky, E. L. (1992). Acquisition and transfer of declarative and procedural knowledge by memory-impaired patients: A computer data-entry task. *Neuropsychologia, 30,* 899–910.

Glover, J. A., & Corkill, A. K. (1987). Influence of paraphrased repetitions on the spacing effect. *Journal of Educational Psychology, 79,* 198–199.

Gluck, M. A., & Bower, G. H. (1988). From conditioning to category learning: An adaptive network model. *Journal of Experimental Psychology: General, 117,* 227–247.

Glucksberg, S., & Danks, J. H. (1968). Effects of discriminative labels and of nonsense labels upon availability of novel function. *Journal of Verbal Learning and Verbal Behavior, 7,* 72–76.

Gnadt, J. W., & Andersen, R. A. (1988). Memory related motor planning activity in posterior parietal cortex of macaque. *Experimental Brain Research, 70,* 216–220.

Godden, D., & Baddeley, A. D. (1975). Context-dependent memory in two natural experiments: On land and under water. *British Journal of Psychology, 66,* 325–331.

Goldinger, S. D., Pisoni, D. B., & Luce, P. A. (1990). Speech perception and spoken word recognition: Research and theory. In N. J. Lass (Ed.), *Principles of experimental phonetics.* Toronto: Decker.

Goldstein, E. B. (1984). *Sensation and perception* (2nd ed.). Belmont, CA: Wadsworth.

Goldstein, E. B. (1989). *Sensation and perception* (3rd ed.). Belmont, CA: Wadsworth.

Goldstein, E., & Farmer, K. (1993). *True stories of false memories.* Boca Raton, FL: SIRS Books.

Golinkoff, R., Hirsh-Pasek, K., Cauley, K., & Gordon, P. (1987). The eyes have it: Lexical and sytactic comprehension in a new paradigm. *Journal of Child Language, 14,* 23–46.

Goodwin, C. (1981). *Conversational organization.* New York: Academic Press.

Goodwin, D. W., Powel, B., Bremer, D., Hoine, H., & Stern, J. (1969). Alcohol and recall: State dependent effects in man. *Science, 163,* 1358–1360.

Gordon, P., Valentine, E., & Wilding, J. M. (1984). One man's memory: A study of a mnemonist. *British Journal of Psychology, 75,* 1–14.

Granrud, C. E., & Yonus, A. (1984). Infants' perception of pictorially specified interposition. *Journal of Experimental Child Psychology, 37,* 500–511.

Grant, D. A., Hake, H. W., & Hornseth, J. P. (1951). Acquisition and extinction of a verbal conditioned response with differing percentages of reinforcement. *Journal of Experimental Psychology, 42,* 1–5.

Gray, J. A., & Wedderburn, A. A. I. (1960). Grouping strategies with simultaneous stimuli. *Quarterly Journal of Experimental Psychology, 12,* 180–184.

Gray, P. (1991). *Psychology.* New York: Worth.

Green, D. M., & Swets, J. A. (1966). *Signal detection theory and psychophysics.* New York: Wiley.

Greene, J. (1972). *Psycholinguistics: Chomsky and psychology.* New York: Penguin.

Greenfield, P. M. (1991). Language, tools, and brain: The ontogeny and phylogeny of hierarchically organized sequential behavior. *Behavioral and Brain Sciences, 14,* 531–595.

Gregory, R. L. (1973). *Eye and brain: The psychology of seeing* (3rd ed.). New York: McGraw-Hill.

Gregory, R. L. (1990). *Eye and brain: The psychology of seeing* (4th ed.). Princeton, NJ: Princeton University Press.

Gregory, R., Harris, J., Heard, P., & Rose, D. (Eds.). (1995). *The artful eye.* New York: Oxford University Press.

Grene, D. (1987). *The History: Herodotus.* Chicago: University of Chicago Press.

Grice, H. P. (1975). Logic and conversation. In P. Cole & J. L. Morgan (Eds.), *Syntax and semantics: Vol. 3, Speech acts* (pp. 41–58). New York: Seminar Press.

Gumperz, J. J. (1962). Types of linguistic communities. *Anthropological Linguistics, 4,* 28–40.

Gustin, W. C. (1985). The development of exceptional research mathematicians. In B. S. Bloom (Ed.), *Developing talent in young people* (pp. 270–331). New York: Ballantine.

Guttentag, R. E. (1985). Memory and aging: Implications for theories of memory development during childhood. *Developmental Review, 5,* 56–82.

Haber, R. N. (1983). The impending demise of the icon: A critique of the concept of iconic storage in visual information processing. *The Behavioral and Brain Sciences, 6,* 1–54.

Hackley, S. A., Woldorff, M., & Hillyard, S. A. (1990). Crossmodal selective attention effects on retinal, myogenic, brainstem, and cerebral evoked potentials. *Psychophysiology, 27,* 195–208.

Hadamard, J. (1945). *The psychology of invention in the mathematical field.* Princeton, NJ: Princeton University Press.

Hale, S. (1990). A global developmental trend in cognitive processing speed. *Child Development, 61,* 653–663.

Hall, J. W., & Tinzmann, M. B. (1989). Sources of improved recall during the school years. *Bulletin of the Psychonomic Society, 27,* 315–316.

Halpern, A. R., & Bower, G. H. (1982). Musical expertise and melodic structure in memory for musical notation. *American Journal of Psychology, 95,* 31–50.

Hamilton, W. (1859). *Lectures on metaphysics and logic.* Edinburgh: Blackwood.

Hammond, K. R. (1988). Judgment and decision making in dynamic tasks. *Information and Decision Technologies, 14,* 3–14.

Hammond, K. R., Stewart, T. R., Brehmer, B., & Steinmann, D. O. (1986). Social judgment theory. In H. R. Arkes & K. R. Hammond (Eds.), *Judgment and decision making: An interdisciplinary reader* (pp. 56–76). Cambridge: Cambridge University Press.

Hancock, L. & Wingert, P. (1996). If you can read this . . . you learned phonics. Or so its supporters say. *Newsweek,* May, p. 75.

Harris, J. B. (1994). Electronic impersonations: Changing the context of teacher-student interaction. *Journal of Computing in Childhood Education, 5,* 241–255.

Hartley, J. T., Stojack, C. C., & Mushaney, T. J., Kiku-Annon, T. A., & Lee, D. W. (1994). Reading speed and prose memory in older and younger adults. *Psychology and Aging, 9,* 216–223.

Hasher, L., Stoltzfus, E. R., Zacks, R. T., & Rypma, B. (1991). Age and inhibition. *Journal of Experimental Psychology: Learning, Memory and Cognition, 17,* 163–169.

Hasher, L., & Zacks, R. T. (1979). Automatic and effortful processes in memory. *Journal of Experimental Psychology: General, 108,* 356–388.

Hasher, L., & Zacks, R. T. (1988). Working memory, comprehension, and aging: A review and new view. In G. H. Bower (Ed.), *The psychology of learning and motivation* (Vol. 22, pp. 193–225). New York: Academic Press.

Haugen, E. (1956). *Bilingualism in the Americas.* University of Alabama: University of Alabama Press.

Haviland, S. E., & Clark, H. H. (1974). What's new? Acquiring new information as a process in comprehension. *Journal of Verbal Learning and Verbal Behavior, 13*, 512–521.

Hawkins, R. D., & Kandel, E. R. (1984). Is there a cell-biological alphabet for simple forms of learning? *Psychological Review, 91*, 375–391.

Hayes, C. (1951). *The ape in our house.* New York: Harper & Row.

Hayes, J. R. (1981). *The complete problem-solver.* Philadelphia: Franklin Institute Press.

Hayes, J. R. (1989). Writing research: The analysis of a very complex task. In D. Klahr & K. Kotovsky (Eds.), *Complex information processing: The impact of Herbert A. Simon* (pp. 209–234). Hillsdale, NJ: Erlbaum.

Hayes, J. R., & Flower, L. S. (1986). Writing research and the writer. *American Psychologist, 41*, 1106–1113.

Hayes, J. R., Scott, L. C., Chemelski, B. E., & Johnson, J. (1987). Physical and emotional states as memory-relevant factors: Cognitive monitoring in young children. *Merrill-Palmer Quarterly, 33*, 473–487.

Heath, R. A. (1992). A general nonstationary diffusion model for two choice decision making. *Mathematical Social Sciences, 23*, 283–310.

Hebb, D. O. (1949). *The organization of behavior.* New York: Wiley.

Hebb, D. (1955). Drives and the CNS (conceptual nervous system). *Psychological Review, 62*, 243–254.

Hebb, D. O. (1961). Distinctive features of learning in the higher animals. In J. F. Delfresnaye (Ed.), *Brain mechanisms and learning.* New York: Oxford.

Helson, H. (1964). *Adaptation-level theory.* New York: Harper & Row.

Herman, L. M., Kuczaj, S. A., II, & Holder, M. D. (1993). Responses to anomalous gestural sequences by a language-trained dolphin: Evidence for processing of semantic relations and syntactic information. *Journal of Experimental Psychology: General, 122*, 184–194.

Herman, L. M., Richards, D. G., & Wolz, J. P. (1984). Comprehension of sentences by bottlenosed dolphins. *Cognition, 16*, 129–219.

Herrmann, D. J. (1982). The history of memory typologies and the semantic-episodic distinction. *Bulletin of the Psychonomic Society, 20*, 207–210.

Hertel, P. T., & Hardin, T. S. (1990). Remembering with and without awareness in a depressed mood: Evidence for deficits in initiative. *Journal of Experimental Psychology: General, 119*, 45–59.

Hertel, P. T., & Rude, S. S. (1991). Depressive effects in memory: Focusing attention improves subsequent recall. *Journal of Experimental Psychology: General, 120*, 301–309.

Heston, L. L., & White, J. A. (1983). *Dementia—A practical guide to Alzheimer's disease and related disorders.* New York: W. H. Freeman.

Hill, A. L., & Black, L. (1978). Bibliography on idiots savants. *Catalog of Selected Documents in Psychology, 8*, MS. 1653.

Hille, B. (1992). *Ionic channels of excitable membranes* (2nd ed.). Sunderland, MA: Sinauer Associates.

Hillyard, S. A., Hink, R. F., Schwent, V. L., & Picton, T. W. (1973). Electrical signs of selective attention in the human brain. *Science, 182*, 177–180.

Hinton, G. E. (1989). Learning distributed representations of concepts. In R. G. M. Morris (Ed.), *Parallel distributed processing: Implications for psychology and neurobiology* (pp. 46–61). Oxford: Clarendon.

Hintzman, D. L. (1978). *The psychology of learning and memory.* San Francisco: Freeman.

Hintzman, D. L. (1988). Judgments of frequency and recognition memory in a multiple-trace memory model. *Psychological Review, 95*, 528–551.

Hirsh, I. J., & Sherrick, C. E. J. (1961). Perceived order in different sense modalities. *Journal of Experimental Psychology, 62*, 423–432.

Hirsch, W. Z. (1952). Manufacturing progress functions. *Review of Economics and Statistics, 34*, 143–155.

Hockett, C. F. (1960a). Logical considerations in the study of animal communication. In W. E. Lanyon & W. N. Tavolga (Eds.), *Animal sounds and communication* (pp. 392–430). Washington, DC: American Institute of Biological Sciences.

Hockett, C. F. (1960b). The origin of speech. *Scientific American, 203*, 89–96.

Hockett, C. F. (1966). The problem with universals in language. In J. H. Greenberg (Ed.), *Universals of language* (2nd ed.) (pp. 1–29). Cambridge, MA: MIT Press.

Hockey, G. R. J. (1986). Changes in operator efficiency as a function of stress, fatigue, and circadian rhythms. In K. R. Boff, L. Kaufman, & J. P. Thomas (Eds.), *Handbook of perception and human performance.* Chichester, England: Wiley.

Hogaboam, T. W. (1983). Reading patterns in eye movement data. In K. Rayner (Ed.), *Eye movements in reading: Perceptual and language processes.* New York: Academic Press.

Hogarth, R., & Einhorn, H. J. (1990). Venture theory: A model of decision weights. *Management Science, 36*, 780–803.

Holden, C. (1987). OTA cites financial disaster of Alzheimer's. *Science, 236*, 253.

Holding, D. H. (1975a). Sensory storage reconsidered. *Memory and Cognition, 3*, 31–41.

Holding, D. H. (1975b). A rejoinder. *Memory and Cognition, 3*, 49–50.

Holender, D. (1986). Semantic activation without conscious identification in dichotic listening, parafoveal vision, and visual masking: A survey and appraisal. *Behavioral & Brain Sciences, 9*, 1–66.

Horgan, D. D., & Morgan, D. (1990). Chess expertise in children. *Applied Cognitive Psychology, 4*, 109–128.

Horn, M. (1993, November 29). Memories lost and found. *U.S. News & World Report,* pp. 52–63.

Hothersall, D. (1984). *History of psychology.* Philadelphia: Temple University Press.

Houston, J. P. (1991). *Fundamentals of learning and memory* (4th ed.). San Diego: Harcourt Brace Jovanovich.

Howard, D. V. (1983). *Cognitive psychology: Memory, language, and thought.* New York: Macmillan.

Howe, M. L., & O'Sullivan, J. T. (1990). The development of strategic memory: Coordinating knowledge, metamemory, and resources. In D. F. Bjorklund (Ed.), *Children's strategies: Contemporary views of cognitive development* (pp. 129–155). Hillsdale, NJ: Erlbaum.

Howe, M. L., & Rabinowitz, F. M. (1989). On the uninterpretability of dual-task performance. *Journal of Experimental Child Psychology, 47*, 32–38.

Howes, D., & Solomon, R. L. (1951). Visual duration thresholds as a function of word probability. *Journal of Experimental Psychology, 41*, 401–410.

Hubel, D. H., & Wiesel, T. N. (1968). Receptive fields and functional architecture of monkey striate cortex. *Journal of Physiology, 195,* 215–243.

Hull, C. L. (1920). Quantitative aspects of the evolution of concepts. *Psychological Monographs, 28.*

Hull, C. L. (1943). *Principles of behavior.* New York: Appleton-Century-Crofts.

Hulme, C., Maughan, S., & Brown, G. D. A. (1991). Memory for familiar and unfamiliar words: Evidence for a long-term memory contribution to short-term memory span. *Journal of Memory and Language, 30,* 668–701.

Hulme, C., Thomson, N., Muir, C., & Lawrence, A. (1984). Speech rate and the development of short-term memory span. *Journal of Experimental Child Psychology, 38,* 241–253.

Hulme, C., & Tordoff, V. (1989). Working memory development: The effects of speech rate, word length, and acoustic similarity on serial recall. *Journal of Experimental Child Psychology, 47,* 72–87.

Hultsch, D. F., & Dixon, R. A. (1990). Learning and memory in aging. *Handbook of psychology of aging* (3rd ed.). New York: Academic Press.

Hultsch, D. F., Hertzog, C., & Dixon, R. A. (1987). Age differences in metamemory: Resolving the inconsistencies. Special issue: Aging and cognition. *Canadian Journal of Psychology, 41,* 193–208.

Humphreys, L. G. (1939). Acquisition and extinction of verbal expectations in a situation analogous to conditioning. *Journal of Experimental Psychology, 25,* 294–301.

Hunt, E. (1980). Intelligence as an information processing concept. *British Journal of Psychology, 71,* 449–474.

Hunt, E., & Agnoli, F. (1991). The Whorfian hypothesis: A cognitive psychology perspective. *Psychological Review, 98,* 377–389.

Hunt, E., & Love, T. (1972). How good can memory be? In A. W. Melton & E. Martin (Eds.), *Coding processes in human memory.* Washington, DC: Winston.

Inhoff, A. W., & Topolski, R. (1994). Seeing morphemes: Loss of visibility during the retinal stabilization of compound and pseudocompound words. *Journal of Experimental Psychology: Human Perception and Performance, 20,* 840–853.

Irion, A. L. (1966). A brief history of research on the acquisition of skill. In E. A. Bilodeau (Ed.), *Acquisition of skill* (pp. 1–46). New York: Academic.

Jacobs, A. M., & Grainger, J. (1994). Models of visual word recognition—Sampling the state of the art. *Journal of Experimental Psychology: Human Perception and Performance, 20,* 1311–1334.

Jacoby, L. L. (1983a). Perceptual enhancement: Persistent effects of experience. *Journal of Experimental Psychology: Learning, Memory, and Cognition, 9,* 21–38.

Jacoby, L. L. (1983b). Remembering the data: Analyzing interactive processes in reading. *Journal of Verbal Learning and Verbal Behavior, 22,* 485–508.

Jacoby, L. L., & Dallas, M. (1981). On the relationship between autobiographical memory and perceptual learning. *Journal of Experimental Psychology: General, 110,* 306–340.

Jacoby, L. L., & Hayman, C. A. G. (1987). Specific visual transfer in word identification. *Journal of Experimental Psychology: Learning, Memory, and Cognition, 13,* 456–463.

Jacoby, L. L., & Witherspoon, D. (1982). Remembering without awareness. *Canadian Journal of Psychology, 36,* 300–324.

Jakobovitz, L. A. (1970). *Foreign language learning: A psycholinguistic analysis of the issues.* Rowley, MA: Newbury House.

James, W. (1890). *Principles of psychology.* New York: Holt.

Jaroff, L. (1993, November 29). Lies of the mind. *Time,* pp. 52–57.

Javal, L. E. (1878). Essai sur la physiologie de la lecture. *Annales d'Oculistique, 82,* 242–253.

Jaynes, J. (1976). *The origin of consciousness in the breakdown of the bicameral mind.* Boston: Houghton Mifflin.

Jenkins, J. J., Strange, W., & Edman, T. R. (1983). Identification of vowels in "vowelless" syllables. *Perception & Psychophysics, 34,* 441–450.

Johnston, W. A., & Heinz, S. P. (1978). Flexibility and capacity demands of attention. *Journal of Experimental Psychology: General, 107,* 420–435.

Jorland, G. (1987). The St. Petersburg paradox 1713–1937. In L. Kruger, L. J. Daston, & M. Heidelberger (Eds.), *The probabilistic revolution: Ideas in history* (Vol. I). Cambridge, MA: MIT Press.

Joseph, G. M., & Patel, V. L. (1990). Domain knowledge and hypothesis generation in diagnostic reasoning. *Journal of Medical Decision Making, 10,* 31–46.

Jost, A. (1897). Die Assoziationsfestigkeit in ihrer Abhangigkeit von der Verteilung der Wiederholungen. *Zeitschrift fur Psychologie, 14,* 436–472.

Julesz, B. (1984). A brief outline of the texton theory of human vision. *Trends in Neuroscience, 7,* 41–45.

Juola, J. F., Fischler, I., Wood, C. T., & Atkinson, R. C. (1971). Recognition time for information stored in long-term memory. *Perception & Psychophysics, 10,* 8–14.

Jusczyk, P. W., Cutler, A., & Redanz, N. (1993). Infants' preference for the predominant stress patterns of English words. *Child Development, 64,* 675–687.

Jusczyk, P. W., Pisoni, D. B., Walley, A. C., & Murray, J. (1980). Discrimination of relative onset time of two-component tones by infants. *Journal of the Acoustical Society of America, 67,* 262–270.

Just, M. A., & Carpenter, P. A. (1992). A capacity theory of comprehension: Individual differences in working memory. *Psychological Review, 99,* 122–149.

Just, M. A., Carpenter, P. A., & Keller, T. A. (1996). The capacity theory of comprehension: New frontiers of evidence and arguments. *Psychological Review, 103,* 773–780.

Kahneman, D. (1973). *Attention and effort.* Englewood Cliffs, NJ: Prentice Hall.

Kahneman, D., & Tversky, A. (1973). On the psychology of prediction. *Psychological Review, 80,* 237–251.

Kail, R. (1986). Sources of age differences in speed of processing. *Child Development, 57,* 969–987.

Kail, R. (1988a). Developmental changes in speed of processing: Central limiting mechanism or skill transfer? Reply to Stigler, Nusbaum, and Chalip. *Child Development, 59,* 1154–1157.

Kail, R. (1988b). Developmental functions for speeds of cognitive processes. *Journal of Experimental Child Psychology, 45,* 339–364.

Kail, R. (1991a). Processing time declines exponentially during childhood and adolescence. *Developmental Psychology, 27,* 259–266.

Kail, R. (1991b). Developmental change in speed of processing during childhood and adolescence. *Psychological Bulletin, 109,* 490–501.

Kail, R. (1991c). Controlled and automatic processing during mental rotation. *Journal of Experimental Child Psychology, 51,* 337–347.

Kail, R., & Hall, L. K. (1994). Processing speed, naming speed, and reading. *Developmental Psychology, 30,* 949–954.

Kail, R., & Park, Y. (1992). Global developmental change in processing time. *Merrill Palmer Quarterly, 38,* 525–541.

Kail, R., & Salthouse, T. A. (1994). Processing speed as a mental capacity. Special issue: Life span changes in human performance. *Acta Psychologica, 86,* 199–225.

Kalinowski, A. G. (1985). The development of Olympic swimmers. In B. S. Bloom (Ed.), *Developing talent in young people* (pp. 139–192). New York: Ballantine.

Kane, M., Hasher, L., Stoltzfus, E. R., Zacks, R. T., & Connelly, S. L. (1994). Inhibitory attentional mechanisms and aging. *Psychology and Aging, 9,* 102–112.

Kanizsa, G. (1976). Subjective contours. *Scientific American, 235,* 48–52.

Kantowitz, B. H., & Sorkin, R. D. (1983). *Human factors: Understanding people-system relationships.* New York: Wiley.

Kanwisher, N. G., Kim, J. W., & Wickens, T. D. (1996). Signal detection analyses of repetition blindness. *Journal of Experimental Psychology: Human Perception and Performance, 22,* 1249–1260.

Karni, A., Meyer, G., Jezzard, P., Adams, M. M., Turner, R., & Ungerleider, L. G. (1995). Functional MRI evidence for adult motor cortex plasticity during motor skill learning. *Nature, 377,* 155–158.

Kausler, D. H., & Puckett, J. M. (1981a). Adult age differences in memory for modality attributes. *Experimental Aging Research, 7,* 117–125.

Kausler, D. H., & Puckett, J. M. (1981b). Adult age differences in memory for sex of voice. *Journals of Gerontology, 36,* 44–50.

Kausler, D. H., Wiley, J. G., & Phillips, P. L. (1990). Adult age differences in memory for massed and distributed repeated practice. *Psychology and Aging, 5,* 530–534.

Kawabata, N. (1984). Perception at the blindspot and similarity grouping. *Perception & Psychophysics, 36,* 151–158.

Kawabata, N. (1990). Structural information processing in peripheral vision. *Perception, 19,* 631–636.

Keeney, T. J., Cannizzo, S. R., & Flavell, J. H. (1967). Spontaneous and induced verbal rehearsal in a recall task. *Child Development, 38,* 953–966.

Keller, F. S. (1958). The phantom plateau. *Journal of the Experimental Analysis of Behavior, 1,* 1–13.

Kelley, H. P. (1964). Memory abilities: A factor analysis. *Psychometric Society Monographs, 11,* 1–53.

Kellman, P. J. (1984). Perception of three-dimensional form by human infants. *Perception & Psychophysics, 36,* 353–358.

Kellogg, R. T. (1987). Effects of topic knowledge on the allocation of processing time and cognitive effort to writing processes. *Memory & Cognition, 15,* 256–266.

Kellogg, R. T. (1990). Effectiveness of prewriting strategies as a function of task demands. *American Journal of Psychology, 103,* 327–342.

Kellogg, W. N., & Kellogg, L. A. (1933). *The ape and the child.* New York: McGraw-Hill.

Kemler-Nelson, D., Hirsh-Pasek, K., Jusczyk, P. W., & Wright Cassidy, K. (1989). How prosodic cues in motherese might assist language learning. *Journal of Child Language, 16,* 55–68.

Kendler, H. H., & Kendler, T. S. (1975). From discrimination learning to cognitive development: A neobehavioristic odyssey. In W. K. Estes (Ed.), *Handbook of Learning and Cognitive Processes.* Hillsdale, NJ: Lawrence Erlbaum Associates.

Kendler, T. S., & Kendler, H. H. (1962a). Vertical and horizontal processes in problem solving. *Psychological Review, 69,* 1–16.

Kendler, T. S., & Kendler, H. H. (1962b). Inferential behavior as a function of subgoal constancy and age. *Journal of Experimental Psychology, 64,* 460–466.

Kennedy, R. S., & Coulter, X. B. (1975). Research note: The interactions among stress, vigilance, and task complexity. *Human Factors, 17,* 106–109.

Keppel, G., & Underwood, B. J. (1962). Proactive inhibition in short-term retention of single items. *Journal of Verbal Learning and Verbal Behavior, 1,* 153–161.

Kess, J. F. (1992). *Psycholinguistics: Psychology, linguistics, and the study of natural language.* Amsterdam: John Benjamins.

Kientzle, M. J. (1946). Properties of learning curves under varied conditions of practice. *Journal of Experimental Psychology, 36,* 187–211.

Kientzle, M. J. (1949). Ability patterns under distributed practice. *Journal of Experimental Psychology, 39,* 532–537.

Kimura, D. (1992). Sex differences in the brain. *Scientific American, 267,* 118–125.

Kinney, G. C., Marsetta, M., & Showman, D. J. (1966). *Studies in display symbol legibility, part XII. The legibility of alphanumeric symbols for digitalized television.* Bedford, MA: Mitre Corp. Cited in Lindsay, P. H., & Norman, D. A. (1972). *Human information processing.* New York: Academic Press.

Kinsbourne, M., & Hicks, R. E. (1978). Functional cerebral space: A model for overflow, transfer and interference effects in human memory: A tutorial review. In J. Requin (Ed.), *Attention and Performance VII.* Hillsdale, NJ: Erlbaum.

Kintsch, W. (1970a). *Learning, memory, and conceptual processes.* New York: Wiley.

Kintsch, W. (1970b). Models for free recall and recognition. In D. A. Norman (Ed.), *Models of human memory* (pp. 331–373). New York: Academic Press.

Kintsch, W. (1974). *The representation of meaning in memory.* Hillsdale, NJ: Erlbaum.

Kintsch, W. (1988). The use of knowledge in discourse processing: A construction-integration model. *Psychological Review, 95,* 163–182.

Kintsch, W., & Buschke, H. (1969). Homophones and synonyms in short-term memory. *Journal of Experimental Psychology, 80,* 403–407.

Kintsch, W., & van Dijk, T. A. (1978). Toward a model of text comprehension and production. *Psychological Review, 85,* 363–394.

Kintsch, W., & Welsch, D. M. (1991). The construction-integration model: A framework for studying memory for text. In W. E. Hockley & S. Lewandowsky (Eds.), *Relating theory and data: Essays on human memory in honor of Bennet B. Murdock* (pp. 367–385). Hillsdale, NJ: Erlbaum.

Kirlik, A. (1995). Requirements for psychological models to support design: Towards ecological task analysis. In J. M. Flach, P. A. Hancock, J. K. Caird, & K. J. Vicente (Eds.), *An ecological approach to human-machine systems I: A global perspective* (pp. 68–120). Hillsdale, NJ: Erlbaum.

Kirlik, A., Miller, R. A., & Jagacinski, R. J. (1993). Supervisory control in a dynamic and uncertain environment: A process model of skilled human-environment interaction. *IEEE Transactions on Systems, Man, and Cybernetics, 23,* 929–952.

Kirlik, A., Walker, N., Fisk, A. D., & Nagel, K. (1996). Supporting perception in the service of dynamic decision making. *Human Factors, 38,* 288–299.

Klein, J. P. (1975). Socratic dialogue vs. behavioral practice in the development of coping skills. *Alberta Journal of Educational Research, 21,* 255–261.

Kleinmuntz, B. (1968). The processing of clinical information by man and machine. In B. Kleinmuntz (Ed.), *Formal representation of human judgment* (pp. 149–186). New York: Wiley.

Kleinmuntz, B. (1984). The scientific study of clinical judgment in psychology and medicine. *Clinical Psychology Review, 4,* 111–126.

Kliegl, R., Smith, J., & Baltes, P. B. (1989). Testing-the-limits and the study of adult age differences in cognitive plasticity of a memory skill. *Developmental Psychology, 25,* 247–256.

Kliegl, R., Smith, J., & Baltes, P. B. (1990). On the locus and process of magnification of age differences during mnemonic training. *Developmental Psychology, 26,* 894–904.

Kluender, K. R., Diehl, R. L., & Killeen, P. R. (1987). Japanese quail can learn phonetic categories. *Science, 237,* 1195–1197.

Knowlton, B. J., Ramus, S. J., & Squire, L. R. (1992). Intact artificial grammar learning in amnesia: Dissociation of classification learning and explicit memory for specific instances. *Psychological Science, 3,* 172–179.

Koch, S. (1954). Clark L. Hull. In A. T. Poffenberger (Ed.), *Modern learning theory: A critical analysis of five examples* (pp. 1–175). New York: Appleton-Century-Crofts.

Koffka, K. (1935). *Principles of Gestalt psychology.* New York: Harcourt Brace.

Köhler, W. (1947). *Gestalt psychology: An introduction to new concepts in modern psychology.* New York: Leveright (Meuter).

Kohonen, T. (1989). *Self-organization and associative memory* (3rd ed.). Berlin: Springer-Verlag.

Kolb, B. (1984). Functions of the frontal cortex of the rat: A comparative review. *Brain Research, 8,* 65–98.

Kolb, B., & Wishaw, I. Q. (1990). *Fundamentals of human neuropsychology.* San Francisco: W. H. Freeman.

Kolers, P. (1975a). Specificity of operations in sentence recognition. *Cognitive Psychology, 7,* 289–306.

Kolers, P. A. (1975b). Memorial consequences of automatized encoding. *Journal of Experimental Psychology: Human Learning and Memory, 1,* 689–701.

Kolers, P. (1976). Reading a year later. *Journal of Experimental Psychology: Human Learning and Memory, 2,* 554–565.

Kolodny, J. A. (1994). Memory processes in classification learning: An investigation of amnesic performance in categorization of dot patterns and artistic styles. *Psychological Science, 5,* 164–169.

Konorski, J. (1967). *Integrative activity of the brain.* Chicago: University of Chicago Press.

Koppenaal, L., & Glanzer, M. (1990). A reexamination of the continuous distractor task and the "long-term recency effect." *Memory & Cognition, 18,* 183–195.

Kornblum, S., Hasbroucq, T., & Osman, A. (1990). Dimensional overlap—a model and taxonomy. *Psychological Review, 97,* 253–270.

Kosslyn, S. M., & Koenig, O. (1995). *Wet mind: The new cognitive neuroscience.* New York: Free Press.

Kramer, A. F., Trejo, L. J., & Humphrey, D. (1995). Assessment of mental workload with task-irrelevant auditory probes. *Biological Psychology, 40,* 83–100.

Krishnan, H. S., & Shapiro, S. (1996). Comparing implicit and explicit memory for brand names from advertisements. *Journal of Experimental Psychology: Applied, 2,* 147–163.

Krogius, N. (1976). *Psychology in chess.* New York: RHM Press.

Kruschke, J. K. (1992). ALCOVE: An exemplar–based connectionist model of category learning. *Psychological Review, 99,* 22–44.

Kruschke, J. K. (1993). Human category learning: Implications for backpropagation models. *Connection Science, 5,* 3–36.

Kuffler, S. W. (1953). Discharge patterns and functional organization of the mammalian retina. *Journal of Neurophysiology, 16,* 37–68.

Kuhl, P. K. (1986). Theoretical contributions of tests on animals to the special-mechanisms debate in speech. *Experimental Biology, 45,* 233–265.

Kuhl, P. K. (1989). On babies, birds, modules, and mechanisms: A comparative approach to the acquisition of vocal communication. In P. Salapatek & L. Cohen (Eds.), *Handbook of infant perception,* Vol. 2 (pp. 275–382). Orlando, FL: Academic Press.

Kutas, M., & Van Petten, C. (1988). Event-related brain potential studies of language. In P. Ackles, J. R. Jennings, & M. Coles (Eds.), *Advances in psychophysiology.* Greenwich, CT: JAI Press.

Lachman, J. L, Lachman, R., & Thronesbery, C. (1979). Metamemory through the adult life span. *Developmental Psychology, 15,* 543–551.

Lachman, R. (1973). Uncertainty effects on time to access the internal lexicon. *Journal of Experimental Psychology, 99,* 199–208.

Lachman, R., Lachman, J. L., & Butterfield, E. C. (1979). *Cognitive psychology and information processing: An introduction.* Hillsdale, NJ: Erlbaum.

Lambert, W. E. (1990). Persistent issues in bilingualism. In B. Harley, P. Allen, J. Cummins, & M. Swain (Eds.), *The development of second language proficiency* (pp. 201–218). Cambridge: Cambridge University Press.

Landauer, T. K. (1986). How much do people remember? Some estimates of the quantity of learned information in long-term memory. *Cognitive Science, 10,* 477–493.

Landauer, T. K., & Bjork, R. A. (1978). Optimal rehearsal patterns and name learning. In M. M. Gruneberg, P. E. Morris, & R. N. Sykes (Eds.), *Practical aspects of memory* (pp. 625–632). London: Academic Press.

Landauer, T. K., & Freedman, J. L. (1968). Information retrieval from long-term memory: Category size and recognition time. *Journal of Verbal Learning and Verbal Behavior, 7,* 291–295.

Landauer, T. K., & Meyer, D. E. (1972). Category size and semantic memory retrieval. *Journal of Verbal Learning and Verbal Behavior, 11,* 539–549.

Lashley, K. (1941). Patterns of cerebral integration indicated by the scotomas of migraine. *Archives of Neurology and Psychiatry, 46,* 331–339.

Lashley, K. S. (1929). *Brain mechanisms and intelligence: A quantitative study of injuries to the brain.* Chicago: University of Chicago Press.

Lashley, K. S. (1951). The problem of serial order in behavior. In L. A. Jeffress (Ed.), *Cerebral mechanisms in behavior* (pp. 112–136). New York: Wiley.

Lassaline, M. E., & Logan, G. D. (1993). Memory-based automaticity in the discrimination of visual numerosity. *Journal of Experimental Psychology: Learning, Memory, and Cognition, 19,* 561–581.

Lee, C. L., & Estes, W. K. (1977). Order and position in primary memory for letter strings. *Journal of Verbal Learning and Verbal Behavior, 16*, 396–418.

Lee, C. L., & Estes, W. K. (1981). Item and order information in short-term memory: Evidence for multilevel perturbation processes. *Journal of Experimental Psychology: Human Learning and Memory, 7*, 149–169.

Legge, G. E., Grossman, C., & Pieper, C. M. (1984). Learning unfamiliar voices. *Journal of Experimental Psychology: Learning, Memory, and Cognition, 10*, 298–303.

Lehman, E. B., & Mellinger, J. C. (1984). Effects of aging on memory for presentation modality. *Developmental Psychology, 20*, 1210–1217.

Lehman, E. B., & Mellinger, J. C. (1986). Forgetting rates in modality memory for young, mid-life, and older women. *Psychology and Aging, 1*, 178–179.

Lenneberg, E. (1967). *The biological foundations of language.* New York: Wiley.

Lesgold, A. M. (1984). Acquiring expertise. In J. R. Anderson and S. M. Kosslyn (Eds.), *Tutorials in learning and memory* (pp. 31–60). San Francisco: W. H. Freeman.

Levelt, W. (1989). *Speaking: From intention to articulation.* Cambridge, MA: MIT Press.

Lewandowsky, S. (1993). The rewards and hazards of computer simulations. *Psychological Science, 4*, 236–243.

Lewandowsky, S., & Li, S.-C. (1994). Memory for serial order revisited. *Psychological Review, 101*, 539–543.

Lewin, K. (1935). *A dynamic theory of personality.* New York: McGraw-Hill.

Lewis, M. W., & Anderson, J. R. (1985). Discrimination of operator schemata in problem-solving: Learning from examples. *Cognitive Psychology, 17*, 26–65.

Liberman, A. M. (1970). The grammars of speech language. *Cognitive Psychology, 1*, 301–323.

Liberman, A. M. (1982). On finding that speech is special. *American Psychologist, 37*, 148–167.

Liberman, A. M., Cooper, F. S., Shankweiler, D. P., & Studdert-Kennedy, M. (1967). Perception of the speech code. *Psychological Review, 74*, 431–461.

Liberman, A. M., Harris, K. S., Hoffman, H. S., & Griffith, B. C. (1957). The discrimination of speech sounds within and across phoneme boundaries. *Journal of Experimental Psychology, 54*, 358–368.

Liberman, A. M., & Mattingly, I. G. (1985). The motor theory of speech perception revised. *Cognition, 21*, 1–36.

Liberman, I. Y. (1989). Phonology and beginning reading revisited. In C. von Euler, I. Lundberg, & G. Lennerstrand (Eds.), *Brain and reading* (pp. 207–220). New York: Stockton Press.

Lickliter, R., & Berry, T. D. (1990). The phylogeny fallacy: Developmental psychology's misapplication of evolutionary theory. *Developmental Review, 10*, 348–364.

Light, L. L. (1991). Memory and aging: Four hypotheses in search of data. *Annual Review of Psychology, 42*, 333–376.

Lindsay, D. S., & Read, J. D. (1994). Psychotherapy and memories of childhood sexual abuse: A cognitive perspective. *Applied Cognitive Psychology, 8*, 281–338.

Lindsley, D. B. (1950). Emotions and the electroencephalogram. In M. L. Reymart (Ed.), *Feelings and emotions: The Mooseheart symposium.* New York: McGraw-Hill.

Link, S. W. (1992). *The wave theory of difference and similarity.* Hillsdale, NJ: Erlbaum.

Linton, M. (1988). The maintenance of knowledge: Some long-term specific and generic changes. In M. M. Gruneberg, P. E. Morris, & R. N. Sykes (Eds.), *Practical aspects of memory: Current research and issues* (Vol. 1, pp. 378–384). New York: Wiley.

Lissauer, H. (1890). Ein fall von seelenblindheit nebst einem Beitrag zur theorie derselben. *Archive. fur Psychiatrie, 21*, 222–270. [Edited and reprinted in translation by Jackson, M. (1988). Lissauer on agnosia. *Cognitive Neuropsychology, 5*, 155–192.]

Locke, E. A., & Latham, G. P. (1990). *A theory of goal setting and task performance.* Englewood Cliffs, NJ: Prentice-Hall.

Loess, H. (1968). Short-term memory and item similarity. *Journal of Verbal Learning and Verbal Behavior, 8*, 240–247.

Loftus, E. F. (1979a). *Eyewitness testimony.* Cambridge, MA: Harvard University Press.

Loftus, E. F. (1979b). The malleability of human memory. *American Scientist, 67*, 312–320.

Loftus, E. F., & Ketcham, K. (1994). *The myth of repressed memory: False memories and allegations of sexual abuse.* New York: St. Martin's.

Loftus, E. F., & Loftus, G. R. (1980). On the permanence of stored information in the human brain. *American Psychologist, 35*, 409–420.

Loftus, E. F., & Palmer, J. C. (1974). Reconstruction of automobile destruction: An example of the interaction between language and memory. *Journal of Verbal Learning and Verbal Behavior, 13*, 585–589.

Loftus, E. F., & Pickerell, J. E. (1995). The formation of false memories. *Psychiatric Annals, 25*, 720–725.

Loftus, G. R. (1983). The continuing persistence of the icon. *The Behavioral and Brain Sciences, 6*, 28.

Loftus, G. R. (1985). On worthwhile icons: Reply to DiLollo and Haber. *Journal of Experimental Psychology: Human Perception and Performance, 11*, 384–388.

Logan, G. D. (1988). Toward an instance theory of automatization. *Psychological Review, 95*, 492–527.

Logan, G. D. (1990). Repetition priming and automaticity: Common underlying mechanisms. *Cognitive Psychology, 22*, 1–35.

Logan, G. D. (1992). Shapes of reaction-time distributions and shapes of learning curves: A test of the instance theory of automaticity. *Journal of Experimental Psychology: Learning, Memory, and Cognition, 18*, 883–914.

Logan, G. D., & Etherton, J. L. (1994). What is learned during automatization? The role of attention in constructing an instance. *Journal of Experimental Psychology: Learning, Memory, and Cognition, 20*, 1022–1050.

Logan, G. D., & Klapp, S. T. (1991). Automatizing alphabet arithmetic: I. Is extended practice necessary to produce automaticity? *Journal of Experimental Psychology: Learning, Memory, & Cognition, 17*, 179–195.

Logan, G. D., Taylor, S. E., & Etherton, J. L. (1996). Attention in the acquisition and expression of automaticity. *Journal of Experimental Psychology: Learning, Memory, and Cognition, 22*, 620–638.

Long, D. L., & Bourg, T. (1996). Thinking aloud: Telling a story about a story. *Discourse Processes, 21*, 329–339.

Long, G. M. (1980). Iconic memory: A review and critique of the study of short-term visual storage. *Psychological Bulletin, 88*, 785–820.

Loomes, G., & Sugden, R. (1982). Regret theory: An alternative theory of rational choice under uncertainty. *Economic Journal, 92,* 805–824.

Loomes, G., & Sugden, R. (1987). Some implications of a more general form of regret theory. *Journal of Economic Theory, 41,* 270–287.

Lopes, L. L. (1976). Model-based decision and inference in stud poker. *Journal of Experimental Psychology: General, 105,* 217–239.

Lopes, L. L. (1987). Between hope and fear: The psychology of risk. In L. Berkowitz (Ed.), *Advances in experimental social psychology* (Vol. 20, pp. 255–295). San Diego: Academic Press.

Lourenco, O., & Machado, A. (1996). In defense of Piaget's theory: A reply to 10 common criticisms. *Psychological Review, 103,* 143–164.

Luce, R. D. (1959). *Individual choice behavior.* New York: Wiley.

Luce, R. D. (1963). Detection and recognition. In R. D. Luce, R. R. Bush, & E. Galanter (Eds.), *Handbook of mathematical psychology* (Vol. 1, pp. 193–243). New York: Wiley.

Luce, R. D. (1977). The choice axiom after twenty years. *Journal of Mathematical Psychology, 15,* 215–233.

Luchins, A. S. (1942). Mechanization in problem solving. *Psychological Monographs, 54,* 1–248.

Luchins, A. S., & Luchins, E. H. (1959). *Rigidity of behavior: A variational approach to the effect of Einstellung.* Eugene: University of Oregon Press.

Luria, A. R. (1968). *The mind of a mnemonist.* New York: Avon.

Lusted, L. B. (1971). Signal detectability and medical decision-making. *Science, 171,* 1217–1219.

Lyon, D. O. (1914). The relation of length of material to time taken for learning and the optimum distribution of time. *Journal of Educational Psychology, 5,* 1–9.

MacCorquodale, K., & Meehl, P. E. (1948). On a distinction between hypothetical constructs and intervening variables. *Psychological Review, 55,* 95–107.

MacDonald, J., & McGurk, H. (1978). Visual influences on speech perception processes. *Perception & Psychophysics, 24,* 253–257.

MacKay, D. G. (1973). Aspects of a theory of comprehension, memory and attention. *Quarterly Journal of Experimental Psychology, 25,* 22–40.

Mackie, R. R., Wylie, C. D., & Smith, M. J. (1994). Countering loss of vigilance in sonar watch standing using signal injection and performance feedback. *Ergonomics, 37,* 1157–1184.

Maclay, H. (1973). Linguistics and psycholinguistics. In B. Kachru (Ed.), *Issues in linguistics* (pp. 569–587). Urbana: University of Illinois Press.

MacLean, P. D. (1949). Psychosomatic disease and the "visceral brain": Recent developments bearing on the Papez theory of emotion. *Psychosomatic Medicine, 11,* 338–353.

MacLeod, C. M. (1991). Half a century of research on the Stroop effect: An integrative review. *Psychological Review, 109,* 163–203.

MacLeod, C. M. (1992). The Stroop task: The "gold standard" of attentional measures. *Journal of Experimental Psychology: General, 121,* 12–14.

MacLeod, C. M. (1997). Is attention under your control? The diabolical Stroop effect. *Psychological Science Agenda, 10,* 6–7.

MacLeod, C. M., & Dunbar, K. (1988). Training and Stroop-like interference: Evidence for a continuum of automaticity. *Journal of Experimental Psychology: Learning, Memory and Cognition, 14,* 126–135.

Macmillan, N. A., & Creelman, C. D. (1991). *Detection theory: A user's guide.* New York: Cambridge University Press.

Malmo, R. B. (1959). Activation: A neuropsychological dimension. *Psychological Review, 66,* 367–386.

Mandler, G. (1970). Words, lists, and categories: An experimental view of organized memory. In J. L. Cowan (Ed.), *Studies in thought and language* (pp. 99–131). Tucson: University of Arizona Press.

Mandler, G. (1972). Organization and recognition. In E. Tulving & W. Donaldson (Eds.), *Organization and memory* (pp. 139–166). New York: Academic Press.

Mandler, G. (1980). Recognizing: The judgment of previous occurrence. *Psychological Review, 87,* 252–271.

Mandler, G. (1991). Your face looks familiar but I can't remember your name: A review of dual process theory. In W. E. Hockley & S. Lewandowsky (Eds.), *Relating theory and data: Essays in honor of Bennet B. Murdock* (pp. 207–225). Hillsdale, NJ: Erlbaum.

Mandler, G., Hamson, C., Overson, C., & Dorfman, J. (1990). Tests of dual process theory: Word priming and recognition. *Quarterly Journal of Experimental Psychology, 42A,* 713–739.

Marbe, K. (1901). *Experimentell-psychologische Untersuchungen uber das Utriel.* Leipzig: Engelmann.

Marcel, A. J. (1980). Conscious and preconscious recognition of polysemous words: Locating the selective effects of prior verbal context. In R. S. Nickerson (Ed.), *Attention and Performance VIII* (pp. 435–457). Hillsdale, NJ: Erlbaum.

Marcel, A. J. (1983a). Conscious and unconscious perception: Experiments on visual masking and word recognition. *Cognitive Psychology, 15,* 197–237.

Marcel, A. J. (1983b). Conscious and unconscious perception: An approach to the relation between phenomenal and perceptual processes. *Cognitive Psychology, 15,* 238–300.

Markman, E. M., & Gorin, L. (1981). Children's ability to adjust their standards for evaluating comprehension. *Journal of Educational Psychology, 73,* 320–325.

Marr, D. (1982). *Vision: A computational investigation into the human representation and processing of visual information.* San Francisco: W. H. Freeman.

Marr, D., & Hildreth, E. (1980). Theory of edge detection. *Proceedings of the Royal Society of London, B207,* 187–217.

Marshal, P. H., & Werder, P. R. (1972). The effects of the elimination of rehearsal on primacy and recency. *Journal of Verbal Learning and Verbal Behavior, 11,* 649–653.

Martin, L. (1986). Eskimo words for snow: A case study in the genesis and decay of an anthropological example. *American Anthropologist, 88,* 418–423.

Martin, R. C. (1993). Short-term memory and sentence processing: Evidence from neuropsychology. *Memory & Cognition, 21,* 176–183.

Martin, R. C. (1996). Heterogeneity of deficits in developmental dyslexia and implications for methodology. *Psychonomic Bulletin and Review, 2,* 494–500.

Martin, R. C., Shelton, J. R., & Yaffee, L. S. (1993). Language processing and working memory: Neuropsychological evidence for separate phonological and semantic capacities. *Journal of Memory and Language.*

Marx, M. H., & Hillix, W. A. (1973). *Systems and theories in psychology* (2nd ed.). New York: McGraw-Hill.

Massaro, D. W. (1979). Letter information and orthographic context in word perception. *Journal of Experimental Psychology: Human Perception and Performance, 5,* 595–609.

Massaro, D. W. (1986). A new perspective and old problems. *Journal of Phonetics, 14,* 69–74.

Massaro, D. W. (1987). *Speech perception by ear and eye: A paradigm for psychological inquiry.* Hillsdale, NJ: Erlbaum.

Massaro, D. W. (1989a). Multiple book review of speech perception by ear and eye: A paradigm for psychological inquiry. *The Behavioral and Brain Sciences, 12,* 741–794.

Massaro, D. W. (1989b). Testing between the TRACE model and the fuzzy logical model of perception. *Cognitive Psychology, 21,* 398–421.

Massaro, D. W. (1992). Broadening the domain of the fuzzy logical model of perception. In H. L. J. Pick, P. van den Broek, & D. C. Knill (Eds.), *Cognition: Conceptual and methodological issues* (pp. 51–84). Washington, DC: APA.

Massaro, D. W. (1995). *A theoretical framework for psychological inquiry.* Paper presented at the Annual Meeting of the Psychonomic Society, Los Angeles.

Massaro, D. W., & Cohen, M. M. (1977). Voice onset time and fundamental frequency as cues to the /zi/-/si/ distinction. *Perception and Psychophysics, 22,* 373–382.

Massaro, D. W., & Friedman, D. (1990). Models of integration given multiple sources of information. *Psychological Review, 97,* 225–252.

Massaro, D. W., Weldon, M. S., & Kitzis, S. N. (1991). Integration of orthographic and semantic information in memory retrieval. *Journal of Experimental Psychology: Learning, Memory, and Cognition, 17,* 277–287.

Masson, M. E. J. (1990). Cognitive theories of skill acquisition. *Human Movement Science, 9,* 221–239.

Matlin, M. W. (1988). *Sensation and perception.* Boston: Allyn and Bacon.

Matlin, M. W. (1993). *Perception.* Boston: Allyn and Bacon.

Matthews, G. (1996). Signal probability effects on high-workload vigilance tasks. *Psychonomic Bulletin & Review, 3,* 339–343.

Maurer, D. (1985). Infants' perception of facedness. In T. M. Field & N. A. Fox (Eds.), *Social perception in infants* (pp. 73–100). Norwood, NJ: Ablex.

May, C. P., Kane, M. J., & Hasher, L. (1995). Determinants of negative priming. *Psychological Bulletin, 118,* 35–54.

Mayer, A., & Orth, J. (1901). Zur Qualitativen Untersuchcung der Association. *Z. Psychol., 26,* 1–13.

Mayer, R. E. (1992). *Thinking, problem solving, cognition.* New York: W. H. Freeman.

Mazziotta, J. (1993). *Enabling technologies in behavioral research.* Paper presented at the 5th Annual Meeting of the American Psychological Society, Chicago, IL.

McCarthy, R. A., & Warrington, E. K. (1986). Visual associative agnosia: A clinical anatomical study of a single case. *Journal of Neurology, Neurosurgery, and Psychiatry, 49,* 1233–1240.

McClelland, J. L., McNaughton, B. L., & O'Reilly, R. C. (1995). Why there are complementary learning systems in the hippocampus and neocortex: Insights from the successes and failures of connectionist models of learning and memory. *Psychological Review, 102,* 419–457.

McClelland, J. L., & Rumelhart, D. E. (1981). An interactive activation model of context effects in letter perception: Part 1. An account of basic findings. *Psychological Review, 88,* 375–407.

McClelland, J. L., & Rumelhart, D. E. (1986). *Parallel-distributed processing: Explorations in the microstructure of cognition.* Cambridge, MA: Bradford.

McClelland, J. L., & Rumelhart, D. E. (1988). *Explorations in parallel distributed processing: A handbook of models, programs, and exercises.* Cambridge, MA: MIT Press.

McCloskey, M. (1991). Networks and theories: The place of connectionism in cognitive science. *Psychological Science, 2,* 387–395.

McCloskey, M., & Cohen, N. J. (1989). Catastrophic interference in connectionist networks: The sequential learning problem. In G. H. Bower (Ed.), *The psychology of learning and motivation* (Vol. 24, pp. 109–165). New York: Academic Press.

McCloskey, M., & Palmer, E. (1996). Visual representation of object location: Insights from localization impairments. *Current Directions in Psychological Science, 5,* 25–28.

McCloskey, M., & Zaragoza, M. (1985). Misleading postevent information and memory for events: Arguments and evidence against memory impairment hypotheses. *Journal of Experimental Psychology: General, 1,* 1–16.

McConkie, G. W. (1979). On the role and control of eye movements during reading. In P. A. Kolers, M. E. Wrolstad, & H. Bouma (Eds.), *Processing of visible language,* Vol. 1. New York: Plenum.

McCormick, D. A. (1990). Membrane properties and neurotransmitter actions. In G. M. Shepherd (Ed.), *The synaptic organization of the brain* (pp. 32–66). Oxford: Oxford University Press.

McCulloch, W. S., & Pitts, W. H. (1943). A logical calculus of the ideas immanent in nervous activity. *Bulletin of Mathematical Biophysiology, 5,* 115–133.

McDaniel, M. A., & Schlager, M. S. (1990). Discovery learning and transfer of problem skills. *Cognition & Instruction, 7,* 129–159.

McDowd, M. J., & Oseas-Kreger, D. M. (1991). Aging, inhibitory processes and negative priming. *Journal of Gerontology: Psychology Sciences, 46,* 340–345.

McElree, B., & Dosher, B. A. (1993). Serial retrieval processes in the recovery of order information. *Journal of Experimental Psychology: General, 118,* 346–373.

McGeogh, J. A. (1927). The acquisition of skill. *Psychological Bulletin, 24,* 437–466.

McGurk, H., & MacDonald, J. (1976). Hearing lips and seeing voices. *Nature, 264,* 746–748.

McKoon, G., & Ratcliff, R. (1981). The comprehension processes and memory structures involved in instrumental inference. *Journal of Verbal Learning and Verbal Behavior, 20,* 671–682.

McKoon, G., & Ratcliff, R. (1986). Inferences about predictable events. *Journal of Experimental Psychology: Learning, Memory, and Cognition, 12,* 82–91.

McLaughlin, B. (1984). *Second language acquisition in childhood* (Vols. 1 and 2, 2nd ed.). Hillsdale, NJ: Erlbaum.

McLaughlin, M. L. (1984). *How talk is organized.* Beverly Hills, CA: Sage.

McNaughton, B. L., & Barnes, C. A. (1990). From cooperative synaptic enhancement to associative memory: Bridging the abyss. *Seminars in the Neurosciences, 2,* 403–416.

McNeill, D. (1985). So you think gestures are nonverbal? *Psychological Review, 92,* 350–371.

Meck, W. H., Church, R. M., & Olton, D. S. (1984). Hippocampus, time, and memory. *Behavioral Neuroscience, 98,* 3–22.

Medin, D. L., & Schaffer, M. M. (1978). Context theory of classification learning. *Psychological Review, 85,* 207–238.

Melton, A. W. (1963). Implications of short-term memory for a general theory of memory. *Journal of Verbal Learning and Verbal Behavior, 2,* 1–21.

Melton, A. W., & Irwin, J. M. (1940). The influence of degree of interpolated learning on retroactive inhibition and the overt transfer of specific responses. *American Journal of Psychology, 53,* 173–203.

Merikle, P. M. (1988). Subliminal auditory messages: An evaluation. *Psychology & Marketing, 5,* 355–372.

Meyer, D. E., & Schvaneveldt, R. W. (1971). Facilitation in recognizing pairs of words: Evidence for a dependence between retrieval operations. *Journal of Experimental Psychology, 90,* 227–234.

Michaels, C. F., & Carello, C. (1981). *Direct perception.* Englewood Cliffs, NJ: Prentice-Hall.

Mill, J. (1829). Analysis of the phenomenon of the human mind. In B. Rand (Ed.), *The classical psychologists* (pp. 463–482). Boston: Houghton Mifflin, 1912.

Miller, G. A. (1951). *Language and communication.* New York: McGraw-Hill.

Miller, G. A. (1981). *Language and speech.* San Francisco: W. H. Freeman.

Miller, G. W. (1956). The magical number seven, plus or minus two: Some limits on our capacity for processing information. *Psychological Review, 63,* 81–97.

Miller, J. D., Wier, C. C., Pastore, R., Kelly, W. J., & Dooling, R. J. (1976). Discrimination and labeling of noise-buzz sequences with varying noise-lead times: An example of categorical perception. *Journal of the Acoustical Society of America, 60,* 410–417.

Miller, L. K. (1989). *Musical savants: Exceptional skill in the mentally retarded.* Hillsdale, NJ: Erlbaum.

Miller, N. E. (1959). Liberalization of basic S-R concepts: Extensions to conflict behavior, motivation, and social learning. In S. Koch (Ed.), *Psychology: A study of a science* (Vol. II). New York: McGraw-Hill.

Miller, P. H. (1990). The development of strategies of selective attention. In D. F. Bjorklund (Ed.), *Children's strategies: Contemporary views of cognitive development.* Hillsdale, NJ: Erlbaum.

Miller, P. H. (1993). *Theories of developmental psychology* (3rd ed.). New York: W. H. Freeman.

Miller, R. R., Kasparow, W. J., & Schactman, T. C. (1986). Retrieval variability: Sources and consequences. *American Journal of Psychology, 99,* 146–218.

Milner, B. (1966). Amnesia following operation on the temporal lobes. In C. Whitty & O. Zangwill (Eds.), *Amnesia* (pp. 109–133). London: Butterworth.

Milon, J. P. (1974). The development of negation in English by a second language learner. *TESOL Quarterly, 8,* 137–143.

Minsky, M., & Papert, S. (1968). *Perceptions: An essay in computational geometry.* Cambridge, MA: MIT Press.

Mitchell, D. C., & Holmes, V. M. (1985). The role of specific information about the verb in parsing sentences with local structural ambiguity. *Journal of Memory and Language, 24,* 542–559.

Miyashita, Y., & Chang, H. S. (1988). Neuronal correlate of pictorial short-term memory in the primate temporal cortex. *Nature, 331,* 68–70.

Modigliani, V., & Hodges, D. G. (1987). Distributed rehearsals and the primacy effect in single-trial free recall. *Journal of Experimental Psychology: Learning, Memory, and Cognition, 13,* 426–436.

Mohanty, A. K. (1992). Bilingualism and cognitive development of Kond tribal children: Studies on metalinguistic hypothesis.

Special issue: Environmental toxicology and social ecology. *Pharmacopsychoecologia, 5,* 57–66.

Mollon, J. D. (1982). Color vision. *Annual Review of Psychology, 33,* 41–85.

Monsaas, J. A. (1986). Talent development: A study of the development of world class tennis players. *Dissertation Abstracts International, 46,* 3660.

Moran, T. P. (1980). *Compiling cognitive skill.* AIP Memo 150, Xerox PARC.

Moray, N. (1959). Attention in dichotic listening: Affective cues and the influence of instructions. *Quarterly Journal of Experimental Psychology, 11,* 56–60.

Moray, N., Bates, A., & Barnett, T. (1965). Experiments on the four-eared man. *Journal of the Acoustical Society of America, 38,* 196–210.

Morris, C. D., Bransford, J. D., & Franks, J. J. (1977). Levels of processing versus transfer appropriate processing. *Journal of Verbal Learning and Verbal Behavior, 16,* 519–533.

Morrison, R. E. (1984). Manipulation of stimulus onset delay in reading: Evidence for parallel programming of saccades. *Journal of Experimental Psychology: Human Perception and Performance, 10,* 667–682.

Morrison, R. E., & Inhoff, A. W. (1981). Visual factors and eye movements in reading. *Visible Language, 15,* 129–146.

Morton, J. (1969). Interaction of information in word recognition. *Psychological Review, 76,* 165–178.

Morton, J. (1970). A functional model of memory. In D. A. Norman (Ed.), *Models of human memory.* New York: Academic Press.

Moruzzi, G., & Magoun, H. W. (1949). Brain stem and reticular formation and activation of the EEG. *Electroencephalography and Clinical Neurophysiology, 1,* 455–473.

Moscovitch, M. (1989). Confabulation and the frontal systems: Strategic versus associated retrieval in neuropsychological theories of memory. In H. L. Roediger & F. I. M. Craik (Eds.), *Varieties of memory and consciousness: Essays in honour of Endel Tulving* (pp. 133–160). Hillsdale, NJ: Erlbaum.

Muller, G. E., & Pilzecker, A. (1900). Experimentelle BeitrÑge zur Lehre vom Gedachtnis. *Z. Psychol., Ergbd. I.*

Murdock, B. B., Jr. (1960). The distinctiveness of stimuli. *Psychological Review, 67,* 16–31.

Murdock, B. B., Jr. (1961). The retention of individual items. *Journal of Experimental Psychology, 62,* 618–625.

Murdock, B. B., Jr. (1962). The serial position effect of free recall. *Journal of Experimental Psychology, 64,* 482–488.

Murdock, B. B., Jr. (1967). Auditory and visual stores in short term memory. *Acta Psychologica, 27,* 316–324.

Murdock, B. B., Jr. (1974). *Human memory: Theory and data.* Hillsdale, NJ: Erlbaum.

Murdock, B. B., Jr. (1983). A distributed memory model for serial-order information. *Psychological Review, 90,* 316–338.

Murdock, B. B., Jr. (1985). The contributions of Herman Ebbinghaus. *Journal of Experimental Psychology: Learning, Memory, and Cognition, 11,* 469–471.

Murdock, B. B., Jr. (1993). TODAM2: A model for the storage and retrieval of item, associative, and order information. *Psychological Review, 100,* 183–203.

Murnane, K., & Phelps, M. P. (1994). When does a different environmental context make a difference in recognition: A global activation model. *Memory & Cognition, 22,* 584–590.

Murnane, K., & Phelps, M. P. (1995). Effects of changes in relative cue strengths on context-dependent memory. *Journal of*

Experimental Psychology: Learning, Memory, and Cognition, 21, 158–172.

Murphy, G. L., & Shapiro, A. M (1994). Forgetting of verbatim information in discourse. *Memory & Cognition, 22,* 85–94.

Murphy, M. D., Schmitt, F. A., Caruso, M. J., Sanders, R. E. Metamemory in older adults: The role of monitoring in serial recall. *Psychology & Aging, 2* (4), 331–339.

Murray, J. E. (1995). Negative priming by rotated objects. *Psychonomic Bulletin and Review, 2,* 534–537.

Myers, J. L., & Duffy, S. A. (1990). Causal relatedness and text memory. In A. C. Graesser & G. H. Bower (Eds.), *The psychology of learning and motivation,* Vol. 25 (pp. 159–173). San Diego: Academic Press.

Myers, J. L., & Katz, L. (1962). Range of payoffs and feedback in risk-taking. *Psychological Reports, 10,* 483–486.

Myers, J. L., O'Brien, E. J., Albrecht, J. E., & Mason, R. A. (1994). Maintaining global coherence during reading. *Journal of Experimental Psychology: Learning, Memory, and Cognition, 20,* 876–886.

Myers, J. L., & Sadler, E. (1960). Effect of range of payoffs as a variable in risk-taking. *Journal of Experimental Psychology, 60,* 306–309.

Myers, J. L., Suydam, M. M., & Gambino, B. (1965). Contingent gains and losses in a risk-taking situation. *Journal of Mathematical Psychology, 2,* 363–370.

Nairne, J. S. (1988). A framework for interpreting recency effects in immediate serial recall. *Memory & Cognition, 16,* 343–352.

Nairne, J. S. (1991). Positional uncertainty in long-term memory. *Memory & Cognition, 19,* 332–340.

Nairne, J. S. (1992). The loss of positional certainty in long-term memory. *Psychological Science, 3,* 199–202.

Nairne, J. S., & Neath, I. (1994). Critique of the retrieval/deblurring assumptions of the theory of distributed associative memory. *Psychological Review, 101,* 528–533.

Navon, D., & Gopher, D. (1979). On the economy of the human information processing system. *Psychological Review, 86,* 214–255.

Neath, I. (1993a). Contextual and distinctive processes and the serial position function. *Journal of Memory and Language, 32,* 820–840.

Neath, I. (1993b). Distinctiveness and serial position effects in recognition. *Memory & Cognition, 21,* 689–698.

Neath, I., & Knoedler, A. J. (1994). Distinctiveness and serial position effects in recognition and sentence processing. *Journal of Memory and Language, 33,* 776–795.

Neath, I., Surprenant, A., & Crowder, R. G. (1993). The context-dependent stimulus suffix effect. *Journal of Experimental Psychology: Learning, Memory, and Cognition, 19,* 698–703.

Neely, J. H. (1977). Semantic priming and retrieval from lexical memory: Roles of inhibitionless spreading activation and limited-capacity attention. *Journal of Experimental Psychology: General, 106,* 226–254.

Neely, J. H. (1989). Experimental dissociations and the episodic/semantic memory distinction. In H. L. Roediger, III, & F. I. M. Craik (Eds.), *Varieties of memory and consciousness: Essays in honour of Endel Tulving* (pp. 229–270). Hillsdale, NJ: Erlbaum.

Neely, J. H. (1991). Semantic priming effects in visual word recognition: A selective review of current findings and theories. In D. Besner & G. W. Humphreys (Eds.), *Basic processes in reading: Visual word recognition* (pp. 264–336). Hillsdale, NJ: Erlbaum.

Neely, J. H., & Durgonoglu, A. Y. (1985). Dissociative episodic and semantic priming effects in episodic recognition and lexical decision tasks. *Journal of Memory and Language, 24,* 466–489.

Neely, J. H., & Payne, D. G. (1983). A direct comparison of recognition failure rates for recallable names in episodic and semantic memory tests. *Memory & Cognition, 11,* 161–171.

Neill, W. T. (1977). Inhibitory and facilitatory processes in attention. *Journal of Experimental Psychology: Human Perception and Performance, 3,* 444–450.

Neill, W. T. (1979). Switching attention within and between categories: Evidence for intracategory inhibition. *Memory & Cognition, 7,* 283–290.

Neill, W. T. (1985). Levels of processing in disruptive effects of prior information. *Memory & Cognition, 13,* 477–484.

Neill, W. T., & Valdes, L. A. (1992). Persistence of negative priming: Steady state or decay? *Journal of Experimental Psychology: Learning, Memory, and Cognition, 18,* 565–576.

Neill, W. T., Valdes, L. A., Terry, K. M., & Gorfein, D. S. (1992). Persistence of negative priming: II. Evidence for episodic trace retrieval. *Journal of Experimental Psychology: Learning, Memory, and Cognition, 18,* 993–1000.

Neisser, U. (1964). Visual search. *Scientific American, 210,* 94–102.

Neisser, U. (1967). *Cognitive psychology.* New York: Appleton-Century-Crofts.

Neisser, U. (1982). John Dean's memory: A case study. In U. Neisser (Ed.), *Memory observed: Remembering in natural contexts* (pp. 139–159). San Francisco: Freeman.

Neisser, U., & Becklen, R. (1975). Selective looking: Attending to visually specified events. *Cognitive Psychology, 7,* 480–494.

Neisser, U., Novick, R., & Lazar, R. (1963). Searching for ten targets simultaneously. *Perceptual and Motor Skills, 17,* 955–961.

Nelson, K. (1986). Event knowledge and cognitive development. In K. Nelson (Ed.), *Event knowledge: Structure and function in development* (pp. 1–20). Hillsdale, NJ: Erlbaum.

Nelson, K. (1992). Emergence of autobiographical memory at age 4. *Human Development, 35,* 172–177.

Nelson, K. (1993a). The psychological and social origins of autobiographical memory. *Psychological Science, 4,* 7–14.

Nelson, K. (1993b). Events, narratives, memory: What develops? In C. A. Nelson (Ed.), *Memory and affect in development: The Minnesota Symposia on Child Psychology* (Vol. 26, pp. 1–24). Hillsdale, NJ: Erlbaum.

Nelson, K., & Gruendel, J. (1981). Generalized event representations: Basic building blocks of cognitive development. In M. E. Lamb & A. L. Brown (Eds.), *Advances in developmental psychology* (Vol. 1, pp. 131–158). Hillsdale, NJ: Erlbaum.

Neves, D. M., & Anderson, J. R. (1981). Knowledge compilation: Mechanisms for the automatization of cognitive skills. In J. R. Anderson (Ed.), *Cognitive skills and their acquisition* (pp. 57–84). Hillsdale, NJ: Erlbaum.

Newell, A. (1980). Reasoning, problem solving, and decision processes: The problem space as a fundamental category. In R. S. Nickerson (Ed.), *Attention and performance VIII* (pp. 693–718). Hillsdale, NJ: Erlbaum.

Newell, A. (1982). The knowledge level. *Artificial Intelligence, 18,* 87–127.

Newell, A. (1992). *Unified theories of cognition.*

Newell, A., & Rosenbloom, P. S. (1981). Mechanisms of skill acquisition and the law of practice. In J. R. Anderson (Ed.), *Cog-*

nitive skills and their acquisition (pp. 1–55). Hillsdale, NJ: Erlbaum.

Newell, A., & Simon, H. A. (1972). *Human problem solving.* Englewood Cliffs, NJ: Prentice-Hall.

Newport, E. L. (1990). Maturational constraints on language learning. *Cognitive Science, 14,* 11–28.

Norman, D. (1968). Toward a theory of memory and attention. *Psychological Review, 75,* 522–536.

Norman, G. R., Brooks, L. R., Coblentz, C. L., & Babcock, C. J. (1992). The correlation of feature identification and category judgments in diagnostic radiology. *Memory & Cognition, 20,* 344–355.

Nosofsky, R. M. (1991). Typicality in logically defined categories: Exemplar-similarity versus rule instantiation. *Memory & Cognition, 19,* 131–150.

Nosofsky, R. M., Kruschke, J. K., & McKinley, S. (1992). Combining exemplar-based category representations and connectionist learning rules. *Journal of Experimental Psychology: Learning, Memory and Cognition, 18,* 211–233.

Nygaard, L. C., & Eimas, P. D. (1990). A new version of duplex perception: Evidence for phonetic and non-phonetic fusion. *Journal of the Acoustical Society of America, 88,* 75–86.

Nygaard, L. C., Sommers, M. S., Pisoni, D. B. (1994) Speech perception as a talker-contingent process. *Psychological Science, 5* (1), 42–46.

O'Brien, E. J., Shank, D. M., Myers, J. L., & Rayner, K. (1988). Elaborative inferences during reading: Do they occur on-line? *Journal of Experimental Psychology: Learning, Memory, and Cognition, 14,* 410–420.

Oden, G. C. (1977). Fuzziness in semantic memory: Choosing exemplars of subjective categories. *Memory & Cognition, 5,* 198–204.

Oden, G. C. (1981). A fuzzy propositional model of concept structure and use: A case study in object identification. In G. W. Lasker (Ed.), *Applied systems and cybernetics:* Vol. VI (pp. 2890–2897). Elmsford, NY: Pergamon.

Oden, G. C. (1984). Dependence, independence, and the emergence of word features. *Journal of Experimental Psychology: Human Perception and Performance, 10,* 394–405.

Oden, G. C., & Massaro, D. W. (1978). Integration of featural information in speech perception. *Psychological Review, 85,* 172–191.

Ofshe, R., & Watters, N. (1994). *Making monsters: False memories, psychotherapy, and sexual hysteria.* New York: Charles Scribner's Sons.

Oldfield, R. C. (1963). Individual vocabulary and semantic currency. *British Journal of Social and Clinical Psychology, 2,* 122–130.

Oldfield, R. C., & Wingfield, A. (1964). The time it takes to name an object. *Nature, 202,* 1031–1032.

Oldfield, R. C., & Wingfield, A. (1965). Response latencies in naming objects. *Quarterly Journal of Experimental Psychology, 17,* 273–281.

Olton, D. S. (1989). Inferring psychological dissociations from experimental dissociations: The temporal context of episodic memory. In H. L. Roediger & F. I. M. Craik (Eds.), *Varieties of memory and consciousness: Essays in honour of Endel Tulving* (pp. 161–178). Hillsdale, NJ: Erlbaum.

Olton, D. S., Becker, J. T., & Handelmann, G. T. (1979). Hippocampus, space, and memory. *The Behavioral and Brain Sciences, 2,* 313–365.

Olton, D. S., Meck, W. H., & Church, R. M. (1987). Separation of hippocampal and amygdaloid involvement in temporal memory dysfunctions. *Brain Research, 404,* 180–188.

Ornstein, P. A., & Naus, M. J. (1978). Rehearsal processes in children's memory. In P. A. Ornstein (Ed.), *Children's memory* (pp. 69–99). Hillsdale, NJ: Erlbaum.

Ornstein, P. A., Naus, M. J., & Liberty, C. (1975). Rehearsal and organizational processes in children's memory. *Child Development, 46,* 818–830.

Osgood, C. E. (1949). The similarity paradox in human learning: A resolution. *Psychological Review, 56,* 132–143.

Osgood, C. E. (1953). *Theory and method in experimental psychology.* New York: Oxford.

Osgood, C. E., & Sebeok, T. A. (1954). *Psycholinguistics: A survey of theory and research problems.* Memoir 10, Indiana University Publications in Anthropology and Linguistics.

O'Sullivan, J. T. (1993). Preschoolers' beliefs about effort, incentives, and recall. *Journal of Experimental Child Psychology, 55,* 396–414.

Owsley, C. (1983). The role of motion in infants' perception of solid shape. *Perception, 12,* 707–717.

Paivio, A. (1969). Mental imagery in associative learning and memory. *Psychological Review, 76,* 241–263.

Palmer, S. (1975). The effects of contextual scenes on the identification of objects. *Memory & Cognition, 3,* 519–526.

Parasuraman, R. (1985). Detection and identification of abnormalities in chest x-rays: Effects of reader skill, disease prevalence, and reporting standards. In R. E. Eberts & C. G. Eberts (Eds.), *Trends in ergonomics/human factors II.* Amsterdam: North-Holland.

Park, D. C., & Puglisi, J. T. (1985). Older adults' memory for the color of pictures and words. *Journals of Gerontology, 40,* 198–204.

Park, K. B., Lee, H., & Lee, S. (1996). Monotonous social environments and the identification of crime suspects: A comparison of police cadets and civilian college students. *Psychological Reports, 79,* 647–654.

Pastore, R. E., & Scheirer, C. J. (1974). Signal detection theory: Considerations for general application. *Psychological Bulletin, 81,* 945–958.

Pastore, R. E., Schmeckler, M. A., Rosenblum, L., & Szczesiul, R. (1983). Duplex perception with musical stimuli. *Perception & Psychophysics, 33,* 469–474.

Patel, V. L., & Groen, G. J. (1991). The general and specific nature of medical expertise: A critical look. In K. A. Ericsson & J. Smith (Eds.), *Toward a general theory of expertise: Prospects and limits* (pp. 93–125). Cambridge: Cambridge University Press.

Patel, V. L., Groen, G. J., & Arocha, J. F. (1990). Medical expertise as a function of task difficulty. *Memory & Cognition, 18,* 394–406.

Paul, H. (1886). *Prinzipien der sprachgeschichte.* Leipzig: Engelmann.

Pavlov, I. P. (1927). *Conditioned reflexes: An investigation of the physiological activity of the cerebral cortex.* London: Oxford University Press.

Payne, D. G. (1987). Hypermnesia and reminiscence in recall: A historical and empirical review. *Psychological Bulletin, 101,* 5–27.

Payne, D. G., & Blackwell, J. M. (1997). Truth in memory from human memory: Caveat emptor. In S. J. Lynn & N. Spanos (Eds.), *Truth in memory.* New York: Guilford Press.

Payne, D. G., Elie, C. J., Blackwell, J. M., & Neuschatz, J. S. (1996). Memory illusions: Recalling, recognizing, and recollecting events that never occurred. *Journal of Memory and Language, 35,* 261–285.

Payne, D. G., Peters, L. J., Birkmire, D. P., Bonto, M. A., Anastasi, J. S., & Wenger, M. J. (1994). Effects of speech intelligibility level on concurrent visual task performance. *Human Factors, 36,* 441–475.

Payne, D. G., & Wenger, M. J. (1992). Improving memory through practice. In D. Herrmann, H. Weingartner, A. Searleman, & C. McEvoy (Eds.), *Memory improvement: Implications for memory theory* (pp. 187–209). New York: Springer-Verlag.

Payne, D. G., & Wenger, M. J. (1996). Practice effects in memory: Data, theory, and unanswered questions. In D. Herrmann, C. McEvoy, C. Herzog, P. Hertel, & M. K. Johnson (Eds.), *Basic and applied memory research: Practical applications* (pp. 123–138). Hillsdale, NJ: Erlbaum.

Pendergast, M. (1995). *Victims of memory: Incest accusations and shattered lives:* Upper Access Books.

Perrett, D. I., Harries, M. H., Mistlin, A. J., Hiatanen, J. K., Benson, P. J., Bevan, R., Thomas, S., Oram, M. W., Ortega, J., & Brierly, K. (1990). Social signals analyzed at the single cell level: Someone is looking at me, something touched me, something moved. *International Journal of Comparative Psychology, 4,* 25–55.

Peterson, L. R., & Gentile, A. (1963). Proactive interference as a function of time between tests. *Journal of Experimental Psychology, 70,* 473–478.

Peterson, L. R., & Peterson, M. J. (1959). Short-term retention of individual verbal items. *Journal of Experimental Psychology, 58,* 193–198.

Peterson, M. A. (1994). Object recognition processes can and do operate before figure-ground organization. *Current Directions in Psychological Science, 3,* 105–111.

Peterson, S. E., Fox, P. T., Posner, M. I., Mintun, M., & Raichle, M. E. (1988). Positron emission tomographic studies of the cortical anatomy of single-word processing. *Nature, 331,* 585–589.

Petry, S., & Meyer, G. E. (1987). *The perception of illusory contours.* New York: Springer-Verlag.

Peverly, S. T. (1991). Problems with the knowledge-based explanation of memory and development. *Review of Educational Research, 61,* 71–93.

Pezdek, K. (1994). The illusion of illusory memory. *Applied Cognitive Psychology, 8,* 339–350.

Piaget, J. (1954). *The construction of reality in the child.* New York: Basic Books.

Pickett, J. M. (1980). *The sounds of speech communication.*

Pillsbury, W. B. (1897). A study in apperception. *American Journal of Psychology, 8,* 315–393.

Pillsbury, W. B. (1908). The effects of training on memory. *Educational Review, 36,* 15–27.

Pinel, J. P. J. (1993). *Biopsychology.* Boston: Allyn and Bacon.

Pinker, S. (1984). *Language learnability and language development.* Cambridge, MA: MIT Press.

Pinker, S. (1990). Language acquisition. In D. N. Osherson & H. Lasnik (Eds.), *Language: An invitation to cognitive science* (Vol. 1, pp. 199–241). Cambridge, MA: MIT Press.

Pinker, S. (1991). Rules of language. *Science, 253,* 530–535.

Pinto, A. D. C., & Baddeley, A. D. (1991). Where did you park your car? Analysis of a naturalistic long-term recency effect. *European Journal of Cognitive Psychology, 3,* 297–313.

Pirolli, P. L., & Anderson, J. R. (1985). The role of practice in fact retrieval. *Journal of Experimental Psychology: Learning, Memory, and Cognition, 11,* 136–153.

Pisoni, D. B. (1977). Identification and discrimination of the relative onset of two-component tones: Implications for voicing perception in stops. *Journal of the Acoustical Society of America, 61,* 1352–1361.

Pisoni, D. B., & Luce, P. A. (1986). Speech perception: Research, theory, and the principle issues. In E. C. Schwab & H. C. Nusbaum (Eds.), *Perception of speech and visual form: Theoretical issues, models and research* (pp. 1–50). New York: Academic Press.

Pisoni, D. B., & Sawusch, J. R. (1975). Some stages of processing in speech perception. In A. Cohen & S. G. Nooteboom (Eds.), *Structure and process in speech perception* (pp. 16–34). Heidelberg: Springer-Verlag.

Pollack, I. (1963). Speed of classification of words into superordinate categories. *Journal of Verbal Learning and Verbal Behavior, 2,* 159–165.

Pollatsek, A., Rayner, K., & Balota, D. A. (1986). Inferences about eye movement control from the perceptual span in reading. *Perception & Psychophysics, 40,* 123–130.

Polster, M. R., Nadel, L., & Schacter, D. L. (1991). A cognitive neuroscience analysis of memory: A historical perspective. *Journal of Cognitive Neuroscience, 3,* 95–116.

Pomerantz, J. R. (1981). Perceptual organization in information processing. In M. Kubovy & J. R. Pomerantz (Eds.), *Perceptual organization.* Hillsdale, NJ: Lawrence Erlbaum Associates.

Posner, M. I. (1973). *Cognition: An introduction.* Glenview, IL: Scott, Foresman and Company.

Posner, M. I. (1982). Cumulative development of attentional theory. *American Psychologist, 37,* 168–179.

Posner, M. I., Goldsmith, R., & Welton, K. E. (1967). Perceived distance and the classification of distorted patterns. *Journal of Experimental Psychology, 73,* 28–38.

Posner, M. I., & Keele, S. W. (1967). Decay of visual information in a single letter. *Science, 158,* 137–139.

Posner, M. I., & Keele, S. W. (1968). On the genesis of abstract ideas. *Journal of Experimental Psychology, 77,* 353–363.

Posner, M. I., & Keele, S. W. (1970). Retention of abstract ideas. *Journal of Experimental Psychology, 83,* 304–308.

Posner, M. I., Peterson, S. E., Fox, P. T., & Raichle, M. E. (1988). Localization of cognitive operations in the human brain. *Science, 240,* 1627–1631.

Posner, M. I., & Raichle, M. E. (1994). *Images of mind.* New York: Scientific American Library.

Posner, M. I., & Snyder, C. R. R. (1975). Information processing and cognition: The Loyola Symposium. In R. Solso (Ed.), *Attention and cognitive control.* Hillsdale, NJ: Erlbaum.

Postman, L. (1975). Verbal learning and memory. *Annual Review of Psychology, 26,* 291–335.

Predebon, J., & Woolley, J. S. (1994). The familiar-size cue to depth under reduced-cue viewing conditions. *Perception, 23,* 1301–1312.

Premack, D. (1971). Language in chimpanzee? *Science, 172,* 808–822.

Pressley, M. (1982). Elaboration and memory development. *Child Development, 53,* 296–309.

Pressley, M., & Van Meter, P. (1994). What is memory development the development of? A 1990s theory of memory and cognitive development 'twixt 2 and 20. In P. Morris & M.

Gruneberg (Eds.), *Theoretical aspects of memory* (2nd ed., pp. 79–129). London: Routledge.

Pribram, K. H., & Tubbs, W. E. (1967). Short-term memory, parsing, and the primate frontal cortex. *Science, 156,* 1765–1767.

Pritchard, R. M. (1961). Stabilized images on the retina. *Scientific American, 204,* 72–78.

Proctor, R. W., & Dutta, A. D. (1995). *Skill acquisition and human performance.* Thousand Oaks, CA: Sage.

Proctor, R. W., & Van Zandt, T. (1994). *Human factors in simple and complex systems.* Boston: Allyn and Bacon.

Puppe, C. (1991). *Distorted probabilities and choice under risk* (Vol. 363). Berlin: Springer-Verlag.

Pyle, W. H. (1913). Economical learning. *Journal of Educational Psychology, 4,* 148–158.

Pyle, W. H. (1914). Concentrated versus distributed practice. *Journal of Educational Psychology, 5,* 247–251.

Quillian, M. R. (1968). Semantic memory. In M. Minsky (Ed.), *Semantic information processing.* Cambridge, MA: MIT Press.

Quinn, P. C., Burke, S., & Rush, A. (1993). Part-whole perception in early infancy: Evidence for perceptual grouping produced by lightness similarity. *Infant Behavior and Development, 16,* 19–42.

Raaijmakers, J. G. W. (1981). Search of associative memory. *Psychological Review, 88,* 93–134.

Rabinowitz, J. C., Ackerman, B. P., Craik, F. I. M., & Hinchley, J. L. (1982). Aging and metamemory: The roles of relatedness and imagery. *Journals of Gerontology, 37,* 688–695.

Radvansky, G. A., Spieler, D. H., & Zacks, R. T. (1993). Mental model organization. *Journal of Experimental Psychology: Learning, Memory, and Cognition, 19,* 95–114.

Radvansky, G. A., & Zacks, R. T. (1991). Mental models and the fan effect. *Journal of Experimental Psychology: Learning, Memory, & Cognition, 17,* 940–953.

Rand, B. (1912). *The classical psychologists.* Boston: Houghton-Mifflin.

Raney, G. E., & Rayner, K. (1993). Event-related brain potentials, eye movements, and reading. *Psychological Science, 4,* 283–286.

Raskin, E. (1936). Comparison of scientific and literary ability: A biographical study of eminent scientists and men of letters of the nineteenth century. *Journal of Abnormal & Social Psychology, 31,* 20–35.

Ratcliff, R. (1978). A theory of memory retrieval. *Psychological Review, 85,* 59–108.

Ratcliff, R., & McKoon, G. (1986). More on the distinction between episodic and semantic memories. *Journal of Experimental Psychology: Learning, Memory, and Cognition, 12,* 312–313.

Ravem, R. (1974). The development of wh- questions in first and second language learners. In J. C. Richards (Ed.), *Error analysis: Perspectives on second language acquisition.* London: Longman.

Rayner, K. (1993). Eye movements in reading: Recent developments. *Current Directions in Psychological Science, 2,* 81–85.

Rayner, K., & Pollatsek, A. (1989). *The psychology of reading.* Englewood Cliffs, NJ: Prentice Hall.

Rayner, K., Pollatsek, A., & Bilsky, A. B. (1996). Can a temporal processing deficit account for dyslexia. *Psychonomic Bulletin and Review, 2,* 501–507.

Rayner, K. (1978). Eye movements in reading and information processing. *Psychological Bulletin, 85,* 618–660.

Reber, A. (1989). Implicit learning and tacit knowledge. *Journal of Experimental Psychology: General, 118,* 219–235.

Reder, L. M., & Anderson, J. R. (1982). Effects of spacing and embellishment for the main points of a text. *Memory & Cognition, 10,* 97–102.

Reese, H. W. (1976). Models of memory development. *Human Development, 19,* 291–303.

Reese, H. W., & Rodeheaver, D. (1985). Problem solving and complex decision making. In J. E. Birren & K. W. Schaie (Eds.), *Handbook of the psychology of aging: The handbooks of aging* (2nd ed.) (pp. 474–499). New York: Van Nostrand Reinhold.

Reicher, G. M. (1969). Perceptual recognition as a function of meaningfulness of stimulus material. *Journal of Experimental Psychology, 81,* 275–280.

Reisberg, D. (1997). *Cognition: Exploring the science of the mind.* New York: W. W. Norton & Co.

Reisen, A. H. (1961). Stimulation as a requirement for growth and function in behavioral development. In D. W. Fiske & J. R. Maddi (Eds.), *Functions of varied experience.* Homewood, IL: Dorsey.

Remez, R. E. (1986). Realism, language, and another barrier. *Journal of Phonetics, 14,* 89–97.

Remez, R. E., Rubin, P. E., Pisoni, D. B., & Carrell, T. D. (1981). Speech perception without traditional speech cues. *Science, 212,* 947–950.

Reynolds, B. (1952). The effect of learning on the predictability of psychomotor performance. *Journal of Experimental Psychology, 44,* 189–198.

Ricciardelli, L. A. (1992). Bilingualism and cognitive development in relation to threshold theory. *Journal of Psycholinguistic Research, 21,* 301–316.

Richardson-Klavehn, A., & Bjork, R. A. (1988). Measures of memory. *Annual Review of Psychology, 39,* 475–543.

Riefer, D. M., & Batchelder, W. H. (1988). Multinomial modeling and the measurement of cognitive processes. *Psychological Review, 95,* 318–339.

Rips, L. J., Shoben, E. J., & Smith, E. E. (1973). Semantic distance and the verification of semantic relations. *Journal of Verbal Learning and Verbal Behavior, 14,* 665–681.

Rochat, P. B., Elliot M., Hoffmeyer, L. B. (1989). Oropharyngeal control of hand-mouth coordination in newborn infants. *Developmental Psychology, 24* (4), 459–463.

Roediger, H. L. (1980a). Memory metaphors in cognitive psychology. *Memory & Cognition, 8,* 231–246.

Roediger, H. L. (1980b). The effectiveness of four mnemonics in ordering recall. *Journal of Experimental Psychology: Human Learning and Memory, 6,* 558–567.

Roediger, H. L. (1996). Memory illusions. *Journal of Memory and Language, 35,* 76–100.

Roediger, H. L., & Blaxton, T. A. (1987). Effects of varying modality, surface features, and retention interval on priming in word-fragment completion. *Memory & Cognition, 15,* 379–388.

Roediger, H. L., & Challis, B. H. (1992). Effects of exact repetition and conceptual repetition on free recall and word-fragment completion. *Journal of Experimental Psychology: Learning, Memory, and Cognition, 18,* 3–14.

Roediger, H. L., & Crowder, R. G. (1976). A serial position effect in recall of United States presidents. *Bulletin of the Psychonomic Society, 8,* 275–278.

Roediger, H. L., & McDermott, K. B. (1995). Creating false memories: Remembering words not presented in lists. *Journal of Ex-*

perimental Psychology: Learning, Memory, and Cognition, 21, 803–814.

Roediger, H. L., & McDermott, K. B. (1996). False perceptions of false memories. *Journal of Experimental Psychology: Learning, Memory, and Cognition, 22,* 814–816.

Roediger, H. L., & Payne, D. G. (1983). Superiority of free recall to cued recall with "strong" cues. *Psychological Research, 45,* 275–286.

Roediger, H. L., Weldon, M. S., & Challis, B. A. (1989). Explaining dissociations between explicit and implicit measures of retention: A processing account. In H. L. Roediger & F. I. M. Craik (Eds.), *Varieties of memory and consciousness: Essays in honor of Endel Tulving* (pp. 3–41). Hillsdale, NJ: Erlbaum.

Roediger, H. L., Weldon, M. S., Stadler, M. L., & Riegler, G. L. (1992). Direct comparison of two implicit memory tests: Word fragment and word stem completion. *Journal of Experimental Psychology: Learning, Memory, and Cognition, 18,* 1251–1269.

Romaine, S. (1989). *Bilingualism.* Oxford: Basil Blackwell.

Rosch, E. H. (1987). Linguistic relativity. *Et cetera, 44,* 254–280.

Rosch, E., & Mervis, C. B. (1975). Family resemblances: Studies in the internal structure of categories. *Cognitive Psychology, 7,* 573–605.

Rosenblatt, F. (1958). The perceptron: A probabilistic model for information storage and organization in the brain. *Psychological Review, 65,* 386–408.

Rosenblatt, F. (1962). *Principles of neurodynamics.* New York: Spartan.

Rosenzweig, M. R., Leiman, A. L., & Breedlove, S. M. (1996). *Biological psychology.* Sunderland, MA: Sinauer Associates.

Ross, D. R., Ceci, S. J., Dunning, D., & Toglia, M. P. (1994). Unconscious transference and mistake identity: When a witness is familiar with an innocent person. *Journal of Applied Psychology, 79,* 918–930.

Rothkopf, E. Z., & Coke, E. U. (1963). Repetition interval and rehearsal method in leaning equivalences from written sentences. *Journal of Verbal Learning and Verbal Behavior, 2,* 406–416.

Rovee-Collier, C. (1989). The joy of kicking: Memories, motives, and mobiles. In P. R. Solomon, G. R. Goethals, C. M. Kelley, & B. R. Stephens (Eds.), *Memory: Interdisciplinary approaches* (pp. 151–180). New York: Springer-Verlag.

Rovee-Collier, C., & Sullivan, M. W. (1980). Organization of infant memory. *Journal of Experimental Psychology: Human Learning and Memory, 6,* 798–807.

Rubenstein, H., Garfield, L., & Millikan, J. A. (1970). Homographic entries in the internal lexicon. *Journal of Verbal Learning and Verbal Behavior, 9,* 487–494.

Rubin, E. (1915/1958). *Synoplevede figurer.* Copenhagen: Clydenalske. [Abridged translation by M. Wertheimer. Figure and ground. In D. C. Beardslee & M. Wertheimer (Eds.), *Readings in perception.* Princeton, NJ: Van Nostrand.]

Rumbaugh, D. M., Gill, T. V., & von Glasersfeld, E. C. (1973). Reading and sentence completion by a chimpanzee (Pan). *Science, 182,* 731–733.

Rumelhart, D. E. (1990). Brain style computation: Learning and generalization. In S. F. Zornetzer, J. L. Davis, & C. Lau (Eds.), *An introduction to neural and electronic networks* (pp. 405–420). San Diego: Academic Press.

Rumelhart, D. E., Hinton, G. E., & Williams, R. J. (1986). Learning internal representations by error propagation. In D. E.

Rumelhart & J. L. McClelland (Eds.), *Parallel distributed processing: Explorations in the microstructure of cognition* (Vol. 1, pp. 318–364). Cambridge, MA: MIT Press.

Rumelhart, D. E., Lindsay, P. H., & Norman, D. A. (1972). A process model for long term memory. In E. Tulving & W. Donaldson (Eds.), *Organization of memory* (pp. 197–246). New York: Academic Press.

Rumelhart, D. E., & McClelland, J. L. (1982). An interactive activation model of context effects in letter perception: Part 2. The contextual enhancement effect and some tests and extensions of the model. *Psychological Review, 89,* 60–94.

Rumelhart, D. E., & McClelland, J. L. (1986). *Parallel distributed processing: Explorations of the microstructure of cognition.* Cambridge, MA: MIT Press.

Rundus, D. (1971). Analysis of rehearsal processes in free recall. *Journal of Experimental Psychology, 89,* 63–77.

Russell, W. A., & Jenkins, J. J. (1954). *The complete Minnesota norms for responses to 100 words from the Kent-Rosanoff Word Association Test* (Technical Report No. 11). University of Minnesota.

Ryan, F. J., & Bilodeau, E. A. (1962). Countertraining of a simple skill with immediate and one-week delays of informative feedback. *Journal of Experimental Psychology, 63,* 19–22.

Sachs, J. S. (1967). Recognition memory for syntactic and semantic aspects of connected discourse. *Perception & Psychophysics, 2,* 437–442.

Sacks, O. (1985). *The man who mistook his wife for a hat and other clinical tales.* New York: Harper & Row.

Sacks, O. (1995). *An anthropologist on Mars.* New York: Alfred A. Knopf.

Sadoski, M., Paivio, A., & Goetz, E. T. (1991). A critique of schema theory in reading and a dual-coding alternative. *Reading Research Quarterly, 26,* 463–484.

Saffran, E. M., & Marin, O. S. M. (1975). Immediate memory for word lists and sentences in a patient with deficient auditory short-term memory. *Brain and Language, 2,* 420–433.

Sagan, C. (1995). *The demon-haunted world: Science as a candle in the dark.* New York: Random House.

Salasoo, A., Shiffrin, R. M., & Feustel, T. C. (1985). Building permanent memory codes: Codification and repetition effects in word identification. *Journal of Experimental Psychology: General, 114,* 50–77.

Salthouse, T. A. (1993). Speed and knowledge as determinants of adult age differences in verbal tasks. *Journals of Gerontology, 48,* 29–36.

Salthouse, T. A. (1996). The processing-speed theory of adult age differences in cognition. *Psychological Review, 103,* 403–428.

Salthouse. T. A., & Coon, V. E. (1993). Influence of task-specific processing speed on age differences in memory. *Journals of Gerontology, 48,* 245–255.

Santrock. J. W. (1996). *Child development* (7th ed.). Dubuque, IA: Brown & Benchmark.

Sattler, J. M. (1982). *Assessment of children's intellectual and special abilities* (2nd ed.). Boston: Allyn and Bacon.

Savage, J. L. (1954). *The foundations of statistics.* New York: Wiley.

Savage-Rumbaugh, E. S., Rumbaugh, D. M., Smith, S. T., & Lawson, J. (1980). Reference: The linguistic essential. *Science, 210,* 922–925.

Sawyer, J. (1966). Measurement and prediction, clinical and statistical. *Psychological Bulletin, 66,* 178–200.

Schacter, D. L. (1987a). Implicit memory: History and current status. *Journal of Experimental Psychology: Learning, Memory, and Cognition, 13,* 501–518.

Schacter, D. L. (1987b). Memory, amnesia, and frontal lobe dysfunction. *Psychobiology, 15,* 21–36.

Schacter, D. L. (1995). Memory distortion: History and current status. In D. L. Schacter, J. T. Coyle, M. M. Fishback, M. M. Mesulam, & L. E. Sullivan (Eds.), *Memory distortion: How minds, brains, and societies reconstruct the past* (pp. 1–65). Cambridge, MA: Harvard University Press.

Schacter, D. L., Reiman, E., Curran, T., Yun, L. S., Bandy, D., McDermott, K. B., & Roediger, H. L. (1996). Neuroanatomical correlates of veridical and illusory recognition memory: Evidence from positron emission tomography. *Neuron, 17,* 267–274.

Schacter, D. L., Rick, S. A., & Stamp, M. S. (1985). Remediation of memory disorders: Experimental evaluation of the spaced retrieval technique. *Journal of Clinical and Experimental Neuropsychology, 7,* 19–26.

Schaeffer, B., & Wallace, R. (1969). Semantic similarity and the comparison of word meanings. *Journal of Experimental Psychology, 82,* 343–346.

Schaffer, H. R. (1984). The child's entry into a social world. *Behavioural Development: A Series of Monographs, 236.*

Schiffman, H. R. (1996). *Sensation and perception* (4th ed.). New York: Wiley.

Schlottmann, A., & Anderson, N. H. (1993). An information integration approach to phenomenal causality. *Memory & Cognition, 21,* 785–801.

Schmidt, R. A., & Bjork, R. A. (1992). New conceptualizations of practice: Common principles in three paradigms suggest new concepts for training. *Psychological Science, 3,* 207–217.

Schmidt, R. A., Young, D. E., Swinnen, S., & Shapiro, D. C. (1989). Summary knowledge of results for skill acquisition: Support for the guidance hypothesis. *Journal of Experimental Psychology: Learning, Memory, and Cognition, 15,* 352–359.

Schneider, W. (1993). Varieties of working memory as seen in biology and in connectionist/control architectures. *Memory & Cognition, 21,* 184–192.

Schneider, W., & Detweiler, M. (1987). A connectionist/control architecture for working memory. In G. H. Bower (Ed.), *The psychology of learning and motivation* (Vol. 21, pp. 53–119). San Diego: Academic Press.

Schneider, W., & Detweiler, M. (1988). The role of practice in dual-task performance: Toward workload modeling in a connectionist/control architecture. *Human Factors, 30,* 539–566.

Schneider, W., Dumais, S. T., & Shiffrin, R. M. (1984). Automatic and control processing and attention. In R. P. &. D. R. Davies (Eds.), *Varieties of attention.* New York: Academic Press.

Schneider, W., & Shiffrin, R. M. (1977). Controlled and automatic human information processing: I. Detection, search, and attention. *Psychological Review, 84,* 1–66.

Schoenfeld, A., & Herrmann, D. (1982). Problem perception and knowledge structure in expert and novice mathematical problem solvers. *Journal of Experimental Psychology: Learning, Memory, and Cognition, 5,* 484–494.

Schooler, C., Neumann, E., Caplan, L. J., & Roberts, B. R. (1997). A time course analysis of Stroop interference and facilitation: Comparing normal individuals and individuals with schizophrenia. *Journal of Experimental Psychology: General, 126,* 19–36.

Schooler, L. J. (1997). Sorting out core memory processes. In M. Oaksford & N. Chater (Eds.), *Rational models of cognition.* Oxford: Oxford University Press.

Schooler, L. J., & Anderson, J. R. (1997). The role of process in the rational analysis of memory. *Cognitive Psychology,* in press.

Schultz, D. (1981). *A history of modern psychology* (3rd ed.). New York: Academic Press.

Schwartz, B., & Reisberg, D. (1991). *Learning and memory.* New York: Norton.

Schweickert, R. (1993). A multinomial processing tree model for degradation and redintegration in immediate recall. *Memory & Cognition, 21,* 168–175.

Schweickert, R., & Boruff, B. (1986). Short-term memory capacity: Magic number or magic spell? *Journal of Experimental Psychology: Learning, Memory, and Cognition, 12,* 419–425.

Schweickert, R., Fisher, D., & Goldstein, W. (1992). *General latent network theory: Structural and quantitative analysis of networks of cognitive processes* (Technical Report No. 92-1). Purdue University Mathematical Psychology Program.

Schweickert, R., Guentert, L., & Hersberger, L. (1990). Phonological similarity, pronunciation rate, and memory span. *Psychological Science, 1,* 74–77.

Scoville, W. B., & Milner, B. (1957). Loss of recent memory after bilateral hippocampal lesions. *Journal of Neurology, Neurosurgery, and Psychiatry, 20,* 11–21.

Scrivner, E., & Safer, M. A. (1988). Eyewitnesses show hypermnesia for details about a violent crime. *Journal of Applied Psychology, 73,* 371–377.

Scurfield, B. K. (1996). Multiple-event forced-choice tasks in the theory of signal detectability. *Journal of Mathematical Psychology, 40,* 253–269.

Seamon, J. G., & Murray, P. (1976). Depth of processing in recall and recognition memory: Differential effects of stimulus meaningfulness and serial position. *Journal of Experimental Psychology: Human Learning and Memory, 8,* 680–687.

Searle, J. R. (1979). *Expression and meaning: Studies in the theory of speech acts.* Cambridge: Cambridge University Press.

Searleman, A. (1977). A review of right hemisphere linguistic capabilities. *Psychological Bulletin, 84,* 503–528.

Searleman, A., & Herrmann, D. (1994). *Memory from a broader perspective.* New York: McGraw-Hill.

Seibel, R. (1963). Discrimination time for a 1,023 alternative task. *Journal of Experimental Psychology, 66,* 215–226.

Seifert, C. M. (1990). Content-based inferences in text. *The psychology of learning and motivation, 25,* 103–122.

Sejnowski, T. J., & Churchland, P. S. (1989). Brain and cognition. In M. I. Posner (Ed.), *Foundations of cognitive science.* Cambridge, MA: MIT Press.

Selfridge, O. (1959). Pandemonium: A paradigm for learning. In *The mechanization of thought processes.* London: H. M. Stationary Office.

Selz, O. (1922). *Zue Psychologie des Produktivens Denkens und des Irrtums.* Bonn: Cohen.

Semon, R. (1921). *The mneme.* London: George Allen & Unwin.

Shaffer, L. H. (1975). Multiple attention in continuous verbal tasks. In S. Dornic (Ed.), *Attention and performance: V.* New York: Academic Press.

Shallice, T., Fletcher, P., Frith, C. D., Grasby, P., Frackowiak, R. S. J., & Dolan, R. J. (1994). Brain regions associated with acquisition and retrieval of verbal episodic memory. *Nature, 368,* 633–635.

Shallice, T., & Vallar, G. (1990). The impairment of auditory-verbal short-term storage. In G. Vallar & T. Shallice (Eds.), *Neuropsychological impairments of short-term memory* (pp. 11–53). Cambridge: Cambridge University Press.

Shallice, T., & Warrington, E. K. (1970). Independent functioning of verbal memory stores: A neuropsychological study. *Quarterly Journal of Experimental Psychology, 22,* 261–273.

Shea, C. H., Kohl, R., & Indermill, C. (1990). Contextual interference: Contributions of practice. *Acta Psychologica, 73,* 145–157.

Shea, J. B., & Morgan, R. L. (1979). Contextual interference effects on acquisition, retention, and transfer of a motor skill. *Journal of Experimental Psychology: Human Learning and Memory, 5,* 179–187.

Shedden, J. M., & Schneider, W. (1990). A connectionist model of attentional enhancement and signal buffering. In *Twelfth Annual Conference of the Cognitive Science Society* (pp. 566–573). Hillsdale, NJ: Erlbaum.

Shepard, R. N. (1958). Stimulus and response generalization: A stochastic model relating generalization to distance in psychological space. *Psychometrika, 22,* 325–345.

Shepard, R. N., Hovland, C. I., & Jenkins, H. M. (1961). Learning and memorization of classifications. *Psychological Monographs, 75.*

Shiffrin, R. M. (1975). The locus and role of attention in memory systems. In P. M. A. Rabbitt & S. Dornic (Eds.), *Attention and performance V.* New York: Academic Press.

Shiffrin, R. M. (1976). Capacity limitations in information processing, attention, and memory. In W. K. Estes (Ed.), *Handbook of learning and cognitive processes,* Vol. 4. Hillsdale, NJ: Erlbaum.

Shiffrin, R. M. (1993). Short-term memory: A brief commentary. *Memory & Cognition, 21,* 193–197.

Shiffrin, R. M., Murnane, K., Gronlund, S., & Roth, M. (1989). On units of storage and retrieval. In C. Izawa (Ed.), *Current issues in cognitive processes: The Tulane Floweree Symposium on Cognition* (pp. 25–68). Hillsdale, NJ: Erlbaum.

Shiffrin, R. M., & Schneider, W. (1977). Controlled and automatic human information processing: II. Perceptual learning, automatic attending, and a general theory. *Psychological Review, 84,* 127–190.

Shiori, W., & Cavanagh, P. (1992). Visual persistence of figures defined by relative motion. *Vision-Research, 32,* 943–951.

Simon, H. A. (1956). Rational choice and the structure of the environment. *Psychological Review, 63,* 129–138.

Simon, H. A. (1972). Theories of bounded rationality. In C. B. Radner & R. Radner (Eds.), *Decision and organization* (pp. 161–176). Amsterdam: North-Holland.

Simon, H. A. (1983). *Reason in human affairs.* Stanford, CA: Stanford University Press.

Simon, H. A. (1986). Alternative visions of rationality. In H. R. Arkes & K. R. Hammond (Eds.), *Judgment and decision making: An interdisciplinary reader* (pp. 97–113). Cambridge: Cambridge University Press.

Simon, H. A., & Chase, W. C. (1973). Skill in chess. *American Scientist, 61,* 394–403.

Singley, M. K., & Anderson, J. R. (1989). *The transfer of cognitive skill.* Cambridge, MA: Harvard University Press.

Skinner, B. F. (1957). *Verbal behavior.* New York: Appleton-Century-Crofts.

Skinner, B. F. (1984). The phylogeny and ontogeny of behavior. *Behavioral and Brain Sciences, 7,* 669–711.

Slamecka, N. J. (1966). Differentiation versus unlearning of verbal associations. *Journal of Experimental Psychology, 71,* 822–828.

Slamecka, N. J. (1985). Ebbinghaus: Some associations. *Journal of Experimental Psychology: Learning, Memory, and Cognition, 11,* 414–435.

Sliwinski, M., Buschke, H., Kuslansky, G., Senior, G., & Scarisbrick, D. (1994). Proportional slowing and addition speed in old and young adults. *Psychology and Aging, 9,* 72–80.

Slobin, D. I. (1973). Cognitive prerequisites for the development of grammar. In C. A. Ferguson & D. I. Slobin (Eds.), *Studies of child language development* (pp. 175–208). New York: Holt, Rinehart & Winston.

Sloboda, J. A. (1991). Music structure and emotional response: Some empirical findings. *Psychology of Music, 19,* 110–120.

Slovic, P., & Lichtenstein, S. (1971). Comparison of Bayesian and regression approaches to the study of information processing in judgment. *Organizational Behavior and Human Performance, 6,* 649–744.

Smith, E. E. (1978). Theories of semantic memory. In W. K. Estes (Ed.), *Handbook of learning and cognitive processes* (Vol. 6). Hillsdale, NJ: Erlbaum.

Smith, E. E., & Medin, D. L. (1981). *Categories and concepts.* Cambridge, MA: Harvard University Press.

Smith, E. E., Shoben, E. J., & Rips, L. J. (1974). Structure and process in semantic memory: A featural model for semantic decisions. *Psychological Review, 1,* 214–241.

Smith, L. B., & Thelen, E. (1993). *A dynamic systems approach to development: Applications.* Cambridge, MA: MIT Press.

Smith, S. M. (1986). Environmental context-dependent recognition memory using a short-term memory task for input. *Memory & Cognition, 14,* 347–354.

Smith, S. M. (1994). Theoretical principles of context-dependent memory. In P. E. Morris & M. Gruneberg (Eds.), *Theoretical aspects of memory* (pp. 168–195). London: Routledge.

Smith, S. M., Glenberg, A., & Bjork, R. A. (1978). Environmental context and human memory. *Memory & Cognition, 6,* 342–353.

Smith, S. M., & Rothkopf, E. Z. (1984). Contextual enhancement and distribution of practice in the classroom. *Cognition and Instruction, 1,* 341–358.

Smotherman, W. P., & Robinson, S. R. (1991). Conditioned activation of fetal behavior. *Physiology and Behavior, 50,* 73–77.

Smyer, M. A., Zarit, S. H., Qualls, S. H. (1990). Psychological intervention with the aging individual. In J. E. Birren, K. W. Schaie, (Eds.) *Handbook of the psychology of aging,* 3rd ed. San Diego: Academic Press, 375–403.

Snoddy, G. S. (1926). Learning and stability. *Journal of Applied Psychology, 10,* 1–36.

Sodorow, L. M. (1995). *Psychology* (3rd ed.). Brown & Benchmark.

Solso, R. L. (1995). *Cognitive psychology* (4th ed.). Boston: Allyn and Bacon.

Sommers, N. I. (1979). The need for theory in composition research. *College Composition and Communication, 30,* 46–49.

Sorkin, R. D., & Dai, H. (1994). Signal detection analysis of the ideal group. *Organizational Behavior & Human Decision Processes, 60,* 1–13.

Sosniak, L. A. (1985). Learning to be a concert pianist. In B. S. Bloom (Ed.), *Developing talent in young people* (pp. 19–67). New York: Ballantine.

Southall, G. H. (1978). *Blind Tom: The post–Civil War enslavement of a Black musical genius.* Minneapolis: Challenge Productions.

Southall, J. C. (1979). A study for the validation of an instructional sequence designed to teach verbal problem solving in elementary mathematics. *Dissertation Abstracts International, 40,* 1935–1936.

Spear, N. E., & Riccio, D. C. (1994). *Memory: Phenomena and principles* (pp. 177–210). Boston: Allyn and Bacon.

Spear-Swerling, L., & Sternberg, R. J. (1994). The road not taken: An integrative theoretical model of reading disability. *Journal of Learning Disabilities, 27,* 91–103.

Spelke, E. S., Breinlinger, K., Macomber, J., & Jacobson, K. (1992). Origins of knowledge. *Psychological Review, 99,* 605–632.

Sperling, G. (1960). The information available in brief visual presentations. *Psychological Monographs, 74* (Whole #498).

Spitz, H. H., & LaFontaine, L. (1973). The digit span of idiots savants. *American Journal of Mental Deficiency, 77,* 757–759.

Spoehr, K. T. (1981). Word recognition in speech and reading: Toward a single theory of language processing. In P. D. Eimas & J. L. Miller (Eds.), *Perspectives on the study of speech* (pp. 239–282). Hillsdale, NJ: Erlbaum.

Springer, S. P., & Deutsch, G. (1993). *Left brain, right brain* (4th ed.). New York: W. H. Freeman.

Spyridakis, J. H., & Wenger, M. J. (1992). Writing for human performance: Relating reading research to document design. *Technical Communication, 39,* 202–215.

Squire, L. R. (1992). Memory and the hippocampus: A synthesis from findings with rats, monkeys, and humans. *Psychological Review, 99,* 195–231.

Squire, L. R., Shimamura, A. P., and Amaral, D. G. (1989). Memory and the hippocampus. In J. H. Byrne and W. O. Berry (Eds.), *Neural models of plasticity: Experimental and theoretical approaches* (p. 227). New York: Academic Press.

Stanovich, K. E., & West, R. F. (1983). On priming by a sentence context. *Journal of Experimental Psychology: General, 112,* 1–36.

Starch, D. (1912). Periods of work in learning. *Journal of Educational Psychology, 3,* 209–213.

Staszewski, J. J. (1988). Skilled memory and expert mental calculation. In M. T. H. Chi, R. Glaser, & M. J. Farr (Eds.), *The nature of expertise* (pp. 71–128). Hillsdale, NJ: Erlbaum.

Staszewski, J. J. (1990). Exceptional memory: The influence of practice and knowledge on the development of elaborative encoding strategies. In W. Schneider & F. E. Weinart (Eds.), *Interactions among aptitudes, strategies, and knowledge in cognitive performance* (pp. 252–285). New York: Springer-Verlag.

Staszewski, J. J. (1993, June). *Skilled memory: Evidence for its generality.* Paper presented at the Annual Convention of the American Psychological Society, Chicago.

Sternberg, R. J. (1985). Human intelligence: The model is the message. *Science, 230,* 1111–1118.

Sternberg, R. J., Conway, B. E., Ketron, J. L., & Bernstein, M. (1981). People's conceptions of intelligence. *Journal of Personality & Social Psychology, 41,* 37–55.

Sternberg, R. J., & Frensch, P. A. (1992). On being an expert: A cost-benefits analysis. In R. R. Hoffman (Ed.), *The psychology of expertise: Cognitive research and empirical AI* (pp. 191–203). New York: Springer-Verlag.

Sternberg, S. (1966). High-speed scanning in human memory. *Science, 153,* 652–654.

Sternberg, S. (1975). Memory scanning: New findings and current controversies. *Quarterly Journal of Experimental Psychology, 27,* 1–32.

Storring, G. (1908). Experimentelle Untersuchung uver einfache Schlussprozesse. *Arhch. ges. Psychol., 11,* 1–127.

Strange, W. (1989a). Dynamic specification of coarticulated vowels spoken in sentence context. *Journal of the Acoustical Society of America, 85,* 2135–2153.

Strange, W. (1989b). Evolving theories of vowel perception. *Journal of the Acoustical Society of America, 85,* 2081–2087.

Strauss, E. (1982). Manual persistence in infancy. *Cortex, 18,* 319–321.

Stroop, J. R. (1935). Studies of interference in serial verbal reactions. *Journal of Experimental Psychology, 18,* 643–662.

Studdert-Kennedy, M., & Mody, M. (1996). Auditory temporal perception deficits in the reading-impaired: A critical review of the evidence. *Psychonomic Bulletin and Review, 2,* 508–514.

Sullivan, M. W., Rovee-Collier, C., & Tynes, D. M. (1979). A conditioning analysis of infant long term memory. *Child Development, 50,* 152–162.

Suppes, P., & Atkinson, R. C. (1960). *Markov learning models for multiperson interactions.* Stanford, CA: Stanford University Press.

Swets, J. A., & Pickett, R. M. (1982). *The evaluation of diagnostic systems.* New York: Academic Press.

Tallal, P. (1984). Temporal or phonetic processing deficit in dyslexia? That is the question. *Applied Psycholinguistics, 5,* 167–169.

Tallal, P., & Curtis, S. (1990). Neurological basis of developmental language disorders. In A. Rothenberger (Ed.), *Brain and behavior in child psychiatry* (pp. 205–216). New York: Springer-Verlag.

Teagle, T. E. (1986). The Socratic method of teaching: Its effect on the development of critical thinking skills of upper grade elementary students. *Dissertation Abstracts International, 47(6-A),* 2011.

Teeter, R. (1987). Scientific origins of adolescent sport. *Adolescence, 22,* 253–257.

Terrace, H. S. (1993). The phylogeny and ontogeny of serial memory: List learning by pigeons and monkeys. *Psychological Science, 4,* 162–169.

Thelen, E. (1992). Development as a dynamic system. *Current Directions in Psychological Science, 1,* 198–193.

Thelen, E. (1995). Motor development: A new synthesis. *American Psychologist, 50,* 79–95.

Thelen, E., & Fisher, D. M. (1982). Newborn stepping: An explanation for a "disappearing" reflex. *Developmental Psychology, 18,* 760–775.

Thelen, E., & Fisher, D. M. (1983). From spontaneous to instrumental behavior: Kinematic analysis of movement changes during very early learning. *Child Development, 54,* 129–140.

Thelen, E., Fisher, D. M., & Ridley-Johnson, R. (1984). The relationship between physical growth and a newborn reflex. *Infant Behavior and Development, 7,* 479–493.

Thelen, E., & Smith, L. B. (1994). *A dynamic systems approach to the development of cognition and action.* Cambridge, MA: Bradford Books/MIT Press.

Thelen, E., & Ulrich, B. D. (1991). A dynamic systems analysis of treadmill stepping during the first year. *Monographs of the Society for Research in Child Development, 56,* 1–104.

Thompson, C. P., Cowan, T., Frieman, J., Mahadevan, R. S., & Vogl, R. J. (1991). Rajan: A study of a memorist. *Journal of Memory and Language, 30,* 702–724.

Thompson, L. A., & Massaro, D. W. (1989). Before you see it, you see its parts: Evidence for feature encoding and integration in preschool children and adults. *Cognitive Psychology, 21,* 334–400.

Thomson, D. M. (1972). Context effects in recognition memory. *Journal of Verbal Learning and Verbal Behavior, 11,* 497–511.

Thorndike, E. L. (1906). *Principles of teaching*. New York: Seiler.

Thorndike, E. L. (1921). *The psychology of learning* (Vol. II). New York: Teachers College, Columbia University.

Thorndike, E. L. (1931). *Human learning*. New York: Century.

Thorndike, E. L. (1932). *The fundamentals of learning*. New York: Teacher's College, Columbia University.

Thorndike, E. L., & Woodworth, R. S. (1901). The influence of improvement in one mental function upon the efficiency of other functions. *Psychological Review, 8,* 247–261.

Thumb, A., & Marbe, K. (1901). *Experimentelle Untersuchungen uber die Psychologischen Grundiagen der Sprachlichen Analogiebildung*. Leipzig: Engelmann.

Tinker, M. A. (1963). *Legibility of print*. Ames: Iowa State University Press.

Tinker, M. A. (1965). *Bases for effective reading*. Minneapolis: University of Minnesota Press.

Tipper, S. P. (1985). The negative priming effect: Inhibitory priming by ignored objects. *Quarterly Journal of Experimental Psychology, 37A,* 571–590.

Tipper, S. P. (1991). Less attentional selectivity as a result of declining inhibition in older adults. *Bulletin of the Psychonomic Society, 29,* 45–47.

Tipper, S. P. (1992). Selection for action: The role of inhibitory mechanisms. *Current Directions in Psychological Science, 1,* 105–109.

Tipper, S. P., & Driver, J. (1988). Negative priming between pictures and words: Evidence for semantic analysis of ignored stimuli. *Memory & Cognition, 16,* 64–70.

Tolman, E. C. (1948). Cognitive maps in rats and men. *Psychological Review, 55,* 189–208.

Townsend, J. T., & Ashby, F. G. (1983). *Stochastic modeling of elementary psychological processes*. New York: Cambridge University Press.

Townsend, J. T., & Busemeyer, J. R. (1989). Approach-avoidance: Return to dynamic decision behavior. In C. Izawa (Ed.), *Current issues in cognitive processes: The Tulane Floweree Symposium on Cognition* (pp. 107–133). Hillsdale, NJ: Erlbaum.

Townsend, J. T., & Kadlec, H. (1990). Psychology and mathematics. In R. E. Mickens (Ed.), *Mathematics and science* (pp. 224–248). Singapore: World Scientific.

Townsend, J. T., & Landon, D. E. (1982). An experimental and theoretical investigation of the constant-ratio rule and other models of visual letter confusion. *Journal of Mathematical Psychology, 25,* 119–162.

Townsend, J. T., & Schweickert, R. (1989). Toward the trichotomy method of reaction times: Laying the foundation of stochastic mental networks. *Journal of Mathematical Psychology, 33,* 309–327.

Trabasso, T. R., & Bower, G. H. (1964). Presolution reversal and dimensional shifts in concept identification. *Journal of Experimental Psychology, 67,* 398–399.

Trabasso, T. R., & Bower, G. H. (1968). *Attention in learning*. New York: Wiley.

Tredgold, A. F., & Tredgold, R. F. (1982). *A textbook of mental deficiency (Amentia)*. Baltimore: Williams & Wilkins.

Treisman, A. M. (1960). Contextual cues in selective listening. *Quarterly Journal of Experimental Psychology, 77,* 533–546.

Treisman, A. M. (1964). Verbal cues, language, and meaning in selective attention. *American Journal of Psychology, 77,* 206–219.

Treisman, M. (1978). A theory of the identification of complex stimuli with an application to word recognition. *Psychological Review, 85,* 525–570.

Treisman, A. M., & Geffen, G. (1967). Selective attention: Perception or response? *Quarterly Journal of Experimental Psychology, 19,* 1–17.

Treisman, A. M., & Gelade, G. L. (1980). A feature integration theory of attention. *Cognitive Psychology, 12,* 97–136.

Treisman, A. M., Russell, R., & Green, J. (1975). Brief visual storage of shape and movement. In P. M. A. Rabbitt & S. Dornic (Eds.), *Attention and performance* (pp. 699–721). New York: Academic Press.

Tsunoda, T. (1985). *The Japanese brain*. Tokyo: Taishukan Publishers.

Tulving, E. (1962). Subjective organization in free recall of "unrelated" words. *Psychological Review, 69,* 344–354.

Tulving, E. (1968). Theoretical issues in free recall. In T. R. Dixon & D. L. Horton (Eds.), *Verbal behavior and general behavior theory*. Englewood Cliffs, NJ: Prentice-Hall.

Tulving, E. (1972). Episodic and semantic memory. In E. Tulving & W. Donaldson (Eds.), *Organization of memory*. New York: Academic Press.

Tulving, E. (1983). *Elements of episodic memory*. Oxford: Oxford University Press.

Tulving, E., & Arbuckle, T. Y. (1963). Sources of intratrial interference in immediate recall of paired associates. *Journal of Verbal Learning and Verbal Behavior, 1,* 321–334.

Tulving, E., & Gold, C. (1963). Stimulus information and contextual information as determinants of tachistoscopic recognition of words. *Journal of Experimental Psychology, 66,* 319–327.

Tulving, E., & Schacter, D. L. (1990). Priming and human memory systems. *Science, 247,* 301–306.

Tulving, E., & Thomson, D. M. (1973). Encoding specificity and retrieval processes in episodic memory. *Psychological Review, 80,* 352–373.

Turner, M. L., & Engle, R. W. (1989). Is working memory capacity task-dependent? *Journal of Memory and Language, 28,* 127–154.

Turvey, M. T., & Kravetz, S. (1970). Retrieval from iconic memory with shape as the selection criterion. *Perception & Psychophysics, 8,* 171–172.

Tversky, A., & Kahneman, D. (1973). Availability: A heuristic for judging frequency and probability. *Cognitive Psychology, 5,* 207–232.

Tversky, A., & Kahneman, D. (1974). Judgment under uncertainty: Heuristics and biases. *Science, 185,* 1124–1131.

Tversky, A., & Kahneman, D. (1986). Rational choice and the framing of decisions. *The Journal of Business, 59,* S251–S278.

Tversky, A., & Shafir, E. (1992). The disjunction effect in choice under uncertainty. *Psychological Science, 3,* 305–309.

Tversky, B. (1996). Memory for pictures, maps, environments, and graphs. In D. G. Payne & F. G. Conrad (Eds.), *Intersections in basic and applied memory research*. Mahwah, NJ: Erlbaum.

Tyler, S. W., Hertel, P. T., McCallum, M. C., & Ellis, H. C. (1979). Cognitive effort and memory. *Journal of Experimental Psychology: Human Learning and Memory, 5,* 607–617.

Underwood, B. J. (1957). Interference and forgetting. *Psychological Review, 64,* 49–60.

Underwood, B. J. (1965). False recognition produced by implicit verbal responses. *Journal of Experimental Psychology, 70,* 122–129.

Underwood, B. J. (1966). *Experimental Psychology* (2nd ed.). New York: Appleton-Century-Crofts.

Underwood, B. J., & Postman, L. (1960). Extraexperimental sources of interference in forgetting. *Psychological Review, 67,* 73–95.

Underwood, G. (1974). Moray vs. the rest: The effects of extended shadowing practice. *Quarterly Journal of Experimental Psychology, 26,* 368–372.

Usher, J. A., & Neisser, U. (1993). Childhood amnesia and the beginnings of memory for four early life events. *Journal of Experimental Psychology: General, 122,* 155–165.

Uttal, W. R., & Smith, P. (1968). Recognition of alphabetic characters during voluntary eye movement. *Perception & Psychophysics, 3,* 257–264.

Van Lehn, K. (1989). Problem solving and cognitive skill acquisition. In M. I. Posner (Ed.), *Foundations of cognitive science* (pp. 527–579). Cambridge, MA: MIT Press.

Vellutino, F. R. (1987). Dyslexia. *Scientific American, 256,* 34–41.

Vildomec, V. (1963). *Multilingualism.* Leyden: A. W. Sythoff.

von Bekesy, G. (1957). The ear. *Scientific American, 197,* 66–78.

von Hofsten, C. (1989). Motor development as the development of systems: Comments on the special section. *Developmental Psychology, 25,* 950–953.

von Neumann, J., & Morganstern, O. (1947). *Theory of games and economic behavior* (2nd ed.). Princeton, NJ: Princeton University Press.

von Wright, J. M. (1968). Selection in visual immediate memory. *Quarterly Journal of Experimental Psychology, 20,* 62–68.

Walk, R. D., & Gibson, E. J. (1961). A comparative and analytic study of visual depth perception. *Psychological Monographs, 75* (Whole no. 519).

Wallingford, R. (1975). Long-distance running. In A. W. Taylor & F. Landry (Eds.), *The scientific aspects of sports training* (pp. 118–130). Springfield, IL: Charles C. Thomas.

Walton, G. E., & Bower, T. G. R. (1993). Newborns form "prototypes" in less than 1 minute. *Psychological Science, 4,* 203–205.

Walton, G. E., Bower, N. J., & Bower, T. G. (1992). Recognition of familiar faces by newborns. *Infant Behavior and Development, 15,* 265–269.

Warrington, E. K., & Shallice, T. (1969). The selective impairment of auditory-verbal short-term memory. *Brain, 92,* 886–896.

Waters, G. S., & Caplan, D. (1996). The capacity theory of sentence comprehension: Critique of Just and Carpenter (1992). *Psychological Review, 103,* 761–772.

Waters, G., Caplan, D., & Hildebrandt, N. (1991). On the structure of verbal short-term memory and its functional role in sentence comprehension: Evidence from neuropsychology. *Cognitive Neuroscience, 8,* 81–126.

Watkins, M. J., & Peynircioglu, Z. F. (1983). Three recency effects at the same time. *Journal of Verbal Learning and Verbal Behavior, 22,* 376–384.

Watkins, O. C., & Watkins, M. J. (1980). The modality effect and echoic persistence. *Journal of Experimental Psychology: General, 109,* 251–278.

Watson, R. I. (1968). *The great psychologists from Aristotle to Freud.* New York: Lippincott.

Watt, H. J. (1905). Experimentelle Beitrage zu einer Theorie des Denkens. *Arch. ges. Psychol., 4,* 289–436.

Waugh, N. C., & Norman, D. A. (1965). Primary memory. *Psychological Review, 72,* 89–104.

Weingartner, H., Miller, H., & Murphy, D. L. (1977). Mood-state dependent retrieval of verbal associations. *Journal of Abnormal Psychology, 86,* 276–284.

Weinstein, A. M. (1995). Visual ERPs evidence for anxious processing of threatening information in anxious university students. *Biological Psychiatry, 37,* 847–858.

Weldon, M. S. (1993). The time course of perceptual and conceptual contributions to word fragment completion priming. *Journal of Experimental Psychology: Learning, Memory, and Cognition, 19,* 1010–1023.

Wellman, H. M. & Gelman, S. A. (1992). Cognitive development: Foundational theories of core domains. *Annual Review of Psychology, 43,* 337–375.

Wenger, M. J. & McKinzie, D. L. (1996). Ontogenetic differences in variability on simple measures of learning: Theoretical and practical implications. *Developmental Psychobiology, 29,* 219–239.

Wenger, M. J., & Payne, D. G. (1995). On the acquisition of mnemonic skill: Application of skilled memory theory. *Journal of Experimental Psychology: Applied, 1,* 194–215.

Wenger, M. J., & Payne, D. G. (1996). Comprehension and retention of nonlinear text: Considerations of working memory and material-appropriate processing. *American Journal of Psychology, 109,* 93–130.

Wenger, M. J., & Payne, D. G. (1997). Cue integration across study tasks and direct and indirect retrieval instructions: Implications for the study of retrieval processes. *Journal of Experimental Psychology: Learning, Memory, and Cognition, 23,* 102–122.

Werker, J., & Lalonde, C. (1988). Cross-language speech perception: Initial capabilities and developmental change. *Developmental Psychology, 24,* 672–683.

Wertheimer, M. (1912). Experimentelle Studien uber das Sehen von Bewegung. *Zeitschrift der Psychologie, 61,* 161–265. [Excerpted in W. S. Sahakian (Ed.), *History of psychology* (pp. 418–422). Itaska, IL: Peacock, 1968.]

Wertheimer, M. (1923). Untersuchungen zur Lehre von Gestalt, II. [Translated as: Laws of organization in perceptual forms. In W. D. Ellis (Ed.), *A source book of Gestalt Psychology* (pp. 301–350). London: Routledge & Kegan Paul.]

Whaley, C. J., & Fisk, A. D. (1993). Effects of part-task training on memory set unitization and retention of memory-dependent skilled search. *Human Factors, 35,* 639–652.

Wheeler, D. D. (1970). Processes in word recognition. *Cognitive Psychology, 1,* 59–85.

Whipple, G. M. (1914). *Manual of mental and physical tests. Part I: Simpler processes.* Baltimore: Warwick & York.

Whitbourne, S. K. (1985). *The aging body.* New York: Springer-Verlag.

Whittlesea, B. W. A. (1993). Illusions of familiarity. *Journal of Experimental Psychology: Learning, Memory, & Cognition, 19,* 1235–1253.

Whittlesea, B. W. A., & Wright, R. L. (1997). Implicit (and explicit) learning: Acting adaptively without knowing the consequences. *Journal of Experimental Psychology: Learning, Memory and Cognition, 23,* 181–200.

Whorf, B. L. (1956). *Language, thought and reality: Selected writings of Benjamin Lee Whorf.* J. B. Carroll (Ed.). New York: Wiley.

Wickelgren, W. A. (1965). Acoustic similarity and intrusion errors in short-term memory. *Journal of Experimental Psychology, 70,* 102–108.

Wickelgren, W. A. (1977). Speed-accuracy tradeoff and information processing dynamics. *Acta Psychologica, 41,* 67–85.

Wickelgren, W. A., & Corbett, A. T. (1977). Associative interference and retrieval dynamics in yes-no recall and recognition.

Journal of Experimental Psychology: Human Learning and Memory, 3, 189–202.

Wickens, C. D. (1976). The effects of divided attention on information processing in tracking. *Journal of Experimental Psychology: Human Perception and Performance, 2,* 1–13.

Wickens, C. D. (1980). The structure of attentional resources. In R. Nickerson (Ed.), *Attention and performance VIII.* Hillsdale, NJ: Erlbaum.

Wickens, C. D. (1984). Processing resources in attention. In R. Parasuraman & R. Davies (Eds.), *Varieties of attention.* New York: Academic Press.

Wickens, C. D. (1992). *Engineering psychology and human performance.* New York: HarperCollins.

Wickens, C. D., Sandry, D., & Vidulich, M. (1983). Compatibility and resource competition between modalities of input, output, and central processing. *Human Factors, 26,* 227–248.

Wickens, D. D. (1970). Encoding categories of words: An empirical approach to meaning. *Psychological Review, 77,* 1–15.

Wickens, D. D. (1972). Characteristics of word encoding. In A. W. Melton & E. Martin (Eds.), *Coding processes in human memory* (pp. 191–215). New York: Winston.

Wickens, D. D. (1987). The dual meanings of context: Implications for research, theory, and applications. In D. S. Gorfein & R. R. Hoffman (Eds.), *Memory and learning: The Ebbinghaus Centennial Conference* (pp. 135–152). Hillsdale, NJ: Erlbaum.

Wickens, D. D., Born, D. G., & Allen, C. K. (1963). Proactive inhibition and item similarity in short-term memory. *Journal of Verbal Learning and Verbal Behavior, 7,* 87–92.

Wightman, D. C., & Lintern, G. (1985). Part-task training for tracking and manual control. *Human Factors, 27,* 267–284.

Willis, S. L. (1996). Everyday cognitive competence in elderly persons: Conceptual issues and empirical findings. *Gerontologist, 36,* 595–601.

Wittgenstein, L. (1958). *Philosophical investigations* (2nd ed.). Oxford: Blackwell.

Woldorff, M. G., Gallen, C. C., Hampson, S. A., Hillyard, S. A., Pantey, C., Sobel, D., & Bloom, F. E. (1993). Modulation of early sensory processing in human auditory cortex. *Proceedings of the National Academy of Science, 90,* 8722–8726.

Wood, C., & Cowan, N. (1995). The cocktail party phenomenon revisited: How frequent are attention shifts to one's name in an irrelevant auditory channel? *Journal of Experimental Psychology: Learning, Memory, and Cognition, 21,* 255–260.

Woodrow, H. (1927). The effect of type of training on transference. *Journal of Educational Psychology, 18,* 159–172.

Woodrow, H. (1938a). The effect of practice on groups of different initial ability. *Journal of Educational Psychology, 29,* 268–278.

Woodrow, H. (1938b). The effect of practice on test intercorrelations. *Journal of Educational Psychology, 29,* 561–572.

Woodrow, H. (1938c). The relation between abilities and improvement with practice. *Journal of Educational Psychology, 29,* 215–230.

Woodruff, G., & Premack, D. (1979). Intentional communication in the chimpanzee: The development of deception. *Cognition, 7* (4), 333–362.

Woodworth, R. S. (1918). *Dynamic psychology.* New York: Columbia University Press.

Wundt, W. (1900). *Die Sprache.* Leipzig: Engelmann.

Yarmey, A. D. (1994). Earwitness evidence: Memory for a perpetrator's voice. In D. F. Ross, J. D. Read, & M. P. Toglia (Eds.), *Adult eyewitness testimony: Current trends and developments* (pp. 101–124). Cambridge: Cambridge University Press.

Yarmey, A. D., & Matthys, E. (1992). Voice identification of an abductor. *Applied Cognitive Psychology, 6,* 367–377.

Yee, P. L. (1991). Semantic inhibition of ignored words during a figure classification task. *Quarterly Journal of Experimental Psychology, 43A,* 127–153.

Yellott, J. I. J., & Curnow, P. F. (1967). Second choices in a visual span of apprehension task. *Perception & Psychophysics, 2,* 307–311.

Yeni-Komshian, G. H. (1993). Speech perception. In J. Berko Gleason & N. Bernstein Ratner (Eds.), *Psycholinguistics.* Fort Worth: Holt, Rinehart and Winston.

Yerkes, R. M., & Dodson, J. D. (1908). The relation of strength of stimulus to rapidity of habit formation. *Journal of Comparative Neurological Psychology, 18,* 459–482.

Yonelinas, A. P., Regeher, G., & Jacoby, L. L. (1996). Incorporating response bias in a dual-process theory of memory. *Journal of Memory & Language, 34,* 821–835.

Yonus, A., Bechtold, A. G., Frankel, D., Gordon, F. R., McRoberts, G., Norcia, A., & Sternfels, S. (1977). Development of sensitivity to information for impending collision. *Perception & Psychophysics, 21,* 97–104.

Young, L. R. (1963). Measuring eye movements. *American Journal of Medical Electronics, 2,* 300–307.

Zechmeister, E. B., & Shaughnessy, J. J. (1980). When you know that you know and when you think that you know but you don't. *Bulletin of the Psychonomic Society, 15,* 41–44.

Zipser, D. (1991). Recurrent network model of the neural mechanism of short-term active memory. *Neural Computation, 331,* 679–684.

Zivian, M. T., & Darjes, R. W. (1983). Free recall by in-school and out-of-school adults: Performance and metamemory. *Developmental Psychology, 19,* 513–520.

Name Index

Subject Index